ACCOUNTING AND FINANCE

ACCOUNTING AND FINANCE

ACCOUNTING AND FINANCE

Michael Jones
University of Bristol

Registered office
John Wiley & Sons Ltd, The Atrium, Southern Gate, Chichester, West Sussex, PO19 8SQ,
United Kingdom

For details of our global editorial offices, for customer services and for information about how
to apply for permission to reuse the copyright material in this book please see our website at
www.wiley.com.

Library of Congress Cataloging-in-Publication Data
Jones, Michael, 1953-
  Accounting and finance / Michael Jones, University of Bristol.
    pages cm
  Includes index.
  ISBN 978-1-118-93207-0 (pbk.)
1. Accounting. 2. Managerial accounting. 3. Business enterprises—Finance. I. Title.
  HF5636.J6596 2014
  657—dc23

                                                                    2014027700

ISBN 978-1-118-93207-0 (pbk)
ISBN 978-1-118-96864-2 (ebk)
ISBN 978-1-118-96865-9 (ebk)

A catalogue record for this book is available from the British Library.

Set in 10/12pt Sabon Roman by Thomson Digital, India
Printed and bound in Great Britain by Bell & Bain Ltd, Glasgow

I would like to dedicate this book to the following people who have made my life richer.

- My father, Donald, who died in 2003

- My mother, Lilian

- My daughter, Katherine

- Tony Brinn (in memoriam)

- All my friends in Hereford, Cardiff and elsewhere

- All my colleagues

- And, finally, my past students!

Contents

About the Author   xv

About the Book   xvii

Acknowledgements   xxiii

1   INTRODUCTION TO ACCOUNTING AND FINANCE   1

Introduction   2
Nature of Accounting and Finance   2
Importance of Accounting and Finance   4
Financial Accounting and Management Accounting   5
Users of Accounts   7
Accounting Context   9
Types of Accountancy   13
Types of Accountant   18
Limitations of Accounting   21
Conclusion   21
Discussion Questions   23

SECTION A: FINANCIAL ACCOUNTING: THE TECHNIQUES   25

2   THE ACCOUNTING BACKGROUND   27

Introduction   28
Financial Accounting   28
Language of Accounting   30
The Process of Accounting   38
The Accounting Equation   38
Student Example   44
Why Is Financial Accounting Important?   48
Accounting Principles   49
Accounting Conventions   49
Conclusion   51
Discussion Questions   52
Numerical Questions   53
Appendix 2.1: Illustration of a Consolidated Income Statement
for Marks & Spencer plc 2010   55
Appendix 2.2: Illustration of a Consolidated Statement of Financial
Position for Marks and Spencer plc 2010   57

Appendix 2.3: Illustration of a Consolidated Statement of Cash
Flows for Marks and Spencer plc 2010   59

Appendix 2.4: Illustration of a Consolidated Income Statement
for Volkswagen 2009   61

Appendix 2.5: Illustration of a Consolidated Balance Sheet
(Statement of Financial Position) for Volkswagen 2009   62

Appendix 2.6: Illustration of a Consolidated Cash Flow
Statement (Statement of Cash Flows) for Volkswagen 2009   64

**3   MAIN FINANCIAL STATEMENTS: THE INCOME
STATEMENT (PROFIT AND LOSS ACCOUNT)   66**

Introduction   67
Context   67
Definitions   69
Layout   71
Main Components   72
Profit   79
Listed Companies   82
Capital and Revenue Expenditure   82
Limitations   83
Interpretation   83
Conclusion   83
Discussion Questions   84
Numerical Questions   84

**4   MAIN FINANCIAL STATEMENTS: THE STATEMENT
OF FINANCIAL POSITION (BALANCE SHEET)   86**

Introduction   87
Context   88
Definitions   89
Layout   90
Main Components   91
Limitations   103
Interpretation   104
Listed Companies   105
Conclusion   105
Discussion Questions   106
Numerical Questions   107
Appendix 4.1: Horizontal Format of Statement of Financial Position   108

5   PREPARING THE FINANCIAL STATEMENTS   109

Introduction   110
Main Financial Statements   110
Trial Balance to the Income Statement (Profit and Loss Account)
and the Statement of Financial Position (Balance Sheet)   112
Adjustments to Trial Balance   116
Comprehensive Example   124
Conclusion   128
Discussion Questions   128
Numerical Questions   129

6   PARTNERSHIPS AND LIMITED COMPANIES   141

Introduction   142
Context   143
Partnerships   144
Limited Companies   150
Distinctive Accounting Features of Limited Companies   154
Accounting Treatment For Limited Companies   163
Limited Company Example: Stevens, Turner Ltd   165
Limited Companies: Published Accounts   170
Conclusion   175
Discussion Questions   176
Numerical Questions   177
Appendix 6.1: Example of an Income Statement (Profit and Loss Account)
Using UK GAAP (Manchester United Ltd)   187
Appendix 6.2: Example of a Statement of Financial Position
(Balance Sheet) Using UK GAAP (Manchester United Ltd)   188

7   MAIN FINANCIAL STATEMENTS: THE STATEMENT
    OF CASH FLOWS   190

Introduction   191
Importance of Cash   192
Context   194
Cash and the Bank Account   194
Relationship between Cash and Profit   198
Preparation of Statement of Cash Flows   200
Conclusion   214
Discussion Questions   214
Numerical Questions   215

Appendix 7.1: Main Headings for the Cash Flow Statement
(Statement of Cash Flows) for Sole Traders, Partnerships
and some Non-Listed Companies under UK GAAP   222

Appendix 7.2: Preparation of a Sole Trader's Cash Flow
Statement Using the Direct Method Using UK Format   223

Appendix 7.3: Preparation of the Cash Flow Statement of
Any Company Ltd Using the Indirect Method Using UK GAAP   224

Appendix 7.4: Example of Statement of Cash Flows
(Cash Flow Statement) Using UK GAAP (Manchester United Ltd)   227

8   INTERPRETATION OF ACCOUNTS   229

Introduction   230
Context   230
Overview   231
Importance of Ratios   233
Closer Look at Main Ratios   234
Worked Example   246
Report Format   254
Holistic View of Ratios   256
Performance Indicators   257
Limitations   258
Conclusion   259
Discussion Questions   260
Numerical Questions   261
Appendix 8.1: John Brown Plc   270
Appendix 8.2: The Cash Flow Ratio Using UK GAAP   272

SECTION B: FINANCIAL ACCOUNTING: THE CONTEXT   273

9   REGULATORY AND CONCEPTUAL FRAMEWORKS   275

Introduction   276
Traditional Corporate Model: Directors,
Auditors and Shareholders   277
Regulatory Framework   282
Regulatory Framework in the UK   288
Corporate Governance   293
Conceptual Framework   298
Conclusion   306
Selected Reading   306
Discussion Questions   308

10 MEASUREMENT SYSTEMS   309

Introduction   310
Overview   310
Measurement Systems   313
Deficiencies of Historical Cost Accounting   315
Illustrative Example of Different Measurement Systems   315
Real Life   318
Conclusion   319
Selected Reading   319
Discussion Questions   320

11 THE ANNUAL REPORT   321

Introduction   322
Definition   322
Context   323
Multiple Roles   324
Main Contents of the Annual Report   329
Presentation   348
Group Accounts   350
Impression Management   352
Conclusion   355
Selected Reading   356
Discussion Questions   357

SECTION C: MANAGEMENT ACCOUNTING   359

12 INTRODUCTION TO MANAGEMENT ACCOUNTING AND FINANCE   361

Introduction   362
Context   363
Relationship with Financial Accounting   364
Relationship between Management Accounting and Finance   366
Overview   366
Cost Minimisation and Revenue Maximisation   374
Use of Computers and Impact of Digital Technology   375
Art not a Science   376
Changing Nature of Management Accounting   377
Conclusion   377
Selected Reading   377
Discussion Questions   379

13 COSTING 380

Introduction	381
Importance of Cost Accounting	382
Types of Cost	383
Traditional Costing	387
Activity-Based Costing	393
Costing for Inventory Valuation	397
Different Costing Methods for Different Industries	401
Target Costing	405
Cost-Cutting	405
Conclusion	406
Discussion Questions	407
Numerical Questions	407

14 PLANNING, CONTROL AND PERFORMANCE: BUDGETING 413

Introduction	414
Management Accounting Control Systems	414
Nature of Budgeting	415
Cash Budget	419
Other Budgets	420
Manufacturing Budgets	423
Comprehensive Budgeting Example	426
Behavioural Aspects of Budgeting	431
Responsibility Accounting	435
Conclusion	437
Discussion Questions	437
Numerical Questions	438

15 PLANNING, CONTROL AND PERFORMANCE: STANDARD COSTING 443

Introduction	444
Nature of Standard Costing	445
Standard Cost Variances	446
Interpretation of Variances	455
Conclusion	456
Discussion Questions	457
Numerical Questions	458

16 SHORT-TERM DECISION MAKING   **462**

Introduction   463
Decision Making   463
Contribution Analysis   465
Decisions, Decisions   469
Throughput Accounting   475
Break-Even Analysis   477
Contribution Graph   481
Conclusion   483
Discussion Questions   484
Numerical Questions   484

SECTION D: BUSINESS FINANCE   **489**

**17 LONG-TERM DECISION MAKING: CAPITAL
     INVESTMENT APPRAISAL**   **491**

Introduction   492
Nature of Capital Investment   492
Capital Investment Appraisal Techniques   496
Payback Period   498
Accounting Rate of Return   500
Net Present Value   504
Profitability Index   507
Internal Rate of Return (IRR)   507
Other Factors   512
Conclusion   512
Discussion Questions   513
Numerical Questions   514
Appendix 17.1: Present Value of £1 at Compound
Interest Rate $(1 + r)$ 517

18 THE SOURCES OF FINANCE   **518**

Introduction   519
Nature of Sources of Finance   519
Long-Term Financing   521
Structure of the Business   534
Cost of Capital   534
Conclusion   537
Discussion Questions   538
Numerical Questions   539

19 THE MANAGEMENT OF WORKING CAPITAL   **540**

    Introduction   541
    Working Capital   541
    Short-Term Financing   544
    Conclusion   556
    Discussion Questions   556
    Numerical Questions   557

Glossary of Key Accounting and Finance Terms   **559**

Appendix: Answers   **591**

Index   **645**

About the Author

Michael Jones has taught accounting to both specialists and non-specialists for 34 years, first at Hereford Technical College, then at Portsmouth Polytechnic (now University) and currently at the School of Economics, Finance and Management, University of Bristol. He has taught accounting at all levels from GCSE level, to final-year degree courses, to MBA and MSc courses as well as supervising accounting PhDs. He has published over 140 articles in both professional and academic journals. These articles cover a wide range of topics such as financial accounting, the history of accounting, social and environmental accounting and international accounting. He has also published *Creative Accounting, Fraud and International Accounting Scandals* and *Accounting for Biodiversity*. The author's main research interest is in financial communication. He was formerly Professor of Financial Reporting at Cardiff Business School and Director of its Financial Reporting and Business Communication Unit. He is currently Professor of Financial Reporting (Head of Department 2009–2014) at the School of Economics, Finance and Management, University of Bristol. He is Chair of the British Accounting and Finance Association's Financial Accounting and Reporting Special Interest Group and was Joint Editor of the *British Accounting Review* (2009–2013).

About the Book

Background

Accounting and finance are key aspects of business. All those who work for, or deal with, businesses, therefore, need to understand these subjects. Essentially, understanding accounting and finance is a prerequisite for understanding business. This book aims to introduce students to accounting and finance and provide them with the necessary understanding of the theory and practice of financial accounting, management accounting and business finance. The book, therefore, is aimed primarily at students studying accounting for the first time and seeks to be as understandable and readable as possible.

The Market

This book is intended as a primary text for students studying accounting and finance for the first time: either those following an undergraduate degree in a business school or non-business studies students studying an accounting course. Thus, this includes students on accounting, accounting and finance, and non-accounting degrees as well as MBA students and MSc students. The book therefore covers, for example, accountants, finance specialists, business, engineers, physicists, hotel and catering, social studies and media-study students. The text aims to produce a self-contained, introductory, one-year course covering the major aspects of accounting and finance. However, it is also designed so that students can progress to more advanced follow-up courses in financial accounting, or management accounting and/or finance. The text is thus well suited as an introduction for mainstream accounting or finance graduates or MBA and MSc students as a basic text. The book should be particularly useful in reinforcing the fundamental theory and practice of introductory accounting and finance.

Scope

The book sets down my acquired wisdom (such as it is) over 34 years and interweaves context and technique. It aims to introduce the topic of accounting and finance to students in a student-friendly way. Not only are certain chapters devoted solely to context, but the key to each particular topic is seen as developing the student's understanding of the underlying concepts. This is a novel approach for this type of book.

The book is divided into 19 chapters within four sections. Section A deals with the context and techniques of basic financial accounting and reporting. Section B looks at the context of financial accounting and reporting. Section C provides an introduction to the context and techniques of management accounting. Then Section D provides an introduction to business finance.

Section A: Financial Accounting: The Techniques

In the first section, after introducing the context and background to accounting, the mechanics of financial accounting are explored; for example, bookkeeping and the preparation of financial statements (such as the income statement and statement of financial position). An income statement and statement of financial position are then prepared. The section continues by explaining the adjustments to financial statements, different enterprises' financial statements, the statement of cash flows statement and the interpretation of accounts.

Section B: Financial Accounting: The Context

The focus in this section is on exploring some wider aspects of external financial reporting. It begins by contextualising financial reporting by looking at the regulatory framework, measurement systems and the annual report.

Section C: Management Accounting

This section begins with an exploration of the main concepts underpinning management accounting. Seven main areas are covered: costing, budgeting, standard costing, short-term decision making, strategic management accounting, capital investment and sources of finance. This section thus provides a good coverage of the basics of costing and management accounting as well as introducing strategic management accounting, a topic which has recently become more prominent. The aim of this section is to introduce students to a wide range of key concepts so that they gain a good knowledge base.

Section D: Business Finance

This section explores some of the fundamentals of business finance. It aims to provide students with an introduction to capital investment appraisal as well as to the sources of capital that a business needs. It focuses on external sources of capital such as share and loan capital as well as on the efficient use of working capital.

Coverage

The issues of double-entry bookkeeping, partnerships, manufacturing accounts, computers, internationalism and the public sector are tricky ones for an introductory text. In this book the basics of double-entry bookkeeping are outlined; however, there is no in-depth coverage. This can be found in more specialist books, such as the companion books *Accounting* and *Financial Accounting* by the same author. This book, after much consideration, focuses on three types of business enterprise: sole traders, partnerships and limited companies. These three enterprises comprise the vast bulk of UK businesses. Indeed, according to the Office of National Statistics (2013), in the UK, 66% of enterprises are companies and public corporations, 22% sole traders and 12% partnerships. The sole trader is the simplest business enterprise. The earlier chapters in Section A, therefore, focus primarily on the sole trader to explain the basics. However, later chapters in Section A are more concerned with companies. A distinction is made throughout the book between the requirements of listed and non-listed companies.

Manufacturing accounts are excluded because I consider them unnecessarily complex for students studying accounting for the first time and also because of their diminishing importance within the UK economy. Indeed, in 2013, only 9% of UK businesses were in manufacturing (Office for National Statistics, 2013). The impact of computers on accounting is covered in the text where appropriate. I consider that the widespread use of computers makes it even more important than before to understand the basics of accounting. Although the primary audience for this textbook is likely to be the UK, I have, where possible, attempted to 'internationalise' it. I have tried to integrate international aspects into the book; for instance, drawing on the International Accounting Standards Board's Statement of Principles. Throughout the book, I use IFRS terminology and format. A decision was taken at an early stage to focus on the private sector rather than the public sector. So when the terms company, firm, enterprise and organisation are used, sometimes interchangeably, generally they refer to private sector organisations. There is some coverage of public sector issues, but in general, students interested in this area should refer to a more specialised public sector textbook. This book introduces students to the basics of business finance. It covers investment appraisal, the external sources of funds and the internal management of working capital. It does not, however, cover topics such as foreign exchange, derivatives, portfolio theory or capital asset pricing. It leaves them for a more advanced textbook.

Special Features

A particular effort has been made to make accounting as accessible as possible to students. There are thus several special features in this book which, taken together, distinguish it from other introductory textbooks.

Blend of Theory and Practice

I believe that the key to accounting is understanding. As a result, the text stresses the underlying concepts of accounting and the context within which accounting operates. The book, therefore, blends practice and theory. Worked examples are supplemented by explanation. In addition, the context of accounting is explored. The aim is to contextualise accounting within a wider framework.

Interpretation

I appreciate the need for students to evaluate and interpret material. There is thus a comprehensive chapter on the interpretation of accounts. Equally important, the book strives to emphasise why particular techniques are important.

Readable and Understandable Presentation

Much of my research has been into readable and understandable presentation. At all times, I have strived to achieve this. In particular, I have tried to present complicated materials in a simple way.

Innovative Presentation

I am very keen to focus on effective presentation. This book, therefore, includes many presentational features which aim to enliven the text. Quotations, extracts from newspapers and journals (real-world views), and extracts from annual reports (company cameras) convey the day-to-day relevance of accounting. I also attempt to use realistic examples. This has not, however, always been easy or practical given the introductory nature of the material. In addition, I have attempted to inject some wit and humour into the text through the use of, among other things, cartoons and soundbites. The cartoons, in particular, are designed to present a sideways, irreverent look at accounting which, hopefully, students will find not only entertaining, but also thought-provoking. Finally, I have frequently used boxes and diagrams to simplify and clarify material. Throughout the text there are reflective questions (pauses for thought). These are designed as places where students may pause briefly in their reading of the text to reflect on a particular aspect of accounting or to test their knowledge.

End-of-Chapter Questions and Answers

There are numerous questions and answers at the end of each chapter which test the student's knowledge. These comprise both numerical and discussion questions. The discussion questions are designed for group discussion between lecturer and students. At the end of the book an outline is provided to, at least, the first discussion question of each chapter. This answer provides some outline points for discussion and allows the students to gauge the level and depth of the answers required. However, it should not be taken as exhaustive or prescriptive. The other discussion answers are to be found on the lecturers' area of the website. The answers to the numerical questions are divided roughly in two. Half of the answers are provided at the back of the book for students to practise the techniques and to test themselves. These questions are indicated by the number being in blue. The other numerical answers are to be found on the lecturers' area of the website. A further testbank is also available to lecturers on the website: **www.wiley.com/college/jones**.

Companion Websites

In addition to the supplementary questions, there are Powerpoint slides available on the lecturers' website (visit **www.wiley.com/college/jones**). On the students' website, there are 190 multiple-choice questions (ten for each chapter) as well as 19 additional questions with answers (one for each chapter). The website also houses an impressive range of interactive concept modules that engage students, helping them to master key accounting concepts.

Overall Effect

Taken together, I believe that the blend of theory and practice, focus on readable and understandable presentation, novel material, interpretative stance and innovative presentation make this a distinctive and useful introductory textbook. Hopefully, readers will find it useful and interesting! I have done my best. Enjoy!

New Developments

Since first publication, the book has been updated to reflect new developments in accounting such as the creation of the new UK Accounting Standards Setting Regime, the creation of limited liability partnerships, the change of certain accounting standards and the evolving nature of the annual report and latest developments in management accounting.

International Financial Reporting Standards (IFRS)

The adoption of IFRS by European listed companies from 1st January 2005 has been fully reflected in this book. The book clearly distinguishes between listed companies that follow

IFRS and non-listed companies that do not. Following discussions and feedback with UK and international scholars, IFRS terminology is used consistently throughout this book for sole traders, partnerships and companies. Therefore, for example, as a rule, after much reflection, the term Income Statement replaces Profit and Loss Account, the Statement of Financial Position replaces Balance Sheet and Statement of Cash Flows replaces Cash Flow Statement. In addition, for the elements of the financial statements I also use IFRS terminology, such as revenue for sales, inventory for stock, and trade receivables and trade payables for debtors and creditors, respectively. This new terminology and the new formats have been used consistently throughout the book, including in the management accounting and business finance sections for consistency and ease of understanding. The consistent use of IFRS has also enabled the book to be more international in outlook; examples of foreign companies such as Nokia and Volkswagen have been used.

Mike Jones
October 2014

Acknowledgements

In many ways writing a textbook of this nature is a team effort. Throughout the time it has taken to write this book, I have consistently sought the help and advice of others in order to improve it. I am, therefore, extremely grateful to a great number of academic staff and students (no affiliation below) whose comments have helped me to improve this book. I list colleagues below who have commented on earlier versions of my textbooks. I then give a special mention to those who have commented on this edition. The errors remain mine.

Malcolm Anderson (Cardiff Business School)
Elizabetta Barone (Kings College London/Henley Business School)
Matt Bamber (University of Bristol)
Tony Brinn (Cardiff Business School, RIP)
Alex Brown
Peter Chidgey (BDO Binder, Hamlyn)
Gin Chong (Prairie View/A&M University)
Mark Clatworthy (Cardiff Business School/University of Bristol)
Christopher Coles (Glasgow University)
Alpa Dhanani (Cardiff Business School)
Mahmoud Ezzamel (Cardiff Business School)
Wayne Fiddler (University of Huddersfield)
Charlotte Gladstone-Miller (Portsmouth Business School)
Paul Gordon (Heriot Watt University)
Tony Hines (Portsmouth Business School)
Deborah Holywell
Carolyn Isaaks (Nottingham Trent University)
Tuomas Korppoo
Margaret Lamb (Warwick Business School)
Andrew Lennard (Accounting Standards Board)
Les Lumsdon (Manchester Metropolitan University)
Claire Lutwyche
Louise Macniven (Cardiff Business School)
Neil Marriott (University of Glamorgan/University of Winchester)
Howard Mellett (Cardiff Business School)
Joanne Mitchell
Peter Morgan (Cardiff Business School)
Barry Morse (Cardiff Business School)
Simon Norton (Cardiff Business School)
Phillip O'Regan (Limerick University)
David Parker (Portsmouth Business School)
Roger Pegum (Liverpool John Moores University)
Maurice Pendlebury (Cardiff Business School)
Elaine Porter (Bournemouth University)

Neil Robson (University of the West of England)
Julia Smith (Cardiff Business School)
Aris Solomon (University of Exeter)
Jill Solomon (Cardiff Business School/Kings College, London/Henley Business School)
Ioannis Tsalavoutas (University of Stirling)
Ricky Tutin (University of Bristol)
Tony Wall (University of Ulster)
Tony Whitford (University of Westminster)
Jason Xiao (Cardiff Business School)

This book is hopefully enlivened by many extracts from books, newspapers and annual reports. This material should not be reproduced, copied or transmitted unless written permission is obtained from the original copyright owner. I am, therefore, grateful to all those who kindly granted the publisher permission to reproduce the copyright material. Accordingly, every effort has been made to trace the original copyrighter owners. Thanks to Deloitte, GlaxoSmithKline, Stagecoach Group, News and Media, and I am also grateful to the British Council, Elsevier, CIMA (Chartered Institute of Management Accountants), Fame Database, IASB, John Wiley & Sons Ltd, the *New Scientist*, the Office for National Statistics, Oxford University Press and Pearson.

I should also like to thank Steve Hardman and his team at John Wiley, particularly Juliet Booker and Georgia King, for their help and support, as well as the proofreader, Pat Winfield. Finally, last but certainly not least, I should like to thank Jan Richards for her patience and hard work in turning my generally illegible scribbling into the final manuscript.

Chapter 1

Introduction to accounting and finance

'One way to cheat death is to become an accountant, it seems. The Norfolk accountancy firm W.R. Kewley announces on its website that it was "originally established in 1982 with 2 partners, one of whom died in 1993. After a short break he re-established in 1997, offering a personal service throughout." He was, feedback presumes, dead only for tax purposes.'

New Scientist, 1 April 2000, vol. 166, no. 2232, p. 96. © Reed Business Information Ltd, England. Reproduced by permission. http:www.newscientist.com/article/mg16622327.100-feedback.html.

Learning Outcomes

After completing this chapter you should be able to:

- Explain the nature and importance of accounting and finance.
- Outline the context which shapes accounting and finance.
- Identify the main users of accounting and discuss their information needs.
- Distinguish between the different types of accountancy and accountant.

Go online to discover the extra features for this chapter at
www.wiley.com/college/jones

Chapter Summary

- Accounting is the provision of financial information to managers or owners so that they can make business decisions.
- Accounting measures, monitors and controls business activities.
- Financial accounting supplies financial information to external users.
- Management accounting serves the needs of managers.
- Finance includes the raising of external funds, investment appraisal and the management of working capital.
- Users of accounting information include shareholders and managers.
- Accounting theory and practice are affected by history, country, technology and organisation.
- Auditing, bookkeeping, financial accounting, financial management, insolvency, management accounting, taxation and management consultancy are all branches of accountancy.
- Accountants may be members of professional bodies, such as the Institute of Chartered Accountants in England and Wales.
- Although very useful, accounting has several limitations such as its historic nature and its failure to measure the non-financial aspects of business.

Introduction

The key to understanding business is to understand accounting and finance. Accounting is central to the operation of modern business. Accounting enables businesses to keep track of their money. If businesses cannot make enough profit or generate enough cash, they will go bankrupt. Finance allows a business to survive and grow. Without the provision of external funds and the efficient use of working capital, businesses would also not survive. Often accounting is called the 'language of business'. It provides a means of effective and understandable business communication. If you understand the language, you will, therefore, understand business. However, like many languages, accounting needs to be learnt. The aim of this book is to teach the language of accounting.

Nature of Accounting and Finance

At its simplest, accounting is all about recording, preparing and interpreting business transactions. Accounting provides a key source of information about a business to those who need it, such as managers or owners. This information allows managers to monitor, plan and control the activities of a business. A knowledge of finance enables managers to raise funds to sustain the business. This enables managers to answer key questions such as:

- How much profit have we made?
- Have we enough cash to pay our employees' wages?
- What level of dividends can we pay to our shareholders?
- Should we expand our product range?
- What is the most efficient way to raise funds?
- How should we best use working capital?

PAUSE FOR THOUGHT 1.1

Some Accounting and Finance Questions

You are thinking of manufacturing a new product, the superwhizzo. What are the main accounting questions you would ask?

The principal questions would relate to sales or revenue, costs, profit and finance. They might be:

- What price are rival products selling at?
- How much raw material will I need? How much will it cost?
- How many hours will it take to make each superwhizzo and how much is labour per hour?
- How much will it cost to make the product in terms of items such as electricity?
- How should I recover general business costs such as business rates, wages and salaries or the cost of machinery wearing out?
- How much profit should I aim to make on each superwhizzo?
- How best should we find the money to make the superwhizzo?

In small businesses, managers and owners will often be the same people. However, in larger businesses, such as public limited companies, managers and owners will not be the same. Managers will run the companies on behalf of the owners. In such cases, accounting information serves a particularly useful role. Managers supply the owners with financial information in the form of an income statement, a statement of financial position and a statement of cash flows. This enables the owners to see how well the business is performing. In companies, the owners of a business are called the shareholders.

Essentially, therefore, accounting is all about providing financial information to managers and owners so that they can make business decisions (see Definition 1.1). The formal definition (given below), although dating from 1966, has stood the test well as a comprehensive definition of accounting.

DEFINITION 1.1

Accounting

Working definition
The provision of information to managers and owners so that they can make business decisions.

Formal definition
'The process of identifying, measuring and communicating economic information to permit informed judgments and decisions by users of the information.'

Source: American Accounting Association (1966), *Statement of Basic Accounting Theory*, p. 1.

Finance is about how the business raises funds to sustain its existence and grow. It covers the sources of external funds, investment appraisal, the management of working capital and investment strategies. In this book, we concentrate on the sources of external funds, investment appraisal and the management of working capital. In Definition 1.2 a working definition is provided.

DEFINITION 1.2

Finance

Working definition
The way in which companies raise funds and the application of those funds.

Importance of Accounting and Finance

Accounting is essential to the running of any business or organisation. Organisations as diverse as Microsoft, Barclays Bank, General Electric Company, Volkswagen, The Royal Society for the Protection of Birds (RSPB) and Manchester United football club all need to keep a close check on their finances.

At its simplest, money makes the world go round and accounting keeps track of the money. Businesses depend on cash and profit. If businesses do not make enough cash or earn enough profit, they will get into financial difficulties, perhaps even go bankrupt. Accounting provides the framework by which cash and profit can be monitored, planned and controlled. It is useful to not only monitor the activities of a business but also to plan for the future.

Unless you can understand accounting, you will never understand business. This does not mean everybody has to be an expert accountant. However, it is necessary to know the language of accounting and to be able to interpret accounting numbers. In some respects, there is a similarity between learning to drive a car and learning about accounting. When you are learning to drive a car, you do not need to be a car mechanic. However, you have to understand the car's instruments, such as a speedometer or fuel gauge. Similarly, with accounting, you do not have to be a professional accountant. However, you do need to understand the basic terminology such as income, expenses, profit, assets, liabilities, equity and cash flow.

Without finance a business would not survive. At its simplest the sources of finance are equity capital and loan capital. However, the world of finance is exceedingly complex, involving the City of London, banks, investment analysts and the international money market. There is truth in the old saying 'Money makes the world go round.'

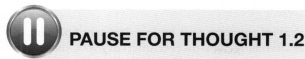

PAUSE FOR THOUGHT 1.2

Manchester United

What information might the board of directors of Manchester United find useful?

Manchester United is both a football club and a thriving business. Indeed, the two go hand in hand. Playing success generates financial success, and financial success generates playing success. Key issues for Manchester United might be:

- How much in gate receipts will we get from our league matches, cup matches and European fixtures?
- How much can we afford to pay our players?
- How much cash have we available to buy rising new stars and how much will our fading old stars bring us?
- How much will we get from television rights and commercial sponsorship?
- How much do we need to finance new capital expenditure, such as building a new stadium?

Financial Accounting and Management Accounting

There is a basic distinction between financial accounting and management accounting. Financial accounting is concerned with information on a business's performance and is targeted primarily at those outside the business (such as shareholders). However, it is also used internally by managers. By contrast, management accounting is internal to a business and used solely by managers. A brief overview is provided in Figure 1.1.

Figure 1.1 Overview of Financial and Management Accounting

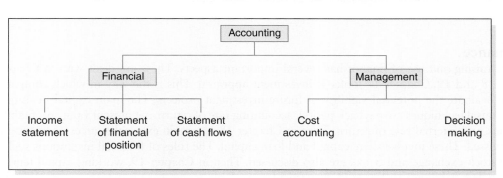

Financial Accounting

Financial accounting is the provision of financial information on a business's recent financial performance targeted at external users, such as shareholders. However, internal users, such as management, may also find it useful. It is required by law. Essentially, it is backward-looking, dealing with past events. Transactions are initially recorded using double-entry bookkeeping. Three major financial statements can then be prepared: the income statement, the statement of financial position and the statement of cash flows (see Chapters 3–7). In this book, I primarily use these three terms. They are the terms used by the International Accounting Standards Board (IASB) in International Financial Reporting Standards (IFRS). IFRS are widely used worldwide; for example, by listed companies in Europe. However, there are also often national reporting rules. In the UK, for example, Generally Accepted Accounting Principles (GAAP) are often used by UK non-listed companies. Alternative terminology is used as follows: income statement (alternative: profit and loss account), statement of financial position (alternative: balance sheet) and statement of cash flows (alternative: cash flow statement). These standards are then interpreted using ratios (see Chapter 8) by users such as shareholders and analysts.

Management Accounting

By contrast, management accounting primarily serves the internal needs of organisations. Management accounting can be divided into cost accounting and decision making. In turn, cost accounting can be split into costing (Chapter 13) and planning, control and performance: budgeting (Chapter 14) and standard costing (Chapter 15). Decision making is covered in Chapter 16.

SOUNDBITE 1.1

Investment Analysts

'Over-paid, under-qualified and inappropriately influential. That seems to be the conventional view of that rampaging beast, the city analyst.'

Source: Damian Wild, *Accountancy Age*, 21 October 2004, p. 14.

Finance

The raising and use of finance has several important aspects. These are dealt with in Chapters 17, 18 and 19. Chapter 17 looks at investment appraisal. This is the way in which companies can evaluate the potential viability of future investment projects. The main capital investment appraisal techniques are payback period, accounting rate of return, net present value, profitability index and internal rate of return. Then in Chapter 18, the main external sources of finance are discussed. These involve share capital and loan capital. The roles of financial institutions such as the stock exchange and banks are also discussed. Then in Chapter 19, working capital (current assets less liabilities) is discussed. In particular, we look at the ways in which companies try to ensure the maximum efficiency of their usage of working capital and short-term external financing.

Users of Accounts

The IASB now takes a relatively narrow view of the users of accounts, identifying only investors, lenders and other creditors in its 2010 conceptual framework. However, there are in fact many more. The users of accounting information may broadly be divided into insiders and outsiders (see Figure 1.2). The insiders are the management and the employees. However, employees are also outsiders in the sense that they often do not have direct access to the financial information. The primary user groups are management and shareholders. Shareholders or investors are often advised by professional financial analysts who work for stockbrokers or big city investment houses. These financial analysts help to determine the share prices of companies quoted on the stock exchange. However, sometimes, they are viewed with mistrust (see Real-World View 1.1).

Figure 1.2 Main Users of Accounting Information

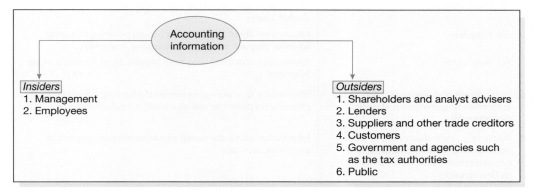

REAL-WORLD VIEW 1.1

Financial Analysts

Working with analysts is a little like being a member of the Magic Circle or the freemasons – those who know how to perform these masterful sleights of hand or arcane rituals are forbidden from ever revealing them to outsiders. Of course, the alternative is that I can't reveal them because I don't understand them myself – I'll let you decide.

Source: James Montier, Showbiz values come to the City, *The Guardian*, 15 January 2000, p. 5. Guardian Newspapers Ltd 2000. Reproduced by permission of James Montier.

The influence of other users (or stakeholders) is growing in importance. Suppliers, customers and lenders have a closer relationship to the company than the government and tax authorities, or the public. These users all need accounting information to help them make business decisions. Usually, the main information requirements concern a company's profits, cash flow, assets and debt (see Figure 1.3).

Figure 1.3 User Information Requirements

User Group	Possible Information Requirements
Internal Users	
1. Management	Information for costing, decision making, planning and control.
2. Employees and employee organisations (Trade Unions)	Information about job security and for collective bargaining.
External Users	
1. Shareholders (current and potential)	Information for buying and selling shares.
2. Analysts, advisers (brokers, dealers)	Information for buying and selling shares.
3. Lenders (bank, creditors)	Information about assets and the company's cash position.
4. Business contacts	
(i) Competitors	Information about revenue and profits so that they can judge market share.
(ii) Suppliers	Information about the company's cash position, to assess whether they will be paid and how long it will take.
(iii) Customers	Information about the long-term prospects and survival of the business.
5. Government and agencies (such as tax authorities or government statistical departments)	Information to enable governmental planning. Information primarily on profits to use as a basis for calculating tax.
6. Public (e.g., individual citizens, local communities, educational groups or non-governmental organisations such as Greenpeace)	Information about the social and environmental impact of corporate activities.

Shareholders, for example, require information so that they can decide whether to buy, hold or sell their shares. The information needs of each group differ slightly and, indeed, may conflict (see Pause for Thought 1.3).

PAUSE FOR THOUGHT 1.3

Conflicting Interests of User Groups

Can you think of an example where the interests of users might actually conflict?

A good example would be in the payment of dividends to shareholders. The higher the dividend, the less money is kept in the company to pay employees or suppliers. Another, more subtle, example is the interests of shareholders and analyst advisers. Shareholders own shares. However, they rely on the advice of analyst advisers such as stockbrokers. Their interests may

PAUSE FOR THOUGHT 1.3 *(continued)*

superficially seem the same (e.g., selling underperforming shares and buying good performers). However, the analyst advisers live by the commission they make. It is in their interests to advise shareholders to buy and sell shares. Unfortunately, it costs money to buy and sell shares; therefore, this may not always be in the potential shareholders' best interests. Shareholders' and employees' interests may also conflict in certain circumstances. For instance, companies with low profits may not have sufficient cash to pay both generous dividends and generous bonuses.

Accounting Context

It is important to realise that accounting is more than just a mere technical subject. Although it is true that at the heart of accounting there are many techniques. However, accounting is also determined by the context in which it operates. Accounting changes as society changes. Accounting in medieval England and accounting today, for example, are very different. Similarly, there are major differences between accounting in Germany and in the United Kingdom. We can see the importance of context if we look briefly at the effects of history, country, technology and organisation (see Figure 1.4).

Figure 1.4 Importance of Accounting Context

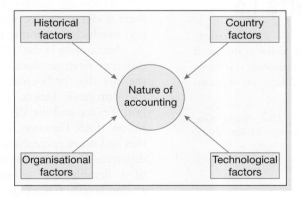

History

Accounting is an integral part of human society. Early societies had accounting systems which, although appearing primitive to us today, served their needs adequately. The Incas in South America, for example, used knotted ropes, called quipus, for accounting. In medieval England notched sticks called tally sticks were used to record transactions.

PAUSE FOR THOUGHT 1.4

The Term 'Accounting'

Why is accounting so called?

....

It is believed that accounting derives from the old thirteenth-century word *aconter*, to count. At its simplest, therefore, accounting means counting. This makes sense as the earliest accountants would have counted sheep or pigs!

Gradually, over time, human society became more sophisticated. A form of accounting called double-entry bookkeeping (every transaction is recorded twice) arose. Emerging from Italy in the fifteenth century, at the same time that Columbus discovered America, double-entry bookkeeping is now the standard way by which accounting transactions are recorded throughout the world.

International Accounting

Double-entry bookkeeping, the income statement (the profit and loss account) and the statement of financial position (balance sheet) are now routine in most major countries. The International Accounting Standards Board (IASB) is also making great efforts to harmonise the disclosure and measurement practices of listed companies worldwide and publishes International Financial Reporting Standards (IFRS). However, there is still great diversity in the broader context in which accounting is carried out.

SOUNDBITE 1.2

'We now operate in a global marketplace, and this is driving the need for universal professional standards and the global qualifications that can deliver them.'

Source: Chris Ward, One World, One Revision, *Accountancy Age*, 11 April 2005, p. 16.

Accounting in the UK, for example, is very different from accounting in France, despite the fact that both countries are members of the European Union. Listed companies in both France and the UK, however, do have to follow IFRS. However, for non-listed companies and other enterprises, the situation is very different. The UK traditionally has been proud of a flexible and self-regulated accounting system largely free of government control. By contrast, the French system has traditionally been very standardised and largely governmentally controlled. In general, as Soundbite 1.2 shows, accounting plays an important role globally.

There are also clear differences between the UK and the US. For example, in the UK, there are Companies Acts, which apply to all UK companies whereas in the US only companies quoted on the stock exchange (i.e., listed companies) are subject to detailed and comprehensive Federal regulations. Also, US listed companies, unlike those in the UK, do not have to comply with IFRS. Unlisted companies are subject only to state regulations, which vary from state to state.

Technology

A rapid change which has affected accounting is computerisation. Up until the advent of computers, accounting was done manually. This was labour-intensive work. Each transaction was entered into the books twice using double-entry bookkeeping. The accounts were then prepared by hand. Similarly, costing, budgeting and decision making were all carried out manually.

Today, almost all businesses use computers. However, they must be used with caution. For the computer, GIGO rules. If you put garbage in, you get garbage out. To avoid GIGO, one needs to understand accounting. In fact, computerisation probably makes it more, rather than less, important to understand the basics.

Organisations

The nature of accounting will vary from business to business. It will depend on the structure of the business and the nature of the business activity.

Structure

If we take the accounts of the three types of business enterprise with which this book deals; a sole trader's accounts will normally be a lot simpler than those of either a partnership or a company. Businesses run by sole traders (usually one person) are smaller, less complicated businesses (for example, a small butcher's shop). Partnerships are multi-owned businesses typically larger in size than sole traders. The sole traders' and partnerships' accounts will normally be less complicated than company accounts as they are prepared for the benefit of active owner-managers rather than for owners who do not actually run the business. Companies are owned by shareholders who own shares, but are run by managers.

Nature of the Business

Every organisation is different. Consequently, every organisation's accounts will differ in certain respects. For example, property companies will own predominantly more land and buildings than non-property companies. Manufacturing companies will have more inventory than non-manufacturing companies.

It is clear from Figure 1.5 that the nature of revenue or sales varies from business to business. In some businesses, a service is provided (e.g., bank, football club, insurance company and plumber).

Figure 1.5 Nature of the Revenue

Business	Nature of Main Revenue
Bank	Interest received
Football club	Gate receipts
Insurance company	Premiums received
Manufacturing company	Sales of goods to retailers
Plumber	Sales of services and other goods
Shop	Sales of goods to customers

Company Snapshot 1.1 shows the sales revenue (sometimes termed turnover) of Manchester United plc, mainly gate receipts, television and merchandising, which is generated by entertaining its customers. In other businesses, the sale is more tangible as goods change hands (for example, manufacturing companies and shops).

Overall, within the UK economy, services are becoming relatively more important and manufacturing industry is declining. In particular, there is an increase in information technology and knowledge-based industries. This trend is set to continue.

COMPANY SNAPSHOT 1.1

Turnover [i.e., revenue or sales]

Turnover, all of which arises from the Group's principal activity, can be analysed into its main components as follows:

	Year ended 30 June 2010 £'000	Year ended 30 June 2009 £'000
Match Day	100,164	108,799
Media	104,814	99,735
Commercial	81,438	69,942
	286,416	278,476

Turnover, all of which originates in the United Kingdom, can be analysed by destination as follows:

	Year ended 30 June 2010 £'000	Year ended 30 June 2009 £'000
United Kingdom	283,552	272,021
Rest of world – tour income	2,864	6,455
	286,416	278,476

Media income from European cup competitions is distributed by the Football Association and is therefore classified as being of United Kingdom origin and destination.

The Group's activities are managed as one business and, as such, the operating expenses are not separately identifiable to any particular segment. As a result, no segmental analysis of operating performance or net assets is provided.

Source: Manchester United Ltd, *Annual Report and Financial Statements for the Year Ended 30 June 2009*, p. 21.

Types of Accountancy

We need to distinguish between the types of accountancy and the types of accountant. Accountancy refers to the process, while accountant refers to the person. In other words, accountancy is what accountants do! In this book, we primarily focus on bookkeeping, financial accounting and management accounting. However, accountants perform other roles such as auditing, financial management, insolvency, fraud detection, taxation and management consultancy. All of these are briefly covered later. Auditors charge management audit and consultancy fees. For example, KPMG, a firm of auditors, charged HSBC Holdings £24.5 million in 2008 for auditing and £17.2 million for consultancy services. Audit fees are shown for the banking system in the UK in 2008 in Real-World View 1.2.

 REAL-WORLD VIEW 1.2

Audit Fees

According to *Accountancy's* most recent survey of auditors' fees, the Big Four made £36.4m in non-audit fees and £90.6m in audit fees from their FTSE 100 banking clients last year.

Bank	Auditor	Audit fee (£m)	Related fee (£m)	Other services (£m)
Barclays	PwC	25.0	4.0	15.0
HBOS	KPMG	8.0	1.0	2.4
HSBC	KPMG	24.5	9.8	7.4
Lloyds TSB	PwC	9.3	3.8	1.5
RBS	Deloitte	17.0	4.9	9.3
StanChart	KPMG	6.8	1.5	0.8

Source: Emily Beattie, Don't Bank on it, *Accountancy Magazine*, June 2009, p. 17. Copyright Wolters Kluwer (UK) Ltd.

Auditing

Auditing is carried out by teams of staff headed by qualified accountants who are independent of the business. Essentially, auditors check that the financial statements, prepared by management, give a true and fair view of the accounts. The auditors do not comment on the efficiency of a company and an audit will not necessarily detect fraud or misstatements as the auditors cannot check every single company transaction. Auditing is normally associated with company accounts. However, the tax authorities or the bank may request an audit of the accounts of sole traders or partnerships. For companies, auditors issue an auditors' report annually to shareholders. Company Snapshot 1.2 provides an auditors' report for J. Sainsbury plc. This is issued after a thorough examination by the auditors of the accounting records and systems of the company.

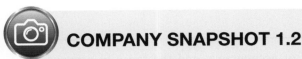

COMPANY SNAPSHOT 1.2

Independent Auditors' report to the members of J Sainsbury plc

We have audited the financial statements of J Sainsbury plc for the 52 weeks ended 20 March 2010 which comprise the Group income statement, the Group and Company Statements of comprehensive income, the Group and Company Balance sheets, the Group and Company Cash flow statements, the Group and Company Statement of changes in equity and the related notes. The financial reporting framework that has been applied in their preparation is applicable law and International Financial Reporting Standards ('IFRSs') as adopted by the European Union and, as regards the Company financial statements, as applied in accordance with the provisions of the Companies Act 2006.

Respective responsibilities of Directors and Auditors

As explained more fully in the Statement of Directors' responsibilities set out on page 43, the Directors are responsible for the preparation of the Annual Report, the Remuneration report and financial statements. The Directors are responsible for being satisfied that the financial statements give a true and fair view. Our responsibility is to audit the financial statements in accordance with applicable law and International Standards on Auditing (UK and Ireland). Those standards require us to comply with the Auditing Practices Board's Ethical Standards for Auditors.

This report, including the opinion, has been prepared for and only for the Company's members as a body in accordance with Chapter 3 of Part 16 of the Companies Act 2006 and for no other purpose. We do not, in giving this opinion, accept or assume responsibility for any other purpose or to any other person to whom this report is shown or into whose hands it may come save where expressly agreed by our prior consent in writing.

Scope of the audit of the financial statements

An audit involves obtaining evidence about the amounts and disclosures in the financial statements sufficient to give reasonable assurance that the financial statements are free from material misstatement, whether caused by fraud or error. This includes an assessment of: whether the accounting policies are appropriate to the Group's and the Company's circumstances and have been consistently applied and adequately disclosed; the reasonableness of significant accounting estimates made by the Directors; and the overall presentation of the financial statements.

Opinion on financial statements

In our opinion:

- the financial statements give a true and fair view of the state of the Group's and of the Company's affairs as at 20 March 2010 and of the Group's profit and the Group's and Company's cash flows for the 52 weeks then ended;
- the Group financial statements have been properly prepared in accordance with IFRSs as adopted by the European Union;
- the Company financial statements have been properly prepared in accordance with IFRSs as adopted by the European Union and as applied in accordance with the provisions of the Companies Act 2006; and
- the financial statements have been prepared in accordance with the requirements of the Companies Act 2006 and, as regards the Group financial statements, Article 4 of the lAS Regulation.

COMPANY SNAPSHOT 1.2 (*continued*)

Opinion on other matters prescribed by the Companies Act 2006
In our opinion:

- the part of the Remuneration report to be audited has been properly prepared in accordance with the Companies Act 2006; and
- the information given in the Directors' report for the financial year for which the financial statements are prepared is consistent with the financial statements.

Matters on which we are required to report by exception
We have nothing to report in respect of the following:

Under the Companies Act 2006 we are required to report to you if, in our opinion:

- adequate accounting records have not been kept by the Company, or returns adequate for our audit have not been received from branches not visited by us; or
- the Company financial statements and the part of the Remuneration report to be audited are not in agreement with the accounting records and returns; or
- certain disclosures of Directors' remuneration specified by law are not made: or
- we have not received all the information and explanations we require for our audit.

Under the Listing Rules we are required to review:

- the Directors' statement, set out on page 28, in relation to going concern; and
- the parts of the Statement of corporate governance relating to the Company's compliance with the nine provisions of the June 2008 Combined Code specified for our review.

Robert Milburn (Senior Statutory Auditor)
for and on behalf of PricewaterhouseCoopers LLP
Chartered Accountants and Statutory Auditors
London
12 May 2010

Source: J. Sainsbury Plc, *Annual Report and Financial Statements 2010*, p. 44. Reproduced by kind permission of Sainsbury's Supermarkets Ltd.

Bookkeeping

Bookkeeping is the preparation of the basic accounts. It involves entering monetary transactions into the books of account. A trial balance is then extracted, and an income statement and statement of financial position are prepared. Nowadays, most companies use computer packages for the basic bookkeeping function, which is often performed by non-qualified accountants.

Financial Accounting

Financial accounting is a wider term than bookkeeping. It deals not only with the mechanistic bookkeeping process, but the preparation and interpretation of the financial accounts. For companies, financial accounting also includes the preparation of the annual report (a document sent annually to shareholders, comprising both financial and non-financial information). In orientation, financial accounting is primarily outward-looking and aimed at providing information for external users. However, monthly financial accounts are often prepared and used internally within a business. Within a company, financial accounting is usually carried out by a company's employees. Smaller businesses, such as sole traders, may use professionally qualified independent accountants.

Finance

An area of growing importance for accountants is finance. This is also often known as financial management. Finance, as its name suggests, is about managing the sources of finance of an organisation. It may, therefore, involve managing the working capital (i.e., short-term assets and liabilities) of a company or finding the cheapest form of borrowing. These topics are examined in Chapters 18 and 19. There is often a separate department of a company called the financial management or treasury department. Finance also includes capital investment appraisal (see Chapter 17).

Insolvency

One of the main reasons for the rise to prominence of professional accountants in the UK was to wind up failed businesses. This is still part of a professional accountant's role. Professional accounting firms are often called in to manage the affairs of failed businesses, in particular to pay creditors (trade payables or banks) who are owed money by the business.

Management Accounting

Management accounting covers the internal accounting of an organisation. There are several different areas of management accounting: costing (see Chapter 13), budgeting (see Chapter 14), standard costing (see Chapter 15), and short-term decision making (see Chapter 16). Essentially, these activities aim to monitor, control and plan the financial activities of organisations. Management uses such information for decisions such as determining a product's selling price or setting the sales budget.

Fraud Detection

Accountants who detect fraud are often called forensic accountants. The frauds they investigate may be personal or corporate and often involve large amounts of money. Real-World View 1.3 shows an interesting example.

 **REAL-WORLD VIEW 1.3**

Forensic Accounting

Case Study: Lust, Lies and the Law
I was once involved in a divorce case, acting on behalf of the wife. We believed her husband was withholding information about assets, and had not disclosed all of his income (wives tend to remember being told these things). We had to get hold of evidence.

REAL-WORLD VIEW 1.3 *(continued)*

We knew that the husband kept a large number of documents in his garage so, accompanied by the local police, the solicitor and I conducted a 6am visit to his house.

The husband's new girlfriend opened the door. Minutes later, she was replaced by a man carrying a shotgun, which he thrust in my face. Luckily, the local sergeant was quite relaxed and talked the man round by assuring him it wasn't worth killing me as I was, after all, 'only a bean counter'. I found out later that the gun wasn't loaded – it didn't make much difference. The husband had originally made an offer of £1m, but the documents we seized proved that he held a lot of assets in Switzerland. He increased the offer to £2.5m, and eventually paid out a total of £3m.

The final ironic twist in the saga was that he dropped his girlfriend and had an inappropriate affair with his solicitor.

The shotgun man was charged with threatening behaviour with a dangerous weapon. In the long term, it all made me more determined to fight for justice.

Steven Redhead is a member of the ICAEW forensic group, interviewed by Ruth Banks.

Source: Ruth Banks, CSI Accountancy, *Accountancy Magazine*, June 2010, p. 106. Copyright Wolters Kluwer (UK) Ltd.

Taxation

Taxation is a complicated area. Professional accountants advise businesses on a whole range of tax issues. Much of this involves tax planning (i.e., minimising the amount of tax that organisations have to pay by taking full advantage of the often complex tax regulations). Thus, for example, Lisa O'Carroll (*Guardian*, 14 October 2011) commented that it had been calculated that over a three-year period, Google had 'saved $3.1 bn in tax revenues using a subsidiary located in Bermuda where the corporate tax rate is zero'. A Google spokesperson told the *Guardian* 'We have an obligation to our shareholders to set up a tax-efficient structure, and our present structure is compliant with the tax rules in all the countries where we operate.' This tax avoidance which operates within the law should be distinguished from tax evasion which is illegal. Professional accountants may also help individuals with a scourge of modern life, the preparation of their annual income tax assessment.

SOUNDBITE 1.3

Management Consultancy

'[Definition of management consultancy] Telling a company what it should already know.'

The Economist (12 September 1987)

Source: The Wiley Book of Business Quotations (1998), p. 359.

Management Consultancy

Management consultancy is a lucrative source of income for accountants (see Real-World View 1.4). However, as Soundbite 1.3 shows, management consultants are often viewed cynically. Management consultancy embraces a whole range of activities such as special efficiency audits, feasibility studies and tax advice. Many professional accounting firms now make more money from management consultancy than from auditing. Examples of management consultancy are investigating the feasibility of a new football stadium or the costing of a local authority's school meals proposals.

REAL-WORLD VIEW 1.4

Management Consultancy

To be fair, many of these issues were problems of success. The accountancy industry had kick-started phenomenal growth and change in the management consultancy services it offered its client base. It was natural to sell those services to its existing clients who eagerly purchased the IT, strategy and financial management consultancy on top of the bog-standard audit and tax services. Suddenly audit became the poor relation, both in terms of excitement and financial return. Audit became a commodity and we all know what happens then – the product becomes devalued and the price goes down.

Source: Peter Williams, How the Brits started the Rot, *Accountancy Age*, 11 November 2004, p. 28.

Types of Accountant

There are several types of accountant. In the UK, for example, the most high-profile are those belonging to the six professionally qualified bodies. In addition to these accountancy bodies, there are other accounting associations in the UK, the most important of which is probably the Association of Accounting Technicians. The web addresses for these institutes are listed at the end of the chapter.

Professionally Qualified Accountants

Chartered Accountants

Six institutions of professionally qualified accountants currently operate in the UK (see Figure 1.6). All jealously guard their independence and the many attempts to merge have all failed (see Real-World View 1.5). 'It's like proposing that Manchester United and Manchester City merge, suggests one indignant ICAEW member, illustrating the strength of feeling' (Michelle Perry, *Accountancy Age*, 22 July 2004, p. 6).

Figure 1.6 Main UK Professional Accountancy Bodies

Body	Main Activities
Institute of Chartered Accountants in England and Wales (ICAEW)	Generally auditing, financial accounting, management consultancy, insolvency and tax advice. However, many work in industry.
Chartered Accountants Ireland (CAI)	Similar to ICAEW.
Institute of Chartered Accountants of Scotland (ICAS)	Similar to ICAEW.
Association of Chartered Certified Accountants (ACCA)	Auditing, financial accounting, insolvency, management consultancy and tax advice. Many train or work in industry.
Chartered Institute of Management Accountants (CIMA)	Management accounting.
Chartered Institute of Public Finance and Accounting (CIPFA)	Accounting within the public sector and privatised industries.

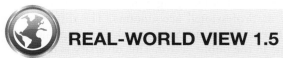

REAL-WORLD VIEW 1.5

Professional Accountancy Bodies

There have been several attempts to persuade the UK's accountancy bodies to merge over the past few years, all without much success. Six accountancy bodies is rather a lot and the government understandably gets exasperated from time to time by six (and sometimes seven) different responses to a consultation paper. But the bodies' members have consistently refused merger initiatives, always citing differing training requirements as a major consideration – and not without justification.

Source: Elizabeth Mackay, Big Five Pressure Gets Results, *Accountancy Age*, 9 March 2000, p. 18.

There are three institutes of chartered accountants: the Institute of Chartered Accountants in England and Wales (ICAEW), the Chartered Accountants Ireland (CAI) and the Institute of Chartered Accountants of Scotland (ICAS). The largest of these three is the ICAEW. Its members were once mainly financial accountants and auditors, but now take part in a whole range of activities. Many leave the professional partnerships with which they train to join business organisations. In fact, qualifying as a chartered accountant is often seen as a route into a business career.

Association of Chartered Certified Accountants (ACCA)

The ACCA's members are not so easy to pigeonhole as the other professionally qualified accountants. They work both in public practice as auditors and as financial accountants. They also have an enormous number of overseas students. Many certified accountants train for their qualification in industry and never work in public practice. The ACCA qualification is very popular overseas.

Chartered Institute of Management Accountants (CIMA)

This is an important body whose members generally train and work in industry. They are found in almost every industry, ranging, for example, from coal mining to computing. They mainly perform the management accounting function.

Chartered Institute of Public Finance and Accountancy (CIPFA)

This institute is smaller than the ICAEW, ACCA or CIMA. It is also much more specialised with its members typically working in the public sector or the newly privatised industries, such as Railtrack. CIPFA members perform a wide range of financial activities within these organisations, such as budgeting in local government.

Second-Tier Bodies

The main second-tier body in the UK is the Association of Accounting Technicians. This body was set up by the major professional accountancy bodies. Accounting technicians help professional accountants, often doing the more routine bookkeeping and costing activities. Many accounting technicians go on to qualify as professional accountants. The different accountancy bodies, therefore, all perform different functions. Some work in companies, some in professional accountancy practices, some in the public sector. This diversity is high-lighted in an original way in Real-World View 1.6.

REAL-WORLD VIEW 1.6

A Sideways Look at the Accounting Profession

Thus, to take parallels from the religious world, we have:

- **the lay priest:** the accountant working for a company;
- **the mendicant priest:** the professional accountant in a partnership;
- **the monastic priest:** the banker, who, while not strictly an accountant, serves much the same ends in a separate and semi-isolated unit;
- **the father confessor:** the auditing accountant to whom everything is (officially) revealed, and who then grants absolution.

Source: Graham Cleverly (1971), *Managers and Magic*, Longman Group Ltd, London, p. 47.

Limitations of Accounting

Accounting, therefore, measures business transactions in numerical terms. It thus provides useful information for managers and other users of accounts. It is, however, important to appreciate certain limitations of accounting. First, accounting tends to measure the cost of past expenditures rather than the current value of assets. There have been attempts to introduce 'fair value' or 'market prices' in some cases. However, this then brings a great deal of subjectivity into accounting. This is dealt with in more detail in Chapter 10. Second, traditional accounting does not capture non-financial aspects of business. Thus, if an industry pollutes the air or the water, this is not recorded in the conventional accounts. Nor does traditional accounting measure the human resources of a business or its knowledge and skills base. The accounts can, thus, only give a partial picture of a business's activities.

SOUNDBITE 1.4

Limitations of Traditional Accounts

'Non-financial items like business opportunities, management strategies and risks have a big effect on company performance and need to be reflected in company reports.'

Mike Starr, Chairman of American Institute of Certified Public Accountants. Committee on Enhanced Business Reporting.

Source: Nicholas Neveling, Consortium Urges Reporting Reforms, *Accountancy Age,* 17 February 2005, p. 11.

Conclusion

Accounting and finance are key business activities. They provide information about a business so that managers or owners (for example, shareholders) can make business decisions. Accounting provides the framework by which cash and profit can be monitored and controlled. A basic distinction is between financial accounting (accounting targeted primarily at those outside the business, but also useful to managers) and management accounting (providing information solely to managers). Finance essentially involves the raising and usage of finance. This covers investment appraisal, sources of external funds and the management of working capital.

Accounting changes as society changes. In particular, it is contingent upon history, country, technology and the nature and type of the organisation. There are at least eight groups which use accounting information, the main ones being managers and shareholders. These user groups require information about, amongst other things, profits, cash flow, assets and debts. There are several types of accountancy and accountant. The types of accountancy include auditing, bookkeeping, financial accounting, financial management, insolvency, management accounting, taxation and management consultancy. The six UK professional accountancy bodies are the Association of Chartered Certified Accountants, the Chartered Institute of Management Accountants, the Chartered Institute of Public Finance and Accountancy, the Institute of Chartered Accountants in England and Wales, the Institute of Chartered Accountants in Ireland and the Institute of Chartered Accountants of Scotland. Although very useful, accounting has certain limitations; for example, its historic nature and its failure to measure non-financial transactions.

 # Websites

A list of useful websites is included below for students interested in a career in accounting and who wish to find out more information.

i) Accountancy Institutes

Association of Chartered Certified Accountants (ACCA)
www.accaglobal.com

Chartered Institute of Management Accountants (CIMA)
www.cimaglobal.com

Chartered Institute of Public Finance and Accounting (CIPFA)
www.cipfa.org.uk

Institute of Chartered Accountants in England and Wales (ICAEW)
www.icaew.co.uk

Chartered Accountants in Ireland (CAI)
www.chartered accountants.ie

Institute of Chartered Accountants of Scotland (ICAS)
www.icas.org.uk

Association of Accounting Technicians (AAT)
www.aat.co.uk

ii) Accounting Firms

PriceWaterhouseCoopers
www.pwcglobal.com

Ernst & Young
www.ey.com

KPMG
www.kpmg.com

Deloitte
www.deloitte.com

Discussion Questions

Questions with numbers in blue have answers at the back of the book.

Q1 What is the importance, if any, of accounting?

Q2 Can you think of three business decisions for which managers would need accounting information?

Q3 What do you consider to be the main differences between financial and management accounting?

Q4 Discuss the idea that as society changes so does accounting.

Q5 'Managers should only supply financial information to the "current" shareholders of companies; no other user groups have any rights at all to information, particularly not the general public or government.' Discuss.

Q6 Why is finance important to a business?

 Go online to discover the extra features for this chapter at
www.wiley.com/college/jones

SECTION A

Financial Accounting: The Techniques

In this section, we look at the accounting techniques which underpin the preparation and interpretation of the financial statements.

In these initial 7 chapters, we focus primarily on the financial statements of the sole trader as these are the most straightforward. Chapter 2 sets the scene for this section, explaining the essential background. It deals with the nature and importance of financial accounting and introduces some of the basic concepts and terminology. We outline the basics of double-entry bookkeeping in Chapter 2, but do not go into depth. This is done in the companion books *Accounting* and *Financial Accounting*. In Chapters 3 and 4, the essential nature, function and contents of the income statement and statement of financial position are discussed. This will enable students more fully to appreciate the importance of the income statement and statement of financial position before their preparation from the trial balance is explained in Chapter 5. In Chapter 6, we prepare the income statement and statement of financial position (balance sheet) of partnerships and limited companies. The final two chapters look at the statement of cash flows (Chapter 7) and the interpretation of accounts (Chapter 8) primarily from the perspective of limited companies. The statement of cash flows is the third most important financial statement for a company. Finally, in Chapter 8 we look at 16 ratios commonly used to assess an organisation's performance.

Chapter 2

The accounting background

'*Living up to his reputation, he brooks no nonsense, adds no frills. A murmured thank you to the chair, then: "Let us never forget that we are all of us in business for one thing only. To make a profit." The hush breaks, the apprehension goes. Audibly, feet slide forward and chairs ease back. Orthodoxy has been established. The incantation has been spoken. No one is going to be forced to query the framework of his world, to face the terrible question, why?'*

Graham Cleverly, *Managers and Magic* (1971), Longman, pp. 25–6.

Learning Outcomes

After completing this chapter you should be able to:

- Explain the nature of financial accounting.
- Appreciate the basic language of accounting.
- Identify the major accounting conventions and concepts.

Go online to discover the extra features for this chapter at
www.wiley.com/college/jones

Chapter Summary

- Financial accounting is about providing users with financial information so that they can make decisions.
- Key accounting terminology includes income, expenses, equity or capital, assets and liabilities.
- The three major financial statements are the income statement (also known as the profit and loss account), statement of financial position (also known as the balance sheet) and statement of cash flows (also known as the cash flow statement).
- The process of accounting consists of the accounting equation, debits and credits and preparing a trial balance.
- The most widely agreed objective is to provide information for decision making.
- The most important external users for companies are the shareholders.
- Four major accounting conventions are entity, money measurement, historic cost and periodicity.
- Three major accounting concepts are going concern, accruals and consistency.
- Prudence is a fourth much-disputed accounting concept.

Introduction

Financial accounting is the process by which financial information is prepared and then communicated to the users. It is a key element in modern business. For limited companies, it enables the shareholders to receive from the managers an annual set of accounts which has been independently checked by auditors. For sole traders and partnerships, it allows the tax authorities to have a set of accounts which is often prepared by independent accountants. There are thus three parties to the production and dissemination of the financial accounts: the preparers, the users and the independent accountants. The broad objective of financial accounting is to provide information for decision making. Its preparation is governed by basic underpinning principles called accounting conventions and accounting concepts.

Financial Accounting

Once a year, company shareholders receive through the post an annual report containing the company's annual accounts. These comprise the key financial statements as well as other financial and non-financial information. Sole traders and partnerships annually prepare a set of financial statements for the tax authorities. Managers will also use these financial statements to evaluate the performance of the business over the past year. The whole process is underpinned by a set of overarching accounting principles (i.e., accounting conventions and accounting concepts) and by detailed accounting measurement and disclosure rules. Essentially, financial accounting is concerned with providing financial information to users so that they can make decisions. Definition 2.1 provides a more formal definition derived from the International Accounting Standards Board (a regulatory body which seeks to set accounting standards which will be used worldwide) applicable to all commercial, industrial and business reporting enterprises as well as a fuller definition from the Chartered Institute of Management Accountants.

DEFINITION 2.1

Financial Accounting

Working definition
The provision of financial information to users for decision making.

Formal definitions
The International Accounting Standards Board broadly sees the objective of financial accounting as the provision of financial information about an organisation that is useful to a range of users, such as existing and potential investors, lenders or creditors, when they are seeking to make decisions. The decisions may be, for example, buying or selling shares or giving loans.

'Classification and recording of the monetary transactions of an entity in accordance with established concepts, principles, accounting standards and legal requirements and their presentation, by means of income statements, balance sheets [statements of financial position] and cash flow statements [statements of cash flow], during and at the end of an accounting period.'

Source: Chartered Institute of Management Accountants (2005), *Official Terminology*. Reproduced by Permission of Elsevier.

SOUNDBITE 2.1

Money

'Money never meant anything to us. It was just sort of how we kept the score.'

Nelson Bunker Hunt, *Great Business Quotations*, R. Barron and J. Fisk

Source: The Book of Business Quotations (1991), p. 155.

Financial accounting meets the common needs of a wide range of users. It does not, however, provide all the information users may need. An important additional role of financial accounting is that it shows the stewardship of management (i.e., how successfully they run the company). Shareholders may use this information to decide whether or not to sell their shares.

At a still broader level, accounting allows managers to assess their organisation's performance. It is a way of seeing how well they have done or, as Soundbite 2.1 shows, of keeping the score. The main financial statements for sole traders, partnerships and companies are the income statement (profit and loss account) and the statement of financial position (balance sheet). These contain details of income, expenses, assets, liabilities and equity or capital. For companies (and often for other businesses), these two statements are accompanied by a statement of cash flows (cash flow statement), which summarises a company's cash flows. Generally, the principal user is assumed to be the shareholder. These three statements are sent to shareholders once a year in a document called an annual report. However, managers need more detailed and more frequent information to run a company effectively. Monthly accounts and accounts for different parts of the business are, therefore, often drawn up.

PAUSE FOR THOUGHT 2.1

Annual Financial Accounts

Why do sole traders, partnerships and limited companies produce financial accounts?

There are several reasons. First, those running the business wish to assess their own performance and regular, periodic accounts are a good way to do this. Second, businesses may need to provide third parties with financial information. In the case of sole traders and partnerships, the tax authorities need to assess the business's profits. Bankers may also want regular financial statements if they have loaned money. Similarly, companies are accountable not only to their shareholders, but to other users of accounts.

Language of Accounting

Accounting is a language. As with all languages, it is important to understand the basics. Five basic accounting terms (income, expenses, assets, liabilities and equity or capital) are introduced here as well as the three main financial statements: the income statement (the profit and loss account), the statement of financial position (balance sheet) and the statement of cash flows (cash flow statement). These concepts are explained more fully later in the book.

Income
Income is essentially the revenue earned by a business. Sales revenue is a good example. Income is income, even if goods and services have been delivered but customers have not yet paid. Income thus differs from cash received. Revenues are closely watched by analysts. Deloitte, a leading professional accountancy firm, for example, analyses football sales annually. An extract from its 2009/10 analysis is given in Real-World View 2.1.

REAL-WORLD VIEW 2.1

Europe's Premier Leagues

- Despite significant economic headwinds, the European football market grew by 4% to €16.3 billion in 2009/10.
- The 'big five' leagues' revenues grew by 5% to €8.4 billion, with all five leagues demonstrating revenue growth. Broadcasting revenue was the main driver of growth (up 8%) and now stands at over €4 billion.
- The Premier League increased its revenue to almost €2.5 billion in 2009/10. The gap to the second highest revenue generating league, the Bundesliga, now exceeds €800m.
- The Bundesliga's revenue grew 6% to €1,664m, driven by an impressive increase in commercial revenues, and the largest average attendance (42,700) in European football.

Source: Deloitte (13 June 2011) as reproduced in www.accountacyageinsight.com/abstract/football-finance-highlights.

Expenses

Expenses are the costs incurred in running a business. Examples are telephone, business rates and wages. The nature of expenses varies from business to business. Real-World View 2.2 shows that the biggest expense for football clubs is their wages. Expenses are expenses, even if goods and services have been consumed but the business has still not paid for them. Expenses are, therefore, different from cash paid.

REAL-WORLD VIEW 2.2

Football Club Expenses

It takes a lot to convince a former Conservative cabinet minister that wage caps are necessary. Yet that is the impact football had on our former chairman, Lord Mawhinney.

Instinctively, I don't believe in salary controls. It is all a little bit too 'Soviet' for my liking. But as far as league football is concerned, it looks like being a necessary evil.

It is necessary because people leave their business brains behind when they enter the emotionally charged world of football. Clubs are chasing a dream – they all want to gain promotion or win something for their fans. In doing so, the usual rules of business go out the window.

REAL-WORLD VIEW 2.2 *(continued)*

At the Football League, we spend a great deal of time devising ways of protecting clubs from themselves.

....

In the Championship during the 2007/08 season, the ratio of total wages against turnover was between 58% and 124%, averaging at 87%, up from 79% in the previous year. Last season's figures are expected to be even higher. It should be, at worst, between 60% and 70%.

Indeed, player wages in the 2008/09 tax year totalled £197m, some 24% higher than in 2007/08 and 45% higher than those in 2006/07.

It is clear to everyone in the game that clubs spend too much of their income on player wages.

Source: Tad Detko, Fever Pitch, *Accountancy Magazine*, May 2010, p. 18. Copyright Wolters Kluwer (UK) Ltd.

Assets

Assets are essentially items owned (or leased) by the business which will bring economic benefits. An example might be a building or inventory awaiting resale. Assets may be held for a long time for use in the business (such as motor vehicles) or alternatively be short-term assets (such as inventory) held for immediate resale. As Real-World View 2.3 shows, a solid asset base often underpins a successful company.

 ## REAL-WORLD VIEW 2.3

Assets

With assets of £2.6 billion and 2,300 staff, Pennon is a 'bog standard' utility with a waste disposal business bolted on the side. For investors this need not be a turn-off. Pennon generates oodles of cash relative to its size, and – like all utilities – gives most of it to shareholders in the form of dividends.

Source: Philip Aldrick, Pennon's Safe Enough but Doesn't Hold Water for Growth Prospects, *Daily Telegraph*, 10 December 2004, p. 36.

Liabilities

Liabilities are amounts the business owes to a third party. An example might be money owed to the bank following a bank loan. Alternatively, the company may owe money to the suppliers of goods (known as trade payables or creditors).

Equity (Capital)

Equity equals the assets of a business less its liabilities to third parties. Equity represents the owner's interest in the business. In effect, equity is a liability as it is owed by the business to the owner. Owners may be sole traders, partners or shareholders. Under IFRS terminology 'equity' is preferred to 'capital'.

Income Statement

An income statement, at its simplest, records the income and expenses of a business over time. Income less expenses equals profit. By contrast, where expenses are greater than income, losses will occur. It is important (as Real-World View 2.4 shows) for even the world's largest companies to ensure that income (or revenue) exceeds expenses (or costs). The net profit (or net loss) in the income statement is added to (or subtracted from) equity in the statement of financial position. Over the years the accepted terminology has changed. The income statement was formally known as the profit and loss account. Under IFRS, there is a separation of profit generated from continuing operations such as sales and other comprehensive income (for example, gains on foreign exchange translations, property valuation and actuarial gains (i.e., from pensions)). IAS 1 permits two presentations. First, one statement called the 'statement of comprehensive income' (this combines both profits from continuing operations (i.e., the buying and selling of goods) and other comprehensive income). Alternatively, two statements can be provided. First, an income statement for continuing operations and then a statement of comprehensive income (i.e., income from other sources, such as profits on the sale of investments). Given the nature of this introductory book, I generally use the income statement as small businesses (sole traders, partnerships and non-listed limited companies) do not usually have other comprehensive income. For listed companies, however, I do sometimes use 'statement of comprehensive income', even though I do not deal in any depth with 'other comprehensive income' in this book. In this book, I follow current usage and reserve statement of comprehensive income for a separate statement showing items such as gains from foreign currency. This is explained more fully in Chapter 6.

REAL-WORLD VIEW 2.4

Revenues and Expenses

HSBC has outlined plans to cut costs by as much as $3.5bn (£2.1bn) over the next three years as part of an attempt to boost its returns to shareholders. ... Analysts at Bank of America, Merrill Lynch, said the envisaged cuts could shave close to 10pc off the bank's total cost base, with HSBC looking to reduce costs as a proportion of revenues from 55.2 pc today to 48pc – 52pc by 2013 ... Among the businesses that will benefit from the plan is wealth management, with HSBC targeting annual revenues of $4bn as it looks to grab a large slice of the profits from managing the money of the world's richest people. HSBC aims to shave costs by up to $3.5bn in three years.

Source: Daily Telegraph, 12 May 2011, p. 1.

PAUSE FOR THOUGHT 2.2

Accounting Terms

Can you think of two examples of income, and three examples of expenses, assets and liabilities which a typical business might have?

These are many and varied. A few examples are given below:

Income	*Expenses*	*Assets*	*Liabilities*
Sales of goods	Telephone	Buildings	Bank loan
Sales of assets	Business rates	Motor cars	Trade payables
Bank interest earned	Electricity	Furniture	
	Repairs	Inventory	
	Petrol consumed	Trade receivables	

Company Snapshot 2.1 shows a reconstruction of the summary consolidated income statement for Marks & Spencer plc in 2010 (see Appendix 2.1 for full statement). From Company Snapshot 2.1 it can be seen that expenses are deducted from revenue and other income to give profit before taxation. Other income is negative because of high financing costs. Once taxation has been deducted, we arrive at the profit for the year (£523 million for 2010 and £507 million for 2009). The 2010 accounts of Marks & Spencer plc follow the IFRS format set out by the International Accounting Standards Board for listed companies. In Appendix 2.4, the income statement for Volkswagen, also prepared using International Accounting Standards, is provided.

Statement of Financial Position (Balance Sheet)

A statement of financial position records the assets, liabilities and equity of a business at a certain point in time. Assets less liabilities will equal equity. Equity is thus the owners' interest in the business. The statement of financial position for Marks & Spencer as at 3rd April 2010 is presented in Company Snapshot 2.2. Here the assets are added together and then the liabilities are taken away. The net assets (i.e., assets less liabilities) equal the total equity employed by the business. A statement of financial position (balance sheet) in a listed company format following international accounting standards is presented for Volkswagen in Appendix 2.5. This is prepared using a format where the total assets are totalled; these then equal total equity and liabilities. This approach is commonly used by non-UK companies under International Financial Reporting Standards. UK companies more typically use a net assets approach as demonstrated already by Marks and Spencer in Appendix 2.2 and in Company Snapshot 6.4 by the British company AstraZeneca. This approach is used in this book.

COMPANY SNAPSHOT 2.1

Marks & Spencer Summarised Consolidated Income Statement

Marks & Spencer
    Summary income statement for the 53 weeks ended 3rd April, 2010

	2010	2009
	£m	£m
Revenue	9,537	9,062
Less: Other income	(149)	(164)
	9,388	8,898
Less: Expenses	(8,685)	(8,192)
Profit before taxation	703	706
Taxation	(180)	(199)
Profit for the year	523	507

Note: The income statement has been simplified and reconstructed. The original summary income statement can be found as Appendix 2.1 at the back of this chapter. Appendix 2.1 also includes the consolidated statement of comprehensive income.

Source: Marks & Spencer plc, *Annual Review and Summary Financial Statements 2010*, p. 78.

COMPANY SNAPSHOT 2.2

Illustration of a Summarised Consolidated Statement of Financial Position

Marks & Spencer
    Summary statement of financial position for the 53 weeks as at 3rd April, 2010

	As at 3 April 2010	As at 29 March 2009 as restated
	£m	£m
ASSETS		
Non-current assets		
Intangible assets	453	400
Property, plant and equipment	4,722	4,834
Other non-current assets	458	634
	5,633	5,868

COMPANY SNAPSHOT 2.2 (*continued*)

	£m	£m
Current assets		
Inventories	613	536
Trade receivables	281	285
Cash	406	423
Other	220	146
	1,520	1,390
Total Assets	7,153	7,258
LIABILITIES		
Current liabilities		
Trade payables	1,154	1,074
Other	736	1,233
	1,890	2,307
Non-current liabilities	3,077	2,850
Total liabilities	4,967	5,157
Net assets	2,186	2,101

	£m	£m
EQUITY		
Equity shareholders' funds	2,169	2,082
Non-equity shareholders' funds	17	19
Total Equity	2,186	2,101

Note: The statement of financial position has been simplified and reconstructed. The original summary statement of financial position can be found as Appendix 2.2 at the back of this chapter.

Source: Marks & Spencer plc, *Annual Report and Financial Statements 2010*, p. 79.

Statement of Cash Flows

A statement of cash flows shows the cash inflows and outflows of the business. These are normally calculated by comparing the statements of financial position for two consecutive years. As Chapter 7 shows, this can be very complicated. The statement of cash flows which deals with actual historic cash flows can be compared to future cash flows that are presented in a cash budget (see Chapter 14). Company Snapshot 2.3 shows a summary statement of cash flows for Marks & Spencer for 2010. Cash flows are split into three categories: operating (such as buying and selling goods or paying wages), investing (such as buying and selling machinery or receiving interest or dividends on investments) and financing (such as borrowing money and paying interest on loans). Overall, Marks & Spencer has a positive net cash flow from operating activities of £1,229 million in 2010. In Appendix 2.3 the statement of cash flows for Marks and Spencer is reproduced. Then in Appendix 2.6, the statement of cash flows (cash flow statement) for Volkswagen, a German listed company following international accounting standards, is presented.

 COMPANY SNAPSHOT 2.3

Illustration of a Summarised Consolidated Statement of Cash Flows

Marks & Spencer
Summary statement of cash flows for the 53 weeks ended 3rd April, 2010

	53 weeks ended 3 April 2010 £m	52 weeks ended 29 March 2009 as restated £m
Cash generated from operations	1,350	1,372
Tax paid	(121)	(81)
Net cash inflow from operating activities	1,229	1,291
Cash flows from investing activities	(530)	(597)
Cash flows from financing activities	(792)	(521)
Exchange rate changes	(2)	7
Net cash (out) inflow from activities	(95)	180
	£m	£m
Opening net cash	298	118
Net cash flow from activities	(95)	180
Closing net cash	203	298

Note: The statement of cash flows has been simplified and reconstructed. The original statement of cash flows can be found as Appendix 2.3 at the back of this chapter.

Source: Marks & Spencer plc, *Annual Report and Financial Statements 2010*, p. 81.

The Process of Accounting

Fundamental to the process of accounting are debits and credits, the accounting equation and double-entry bookkeeping. These concepts are outlined briefly below. Students wishing to study these topics in more depth are referred to Chapter 3 of the more specialist books on *Accounting* (3rd edition), or *Financial Accounting* by Michael Jones.

Businesses make thousands, if not millions, of transactions every year. There needs to be a coherent and standardised way of doing this. In effect, this is what bookkeeping represents.

In a way it is like a business diary where all the financial transactions are recorded. Therefore, in essence, double-entry bookkeeping is the systematic recording of income, expenses, assets, liabilities and equity. Double-entry bookkeeping is a way of systematically recording the financial transactions of a company so that each transaction is recorded twice. Double-entry bookkeeping's importance lies in the fact that the income statement (also known as the profit and loss account) and statement of financial position (also known as the balance sheet) are prepared only after the accounting transactions have been recorded. The accounting equation and double-entry bookkeeping apply to all businesses. In this chapter, unless otherwise specified, the terminology used applies to sole traders, partnerships and non-listed companies.

The Accounting Equation

At the heart of the double-entry system is the accounting equation. This starts from the basic premise that assets equal liabilities. Liabilities are, in effect, claims that somebody has over assets. It then logically builds up in complexity, as follows:

Step 1. | Assets = Liabilities |

If there is an asset of £1, then somebody must have a claim over that £1. This can either be a third party (such as the bank) or the owner of the business. There is thus a basic equality. For every asset, there is a liability.

Step 2. It should be appreciated that equity is a distinct type of liability because it is owed to the owner of a business. If we expand our accounting equation to formally distinguish between claims which owners have over a business (i.e., equity) and claims which others have over the business (i.e., third-party liabilities), we now have:

| Assets = Liabilities + Equity |

Accountants sometimes use the term 'Capital' to describe the amount invested by the owner. However, for consistency in this book the term equity is used. In a company, like Tesco, the equity is share capital and will have been invested by shareholders.

Step 3. | Assets = Liabilities + Equity + Profit |

When an organisation earns a profit, its assets increase. Profit is on the same side as liabilities because profit is owed to the owner. Profit thus also increases the owner's share in the business. If a loss is made, assets will decrease, but the principle of equality still holds.

Step 4. $\boxed{\text{Assets} = \text{Liabilities} + \text{Equity} + (\text{Income} - \text{Expenses})}$

All we have done is broken down profit into its constituent parts (i.e., income less expenses). We have still maintained the basic equality.

Step 5. $\boxed{\text{Assets} + \text{Expenses} = \text{Liabilities} + \text{Equity} + \text{Income}}$

We have now rearranged the accounting equation by adding expenses to assets. We have still preserved the accounting equation.

Step 6. In accounting terms, **assets** and **expenses** are recorded using **debit entries** and **income, liabilities** and **equity** are recorded using **credit entries**. Each page of each book of account has a debit side (left-hand side) and a credit side (right-hand side).

 PAUSE FOR THOUGHT 2.3

The Accounting Equation

John decides to start a business and puts £10,000 into a business bank account. He also borrows £5,000 from the bank. How does this obey the accounting equation?

The asset here is easy. It is £15,000 cash. There is also clearly a £5,000 liability to the bank. However, the remaining £10,000, at first glance, is more elusive. A liability does, however, exist. This is because of the entity concept where the business and John are treated as different entities. Thus, the business owes John £10,000. We therefore have:

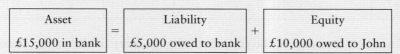

Asset		Liability		Equity
£15,000 in bank	=	£5,000 owed to bank	+	£10,000 owed to John

Where a business has a liability to its owner, this is known as equity.

This division of the page is called a 'T' account, with debits being on the left and credits on the right. Thus:

'T' Account (ledger account)	
Assets and expenses on the left-hand side DEBIT	Incomes, liabilities and equity on the right-hand side CREDIT

PAUSE FOR THOUGHT 2.4

Illustration of Accounting Equation

A firm starts the year with £10,000 assets and £10,000 liabilities (£6,000 third-party liabilities and £4,000 owner's equity). During the year, the firm makes £5,000 profit (£9,000 income, £4,000 expenses). Show how the accounting equation works.

	Accounting equation	Transaction
(1)	Assets = Liabilities	£10,000 = £10,000
(2)	Assets = Liabilities + Equity	£10,000 = £6,000 + £4,000
(3)	Assets = Liabilities + Equity + Profit	£15,000 = £6,000 + £4,000 + £5,000
(4)	Assets = Liabilities + Equity + (Income − Expenses)	£15,000 = £6,000 + £4,000 + (£9,000 − £4,000)
(5)	Assets + Expenses = Liabilities + Capital + Income	£15,000 + £4,000 = £6,000 + £4,000 + £9,000

'T' Account		'T' Account	
Assets + Expenses	Liabilities + Equity + Income	£15,000 + £4,000	£6,000 + £4,000 + £9,000

The 'T' account is central to the concept of double-entry bookkeeping. In turn, double-entry bookkeeping is the backbone of financial accounting. As Helpnote 2.1 shows, it is underpinned by three major rules.

HELPNOTE 2.1

Basic Rules of Double-Entry Bookkeeping

1. For every transaction, there must be a *debit and a credit entry*.
2. These debit and credit entries are *equal* and *opposite*.
3. In the *cash book* all accounts *paid in* are recorded on the *debit* side, whereas all amounts *paid out* are recorded on the *credit* side.

In practice, there are many types of asset, liability, equity, income and expense. Figure 2.1 provides a brief summary of some of these.

Figure 2.1 does not provide an exhaustive list of all assets and liabilities. For instance, it only deals with tangible assets (literally assets you can touch). It thus ignores intangible assets (literally assets you cannot touch) such as royalties or goodwill. However, for now, this provides a useful framework. Intangible assets are most often found in the accounts of companies and are discussed later. More detail on the individual items in Figure 2.1 is provided in later chapters.

Figure 2.1 Summary of Some of the Major Types of Assets, Liabilities and Equity, Income and Expenses

---

Four Major Types of Items

1. Assets
2. Liabilities and equity
3. Income
4. Expenses

1. Assets
Essentially items owned or leased by a business which will bring economic benefits. Two main sorts of tangible assets (i.e., assets with a physical existence):

I. _Non-current assets_
These can be divided into intangible assets such as patents or goodwill and tangible assets: property, plant and equipment. These are infrastructure assets _not_ used in day-to-day trading. They are assets in use usually over a long period of time.

      i. Motor vehicles
      ii. Land and buildings
      iii. Fixtures and fittings
      iv. Plant and machinery

II. _Current assets_
These are assets used in day-to-day trading

      i. Inventory (Stock)
      ii. Trade receivables (Debtors)
      iii. Cash

2. Liabilities
Essentially these can be divided into:
I. Short-term and long-term third-party liabilities; and
II. Equity which is a liability owed by the business to the owner.

I. _Third-party liabilities_
(a) **_Short-term (current liabilities)_**

      (i) Trade payables (creditors)
      (ii) Bank overdraft
      (iii) Proposed taxation (companies only)

(b) **_Long-term (non-current liabilities)_**

      (i) Bank loan repayable after several years
      (ii) Mortgage loan

II. _Equity_
Equity is a liability because the business owes it to the owner. Owner's equity (capital) is increased by profits, but reduced by losses.

3. Income
This is the day-to-day revenue earned by the business, e.g., revenue or sales.

4. Expenses
These are the day-to-day costs of running a business, e.g., rent and rates, electricity, wages.

Once the transactions have been entered into the books, there are, as Figure 2.2 shows, two more stages: balancing off and the trial balance. Balancing off simply means working out how much money is in an individual account. So, for example, if there was £8,000 on the debit side of a cash account and £6,000 on the credit side, the overall balance would be £2,000 credit (in other words the company would be overdrawn by £2,000). Once the accounts have been balanced off, then a trial balance is prepared.

Figure 2.2 Recording the Transactions

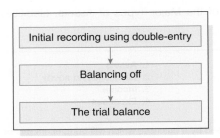

A trial balance is simply a listing of all the balances of the individual accounts ('T' accounts) that a company has drawn up.

 PAUSE FOR THOUGHT 2.5

The Trial Balance I

Why should the trial balance balance?

A trial balance is simply a list of all the balances on the individual accounts. If the double-entry process has been completed correctly, each debit will be matched by an equal and opposite credit entry. There will thus be equal amounts on the debit and credit sides. If the trial balance fails to balance – and it often will, even for experts – then you know a mistake has been made in the double-entry process. You need, therefore, to find it. This process of trial and error is the reason why a trial balance is so called.

If, for example, we had a small business (Armstrong) with the following balances as at 30 March, we could draw up the trial balance in Figure 2.3.

Hotel	£80,000	Wages	£3,000
Van	£50,000	Other Expenses	£4,500
Revenue	£17,000	Trade Receivables	£6,000
Purchases	£13,000	Trade Payables	£3,000
Bank	£20,000	Equity	£156,500

Figure 2.3 Armstrong's Trial Balance as at 30 March

	Debit £	Credit £
Hotel	80,000	
Van	50,000	
Revenue		17,000
Purchases	13,000	
Bank	20,000	
Wages	3,000	
Other Expenses	4,500	
Trade Receivables	6,000	
Trade Payables		3,000
Equity		156,500
	176,500	176,500

We can break these balances down in Figure 2.4 into the elements of the accounting equation.

Figure 2.4 Analysis of Armstrong's Trial Balance

Assets	Hotel, Van, Bank, Trade Receivables
Expenses	Purchases, Wages, Other Expenses
Income	Revenue
Liabilities	Trade Payables
Equity	Equity

From the trial balance, we can then prepare two main financial statements: the income statement (income and expenses) and the statement of financial position (assets, liabilities and equity). The next three chapters deal with these. In Chapter 3, we look at the income statement. Chapter 4 deals with the statement of financial position. And then, finally, the main financial statements (income statement and statement of financial position) are prepared from the trial balance.

We will now look at three summary financial statements for a business called Gavin Stevens. Gavin Stevens runs a hotel and summary details of his income, expenses, assets, liabilities and equity are given. At this stage, the financial statements for Gavin Stevens (see Figure 2.5) and for Simon Tudent (see Figure 2.6) are drawn up using only broad general headings. More detailed presentation is covered in later chapters.

Figure 2.5 Preparation of Summary Income Statement, Statement of Financial Position and Statement of Cash Flows for Gavin Stevens

Financial Information

Income	£8,930	Liabilities	£1,350
Expenses	£5,600	Opening equity	£200,000
Assets	£204,680	Closing equity	£203,330
Cash inflows	£204,465	Cash outflows	£117,550

(i) Income Statement (Profit and Loss Account)

Here we are concerned with determining profit by subtracting expenses from income. We call the profit, net profit.

	£
Income	8,930
Less: *Expenses*	5,600
Net Profit	3,330

(ii) Statement of Financial Position (Balance Sheet)

Here we deduct the assets from the liabilities to give net assets. This represents the owner's equity employed in the business.

	£
Assets	204,680
Liabilities	(1,350)
Net Assets	203,330

	£
Opening equity	200,000
Add: Profit	3,330
Closing equity	203,330

(iii) Statement of Cash Flows

	£
Cash Inflows	204,465
Cash Outflows	(117,550)
Net cash inflow	86,915

We have a positive cash flow. In other words, our cash has increased by £86,915 over the year. Note that in accounting when figures such as liabilities and cash outflows are subtracted it is common to use brackets if the word 'less' is not used.

Student Example

In order to give a further flavour of the nature of the main accounting terms, this section presents the income and expenditure of Simon Tudent. Simon is a student.

From S. Tudent's financial statements, it can thus be seen that the net deficit (£2,550) occurs twice: in the income statement and in the capital employed section of the statement of financial position. This figure thus provides a link between these two statements. The closing figure of the bank balance in the statement of cash flows also appears under current assets in

Figure 2.6 A Student's Financial Statements

Simon has collected the following details of his finances for his first year at university and possessions on 31 December. He has already divided them into income, expenses, assets and liabilities.

Income	£	*Assets*	£
Wages received from working in Student Union (38 weeks at £50 per week)	1,900	Second-hand car worth probably	700*
		Cash at bank at start of year	2,500*
Gift from grandparents	12,000	Computer worth about	150*
		CD player worth about	200*
Wages owing from Student Union (2 weeks at £50 per week – also an asset because he is owed it)	100	*All possessions at start of year.	

Expenses	£	*Liabilities*	£
University tuition fees	9,000	Owes parents £150 for loan	150
Hall of residence fees	3,000	Student loan from Government	9,000
Money spent on books	600	Maintenance loan	4,300
Money spent on entertainment	1,000		
Petrol used in car	500		
Phone calls	100		
Car repairs	1,000		
Car expenses	1,200		
General	150		

Note: Simon's opening equity is simply his opening assets less any opening liabilities. For simplicity, we assume that they are worth the same as at the start and as at the end of the year (except for cash at bank).

From the information shown above, we can present three financial statements, shown below and on the next page.

1. An income statement or profit and loss account (strictly, for a student we should call this an income and expenditure statement).
2. A statement of financial position or balance sheet (strictly, for a student we should call this an assets and liabilities statement).
3. A statement of cash flows or cash flow statement.

S. Tudent
Income Statement (profit and loss account) for the Year Ended 31 December

Income	£	£
Student Union wages (note: includes £100 owing)		2,000
Gift from grandparents		12,000
		14,000

Figure 2.6 A Student's Financial Statements (*continued*)

	£	£
Less Expenses		
University tuition fees	9,000	
Hall of residence fees	3,000	
Books	600	
Entertainment	1,000	
Petrol	500	
Phone calls	100	
Car repairs	1,000	
Car expenses	1,200	
General	150	16,550
Net Deficit		(2,550)

Note that this statement deals with all income and expenses earned and incurred, not just with cash paid and received. We deduct all the expenses from the income and ascertain that S. Tudent has a net deficit. In business, this would be called a net loss.

....

S. Tudent
Statement of Financial Position (Balance Sheet) as at 31 December

	£	£
Assets		
Cash at bank		
(balance from statement of cash flows)		13,300
Second-hand car		700
Computer		150
CD player		200
Owed by Student Union		100
Total Assets		14,450
Liabilities		
Parental Loan	(150)	
Government loans (9,000 + 4,300)	(13,300)	
Total Liabilities		(13,450)
Net Assets		1,000*
Capital Employed		£
Opening equity		3,550*
Net deficit		(2,550)
Closing equity		1,000*

Note: these two figures balance

*Opening possessions (£700 + £2,500 + £150 + £200)

We are simply listing the assets and liabilities. The assets less liabilities give net assets. This also equals equity, also known as capital employed. The opening equity is simply opening assets less opening liabilities. Note that opening equity less the net deficit gives closing equity. A student loan is a liability because it is owed to the government. It is not income. In this case, as with many students, the position for the year is that the student has a net deficit. However, this can be seen as a current sacrifice for future benefits. In fact, this student is lucky for without the grandparents' contribution his net position would be of net liabilities.

....

Figure 2.6 A Student's Financial Statements (*continued*)

S. Tudent
Statement of Cash Flows (Cash Flow Statement) Year ended 31 December

	£	£
Bank balance at start of year		2,500
Add Receipts:		
Maintenance loan	4,300	
Student loan	9,000	
Student Union	1,900	
Loan from parents	150	
Gift from grandparents	12,000	27,350
		29,850
Less Payments:		
Books	600	
Entertainment	1,000	
Petrol used	500	
Phone calls	100	
Car repairs	1,000	
Car expenses	1,200	
General	150	
Hall fees	3,000	
University fees	9,000	16,550
Bank balance at end of year (balancing figure)		13,300

Note that we are simply recording all cash received and paid. We were not given the closing bank figure. However, it must be £13,300: opening cash of £2,500 plus receipts of £27,350 gives £29,850 less £16,550 payments.

the statement of financial position. It should be noted that although most of the individual items of payments and expenses are the same in this example, normally they will not be – it is just that for simplification we have assumed that there are no amounts owing.

 PAUSE FOR THOUGHT 2.6

Student Loan

Students are often granted loans by the government. Why would a student loan from the government or a loan from one's parents be a liability, but a gift from parents be income?

PAUSE FOR THOUGHT 2.6 (*continued*)

This is because the loans must be repaid. They are, therefore, liabilities. When they are repaid, in part or in full, the liability is reduced. By contrast, a gift will be income as it does not have to be repaid.

Why Is Financial Accounting Important?

Financial accounting is a key control mechanism. All businesses prepare and use financial information in order to help them measure their performance. It is also useful in a business's relationship with third parties. It enables sole traders and partnerships to provide accounting information to the tax authorities or bank. For the limited company, it makes company directors accountable to company shareholders. For small businesses, the accounts are normally prepared by independent qualified accountants. In the case of large businesses, such as limited companies, the accounts are normally prepared by the managers and directors, but then audited by professional accountants. Auditing means checking the accounts are 'true and fair'. This term 'true and fair' is elusive and slippery. It is probably best considered to mean faithfully representing the underlying economic transactions of a business. The independent preparation and/or auditing of the financial accounts by accountants and auditors is an essential task in the protection of the users. The tax authorities need to ensure that the sole traders and partnership accounts have been properly prepared by an expert. Similarly, the shareholders need to have confidence that the managers have prepared a 'true and fair' account. For shareholders, this is particularly important as they are not usually directly involved in running the business. They provide the money, then stand back and allow the managers to run the company. So how can shareholders ensure that the managers are not abusing their trust? Bluntly, how can the shareholders make sure they are not being 'ripped off' by the managers? Auditing is one solution.

 ## PAUSE FOR THOUGHT 2.7

Directors' Self-Interest

How might the directors of a company serve their own interests rather than the interests of the shareholders?

Both directors and shareholders want to share in a business's success. Directors are rewarded by salaries and other rewards, such as company cars, profit-related bonuses or lucrative pensions. Shareholders are rewarded by receiving cash payments in the form of dividends or an increase in share price. The problem is that the more the directors take for themselves, the less there will be left for the shareholders. So if directors pay themselves large bonuses, the shareholders will get smaller dividends.

Accounting Principles

There are several accounting principles which underpin the preparation of the accounts. For convenience, we classify them here into accounting conventions and accounting concepts (see Figure 2.7). Essentially, conventions concern the whole accounting process, while concepts are assumptions which underpin the actual accounts preparation. There are four generally recognised accounting conventions and four generally recognised 'potential' accounting concepts.

Figure 2.7 Accounting Principles

Accounting Conventions	*Accounting Concepts*
• Entity	• Going concern
• Monetary measurement	• Matching (or accruals)
• Historic cost	• Consistency
• Periodicity	• Prudence (a disputed and controversial concept)

Accounting Conventions

Entity
The entity convention simply means that a business has a distinct and separate identity from its owners. This is fairly obvious in the case of a large limited company where shareholders own the company and managers manage the company. However, for a sole trader, such as a small baker's shop, it is important to realise that there is a theoretical distinction between personal and business assets. The business is treated as a separate entity from the owner. The business's assets less third-party liabilities represent the owner's equity or capital.

Monetary Measurement
Under this convention only items which can be measured in financial terms (for example, in pounds or dollars) are included in the accounts. If a company pollutes the atmosphere, this is not included in the accounts, since this pollution has no measurable financial value. However, a fine imposed for pollution is measurable and should be included in the accounts. A recent innovation in accounting is that a market in carbon emissions is emerging.

Historical Cost
Businesses may trade for many years. The historical cost convention basically states that the amount recorded in the accounts will be based on the *original* amount paid for a good or service. If, for example, we purchased a building for £1 million in 1970, that is the cost recorded, even though it might now be worth £10 million. Nowadays, in the UK, and under International Financial Reporting Standards (IFRS), there are frequent departures from historical cost. For example, many companies remeasure land and buildings to reflect their increase in value. Company Snapshot 2.4 shows that Tesco plc prepared its accounts using the historical cost convention. It also shows that it used fair value (which is effectively a market value) for some financial assets and liabilities.

COMPANY SNAPSHOT 2.4

Historical Cost Convention: Basis of Preparation of Financial Statements

The financial statements are presented in Pounds Sterling, generally rounded to the nearest million. They are prepared on the historical cost basis, except for certain financial instruments, share-based payments, customer loyalty programmes and pensions that have been measured at fair value.

Source: Tesco Plc, *Annual Report and Financial Statements 2010,* p. 10.

Periodicity

This simply means that accounts are prepared for a set period of time. Audited financial statements are usually prepared for a year. Financial statements prepared for internal management are often drawn up more frequently. This means, in effect, that sometimes rather arbitrary distinctions are made about the period in which accounting items are recorded.

Accounting Assumptions or Concepts

There are four generally recognised potential accounting concepts. The International Accounting Standards Board recognises two overriding underlying assumptions (going concern and accruals). The UK Companies Act, however, recognises in addition two extra assumptions: consistency and prudence. However, the IASB has severe reservations about prudence, which is the most contentious of the concepts.

Going Concern

This concept assumes the business will continue into the foreseeable future. Assets, liabilities, income and expenses are thus calculated on this basis. If you are valuing a specialised machine, for example, you will value the machine at a higher value if the business is ongoing than if it is about to go bankrupt. If it were bankrupt, the machine would only have scrap value. In Company Snapshot 2.5, we can see that J.D. Wetherspoon's directors have assured themselves that the company is a going concern.

COMPANY SNAPSHOT 2.5

Going Concern

The Directors have made enquiries into the adequacy of the Company's financial resources, through a review of the Company's budget and medium-term financial plan, including capital expenditure plans, cash flow forecasts; they have satisfied themselves that the Company will continue in operational existence for the foreseeable future. For this reason, they continue to adopt the going-concern basis in preparing the Company's financial statements.

Source: J.D. Wetherspoon plc, *Annual Report 2010,* p. 55.

Accruals

The accruals concept (often known as the matching concept) recognises income and expenses when they are accrued (i.e., earned or incurred) rather than when the money is received or paid. Income is matched with any associated expenses to determine the appropriate profit or loss. A telephone bill owing at the accounting year end is thus treated as an expense for this year even if it is paid in the next year. If the telephone bill is not received by the year end, then the amount of telephone calls will be estimated. Alternatively, if rent is paid in advance, it will be treated as a prepayment rather than an annual expense.

Consistency

This concept states that similar items will be treated similarly from year to year. Thus consistency attempts to stop companies choosing different accounting policies in different years. If they do this, then it becomes more difficult to compare the results of one year to the next.

Prudence

This is the most contentious of the four accounting concepts. Indeed, the IASB in the latest version of its Conceptual Framework in 2010 has replaced it completely. Prudence introduces an element of caution into accounting. Income and profits should only be recorded in the books when they are *certain* to result in an inflow of cash. By contrast, provisions or liabilities should be made *as soon as they are recognised*, even though their amount may not be known with certainty. Prudence is contentious because it introduces an asymmetry into the accounting process. Potential incomes are treated differently from potential liabilities. Some accountants believe that prudence is an out-of-date concept, while others feel that it is needed to stop management providing an over-optimistic view of the accounts. However, the IASB feels that prudence conflicts with a neutral view of accounts. It is, therefore, undesirable as it introduces bias into accounting.

PAUSE FOR THOUGHT 2.8

Personal Finances

Draw up a set of financial statements for yourself for the last twelve months.

I hope they are not too gruesome!

Conclusion

Financial accounting, along with management accounting, is one of the two main branches of accounting. Its main objective is to provide financial information to users for decision making. Some of the major elements of accounting are income, expenses, assets, liabilities and equity. The process of accounting consists of recording transactions using debits and credits. A trial balance is prepared and then from the trial balance an income statement and statement of financial position. Shareholders, for example, are provided with information to assess the stewardship of managers so that they can then make decisions such as whether to buy or sell their shares. Understanding the accounting language is a key requisite to understanding accounting itself. Four accounting conventions (entity, money measurement, historical cost and periodicity) and three accounting concepts (going concern, accruals and consistency) underpin financial accounting. In addition, many people believe prudence is an important accounting concept.

Discussion Questions

Questions with numbers in blue have answers at the back of the book.

Q1 What is financial accounting and why is its study important?

Q2 **Formal definitions**

The International Accounting Standards Board broadly sees the objective of **financial accounting** as the provision of **financial information about an organisation** that is useful to a range of users, such as existing and potential investors, lenders or creditors, when they are seeking to make decisions. The decisions may be, for example, buying or selling shares or giving loans.

Discuss the key aspects *highlighted in bold* of this definition of the objective of general purpose financial reporting based on that formulated by the IASB in its conceptual framework in 2010.

Q3 Sole traders, partnerships and limited companies all have different users who need financial information for different purposes. Discuss.

Q4 Classify the following as an income, an expense, an asset or a liability:
  (a) Friend owes business money
  (b) Football club's gate receipts
  (c) Petrol used by a car
  (d) Photocopier
  (e) Revenue or Sales
  (f) Telephone bill outstanding
  (g) Long-term loan
  (h) Cash
  (i) Wages
  (j) Equity or capital

Q5 Why is double-entry bookkeeping important?

Q6 State whether the following are true or false. If false, explain why.
  (a) Assets and liabilities show how much the business owns and owes.
  (b) The income statement shows the income, expenses and thus the net assets of a business.

(c) Stewardship is now recognised as the primary objective of financial accounting.
(d) When running a small business, the owner must be careful to separate business from private expenditure.
(e) The matching and prudence accounting concepts sometimes conflict.
(f) All accounting transactions are entered into the books of accounts using debits and credits.

 Numerical Questions

Questions with numbers in blue have answers at the back of the book.

Q1 Sharon Taylor has the following financial details:

Revenue	£8,000	Assets	£15,000
General expenses	£4,000	Liabilities	£3,000
Trading expenses	£3,000	Cash outflows	£12,000
Cash inflows	£10,000	Closing equity	£12,000
Opening equity	£11,000		

Required: Prepare Sharon Taylor's
(a) Income Statement (Profit and Loss Account)
(b) Statement of Financial Position (Balance Sheet)
(c) Statement of Cash Flows

Q2 Priya Patel is an overseas student studying at a British University. Priya has the following financial details:

	£		£
Tuition fees paid	16,840	Food paid	550
Hall of residence fees paid	8,000	General expenses paid	180
Money spent on books	160	Parental loan	5,000
Money spent on entertainment	500	during year	
		Gift from grandparents	15,000
Money earned from part-time job	4,800	*State of affairs at the start of the year:*	
Phone calls paid	100	Cash at bank	8,600
		Music system*	200

*Still worth £200 at end of year.

Required: Priya's:
(a) Income Statement (Profit and Loss Account)
(b) Statement of Financial Position (Balance Sheet)
(c) Statement of Cash Flows

Q3 From the following accounting figures show the six steps in the accounting equation:
opening assets £25,000, opening liabilities £25,000 (£15,000 third party and £10,000 equity), profit £15,000 (income £60,000, expenses £45,000).

Q4 Show the debit and credit accounts of the following transactions in the ledger and what effect (i.e., increase/decrease) they have on assets, liabilities, equity, income and expenses.
The first one is done as an illustration.
(a) Pay wages of £7,000
Debit effect   *Credit effect*
Wages: increases an expense   Bank: decreases an asset
(b) Introduces £10,000 equity by way of a cheque.
(c) Buys a car for £9,000 by cheque.
(d) Pays electricity bill of £300.
(e) Sales for £9,000 cash.
(f) Purchases £3,000 on credit from A. Taylor.

Appendix 2.1: Illustration of a Consolidated Income Statement for Marks & Spencer plc 2010

Consolidated income statement

	Notes	53 weeks ended 3 April 2010 £m	52 weeks ended 28 March 2009 £m
Revenue	2, 3	9,536.6	9,062.1
Operating profit	2, 3	852.0	870.7
Finance income	6	12.9	50.0
Finance costs	6	(162.2)	(214.5)
Profit on ordinary activities before taxation	4	702.7	706.2
Analysed between:			
Before property disposals and exceptional items		694.6	604.4
Profit on property disposals	2, 3	8.1	6.4
Exceptional costs	5	—	(135.9)
Exceptional pension credit	5, 11	—	231.3
Income tax expense	7	(179.7)	(199.4)
Profit for the year		523.0	506.8
Attributable to:			
Equity shareholders of the Company		526.3	508.0
Minority interests		(3.3)	(1.2)
		523.0	506.8
Basic earnings per share	8A	33.5p	32.3p
Diluted earnings per share	8B	33.2p	32.3p
Non-GAAP measure:			
Adjusted profit before taxation (£m)	1	694.6	604.4
Adjusted basic earnings per share	8A	33.0p	28.0p
Adjusted diluted earnings per share	8B	32.7p	28.0p

Appendix 2.1 Marks & Spencer Income Statement (*continued*)

Consolidated statement of comprehensive income

	53 weeks ended 3 April 2010 £m	52 weeks ended 28 March 2009 £m
Profit for the year	523.0	506.8
Other comprehensive income:		
Foreign currency translation differences	(17.4)	33.1
Actuarial losses on retirement benefit schemes	(251.6)	(927.1)
Deferred tax on retirement benefit scheme	71.7	254.9
Cash flow and net investment hedges		
– fair value movements in equity	52.1	304.8
– reclassified and reported in net profit	(119.8)	(206.8)
– amount recognised in inventories	4.8	(8.6)
Tax on cash flow hedges and fair hedges	25.9	(29.3)
Other comprehensive income for the year, net of tax	(234.3)	(579.0)
Total comprehensive income/(loss) for the year	288.7	(72.2)
Attributable to:		
Equity shareholders of the Company	292.0	(71.0)
Minority interests	(3.3)	(1.2)
	288.7	(72.2)

Source: Marks and Spencer plc, *Annual Report and Financial Statements 2010*, p. 78.

Appendix 2.2: Illustration of a Consolidated Statement of Financial Position for Marks and Spencer plc 2010

Consolidated statement of financial position

	Notes	As at 3 April 2010 £m	Restated as at 28 March 2009 £m
Assets			
Non-current assets			
Intangible assets	13	452.8	400.3
Property, plant and equipment	14	4,722.0	4,834.0
Investment property	15	22.4	24.8
Investment in joint ventures	16	11.5	13.8
Other financial assets	17	3.0	3.0
Trade and other receivables	18	287.7	336.8
Derivative financial instruments	22	132.9	254.0
Deferred tax assets	24	0.7	1.6
		5,633.0	5,868.3
Current assets			
Inventories		613.2	536.0
Other financial assets	17	171.7	53.1
Trade and other receivables	18	281.4	285.2
Derivative financial instruments	22	48.1	92.6
Cash and cash equivalents	19	405.8	422.9
		1,520.2	1,389.8
Total assets		7,153.2	7,258.1
Liabilities			
Current liabilities			
Trade and other payables	20	1,153.8	1,073.5
Borrowings and other financial liabilities	21	482.9	942.8
Partnership liability to the Marks & Spencer UK Pension Scheme	21	71.9	71.9
Derivative financial instruments	22	27.1	76.2
Provisions	23	25.6	63.6
Current tax liabilities		129.2	78.9
		1,890.5	2,306.9

Appendix 2.2 Marks and Spencer Statement of Financial Position (*continued*)

		£m	£m
Non-current liabilities			
Retirement benefit deficit	11	**366.5**	152.2
Trade and other payables	20	**280.3**	243.8
Borrowings and other financial liabilities	21	**2,278.0**	2,117.9
Partnership liability to the Marks & Spencer UK Pension Scheme	21	**—**	68.0
Derivative financial instruments	22	**—**	3.0
Provisions	23	**25.5**	40.2
Deferred tax liabilities	24	**126.5**	225.5
		3,076.8	2,850.6
Total liabilities		**4,967.3**	5,157.5
Net assets		**2,185.9**	2,100.6
Equity			
Called-up share capital – equity	25	**395.5**	394.4
Share premium account		**247.5**	236.2
Capital redemption reserve		**2,202.6**	2,202.6
Hedging reserve		**11.6**	62.6
Other reserve		**(5,970.5)**	(5,970.5)
Retained earnings		**5,281.9**	5,156.4
Total shareholders' equity		**2,168.6**	2,081.7
Minority interests in equity		**17.3**	18.9
Total equity		**2,185.9**	2,100.6

The financial statements were approved by the Board and authorised for issue on 24 May 2010. The financial statements also comprise the notes on pages 82 to 111.

Stuart Rose   **Ian Dyson**
Chairman   Group Finance and Operations Director

Source: Marks and Spencer plc, *Annual Report and Financial Statements 2010*, p. 79.

Appendix 2.3: Illustration of a Consolidated Statement of Cash Flows for Marks and Spencer plc 2010

Consolidated cash flow information

Illustration of Statement of cash flows
Marks and Spencer plc for 2010

	Notes	53 weeks ended 3 April 2010 £m	52 weeks ended 28 March 2009 £m
Consolidated statement of cash flows			
Cash flows from operating activities			
Cash generated from operations	28	**1,349.7**	1,371.9
Tax paid		**(120.7)**	(81.3)
Net cash inflow from operating activities		**1,229.0**	1,290.6
Cash flows from investing activities			
Acquisition of subsidiaries, net of cash acquired		**(5.4)**	—
Purchase of property, plant and equipment		**(352.0)**	(540.8)
Proceeds from sale of property, plant and equipment		**20.9**	58.3
Purchase of intangible assets		**(77.5)**	(121.6)
Purchase of non-current financial assets		**—**	(4.4)
Purchase of current financial assets		**(118.3)**	(1.1)
Interest received		**2.7**	12.7
Net cash outflow from investing activities		**(529.6)**	(596.9)
Cash flows from financing activities			
Interest paid		**(163.4)**	(197.1)
Cash inflow/(outflow) from borrowings		**30.7**	(25.8)
(Repayment)/drawdown of syndicated bank facility		**(529.4)**	108.1
Issue of medium-term notes		**397.2**	—
Redemption of medium-term notes		**(200.4)**	—
Payment of liability to the Marks & Spencer UK Pension Scheme		**(68.0)**	(15.1)
Decrease in obligations under finance leases		**(17.0)**	(1.0)
Equity dividends paid		**(236.0)**	(354.6)
Shares issued on exercise of employee share options		**12.4**	5.3
Shares purchased in buy back		**—**	(40.9)
Purchase of own shares by employee trust		**(19.0)**	—
Net cash outflow from financing activities		**(792.9)**	(521.1)

Appendix 2.3 Marks & Spencer Statement of Cash Flows (*continued*)

		£m	£m
Net cash (outflow)/inflow from activities		(93.5)	172.6
Effects of exchange rate changes		(2.1)	7.8
Opening net cash		298.3	117.9
Closing net cash	29	**202.7**	298.3

	Notes	53 weeks ended 3 April 2010 £m	52 weeks ended 28 March 2009 £m
Reconciliation of net cash flow to movement in net debt			
Opening net debt		**(2,490.8)**	**(3,077.7)**
Net cash (outflow)/inflow from activities		(93.5)	172.6
Increase in current financial assets		118.3	1.1
Decrease/(increase) in debt financing		386.9	(66.2)
Partnership liability to the Marks & Spencer UK Pension Scheme (non-cash)		—	539.6
Exchange and other non-cash movements		10.7	(60.2)
Movement in net debt		**422.4**	**586.9**
Closing net debt	29	**(2,068.4)**	**(2,490.8)**

Source: Marks and Spencer plc, *Annual Report and Financial Statements 2010*, p. 81.

Appendix 2.4: Illustration of a Consolidated Income Statement for Volkswagen 2009

Consolidated Financial Statements of the Volkswagen Group

Income Statement of the Volkswagen Group
for the Period January 1 to December 31, 2009

€ million	Note	2009	2008
Sales revenue	1	105,187	113,808
Cost of sales	2	−91,608	−96,612
Gross profit		13,579	17,196
Distribution expenses	3	−10,537	−10,552
Administrative expenses	4	−2,739	−2,742
Other operating income	5	7,904	8,770
Other operating expenses	6	−6,352	−6,339
Operating profit		1,855	6,333
Share of profits and losses of equity-accounted investments	7	701	910
Finance costs	8	−2,268	−1,815
Other financial result	9	972	1,180
Financial result		−595	275
Profit before tax		1,261	6,608
Income tax income/expense	10	−349	−1,920
current		−1,145	−2,338
deferred		796	418
Profit after tax		911	4,688
Minority interests		−49	−65
Profit attributable to shareholders of Volkswagen AG		960	4,753
Basic earnings per ordinary share in €	11	2.38	11.92
Basic earnings per preferred share in €	11	2.44	11.98
Diluted earnings per ordinary share in €	11	2.38	11.88
Diluted earnings per preferred share in €	11	2.44	11.94

Source: *Volkswagen Group Annual Report 2009*, p. 204. Copyright Volkswagen AG (Investor Relations).

Appendix 2.5: Illustration of a Consolidated Balance Sheet (Statement of Financial Position) for Volkswagen 2009

Balance Sheet of the Volkswagen Group as of December 31, 2009

€ million	Note	Dec. 31, 2009	Dec. 31, 2008
Assets			
Noncurrent assets			
Intangible assets	12	12,907	12,291
Property, plant and equipment	13	24,444	23,121
Leasing and rental assets	14	10,288	9,889
Investment property	14	216	150
Equity-accounted investments	15	10,385	6,373
Other equity investments	15	543	583
Financial services receivables	16	33,174	31,855
Other receivables and financial assets	17	3,747	3,387
Noncurrent tax receivables	18	685	763
Deferred tax assets	18	3,013	3,344
		99,402	91,756
Current assets			
Inventories	19	14,124	17,816
Trade receivables	20	5,692	5,969
Financial services receivables	16	27,403	27,035
Other receivables and financial assets	17	5,927	10,068
Current tax receivables	18	762	1,024
Marketable securities	21	3,330	3,770
Cash and cash equivalents	22	20,539	9,474
Assets held for sale	23	—	1,007
		77,776	76,163
Total assets		177,178	167,919
Equity and Liabilities			
Equity	24		
Subscribed capital		1,025	1,024
Capital reserves		5,356	5,351
Retained earnings		28,901	28,636
Equity attributable to shareholders of Volkswagen AG		35,281	35,011
Minority interests		2,149	2,377
		37,430	37,388

Appendix 2.5 Volkswagen Balance Sheet (*continued*)

Noncurrent liabilities			
Noncurrent financial liabilities	25	36,993	33,257
Other noncurrent liabilities	26	3,028	3,235
Deferred tax liabilities	27	2,224	3,654
Provisions for pensions	28	13,936	12,955
Provisions for taxes	27	3,946	3,555
Other noncurrent provisions	29	10,088	9,073
		70,215	65,729
Current liabilities			
Current financial liabilities	25	40,606	36,123
Trade payables	30	10,225	9,676
Current tax payables	27	73	59
Other current liabilities	26	8,237	8,545
Provisions for taxes	27	973	1,160
Other current provisions	29	9,420	8,473
Liabilities associated with assets held for sale	23	—	766
		69,534	64,802
Total equity and liabilities		177,178	167,919

Source: Volkswagen Group Annual Report 2009, p. 206. Copyright Volkswagen AG (Investor Relations).

Appendix 2.6: Illustration of a Consolidated Cash Flow Statement (Statement of Cash Flows) for Volkswagen 2009

Cash Flow Statement of the Volkswagen Group for the Period January 1 to December 31, 2009

€ million	2009	2008
Cash and cash equivalents at beginning of period (excluding time deposit investments)	**9,443**	**9,914**
Profit before tax	1,261	6,608
Income taxes paid	−529	−2,075
Depreciation and amortization of property, plant and equipment, intangible assets and investment property[1]	5,028	5,198
Amortization of capitalized development costs[1]	1,586	1,392
Impairment losses on equity investments[1]	16	32
Depreciation of leasing and rental assets[1]	2,247	1,816
Gain/loss on disposal of noncurrent assets	−547	37
Share of profit or loss of equity-accounted investments	−298	−219
Other noncash expense/income	727	765
Change in inventories	4,155	−3,056
Change in receivables (excluding financial services)	465	−1,333
Change in liabilities (excluding financial liabilities)	260	815
Change in provisions	1,660	509
Change in leasing and rental assets	−2,571	−2,734
Change in financial services receivables	−719	−5,053
Cash flows from operating activities	**12,741**	**2,702**
Investments in property, plant and equipment, intangible assets and investment property	−5,963	−6,896
Additions to capitalized development costs	−1,948	−2,216
Acquisition of equity investments	−3,989	−2,597
Disposal of equity investments	1,320	−1
Proceeds from disposal of property, plant and equipment, intangible assets and investment property	153	95
Change in investments in securities	989	2,041
Change in loans and time deposit investments	−236	−1,611

Appendix 2.6 Volkswagen Cash Flow Statement (*continued*)

Cash flows from investing activities	–9,675	–11,183
Capital contributions	4	218
Dividends paid	–874	–722
Capital transactions with minority interests	–392	–362
Other changes	23	–3
Proceeds from issue of bonds	15,593	7,671
Repayment of bonds	–10,202	–8,470
Change in other financial liabilities	1,405	9,806
Finance lease payments	–23	–15
Cash flows from financing activities	5,536	8,123
Effect of exchange rate changes on cash and cash equivalents	190	–113
Net change in cash and cash equivalents	8,792	–471
Cash and cash equivalents at end of period (excluding time deposit investments)	18,235	9,443
Cash and cash equivalents at end of period (excluding time deposit investments)	18,235	9,443
Securities and loans (including time deposit investments)	7,312	7,875
Gross liquidity	25,547	17,318
Total third-party borrowings	–77,599	–69,555
Net liquidity	–52,052	–52,237

[1] Net of impairment reversals.
[2] Prior-period amount adjusted.
Source: *Volkswagen Group Annual Report 2009*, p. 208. Copyright Volkswagen AG (Investor Relations).

Go online to discover the extra features for this chapter at
www.wiley.com/college/jones

Chapter 3

Main financial statements: The Income Statement (Profit and Loss Account)

'*Around here you're either expense or you're revenue.*'

Donna Vaillancourt, Inc. (March 1994) *The Wiley Book of Business Quotations* (1998), p. 90.

Learning Outcomes

After completing this chapter you should be able to:

- Explain the nature of the income statement.
- Understand the individual components of the income statement.
- Outline the layout of the income statement.
- Evaluate the nature and importance of profit.

Go online to discover the extra features for this chapter at
www.wiley.com/college/jones

Chapter Summary

- One of three main financial statements.
- Consists of revenue, cost of sales and other expenses.
- Cost of sales is essentially opening inventory plus purchases less closing inventory.
- Gross profit is revenue less cost of sales.
- Net profit is income less cost of sales less other expenses.
- Profit is determined by income earned less expenses incurred, not by cash received less cash paid.
- Profit is an elusive concept.
- Capital expenditure (i.e., on non-current assets such as motor vehicles) is treated differently to revenue expenditure (i.e., an expense such as telephone line rental).
- Profit is useful when evaluating an organisation's performance.

Introduction

The income statement (often known as profit and loss account, or sometimes as statement of comprehensive income in a listed company) is one of the three most important financial statements. Effectively, it records an organisation's income and expenses and is prepared from the trial balance. For UK companies, it is required by the Companies Act 2006. An income statement seeks to determine an organisation's profit (i.e., income less expenses) over a period of time. It is thus concerned with measuring an organisation's performance. Different organisations will have different income statements. Indeed, they also have slightly different names. In this chapter, we focus on understanding the purpose, nature, contents and layout of the income statement of the sole trader. The preparation of the income statement of the sole trader from the trial balance is covered in Chapter 5. In Chapter 6 we investigate the preparation of the income statements of partnerships and limited companies. In this chapter, I have used the term 'income statement', which is recommended by the International Accounting Standards Board. I prefer this to the term statement of comprehensive income, which is also international accounting terminology, as the latter includes items such as gains on foreign exchange, which is outside the scope of this book. Sometimes the term profit and loss account is used for sole traders, partnerships or non-listed companies. However, to avoid confusion I use the term 'income statement' for all those business enterprises.

Context

The income statement, along with the statement of financial position and statement of cash flows, is one of the three major financial statements. It is prepared from the trial balance and presents an organisation's income and expenses over a period of time. This period may vary. Many businesses prepare a monthly income statement for internal management purposes.

Annual accounts are prepared for external users like shareholders or the tax authorities. From now on we generally discuss a yearly income statement. By contrast, the statement of financial position presents an organisation's assets, liabilities and equity and is presented at a particular point in time. The statement of cash flows shows the cash inflows and outflows of a business.

SOUNDBITE 3.1

Profits

'You must deodorise profits and make people understand that profit is not something offensive, but as important to a company as breathing.'

Sir Peter Parker, quoted in the *Sunday Telegraph* (5 September 1976)

Source: The Book of Business Quotations (1991), p. 183.

The major parts of the income statement are:

$$\text{Income} - \text{Expenses} = \text{Profit}$$

As Soundbite 3.1 above shows, profits are central to evaluating an organisation's performance. The profit figure is extremely important as it is used for a variety of purposes. It is used as an overall measure of performance and for more specific purposes, such as the basis by which companies distribute dividends to shareholders or as a starting point for working out taxation payable to the government. An organisation's profit performance is closely followed by analysts and by the press. In Real-World View 3.1, for example, HSBC have produced record results.

REAL-WORLD VIEW 3.1

Profit Performance

HSBC Enters History Books with £10 Billion Profit
Banking group HSBC stepped into another row about profits yesterday when it announced the largest earnings in British corporate history, alongside bumper payouts for its top executives. The company said it made pre-tax profits of £10 billion last year – 35pc more than in 2003 and higher than the £9.3 billion profits declared by oil giant Shell last month.

Source: Andrew Cave, *Daily Telegraph*, 1 March 2005, p. 38.

Definitions

As Definition 3.1 indicates, an income statement represents the income less the expenses of an organisation. Essentially, income represents money earned by the organisation (for example, revenue or sales), while expenses represent the costs of generating these sales (for example, purchases) and of running the business (for example, telephone expenses). Definition 3.1 gives a working and a formal definition of an income statement and an official definition from the Chartered Institute of Management Accountants.

DEFINITION 3.1

Definition of an Income Statement (Profit and Loss Account)

Working definition
The statement detailing the income less the expenses of an organisation over a period of time, giving profit.

Formal definition
'A key financial statement which represents an organisation's income less its expenses over a period of time and thus determines its profit so as to give a 'true and fair' view of an organisation's financial affairs.'

Formal definition (CIMA (2005) *Official Terminology*)
'Financial statement including all the profits and losses recognised in a period, unless an accounting standard requires inclusion elsewhere.'

Source: Chartered Institute of Management Accountants (2000), *Official Terminology*. Reproduced by Permission of Elsevier.

Broadly, a working definition of income is the revenue and other gains earned by a business, while expenses are the costs incurred running a business. The International Accounting Standards Board formally defines income and expenses using the concept of an increase or a decrease in economic benefit (i.e., does it increase the wealth of the business). Incomes are thus increases in economic benefit (i.e., inflows or increases in assets or decreases in third-party liabilities) which increase owners' equity. Expenses are decreases in economic benefit (i.e., outflows or decreases in assets or increases in third-party liabilities) that decrease owners' equity. Working definitions are provided in Definition 3.2.

DEFINITION 3.2

Income

Working definition
Revenue and other gains earned by a business recorded in the income statement. In effect, these increase an organisation's assets or decrease its liabilities.

Expenses

Working definition
Costs incurred running a business recorded in the income statement. In effect, these decrease an organisation's assets or increase its liabilities.

PAUSE FOR THOUGHT 3.1

Limited Companies' Income Statement (Profit and Loss Account)

Why do you think limited companies produce only abbreviated figures for their shareholders?

The answer to this is twofold. First of all, many limited companies are large and complicated businesses. They need to simplify the financial information provided. Otherwise, the users of the accounts might suffer from information overload. Second, for public limited companies, there is the problem of confidentiality. Remember that a company is owned by shareholders. Anybody can buy shares. A competitor, for example, could buy shares in a company. Companies would not wish to give away all the details of their revenue and expenses to a potential competitor. Therefore, they summarise and limit the amount of information they provide. Limited companies, therefore, publicly provide abridged (or summarised) accounts rather than full ones using all the figures from the trial balance.

Layout

The income statement is nowadays conventionally presented in a vertical format (such as in Figure 3.1 below). Here we begin with revenue (sales) and then deduct the expenses. In the UK, the 2006 Companies Act sets out several possible formats, which are broadly followed. For sole traders or partnerships, a full income statement is sometimes prepared using all the figures from the trial balance. Often, however, the income statement is presented in summary form, with many individual revenues and expenses grouped together.

Figure 3.1 Sole Trader's Income Statement

	£	£
R. Beer		
Income Statement for the Year Ended 31 March 2014		
Revenue		100,425
Less *Cost of Sales*		
Opening inventory	3,590	
Add Purchases	58,210	
	61,800	
Less Closing inventory	2,200	59,600
Gross Profit		40,825
Add *Other Income*		
Gaming machine		2,000
		42,825
Less *Expenses*		
Wages	8,433	
Rates and water	3,072	
Insurance	397	
Electricity	2,714	
Telephone	292	
Advertising	172	
Motor expenses	530	
Darts team expenses	1,865	
Repairs and renewals	808	
Laundry	1,174	
Music and entertainment	3,095	
Licences	604	
Guard dog expenses	385	
Garden expenses	1,716	
Sundry expenses	1,648	
Accounting	800	
Depreciation	6,770	34,475
Net Profit		8,350

For companies presenting their results to the shareholders in the annual report, the exact relationship to the original trial balance is often unclear. Examples of Marks & Spencer plc and AstraZeneca plc income statements (profit and loss accounts) are given in Company Snapshots 2.1 (in Chapter 2) and 6.3 in Chapter 6 respectively.

By contrast the income statement (sometimes called the trading and profit and loss account) of the sole trader is more clearly derived from the trial balance. In this section we explain the theory behind this in more detail. In the following section the main terminology is explained. In order to be more realistic, we use the adapted income statement of a real person, a sole trader who runs a public house (pub). This is presented in Figure 3.1.

The corresponding statement of financial position (balance sheet) for R. Beer is presented in the next chapter in Figure 4.2. In Chapter 5, we show how to prepare an income statement from the trial balance.

Main Components

Figure 3.2 shows the six main components of the income statement (revenue or sales, cost of sales, gross profit, other income, expenses and net profit) of a sole trader.

These six components are shown in Figure 3.3. In the first column, an overview definition is provided. This is followed by some general examples and then, whenever possible, a specific example. These components are then discussed in more detail in the text. The same order is used as for R. Beer's income statement.

Revenue or Sales

Generating sales is a key ingredient of business success. However, the nature of sales varies considerably from organisation to organisation. For companies, the word 'revenue' or sometimes 'turnover' is used for sales. In this book, for consistency, we use the term revenue in the financial statements and sales more generally. In the Management Accounting section, we keep return on sales and sales variances rather than return on revenue and revenue variances as this is customary usage. We do, however, use contribution/revenue ratio as this seems more consistent. However, practice in this area is variable. Essentially, revenue is the income that an organisation generates from its operations. For example, Brook Brothers in Real-World View 3.2 sold clothes.

Figure 3.2 Overview of Income Statement

Revenue

Less

Cost of Sales

Equals

Gross Profit

Add

Other Income

Less

Other Expenses

Equals

Net Profit

Figure 3.3 Main Components of the Income Statement (Trading and Profit and Loss Account)

	Overview	*General Examples*	*Specific Examples*
Revenue (sales)	Income earned from selling goods (may be reduced by revenue returns, i.e., goods returned by customers)	Sales	e.g., Sales of beer, food
Cost of Sales	The costs directly incurred in selling goods	1. Opening inventory 2. Purchases (may be reduced by purchases returns, i.e., goods returned to supplier) 3. Closing inventory	e.g., Barrels of beer a pub has at start of year e.g., Purchases of beer e.g., Barrels of beer a pub has left at end of year
Gross Profit	Revenue less cost of sales	Measures gain of organisation from buying and selling	e.g., The direct profit a pub makes by reselling the beer
Other Income	Non-trading income which a firm has earned	1. Income from investments 2. Income from sale of property, plant and equipment	e.g., Interest received from deposit account at bank e.g., Profit on selling a car for more than it was recorded in the accounts
Expenses	Items indirectly incurred in selling the goods	1. Light and heat 2. Employees' pay	e.g., Electricity e.g., Wages and salaries
Net Profit	Sales less cost of sales less expenses	Measures gain of organisation from all business activities	e.g., The profit a pub makes after taking into account all the pub's expenses

REAL-WORLD VIEW 3.2

Revenue

In 1964 the lower Manhattan branch of Brook Brothers was robbed, and the thieves got away with clothes worth $200,000. One clerk remarked: 'If they had come during our sale two weeks ago, we could have saved 20 percent.'

Source: Peter Hay (1988), *The Book of Business Anecdotes*, Harrap Ltd, London, p. 100.

Sales may be made for credit or for cash. Credit sales create debtors, who owe the business money. A business reports the balance that these debtors owe as an asset called 'trade receivables'. Some businesses, such as supermarkets, have predominantly cash customers. By contrast, manufacturing businesses will have largely credit customers. A further distinction is

COMPANY SNAPSHOT 3.1

Stagecoach Plc

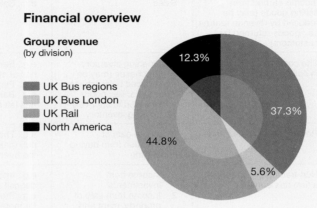

Financial overview

Group revenue
(by division)

- UK Bus regions
- UK Bus London
- UK Rail
- North America

12.3%

37.3%

5.6%

44.8%

Source: Stagecoach Group plc, *Annual Report and Financial Statements*, 2011.

between businesses that primarily sell goods (for example, supermarkets which supply food) and those which supply services (for example, a bank). Revenue is very diverse. In Company Snapshot 3.1, for example, Stagecoach Plc's revenue for 2011 is shown divided up into UK Bus and Rail, and North America.

In the modern world, both developed and developing countries have varied businesses with varied revenue. For example, banks can have interest earned, football clubs gate receipts, merchandising and television broadcasts. Companies like the UK's Independent Television (ITV) are dependent on advertising revenues. If revenues increase or decrease then this can affect their share price quite dramatically as is the case in Real-World View 3.3.

REAL-WORLD VIEW 3.3

Revenue and Share Price

ITV was yesterday's worst performer in the FTSE100 after it said advertising revenues could fall by as much as 20pc in June. Adam Crozier, ITV's chief executive, said advertising revenues plunged by 9pc in May and predicted a fall of between 15pc and 20pc in June, blaming 'continued economic uncertainty' and tough comparatives with last year's World Cup.

Source: Amanda Andrews, ITV June ad sales may fall by 20pc, *Daily Telegraph*, 12 May 2011, p. 33.

Figure 3.4 Selected Industrial Sectors for 2010

Sector	Example of Revenue	Credit/cash	Goods/services
Agriculture, forestry and fishing	Farm produce	Credit	Goods
Manufacturing	Manufactured goods	Credit	Goods
Construction	Buildings	Credit	Goods
Motor trade	New cars or car repairs	Cash and credit	Goods
Wholesale*	Food wholesaler*	Credit	Goods
Retail	Supermarket	Cash and credit card	Goods
Hotels and catering	Hotels	Cash and credit card	Services
Transport and storage	Taxi fares	Cash	Services
Finance and income	Interest earned	Not applicable	Services
Property and business services	Rents	Cash and credit	Services

*Wholesale businesses act as middlemen between manufacturers and customers. They buy from manufacturers and sell on to retailers

Source: Office for National Statistics licensed under the Open Government Licence v.1.0.

Revenue recognition is a topic that has concerned accountants for generations. In many cases, it is not straightforward to determine the exact timing or nature of a sale. An illustration of this is when should a sale be recognised on a leasing contract? There are many similar examples which accountants continue to wrestle with.

The great variety of revenue is indicated in Figure 3.4 which provides an overview of the different types of revenue. This figure is for guidance only. The division between credit and cash is, in particular, very rough and ready.

Revenue is reduced by sales returns. These are simply goods which are returned by customers, usually because they are faulty or damaged.

Cost of Sales

Cost of sales is essentially the expense of directly providing the goods for sale. Cost of sales is normally primarily found in businesses which buy and sell goods rather than those which provide services. The main component of cost of sales is purchases. However, purchases are adjusted for other items such as purchases returns (goods returned to suppliers), carriage inwards (i.e., the cost of delivering the goods from the supplier), and, of particular importance, inventory. Company Snapshot 3.2 shows the cost of sales for J. Sainsbury plc.

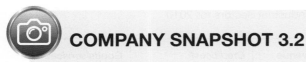

COMPANY SNAPSHOT 3.2

Cost of Sales

Cost of sales consists of all costs to the point of sale including warehouse and transportation costs and all the costs of operating retail outlets.

Supplier incentives, rebates and discounts are recognised within cost of sales based on the expected entitlement at the balance sheet date. The accrued value at the reporting date is included in prepayments and accrued income.

Source: J. Sainsbury plc, *Annual Report and Financial Statements 2010*, p. 53. Reproduced by kind permission of Sainsbury's Supermarkets Ltd.

In businesses that manufacture products, rather than buy and sell goods, the cost of revenue is more complicated. It will contain, for example, those costs which can be directly related to manufacturing. Figure 3.5 presents a detailed example of cost of sales.

Figure 3.5 Cost of Sales

John Green, a retailer, runs a small business. He has the following details of a week's trading: Opening inventory £2,000, carriage inwards £100, purchases £9,000, purchases returns £300, closing inventory £3,800.
(i) What is his cost of sales? (ii) Why do we adjust for inventory?

	£	£
Cost of Sales:		
Opening inventory		2,000
Add Purchases	9,000	
Less Purchases returns	300	
	8,700	
Add Carriage inwards	100	8,800
		10,800
Less Closing inventory		3,800
Cost of Sales		7,000

i.   Cost of sales is thus £7,000. Note that we have adjusted (i) for goods returned to the supplier £300, (ii) for carriage inwards which is the cost of delivering the goods from the supplier (i.e., like 'postage' on goods), and (iii) for closing inventory.

ii. We need to match the revenue with the actual costs directly incurred in generating them. Essentially, opening inventory represents purchases made last period, but not used. They were not, therefore, directly involved in generating last period's revenue. Similarly, closing inventory represents this year's purchases which have not been used. They will, therefore, be used to generate the next period's, rather than this period's, revenue.

Helpnote: When presenting cost of sales we subtract purchases returns and closing inventory. We indicate this using the word 'less'. As a result, we do not put these figures in brackets.

Gross Profit

Gross profit is simply revenue (sales) less cost of sales. It is a good measure of how much an organisation makes for every £1 of goods sold. In other words, the mark-up an organisation is making. Mark-ups and margins are discussed in Pause for Thought 3.2.

 PAUSE FOR THOUGHT 3.2

Gross Profit

A business operates on a mark-up of 50% on cost of sales. If its cost of sales was £60,000, how much would you expect gross profit to be?

	Mark-up		Gross margin
	%	£	%
Revenue	150	90,000	100
Cost of sales	100	60,000	67
Gross profit	50	30,000	33

Alternatively, a business might talk in terms of gross margin. This is a percentage of revenue **not** of cost of sales. As we can see above, both mark-up and gross margin are different ways of expressing the same thing.

Businesses watch their cost of sales and their gross profit margins very closely. Gross profit is determined by taking cost of sales from revenue (this section of the income statement is sometimes called the trading account).

Other Income

This is basically income from activities other than trading. So it might be interest from money in a bank or building society (interest received). Or it might be dividends received from an investment or profit on the sale of a particular item of plant, property and equipment. In the case of the R. Beer example it was income gained from the profit made when selling the gaming machine. Sometimes organisations report operating profits. Operating profit is concerned with trading activities (e.g., revenue, purchases and expenses). Other income would be excluded.

Expenses

Expenses are many and varied. They are simply the costs incurred in meeting revenue. Some companies itemise their expenses in their accounts. For example, British Airways in 2009 list

PAUSE FOR THOUGHT 3.3

Trading Account

In the accounts of sole traders, the income statement is often presented using a fully una-bridged format. The income statement is sometimes called the trading, profit and loss account.

This begs the question:

What actually is the trading account and why is it so called?

The trading account is the initial part of the sole trader's income statement (or trading and profit and loss account). In other words, revenue less cost of sales. As we can see below, it deals with the revenue and purchases of goods and gives gross profit.

	£	£	£
Revenue			100,000
Less Revenue returns			10,000
			90,000
Less *Cost of Sales*			
Opening inventory		8,000	
Add Purchases	50,000		
Less Purchases returns	4,000	46,000	
		54,000	
Less Closing inventory		2,000	52,000
Gross Profit			38,000

It is termed a trading account because it gives details of an organisation's direct trading income (i.e., buying and selling goods) rather than non-trading income (e.g., bank interest) or expenses. Nowadays, because of the growth of businesses which have little inventory (e.g., service companies), the trading account is becoming less important.

their main expenses in their income statement (see Company Snapshot 3.3). Some common expenses are listed below.

- Accountants' fees
- Advertising
- Insurance
- Light and heat
- Petrol consumed

- Sales commission
- Business rates
- Rent paid
- Repairs and renewals
- Telephone bill

COMPANY SNAPSHOT 3.3

Expenses

Employee costs (£ million)	2,166	2,277
Depreciation, amortisation and impairment	692	714
Aircraft operating lease costs	68	81
Fuel and oil costs	2,055	1,931
Engineering and other aircraft costs	451	414
Landing fees and en route charges	528	517
Handling charges, catering and other operating costs	977	930
Selling costs	359	436
Currency differences	6	18
Accommodation, ground equipment and IT costs	576	618
Total expenditure on operations before non-recurring items	7,878	7,936

Source: British Airways Annual Report 2007/8, p. 78. Reproduced by Permission.

Most expenses *are* a result of a cash payment (e.g., rent paid) or *will* result in a cash payment (e.g., rent owing). However, depreciation is a non-cash payment. It represents the expense of using property, plant and equipment, such as motor vehicles, which wear out over time. The topic of depreciation is dealt with in more detail in Chapter 4.

Net Profit

Net profit is simply the amount left over after costs of sales and expenses have been deducted from revenue. It is a key method of measuring a business's performance. It is often expressed as a percentage of revenue, giving a net profit to revenue ratio.

Profit

The concept of profit seems a simple one, at first. Take a barrow boy, Jim, selling fruit and vegetables from his barrow in Manchester. If he buys £50 of fruit and vegetables in the morning and by the evening has sold all his goods for £70, Jim has made a profit of £20. However, in practice profit measurement is much more complicated and often elusive. Although there is a set of rules which guide the determination of income and expenses, there are also many assumptions which underpin the calculation of profit. The main factors which complicate matters are:

- the accruals or matching concept
- estimation
- changing prices
- the wearing out of assets

Soundbite 3.2 shows that profit, and profit generation, is central to any successful business.

SOUNDBITE 3.2

Successful Profit Generation

'Mining companies with strong balance sheets invariably turn to acquisitions and BHP, after the rebound in commodity prices in 2009, has an embarrassment of riches. The company has little debt and was generating profits at a rate of £20m a day in its last reporting period.'

Source: Nils Pratley, Viewpoint, *The Guardian*, 18 August 2012, p. 25.

Accruals or Matching Concept

It is essential to appreciate that the whole purpose of the income statement is to match income earned and expenses incurred. This is the accruals or matching concept which we saw in Chapter 2. Income earned and expenses incurred are not the same as cash paid and cash received. We have already seen that depreciation is a non-cash item. However, it is also important to realise that for many other income and expense items the cash received and paid during the year are not the same as income earned and expenses incurred. When we are attempting to arrive at income earned and expenses incurred, we have to estimate certain items such as amounts owing (known as accruals). We also need to adjust for items paid this year which will, in fact, be incurred next year (for example, rent paid in advance).

Estimating

Accounting is often about estimation. This is because we often have uncertain information. For example, we may estimate the outstanding telephone bill or the value of closing inventory.

Changing Prices

If the price of a non-current asset (such as property, plant and equipment) rises then we have a gain from holding that asset. Indeed, property is often revalued. Is this gain profit? Well yes, in the sense that the organisation has gained. But no, in that it is not a profit from trading. This whole area is clouded with uncertainty. There are different views. Normally such property, plant and equipment gains are only included in the accounts when the plant, property and equipment are sold.

Wearing Out of Assets

Assets wear out and this is accounted for by the concept of depreciation. However, calculating depreciation involves a lot of assumptions; for example, length of asset life. Profit is thus contingent upon many adjustments, assumptions and estimates. All in all, therefore, the determination of profit is more an art than a science.

It is true to say that different accountants will calculate different profits. And they might all be correct! It is, however, also true that despite the assumptions needed to arrive at profits, profits are a key determinant by which businesses of all sorts are judged. Real-World View 3.4, for example, shows the profits of leading UK football clubs in 2008.

REAL-WORLD VIEW 3.4

Football Clubs' Profits

Top 20 Premier League Clubs' Financial Information 2008

Club	Revenue £'000	Operating profit/(loss) before player trading £'000	Net funds/ (debt) £'000
Arsenal	209,294	48,473	(318,073)
Aston Villa	75,639	4,821	(72,261)
Birmingham City	49,836	12,829	2,414
Blackburn Rovers	56,395	6,567	(16,918)
Bolton Wanderers	59,072	(5,002)	(53,542)
Chelsea	213,648	(30,878)	(710,562)
Derby County	48,558	12,328	(21,811)
Everton	75,650	6,809	(36,752)
Fulham	53,670	(1,979)	(192,823)
Liverpool	164,222	28,350	(299,838)
Manchester City	82,295	(1,598)	(137,532)
Manchester United	257,116	71,758	(649,429)
Middlesbrough	47,952	(1,826)	(93,842)
Newcastle United	100,866	(11,692)	(245,053)
Portsmouth	71,556	(6,323)	(50,106)
Reading	58,023	12,529	(42,313)
Sunderland	63,597	11,142	(71,231)
Tottenham Hotspur	114,788	27,461	(29,702)
West Ham United	n/a	n/a	n/a
Wigan Athletic	43,455	(2,805)	(66,412)
Totals	**1,845,632**	**180,964**	**(3,105,786)**

Source: Deloitte *Annual Review of Football Finance* (2009).

Sometimes, an asset will have lost more value than is accounted for via depreciation. In this case, the value of the asset may be written down. This is called impairment.

Listed Companies

Listed companies in Europe follow International Financial Reporting Standards (IFRS) for their group accounts. Under IFRS, companies should present an income statement (sometimes called the Statement of Comprehensive Income). Under IFRS, sales are conventionally termed revenue. The listed company is covered in depth in Chapter 6.

Capital and Revenue Expenditure

One example of the many decisions which an accountant must make is the distinction between capital and revenue expenditure. Capital expenditure is usually associated with items in the statement of financial position, such as property, plant and equipment; in other words, assets which may last for more than one year (e.g., land and buildings, plant and machinery, motor vehicles, and fixtures and fittings). By contrast, revenue expenditure is usually associated with income statement items such as telephone, light and heat or purchases. This appears simple, but sometimes it is not. For example, to a student, is this book a capital or a revenue expenditure? Well, it has elements of both. A capital expenditure in that you may keep it for reference. A revenue expenditure in that its main use will probably be over a relatively short period of time. So we can choose! Often when there is uncertainty, small-value items are charged to the profit and loss account. Interestingly, the WorldCom accounting scandal involved WorldCom incorrectly treating £2.5 billion of revenue expenditure as capital expenditure. This had the effect of increasing profit by £2.5 billion.

DEFINITION 3.3

Capital and Revenue Expenditure

Capital expenditure
A payment to purchase an asset with a continuing use in the business such as an item of property, plant and equipment.

Revenue expenditure
A payment for a current year's good or services such as purchases for resale or telephone expenses.

Limitations

So does the income statement provide a realistic view of the performance of the company over the year, especially of profit? The answer is, maybe! The income statement does list income and expenses and thus arrives at profit. However, there are many estimates, which means that the profit figure is inherently subjective. At the end of a year, for example, there is a need to estimate the amount of phone calls made. This brings subjectivity into the estimation of profit. Another example is that the loss in value of property, plant and equipment is not accurately measured. Similarly, the valuation of inventory is very subjective. It should be noted that given the wealth of detail in companies' accounts, the figures presented are generally summarised.

Interpretation

The income statement, despite its limitations, is often used for performance comparisons between companies and for the same company over time. These performance comparisons can then be used as the basis for investment decisions. Profitability ratios are often used to assess a company's performance over time or relative to other companies (for example, profit is often measured against revenue or capital employed). Ratios are more fully explained in Chapter 8.

Conclusion

The income statement presents an organisation's income and expenses over a period. It allows the determination of both gross and net profit. In many ways, making a profit is the key to business success (as Soundbite 3.3 shows). Gross profit is essentially an organisation's profit from trading. Net profit represents profit after all expenses have been taken into account. It is important to realise that the income statement is concerned with matching revenues earned with expenses incurred. It is not, therefore, a record of cash paid less cash received. Profit is not a precise absolute figure: it depends on many estimates and assumptions. However, despite its subjectivity, profit forms a key element in the performance evaluation of an organisation.

SOUNDBITE 3.3

Profits

'Nobody ever got poor taking a profit.'

Cary Reich, *Financier: André Meyer*, p. 119

Source: The Executive's Book of Quotations (1994), p. 233.

Discussion Questions

Questions with numbers in blue have answers at the back of the book.

Q1 Why is the income statement such an important and useful financial statement to such a variety of users?

Q2 'There is not just one profit, there are hundreds of profits.' Do you agree with this statement, taking into account the subjectivity inherent in calculating profit?

Q3 The matching principle is essential to the calculation of accounting profit. Discuss.

Q4 Over time, with the decline of the manufacturing company and rise of the service company, inventory, cost of sales and gross profit are becoming less important. Discuss.

Q5 State which of the following statements is true and which false? If false, explain why.
(a) Profit is income earned less expenses paid.
(b) Revenue less cost of sales less expenses will give net profit.
(c) Revenue returns are returns by suppliers.
(d) If closing inventory increases so will gross profit.
(e) The purchase of an item of property, plant or equipment is known as a capital expenditure.

Numerical Questions

Questions with numbers in blue have answers at the back of the book.

Q1 Joan Smith has the following details from her accounts year ended 31 December 2013.

Revenue	£100,000	Purchases	£60,000	General expenses	£10,000
Opening Inventory	£10,000	Closing Inventory	£5,000	Other expenses	£8,000

Required: Draw up Joan Smith's income statement (trading and profit and loss account) for the year ended 31 December 2013.

Q2 Dale Reynolds has the following details from his accounts for the year ended 31 December 2013.

	£		£
Opening inventory	5,000	Closing inventory	8,000
Purchases	25,000	Purchases returns	2,000
Revenue	50,000	Revenue returns	1,000
Carriage inwards	1,000		

Required: Draw up Dale Reynolds' trading account for the year ended 31 December 2013.

Q3 Mary Scott has the following details for the year to 31 December 2013.

	£		£
Revenue	200,000	Income from investments	3,000
Opening inventory	5,000	Wages	4,000
Purchases	100,000	Insurance	2,500
Closing inventory	3,000	Electricity	3,500
Advertising	3,500	Telephone	4,000
Motor expenses	1,500	Purchases returns	1,000
Repairs	800	Revenue returns	2,000
Sundry expenses	2,400		

Required: Draw up Mary Scott's income statement (trading and profit and loss account) for the year ended 31 December 2013.

Q4 Given the following different scenarios, calculate revenue, gross profit and cost of sales from the information available.
(a) Revenue £100,000, gross margin 25%.
(b) Revenue £200,000, mark-up 30%.
(c) Cost of sales £50,000, gross margin 25%.
(d) Cost of sales £40,000, mark-up 20%.

Go online to discover the extra features for this chapter at
www.wiley.com/college/jones

Chapter 4

Main financial statements: The statement of financial position (balance sheet)

'Creative accounting practices gave rise to the quip: "A balance sheet is very much like a bikini bathing suit. What it reveals is interesting, what it conceals is vital."'

Abraham Briloff, *Unaccountable Accounting*, Harper & Row (1972). *The Wiley Book of Business Quotations* (1998), p. 351.

Statements of Financial Position are like icebergs. What they reveal is important, but what they conceal can be essential.

They reveal the assets, liabilities and therefore the equity.

Unfortunately the assets and liabilities are often outdated, understated and incomplete.

©MMI Mike Jones

Learning Outcomes

After completing this chapter you should be able to:

- Explain the nature of a statement of financial position.
- Understand the individual components of a statement of financial position.
- Outline the layout of a statement of financial position.
- Evaluate the usefulness of a statement of financial position.

Go online to discover the extra features for this chapter at
www.wiley.com/college/jones

Chapter Summary

- One of three main financial statements.
- Consists of assets, liabilities and equity.
- Assets are most often non-current (e.g., property, plant and equipment such as land and buildings, plant and machinery, motor vehicles, and fixtures and fittings) or current (e.g., inventory, trade receivables, cash).
- Liabilities can be current (e.g., trade payables, short-term loans) or non-current (e.g., long-term loans).
- Current assets less current liabilities represents a company's net current assets or working capital.
- Listed companies have a special terminology and presentational format for the statement of financial position.
- A sole trader's equity is opening equity plus profit for the period less drawings.
- In modern statements of financial position, a vertical format is most popular.
- A statement of financial position's usefulness is limited by missing assets and inconsistent valuation.
- Different business organisations will have differently structured statements of financial position (e.g., sole traders and limited companies).
- Statements of financial position are used as a basis for determining liquidity.

Introduction

The statement of financial position, along with the income statement and statement of cash flows, is one of the most important financial statements. However, it is only in the last century that the income statement or profit and loss account gained in importance. Before then, the statement of financial position ruled supreme. There is great debate on whether you should give pre-eminence to the statement of financial position so that the income statement becomes the secondary statement or vice versa. The statement of financial position is prepared from an organisation's trial balance. It consists of assets, liabilities and equity. For UK companies, it is required by the Companies Act 2006. The statement of financial position seeks to measure an organisation's net assets at a particular point in time. It developed out of concepts of stewardship and accountability. Although useful for assessing liquidity, statements of financial position do not actually represent an organisation's market value. In this chapter, the primary focus will be on understanding the purpose, nature and contents of the statement of financial position. The preparation of the statement of financial position of sole traders, partnerships and limited companies from the trial balance is covered in depth in Chapters 5 and 6, respectively. For listed companies, a different terminology and presentation is adopted. This is mentioned in this chapter, but dealt with in more depth in Chapter 6.

Context

The statement of financial position is one of the key financial statements. It is prepared from the trial balance at a particular point in time, which can be any time during the year. The statement of financial position is usually prepared for shareholders at either 31 December or 31 March. The statement of financial position has three main elements: assets, liabilities and equity. Essentially, the assets less the third-party liabilities (i.e., net assets) equal the owner's equity. Thus,

$$\boxed{\text{Assets} - \text{Liabilities} = \text{Equity}}$$

Alternatively:

$$\boxed{\text{Assets} = \text{Liabilities} + \text{Equity}}$$

The statement of financial position and income statement are complementary (see Figure 4.1). The income statement shows an organisation's performance over the accounting period, normally a year. It is thus concerned with income, expenses and profit. A statement of financial position, by contrast, is a snapshot of a business at a particular point in time. It thus focuses on assets, liabilities and equity.

As Soundbite 4.1 shows, the statement of financial position provides basic information which helps users to judge the value of a company.

SOUNDBITE 4.1

Statement of Financial Position

'The market is mostly a matter of psychology and emotion, and all that you find in the statement of financial position [balance sheets] is what you read into them; we've all guessed to one extent or another, and when we guess wrong they say we're crooks.'

Major L.L.B. Angas, *Stealing the Market*, p. 15

Source: The Executive's Book of Quotations (1994), p. 179.

Figure 4.1 Comparison of Income Statement and Statement of Financial Position

	Income Statement (Profit and Loss Account)	Statement of Financial Position (Balance Sheet)
Preparation source	Trial balance	Trial balance
Main elements	Income, expenses, profit	Assets, liabilities, equity
Period covered	Usually a year	A point in time
Main focus	Profitability	Net assets

Definitions

As Definition 4.1 shows, a statement of financial position is essentially a collection of the assets, liabilities and equity of an organisation at a point in time. It is prepared so as to provide a true and fair view of the organisation.

DEFINITION 4.1

Statement of Financial Position (Balance Sheet)

Working definition
A collection of the assets, liabilities and equity of an organisation at a particular point in time.

Formal definition
'Statement of the financial position of an entity at a given date disclosing the assets, liabilities and accumulated funds (such as shareholders' contributions and reserves) prepared to give a true and fair view of the financial state of the entity at that date.'

Source: Chartered Institute of Management Accountants (2005), *Official Terminology.* Reproduced by Permission of Elsevier.

PAUSE FOR THOUGHT 4.1

Net Assets

If the assets were £20,000 and the liabilities to third parties were £10,000, what would (a) net assets and (b) equity be?

The answer would be £10,000 for both. This is because net assets equals assets less liabilities and equity equals net assets.

Broadly, assets are the things an organisation owns or leases; liabilities are things it owes. Assets can bring economic benefits by either being sold (for example, inventory) or being used (for example, a car). Equity (sometimes known as ownership interest) is accumulated wealth. Equity is effectively a liability of the business because it is 'owed' to the owner: standard setters more formally define assets in terms of rights to future economic benefits and liabilities as obligations. Equity (ownership interest) is what is left over. In other words, assets less third-party liabilities equal owner's equity. By formally defining assets and liabilities, the statement of financial position tends to drive the income statement. In the statement of financial position, as we will see in Figure 4.2, an individual's closing equity is represented by opening equity plus net profit less drawings (i.e., money taken out of a business by the owner). In Definition 4.2 we present the working definitions of assets, third-party liabilities and equity (ownership interest). The IASB sees both assets and liabilities as arising from past events which will lead to future economic benefits or future obligations respectively.

DEFINITION 4.2

Assets

Working definition
Items owned or leased by a business from which future economic benefits are expected to arise.

Liabilities

Working definition
Items owed by a business which are expected to lead to future payments.

Equity (Capital or Ownership Interest)

Working definition
The funds (assets less liabilities) belonging to the owner(s).

Layout

Traditionally, the statement of financial position was always arranged with the assets on the right-hand side of the page and the liabilities on the left-hand side of the page. However, more recently, the vertical format has become most popular. For UK companies, the use of the vertical format was set out by the 1985 Companies Act. Examples of Marks & Spencer plc's and AstraZeneca plc's statements of financial position are given in Company Snapshots 2.2 (in Chapter 2) and 6.4 (in Chapter 6), respectively. However, many other organisations which are not companies now commonly use the vertical format. This sets out the assets and liabilities at the top. The equity employed is then put at the bottom. This modern format is the one which this book will use from now on. However, Appendix 4.1 (at the end of this chapter) gives an example of the traditional 'horizontal' format which readers may occasionally encounter.

In order to be more realistic, we continue to use the adapted statement of financial position of a real person, a sole trader, R. Beer, who runs a public house. This is given in Figure 4.2. In Chapter 5, we show the mechanics of the preparation of the statement of financial position from the trial balance. The purpose of this section is to explain the theory behind the presentation.

Figure 4.2 Sole Trader's Statement of Financial Position

R. Beer	
Statement of Financial Position as at 31 March 2014	
ASSETS	
Non-Current Assets	
Property, Plant and Equipment	£
Land and buildings	71,572
Plant and machinery	3,500
Furniture and fittings	5,834
Motor car	3,398
Total non-current assets	84,304
Current Assets	
Inventory	2,200
Trade receivables	100
Prepayments	50
Bank	3,738
Cash	340
Total current assets	6,428
Total Assets	90,732
LIABILITIES	
Current Liabilities	
Trade payables	(3,900)
Accruals	(91)
Short-term loans	(1,000)
Total current liabilities	(4,991)
Non-current Liabilities	(6,500)
Total Liabilities	(11,491)
Net Assets	79,241
EQUITY	£
Opening equity	80,257
Add Net profit	8,350
	88,607
Less Drawings	9,366
Closing equity	79,241

Main Components

Figure 4.3 lists the main components commonly found in the statement of financial position of a sole trader. It provides some general examples and, wherever possible, a specific example. The main components of the statement of financial position are then discussed in the text. The same order is used as for R. Beer's statement of financial position.

Figure 4.3 Main Components of the Statement of Financial Position

	Overview	General Examples	Specific Examples
Non-current Assets (Property, plant and equipment)	Assets used to run the business long-term	1. Land and buildings 2. Plant and machinery 3. Fixtures and fittings 4. Motor vehicles	Public house, factory Lathe Computer, photocopier Car, van
Current Assets (i.e., short-term assets) (i) Inventories	Goods purchased and awaiting use or produced awaiting sale	1. Finished goods 2. Work in progress 3. Raw materials	Tables manufactured and awaiting sale Half-made tables Raw wood awaiting manufacture
(ii) Trade Receivables	Amounts owed to company	Trade receivables	Customers who have received goods, but not yet paid
(iii) Prepayments	Amounts paid in advance	Prepayments for services	Insurance prepaid
(iv) Cash and bank	Physical cash Money deposited on short-term basis with a bank	Cash in till Cash and bank deposits	Petty cash Current account in credit
Current Liabilities (i.e., amounts falling due within one year) (i) Trade Payables	Money owed to suppliers	Trade payables	Amounts owing for raw materials
(ii) Accruals	Amounts owed to the suppliers of services	Accruals for services	Amounts owing for electricity or telephone
(iii) Loans	Amounts borrowed from third parties and repayable within a year	Short-term loans from financial institutions	Bank loan
Non-current liabilities	Amounts borrowed from third parties and repayable after a year	Long-term loans from financial institutions	Loan secured, for example, on business property
Equity (Owner's Capital Employed)	Originally, the money the sole trader introduced into the business. Normally represents the net assets (i.e., assets less liabilities)	The equity at the start of the year and equity at the end of the year are generally known as opening and closing equity	The opening and closing equity represent the opening and closing net assets
(i) Profit	The profit earned during the year	Taken from the income statement, represents income less expenses	Net profit for year
(ii) Drawings	Money taken out of the business by the owner. A reduction of owner's equity	Living expenses	Owner's salary or wages

Finally, in Figure 4.6 on page 98, we summarise the major valuation methods used for the main assets. An overview of the structure of the statement of financial position is shown in Figure 4.4.

Figure 4.4 Overview of a Statement of Financial Position

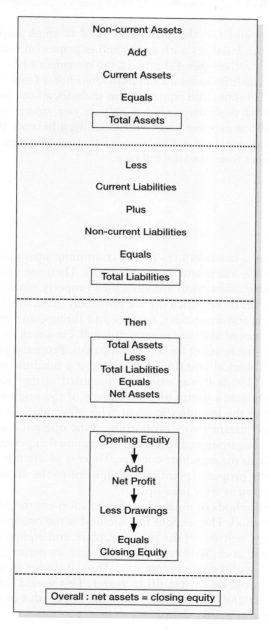

PAUSE FOR THOUGHT 4.2

Statement of Financial Position

Why does a balance sheet (i.e., statement of financial position) balance?

This is a tricky question! For the answer we need to think back to the trial balance. The trial balance balances with assets and expenses on one side and income, liabilities and equity on the other. Essentially, the statement of financial position is a rewritten trial balance. It includes all the individual items from the trial balance in terms of the assets, liabilities and equity. It also includes all the income and expense items. However, all of these are included only as one figure: 'profit' (i.e., all the income items less all the expense items). Incidentally, a balance sheet was probably originally called a balance sheet not because it balances, but because it is a list of all the individual balances from the trial balance.

Non-current Assets

These are the assets that a business uses for its continuing operations. Non-current assets can be divided into tangible assets and intangible assets. There are generally recognised to be four main types of tangible assets, more usually called property, plant and equipment or fixed assets (intangible assets, i.e. those which do not physically exist, are discussed in Chapter 6): land and buildings, plant and machinery, fixtures and fittings, and motor vehicles. For sole traders, these different types of asset are separately listed. However, for presentation purposes they are aggregated into one heading for listed companies. Property, plant and equipment are traditionally valued at historical cost. In other words, if a machine was purchased 10 years ago for £100,000, this £100,000 was originally recorded in the books. Every year of the property, plant and equipment's useful life, an amount of the original purchase cost will be allocated as an expense in the income statement. This allocated cost is termed depreciation. Thus, depreciation simply means that a proportion of the original cost is spread over the life of the property, plant and equipment and treated as an annual expense. In essence, this allocation of costs relates back to the matching concept. There is an attempt to match a proportion of the original cost of the property, plant and equipment to the accounting period in which property, plant and equipment were used up.

The most common methods of measuring depreciation are the straight line method and the reducing balance method. The straight line method is the one used in Figure 4.5. Essentially, the same amount is written off the property, plant and equipment every year over the estimated useful life of the asset. With reducing balance, a set percentage is expensed or written off the net book value of the asset every year. Thus, if the set percentage was 20%, then in Figure 4.5 £20,000 would be written off in year 1. This would leave a net book value of £80,000 (£100,000 − £20,000). Then 20% of the net book value of £80,000 (i.e., £16,000) would be written off in year 2, and so on.

Figure 4.5 Illustrative Example on Depreciation

A machine was purchased 10 years ago for £100,000. Estimated useful life 20 years. The machine will then have no scrap value. We will assume the depreciation is equally allocated over 20 years. What would be the total depreciation (known as accumulated depreciation) after 12 years and at how much would the machine be recorded in the statement of financial position?

Statement of Financial Position

Non-current Assets	Cost	Accumulated depreciation	Net book value
	£	£	£
Property, Plant and Equipment	100,000	(60,000)	40,000

In the statement of financial position, the original cost (£100,000) is recorded, followed by accumulated depreciation (i.e., depreciation over the 12 years: $12 \times £5,000 = £60,000$). The term 'net book value' simply means the amount left in the books after writing off depreciation. It is important to note that the net book value does not equal the market value. Indeed, it may be very different. In the income statement only one year's depreciation (£100,00 ÷ 20 years) of £5,000 is recorded each year.

Note: This topic is discussed more fully in Chapter 5.

Companies have great flexibility when choosing appropriate rates of depreciation. These rates should correspond to the useful lives of the assets. So, for example, if the directors believe an item of property, plant and equipment has a useful life of five years, they would choose a straight line rate of depreciation of 20%. Company Snapshot 4.1 gives the rates of depreciation used by Manchester United plc.

COMPANY SNAPSHOT 4.1

Depreciation

Depreciation is provided on tangible assets at annual rates appropriate to the estimated useful lives of the assets, as follows:

	Reducing Balance	Straight Line
Freehold buildings	1.33%	75 years
Computer equipment and software (included within plant and machinery)	33%	3 years
Plant and machinery	20–25%	4–5 years
General fixtures and fittings	15%	7 years

Tangible fixed assets acquired prior to 31 July 1999 are depreciated on a reducing balance basis at the rates stated above.

Tangible fixed assets acquired after 1 August 1999 are depreciated on a straight line basis at the rates stated above.

Source: Manchester United Ltd, *Annual Report 2010*, p. 60.

Interestingly, up until 1999 the club used the reducing balance method, which is relatively uncommon in the UK. However, it has now changed to the more conventional straight line depreciation.

Finally, it is important to realise that nowadays, many businesses regularly revalue some non-current assets such as property, plant and equipment, for example, every five years. Businesses can also revalue their non-current assets whenever they feel it is necessary (or, alternatively, devalue them if they have lost value). Where revaluations occur, the depreciation is based on the revalued amount. A devaluation of non-current assets is generally called an impairment. Indeed, the term impairment is used more generally for the loss of value of assets.

Current Assets

Current assets are those assets which a company owns which are essentially short-term. They are normally needed to perform the company's day-to-day operations. The five most common forms of current assets are inventories, trade receivables, prepayments, cash and bank.

1. Inventories (Stocks)

Inventories are an important business asset. This is especially so in manufacturing businesses. Inventories can be divided into three categories: raw materials, work-in-progress and finished goods (see, for example, Company Snapshot 4.2).

COMPANY SNAPSHOT 4.2

Inventories (Stocks)

	2010	2009
	EURm	EURm
Raw materials, supplies and other	326	346
Work in progress	477	435
Finished goods	502	388
Total	1,305	1,169

Source: Nokia, *Annual Report 2010*, p. 45.

HELPNOTE 4.1

Inventory or Inventories or Stock

The terminology in this area can be difficult and often confusing. Generally, inventories or inventory is the terminology used under IFRS. In this book, I try to be consistent. I use inventory in general discussion and for sole traders and partnerships as they are likely to have only 'one' sort of inventory. For limited companies, I generally use inventories as they may carry multiple stocks. In the management accounting section I use inventory. I hope I am consistent!

Each category represents a different stage in the production process.

- *Raw materials.* These are the inventories a company has purchased and are ready for use. A carpenter, for example, might have wood awaiting manufacture into tables.
- *Work-in-progress.* These are partially completed inventories, sometimes called inventories in process. They are neither raw materials nor finished goods. They may represent partly manufactured goods such as tables with missing legs. Some of the costs of making the tables should be included.
- *Finished goods.* These represents inventories at the other end of the manufacturing process; for example, finished tables. Cost includes materials and other manufacturing costs (e.g., labour and manufacturing overheads).

Inventories at the year-end are often determined after a stocktake. As Real-World View 4.1 shows, inventories can often represent a substantial percentage of a company's net assets. This is especially true for Rolls-Royce, a manufacturing company. By contrast, Vodafone and Nokia carry relatively little inventories.

 REAL-WORLD VIEW 4.1

The Importance of Inventories (Stock) Valuation

Company	Inventories Value £m[1]	Net Assets £m[1]	Inventories ÷ Net Assets %
Nokia	€2,523	39,123	6.4
Astra Zeneca	$1,750	$20,821	8.0
Tesco	2,729	14,681	18.5
Sainsbury	702	4,966	14.1
Marks & Spencer	613	2,186	28.0
Rolls-Royce	2,432	3,782	64.3
Vodafone	433	90,810	0.004
J.D. Wetherspoon	20	162	12.3
Volkswagen	€14,124	€37,430	37.8

Source: 2009/10 Annual Reports.

1. Unless indicated Astra Zeneca, Volkswagen and Nokia report in $ or €.

Generally, inventories are valued at the lower of cost or net realisable value (i.e., the value they could be sold for). In the case of work-in-progress and finished goods, cost could include some overheads (i.e., costs associated with making the tables). In Chapter 13, we will look at several different ways of calculating cost (e.g., FIFO and AVCO).

Figure 4.6 Summary of the Valuation Methods Used for Property, Plant and Equipment and Inventories

Property, Plant and Equipment	Normally valued at historical cost or revaluation less depreciation. Historical cost is the original purchase price of the assets. Revaluation is the value of the property, plant and equipment as determined, usually by a surveyor, at a particular point in time.
Inventories	Inventories are generally valued at the lower of cost (i.e., what a business paid for it) and the amount one would realise if one sold it (called net realisable value). For a business with work-in-progress or finished goods inventories, an appropriate amount of overheads is included.

2. Trade Receivables (Debtors)

Trade receivables are sales which have been made, but for which the customers have not yet paid. If all transactions were in cash, there would be no trade receivables. Trade receivables at the year end are usually adjusted for those customers who it is believed will not pay. These debts are called a variety of terms such as bad and doubtful debts, impaired receivables, irrecoverable debts. In this book, for consistency, we use provision for the impairment of receivables. Bad debts are those debts which will definitely not be paid. Doubtful debts have an element of uncertainty to them. Usually, businesses estimate a certain proportion of their debts as doubtful debts. These bad and doubtful debts are also included in the income statement.

PAUSE FOR THOUGHT 4.3

Bad and Doubtful Debts

Can you think of any reasons why bad and doubtful debts might occur?

There may be several reasons; for example, bankruptcies, disputes over the goods supplied or cash flow problems. Most businesses constantly monitor their trade receivables to ensure that bad debts are kept to a minimum.

3. Prepayments

Prepayments are those items where a good or service has been paid for in advance. A common example of this is insurance. A business might, for example, pay £1,000 for a year's property insurance on 1 October. If the accounts are drawn up to 31 December, then at 31 December there is an asset of nine months' insurance (January–September) paid in advance, which is £750. The £750 represents an asset as it represents a future benefit to the firm.

4. Cash and bank

This is the actual money held by the business. Cash comprises petty cash and unbanked cash. Bank comprises money deposited at the bank or on short-term loan. For limited companies the term cash and cash equivalents is often used. This recognises that sometimes businesses own assets that can be turned into cash at relatively short notice, such as short-term deposits. As Soundbite 4.2 shows, money has long been the topic of humour.

SOUNDBITE 4.2

Money

They say money can't buy happiness, but it can facilitate it. I thoroughly recommend having lots of it to anybody.

Malcolm Forbes (*Daily Mail*, 20 June 1988)

Source: The Book of Business Quotations (1991), p. 158.

Current Liabilities

These are the amounts which the organisation owes to third parties. For a sole trader, there are three main types.

1. Trade Payables (Creditors)

These are the amounts which are owed to suppliers for goods and services received, but not yet paid (for example, raw materials). They provide a source of finance to a company and are discussed in detail in Chapter 19.

2. Accruals

'Accruals' is accounting terminology for expenses owed at the financial reporting date. Accruals comply with the basic accounting concept of matching. In other words, because an expense has been incurred, but not yet paid, there is no reason to exclude it from the income statement. Accruals are amounts owed, but not yet paid, to suppliers for services received. Accruals relate to expenses such as telephone or light and heat. For example, we might have paid the telephone bill up to 30 November. However, if our year end was 31 December then we might owe, say, another £250 for telephone. Importantly, accruals do *not* relate to purchases of trade goods owing: these are trade payables.

3. Short-term Loans

Loans are the amounts which a third party, such as a bank, has loaned to the company on a short-term basis and which are due for repayment within one year.

The current assets less the current liabilities is, in effect, the operating capital of the business. It is commonly known as a business's working capital. Businesses try to manage their working capital as efficiently as possible (see Chapter 19). A working capital cycle exists (see Figure 4.7), where cash is used to purchase goods which are then turned into inventory. This

Figure 4.7 The Working Capital Cycle

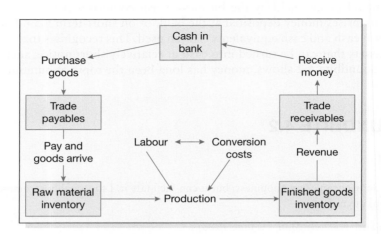

inventory is then sold and cash is generated. Successful businesses will sell their goods for more than their total cost, thus generating a positive cash flow. In most businesses, current assets will be greater than current liabilities. Current assets less current liabilities is known as net current assets. In some cases, a business may have more current liabilities than current assets. Instead of being net current assets, this section becomes net current liabilities. This is the situation with Tesco in 2005; see Company Snapshot 4.3.

COMPANY SNAPSHOT 4.3

Current Assets and Current Liabilities

Current assets	£m	£m	£m	£m
Inventories	1,309	—	1,309	1,199
Trade and other receivables	1,002	(233)	769	811
Cash and cash equivalents	1,146	—	1,146	1,100
	3,457	(233)	3,224	3,110
Current liabilities				
Trade and other payables	(5,374)	417	(4,957)	(3,986)
Short-term borrowings	(477)	(5)	(482)	(847)
Current tax payable	(221)	—	(221)	(308)
	(6,072)	412	(5,660)	(5,141)
Net current liabilities	(2,615)	179	(2,436)	(2,031)

Source: Tesco, 2004/5 Restatement of Financial Information under International Financial Reporting Standards (IFRS), p. 7.

Loans give rise to debt. Many leading companies have large debts. As Soundbite 4.3 shows, debt is a particular problem for football clubs globally, especially in the English Premier League.

SOUNDBITE 4.3

Debts

Liverpool and Manchester United, English football's two most successful clubs, have a combined net debt of nearly £1bn. In March, Sepp Blather, President of FIFA (Fédération Internationale de Football Association) summed it up succinctly when he said: 'I think something is wrong with the Premier League'.

Source: Accountancy Magazine, Alex Blyth, Game Over, May 2010, p. 20.

Non-current Liabilities

Non-current liabilities are liabilities that the organisation owes and must repay after more than one year. Put simply, they are a company's borrowings. The most common are long-term loans. These represent sources of finance to the company and are discussed in detail in Chapter 18. The total assets of a business less current liabilities and non-current liabilities give the total net assets of the business. Total net assets represent the total equity employed by a business.

Contingent Liabilities

These are liabilities that sometimes occur in organisations. They are contingent because they are dependent on the occurrence of an event (for example, the outcome of a law suit). As they may or may not happen, they are not included in the double-entry process, but included in the notes to accounts.

Equity (Capital Employed)

For a sole trader the owner's equity or capital employed is opening equity plus profit less drawings. Thus for R. Beer it is:

Equity	£
Opening equity	80,257
Add Profit	8,350
	88,607
Less Drawings	9,366
Closing equity	79,241

Opening equity is that equity at the start of the year (e.g., 1 April 2014). In essence, it represents the total net assets at the start of the year (i.e., all the assets less all the liabilities). If the business had made a loss, opening equity would have been reduced. It is important to realise that the profit (or loss) recorded under owner's equity represents the net profit (or loss) as determined from the income statement. It is, thus, a linking figure.

PAUSE FOR THOUGHT 4.4

Equity (Capital)

A chip shop owner, B. Atter, has opening equity of £19,500. His income is £100,000 and expenses are £90,000. He has taken out £15,000 to live on. His financial position has improved over the year. True or false?

Unfortunately, for B. Atter, the answer is false. If we quickly draw up his capital employed:

Equity (Owner's capital employed)	£
Opening equity	19,500
Add Profit (i.e., income less expenses)	10,000
	29,500
Less Drawings	15,000
Closing equity	14,500

His capital has declined by £5,000 over the year.

SOUNDBITE 4.4

Capital

'Capital isn't scarce; vision is.'

Michael Milken (junk-bond creator)

Source: The Executive's Book of Quotations (1994), p. 47.

Profit is the profit as determined from the income statement (i.e., revenue less cost of sales and other expenses). Drawings is the money that R. Beer has taken out of the business for his own personal spending. Finally, closing equity is equity at the statement of financial position date. It must be remembered at all times that:

$$\text{Assets} - \text{Liabilities} = \text{Equity}$$

Businesses need capital to operate. However, the capital needs to be used wisely (see Soundbite 4.4).

PAUSE FOR THOUGHT 4.5

Financial Position

Angela Roll, a baker, has the following assets and liabilities. Non-current assets £59,000, current assets £12,000, current liabilities £8,000 and non-current liabilities £7,000. What are her net assets? Is it true that her total assets are £50,000?

....

Net assets are £56,000:

	£
Non-current Assets	59,000
Current Assets	12,000
Total Assets	71,000
Current Liabilities	(8,000)
Non-current Liabilities	(7,000)
Total Liabilities	(15,000)
Net Assets	56,000

Total assets are £71,000

Limitations

To the casual observer, it looks as if the statement of financial position places a market value on the net assets of the organisation. Unfortunately, this is wrong. Very wrong! To understand why, one must look at the major components of the statement of financial position. The statement of financial position is a collection of individual assets and liabilities. These individual assets and liabilities are usually not valued at a real-world market value, so neither is the statement of financial position as a whole. Taking the property, plant and equipment, for example, only selected property, plant and equipment are revalued. These valuations are neither consistent nor necessarily up to date. There is, therefore, a considerable amount of subjectivity involved in their valuation. Also depreciation does not accurately measure the loss in value of property, plant and equipment (nor is it supposed to). The statement of financial position is thus a tangle of assets all measured in different ways.

Another problem, especially for companies, is that significant assets are not shown in the statement of financial position. All the hard work of an owner to generate revenue and goodwill will only be recognised when the business is sold. Many key items that drive corporate value, such as know-how and market share, are also not recorded (see Real-World View 4.2). Neither is the value of human assets recorded! For example, what is the greatest asset of football clubs? You might think it was the footballers like David Beckham, Wayne Rooney or Andy Carroll. However, conventionally these players would not be valued as assets on the statement of financial position unless they have been transferred from another club. Nor, in the case of zoos, would the animals bred in captivity be valued.

REAL-WORLD VIEW 4.2

Missing Assets

In many respects, the current reporting model is more suited to a manufacturing economy than one based on services and knowledge. For example, it does a good job measuring historical costs of physical assets, like plant and equipment. But it ignores many of the key drivers of corporate value, such as know-how and market share. The result is incomplete, or distorted, information about a company's worth, and diminished relevance to investors.

Source: Dennis M. Nally, *The Future of Financial Reporting* (1999), International Financial Reporting Conference From Web http://www.amazon.co.uk/exec/abidos/ASIN.

In addition to these assets which are not required to be shown on the statement of financial position, there is concern that many companies are deliberately omitting assets and, more importantly, liabilities from their financial statements. This is shown in Soundbite 4.5.

SOUNDBITE 4.5

Off-Balance Sheet Financing

'It is child's play, particularly for bankers who devised complex structures to keep assets and, more importantly, the related liabilities off the balance sheet [statement of financial position].'

Source: David Cairns, Accounting Standards and the Financial Crisis, *Accountancy Magazine*, March 2010, p. 67.

Interpretation

Given the above limitations, any meaningful interpretation of amounts recorded in the statement of financial position is difficult. However, there are ratios which are derived from the statement of financial position which are used to assess and better understand the financial position of a business. These ratios are dealt with in more depth in Chapter 8. Here we just briefly comment on liquidity (i.e., cash position) and long-term capital structure.

The statement of financial position records both current assets and current liabilities. These can be used to assess the short-term liquidity (i.e., short-term cash position) of a business. There are a variety of ratios such as the current ratio (current assets divided by current liabilities) and quick ratio (current assets minus inventories then divided by current liabilities) which do this. In addition, the statement of financial position records the long-term capital structure of a business. It is particularly useful in determining how dependent a business is on external borrowings. In Soundbite 4.6, for example, excessive borrowing created a statement of financial position where there was negative net worth.

SOUNDBITE 4.6

Statement of Financial Position (Balance Sheet)

MCI's balance sheet [statement of financial position] looked like Rome after the Visigoths had finished with it. We had a $90-million negative net worth, and we owed the bank $100 million, which was so much that they couldn't call the loan without destroying the company.

W.G. McGowgan, *Henderson Winners*, p. 187

Source: The Executive's Book of Quotations (1994), p. 81.

Listed Companies

Listed Companies in Europe follow International Financial Reporting Standards. Their statements of financial position are presented differently from those of sole traders or partnerships. Several examples of listed companies' statements of financial position are given in this book (see, for example, Marks and Spencer in Appendix 2.2, Volkswagen in Appendix 2.5 and AstraZeneca in Company Snapshot 6.4). They are all slightly different as there is no standardised format.

In this book, we use a standardised terminology for simplification and ease of understanding. Therefore, we use the listed companies' terminology throughout. However, sometimes an alternative terminology is used. We present this in Figure 4.8. For sole traders and partnerships traditionally more detail is given. Listed companies are covered in more depth in Chapter 6.

Conclusion

The statement of financial position is a key financial statement. It shows the net assets of a business at a particular point of time. The three main constituents of the statement of financial position are assets (non-current and current), liabilities (current and non-current) and

Figure 4.8 Terminology

Terminology for Listed Companies	Sole Traders, Partnerships, Non-Listed Companies (alternative terminology permissible)
Property, plant and equipment	Fixed assets
Inventories	Stocks
Trade receivables	Debtors
Trade payables	Creditors
Equity	Capital and reserves/Ownership interest
Non-current liabilities	Long-term liabilities

equity. Normally a vertical statement of financial position is used to portray these elements. The statement of financial position itself is difficult to interpret because of missing assets and inconsistently valued assets. However, it is commonly used to assess the liquidity position of a firm.

Discussion Questions

Questions with numbers in blue have answers at the back of the book.

Q1 The statement of financial position and income statement provide complementary, but contrasting information. Discuss.

Q2 What are the main limitations of the statement of financial position and how can they be overcome?

Q3 Is the statement of financial position of any use?

Q4 Are the different elements of the statement of financial position changing over time; for example, as manufacturing industry gives way to service industry?

Q5 State whether the following are true or false. If false, explain why.
(a) A statement of financial position is a collection of assets, liabilities and equity.
(b) Inventory, bank and trade payables are all current assets.
(c) Total net assets are property, plant and equipment plus current assets less current liabilities.
(d) Total net assets equal closing equity.
(e) An accrual is an amount prepaid; for example, rent paid in advance.

Numerical Questions

Questions with numbers in blue have answers at the back of the book.

Q1 The following financial details are for Jane Bricker as at 31 December 2013.

	£		£
Equity 1 January 2013	5,000	Profit	12,000
Drawings	7,000		

Required: Jane Bricker's capital employed as at 31 December 2013.

Q2 Alpa Shah has the following financial details as at 30 June 2014.

	£		£
Non-current assets	100,000	Current liabilities	30,000
Current assets	50,000	Non-current liabilities	20,000

Required: Alpa Shah's total net assets as at 30 June 2014.

Q3 Jill Jenkins has the following financial details as at 31 December 2013.

	£		£
Inventory	18,000	Cash	4,000
Trade receivables	8,000	Trade payables	12,000

Required: Jill Jenkins' net current assets as at 31 December 2013.

Q4 Janet Richards has the following financial details as at 31 December 2013.

	£		£
Land and buildings	100,000	Trade payables	15,000
Plant and machinery	60,000	Long-term loan	15,000
Inventory	40,000	Opening equity	200,000
Trade receivables	30,000	Net profit	28,000
Cash	20,000	Drawings	8,000
		Closing equity	220,000

Required: Janet Richards' Statement of financial position as at 31 December 2013.

Appendix 4.1: Horizontal Format of Statement of Financial Position

R. Beer's Statement of Financial Position as at 31 March 2014 (presented in horizontal format)

	£	£		£	£
Equity			**Non-Current Assets**		
Opening equity		80,257	Property, Plant and Equipment		
Add Profit		8,350	Land and buildings		71,572
		88,607	Plant and machinery		3,500
Less Drawings		9,366	Furniture and fittings		5,834
Closing equity		79,241	Motor vehicles		3,398
Long-term loan		6,500	*Total Non-current assets*		84,304
		85,741			
Current Liabilities			**Current Assets**		
Trade payables	3,991		Inventory	2,200	
Loan	1,000	4,991	Trade receivables	100	
			Prepayments	50	
			Bank	3,738	
			Cash	340	6,428
		90,732			90,732

Go online to discover the extra features for this chapter at
www.wiley.com/college/jones

Chapter 5

Preparing the financial statements

'Mr Evans was the chief accountant of a large manufacturing concern. Every day, on arriving at work, he would unlock the bottom drawer of his desk, peer at something inside, then close and lock the drawer. He had done this for 25 years. The entire staff was intrigued but no one was game to ask him what was in the drawer. Finally, the time came for Mr Evans to retire. There was a farewell party with speeches and a presentation. As soon as Mr Evans had left the buildings, some of the staff rushed into his office, unlocked the bottom drawer and peered in. Taped to the bottom of the drawer was a sheet of paper. It read, "The debit side is the one nearest the window".'

R. Andrews, *Funny Business, C.A. Magazine*, April 2000, p. 26. Copyright The Institute of Chartered Accountants of Scotland.

Learning Outcomes

After completing this chapter you should be able to:

- Show how the trial balance is used as a basis for preparing the financial statements.
- Prepare the income statement (profit and loss account) and the statement of financial position (balance sheet).
- Understand the post-trial balance adjustments commonly made to the accounts.
- Prepare the income statement (profit and loss account) and the statement of financial position (balance sheet) using post-trial balance adjustments.

Go online to discover the extra features for this chapter at
www.wiley.com/college/jones

Chapter Summary

- The trial balance when rearranged creates an income statement and a statement of financial position.
- The income statement presents revenue, cost of sales, other income and other expenses.
- The statement of financial position consists of assets, liabilities and equity.
- Revenue less cost of sales less other expenses gives net profit.
- There are five main post-trial balance adjustments to the accounts: closing inventory, accruals, prepayments, depreciation, and bad and doubtful debts.
- All five adjustments are made twice to maintain the double-entry: first, in the income statement and second, in the statement of financial position.

Introduction

A trial balance is prepared after the bookkeeping process of recording the financial transactions in a double-entry form. The bookkeeping stage is really one of aggregating and summarising the financial information. The next step is to prepare the income statement (profit and loss account) and the statement of financial position (balance sheet) from the trial balance. In essence, the income statement sets out income less expenses and thus determines profit. Meanwhile, the statement of financial position presents the assets and liabilities, including equity. The two statements are seen as complementary. Chapters 3 and 4 discussed the nature and purpose of the income statement and the statement of financial position. This present chapter looks at the mechanics of how we prepare the final accounts from the trial balance. These mechanics are the same for sole traders, partnerships and companies. However, in companies the final unabridged accounts are then used to provide summarised accounts for publication.

Main Financial Statements

Essentially, the two main financial statements rearrange the items in the trial balance. The profit for the year effectively links the income statement and the statement of financial position. In the **income statement profit is income less expenses paid**, while in the **statement of financial position, closing equity add drawings less opening equity gives profit**. Looked at another way, profit represents the increase in equity over the year. Profit is a key figure in the accounts and plays a vital part in linking the income statement to the statement of financial position. Profit is often reported graphically by companies in their annual reports. Stage Coach plc's profit figure is given in Company Snapshot 5.1.

COMPANY SNAPSHOT 5.1

Operating Profit

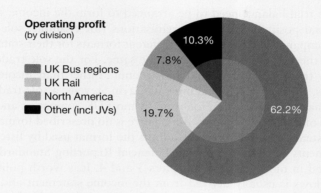

Operating profit
(by division)

- UK Bus regions
- UK Rail
- North America
- Other (incl JVs)

10.3%
7.8%
62.2%
19.7%

Source: Stagecoach Group plc, *Annual Report and Financial Statements 2011.*

PAUSE FOR THOUGHT 5.1

Accounting Equation and Financial Statements

What is the relationship between the accounting equation, income statement and statement of financial position?

In essence, the accounting equation develops into the financial statements. Remember from Chapter 2 that the expanded accounting equation was:

$$\text{Assets} + \text{Expenses} = \text{Liabilities} + \text{Equity} + \text{Income}$$

Rearrange thus:

$$\text{Assets} - (\text{Liabilities} + \text{Equity}) = \text{Income} - \text{Expenses}$$

↓ ↓

Statement of financial position   Income statement

Trial Balance to the Income Statement (Profit and Loss Account) and the Statement of Financial Position (Balance Sheet)

The elements of the trial balance need to be arranged to form the income statement and the statement of financial position. Different organisations (for example, sole traders, partnerships and limited companies) all have slightly different formats for their statement of financial position. However, the basic structure remains the same. For the sole trader, sometimes the terminology used is 'trading and profit and loss account', rather than 'income statement'. For illustrative purposes, we continue the example of Gavin Stevens, a sole trader, who is setting up a hotel. The format used here is that followed by most UK companies and broadly adheres to the requirements of the UK Companies Acts. There is **no prescribed format** for sole traders, therefore, **for consistency this book broadly adopts the format used by listed companies that follow the requirements of the International Financial Reporting Standards.** The individual items were explained in more detail in Chapters 3 and 4. It is worth pointing out that the statement of cash flows is usually derived from the income statement and the statement of financial position once they have been prepared and *not* from the trial balance (see Chapter 7).

Gavin Stevens, Continued

In Chapter 2, we looked at the trial balance. We now can use this to prepare the income statement and the statement of financial position. However, when we prepare the financial accounts we also need to collect information on the amount of inventory and on any expenses which are yet to be paid or have been paid in advance. In this example, we set out more details about inventory, amounts owing for telephone and amounts prepaid for electricity in the notes to the trial balance. It is important to realise that none of these items has so far been entered into the books. We deal with these adjustments in more depth later in this chapter.

Gavin Stevens
Trial Balance as at 7 January

		Debit £	Credit £
Hotel		610,000	
Van		3,000	
Revenue			9,000
Purchases		5,000	
Equity			700,000
Revenue returns		70	
Purchases returns			500
Bank		86,915	
Electricity		300	
Wages		1,000	
Trade receivables	Ireton	1,965	
	Hepworth	2,500	
Trade payables	Hogen		250
	Lewis		1,000
		710,750	710,750

Notes:
1. Gavin Stevens does not use all the catering supplies. He estimates that the amount of catering supplies left as closing inventory is £50.
2. There is a special arrangement with the electricity company in which Gavin Stevens pays £300 in advance for a quarter. By 7 January he has used £50 which means he has prepaid £250. This is known as a prepayment.
3. There is a telephone bill yet to be received. However, Gavin Stevens estimates that he owes £100. This is known as an accrual.

We now prepare the income statement following the steps in Helpnote 5.1.

HELPNOTE 5.1

Presentational Guide to the Four Steps (Given as A–D in Gavin Stevens' Income Statement (Trading and Profit and Loss Account))

In terms of presentation, we should note:

- We must first determine cost of sales (Step A). This is, at its simplest, opening inventory add purchases less closing inventory. Purchases must be adjusted for purchases returns.
- Revenue less cost of sales gives gross profit (Step B). Revenue must be adjusted for revenue returns.
- We list and total all expenses (Step C).
- We determine net profit (Step D) by taking expenses away from gross profit.

Gavin Stevens
Income Statement (Trading and Profit and Loss Account) for the Week Ended 7 January

	£	£	£		
Revenue			9,000		
Less Revenue returns			70		
			8,930		
Less *Cost of Sales*				A	
Opening inventory		–			Trading
Add Purchases	5,000				account
Less Purchases returns	500	4,500			
Less Closing inventory		50	4,450		
Gross Profit			4,480	B	
Less *Expenses*				C	
Electricity		50			
Wages		1,000			Profit and
Telephone		100	1,150		loss account
Net Profit			3,330	D	

Points to notice:

1. All the figures are from the trial balance except for closing inventory £50, electricity £50 and telephone £100 (calculated from notes) and profit £3,330 (calculated).
2. The first part of the statement down to gross profit (B) (revenue less cost of sales (A)) is sometimes called the trading account. It deals with revenue and purchases. Essentially revenue returns and purchases returns are deducted from revenue and purchases, respectively. Inventory is simply unsold purchases.
3. Gross profit (B) is revenue minus cost of sales.
4. Net profit (D) is revenue minus cost of sales minus other expenses (C).
5. Net profit of £3,330 increases equity in the statement of financial position. It is the balancing item, simply income minus expenses.

We now prepare the statement of financial position following the steps in Helpnote 5.2.

HELPNOTE 5.2

Presentational Guide to the Five Steps (Given as A–E in Gavin Stevens' Statement of Financial Position (Balance Sheet))

In terms of presentation, we should note:

- All the property, plant and equipment (i.e., tangible non-current assets) are added together (Step A).
- Total assets (non-current assets and current assets) are determined next. This will give total assets (Step B).
- The total liabilities are determined. This is current liabilities and non-current liabilities added together (Step C).
- Total assets less total liabilities gives net assets (Step D).
- Equity is determined. Effectively, net profit is added to opening equity to give closing equity (Step E).

Gavin Stevens
Statement of Financial Position (Balance Sheet) as at 7 January

TOTAL ASSETS
Non-current Assets

	£	
Property, plant and equipment		
Hotel	610,000	
Van	3,000	
Total non-current assets	613,000	A
Current Assets		
Inventory	50	
Trade receivables (£1,965 + £2,500)	4,465	

Electricity prepayment	250	
Bank	86,915	
Total current assets	91,680	
Total Assets	704,680	B
TOTAL LIABILITIES		
Current Liabilities		
Trade payables (£250 + £1,000)	(1,250)	
Telephone bill accrued	(100)	
Total Liabilities	(1,350)	C
Net Assets	703,330	D
EQUITY	£	
Opening equity	700,000	
Add Net profit	3,330	
Closing equity	703,330	E

Points to notice:

1. Thus, in this example we have:
   A = The sum total of the non-current assets (property, plant and equipment) £613,000.
   B = The total assets £704,680 (£613,000 non-current assets plus £91,680 current assets).
   C = Total liabilities (in this case the current liabilities of £1,350 as there are no non-current liabilities).
   D = Net assets £703,330 (total assets £704,680 (B) less total liabilities £1,350 (C)).
   E = Equity £703,330 (opening equity plus net profit).
2. All figures are from the trial balance except for closing inventory £50, electricity prepayment £250, telephone bill (from notes) and profit £3,330 (balancing figure). Except for electricity, all *these* figures are the same in the income statement. Electricity is different because, in effect, we are splitting up £300. Thus:
   Total paid £300 = £50 used up as an expense in the income statement, and £250 not used up recorded as an asset in the statement of financial position.
3. Our statement is divided into non-current assets, current assets, current liabilities and equity.
4. The trade receivables are the trial balance figures for Ireton and Hepworth; the trade payables are those for Hogen and Lewis.
5. Our opening equity plus our net profit gives us our closing equity. In other words, the business 'owes' Gavin Stevens £700,000 at 1 January, but £703,330 at 7 January.
6. Net profit of £3,330 is found in the income statement. It is the balancing item. As we saw from Pause for Thought 5.1, the profit can be seen as the increase in net assets over the year. Or, alternatively, it can be viewed as assets less liabilities less opening equity.
7. The statement of financial position balances. In other words, total net assets equals closing equity.

PAUSE FOR THOUGHT 5.2

Accounting Equation and Gavin Stevens

How does the Gavin Stevens example we have just completed fit the accounting equation?

....

If we take our expanded accounting equation:

Assets + Expenses = Liabilities + Equity + Income

and rearrange it,

Assets − (Liabilities + Equity) = Income − Expenses

Now, if we substitute the figures from Gavin Stevens, we have:

Non-current assets (£613,000) + Current assets (£91,680) − ((Current liabilities (£1,350) + Opening equity (£700,000)) = Income (£8,930) − (Cost of sales (£4,450) + Expenses (£1,150))

∴ £613,000 + £91,680 − (£1,350 + £700,000) = £8,930 − (£4,450 + £1,150)
∴ £704,680 − £701,350 = £8,930 − £5,600
∴ £3,330 = £3,330

The £3,330 represents net profit. This net profit, therefore, provides a bridge between the statement of financial position and the income statement.

Adjustments to Trial Balance

The trial balance is prepared from the books of account and is then adjusted for certain items. These items represent estimates or adjustments which typically do not form part of the initial double-entry process. Five of the main adjustments are **closing inventory, accruals, prepayments, depreciation,** and **bad and doubtful debts.** The mechanics of their accounting treatment is discussed here. However, the items themselves are discussed in more depth in Chapters 3 and 4 on the income statement and the statement of financial position.

Inventories (Stock)

Inventories are an important asset to any business, especially manufacturing businesses. Stock control systems in large businesses can be very complex and sophisticated. In most sole traders and in many other businesses it is normal not to record the detailed physical movements (i.e., purchases and sales of inventory). Inventory is not, therefore, formally recorded in these organisations in the double-entry process. However, at the financial reporting date inventory is counted, valued and the accounting records updated. To maintain the double-entry, the asset of inventory is entered twice: *first* in the trading part of the income statement; and *second*, in the current assets section of the statement of financial position. These two figures for accounting purposes cancel out and thus the double-entry is maintained. Last year's closing inventory figure becomes the current year's opening inventory figure. The term inventories is often used in listed company accounts to denote the fact that a company may have many individual inventories. An alternative commonly used term is stock.

Accruals

Accruals are the amounts we owe to the suppliers of services such as the telephone or light and heat. In small businesses, accruals are normally excluded from the initial double-entry process. We adjust for accruals so that we will arrive at the expenses incurred for the year not just the amount paid. Accruals appear in the final accounts in two places. *First*, the amount owing is included in the income statement under expenses. *Second*, a matching amount is included under current liabilities in the statement of financial position. The double-entry is thus maintained. Figure 5.1 gives an example of accruals and prepayments (payments in advance for services).

Figure 5.1 Accruals and Prepayments

From the following information calculate the income statement and the statement of financial position entries for:

1. Electricity

Mary Christmas has received and paid three electricity bills for the year (£300, £400, £550). Another bill is due relating to the year, which is estimated at £600.

2. Rent

The quarterly rent for Mary Christmas's offices is £300 payable in advance. The first payment is made on 1st January when the business starts, the last on 31st December.

1. Electricity

Effectively, the total bill incurred for the year is the amount paid (£300 + £400 + £550) £1,250 and the amount due £600. Therefore, the total bill is £1,850; this is included in the income statement. In the statement of financial position, £600 is included as an accrual.

2. Rent

The amount paid is 5 × £300 = £1,500.

However, only £1,200 relates to this year and should go in the income statement. The £300 balance is a prepayment in the statement of financial position.

Income Statement		Statement of Financial Position	
EXPENSES	**£**	**ASSETS**	**£**
Electricity	1,850	**Current Assets**	
Rent	1,200	Rent prepaid	300
		LIABILITIES	
		Current Liabilities	
		Electricity owing	600

Prepayments

Prepayments represent the amount paid in advance to the suppliers of services; for example, rent paid in advance. In many ways, prepayments are the opposite of accruals. Whereas accruals must be added to the final accounts to achieve the matching concept, a prepayment must be deducted. The amount paid in advance is treated as an asset which will be used up at a future date. We adjust for prepayments so that we will arrive at the expenses incurred for the year and not include payments for future years.

PAUSE FOR THOUGHT 5.3

Accruals and Prepayments

Can you think of four examples of accruals and prepayments?

We might have, for example:

Accruals	*Prepayments*
Electricity owing	Rent paid in advance
Business rates owing	Prepaid electricity on meter
Rent owing	Prepaid standing charge for telephone
Telephone owing	Insurance paid in advance

Depreciation

As we saw in Chapter 4, property, plant and equipment wear out over time and depreciation seeks to recognise this. Depreciation in the accounts is simply recording this – twice. *First*, a proportion of the original cost is allocated as an expense in the income statement. *Second*, an equivalent amount is deducted from the property, plant and equipment in the statement of financial position (see Figure 5.2).

Rentokil Initial plc's property, plant and equipment (as recorded in its 2009 statement of financial position) are given as an illustration in Company Snapshot 5.2. As you can see, they can be quite complex. In essence, however, two years' accounts are shown: 2008 and 2009. The amounts recorded at cost are shown and then adjusted for additions and disposals at cost. Adjustments for depreciation and impairment (where there is a write-down in the value of an asset over and above depreciation) are shown. The cost less the depreciation and impairment equals the net book value.

Figure 5.2 Example of Depreciation

A business has five assets shown at cost. Ten per cent of the original cost of each asset has been allocated as depreciation. Record the transactions in the accounts.

	£
Premises	80,000
Machine	75,000
Office furniture	12,000
Computer	1,500
Motor van	6,000

There are two parts to this. **First**, we record 10% of the original cost as an expense in the expenses section of the income statement (for example, premises: 10% £80,000 = £8,000).

Figure 5.2 Example of Depreciation (*continued*)

Income Statement (Year 1)

Expenses	£
Depreciation on premises	8,000
Depreciation on machine	7,500
Depreciation on office furniture	1,200
Depreciation on computer	150
Depreciation on motor van	600

Second, we record the original cost, total depreciation (called accumulated depreciation) and net book value (original cost less depreciation) in the statement of financial position. Note that accumulated depreciation is recorded in brackets – this shows it is being taken away.

Statement of Financial Position (Year 1)

Property, Plant and Equipment	£ Cost	£ Accumulated depreciation	£ Net book value
Premises	80,000	(8,000)	72,000
Machine	75,000	(7,500)	67,500
Office furniture	12,000	(1,200)	10,800
Computer	1,500	(150)	1,350
Motor van	6,000	(600)	5,400
	174,500	(17,450)	157,050

In next year's trial balance, the cost and accumulated depreciation figures would be recorded. The *accumulated depreciation* is often called *provision for depreciation*. This example records only one year's depreciation. However, in future years, there will be more depreciation, which is why it is called accumulated depreciation. In the following year, we also have 10% depreciation. The income statement is thus the same.

Income Statement (Year 2)

Expenses	£
Depreciation on premises	8,000
Depreciation on machine	7,500
Depreciation on office furniture	1,200
Depreciation on computer	150
Depreciation on motor van	600

In the statement of financial position, however, we *add* this year's depreciation to the accumulated depreciation figure. Thus, for premises we add £8,000 and £8,000 to arrive at £16,000. We, therefore, have:

Statement of Financial Position (Year 2)

Property, Plant and Equipment	£ Cost	£ Accumulated depreciation	£ Net book value
Premises	80,000	(16,000)	64,000
Machine	75,000	(15,000)	60,000
Office furniture	12,000	(2,400)	9,600
Computer	1,500	(300)	1,200
Motor van	6,000	(1,200)	4,800
	174,500	(34,900)	139,600

In essence, we have merely added the two years' depreciation figures. Thus, for premises, our opening figure for accumulated depreciation was £8,000. We then added this year's depreciation to arrive at £16,000. The net book value is simply the residual figure.

For ease of understanding these same figures are used in our comprehensive example, Live Wire, later in this chapter.

Tutorial Note: Exchange differences arise, for example, when transactions are carried out in different currencies or company results of overseas subsidiaries are translated from one currency to another.

Bad and Doubtful Debts

This is the last of the five adjustments. Bad and doubtful debts are also considered in Chapter 4 on the statement of financial position. Essentially, some debts *may* not be collected. These are termed doubtful debts.

COMPANY SNAPSHOT 5.2

Property, Plant and Equipment

	Land and Buildings £m	Equipment for rental £m	Other plant and equipment £m	Vehicles and office equipment £m	Total £m
Cost					
At 1 January 2008	182.5	463.0	266.2	212.2	1,123.9
Exchange differences	40.2	137.9	61.0	47.2	286.3
Additions	13.3	136.8	29.9	49.6	229.6
Disposals	(9.6)	(64.6)	(30.8)	(52.3)	(157.3)
Acquisition of companies and businesses[1]	(1.0)	0.1	0.5	1.2	0.8
Reclassifications	(4.1)	—	2.3	1.8	—
At 31 December 2008	221.3	673.2	329.1	259.7	1,483.3
At 1 January 2009	221.3	673.2	329.1	259.7	1,483.3
Exchange differences	(12.2)	(37.2)	(19.1)	(10.1)	(78.6)
Additions	4.1	122.1	16.4	33.0	175.6
Disposals	(6.5)	(93.4)	(17.5)	(43.4)	(160.8)
Acquisition of companies and businesses[1]	—	—	—	0.2	0.2
Disposal of companies and businesses	—	(3.4)	(0.4)	(1.1)	(4.9)
Reclassifications	(0.2)	—	—	0.2	—
At 31 December 2009	206.5	661.3	308.5	238.5	1,414.8
Accumulated depreciation and impairment					
At 1 January 2008	(35.5)	(251.4)	(166.8)	(109.0)	(562.7)
Exchange differences	(10.6)	(78.0)	(38.3)	(26.6)	(153.5)
Disposals	4.8	63.2	28.7	44.0	140.7
Reclassifications	0.1	—	—	(0.1)	—
Depreciation charge	(6.2)	(115.7)	(23.4)	(41.3)	(186.6)
At 31 December 2008	(47.4)	(381.9)	(199.8)	(133.0)	(762.1)
At 1 January 2009	(47.4)	(381.9)	(199.8)	(133.0)	(762.1)
Exchange differences	3.1	21.1	12.0	6.3	42.5
Disposals	2.8	91.6	14.9	38.0	147.3
Disposal of companies and businesses	—	3.2	0.4	0.8	4.4
Depreciation charge	(8.1)	(133.5)	(26.0)	(43.0)	(210.6)
At 31 December 2009	(49.6)	(399.5)	(198.5)	(130.9)	(778.5)

COMPANY SNAPSHOT 5.2 (*continued*)

Net Book Value	£m	£m	£m	£m	£m
At 1 January 2008	147.0	211.6	99.4	103.2	561.2
At 31 December 2008	173.9	291.3	129.3	126.7	721.2
At 31 December 2009	156.9	261.8	110.0	107.6	636.3

The net carrying amounts of assets held under finance leases are as follows:

At 31 December 2008	10.2	—	0.3	15.2	25.7
At 31 December 2009	3.9	0.4	0.4	14.1	18.8

[1]*Included within acquisition of companies and businesses are fair value adjustments to prior periods of (£0.1 million)(2008: £0.6 million). Refer to note 30 for further details on fair value adjustments.*

The category of equipment for rental consists of equipment leased by the group to third parties under operating leases.

Source: Rentokil Initial plc, *Annual Report 2009*, p. 62.

Other debts *will almost certainly not* be collected; they are called bad or irrecoverable debts. The accounting entries to record this are in the income statement as an expense and in the statement of financial position as a reduction in trade receivables. Some businesses, such as building societies and banks, typically carry a high level of bad and doubtful debts. Company Snapshot 5.3 shows the bad and doubtful debts for Vodafone, the UK mobile phone company.

COMPANY SNAPSHOT 5.3

Doubtful Debts

The Group's trade receivables are stated after allowances for bad and doubtful debts based on management's assessment of creditworthiness, an analysis of which is as follows:

	2010 £m	2009 £m
1 April	874	664
Exchange movements	(27)	101
Amounts charged to administrative expenses	465	423
Trade receivables written off	(383)	(314)
31 March	**929**	**874**

The carrying amounts of trade and other receivables approximate their fair value. Trade and other receivables are predominantly non-interest bearing.

Source: Vodafone Group plc, *Annual Report 2010*, p. 99.

When considering the accounting treatment of bad and doubtful debts, it is crucial to distinguish between bad and doubtful debts.

1. Bad Debts

Bad debts are recorded as an expense in the income statement and written off trade receivables in the statement of financial position (see Figure 5.3).

Figure 5.3 Illustrative Example of Bad Debts

A business has trade receivables of £4,800, but estimates that bad debts will be £320.	
Income Statement	£
Expenses	
Bad debts	320
Statement of Financial Position	
ASSETS	
Current Assets	
Trade receivables less bad debts	
(£4,800 - £320)	4,480

For ease of understanding, these same figures are used in our comprehensive example, Live Wire, later in this chapter.

2. Provision for the impairment of receivables

A 'provision for the impairment of receivables' is set up by a business for those debts it is dubious about collecting. The word 'impairment' indicates that it is doubtful whether the full money will be recovered for the trade receivables. This provision is *always* deducted from trade receivables in the statement of financial position. However, only **increases or decreases** in the provision are entered in the income statement. An *increase* is recorded as an *expense* and a *decrease* as an *income* (see Figure 5.4). Where there are both bad and doubtful debts

Figure 5.4 Illustrative Example of Doubtful Debts

A business has trade receivables of £4,800. There is a provision for the impairment of receivables of 10% of trade receivables. Last year trade receivables were £2,400 and the provision for the impairment of receivables was £240 (£480 - £240).	
Income Statement	£
Expenses	
Increase in provision for the impairment of receivables	240
Statement of Financial Position	
ASSETS	
Current Assets	
Trade receivables	4,800
Provision for the impairment of receivables	(480)
Net trade receivables	4,320

For ease of understanding, these same figures are used in our comprehensive example, Live Wire, later in this chapter.

SOUNDBITE 5.1

Debts

'A small debt makes a man your debtor, a large one makes him your enemy.'

Seneca (Ad Lucilium xix)

Source: The Executive's Book of Quotations (1994), p. 80.

then either the provision for the impairment of trade receivables is calculated first and then bad debts are deducted or vice versa. There are arguments both ways. In this example the provision for the impairment of receivables is calculated first. In effect, using this method, bad debts are those debts which are definitely irrecoverable.

It is now time to introduce some items commonly found in accounts. These are briefly explained in Figure 5.5. Mainly we focus on the accounts of a sole trader. Goodwill and other intangible assets (i.e., assets that we cannot touch) such as brands are discussed in more detail in Chapter 11.

Figure 5.5 Introducing Common Items Found in the Final Accounts

Item	Explanation	Location
Bank overdraft	This is where the business owes the bank money. Too many students are in this position!	Statement of financial position Current liabilities
Carriage inwards	This is usually found in manufacturing businesses. It is a cost of purchasing raw materials. It refers to the days when goods were brought in by horse and carriage.	Income statement Trading account Added to purchases
Carriage outwards	Similar to carriage inwards, except that it is an expense incurred by the business when selling goods.	Income statement Profit and loss account Expenses
Discount allowed	This is discount allowed by the business to customers for prompt payment. In other words, instead of paying, say £100, the customer pays £95. The sale £100 is recorded as normal, but discount allowed is recorded separately.	Income statement Profit and loss account Expenses
Discount received	Similar to discount allowed. However, it is received by the business from the supplier for paying promptly. The business, therefore, pays less. The purchase is recorded as normal, the discount received is recorded separately.	Income statement Profit and loss account Other income
Drawings	This is money which the sole trader or owner takes out for his or her living expenses. It is, in effect, the owner's salary. It is really a withdrawal of equity.	Statement of financial position Capital employed **Note:** Do *not* put in expenses
Income receivable*	This is income which is received by the business from a third party. Examples include dividends receivable from companies or interest receivable from the bank. Income received is a narrower term found in the statement of cash flows.	Income statement Profit and loss account Other income

Figure 5.5 Introducing Common Items Found in the Final Accounts (*continued*)

Interest payable*	This is the reverse of income receivable. It is interest payable by the business to outsiders, especially on bank loans. Interest paid is a narrower term found in the statement of cash flows.	Income statement Profit and loss account Expenses
Long-term loan	This is a loan not repayable within a year. The loan may be with a bank or other organisation. Sometimes long-term loans are called debentures.	Statement of financial position Non-current liabilities

* Income receivable and interest payable are broader phrases than interest received and interest paid. They include interest earned yet to be received and interest incurred yet to be paid, respectively.

Note: We have divided the income statement into two parts, a trading account and a profit and loss account. These terms are sometimes used in the accounts of sole traders and partnerships and in the unabridged income statements of companies.

Comprehensive Example

We now close this chapter with a comprehensive example. This example includes most items normally found in the accounts of a sole trader. We use the example of a small engineering business run by Live Wire, which buys and sells electrical products. The trial balance is provided in Figure 5.6(a), and then in Figure 5.6(b) are the income statement, the statement of financial position and the explanatory notes.

Figure 5.6 Worked Example of a Sole Trader's Accounts

(a)

Live Wire
Trial Balance as at 31 December 2013

	Debit £	Credit £
Revenue		250,000
Revenue returns	800	
Purchases	100,000	
Purchases returns		600
Carriage inwards	200	
Carriage outwards	300	
Discounts allowed	150	
Discounts receivable		175
Dividends receivable		225
Interest receivable		100

Figure 5.6 Worked Example of a Sole Trader's Accounts (*continued*)

	£	£
Drawings	26,690	
Advertising	1,250	
Telephone	2,150	
Wages	27,000	
Electricity	3,700	
Business rates	1,500	
Travelling expenses	1,200	
Van repairs	650	
Petrol	3,800	
General expenses	1,200	
Insurance	1,500	
Premises at cost	80,000	
Accumulated depreciation as at 1 January 2013		8,000
Machine at cost	75,000	
Accumulated depreciation as at 1 January 2013		7,500
Office furniture at cost	12,000	
Accumulated depreciation as at 1 January 2013		1,200
Computer at cost	1,500	
Accumulated depreciation as at 1 January 2013		150
Motor van at cost	6,000	
Accumulated depreciation as at 1 January 2013		600
Opening inventory	9,000	
Cash at bank	7,050	
Bank overdraft		3,600
Trade receivables	4,800	
Provision for the impairment of receivables as at 1 January 2013		240
Trade payables		9,800
Long-term loan		15,600
Interest payable	1,150	
Equity		70,800
	368,590	368,590

You have the following extra information:

(i)   Closing inventory at 31 December 2013 was £8,600.

(ii) Of the insurance £500 was paid in advance.

(iii) Live Wire still owes £450 for the telephone.

(iv) Depreciation is charged at 10% on the cost of the property, plant and equipment (i.e., £8,000 for premises, £7,500 for machine, £1,200 for office furniture, £150 for computer and £600 for motor van). The accumulated depreciation is the depreciation charged to date.

(v) Bad debts are £320. They have not yet been written off. The provision for the impairment of receivables has increased from £240 to £480 and is 10% of trade receivables.

Required: Live Wire's Income Statement for year ended 31 December 2013 and Statement of Financial Position as at 31 December 2013.

Figure 5.6 Worked Example of a Sole Trader's Accounts (*continued*)

(b)

Live Wire
Income Statement Year Ended 31 December 2013

	£	£	£
Revenue			250,000
Less Revenue returns			800
			249,200
Less *Cost of Sales*			
Opening inventory		9,000	
Add Purchases	100,000		
Carriage inwards	200		
	100,200		
Less Purchases returns	600	99,600	
		108,600	
Less Closing inventory (Note 2)		8,600	100,000
Gross Profit			149,200
Add *Other Income*			
Discounts receivable		175	
Dividends receivable		225	
Interest receivable		100	500
			149,700
Less *Expenses*			
Carriage outwards		300	
Discounts allowed		150	
Advertising		1,250	
Telephone (Note 3)		2,600	
Wages		27,000	
Electricity		3,700	
Business rates		1,500	
Travelling expenses		1,200	
Van repairs		650	
Petrol		3,800	
General expenses		1,200	
Insurance (Note 4)		1,000	
Interest payable		1,150	
Depreciation (Note 5)			
Premises		8,000	
Machine		7,500	
Office furniture		1,200	
Computer		150	
Motor van		600	
Bad debts (Note 6)		320	
Provision for the impairment of receivables (Note 7)		240	63,510
Net Profit			86,190

Figure 5.6 Worked Example of a Sole Trader's Accounts (*continued*)

Live Wire

Statement of Financial Position as at 31 December 2013

	£	£	£
		Accumulated depreciation	Net book
ASSETS	Cost	(Note 5)	value
Non-current assets			
Property, plant and equipment			
Premises	80,000	(16,000)	64,000
Machine	75,000	(15,000)	60,000
Office furniture	12,000	(2,400)	9,600
Computer	1,500	(300)	1,200
Motor van	6,000	(1,200)	4,800
	174,500	(34,900)	139,600
Current Assets			
Inventory (Note 2)		8,600	
Trade receivables less provision for the impairment of receivables (Notes 6, 7)		4,000	
Prepayments (Note 4)		500	
Cash at bank		7,050	20,150
Total Assets			159,750
LIABILITIES			
Current Liabilities			
Trade payables		(9,800)	
Bank overdraft		(3,600)	
Accruals (Note 3)		(450)	(13,850)
Non-current Liabilities			(15,600)
Total Liabilities			(29,450)
Net Assets			130,300
EQUITY			£
Opening equity			70,800
Add Net profit			86,190
			156,990
Less Drawings			(26,690)
Closing equity			130,300

Notes:

1. All the figures in Live Wire's accounts, except for closing inventory, telephone, insurance, depreciation, and bad and doubtful debts are as listed in the trial balance. The figures for profit and closing equity are calculated as balancing figures.

2. Closing inventory of £8,600 is recorded in the trading account (top part of the income statement) and in the statement of financial position.

Figure 5.6 Worked Example of a Sole Trader's Accounts (*continued*)

3. The telephone expense is adjusted for the £450 owing. In the income statement, the expense increases to £2,600 (£2,150 + £450). In the statement of financial position, the £450 owing becomes an accrual.

4. The insurance is adjusted for the £500 paid in advance. The expense in the income statement thus becomes £1,000 (£1,500 − £500). The £500 is recorded as a prepayment in current assets in the statement of financial position.

5. The depreciation for the year, which was the same as in Figure 5.2, has been recorded twice: *first,* under expenses in the income statement, and *second*, in the statement of financial position under property, plant and equipment. The double-entry is thus maintained.

6. The £320 for bad debts has been recorded twice: *first*, under expenses in the income statement, and *second*, under current assets (trade receivables) in the statement of financial position. The double-entry is thus completed (see also Figure 5.3).

7. Doubtful debts represents the increase in the provision for the impairment of receivables from £240 to £480. The increase of £240 is recorded twice. *First*, under expenses in the income statement, and *second*, as part of the £480 deduction from trade receivables under current assets in the statement of financial position. The double-entry is thus completed (see also Figure 5.4).

Conclusion

The two main financial statements – the income statement and the statement of financial position – are both prepared from the trial balance. The income statement focuses on income, such as revenue or dividends receivable, and expenses, such as telephone or electricity. The statement of financial position, by contrast, focuses on assets, liabilities and owner's capital or equity. In both financial statements, profit becomes the balancing figure. After the trial balance has been prepared, the accounts are often adjusted for items such as closing inventory, accruals (amounts owing), prepayments (amounts prepaid), depreciation (the wearing out of property, plant and equipment), and bad and doubtful debts. In each case, we adjust the accounts twice: *first* in the income statement and *second* in the statement of financial position. The double-entry and the symmetry of the accounts are thus maintained.

 # Discussion Questions

Questions with numbers in blue have answers at the back of the book.

Q1 What is a sole trader and why is it important for the sole trader to prepare a set of financial statements?

Q2 'Profit is the figure which links the income statement and the statement of financial position.' Discuss.

Q3 Why do we need to carry out post-trial balance adjustments when we are preparing the final accounts?

Numerical Questions

The numerical questions which follow are graded in difficulty. Those at the start are about as complex as the illustrative example, Gavin Stevens. They gradually become more complex, until the final questions equate to the illustrative example, Live Wire.

Questions with numbers in blue have answers at the back of the book.

Q1 Michael Anet has the following trial balance.

M. Anet
Trial Balance as at 31 December 2013

	Debit £	Credit £
Hotel	40,000	
Van	10,000	
Revenue		25,000
Purchases	15,000	
Equity		51,900
Bank	8,000	
Electricity	1,500	
Wages	2,500	
A. Brush (Trade receivable)	400	
A. Painter (Trade payable)		500
	77,400	77,400

Required: Prepare Michael Anet's income statement for the year ended 31 December 2013 and statement of financial position as at 31 December 2013.

Q2 Paul Icasso has the following trial balance.

P. Icasso
Trial Balance as at 31 March 2014

	Debit £	Credit £
Hotel	50,000	
Van	8,000	
Revenue		35,000
Purchases	25,000	
Revenue returns	3,000	
Purchases returns		4,000
Equity		60,050
Bank	9,000	
Electricity	1,000	
Advertising	800	
Trade receivable Shah	1,250	
Trade receivable Chan	2,250	
Trade payable Jones		1,250
	100,300	100,300

Required: Prepare Paul Icasso's trading and income statement for the year ended 31 March 2014 and a statement of financial position as at 31 March 2014.

Q3 Rose Ubens buys and sells goods. Her trial balance is presented below.

R. Ubens
Trial Balance as at 31 December 2013

	Debit £	Credit £
Opening inventory	3,600	
Building	20,400	
Motor van	3,500	
Trade receivables	2,600	
Trade payables		3,800
Cash at bank	4,400	
Electricity	1,500	
Advertising	300	
Printing and stationery	50	
Telephone	650	
Rent and rates	1,200	
Postage	150	
Drawings	7,800	
Equity		19,950
Revenue		88,000
Purchases	66,000	
Revenue returns	800	
Purchases returns		1,200
	112,950	112,950

Note:
1. Closing inventory is £4,000

Required: Prepare Rose Ubens' income statement for the year ended 31 December 2013 and a statement of financial position as at 31 December 2013.

Q4 Clara Onstable has prepared her trial balance as at 31 December. She has the following additional information.

(a) She pays £240 rent per month. She has paid £3,600, the whole year's rent plus three months in advance.

(b) She has paid insurance costs of £480. However, she has paid £120 in advance.

Required: Prepare the extracts for the final accounts.

Q5 Vincent Gogh, a shopkeeper, has the following trial balance.

V. Gogh
Trial Balance as at 31 December 2013

	Debit £	Credit £
Revenue		40,000
Revenue returns	500	
Purchases	25,000	
Purchases returns		450
Opening inventory	5,500	
Trade receivables	3,500	
Trade payables		1,500
Cash at bank	1,300	
Long-term loan		3,700
Motor car	8,500	
Shop	9,000	
Business rates	1,000	
Rent	600	
Electricity	350	
Telephone	450	
Insurance	750	
General expenses	150	
Wages	10,500	
Drawings	12,900	
Equity		34,350
	80,000	80,000

You also have the following additional information.
1. Closing inventory as at 31 December 2013 is £9,000.
2. V. Gogh owes £350 for electricity.
3. £200 of the rent is paid in advance.

Required: Prepare V. Gogh's income statement for the year ended 31 December 2013 and a statement of financial position as at 31 December 2013.

Q6 Leonardo Da Vinci, who sells computers, has extracted the following balances from the accounts.

L. Da Vinci
Trial Balance as at 30 September 2014

	Debit £	Credit £
Revenue		105,000
Revenue returns	8,000	
Purchases	70,000	
Purchases returns		1,800
Opening inventory of computers	6,500	
Drawings	8,500	
Trade receivables	12,000	
Trade payables		13,000
Cash at bank	1,800	
Long-term loan		6,600
Discounts allowed	300	
Carriage inwards	250	
Business premises	18,000	
Motor van	7,500	
Computer	1,500	
Wages	32,500	
Electricity	825	
Telephone	325	
Insurance	225	
Rent	1,250	
Business rates	1,000	
Equity		44,075
	170,475	170,475

You have the following additional information.
1. Closing inventory of computers as at 30 September 2014 is £7,000.
2. Da Vinci owes £175 for the telephone and £1,200 for electricity.
3. The prepayments are £25 for insurance and £250 for rent.

Required: Prepare Da Vinci's income statement for the year ended 30 September 2014 and a statement of financial position as at 30 September 2014.

Q7 Helen Ogarth is preparing her accounts for the year to 31 December 2013. On 1 January 2013 she purchased the following property, plant and equipment.

	£
Buildings	100,000
Machine	50,000
Motor van	20,000

She wishes to write off the following amounts for depreciation.

	£
Buildings	10,000
Machine	3,000
Motor van	2,000

Required: Prepare the appropriate extracts for the statement of financial position and income statement.

Q8 Michael Atisse, a carpenter, has the following trial balance as at 31 December 2013.

	Debit £	Credit £
Work done		50,000
Purchases of materials	25,000	
Opening inventory of tools	650	
Motor expenses	3,550	
Trade receivables	1,000	
Trade payables		4,000
Cash at bank	3,600	
Long-term loan		16,800
Building at cost	52,300	
Motor car at cost	8,000	
Computer at cost	6,300	
Office equipment at cost	10,200	
Business rates	1,300	
Electricity	900	

Q8 Michael Atisse (*continued*)

	Debit £	Credit £
Interest on loan	1,600	
Drawings	5,200	
Telephone	1,200	
Equity		50,000
	120,800	120,800

You have the following additional information.
1. Closing inventory of tools   £4,500
2. Depreciation is to be written off the property, plant and equipment as follows:

Buildings	£3,000
Motor car	£2,000
Computer	£1,400
Office equipment	£1,800

Required: Prepare M. Atisse's income statement for the year ended 31 December 2013 and the statement of financial position as at 31 December 2013.

Q9 Clare Analetto, an antiques dealer, has the following trial balance as at 31 December 2013.

	Debit £	Credit £
Revenue		100,000
Revenue returns	5,000	
Purchases	70,000	
Purchases returns		6,000
Opening inventory of antiques	9,000	
Trade receivables	16,800	
Business rates	800	
Trade payables		14,000
Cash at bank	17,100	
Long-term loan		12,000
Bank interest receivable		850
Rent	2,050	
Electricity	1,950	

Q9 Claire Analetto (*continued*)

	Debit £	Credit £
Insurance	1,250	
Loan interest	1,200	
General expenses	1,025	
Motor van expenses	1,800	
Premises at cost	60,000	
Machinery at cost	16,500	
Office equipment at cost	1,750	
Motor car at cost	2,050	
Drawings	8,200	
Repairs to antiques	1,300	
Telephone	500	
Equity		85,425
	218,275	218,275

You also have the following notes to the accounts.
1. Closing inventory of antiques is £7,000.
2. Depreciation for the year is to be charged at 2% on premises, 10% on machinery, 15% on office equipment and 25% on the motor car.

Required: Prepare C. Analetto's income statement for the year ended 31 December 2013 and the statement of financial position as at 31 December 2013.

Q10 Michelle Angelo has trade receivables of £40,000 at the year end. However, she feels that £4,000 is irrecoverable.

Required: Prepare the appropriate statement of financial position and income statement extracts.

Q11 Simon Eurat, who runs a taxi business, has the following trial balance.

S. Eurat
Trial Balance as at 30 June 2014

	Debit £	Credit £
Cash overdrawn at bank		1,500
Long-term loan		3,550
Receipts		28,300
Diesel and oil	8,250	
Taxi repairs and service	3,950	
Radio hire	3,400	
Road fund licences	2,300	
Buildings at cost	68,000	
Taxis at cost	34,500	
Business rates	450	
Electricity	1,300	
Telephone	1,250	
Trade receivables	100	
Trade payables for motor repairs		1,800
Insurance on buildings	1,300	
General expenses	850	
Drawings	9,600	
Bank interest	150	
Equity		103,250
Wages	3,000	
	138,400	138,400

You have the following additional information.
1. 10% of the trade receivables are definitely considered irrecoverable.
2. £800 of the insurance is prepaid.
3. There is £250 owing for electricity and £300 owing for telephone.
4. Depreciation on taxis is to be 25% on cost and on buildings 2% on cost.

Required: Prepare S. Eurat's income statement for the year ended 30 June 2014 and statement of financial position as at 30 June 2014.

Q12 Rebecca Odin has the following details of her property, plant and equipment.

	Cost	Accumulated depreciation as at 31 December 2012
	£	£
Buildings	102,000	8,000
Machinery	65,000	6,500
Motor car	8,000	4,000
Computer	9,000	2,700

She charges depreciation at 2% per annum on cost for buildings, 10% per annum on cost for machinery, 25% per annum on cost for the motor car and 15% per annum on cost for the computer.

Required: Prepare the appropriate extracts for:
(a) the statement of financial position as at 31 December 2012.
(b) the income statement for year ended 31 December 2013 and for the statement of financial position as at 31 December 2013.

Q13 Deborah Urer owns a small bar. Her trial balance as at 30 June 2014 is set out below.

	Debit £	Credit £
Takings from sales of beer, wine and spirits		145,150
Purchases of beer, wine and spirits	83,250	
Discounts receivable		450
Dividends receivable		150
Drawings	26,400	
Advertising	3,600	
Motor expenses	1,750	
Telephone	2,800	
Electricity	1,250	
Insurance	1,900	
General expenses	2,250	
Repairs	350	
Premises at cost	20,340	
Accumulated depreciation as at 1 July 2013		6,300
Bar equipment at cost	8,200	
Accumulated depreciation as at 1 July 2013		2,500

Q13 D. Urer (*continued*)

	Debit £	Credit £
Bar furniture at cost	5,600	
Accumulated depreciation as at 1 July 2013		1,800
Motor car at cost	3,600	
Accumulated depreciation as at 1 July 2013		2,000
Trade receivables	220	
Provision for the impairment of receivables		20
Loan interest	650	
Trade payables		3,650
Cash at bank	4,350	
Long-term loan		6,500
Wages	2,560	
Business rates	2,450	
Opening inventory	5,500	
Equity		8,500
	177,020	177,020

You also have the following additional information.
1. Closing inventory is £6,250.
2. There is £200 owing for electricity and £300 of the insurance is prepaid.
3. Bad debts are £25 to be written off this year.
4. The provision for the impairment of receivables is to be increased to £25 on 30 June 2014.
5. There are the following depreciation charges:
   2% on premises
   10% on bar equipment and bar furniture
   25% on motor car

Required: Prepare D. Urer's income statement for the year ended 30 June 2014 and the statement of financial position as at 30 June 2014.

Q14 Bernard Ruegel has drawn up a trial balance which is presented below.

B. Ruegel
Trial Balance as at 30 September 2014

	Debit £	Credit £
Carriage inwards	350	
Carriage outwards	180	
Discounts allowed	80	
Discounts receivable		75
Revenue		208,275
Revenue returns	185	
Purchases	110,398	
Drawings	38,111	
Purchases returns		98
Interest receivable		790
Advertising	1,987	
Telephone	476	
Wages and salaries	10,298	
Electricity	1,466	
Rent	2,873	
Cash at bank	21,611	
Travelling expenses	1,288	
Van repairs	1,471	
Petrol	2,187	
Business rates	2,250	
General expenses	1,921	
Insurance	1,100	
Premises at cost	50,981	
Accumulated depreciation as at 1 October 2013		28,300
Machine at cost	21,634	
Accumulated depreciation as at 1 October 2013		8,200
Office furniture at cost	8,011	
Accumulated depreciation as at 1 October 2013		2,386
Computer at cost	2,980	
Accumulated depreciation as at 1 October 2013		1,200
Motor van at cost	2,725	
Accumulated depreciation as at 1 October 2013		1,725
Accumulated depreciation as at 1 October 2013		1,980

Q14 B. Ruegel (*continued*)

	Debit £	Credit £
Opening inventory	11,211	
Loan interest	1,500	
Bank overdraft		8,933
Trade receivables	11,000	
Provision for the impairment of receivables		850
Trade payables		4,279
Long-term loan		14,811
Equity		31,758
	313,660	313,660

You have the following extra information:
1. Closing inventory is £13,206.
2. There are the following amounts owing: advertising £325, telephone £125, carriage outwards £20, general expenses £37, wages and salaries £560.
3. The following amounts are prepaid: travelling expenses £288, electricity £76, insurance £250.
4. It is business policy to treat 10% of total trade receivables as doubtful.
5. There is a bad debt of £600 to be provided in addition to the provision.
6. It has been decided to write down the property, plant and equipment to the following net book value amounts as at 30 September 2014.

	£
Premises	21,081
Machine	12,434
Office furniture	4,151
Computer	125
Motor van	275
Motor car	1,599

Required: Prepare, taking the necessary adjustments into account, the income statement for the year ended 30 September 2014 and the statement of financial position as at 30 September 2014.

Go online to discover the extra features for this chapter at
www.wiley.com/college/jones

Chapter 6

Partnerships and limited companies

'Corporation, [i.e. Company] An ingenious device for obtaining individual profit without individual responsibility.'

Ambrose Bierce, *The Devil's Dictionary*, p. 29.

Learning Outcomes

After completing this chapter you should be able to:

- Explain the nature of partnerships and limited companies.
- Outline the distinctive accounting features of partnerships and limited companies.
- Demonstrate how to prepare the accounts of partnerships and limited companies.
- Understand the differences between listed and non-listed companies preparing accounts under IFRS for SMEs.

Go online to discover the extra features for this chapter at
www.wiley.com/college/jones

Chapter Summary

- Sole proprietors, partnerships and limited companies are the main forms of business enterprise.
- A partnership is more than one person working together.
- Partnership accounts must share out the profit and equity between the partners.
- Sharing out profit, capital and current accounts are special partnership features.
- A limited company is based on the limited liability of the shareholders (i.e., they lose only their initial investment if things go wrong).
- A limited company's special features are taxation, dividends and equity employed split between share capital and reserves.
- In company accounts it is common to find intangible assets (i.e., assets you cannot touch) such as goodwill or patents.
- Limited companies may be private or public.
- A listed company's accounts will follow International Financial Reporting Standards.
- Annual reports are sent to shareholders. They are also increasingly put on a company's website.

Introduction

The three most common types of business enterprise are sole traders, partnerships and public corporations. For example, in 2013, in the UK, there were about 449,525 sole proprietors (or sole traders), 243,235 partnerships and 1,701,740 companies and public corporations (Office for National Statistics, 2013). Of these about 1,300 were listed companies. So far in this book, we have focused on sole traders. Sole traders are, typically, relatively small enterprises owned by one person. Their businesses and accounts tend to be less complicated than those of either partnerships or companies. They are thus ideal for introducing the basic principles behind bookkeeping and final accounts. In this chapter, we now look at the income statement and the statement of financial position of partnerships and limited companies. The statement of cash flows prepared by companies is covered in Chapter 7. Partnerships are normally larger than sole traders. However, basically their accounts are similar to those of the sole trader. This reflects the fact that partners, like sole traders, generally own and run their own businesses. For companies, however, the owners provide the equity, but the directors run the company. This divorce of ownership and management is reflected in the accounts of limited companies. In certain respects, particularly the equity or capital employed, the accounts of limited companies thus appear quite different to those of partnerships and sole traders. From 1 January 2005, listed companies (i.e., companies quoted on a national stock exchange) in the UK and other European Union countries had to follow accounting standards set by the International Accounting Standards Board. From 2015, small and medium-sized non-listed companies in the UK will follow FRS102, UK GAAP, which is based on IFRS for small and medium-sized entities.

Context

In this section, we briefly set out the main features of sole traders, partnerships and limited companies. The main points are summarised in Figure 6.1 using the UK as an example. In essence, the differences between these three types of business enterprise can be traced back to size and capital structure. In terms of size, sole traders are normally smaller than partnerships, which are usually smaller than companies. This greater size causes accounting to be more complicated for companies than for sole traders.

Figure 6.1 Sole Traders, Partnerships and Limited Companies Compared

Feature	Sole Traders	Partnerships	Limited Companies
Business			
(i) Owners	Sole traders	Partners	Shareholders
(ii) Run company	Sole traders	Partners	Directors
(iii) Statutory accounting legislation	No specific act	Partnership Act, 1890	Companies Acts
(iv) Number of owners	1	Since 2002 no restriction on numbers	Private 1–50; Public 2 upwards
(v) Liability	Unlimited	Unlimited, except for limited partners	Limited
(vi) Approximate number in UK* in 2009	449,800	277,200	1,236,900
(vii) Size of turnover in UK*	(a) 64% under £100,000 (b) 1% over £1m	(a) 33% under £100,000 (b) 7% over £1m	(a) 33% under £100,000 (b) 22% over £1m
Accounting			
(i) Main external users of accounts	Tax authorities, bank	Tax authorities, bank	Tax authorities for small, private companies, shareholders for public companies
(ii) Main financial statements	Income statement (also called trading and profit and loss account) and statement of financial position (also called balance sheet)	Income statement (also called trading and profit and loss and appropriation account) and statement of financial position (also called balance sheet)	Income statement, statement of financial position and statement of cash flows
(iii) Main differences in income statement from sole trader	–	Appropriation account shares out profit	Income statement has dividends and taxation (IFRS for SMEs) or taxation but not dividends (full IFRS)
(iv) Main differences in net assets from sole trader	–	None	Companies, when in groups, may have goodwill. They are also likely to have other intangible assets such as patents or brands. In current liabilities, taxation payable
(v) Main differences in equity or owners' capital from sole trader		Capital and current accounts record partners' share of equity invested and profit	Equity essentially divided into share capital and reserves
*From Office for National Statistics, UK Business: activity, size and location, 2009			

An important distinction between the three businesses is the capital structure. Sole traders and most partners own and run their businesses. They provide the capital, although they may borrow money. The main problem for partnerships is simply the fair allocation of both the equity and profit to the partners. For companies, the owners provide the equity whereas the directors run the company. The concept of limited liability for companies means that shareholders can only lose the money they initially invested. This is the great advantage that companies have over sole traders and partnerships. Many small businesses, therefore, prefer to convert from sole traders or partnerships to unlisted companies. They then gain potential protection from their creditors should the businesses fail. These unlisted companies are generally not listed and their shares are not publicly traded on the stock market.

Partnerships

Introduction

Partnerships may be seen as sole traders with multiple owners. Many sole traders take on partners to help them finance and run their businesses. As in all human relationships, when partners are well matched, partnerships can prove very successful businesses. However, when they are ill-suited, problems can occur (see Soundbite 6.1). Except for certain occupations (such as firms of accountants or solicitors) the maximum number of partners in the UK is 20. An important aspect of both sole traders and partnerships is that liability is generally unlimited. (There is an exception, if you are a limited partner. Limited partners can lose only the equity invested. However, they do not participate in running the company and there must be at least one unlimited liability partner.) In other words, if a business goes bankrupt the personal assets of the owners are *not* ring-fenced. Bankrupt partners may have to sell their houses to pay their creditors. Recently, however, for professional partnerships, particularly accounting partnerships, a new organisational form, the limited liability partnership (LLP), has been created. For these organisations, liability is capped.

Sole traders and partners prepare accounts for use in their own personal internal management, but also for external users, such as the tax authorities and banks. The key issue which underpins partnerships is how the partners should split any profits. The ratio in which the profits are split is called the profit sharing ratio or PSR. Partnerships traditionally have used the terms 'trading and profit and loss and appropriation account'

SOUNDBITE 6.1

Partners

'The history of human achievement is rich with stories of successful partnerships – while the history of human failure is rife with tales of fruitless competition and wilful antagonisms.'

Margaret E. Mahoney, *The Commonwealth Fund* (Annual Report 1987)

Source: The Executive's Book of Quotations (1994), p. 212.

and 'balance sheet' for their financial statements. However, for consistency with the rest of the book I use the terms 'income statement' and 'statement of financial position'. I also use equity rather than capital. However, I still refer to the appropriation account as a section at the bottom of the partnership income statement.

It is in the appropriation account that the allocation of profits between the partners is presented. The appropriation, or 'sharing out', account appears after the calculation of net profit. In other words, we add a section at the bottom of the income statement.

REAL-WORLD VIEW 6.1

Partnerships

Occasionally partners have more in common than business interests: their names seem to complement each other. The following curious and apt names of partnerships were collected from old English signs and business directories: Carpenter & Wood; Spinage & Lamb; Sage & Gosling; Rumfit & Cutwell, and Greengoose & Measure, both tailors; Single & Double; Foot and Stocking, Hosiers. One is not quite sure whether to believe that Adam & Eve were two surgeons who practised in Paradise Row, London, though Buyers & Sellers did have a shop in Holborn.

'Sometimes the occupation of persons harmonizes admirably with their surnames,' a nineteenth-century antiquarian continues: Gin & Ginman are innkeepers; so is Alehouse; Seaman is the landlord of the Ship Hotel, and A. King holds the 'Crown and Sceptre' resort in City Road. Portwine and Negus are licensed victuallers, one in Westminster and the other in Bishopsgate Street. Mixwell's country inn is a well-known resort. Pegwell is a shoemaker, so are Fitall and Treadaway, likewise Pinch; Tugwell is a noted dentist; Bird an egg merchant; Hemp a sherriff's officer; Captain Isaac Paddle commands a steamboat; Mr. Punt is a favourite member of the Surrey wherry [rowing] club; Laidman was formerly a pugilist; and Smooker or Smoker a lime burner; Skin & Bone were the names of two millers in Manchester; Fogg and Mist china dealers in Warwick street: the firm afterward became Fogg & Son, on which it was naturally enough remarked that the 'son had driven away the mist.' Mr. I. Came, a wealthy shoemaker in Liverpool, who left his immense property to public charities, opened his first shop on the opposite side of the street to where he had started as a servant, and inscribed a sign: 'I CAME from over the way.'

Finally, Going & Gonne was the name of a well-known banking house in Ireland, and on their failure in business someone wrote:

'Going & Gonne are now both one
For Gonne is going and Going's gone.'

Source: Peter Hay (1988), *The Book of Business Anecdotes*, Harrap Ltd, London, pp. 119–20.

The main elements of the basic appropriation account are salaries and the sharing of the profit. Salaries are allocated to the partners before the profit is shared out. Note that for partners, salaries are an appropriation *not* an expense. Figure 6.2 demonstrates the process.

Figure 6.2 Main Elements in the Partnership Appropriation Account

Main Elements	Explanation	Layout		
			£	£
Net Profit	Profit as calculated from income statement	Net profit before appropriation		18,000
		Less:		
Salaries	The amount which each partner earns must be deducted from net profit before profit sharing	Salaries A	5,500	
		B	3,500	9,000
				9,000
Residual Profit	The profit share for each individual	Profit A	6,000	
		B	3,000	9,000

Two partners, A and B, share £18,000 net profit. The profit sharing ratio is 2:1. Their salaries are £5,500 and £3,500, respectively. The example is continued in Figure 6.3.

Partners' equity can be divided into two parts: capital accounts and current accounts. Each partner needs to keep track of his or her own equity.

PAUSE FOR THOUGHT 6.1

Partners' Profit Sharing

Why are profits not just split equally between partners?

Superficially, it might seem that the partners might just split the profit equally between them. So if a partnership of two people earns £30,000, each partner's share is £15,000. Unfortunately, life is not so simple! In practice, profit sharing is determined by a number of factors, such as how hard each partner works, their experience and the equity each partner has contributed. It might, therefore, be decided that the profit sharing ratio or PSR was 2:1. In this case, one partner would take £20,000; the second would take £10,000.

Capital Accounts

These accounts represent the long-term capital invested into the partnership by the individual partners. When new partners join a partnership, it is conventional for them to 'buy their way' into the partnership. This initial equity introduced can be seen as purchasing their share of the net assets of the business they have joined. This initial equity remains unchanged in the accounts unless the partners specifically introduce or withdraw long-term equity. It represents the amount which the business 'owes' the partners.

Figure 6.3 Main Elements in Partners' Current Accounts

Main Elements	Explanation	Layout		
			A £	B £
Opening Balances	Amount of profits brought forward from last year. Normally a credit balance, and is the amount the business owes the partner	Opening balances	7,000	6,000
Salaries	The amount which the partners earn by way of salary	Add: Salaries	5,500	3,500
Profit Share	Amount of the profit attributable to partner. Determined by profit sharing ratio	Profit	6,000 18,500	3,000 12,500
Drawings	Amount the partners take out of the business to live on	Less: Drawings	12,000	10,000
Closing Balances	The amount of profits carried forward to next year. This is usually the balance owed to the partner	Closing balances	6,500	2,500

Current Accounts

In contrast to the capital accounts, current accounts are not fixed. Essentially, they represent the partners' share of the profits of the business since they joined, less their withdrawals. In basic current accounts, the main elements are the opening balances, salaries, profit for year, drawings and closing balances. These elements are set out in Figure 6.3. This continues Figure 6.2, with drawings of £12,000 for A and £10,000 for B. It is important to realise that the salaries are credited (or added) to the partners' current account rather than physically paid. The partners physically withdraw cash, which is known as drawings. Drawings are essentially sums taken out of the business by the partners as living expenses.

PAUSE FOR THOUGHT 6.2

Debit Balances on Current Accounts

What do you think a negative or debit balance on a partner's current account means?

This means that the partner owes the partnership money! A current account represents the partner's account with the business. It is increased by or credited with (i.e., the business owes the partner money) the partner's salary and share of profit. The account is then debited (or reduced) when the partner takes money out (i.e., drawings). If the partner takes out more funds than are covered by the salary and profit share, a debit balance is created. It is, in effect, like going overdrawn at the bank. A partner with a debit balance owes, rather than is owed, capital.

Partnership Example: Stevens and Turner

Let us imagine that Gavin Stevens has traded for several years. The year is now far into the future 20XX. He has now teamed up with Diana Turner. Both partners have invested £135,000 equity into their capital accounts. Their salaries are £12,000 for Stevens and £6,000 for Turner. Their current accounts stand at £8,000 (credit) Stevens, £9,000 (credit) Turner. They share residual profits in Stevens' favour 2:1. Their opening trial balance is below.

Stevens and Turner: Partnership Trial Balance as at 31 December 20XX

		£	£
Capital accounts	Stevens		135,000
	Turner		135,000
Current accounts	Stevens		8,000
	Turner		9,000
Drawings	Stevens	18,000	
	Turner	13,500	
Hotel		610,000	
Vans		30,200	
Opening inventory		5,000	
Trade receivables		15,000	
Trade payables			20,000
Bank		20,300	
Electricity		1,850	
Wages		12,250	
Telephone		350	
Long-term loan			350,000
Revenue			270,000
Purchases		195,000	
Other expenses		5,550	
		927,000	927,000

Notes:
1. Closing inventory is £10,000.
2. For simplicity, we are ignoring all other post-trial balance adjustments such as depreciation, bad and doubtful debts, accruals and prepayments.
3. Salaries are £12,000 for Stevens and £6,000 for Turner. These are 'notional' salaries in that the money is not actually paid to the partners. Instead it is credited to their accounts.

Using this trial balance we now prepare, in Figure 6.4, the income statement (with an appropriation account) and the statement of financial position.

Figure 6.4 Stevens and Turner Partnership Accounts Year Ended 31 December 20XX

Stevens and Turner
Income Statement for the Year Ended
31 December 20XX

	£	£
Revenue		270,000
Less Cost of Sales		
Opening inventory	5,000	
Add Purchases	195,000	
	200,000	
Less Closing inventory	10,000	190,000
Gross Profit		80,000
Less Expenses		
Electricity	1,850	
Wages	12,250	
Telephone	350	
Other expenses	5,550	20,000

* *

Net profit before appropriation		60,000
Less Salaries		
Stevens	12,000	
Turner	6,000	18,000
		42,000
Profits:		
Stevens	28,000	
Turner	14,000	
Net Profit		42,000

* *

Note: The net profit is calculated as for a sole trader. The profit is then shared out between the partners. This appropriation is shown between the asterisks.

Stevens and Turner
Statement of Financial Position as at 31 December 20XX

ASSETS	£
Non-current Assets	
Property, Plant and Equipment	
Hotel	610,000
Vans	30,200
Total non-current assets	640,200

Figure 6.4 Stevens and Turner Partnership Accounts Year Ended 31 December 20XX (*continued*)

Current Assets			£
Inventory			10,000
Trade receivables			15,000
Bank			20,300
Total current assets			45,300
Total Assets			685,500
LIABILITIES			
Current Liabilities			
Trade payables			(20,000)
Non-current Liabilities			(350,000)
Total Liabilities			(370,000)
Net Assets			315,500

	Stevens	Turner	
	£	£	£
EQUITY			
Capital Accounts	135,000	135,000	270,000
Current Accounts			
Opening balances	8,000	9,000	
Add			
Salaries	12,000	6,000	
Profit share	28,000	14,000	
	48,000	29,000	
Less Drawings	18,000	13,500	
Closing balances	30,000	15,500	45,500
Total Partners' Funds			315,500

Note: The total net assets part of the statement of financial position is drawn up as for a sole trader. The capital and current accounts show the amounts due to the partners. They are distinctive to partnership accounts and are shown between the asterisks.

Limited Companies

The Basics

Limited companies are a popular form of legal business entity. As Real-World View 6.2 indicates, in actual fact a 'company' does not physically exist. It is a collection of people and assets. However, companies do have a legal existence. The essence of limited companies lies in the fact that the shareholders' (i.e., owners') liability is limited. This means that owners are only liable to lose the amount of money they have initially invested. For example, if a shareholder invests £500 in a company and the company goes bankrupt, then £500 is all the shareholder will lose. All the shareholder's personal possessions (for example, house or car) are safe! This is a great advantage over partnerships and sole traders where the liability is unlimited.

REAL-WORLD VIEW 6.2

The Company

A second major feature of the orthodox creed is the ascription of supernatural existence to the 'company'. Objectively and rationally speaking, the 'company' does not exist at all, except in so far as it is a heterogeneous collection of people. In order to facilitate the mutual ownership and use of assets, and for other technical reasons, the corporation is treated in law as a person. It is a legal fiction, but a fiction nonetheless.

Source: Graham Cleverly (1971), *Managers and Magic*, Longman Group Limited, London, p. 31.

PAUSE FOR THOUGHT 6.3

Limited Liability

For suppliers, and particularly lenders, limited liability can be bad news as their money may be less secure. Can you think of any ways they may seek to counter this?

A fact that is often overlooked is that in small companies, limited liability is often not seen as a bonus to those who have close connections with the company. Suppliers may be less certain that they will be paid and bankers more worried about making loans. In many cases, unlimited liability is replaced by other control mechanisms. For example, suppliers may want to be paid in cash or have written guarantees of payment. Bankers will often secure their loans against the property of the business and, in many cases, against the personal assets of the owners. So the owners may not avoid losing their personal possessions in a bankruptcy after all.

The mechanism underpinning a limited liability company is the share. The total equity of the business is divided into these shares (literally a 'share' in the equity of the business). For instance, a business with share capital of £500,000 might divide this share capital into 500,000 shares of £1 each. These shares may then be bought and sold. Subsequently, they will probably be bought or sold for more or less than £1. For instance, Sheilah might sell 50,000 £1 shares to Mary for £75,000. There is thus a crucial difference between the face value of the shares (£1 each in this case) and their trading value (£1.50 each in this case).

The face value of the shares is termed **nominal value**. The trading value is termed **market price**. If market price increases, it is the individual shareholder *not* the company that benefits.

The risk for the shareholders is that they will lose the equity they have invested. The reward is twofold. First, shareholders will receive dividends (i.e., annual payments based on profits) for investing their capital. The dividends are the reward for investing their money in the company rather than, for example, investing in a bank or building society where it would earn interest. The second reward is any potential growth in share price. For example, if Sheilah originally purchased the shares for £50,000, she would gain £25,000 when she sold them to Mary for £75,000.

It is important to realise that the shareholders own the company; they do not run the company. Running the company is the job of the directors. This division is known as the 'divorce of ownership and control'. In many small companies, however, the directors own most of the shares. In this case, although in theory there is a separation of ownership and control, in practice there is not.

There are two types of company in the UK. The private limited company and the public limited company. The main features are outlined in Figure 6.5.

Figure 6.5 Features of Private Limited Companies (Ltds) and Public Limited Companies (plcs) in the UK

Feature	Private Limited Company	Public Limited Company
Names	Ltd after company name	PLC after company name
Number of shareholders	1 upwards	2 to unlimited
Share trading	Restricted	Unrestricted
Stock market listing	No	Usually
Authorised share capital	No minimum	At least £50,000
Size	Usually small to medium enterprises	Usually medium to large enterprises
Accounts	Follow National Standards	Follow International Accounting Standards

The essential difference is that private limited companies are usually privately controlled and owned whereas public limited companies are large corporations usually trading on the stock market. Their shares can thus be bought and sold by individuals external to the companies themselves. The major companies world wide such as British Petroleum, Toyota and Coca-Cola are all, in essence, public limited companies. (Even though laws vary from country to country, they are broadly equivalent.) In these large companies, the managers are, in theory, accountable to the shareholders. In practice, many commentators doubt this accountability.

There are several reasons why companies prepare accounts. First, the detailed accounts (normally comprising an income statement, a statement of financial position and a statement of cash flows) will be used by management for internal management purposes. They will often be prepared monthly. The published accounts which are sent to the shareholders will usually be prepared annually.

The second reason is to comply with the Companies Act 2006. This lays down certain minimum statutory requirements which are supplemented by accounting standards and stock exchange regulations. Companies following these accounting requirements will normally prepare and send their shareholders published accounts containing an income statement, statement of financial position and (except for small companies which are exempt) a statement of cash flows.

These accounts are prepared using a standardised format. For large companies, these accounts are sent out to shareholders as part of the annual reporting package. This is dealt with in detail in Chapter 11; however, it is briefly introduced later in this chapter. Companies, as part of their statutory reporting requirements, will also submit a set of accounts to the Registrar of Companies.

Third, as well as preparing accounts for shareholders, companies may also provide accounts to other users who have an interest in the company's affairs. Of particular importance is the role of corporation tax. The statutory accounts are usually used as the starting point for assessing this tax, which was introduced in 1965 and is payable by companies on their profits. It is calculated according to a complicated, and often-changing, set of tax rules. 'Accounting' profit is usually adjusted to arrive at 'taxable' profit. Unlike partnerships and sole traders, who are assessed for income tax as individuals, companies are assessed for corporation tax as taxable entities themselves.

Finally, especially for large companies, there may be a wide range of potential users of the accounts such as employees, customers, banks and suppliers. Their information needs were discussed in Chapter 1. The accounts of medium and large companies are usually prepared by the directors and then audited by independent accountants. This is so that the shareholders and other users can be assured that the accounts are 'true and fair'. The auditors' report is a badge of quality.

PAUSE FOR THOUGHT 6.4

Abridged Company Accounts

Companies often prepare a full, detailed set of accounts for their internal management purposes. Why would they not wish to supply these to their shareholders?

....

For internal management purposes, detailed information is necessary to make decisions. However, in the published accounts, directors are careful what they disclose. In a public limited company, anybody can buy shares and thus receive the published accounts. Directors do not wish to give away any secrets to potential competitors just because they own a few shares. In actual fact, the Companies Acts requirements allow the main details to be disclosed in a way that is sometimes not terribly informative. There are many levels at which accounts can be summarised. Figure 6.8 shows a very high level of summary, while Figure 6.17 is more like the level of detail which companies typically supply in their annual reports.

A distinctive feature of many companies is that they are organised into groups. This book does not cover the preparation of group accounts (which are often complex and complicated and best left to more specialist textbooks). Interested readers might try Alexander, Britton and Jorissen (2011) *International Financial Reporting and Analysis*. For now we merely note that many medium and large companies are not, in fact, single entities, but are really many individual companies working together collectively. There is, usually, one overall company which is the controlling company. This is further discussed in Chapter 11.

Distinctive Accounting Features of Limited Companies

The essence of the income statements of sole traders, partnerships and limited companies is the same. However, there are some important differences. The most important difference between a sole trader and a partnership is that for partnerships the profit is divided (this is formally known as appropriated) between the partners. Many UK companies still follow UK GAAP. Manchester United is a good example and its income statement and statement of financial position (balance sheet) are presented in Appendices 6.1 and 6.2 at the end of this chapter. As you will see, these statements use UK GAAP terminology such as stock for inventories. Many people in the UK still prefer these terms.

For limited companies, there is an abridged, standardised format set out by the 2006 Companies Act for non-listed companies. For listed companies, the format is similar, but is prepared under International Financial Reporting Standards. An illustration of the formats for the four business entities is given in Figure 6.6.

Figure 6.6 Differences between Income Statements of Sole Traders, Partnerships and Limited Companies

Sole Traders: Income Statement (also known as Trading and Profit and Loss Account)		Partnerships: Income Statement (also known as Trading and Profit and Loss and Appropriation Account)		Non-Listed Limited Companies: Income Statement reporting under IFRS for SMEs		Listed Companies: Income Statement	
	£		£		£		£
Revenue	200,000	Revenue	200,000	Revenue	200,000	Revenue	200,000
Cost of Sales	(100,000)	Cost of Sales	(100,000)	Cost of Sales	(100,000)	Cost of Sales	(100,000)
Gross Profit	100,000	Gross Profit	100,000	Gross Profit	100,000	Gross Profit	100,000
Other Income	10,000	Other Income	10,000	Other Income	10,000	Other Income	10,000
	110,000		110,000		110,000		110,000
Expenses	(60,000)	Expenses	(60,000)	Expenses	(60,000)	Expenses	(60,000)
Net Profit	50,000	Net Profit	50,000	Profit before Tax	50,000	Profit before Tax	50,000
				Taxation	(20,000)	Taxation	(20,000)
		Partner A	25,000	Profit after Tax	30,000	Profit for the period	30,000
		Partner B	25,000	Dividends	(15,000)		
				Retained Profit	15,000		
			50,000				

Be careful of the limited companies' format. There are several possible variations and the examples in Figure 6.6 have been grossly simplified for comparison purposes. The income statements of listed companies may be called by a variety of names. For small and medium-sized entities (SMEs), they may be called the Statement of Comprehensive Income and Retained Earnings. This may include dividends. For listed companies, there may be an income statement and then a separate Statement of Other Comprehensive Income dealing with non-operating income such as property revaluations or foreign exchange differences. Alternatively, the limited company may produce a Statement of Comprehensive Income which combines both statements. Dividends will be recorded separately. Generally in this book we will use the term 'the income statement' for ease of understanding. I do, however, use Statement of Comprehensive Income for the published accounts of limited companies.

The special nature of limited companies leads to several distinctive differences between the accounts of limited companies and those of sole traders and partnerships, both in the income statement and in the statement of financial position. We now deal with four special features of a company: taxation, dividends, the formats and long-term capital. We also discuss intangible assets which can occur in the accounts of sole traders and partnerships, but are much more common in company accounts.

1. Taxation

As previously noted, companies pay corporation tax. As Soundbite 6.2 shows, taxation has never proved very popular. For companies, taxation is assessed on annual taxable profits. Essentially, these are the accounting profits adjusted to comply with taxation rules. The accounting consequences of taxation on the income statement and statement of financial position are twofold.

SOUNDBITE 6.2

Taxation

'The art of taxation consists in so plucking the goose as to obtain the largest possible amount of feathers with the smallest possible amount of hissing.'

Jean-Baptiste Colbert

Source: The Book of Business Quotations (1998), p. 257.

- In the income statement, *the amount for taxation for the year is recorded*.
- In the statement of financial position, under current liabilities, *the liability for the year is recorded as proposed taxation*.

It is important to note that for companies there is no direct record of taxation paid in the income statement or statement of financial position. Taxation paid appears in the statement of cash flows. This is illustrated in Pause for Thought 6.5 (see page 157).

2. Dividends

A reward for shareholders for the capital they have invested is the dividends they receive. Recent changes in accounting treatment have led to the virtual elimination of proposed dividends from the accounts. Therefore, in this book, for consistency, all dividends will be treated as paid. In the case of non-listed companies which are reporting under IFRS for SMEs, the following treatment is used. *All dividends for the year are recorded in the income statement*. This feeds into the retained earnings at the end of the year. There is thus no separate disclosure in the statement of financial position. However, in some cases a statement of changes in equity may be prepared.

Note that for listed companies or companies reporting under full IFRS, *no* dividends are recorded in the income statement. There are two possible ways of treating these in the statement of financial position. First, they may be deducted from shareholders' equity in the statement of financial position. Alternatively, and more usually, they may be recorded in a statement of changes in equity. These alternatives are shown in Figure 6.7 below.

Figure 6.7 Treatment of Dividends Paid in the Statement of Financial Position for a Listed Company under IFRS

Tutin Plc has opening retained earnings of £250,000, a profit for the year of £100,000 with preference dividends and ordinary dividends paid of £8,000 and £6,000, respectively, for the year ended 31 December 2012. Other reserves are £300,000.

i) Deduction from reserves.

Statement of Financial Position for Tutin Plc as at 31 December 2013

Reserves	£	£	£
Capital reserves			300,000
Other reserves			
Opening retained earnings		250,000	
Retained earnings for year	100,000		
Less: Dividends paid	(14,000)	86,000	
Closing retained earnings			336,000
Total Equity			636,000

ii) Separate Statement of Changes in Equity

Statement of Changes in Equity for Tutin Plc for the year ended 31 December 2013

	£	£
Opening retained earnings		250,000
Retained earnings for year	100,000	
Less: Dividends Paid	(14,000)	86,000
Closing retained earnings		336,000

This is then taken to the statement of financial position as shown below

Statement of Financial Position for Tutin Plc as at 31 December 2012

	£
Reserves	
Capital Reserves	
Other reserves	300,000
Retained earnings	336,000
Total Equity	636,000

Many companies, like J. Sainsbury plc (the UK supermarket group) pay interim dividends as payments on account during the accounting year and then final dividends once the accounts have been prepared and the actual profit is known. Only the paid dividends are recognised in the financial statements as is illustrated in Company Snapshot 6.1.

COMPANY SNAPSHOT 6.1

Dividends

	2010 pence per share	2009 pence per share	2010 £m	2009 £m
Amounts recognised as distributions to equity holders in the year:				
Final dividend of prior financial year	**9.60**	9.00	**167**	155
Interim dividend of current financial year	4.00	3.60	74	63
	13.60	12.60	241	218

After the balance sheet date, a final dividend of 10.20 pence per share (2009:9.60 pence per share) was proposed by the Directors in respect of the 52 weeks to 20 March 2010, resulting in a total final proposed dividend of £189 million (2009: £167 million). The proposed final dividend has not been included as a liability at 20 March 2010.

Source: J. Sainsbury plc, *Annual Report and Financial Statements 2010*, p. 63. Reproduced by kind permission of Sainsbury's Supermarkets Ltd.

PAUSE FOR THOUGHT 6.5

Taxation Paid

If you have details of the income statement charge for taxation and the opening and closing liabilities, how do you calculate the amount actually paid?

....

One becomes a detective. Take this example: opening taxation payable £800, closing taxation payable £1,000, income statement taxation expense £3,000. Our opening liability of £800 plus this year's charge of £3,000 equals £3,800. At the end of the year, however, we only owe £1,000. We must, therefore, have paid £2,800. This logic underpins the calculation of tax paid in the statement of cash flows, covered in Chapter 7.

3. Formats and Terminology

There are, rather confusingly, a variety of formats used by companies. Non-listed companies may follow either IFRS format, or national UK standards under FRS102 based on IFRS for SMEs. These were covered in Figure 6.6.

The presentational formats for IFRS can be broadly categorised as falling into (1) a total assets and a total equity and liabilities format followed by most European companies and (2) a net assets format followed by most UK companies. These different formats are outlined in Figure 6.8.

Figure 6.8 Different Statement of Financial Position Structures for Sole Traders, Partnerships and Limited Companies

Sole Traders and Partnerships		Companies (1) Net Assets Format		Companies (2) Assets and Liabilities Format	
	£		£		£
ASSETS		**ASSETS**		**ASSETS**	
Non-current Assets	80,000	**Non-current Assets**	80,000	**Non-current Assets**	80,000
Current Assets	80,000	**Current Assets**	80,000	**Current Assets**	80,000
Total Assets	160,000	*Total Assets*	160,000	*Total Assets*	160,000
LIABILITIES		**LIABILITIES**		**EQUITY AND LIABILITIES**	
Current Liabilities	(20,000)	**Current Liabilities**	(20,000)	Equity*	120,000
Non-Current Liabilities	(20,000)	**Non-Current Liabilities**	(20,000)	Non-current Liabilities	20,000
Total Liabilities	(40,000)	*Total Liabilities*	(40,000)	*Total Liabilities*	20,000
Net Assets	120,000	*Net Assets*	120,000		
Equity*	120,000	Equity*	120,000	**Total Equity and Liabilities**	160,000
		Approach used in this book for sole traders, partnerships and companies			

Note: * A breakdown of the Equity figure for the three business types is presented in Figure 6.11.

UK listed companies prefer to subtract total liabilities from total assets to arrive at net assets which equals equity (Assets − Liabilities = Equity). By contrast, European listed companies prefer to record total assets and then to add equity to liabilities (Assets = Equity and Liabilities). Although the totals are different, the individual figures are the same. Examples of the two different approaches are given in Company Snapshot 6.4 on page 172 (net assets equals equity approach) and Appendix 2.5 in Chapter 2 (total assets equals total equity and liabilities approach). The situation is further complicated by the fact that instead of totalling all the assets and liabilities and then striking a balance, some UK companies present a net figure for net current assets. This is illustrated below.

	£	£
Non-current assets		80,000
Current assets	80,000	
Current liabilities	(20,000)	
Net current assets		60,000
Non-current liabilities		(20,000)
Net assets		120,000

In this book, the net assets approach has been used for sole traders, partnerships and companies as followed by UK listed companies as presented in Figure 6.8. This is considered the simplest and easiest to understand.

In terms of terminology, there is a variety of usages. For limited companies, for consistency, and to reflect better the real economic situation, I use inventories not inventory. Also under equity, I use the sub-heading capital and reserves.

4. Long-Term Capital

The long-term capital of a company can be categorised into share capital (comprising ordinary and preference shares) and loan capital (often called debentures). We can see the differences between these in Figure 6.9. This is portrayed diagrammatically in Figure 6.10.

Figure 6.9 Different Types of Long-Term Capital of a Company

Features	Ordinary Shareholders	Preference Shareholders	Debenture holders
Type of capital	Share	Share	Loan
Ownership	Own company	Do not own company	Do not own company
Risk	Lose money invested first	Lose money invested after ordinary shareholder	Often loans secured on assets
Reward	Dividends and growth in the market value of the share	Usually fixed dividends	Interest payable
Accounting treatment for non-listed companies	Under Equity	Under Equity	Under Liabilities as a non-current liability
Accounting treatment for listed companies	Under Equity	Under Equity	Deducted from net assets

Figure 6.10 Long-Term Capital Structure of a Company

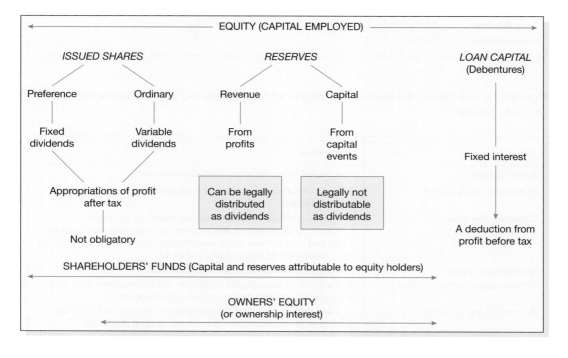

In terms of capital structure, the basic financing structure of a company can be split into that owned by the shareholders in terms of capital and reserves and that provided by debentures in terms of loan capital. The ordinary shareholders' equity is represented by ordinary shares and reserves.

Essentially, ordinary shareholders own the company by way of owning shares and, therefore, take the most risk and, potentially, gain the most reward. The risk is that the company may fail and they may therefore lose their money, while the reward is in terms of dividends and an increase in the value of their shares if they wished to sell. Preference shareholders normally receive a fixed dividend, whereas debenture holders receive interest. Debentures are long-term loans. Neither preference shareholders nor debenture holders are owners of the company.

As Figure 6.11 below shows, the limited company's equity (capital employed) is presented differently from that of the sole trader or partnership. For a limited company, the equity is not adjusted for drawings. Excluding long-term capital, a company's equity is essentially represented by share capital and reserves.

Unfortunately, there are many different types of share capital and reserves. Figure 6.12 below provides a quick overview of these.

Figure 6.11 Owner's Equity (Capital Employed) for Sole Trader, Partnerships and Limited Companies

Sole Trader		Partnership		Limited Company	
	£		£		£
Opening equity	100,000	Capital Accounts	100,000	Share Capital	100,000
Add Net Profit	50,000	Current Accounts	20,000	Reserves	20,000
	150,000	Total Partners' Funds	120,000	Total Equity (total shareholders' funds)	120,000
Less Drawings	30,000				
Closing Equity	120,000				

Figure 6.12 Overview of the Main Terminology of a Limited Company's Share Capital and Reserves, and Loan Capital

Term	Explanation
Share Capital	The capital of the company divided into shares.
Authorised share capital	The amount of share capital that a company is allowed to issue to its shareholders.
Called-up share capital	The amount of issued capital that has been fully paid to the company by shareholders. For example, a share may be issued for £1.50 and paid in three equal installments. After two installments are paid, the called-up share capital will be £1.
Issued share capital	The amount of share capital actually issued.
Ordinary (equity) share capital	The amount of share capital relating to the shareholders who own the company and are entitled to ordinary dividends.
Preference share capital	The amount of share capital relating to shareholders who are not owners of the company and are entitled to fixed dividends.

Figure 6.12 Overview of the Main Terminology of a Limited Company's Share Capital and Reserves, and Loan Capital (*continued*)

Market value	The value the shares will fetch on the open market. This may differ significantly from their nominal value.
Nominal value	The face value of the shares, usually their original issue price.
Reserves	The accumulated profits (revenue reserves) or capital gains (capital reserves) to shareholders.
Capital reserves	Reserves which are not distributable to shareholders as dividends; for example, the share premium account or revaluation reserve.
General reserve	A reserve created to deal with general, unspecified contingencies such as inflation.
Retained earnings	The accumulated profits of a listed company.
Revaluation reserve	A capital reserve created when Property, Plant and Equipment are revalued at more than the original purchase cost. The revaluation is a gain to the shareholders.
Revenue reserves	Reserves that are distributable to shareholders as dividends; for example, the income statement, general reserve.
Share premium account	A capital reserve created when new shares are issued for more than their nominal value. For example, if shares were issued for £150,000 and the nominal value was £100,000, the share premium account would be £50,000.
Total equity	The share capital and reserves which are owned by ordinary and preference shareholders.
Loan capital	Money loaned to the company by third parties. They are not owners of the company and are entitled to interest not dividends.
Debentures	Just another name for a long-term loan. Debentures may be secured or unsecured.
Secured and unsecured loans	Secured loans are loans which are secured on (or guaranteed by) the assets of the company. Unsecured loans are loans which are not secured on the assets.

Share capital represents the amount that the shareholders have directly invested. The amount a company is allowed to issue (authorised share capital) is determined in a company document called the Memorandum of Association. The amount actually issued is the issued share capital. It is important to emphasise that the face value for the shares is not their market value. If you like, it is like buying and selling stamps. The Penny Black, a rare stamp, was issued at one penny (nominal value), but you would have to pay a fortune for one today (market value). Shareholders' funds is an important figure in the statement of financial position and is equivalent to net assets (Company Snapshot 6.2 shows the shareholders' funds for Tesco PLC).

COMPANY SNAPSHOT 6.2

Fame - company report of Tesco PLC

Tesco PLC

Waltham Cross, EN8 9SL (England)

Registered no	00445790
Status	Active

Publicly quoted
This company is the GUO of the Corporate Group

Evolution of: Shareholders' Funds (2001–2010)

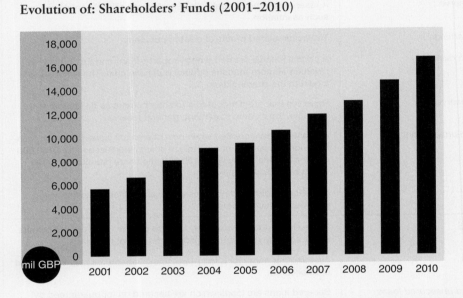

Source: Fame Database. Company report of Tesco PLC. Evolution of: Shareholders' Funds (2001–2010) published by Bureau van Dijk.

Reserves are essentially gains to the shareholder. Capital reserves are gains from activities such as issuing shares at more than the nominal value (share premium account) or revaluing property, plant and equipment (revaluation reserve). They cannot be paid out as dividends. By contrast, revenue reserves, essentially accumulated profits, are distributable.

5. Intangible Assets

Intangible assets are literally non-current assets one cannot touch. They are thus in direct contrast to tangible non-current assets (plant, property and equipment) such as land and buildings, plant and machinery, fixtures and fittings and motor vehicles which are highly visible. They can occur in all businesses, but are most common in companies. Intangible assets are increasing in value and frequency as organisations become more knowledge-based. As the old manufacturing firms which are heavily dependent on property, plant and equipment decline

PAUSE FOR THOUGHT 6.6

The Nature of Reserves

Can you spend reserves?

No! Reserves are not cash. Reserves are in fact amounts which the business owes to the share-holders. They represent either accumulated profits (retained earnings) or gains to the shareholders such as an issue of shares above the nominal value (share premium account) or the revaluation of property, plant and equipment (revaluation account). Reserves are represented by net assets. However, these assets may be non-current assets or current assets. They do not have to be cash. They may, for example, represent intangible assets such as goodwill. If they are not cash, they obviously cannot be spent as cash, although they may be used for certain treasury transactions such as buying back shares.

and the new information technology businesses arise, the balance of assets in companies changes. There are now many types of intangible assets, such as goodwill. Goodwill is covered in more depth in Chapter 11.

PAUSE FOR THOUGHT 6.7

Intangible Assets

Apart from goodwill, can you think of any other intangible assets?

There are many, but four of the most common are brands, copyrights, patents and software development costs. Perhaps the most frequently occurring of these is patents. A patent is an intangible asset which represents the amount a firm has paid to register a patent or has paid to purchase a patent from another business or individual. A patent itself is the right of the patent's owner to exploit the invention for a period of time. Patents are recorded in the statement of financial position under intangible assets.

Accounting Treatment For Limited Companies

Income Statement

Essentially, the income statement is calculated as normal. We then have to appropriate (or distribute) some of the profit to the government by way of tax. In addition, non-listed companies preparing a statement of comprehensive income and retained earnings under IFRS for SMEs distribute dividends to their shareholders. For listed companies and companies following IFRS, dividends are not recorded in the income statement. This is demonstrated in Figure 6.13.

Figure 6.13 Limited Companies' Appropriation Account Format

The income statement was prepared as normal. The profit was £100,000. The tax for the year was £40,000 and dividends are £25,000.

Unlisted Limited Co. Ltd (following IFRS for SMEs) Income Statement (extract)		Unlisted and Listed Limited Co. Ltd (following IFRS) Income Statement (extract)	
	£		£
Profit before Taxation (calculated as normal)	100,000	*Profit before Taxation (calculated as normal)*	100,000
Taxation	(40,000)	Taxation	(40,000)
Profit after Taxation	60,000	*Profit for the year*	60,000
Dividends for year	(25,000)		
Retained Profit	35,000		

Statement of Financial Position

In the statement of financial position, the main differences between a sole trader or partnership and a company are (i) that taxation payable is recorded under current liabilities; (ii) in the presentation of equity (capital employed); and (iii) that limited companies are more likely than sole traders or partnerships to have intangible assets such as goodwill or patents. The current liabilities presentation is relatively straightforward, so only the presentation of equity format is given here (see Figure 6.14).

Intangible assets are recorded in the statement of financial position under non-current assets. The more conventional non-current assets, such as land and buildings, are then recorded as property, plant and equipment.

Figure 6.14 Limited Companies Equity (Capital Employed) Format

Limited Co. Ltd has the following details of equity.			
Ordinary share capital	£100,000	*Retained earnings*	£15,000
Preference share capital	£50,000	*Share premium account*	£5,000
		Revaluation reserve	£6,000
EQUITY		£	£
Capital and Reserves			
Share Capital			
Ordinary share capital			100,000
Preference share capital			50,000
			150,000
Reserves			
Capital reserves			
Share premium account		5,000	
Other reserves			
Revaluation reserve		6,000	
Retained earnings		15,000	26,000
Total Equity			176,000

Limited Company Example: Stevens, Turner Ltd

In order to demonstrate a more comprehensive example of the preparation of a limited company's accounts, we now turn again to the accounts of Gavin Stevens. When we last met Gavin Stevens he had formed a partnership with Diana Turner and they were trading as a partnership, Stevens and Turner (see Figure 6.4). We now assume that many years into the future in the year 20X1, the partnership has turned into a non-listed company. The trial balance is listed below.

Stevens, Turner Ltd: Trial Balance as at 31 December 20X1

	£000	£000
Ordinary share capital (£1 each)		300
Preference share capital (£1 each)		150
Share premium account		25
Revaluation reserve		30
General reserve		20
Retained earnings as at 1 January 20X1		50
Long-term loan		80
Land and buildings	550	
Patents	50	
Motor vehicles	50	
Opening inventories	10	
Trade receivables	80	
Trade payables		54
Bank	75	
Electricity	8	
Ordinary dividends	6	
Preference dividends	3	
Wages	50	
Telephone	7	
Revenue		350
Purchases	150	
Loan interest	8	
Other expenses	12	
	1,059	1,059

Notes:
1. Closing inventories are £25,000.
2. For simplicity, we are ignoring all other post-trial balance adjustments such as depreciation, bad and doubtful debts, accruals and prepayments.
3. Also for ease of understanding, we do not include non-operating items here such as revaluation of property, plant and equipment and gains or losses from foreign currency.
4. The following is not recorded in the trial balance: taxation payable £26,000.

We will now prepare the company accounts (see Figure 6.15). **The distinctive elements of a limited company's accounts are bordered by asterisks.** It is important to realise that in this section we are preparing the **full accounts for internal management purposes.** We are preparing the accounts here assuming Gavin Stevens is a non-listed company following IFRS for SMEs in Figure 6.15. However, in Figure 6.16 we present the accounts of the company as if it were a listed company following full IFRS. You will note that only the treatment of dividends is different. These are listed separately in bold at the bottom of Figure 6.15 in the statement of comprehensive income and retained earnings. Also, in the case of a listed company in Figure 6.16, we adjust for dividends in a statement of changes in equity. We could have prepared a separate statement of changes in equity in Figure 6.15. However, given its simplicity, we recorded the opening and closing retained earnings in the statement of financial position. These are, in effect, alternative treatments. In Figure 6.17, we show the published accounts of Stevens, Turner assuming they are a public limited company.

I. Presentation as the accounts of a non-listed company following IFRS for SMEs (unabridged)

Figure 6.15 Stevens, Turner Ltd: Accounts for Year Ended 31 December 20X1

Stevens, Turner Ltd Statement of Comprehensive Income and Retained Earnings for the Year Ended 20X1		
	£000	£000
Revenue		350
Less Cost of Sales		
Opening Inventories	10	
Add Purchases	150	
	160	
Less Closing Inventories	25	135
Gross Profit		215
Less Expenses		
Electricity	8	
Wages	50	
Telephone	7	
Loan Interest	8	
Other expenses	12	85
Profit before Taxation		130
Taxation[1]		(26)
Profit after Taxation		104
Ordinary dividends		(6)
Preference dividends		(3)
Retained Profit		95

Figure 6.15 Stevens, Turner Ltd: Accounts for Year Ended 31 December 20X1 (*continued*)

Stevens, Turner Ltd
Statement of Financial Position as at 31 December 20X1

	£000	£000
ASSETS		
Non-current Assets		
Intangible Assets		
Patents		50
Property, Plant and Equipment		
Land and buildings		550
Motor vehicles		50
		600
Total non-current assets		650
Current Assets		
Inventory		25
Trade receivables		80
Bank		75
Total current assets		180
Total Assets		830
LIABILITIES		
Current Liabilities		
Trade payables		54
Taxation payable[1]		26
Total Current Liabilities		80
Non-current Liabilities		80
Total Liabilities		160
Net Assets		670

	£000	£000	£000
EQUITY			
Capital and Reserves			
Share Capital		Authorised	Issued
Ordinary share capital		350	300
Preference share capital		200	150
		550	450

Figure 6.15 Stevens, Turner Ltd: Accounts for Year Ended 31 December 20X1 (*continued*)

Reserves	£000	£000	£000
Capital reserves			
Share premium account		25	
Other reserves			
Revaluation reserve		30	
General reserve		20	
Opening retained earnings	50		
Retained earnings for year	95		
Closing retained earnings		145	220
Total Equity			670

Note 1: In this case, the amount payable equals the charge for the year. This will not always be so.

II. Presentation as the accounts of a listed company following IFRS (unabridged)

Figure 6.16 Stevens, Turner Plc: Accounts for the Year Ended 31 December 20X1

Stevens, Turner plc		
Income Statement for the Year Ended 20X1		
	£000	£000
Revenue		350
Less Cost of Sales		
Opening Inventories	10	
Add Purchases	150	
	160	
Less Closing Inventories	(25)	(135)
Gross Profit		215
Less Expenses		
Electricity	8	
Wages	50	
Telephone	7	
Loan Interest	8	
Other expenses	12	(85)
Profit before Taxation		130
Taxation[1]		(26)
Profit for the year		104

Figure 6.16 Stevens, Turner Plc: Accounts for the year ended 31 December 20X1 (*continued*)

Stevens, Turner plc Statement of Financial Position as at 31 December 20X1		
		£000
ASSETS		
Non-current Assets		
Intangible Assets		
Patents		50
Property, plant and equipment		
Land and buildings		550
Motor vehicles		50
		600
Total non-current assets		650
Current Assets		
Inventory		25
Trade receivables		80
Bank		75
Total current assets		180
Total Assets		830
LIABILITIES		
Current Liabilities		
Trade payables		54
Taxation payable[1]		26
Total current liabilities		80
Non-current Liabilities		80
Total Liabilities		160
Net Assets		670
EQUITY		
Capital and Reserves	£000	£000
Share Capital	*Authorised*	*Issued*
Ordinary share capital	350	300
Preference share capital	200	150
	550	450

Figure 6.16 Stevens, Turner Plc: Accounts for the Year Ended 31 December 20X1 (*continued*)

Reserves	£000	£000
Capital reserves		
Share premium account	25	
Other reserves		
Revaluation reserve	30	
General reserve	20	
Retained earnings	<u>145</u>	<u>220</u>
Total Equity		<u>670</u>

Note 1:

In this case, the amount payable equals the charge for the year. This will not always be so.

Stevens, Turner plc

Statement of Changes in Equity for the year ended 31 December 20X1

	£000	£000
Opening Retained Earnings		50
Profit for year	104	
Less Dividends	(9)	95
Closing Retained Earnings		<u>145</u>

Limited Companies: Published Accounts

The internal company accounts are not suitable for external publication. The published accounts which are sent to shareholders are incorporated in a special document called an annual report and have several special features: they are standardised and abridged and have supplementary notes.

- *Standardised*. Published accounts use special Companies Acts' formats. In actual fact, these formats are broadly used throughout this book for consistency and to aid understanding.
- *Abridged*. The Companies Acts' formats mean that the details are summarised.
- *Supplementary notes*. Supplementary notes are used to flesh out the details of the main accounts.
- *Annual report*. In the case of public limited companies, an annual report is sent to shareholders. Increasingly, the annual report is also put onto a company's website. The website will include the financial statements, but also much more information. A separate chapter is devoted to the annual report (Chapter 11), given its importance, with Figure 11.4 providing some corporate website addresses.

Company Snapshots 6.3 and 6.4 that follow on pages 171 and 172 show the income statement and statement of financial position for a UK company, AstraZeneca, in 2009. They have been prepared using International Financial Reporting Standards and using dollars rather than pounds.

COMPANY SNAPSHOT 6.3

Income Statement for a Limited Company

Consolidated Statement of Comprehensive Income for the year ended 31 December

	Notes	2009 $m	2008 $m	2007 $m
Revenue	1	32,804	31,601	29,559
Cost of sales		(5,775)	(6,598)	(6,419)
Gross profit		27,029	25,003	23,140
Distribution costs		(298)	(291)	(248)
Research and development		(4,409)	(5,179)	(5,162)
Selling, general and administrative costs	2	(11,332)	(10,913)	(10,364)
Other operating income and expense	2	553	524	728
Operating profit	2	11,543	9,144	8,094
Finance income	3	462	854	959
Finance expense	3	(1,198)	(1,317)	(1,070)
Profit before tax		10,807	8,681	7,983
Taxation	4	(3,263)	(2,551)	(2,356)
Profit for the period		7,544	6,130	5,627
Other Comprehensive Income:				
Foreign exchange arising on consolidation		388	(1,336)	492
Foreign exchange differences on borrowings forming net investment hedges		(68)	291	(40)
Gain/(loss) on cash flow hedge in connection with debt issue		1	1	(21)
Net available for sale gains/(losses) taken to equity		2	2	(9)
Actuarial loss for the period		(569)	(1,232)	(113)
Income tax relating to components of Other Comprehensive Income	4	192	368	33
Other Comprehensive Income for the period, net of tax		(54)	(1,906)	342
Total Comprehensive income for the period		7,490	4,224	5,969
Profit attributable to:				
Owners of the Parent		7,521	6,101	5,595
Non-controlling interests		23	29	32
Total Comprehensive income attributable to:				
Owners of the Parent		7,467	4,176	5,934
Non-controlling interests		23	48	35
Basic earnings per $0.25 Ordinary Share	5	$5.19	$4.20	$3.74
Diluted earnings per $0.25 Ordinary Share	5	$5.19	$4.20	$3.73

COMPANY SNAPSHOT 6.3 (continued)

	Notes	2009 $m	2008 $m	2007 $m
Weighted average number of Ordinary Shares in issue (millions)	5	1,448	1,453	1,495
Diluted weighted average number of Ordinary Shares in issue (millions)	5	1,450	1,453	1,498
Dividends declared and paid in the period	21	3,026	2,767	2,658

All activities were in respect of continuing operations.
$m means millions of US dollars.

Source: AstraZeneca PLC, *Annual Report and Form 20-F information 2009*, p. 124.

The specific requirements for published company accounts are complex and beyond the scope of this book. All European listed companies must prepare their accounts in accordance with International Financial Reporting Standards. The presentation of the accounts differs from that conventionally used for sole traders and partnerships. However, Figure 6.17 on page 174 is a summary of what Stevens, Turner plc might look like. It is prepared using the same information from the trial balance for Stevens Turner Ltd presented earlier in this chapter.

COMPANY SNAPSHOT 6.4

Statement of Financial Position for a Limited Company

Consolidated Statement of Financial Position at 31 December

	Notes	2009 $m	2008 $m	2007 $m
Assets				
Non-current assets				
Property, plant and equipment	7	7,307	7,043	8,298
Goodwill	8	9,889	9,874	9,884
Intangible assets	9	12,226	12,323	11,467
Derivative financial instruments	16	262	449	117
Other investments	10	184	156	182
Deferred tax assets	4	1,292	1,236	1,044
		31,160	31,081	30,992
Current assets				
Inventories	11	1,750	1,636	2,119
Trade and other receivables	12	7,709	7,261	6,668

COMPANY SNAPSHOT 6.4 *(continued)*

Other investments	10	**1,484**	105	91
Derivative financial instruments	16	**24**	—	—
Income tax receivable		**2,875**	2,581	2,251
Cash and cash equivalents	13	**9,918**	4,286	5,867
		23,760	15,869	16,996
Total assets		**54,920**	46,950	47,988
Liabilities				
Current liabilities				
Interest-bearing loans and borrowings	14	**(1,926)**	(993)	(4,280)
Trade and other payables	17	**(8,687)**	(7,178)	(6,968)
Derivative financial instruments	16	**(90)**	(95)	(31)
Provisions	18	**(1,209)**	(600)	(387)
Income tax payable		**(5,728)**	(4,549)	(3,552)
		(17,640)	(13,415)	(15,218)
Non-current liabilities				
Interest-bearing loans and borrowings	14	**(9,137)**	(10,855)	(10,876)
Derivative financial instruments	16	**—**	(71)	—
Deferred tax liabilities	4	**(3,247)**	(3,126)	(4,119)
Retirement benefit obligations	23	**(3,354)**	(2,732)	(1,998)
Provisions	18	**(477)**	(542)	(633)
Other payables	17	**(244)**	(149)	(229)
		(16,459)	(17,475)	(17,855)
Total liabilities		**(34,099)**	(30,890)	(33,073)
Net assets		**20,821**	16,060	14,915
Equity				
Capital and reserves & attributable to equity holders of the Company				
Share capital	20	**363**	362	364
Share premium account	19	**2,180**	2,046	1,888
Capital redemption reserve	19	**94**	94	91
Merger reserve	19	**433**	433	433
Other reserves	19	**1,392**	1,405	1,378
Retained earnings	19	**16,198**	11,572	10,624
		20,660	15,912	14,778
Non-controlling interests	19	**161**	148	137
Total equity	19	**20,821**	16,060	14,915

The Financial Statements on pages 124 to 186 were approved by the Board of Directors on 28 January 2010 and were signed on its behalf by:

David R Brennan Simon Lowth
Director   Director

Source: AstraZeneca PLC, *Annual Report and Form 20-F Information 2009*, p. 125.

Figure 6.17 Stevens, Turner Ltd: Accounts Presented as Published Accounts of a Public Limited Company

	Notes	£000
Stevens, Turner plc		
Statement of Comprehensive Income for the year ended 31 December 20X1		
Revenue[1]		350
Cost of Sales		(135)
Gross Profit		215
Administrative expenses		(85)
Profit before Taxation		130
Taxation		(26)
Profit for year[2,3]		104

	Notes	£000
Stevens, Turner plc		
Statement of Financial Position as at 31 December 20X1		
ASSETS		
Non-current assets		
Property, plant and equipment	1	600
Goodwill and intangible assets		50
Total non-current assets		650
Current Assets		
Inventory		25
Trade receivables		80
Bank		75
Total current assets		180
Total Assets		830
LIABILITIES		
Current Liabilities	2	80
Non-current Liabilities		80
Total Liabilities		160
Net Assets		670
EQUITY		£000
Capital and Reserves		
Called-up share capital[4]	3	450
Share premium account		25
Other reserves	4	50
Retained earnings		145
Total Equity		670

Figure 6.17 Stevens, Turner Ltd: Accounts Presented as Published Accounts of a Public Limited Company (*continued*)

Stevens, Turner plc Statement of Changes in Equity for the year ended 31 December 20X1		
	£000	£000
Opening Retained Earnings		50
Profit for year	104	
Less Dividends	(9)	95
Closing Retained Earnings		145

Notes to the accounts

1. Property, Plant and Equipment	£000	3. Called-up Share Capital[3]	£000
Land and buildings	550	Ordinary share capital	300
Motor vehicles	50	Preference share capital	150
	600		450
2. Current Liabilities		**4. Other Reserves**	
Trade receivables	54	Revaluation reserve	30
Taxation payable	26	General reserve	20
	80		50

We have thus summarised the accounts of Stevens, Turner plc and supplemented them with notes to the accounts. The main figures can thus easily be identified. There are some points of interest, indicated by the superscript notes in Figure 6.17.

1. Revenue may also be called 'sales' or 'turnover'.
2. No dividends are shown in the income statement. Dividends paid are deducted in the statement of changes in equity. Dividends proposed are not recorded.
3. There is no non-operating income recorded here. If there were, it would be either recorded as other comprehensive income under profit for the year or alternatively in a second statement called Statement of Other Comprehensive Income.
4. Called-up share capital has a technical meaning (see Figure 6.12). However, for convenience, it can be taken here as issued share capital.

Conclusion

Partnerships and limited companies are important types of business organisation. Partnerships are broadly similar to sole traders, except that there is the problem of how to divide the equity and profit between the partners. Limited companies, unlike partnerships or sole traders, are based on the concept of limited liability. The principal differentiating features in the accounts of companies are corporation tax, dividends and the division of equity (capital employed) into share capital and reserves. Limited companies may be either private limited companies or public limited companies. It is the latter which are quoted on the stock exchange. The presentation and format of published public limited companies differ from those of the other types of business organisation.

 ## Discussion Questions

Questions with numbers in blue have answers at the back of the book.

Q1 Why do you think that three different types of business enterprise (sole traders, partnerships and limited companies) exist?

Q2 Discuss the view that the accounts of partnerships are much like those of sole traders except for the need to share out the equity and profit between more than one partner.

Q3 Distinguish between a private limited company and a public limited company. Is there any difference between the users of the accounts of each type of company?

Q4 Why is the distinction between capital and revenue reserves so important for a company?

Q5 State whether the following are true or false. If false, explain why.
  (a) Drawings are an expense recorded in the partners' trading, profit and loss and appropriation account (i.e., a separate section of the income statement called the appropriation account).
  (b) Partners' current accounts report the yearly short-term movements in partners' equity or capital.
  (c) The nominal value of a company's shares is the amount the shares will fetch on the stock market.
  (d) An unsecured loan is secured on specific assets such as the company's machinery.
  (e) Reserves can be spent on the purchase of property, plant and equipment.

Numerical Questions

These questions are separated into those on (A) partnerships and (B) limited companies. Within each section, they are graded in difficulty.

Questions with numbers in blue have answers at the back of the book.

A Partnerships

Q1 Two partners, Peter Tom and Sheila Thumb, have the following details of their accounts for the year ended 31 December 2013.

			£	
Net profit before appropriation: £100,000	Capital accounts:	Tom	8,000	
Profit sharing ratio: 3 Tom, 1 Thumb		Thumb	6,000	
Salaries: Tom £10,000, Thumb £30,000	Current accounts:	Tom	3,000	cr
Drawings: Tom £25,000, Thumb £30,000		Thumb	1,000	dr

Required: Prepare the relevant income statement and statement of financial position extracts.

Q2 J. Waite and P. Watcher's trial balance as at 30 November 2014 is set out below.

		£	£
Capital accounts:	Waite		88,000
	Watcher		64,000
Current accounts:	Waite	2,500	
	Watcher		12,000
Drawings:	Waite	13,300	
	Watcher	6,300	
Land and buildings at cost		166,313	
Motor vehicles at cost		65,000	
Opening inventory		9,000	
Trade receivables		12,000	
Trade payables			18,500
Bank		6,501	
Electricity		3,406	
Wages		14,870	
Telephone		1,350	
Rent and business rates		6,660	
Long-term loan			28,000
Revenue			350,000
Purchases		245,000	
Interest on loan		2,800	
Other expenses		5,500	
		560,500	560,500

Q2 Waite and Watcher (*continued*)

Notes:
1. Closing inventory is £15,000.
2. Salaries are £18,000 for Waite and £16,000 for Watcher.
3. There is £300 owing for rent.
4. Depreciation for the year is £2,000 on land and buildings and £3,000 on motor vehicles. The business was started on 1 December 2013.
5. The split of profits is 3 Watcher:2 Waite.

Required: Prepare the income statement for year ended 30 November 2014 and the statement of financial position as at 30 November 2014.

Q3 Cherie and Tony's trial balance as at 31 December 2013 is set out below.

		£	£
Capital accounts:	Cherie		30,000
	Tony		35,000
Current accounts:	Cherie		26,000
	Tony		18,500
Drawings	Cherie	21,294	
	Tony	18,321	
Land and buildings at cost		203,500	
Plant and machinery at cost		26,240	
Land and buildings accumulated depreciation as at 1 January 2013			12,315
Plant and machinery accumulated depreciation as at 1 January 2013			9,218
Trade receivables		18,613	
Trade payables			2,451
Bank		25,016	
Electricity		1,324	
Wages		12,187	
Telephone		1,923	
Insurance		1,318	
Long-term loan			83,000
Revenue			251,800
Revenue returns		340	
Purchases		128,317	
Purchases returns			206
Other expenses		1,497	
Opening inventory		8,600	
		468,490	468,490

Q3 Cherie and Tony (*continued*)
Notes:
1. Closing inventory is £12,000.
2. £197 of the other expenses was prepaid and £200 is owed for the telephone.
3. Salaries will be £12,000 for Cherie and £10,000 for Tony.
4. Depreciation is fixed at 2% on the cost of land and buildings and 10% on the cost of plant and machinery.
5. Profits are shared in the ratio 2 for Cherie and 1 for Tony.

Required: Prepare the income statement for the year ended 31 December 2013 and the statement of financial position as at 31 December 2013.

Q4 Sister and Sledge are trading in partnership, sharing profits and losses in the ratio of 2:1, respectively. The partners are entitled to salaries of Sister £6,000 per annum and Sledge £5,000 per annum. There is the following additional information:
(1) Inventory as at 31 December 2013 was valued at £8,800.
(2) Staff salaries owing £290.
(3) Advertising paid in advance £200.
(4) Provision for the impairment of receivables to be increased to £720.
(5) Provision should be made for depreciation of 2% on land and buildings on cost, and for fixtures and fittings at 10% on cost.

Trial Balance as at 31 December 2013

	£	£
Capital accounts:		
Sister		12,500
Sledge		5,000
Current accounts:		
Sister		1,500
Sledge	600	
Drawings:		
Sister	9,800	
Sledge	6,700	
Long-term loan		40,250
Land and buildings at cost	164,850	
Inventory as at 1 January 2013	9,500	
Fixtures and fittings at cost	12,500	
Purchases	126,000	
Cash at bank	3,480	
Revenue		305,400
Trade receivables	9,600	
Carriage inwards	200	
Carriage outwards	300	
Staff salaries	24,300	
Trade payables		26,300

Q4 Sister and Sledge (*continued*)

General expenses	18,200	
Provision for the impairment of receivables		480
Advertising	5,350	
Discounts receivable		120
Discounts allowed	350	
Rent and business rates	2,850	
Land and buildings accumulated depreciation as at 1 January 2013		9,750
Fixtures and fittings accumulated depreciation as at 1 January 2013		3,500
Electricity	4,500	
Telephone	5,720	
	404,800	404,800

Required: Prepare the income statement for the year ended 31 December 2013 and the statement of financial position as at 31 December 2013.

B Limited Companies

i Non-Listed Companies Reporting under IFRS for SMEs

Q5 Red Devils Ltd has the following extracts from its accounts.

Red Devils Ltd
Trial Balance as at 30 November 2014

	£	£
Gross profit for year		150,000
7% Debentures		200,000
6% Preference share capital (£150,000 authorised)		150,000
£1 Ordinary share capital (£400,000 authorised)		250,000
Share premium account		55,000
Property, plant and equipment	680,900	
Ordinary dividends	25,000	
Preference dividends	9,000	
General expenses	22,100	
Directors' fees	19,200	
Trade receivables	4,700	
Trade payables		46,200
Bank	5,300	
	£	£
Retained earnings as at 1 December 2013		9,000
General reserve as at 1 December 2013		11,000
Inventories as at 30 November 2014	105,000	
	871,200	871,200

Q5 Red Devils (*continued*)
Notes:
1. An audit fee is to be provided of £7,500.
2. The debenture interest for the year has not been paid.
3. The directors propose to transfer £3,500 to the general reserve. (Note: transfers are recorded in the statement of comprehensive income.)
4. Corporation tax of £17,440 is to be provided on the profit for the year.

Required: Prepare for internal management purposes:
(a) The statement of comprehensive income and retained earnings (income statement) for the year ended 30 November 2014.
(b) The statement of financial position as at 30 November 2014.

Q6 Superprofit Ltd.

Trial Balance as at 31 December 2013

	£000	£000
Ordinary share capital		210
Preference share capital		25
Share premium account		40
Revaluation reserve		35
General reserve		15
Retained earnings as at 1 January 2013		28
Long-term loan		32
Land and buildings	378	
Patents	12	
Motor vehicles	47	
Opening inventories	23	
Trade receivables	18	
Trade payables		45
Bank	31	
Electricity	12	
Insurance	3	
Wages	24	
Ordinary dividends	9	
Preference dividends	3	
Telephone	5	
Light and heat	8	
Revenue		351
Purchases	182	
Other expenses	26	
	781	781

Q6 Superprofit Ltd. (*continued*)

Notes (all figures in £000s):
1. Closing inventories are £26.
2. The following had not yet been recorded in the trial balance:
(a) Taxation payable £13
(b) Interest on long-term loan £4
(c) Auditors' fees £2
(d) The authorised share capital is ordinary share capital £250, preference share capital £50.
3. The business started trading on 1 January 2013. Depreciation for the year is £18 for land and buildings and £7 for motor vehicles.

Required: Prepare for *internal management purposes* the income statement for year ended 31 December 2013 and the statement of financial position as at 31 December 2013.

ii Companies Reporting under Full IFRS

Q7 Lindesay Trading plc

Trial Balance as at 31 March 2014

	£000	£000
Ordinary share capital		425
Preference share capital		312
Share premium account		18
Revaluation reserve		27
General reserve as at 1 April 2013		13
Retained earnings as at 1 April 2013		17
Long-term loan		87
Land and buildings at cost	834	
Patents	25	
Motor vehicles at cost	312	
Opening inventories as at 1 April 2013	10	
Trade receivables	157	
Trade payables		121
Ordinary dividends	19	
Preference dividends	9	
Bank	186	
Electricity	12	
Wages and salaries	183	

Q7   Lindesay Trading plc (*continued*)

	£000	£000
Telephone	5	
Revenue		1,500
Insurance	6	
Purchases	750	
Other expenses	125	
Land and buildings accumulated depreciation as at 1 April 2013		25
Motor vehicles accumulated depreciation as at 1 April 2013		88
	2,633	2,633

Notes (all figures in £000s):
1. Closing inventories are £13.
2. The following are not recorded in the trial balance: Taxation payable £58.
3. Authorised share capital was £500 for ordinary share capital and £400 for preference share capital.
4. There was £45 owing for wages and salaries.
5. Debenture interest was £8.
6. Of the insurance £1 was prepaid.
7. The proposed auditors' fees are £3.
8. A transfer to the general reserve was made of £16.
9. Depreciation is to be £17 on land and buildings and £60 on motor vehicles.

Required: Prepare for *internal management purposes* the income statement for the year ended 31 March 2014 and the statement of financial position as at 31 March 2014.

Q8 The following trial balance was extracted from the books of Leisureplay plc, a listed company, for the year ended 31 December 2013.

	£000	£000
Ordinary share capital (£1 each)		700,000
Preference share capital (£1 each)		80,000
Debentures		412,000
Retained earnings as at 1 January 2013		98,000
Share premium account		62,000
Revaluation reserve		70,000
General reserve		18,000
Freehold premises at cost	1,550,000	
Motor vehicles at cost	18,000	
Furniture and fittings at cost	8,000	
Freehold premises accumulated depreciation as at 1 January 2013		102,000
Motor vehicles accumulated depreciation as at 1 January 2013		9,350
Furniture and fittings accumulated depreciation as at 1 January 2013		1,100
Inventories as at 1 January 2013	5,000	
Cash at bank	183,550	
Provision for the impairment of receivables		1,000
Purchases/revenue	500,000	800,000
Trade receivables/payables	28,900	7,000
Revenue returns/purchases returns	3,500	3,800
Carriage inwards	60	
Carriage outwards	70	
Bank charges	20	
Rates	4,280	
Salaries	5,970	
Wages	3,130	
Travelling expenses	1,980	

Q8 Leisureplay plc (*continued*)

	£000	£000
Preference dividends	5,000	
Ordinary dividends	25,000	
Discount allowed	20	
Discount received		15
General expenses	8,100	
Gas, electricity	9,385	
Printing, stationery	1,850	
Advertising	2,450	
	2,364,265	2,364,265

Notes (all figures are in 000s):
(a) Inventories as at 31 December 2013 are £12,000
(b) Depreciation is to be charged as follows:
    (i)   Freehold premises 2% on cost
    (ii) Motor vehicles 10% on cost
    (iii) Furniture and fittings 5% on cost
(c) There is the following payment in advance:
    General expenses   £500
(d) There are the following accrued expenses:
    Business rates   £300
    Advertising   £550
    Auditors' fees   £250
(e) Authorised ordinary share capital is £1,000,000 £1 shares, and authorised preference share capital is 100,000 £1 shares.
(f) Taxation has been calculated as £58,500.
(g) Debenture interest should be charged at 10%.
(h) Provision for the impairment of receivables is increased to £1,600 and a bad debt of £400 is to be written off. You should calculate out the provision first.
(i) The ordinary and preference dividends should be deducted from retained earnings.

Required: Prepare for *internal management purposes* the income statement for Leisureplay plc for the year ended 31 December 2013 and statement of financial position as at 31 December 2013 using International Financial Reporting Standards.

Q9 You have the following summarised trial balance for Stock High plc as at 31 March 2014. Further details are provided in the notes.

	£000	£000
Revenue		1,250
Cost of sales	400	
Administrative expenses	200	
Distribution expenses	150	
Patents	50	
Land and buildings at cost	800	
Motor vehicles at cost	400	
Land and buildings accumulated depreciation as at 1 April 2013		140
Motor vehicles accumulated depreciation as at 1 April 2013		150
Long-term loan		60
Retained earnings as at 1 April 2013		36
Share premium account		25
Revaluation reserve		30
General reserve		25
Ordinary share capital		450
Preference share capital		100
Taxation paid	86	
Ordinary dividends paid	50	
Trade payables		12
Inventories as at 31 March 2014	20	
Trade receivables	100	
Cash	22	
	2,278	2,278

Notes (in £000s except for note 3):
1. At the statement of financial position date £8 is owing for taxation.
2. Depreciation is to be charged at 2% on cost for land and buildings (used for administration) and 20% on cost for motor vehicles (used for selling and distribution).
3. Authorised share capital is 600,000 £1 ordinary shares and £150,000 £1 preference shares.

Required: Prepare the statement of comprehensive income and statement of changes in equity for the year ended 31 March 2014 and the statement of financial position for the year ended 31 March 2014 as they would appear in the published accounts prepared under International Financial Reporting Standards.

Appendix 6.1: Example of an Income Statement (Profit and Loss Account) Using UK GAAP (Manchester United Ltd)

Manchester United Limited

Consolidated profit and loss account

	Note	Year ended 30 June 2009 £'000	Year ended 30 June 2008 £'000
Turnover: Group and share of joint venture		278,476	257,116
Less: Share of joint venture		—	(877)
Group turnover	2	278,476	256,239
Operating expenses–other	3	(230,481)	(212,928)
Operating expenses–exceptional items	4	(837)	(490)
Total operating expenses		(231,318)	(213,418)
Group operating profit		47,158	42,821
Analysed as:			
Group operating profit before depreciation and amortisation of players' registrations and goodwill		92,789	86,005
Depreciation		(7,427)	(7,271)
Amortisation of players' registrations		(37,641)	(35,481)
Amortisation of goodwill		(563)	(432)
		47,158	42,821
Share of operating profit in:			
- Joint venture		—	2
- Associate		—	91
Total operating profit: Group and share of joint venture and associate		47,158	42,914
Profit on disposal of associate		—	1,209
Profit on disposal of players		80,724	21,831
Profit before interest and taxation		127,882	65,954
Net interest (payable)/receivable	5	(236)	462
Profit on ordinary activities before taxation		127,646	66,416
Tax on profit on ordinary activities	7	(34,768)	(19,916)
Profit on ordinary activities after taxation		92,878	46,500
Equity minority interest		83	254
Profit for the financial year	21	92,961	46,754

Source: Manchester United Limited, *Annual Report and Financial Statements for the year end 30 June 2009*, p. 9.

Appendix 6.2: Example of a Statement of Financial Position (Balance Sheet) Using UK GAAP (Manchester United Ltd)

Manchester United Limited

Consolidated balance sheet

	Note	At 30 June 2009 £'000	At 30 June 2008 £'000
Fixed assets			
Intangible assets – goodwill	9a	7,337	7,900
Intangible assets – players' registrations	9b	113,406	92,739
Tangible assets	10	160,683	166,813
		281,426	267,452
Current assets			
Stock	12	279	283
Debtors – amounts falling due within one year	13	174,094	118,748
Debtors – amounts falling due after more than one year	13	12,650	10,460
Cash at bank and in hand		150,530	49,745
		337,553	179,236
Creditors – amounts falling due within one year	14	(88,409)	(65,487)
Net current assets		249,144	113,749
Total assets less current liabilities		530,570	381,201
Creditors – amounts falling due after more than one year	15	(17,877)	(15,934)
Provision for liabilities and charges			
Deferred taxation	17a	(17,568)	(351)
Other provisions	17b	(1,091)	(1,335)
Accruals and deferred income			
Deferred grant income	18	(380)	(448)
Other deferred income	19	(111,757)	(71,976)
Net assets		381,897	291,157
Capital and reserves			
Called up share capital	20	26,519	26,519
Share premium reserve	21	7,756	7,756
Other reserves	21	1,674	3,696
Profit and loss reserve	21	348,892	256,047
Total shareholders' funds	22	384,841	294,018
Minority interests		(2,944)	(2,861)
Capital employed		381,897	291,157

Manchester United Statement of Financial Position (*continued*)

The financial statements on pages 9 to 40 were approved by the board of directors on 30 September 2009 and signed on its behalf by:

M Bolingbroke
Director

Source: Manchester United Limited, *Annual Report and Financial Statements for the year end 30 June 2009*, p. 11.

Go online to discover the extra features for this chapter at
www.wiley.com/college/jones

Chapter 7

Main financial statements: The statement of cash flows

'Cash is King. It is relatively easy to "manufacture" profits but creating cash is virtually impossible.'

UBS Phillips and Drew (January 1991), *Accounting for Growth*, p. 32.

Learning Outcomes

After completing this chapter you should be able to:

- Explain the nature of cash and the statement of cash flows.
- Demonstrate the importance of cash flow.
- Investigate the relationship between profit and cash flow.
- Outline the direct and indirect methods of the statement of cash flows preparation.

Go online to discover the extra features for this chapter at
www.wiley.com/college/jones

Chapter Summary

- Cash is key to business success.
- Cash flow is concerned with cash received and cash paid, unlike profit which deals with income earned and expenses incurred.
- Reconciling profit to cash flow means adjusting for movements in working capital and for non-cash items, such as depreciation.
- Large companies provide a statement of cash flows as the third major financial statement.
- Sole traders, partnerships and small companies may, but are not required to, prepare a statement of cash flows.
- The two ways of preparing a statement of cash flows are the direct and the indirect methods.
- Most companies use the indirect method of preparing a statement of cash flows.
- Listed companies use a different format than other business organisations.

Introduction

Cash is king. It is the essential lubricant of business. Without cash, a business cannot pay its employees' wages or pay for goods or services. As Real-World View 7.1 shows, at its most extreme, this can lead to the failure of a business. A business records cash in the bank account in the books of account. Small businesses may sometimes prepare a statement of cash flows directly from the bank account. More usually, however, the statement of cash flows is prepared indirectly by deducing the figures from the income statement and the statement of financial position. The statement of cash flows, at its simplest, records the cash inflows and cash outflows classified under certain headings such as cash flows from operating (i.e., trading) activities. All companies (except small ones) must prepare a statement of cash flows in line with

REAL-WORLD VIEW 7.1

Cash Bloodbath

With last week's collapse of Boo.com – the first big liquidation of a dot.com company in Europe – the internet gold rush has taken on the appearance of a bloodbath. The company's principal failing – and there were many, it was burning cash at a rate of $1m a week – was to forget that in the new economy the old rules still apply.

Source: Accountancy Age, 25 May 2000, p. 26.

financial reporting regulations. However, some sole traders, partnerships and smaller companies also provide them, often at the request of their bank. As Real-World View 7.2 shows, banks are well aware of the importance of cash. As well as preparing the statement of cash flows on the basis of past cash flows, businesses will continually monitor their day-to-day cash inflows and outflows. Statements of cash flows essentially record what has happened over the reporting period. As we shall see in Chapter 14, companies also prepare cash budgets which look to the future. Cash management, therefore, concerns the past, present and future activities of a business.

REAL-WORLD VIEW 7.2

Cash Flow

Bankers *do* know about cash flow. They have to live with it on Friday, every Friday, in any number of companies up and down the country. Where there is insufficient cash to pay the wages, really agonising decisions result. Should the company be closed, with all the personal anguish it will cause, or should it be allowed to limp on, perhaps to face exactly the same agonising dilemma in as little as a week's time?

Source: B. Warnes (1984), *The Genghis Khan Guide to Business*, Osmosis Publications, London, p. 6.

Importance of Cash

Cash is the lifeblood of a business. Cash is needed to pay the wages, to pay the day-to-day running costs, to buy inventory and to buy new property, plant and equipment. The generation of cash is, therefore, essential to the survival and expansion of businesses. Money makes the world go round! In many ways, the concept of cash flow is easier to understand than that of profit. Most people are more familiar with cash than profit. Cash is, after all, what we use in our everyday lives. At its most stark, if a business runs out of cash it will not be able to pay its trade payables and it will cease trading. As Jack Welch, a successful US businessman, has said, 'There's one thing you can't cheat on and that's cash and Enron didn't have any cash for the last three years. Accounting is odd, but cash is real stuff. Follow the cash' (*The Guardian*, 27 February 2002, p. 23). Ken Lever, a member of the UK's Accounting Standards Board agrees (*Accountancy Age*, 24 February 2011, p. 5). Cash flow is the key. 'A lot of businesses see cash as an afterthought. There is a tendency to get sidetracked by accounting metrics.'

It is far easier to manipulate profit than it is to manipulate cash flow. This is highlighted by Real-World Views 7.3 and 7.4. In Real-World View 7.3, Phillips and Drew, a firm of city fund managers (now called UBS Global Management), basically state that cash is essential to business success.

REAL-WORLD VIEW 7.3

Importance of Cash I

In the end, investment and accounting all come back to cash. Whereas "manufacturing" profits is relatively easy, cash flow is the most difficult parameter to adjust in a company's accounts. Indeed, tracing cash movements in a company can often lead to the identification of unusual accounting practices. The long term return of an equity investment is determined by the market's perception of the stream of dividends that the company will be able to pay. We believe that there should be less emphasis placed on the reported progression of earnings per share and more attention paid to balance sheet movements, dividend potential and, most important of all, cash.

Source: UBS Phillips and Drew (January 1991), *Accounting for Growth*, p. 1.

This was as true in 1991 as it was in 2011, as Real-World View 7.4 shows.

REAL-WORLD VIEW 7.4

Importance of Cash II

Even more important than earnings coverage, though, is free cash flow coverage. Whereas earnings are in some part an accounting fiction, free cash flow is cold, hard fact. Free cash flow can be used for real purposes, including paying debts, investing in new capacity and paying dividends. Therefore, we tried to pick out companies whose free cash flow had improved or was stable over recent years – as well as those in the opposite situation.

Source: D.M. Hand, Die hard dividends, *Investors Chronicle*, 21–27 October 2011, p. 24. Financial Times Ltd.

HELPNOTE

Free cash flow is defined as:

'Cash flow from operations after deducting interest, tax, preference dividends and ongoing capital expenditure, but excluding capital expenditure associated with strategic acquisitions and/or disposals and ordinary share dividends' (CIMA, 2009, *Official Terminology*).

Context

The statement of cash flows is the third of the key financial statements which medium and large companies provide. It summarises the company's cash transactions over time. At its simplest, the cash flow is related to the opening and closing cash balances:

Opening cash + Inflows − Outflows = Closing cash

Cash inflows are varied, but may, for example, be receipts from sales or interest from a bank deposit account. Cash outflows may be payments for goods or services, or for capital expenditure items such as motor vehicles.

All *large* companies are required to provide a statement of cash flows. There are two methods of preparation. The first is the **direct method**, which categorises cash flow by function; for example, receipts from sales. A statement of cash flows, using the direct method, can be prepared from the bank account and is the most readily understandable. The second method is the **indirect method**. This uses a 'detective' approach. It deduces cash flow from the existing statements of financial position and income statement and reconciles operating profit to operating cash flow. The statement of cash flows, using the indirect method, is not so readily comprehensible. Unfortunately, this is the method most often used.

 PAUSE FOR THOUGHT 7.1

Yes, But What Exactly is Cash?

Cash is cash! However, there are different types of cash, such as petty cash, cash at bank, bank deposit accounts, or deposits repayable on demand or with notice. How do they all differ?

The basic distinction is between cash and bank. However, the terms are often used loosely and interchangeably. Cash is the cash available. In other words, it physically exists; for example, a fifty-pound note. Petty cash is money kept specifically for day-to-day small expenses, such as purchasing coffee. Cash at bank is normally kept either in a current account (which operates via a cheque book for normal day-to-day transactions) or in a deposit account (basically a store for surplus cash). The term cash and cash equivalents is often used to refer to cash at bank and that held in short-term (say up to 30 days) deposit accounts. Deposits repayable on demand are very short-term investments which can be repaid within one working day. Deposits requiring notice are accounts where the customer must give a period of notice for withdrawal (for example, 30 days).

Cash and the Bank Account

Cash is initially recorded in the bank account. In large businesses, a separate book is kept called the cash book. Debits are essentially good news for a company in that they increase cash in the bank account, whereas credits are bad news in that they decrease cash in the bank account. For an individual looking at their bank statements, however, it is the other way round. From the bank account it is possible to prepare a simple statement of cash flows.

PAUSE FOR THOUGHT 7.2

Cash Inflows and Outflows

What might be some examples of the main sources of cash inflow and outflow for a small business?

Cash Inflow	Cash Outflow
Cash from customers for goods	Payments to suppliers for goods
Interest received from bank deposit account	Payments for services; e.g., telephone, light and heat
Cash from sale of property, plant and equipment	Repay bank loans
Cash introduced by owner	Payments for property, plant and equipment; e.g., motor vehicles
Loan received	Interest paid on bank loan

Let us take the example once more of Gavin Stevens' bank account (see Figure 7.1). As Figure 7.1 shows, we have essentially summarised the figures from the bank account and reclassified them under certain headings.

For sole traders and partnerships, there is no regulatory requirement for a statement of cash flows in the UK. Small companies are also exempt. Many organisations do, nevertheless, prepare one. UK non-listed companies are regulated by an accounting standard, Chapter 7 in FRS102. However, UK listed companies, like all European listed companies, follow International Accounting Standard IAS 7. The objective of this standard is to require the provision of information about the historical changes in cash and cash equivalents of an entity by means of a statement of cash flows which classifies cash flows during the period as operating, investing and financing activities. The statement of cash flows is a primary financial statement and ranks along with the statement of financial position and income statement. These standards lay down certain main headings for categorising cash flows (see Figure 7.2).

In Appendix 7.1, the main headings for the cash flow statement (note it is called the cash flow statement rather than the statement of cash flows) as required by the UK's accounting standards are given. This can be used by sole traders, partnerships and some non-listed companies.

We use three headings for listed companies (see Figure 7.2 on page 197): (1) Cash flows from operating activities (which covers flows from operating activities and taxation); (2) Cash flows from investing activities (which covers capital expenditure and financial

Figure 7.1 Simple Statement of Cash Flows for Gavin Stevens

Taking Gavin Stevens' bank account:

Bank

	£		£
1 Jan. Equity	700,000	2 Jan. Hotel	610,000
7 Jan. Ireton	1,965	2 Jan. Van	3,000
7 Jan. Hepworth	2,500	2 Jan. Purchases	2,000
		4 Jan. Electricity	300
		4 Jan. Wages	1,000
		7 Jan. Hogen	250
		7 Jan. Lewis	1,000
		7 Jan. Bal. c/f	86,915
	704,465		704,465
8 Jan. Bal. b/f	86,915		

From the bank account, we can summarise the main cash flows and record them in a statement of cash flows, as follows:

Gavin Stevens
Statement of Cash Flows up to 7 January

	£	£
Opening Cash Balance		–
Add *Inflows*		
Capital invested (1)	700,000	
Trading (2)	4,465	704,465
Less *Outflows*		
Capital expenditure (3)	613,000	
Trading (4)	4,550	617,550
Closing Cash Balance		86,915

Notes:
(1) Represents the initial capital investment. Often termed a 'financing' cash flow.
(2) Represents money received from trade receivables (Ireton £1,965 and Hepworth £2,500). Often termed cash inflow from a 'trading' or 'operating' activity.
(3) Represents the purchase of property, plant and equipment (hotel £610,000 and van £3,000). Often termed cash outflow from 'investing' activities.
(4) Represents the money paid for goods and services (purchases £2,000, electricity £300, wages £1,000, Hogen £250, Lewis £1,000). Often termed cash outflow from a 'trading' or 'operating' activity.

investment, acquisitions and disposals, interest received and dividends received); and (3) Cash flows from financing activities. Unfortunately, these headings are very cumbersome and often lack transparency.

Figure 7.2 Main Headings for the Statement of Cash Flows using IFRS

	Simplified Meaning	Examples of Inflows	Examples of Outflows
Cash flows from operating activities	i. Cash flows from the normal trading activities of a business ii. Cash paid to government for taxation	i. Cash for sale of goods. ii. Taxation refunds	i. Payment for purchases of goods ii. Expenses paid iii. Taxation paid

Cash flows from investing activities	i. Cash flows relating to the purchase and sale of
	  a. property, plant and equipment
	  b. investments
	ii. Payments for the purchase or sale of other companies.
		i. Interest received
		ii. Dividends received
		iii. Receipts for sale of property, plant and equipment e.g. motor vehicles
		iv. Sale of investments
		v. Cash received for sale of another company
			i. Payments for property, plant and equipment e.g. motor vehicles.
			ii. Purchase of investments
			iii. Cash paid to buy another company

Cash flows from financing activities	i. Cash received from shareholders
	ii. Cash flows relating to the issuing or buying back of shares or loan capital
	iii. Dividends companies pay to shareholders
		i. Cash received from the issue of:
		  a. shares
		  b. loans
			i. Cash paid to buy back shares or to repay loans
			ii. Dividends paid
			iii. Interest paid

The details of IAS 7 are well summarised in Real-World View 7.5 by Paul Klumpes and Peter Welch.

REAL-WORLD VIEW 7.5

Cash Flow Statements

According to the International Accounting Standards Committee Foundation's Technical Summary of IAS 7: 'The objective of this standard is to require the provision of information about the historical changes in cash and cash equivalents of an entity by means of a statement of cash flows which classifies cash flows during the period as operating, investing and financing activities.'

Summarising the three cashflow categories:

- Operating: principal revenue-producing activities of the entity.
- Investing: acquisition and disposal of long-term assets and other investments (including subsidiaries).
- Financing: activities that result in changes in the size and composition of equity and borrowings.

REAL-WORLD VIEW 7.5 *(continued)*

Crucially, IAS 7 allows two options for the reporting of operating activities:

- Direct method: major classes of gross cash receipts and payments are disclosed.
- Indirect method: profit and loss adjusted for the effects of non-cash transactions, any deferrals/accruals of operating cashflows and any income and expense items associated with investing or financing cashflows.

The operating section of a bank's cashflow statement is more complex than that of a non-financial firm. A bank's core services – taking in deposits and other funds and using those funds to make loans and investments – are themselves cashflows. These are also captured in the operating segment as operating asset and liability flows. In broad terms, a bank's operating cashflow is therefore made up of two main components:

- The adjustment of profit (normally profit before tax) for non-cash items, tax paid, etc.
- The operating asset and liability flows – the asset-related movements in loans and investments, and liability-related movements in deposits and wholesale funding such as debt securities.

Despite their importance to understanding a bank's financial health, all the UK and Eurozone banks we surveyed were using the indirect method to report their operating asset and liability flows on a net basis. Yet in most cases, the net change can already be calculated or estimated, by comparing the value of the item (for example, loans and advances to customers) in the end period balance sheet with its value in the preceding period balance sheet. This leaves the cashflow statement communicating little new information.

Source: Paul Klumpes and Peter Welch, Call for Clarity, *Accountancy Magazine*, October 2009, pp. 34–5. Copyright Wolters Kluwer (UK) Ltd.

Tutorial Note: Cash equivalents are short-term, highly liquid assets such as one-year bonds.

Relationship between Cash and Profit

Cash and profit are fundamentally different. In essence, cash flow and profit are based on different principles. Cash flow is based on cash received and cash paid (see Figure 7.3). By contrast, profit is concerned with income earned and expenses incurred.

Figure 7.3 Cash Flow and Profit

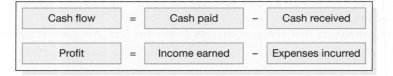

In a sense, the difference between the two merely results from the timing of the cash flows. For example, a telephone bill owing at the year end is included as an accrued expense in the income statement, but is not counted as a cash payment. However, next year the situation will reverse and there will be a cash outflow, but no expense.

An important difference between profit and cash flow is depreciation. Depreciation is a non-cash flow item. The related cash flows occur only when property, plant or equipment is bought or sold. Real-World View 7.6 demonstrates this.

REAL-WORLD VIEW 7.6

Cash Loss vs. Stated Loss

As always, there is the need to distinguish between a stated loss, per the profit and loss account [income statement] and a cash loss. One company the author handled was running at an apparently frightening loss of £25,000 per month, but on closer examination there was not too much to worry about. It had a £30,000 monthly depreciation provision. It was in reality producing a cash-positive profit of £5,000 per month. It had *years* of life before it. This gave all the time needed to get the operation right.

Source: B. Warnes (1984) *The Genghis Khan Guide to Business*, Osmosis Publications, London, p. 63.

Figure 7.4 shows how some common items are treated in the income statement and statement of cash flows. Some items, such as sale of goods for cash, appear in both. However, amounts owing, such as a telephone bill, appear only in the income statement. By contrast, money received from a loan only affects the statement of cash flows.

Figure 7.4 Demonstration of How Some Items Affect the Income Statement and Some Affect the Statement of Cash Flows

	Transaction	In Income Statement	In Statement of Cash Flows
i.	Sale of goods for cash	Yes	Yes
ii.	Sale of goods on credit	Yes	No
iii.	Telephone bill for year owing	Yes	No
iv.	Telephone bill for year paid	Yes	Yes
v.	Cash purchase of property, plant and equipment	No	Yes
vi.	Profit on sale of property, plant and equipment	Yes	No
vii.	Cash from sale of property, plant and equipment	No	Yes
viii.	Money received from a loan	No	Yes
ix.	Bank interest received for a year	Yes	Yes

Sometimes, a business may make a profit, but run out of cash. This is called overtrading and happens especially when a business starts trading.

PAUSE FOR THOUGHT 7.3

Overtrading, Cash Flow vs. Profit

A company, Bigger is Better, doubles its revenue every month.

Month	1	2	3	4
	£000	£000	£000	£000
Revenue	10	20	40	80
Purchases	(8)	(16)	(32)	(64)
Profit	2	4	8	16

It pays its purchases at once, but has to wait two months for its customers to pay for the revenue. The bank, which has loaned £10,000, will close down the business if it is owed £50,000. What happens?

Month	1	2	3	4
	£000	£000	£000	£000
Cash at bank	10	2	(14)	(36)
Cash in	–	–	10	20
Cash out	(8)	(16)	(32)	(64)
Cash at bank	2	(14)	(36)	(80)

The result: Bye-bye, Bigger is Better. Even though the business is trading profitably, it has run out of cash. This is because the first cash is received in month 3, but the cash outflows start at once.

Preparation of Statement of Cash Flows

In this section, we present the two methods of preparing a statement of cash flows (the direct and indirect methods). In Figure 7.5 and Appendix 7. 2, a statement of cash flows is prepared for a sole trader using the **direct method**, which classifies *operating* cash flows by function or type of activity (e.g., receipts from customers). In Figure 7.5 the statement of cash flows is prepared using IFRS while Appendix 7.2 illustrates UK GAAP. In essence, this resembles the statement of cash flows for Gavin Stevens in Figure 7.1. We assume a bank has requested a statement of cash flows and that it is possible to extract the figures directly from the company's accounting records. Figure 7.6 then compares the direct and indirect methods of preparing the statement of cash flows. In Figure 7.7 we then look at some of the adjustments made to profit to arrive at cash flow. This is followed with an illustrative example in Figure 7.8, Collette Ash. We then present the statement of cash flows for a company using the more conventional **indirect method used by most companies** in Figure 7.9, following IFRS format. In Appendix 7.3, we prepare the statement of cash flows using UK GAAP. In this case, we derive the operating cash flow from the income statement and the statement of financial position.

In this book we focus on presentation using IFRS, but it is worth briefly comparing the UK and IFRS cash flow statements. The primary difference between the two is in the main headings. In the most commonly used indirect method, there are six main headings under which the cash flows are classified using UK GAAP, but only three using IFRS.

UK GAAP

1. Net cash flows from operating activities
2. Returns on investment and servicing of finance
3. Taxation
4. Capital expenditure and financial investment
5. Equity dividends paid
6. Financing

IFRS

1. Cash flows from operating activities
2. Cash flows from investing activities
3. Cash flows from financing activities

In particular, under UK GAAP dividends and taxation are separately disclosed.

Figure 7.5 Preparation of a Sole Trader's Statement of Cash Flows Using the Direct Method Using IFRS Format

You have extracted the following aggregated cash figures from the accounting records of Richard Hussey, who runs a book shop. The bank has requested a statement of cash flows. Prepare Hussey's statement of cash flows for the year ended 31 December 2013.

	£		£
Cash receipts from customers	150,000	Interest received	850
Cash payments to suppliers	60,000	Interest paid	400
Cash payments to employees	30,000	Cash from sale of motor car	3,000
Cash expenses	850	Payment for new motor car	4,350
Loan received and paid into the bank	8,150		

Richard Hussey
Statement of Cash Flows for the Year Ended 31 December 2013

Cash Flows from Operating Activities	£	£
Receipts from customers	150,000	
Payments to suppliers	(60,000)	
Payments to employees	(30,000)	
Expenses	(850)	59,150
Cash Flows from Investing Activities		
Interest received	850	
Sale of motor car	3,000	
Purchase of motor car	(4,350)	(500)
Cash Flows from Financing Activities		
Interest paid	(400)	
Loan	8,150	7,750
Increase in Cash		66,400

Direct Method

This method of preparing statements of cash flows is relatively easy to understand. However, in practice it is used far less than the indirect method. It is made of functional flows such as payments to suppliers or employees. These are usually extracted from the cash book or bank account. Figure 7.5 demonstrates the direct method using IFRS format.

We used the headings in Figure 7.2 which relate to the presentation of the statement of cash flows using IFRS. We use this as the main presentational format for ease of understanding. However, Appendix 7.2 gives the traditional format using UK Accounting Standards. The **net cash inflow from operating activities** represents all the cash flows relating to trading activities (e.g., buying or selling goods). By contrast, **returns on investments and servicing of finance** deals with interest received or paid, resulting from money invested or money borrowed. **Capital expenditure and financial investment** are concerned with the cash spent on, or received from, buying or selling property, plant or equipment. Finally, **financing** represents a loan paid into the bank.

PAUSE FOR THOUGHT 7.4

Profit and Positive Cash Flow

If a company makes a profit, does this mean that it will have a positive cash flow?

No! Not necessarily. A fundamental point to grasp is that if a company makes a profit this means that its assets *will increase*, but this increase in assets *will not necessarily be in the form of cash*. Assets other than cash may increase (e.g., property, plant and equipment, inventory or trade receivables) or liabilities may decrease. This can be shown by a quick example. Noreen O. Cash has two assets: inventories £25,000 and cash £50,000. Noreen makes a profit of £25,000, but invests it all in inventories. We can, therefore, compare the two statements of financial position.

	Before £	After £		Before £	After £
Inventories	25,000	50,000	Equity	75,000	75,000
Cash	50,000	50,000	Profit	–	25,000
	75,000	100,000		75,000	100,000

There is a profit, but it does not affect cash. The increase in profit is reflected in the increase in inventories.

From Richard Hussey's statement of cash flows in Figure 7.5, it is clear that cash has increased by £66,400. However, the statement also clearly shows the separate components such as a positive operating cash flow of £59,150. By looking at the statement of cash flows, Richard Hussey can quickly gain an overview of where his cash has come from and where it has been spent. The principles underlying the direct method of preparation are similar to those used in the construction of a cash budget (see Chapter 14).

Indirect Method

The most common method of preparing the statement of cash flows is the indirect method. This method, which can be more difficult to understand than the direct method, has three steps.

- First, *we must adjust profit before taxation to arrive at operating profit.*
- Second, *we must reconcile operating profit to operating cash flow by adjusting for changes in working capital and for other non-cash flow items such as depreciation.* By adjusting the operating profit to arrive at operating cash flow, we effectively bypass the bank account. Instead of directly totalling all the operating cash flows from the bank account, we work indirectly from the figures in the income statement and the opening and closing statements of financial position. *This reconciliation is done either as a separate calculation or in the statement of cash flows.*
- Third, *we can prepare the statement of cash flows.*

These steps are outlined in Figure 7.6 and the direct and indirect methods are compared.

We will now look in more detail at the first two steps. Figure 7.7 summarises these adjustments and then Figure 7.8, Collette Ash, illustrates them. We then work through a full example, Any Company plc, in Figure 7.9. Figure 7.9 uses the IFRS format while in Appendix 7.3 we present the statement of cash flows using the more traditional UK format. Essentially, the method of preparation in the two figures is identical, but the presentation differs.

Figure 7.6 Comparison of Direct and Indirect Methods of Preparing Statement of Cash Flows

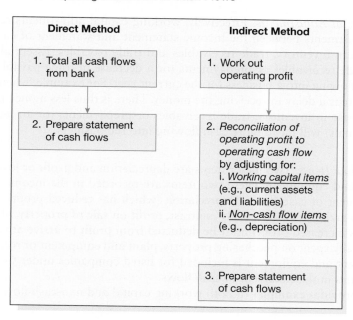

1. Calculation of Operating Profit by Adjusting Profit before Taxation

In the indirect method, we need to calculate operating cash flow (i.e., net cash flow from operating activities). To do this we need to first calculate operating profit so that we can reconcile operating profit to operating cash flow. Operating profit is calculated by *adjusting profit before taxation to operating profit*. The profit before tax figure must be adjusted by adding interest paid and deducting interest received. (Strictly, these items are called interest payable and interest receivable; for simplicity we call them in this section interest paid and interest received: see Figure 5.5 for an explanation of this.) These items can, under IAS 7, be treated as either (i) operating activities or (ii) interest paid as a financing activity and interest received as an investing activity. In either case they must be separately disclosed. In this book I treat them as financing and investing flows respectively, as that seems most logical. Thus, they will appear in our statement of cash flows as follows: interest received under cash flows from investing activities and interest paid under cash flows from financing activities. For listed companies, this adjustment is recorded under the heading *Cash Flows from Operating Activities*.

2. Reconciliation of Operating Profit to Operating Cash Flow

It is possible to identify two main types of adjustment needed to adjust operating profit to operating cash flow: (i) *working capital adjustments* and (ii) *non-cash flow items*, such as depreciation. It is important to emphasise that we need to consider operating cash flow and operating profit. The term 'operating' is used in accounting broadly to mean trading activities such as buying or selling goods or services. For listed companies, we start from profit before taxation not operating profit. Taxation paid is also deducted under *Cash Flow from Operating Activities*.

(i) Working Capital Adjustments. Effectively, working capital adjustments represent short-term timing adjustments between the income statement and statement of cash flows. They principally concern inventory, trade receivables and trade payables. Essentially, an increase in inventory, trade receivables or prepayments (or a decrease in trade payables or accruals) means less cash flowing into a business for the current year. For example, when trade receivables increase there is a delay in receiving the money. There is thus less money in the bank. By contrast, a decrease in inventory, trade receivables or prepayments (or an increase in trade payables or accruals) will mean more cash flowing into the business.

(ii) Non-Cash Flow Items. Two major items are depreciation and profit or loss on the sale of property, plant and equipment. These two items are recorded in the income statement, but not in the statement of cash flows. **Depreciation** (which has reduced profit) must be **added back to profit** to arrive at cash flow. By contrast, **profit on sale of property, plant and equipment** (which has increased profit) must be **deducted from profit** to arrive at *Operating Cash Flow*. Cash actually spent on purchasing property, plant and equipment or received from selling property, plant and equipment is included for listed companies under *Cash Flows from Investing Activities* in the statement of cash flows.

Figure 7.7 provides examples of both working capital and non-cash flow adjustments.

Figure 7.7 Summary of Adjustments Made to Profit to Arrive at Cash Flow

Item	Effect on Cash Flow	Adjustment
i. Working Capital (Source: **Comparison of opening and closing statements of financial position**) Increase in inventories Increase in trade receivables Increase in prepayments Decrease in trade payables Decrease in accruals	All of these **reduce** cash flow as more 'cash' is tied up in working capital (i.e., current assets less current liabilities)	**Deduct from profit** to arrive at cash flow
Decrease in inventories Decrease in trade receivables Decrease in prepayments Increase in trade payables Increase in accruals	All of these **increase** cash flow as less cash is tied up in working capital (i.e., current assets less current liabilities)	**Add to profit** to arrive at cash flow
ii. Non-Cash Flow Items (Source: **Income statement**) Depreciation Loss on sale of property, plant and equipment	Have **no effect** on cash flow, but were deducted from profit as expenses	**Add back to profit** to arrive at cash flow
Profit on sale of property, plant and equipment	Has **no effect** on cash flow, but increased profit as other income	**Deduct from profit** to arrive at cash flow

Figure 7.8, Collette Ash, on the next page now demonstrates the first two steps (calculation of operating profit and reconciliation of operating profit to operating cash flow). *The increases or decreases in working capital items are established by comparing the individual current assets and current liabilities in the opening and closing statement of financial position. By contrast, the non-cash flow items (depreciation and profit on sale of property, plant and equipment) are taken from the income statement.*

In straightforward cases this can be done in the statement of cash flows itself. Otherwise, as here, it can be done separately and the net figure, in this case £100,950, is taken to the statement of cash flows.

Figure 7.8 Illustration of Profit Adjustments

Collette Ash has the following extracts from her business income statement for the year ending 31 December 2013 and the statements of financial position as at 31 December 2012 and 31 December 2013. Reconcile her operating profit to her operating statement of cash flows.

Income Statement	£	Statements of Financial Position	31.12.2012	31.12.2013
Profit before Taxation	95,000	Current Assets	£	£
After deducting:		Inventory	4,000	5,300
Depreciation	3,000	Trade receivables	3,250	3,000
Interest paid	10,000	Prepayments	350	300
After adding:		Cash	6,300	10,500
Profit from sale of property,	1,000	Current Liabilities	(1,850)	(1,750)
plant and equipment	5,000	Trade payables	(650)	(700)
Interest received		Accruals		

i. Calculation of Operating Profit

Before reconciling operating profit to operating cash flow, we must adjust our profit before taxation for interest paid and interest received, which are financing and investment rather than operating items. As explained above they can both be treated as either operating activities **or** interest paid as a financing activity and interest received as an investing activity. In this book I treat them as financing and investing flows respectively. Interest paid has already been deducted in calculating profit before taxation and interest received has already been credited to profit. We must reverse these entries. We, therefore, have:

	£
Profit before Taxation	95,000
Add Interest paid	10,000
Less Interest received	(5,000)
Operating Profit	100,000

ii. Reconciliation of Operating Profit to Operating Cash Flow

We are now in a position to adjust the operating cash flow for all changes in working capital and for all non-cash flow items (i.e., depreciation and profit on sale of property, plant and equipment).

C. Ash
Reconciliation of Operating Profit to Operating Cash Flow

	£	£
Operating Profit		100,000
Add:		
Decrease in trade receivables	250	
Decrease in prepayments	50	
Increase in accruals	50	
Depreciation	3,000	3,350
Deduct:		
Increase in inventory	(1,300)	
Decrease in trade payables	(100)	
Profit on sale of property, plant and equipment	(1,000)	(2,400)
Cash Flows from Operating Activities		100,950

The three-stage process is now illustrated in Figure 7.9, which shows the calculation of a statement of cash flows for Any Company plc. The income statement and statement of financial position are provided. This is done by following IFRS. A statement of cash flows prepared under UK GAAP is recorded as Appendix 7.2. Then steps 1–3 which follow show how a statement of cash flows would be prepared using the indirect method.

Figure 7.9 Preparation of the Statement of Cash Flows of Any Company plc using the Indirect Method Using IFRS

Any Company plc
Income Statement for the Year Ended 31 December 2013

	£000
Profit before Taxation (see note below)	150
Taxation	(30)
Profit for year	120

Note: This is after having added interest received of £15,000 to profit and having deducted interest paid of £8,000 from profit.

Statements of Financial Position

	31 December 2012		31 December 2013	
	£000	£000	£000	£000
ASSETS				
Non-current Assets				
Patents		30		50
Property, plant and equipment				
Cost	300		500	
Accumulated depreciation	(50)	250	(60)	440
Total non-current assets		280		490
Current Assets				
Inventories	50		40	
Trade receivables	20		45	
Prepayments	25		30	
Cash	45	140	40	155
Total Assets		420		645
LIABILITIES				
Current Liabilities				
Trade payables	(35)		(15)	
Accruals	(5)	(40)	(10)	(25)
Non-current Liabilities		(80)		(110)
Total Liabilities		(120)		(135)
Net Assets		300		510
EQUITY				
Capital and Reserves		£000		£000
Ordinary share capital		250		360
Retained earnings		50		150
Total Equity		300		510

Notes:

1. There are no disposals of property, plant and equipment. Therefore, the increases in property, plant and equipment between 2012 and 2013 are purchases of property, plant and equipment.
2. Taxation in the income statement equals the amounts actually paid. This will not always be so.
3. Dividends paid for the year were £20,000.

Figure 7.9 Preparation of the Statement of Cash Flows of Any Company plc using the Indirect Method Using IFRS (*continued*)

Any Company plc Income Statement for the Year Ended 31 December 2013		
Cash Flows from Operating Activities	£000	£000
Net Profit before Taxation		150
Add:		
Interest paid (1)	8	
Decrease in inventories (2)	10	
Increase in accruals (2)	5	
Depreciation (3)	10	33
Deduct:		
Interest received (1)	(15)	
Increase in trade receivables (2)	(25)	
Increase in prepayments (2)	(5)	
Decrease in trade payables (2)	(20)	
Taxation paid (4)	(30)	(95)
Net Cash from Operating Activities		88
Cash Flows from Investing Activities		
Patents purchased	(20)	
Plant and machinery purchased	(200)	
Interest received	15	
Net Cash used in Investing Activities		(205)
Cash flows from Financing Activities		
Increase in non-current liabilities	30	
Interest paid	(8)	
Increase in share capital	110	
Equity dividends paid	(20)	
Net Cash from Financing Activities		112
Net Decrease in Cash		(5)
		£000
Opening Cash and Cash Equivalent(5)		45
Decrease in cash		(5)
Closing Cash and Cash Equivalent(5)		40

Some explanatory help:
1. Interest paid and interest received are added back and deducted, respectively, under operating activities. Interest received is then treated as a cash flow from investing activities and interest paid as a cash flow from financing activities. Note that interest paid can also be treated as an operating flow. Also note the different treatment from a non-listed company prepared under UK GAAP where they are both recorded under Returns on Investments and Servicing of Finance.
2. These items are all movements in working capital taken as the increase or decrease from the statement of financial position.
3. Depreciation is a non-cash flow item taken from increase in accumulated depreciation in the statement of financial position.
4. Taxation paid is recorded under operating activities not under *Taxation* as per a non-listed company using UK GAAP.
5. Cash and cash equivalents represents cash in hand, balances with banks as well as short-term investments.

An example of a statement of cash flows for AstraZeneca, a UK listed company, is given in Company Snapshot 7.1. There is also a statement of cash flows for Manchester United prepared under UK GAAP in Appendix 7.3. This has a very different format from the format of AstraZeneca that is prepared under IFRS.

COMPANY SNAPSHOT 7.1

Statement of Cash Flows for AstraZeneca, a Limited Company

Consolidated Statement of Cash Flows for the year ended 31 December

	Notes	2009 $m	2008 $m	2007 $m
Cash flows from operating activities				
Profit before tax		10,807	8,681	7,983
Finance income and expense	3	736	463	111
Depreciation, amortisation and impairment		2,087	2,620	1,856
Increase in trade and other receivables		(256)	(1,032)	(717)
Decrease in inventories		6	185	442
Increasel(decrease) in trade and other payables and provisions		1,579	637	(168)
Other non-cash movements		(200)	87	901
Cash generated from operations		14,759	11,641	10,408
Interest paid		(639)	(690)	(335)
Tax paid		(2,381)	(2,209)	(2,563)
Net cash inflow from operating activities		11,739	8,742	7,510
Cash flows from investing activities				
Acquisitions of business operations	22	–	–	(14,891)
Movement in short term investments and fixed deposits		(1,371)	1	894
Purchase of property, plant and equipment		(962)	(1,095)	(1,130)
Disposal of property, plant and equipment		138	38	54
Purchase of intangible assets		(624)	(2,944)	(549)
Disposal of intangible assets		269	–	–
Purchase of non-current asset investments		(31)	(40)	(35)
Disposal of non current asset investments		3	32	421
Interest received		113	149	358

COMPANY SNAPSHOT 7.1 (*continued*)

	$m	$m	$m
Payments made by subsidiaries to non-controlling interests	(11)	(37)	(9)
Net cash outflow from investing activities	(2,476)	(3,896)	(14,887)
Net cash inflow/outflow before financing activities	9,263	4,846	(7,377)
Cash flows from financing activities			
Proceeds from issue of share capital	135	159	218
Re-purchase of shares	–	(610)	(4,170)
Issue of loans	–	787	9,692
Repayment of loans	(650)	–	(1,165)
Dividends paid	(2,977)	(2,739)	(2,641)
Movement in short term borrowings	(137)	(3,959)	4,117
Net cash (outflow)/inflow from financing activities	(3,629)	(6,362)	6,051
Net increase/(decrease) in cash and cash equivalents in the period	5,634	(1,516)	(1,326)
Cash and cash equivalents at beginning of the period	4,123	5,727	6,989
Exchange rate effects	71	(88)	64
Cash and cash equivalents at the end of the period 13	9,828	4,123	5,727

Source: AstraZeneca plc, *Annual Report and Form 20-F Information 2009*, p. 127.

All the adjusted figures, therefore, involved comparing the two statements of financial position or taking figures directly from the income statement. In Figures 7.8 and 7.9, the *taxation* in the income statement was *assumed to be the amounts paid*. This will not always be so. Where this is not the case, it is necessary to do some detective work to arrive at cash paid! This is illustrated for tax paid in Figure 7.10.

Sometimes there may be cases where a dividend has been declared, but not paid during the year. In this case, one would do a similar exercise. However, given the rarity of this, it is not considered here in detail.

Essentially, we find the total liability by adding the amount owing at the start of the year to the amount incurred during the year recorded in the income statement. If we then deduct the amount owing at the end of the year, we arrive at the amount paid.

Figure 7.10 Deducing Cash Paid for Tax – the Sherlock Holmes Approach

If we have only details of tax payable and the amount for the year, *we need to deduce* tax paid by a bit of detective work. For example, S. Holmes Ltd has the following information:

Income Statement (extracts)   **Statements of Financial Position** (extracts)

			Opening	Closing
	£		£	£
Tax	9,000	Tax payable	6,500	7,500

How much did S. Holmes pay for taxation?

Effectively, we know the opening and closing amounts owing and the income statement expense. The amount paid is the balance figure, which is £8,000.

Opening liability	+	Income statement	−	Amount paid	=	Closing liability
£6,500	+	£9,000	−	£8,000	=	£7,500

Or for those who like 'T' accounts.

Tax account

	£		£
Amount paid	8,000	Opening liability	6,500
Closing liability	7,500	Income statement	9,000
	15,500		15,500

In Company Snapshot 7.2, J.D.Wetherspoon's 2010 statement of cash flows is presented. We can see that in 2010 there was a cash inflow from operating activities of £110.4 million. There was also a net investment in new pubs of £53.8 million (under cash flows from investing activities). Finally, Wetherspoon financed its operations mainly by bank loans of £87.6 million. Overall, Wetherspoon's cash increased by £2.5 million. Wetherspoon also reports its free cash flow (£71.3 million). Essentially, this is a company's cash flow from ongoing activities excluding financing. Cash flow statements can thus provide important insights into a business's inflows and outflows of cash. In Chapter 9, we cover the interpretation of the cash flow statement.

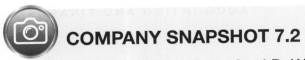

COMPANY SNAPSHOT 7.2

Statement of Cash Flows for J.D. Wetherspoon plc

J D Wetherspoon plc, company number: 1709784

	Notes	52 weeks ended 25 July 2010 £000	52 weeks ended 25 July 2010 £000	52 weeks ended 26 July 2009 £000	52 weeks ended 26 July 2009 £000
Cash flows from operating activities					
Cash generated from operations	8	153,405	153,405	171,850	171,850
Interest received		9	9	460	460
Interest paid		(30,252)	(30,252)	(35,317)	(35,317)
Corporation tax paid		(21,617)	(21,617)	(20,497)	(20,497)
Gaming machine VAT receipt		14,941		–	
Purchase of own shares for share-based payments		(6,129)	(6,129)	(6,003)	(6,003)
Net cash inflow from operating activities		110,357	95,416	110,493	110,493
Cash flows from investing activities					
Purchase of property, plant and equipment		(21,778)	(21,778)	(9,546)	(9,546)
Purchase of intangible assets		(2,294)	(2,294)	(1,453)	(1,453)
Proceeds on sale of property, plant and equipment		170		495	
Investment in new pubs and pub extensions		(53,804)		(36,899)	
Purchase of lease premiums		(3,935)		(931)	
Net cash outflow from investing activities		(81,641)	(24,072)	(48,334)	(10,999)
Cash flows from financing activities					
Equity dividends paid	10	(26,174)		(10,439)	
Proceeds from issue of ordinary shares		523		580	
Advances/(repayments) under bank loans	9	87,586		(44,051)	
Repayment of US private placement	9	(86,742)		–	
Advances under finance leases	9	9,092		–	
Finance costs on new loan	9	(7,626)		(208)	
Finance lease principal payments	9	(2,898)		(889)	
Net cash outflow from financing activities		(26,239)		(55,007)	
Net increase in cash and cash equivalents	9	2,477		7,152	
Opening cash and cash equivalents	17	23,604		16,452	
Closing cash and cash equivalents	17	26,081		23,604	
Free cash flow	7		71,344		99,494
Free cash flow per ordinary share	7		51.3p		71.7p

Source: J.D. Wetherspoon plc, *Annual Report and Accounts 2010*, p. 11.

Most companies comment on their cash flow in their annual reports. Sainsbury's, for example, summarises and comments on its cash flow activities in Company Snapshot 7.3.

COMPANY SNAPSHOT 7.3

Cash Flows from Operating Activities

Net debt and cash flow

Sainsbury's net debt as at 20 March 2010 was £1,549 million (March 2009: £1,671 million), a reduction of £122 million from the 2009 year-end position. The reduction was driven by the cash generated from the capital raised in June 2009 and strong operational cash flows, including another good working capital performance, offset by capital expenditure on the acceleration of the store development programme and outflows for taxation, interest and dividends. The resolution of a number of outstanding items contributed to a lower tax payment than in 2008/09, and interest payments benefited from lower interest rates on inflation linked debt as a result of a lower RPI than last year.

Sainsbury's expects year-end net debt to increase to around £1.9 billion in 2010/11, in line with its increased capital expenditure from the plan to deliver 15 per cent space growth in the two years to March 2011.

Summary cash flow statement for the 52 weeks to 20 March 2010	2009/10 £m	2008/09 £m
Operating cash flows before changes in working capital	1,114	1,039
Changes in working capital	92	167
Cash generated from operations	1,206	1,206
Net interest paid	(96)	(118)
Corporation tax paid	(89)	(160)
Cash flow before appropriations	1,021	928
Purchase of non-current assets	(1,057)	(994)
Investment in joint ventures	(2)	(291)
Disposal of non-current assets	139	390
Proceeds from issue of shares	250	15
Receipt of new debt	123	165
Net dividends paid	(239)	(215)
Increase/(decrease) in cash and cash equivalents	235	(2)
Increase in debt	(115)	(157)
IAS 32 and IAS 39 adjustments and other movements	2	(9)
Movement in net debt	122	(168)
Opening net debt	(1,671)	(1,503)
Closing net debt	(1,549)	(1,671)

COMPANY SNAPSHOT 7.3 (*continued*)

Working capital

Sainsbury's has continued to manage working capital closely and cash generated from operations includes a further year-on-year improvement in working capital of £92 million. This has been achieved through tight management of inventories, which are up less than two per cent on last year, and continued improvement of trade cash flows.

Source: J. Sainsbury plc, *Annual Report 2010*, p. 19. Reproduced by kind permission of Sainsbury's Supermarkets Ltd.

Conclusion

Cash and cash flow are at the heart of all businesses. Cash flow is principally concerned with cash received and cash paid. It can thus be contrasted with profit, which is income earned less expenses incurred. Cash is initially entered into the bank account or cash book. Companies usually derive the statement of cash flows from the income statement and statements of financial position, not the cash book. This is known as the indirect method of cash flow preparation. The statement of cash flows, after the income statement and the statement of financial position, is the third major financial statement. As well as preparing a statement of cash flows based on past cash flows, managers will constantly monitor current cash flows and forecast future cash flows. Cash is much harder to manipulate than profits. 'Accounting sleight of hand might shape profits whichever way a management team desires, but it is hard to deny that a cash balance is what it is. No more, no less' (E. Warner, *The Guardian*, 16 February 2002, p. 26).

Discussion Questions

Questions with numbers in blue have answers at the back of the book.

Q1 At the start of this chapter, it was stated that 'cash is king' and that it is relatively easy 'to manufacture profits, but virtually impossible to create cash'. Discuss this statement.

Q2 What is the relationship between profit and cash flow?

Q3 The direct method of preparing the statement of cash flows is the easiest to understand, but most companies use the indirect method. Why do you think this might be so?

Q4 Preparing a statement of cash flows using the indirect method is like being an accounting detective. Discuss this view.

Q5 State whether the following are true or false. If false, explain why.
- (a) Depreciation and profit from sales of property, plant and equipment are both non-cash flow items and must be added back to operating profit to arrive at operating cash flow.
- (b) Inventory, trade receivables and property, plant and equipment are all items of working capital.
- (c) Decreases in current assets such as inventory, trade receivables and prepayments must be added back to profit to arrive at cash flow.
- (d) We need to adjust profit before taxation for non-operating items (such as interest paid or received) to arrive at operating profit for non-listed companies.
- (e) The indirect method of preparing the statement of cash flows is seldom used by large companies.

 Numerical Questions

These questions are designed to gradually increase in difficulty. Questions with numbers in blue have answers at the back of the book. For consistency and ease of understanding, students should use the format required under International Reporting Standards for all questions whether they relate to sole traders, partnerships or companies.

Q1 Bingo has the following items in its accounts:
- (a) Dividends paid
- (b) Cash from loan
- (c) Sale of goods on credit
- (d) Purchase of goods for cash
- (e) Cash purchase of property, plant and equipment
- (f) Cash on sale of motor car
- (g) Loan repaid
- (h) Taxation payable
- (i) Receipts from share capital issue
- (j) Bank interest paid

Required: Are the above items recorded in the income statement, the statement of cash flows, or both? If these items appear in the statement of cash flows, state which heading would be most appropriate when using the direct method (e.g., net cash inflow from operating activities) under IFRS.

Q2 The cash flows below were extracted from the accounts of Peter Piper, a music shop owner.

	£		£
Loan repaid	25,000	Purchase of office equipment	15,000
Sale of property	25,000	Interest paid	350
Interest received	1,150	Payments to suppliers	175,000
Payments to employees	55,000	Expenses paid	10,000
Receipts from customers	250,000		

Required: Prepare a statement of cash flows using the **direct** method for the year ended 31 December 2013. Prepare a separate reconciliation statement from operating profit to operating cash flow.

Q3 The *cash flows* below were extracted from the accounts of Picasso and Partners, a painting and decorating business.

	£		£
Bank interest paid	1,000	Purchase of a building	88,000
Loan received	9,000	Sale of office furniture	2,300
Cash for sale of a motor car	4,000	Payment for a motor car	12,000
Interest received	300		

Required: Prepare a statement of cash flows under the **indirect** method for the year ended 31 December 2013. Prepare a separate reconciliation statement from operating profit to operating cash flow. You know that the operating profit was £111,000 with £75,000 of working capital adjustments to be deducted and £15,000 of non-cash adjustments to be added back to arrive at operating cash flow. The operating profit has already been adjusted for the interest paid and received (so do not adjust again!).

Q4 Diana Rink Ltd, a chain of off-licences, has the following extracts from the accounts.

Income Statement for 2013		Statements of Financial Position as at 31 December		
			2012	2013
	£		£	£
Operating profit	95,000	**Current Assets**		
Depreciation for year	8,000	Inventories	19,000	16,000
Profit on sale of property, plant and equipment	3,500	Trade receivables	10,000	11,150
		Prepayments	5,000	3,500
		Cash	10,000	3,250
		Current Liabilities		
		Trade payables	1,700	2,000
		Accruals	750	1,000

Required: Prepare a statement which reconciles operating profit to operating cash flow.

Q5 Brian Ridge Ltd, a construction company, has extracted the following *cash flows* from its books as at 30 November 2014.

	£		£
Operating profit	25,000	Interest paid	500
Increase in inventories over year	3,500	Increase in non-current liabilities	4,600
Increase in trade receivables over year	1,300	Purchase of plant and machinery	18,350
Increase in trade payables over year	800	Share capital issued	3,200
		Dividends paid	550
Depreciation for year	6,000	Purchase of patents	1,650
Tax paid	23,500		
Interest received	3,000		

Required: Prepare a statement of cash flows using the indirect method. The operating profit has already been adjusted for the interest paid and received (so do not adjust again!). You should first prepare a reconciliation of operating profit to operating cash flow.

Q6 You have the following extracts from the income statement account and statement of financial position for Grow Hire Ltd, a transport company.

Grow Hire Ltd
Income Statement Year Ended 31 December 2013 (extracts)

	£000
Profit before Taxation (Note)	112,000
Taxation paid	(33,600)
Profit for year	78,400

Grow Hire Ltd
Statements of Financial Position as at 31 December 2012 and 31 December 2013

	2012		2013	
ASSETS	£000	£000	£000	£000
Non-Current Assets				
Patents		8,000		42,200
Property, plant and equipment				
Cost	144,000		164,000	
Accumulated depreciation	(28,000)	116,000	(44,000)	120,000
Total non-current assets		124,000		162,200
Current Assets				
Inventory	112,000		110,000	
Trade receivables	18,000		11,000	
Cash	7,000	137,000	10,000	131,000
Total Assets		261,000		293,200
LIABILITIES				
Current Liabilities				
Trade payables	(45,000)		(20,000)	
Accruals	(4,000)	(49,000)	(5,000)	(25,000)
Non-Current Liabilities		(16,000)		(28,000)
Total Liabilities		(65,000)		(53,000)
Net Assets		196,000		240,200
Capital and Reserves		£000		£000
Share capital		177,000		178,600
Retained earnings		19,000		61,600
Total shareholders' funds		196,000		240,200

Q6 Grow Hire Ltd (*continued*)

There were no sales of property, plant and equipment during the year.

Notes (in £000s):
1. Profit is after adding interest received £13,000 and deducting interest paid £6,500.
2. Dividends paid were £35,800.
3. There were no sales of property, plant and equipment during the year.

Required: Prepare a statement of cash flows using the indirect method for the year ended 31 December 2013.

Q7 You have the following information regarding taxation for Brain and Co., a software house:

Income Statement (Extract)
From Year to 31 December 2013

Statement of Financial Position (Extracts)
as at 31 December

	£		2012 £	2013 £
Profit before Taxation	106,508	**Current Liabilities**		
Taxation	(51,638)	Tax payable	50,320	65,873
Profit for year	54,870			

Required: Calculate tax paid.

Q8 A construction company, Expenso plc, has the following summaries from the income statement and statement of financial position for the year ended 30 September 2014:

	£000
Revenue	460,750
Cost of Sales	(328,123)
Gross Profit	132,627
Other Income	
Interest received	868
	133,495
Expenses includes interest paid £85,000	(123,478)
Profit before Taxation	10,017
Taxation	(3,005)
Profit for Year	7,012

Expenso plc
Statement of Financial Position as at 30 September

	2013 £000	2013 £000	2014 £000	2014 £000
ASSETS				
Non-current Assets				
Property, Plant and Equipment				
Land and buildings:				
Cost	20,000		26,000	
Accumulated depreciation	(7,000)		(8,000)	
Net book value	13,000		18,000	
Plant and machinery:				
Cost	25,000		30,000	
Accumulated depreciation	(8,500)		(10,000)	
Net book value	16,500	29,500	20,000	38,000
Intangible Assets				
Patents		4,000		4,500
Total non-current assets		33,500		42,500
Current Assets				
Inventories	2,800		6,400	
Trade receivables	3,200		4,500	
Cash	8,800	14,800	1,500	12,400
Total Assets		48,300		54,900

Q8 Expenso Ltd (*continued*)

	2013		2014	
	£000	£000	£000	£000
LIABILITIES				
Current Liabilities				
Trade payables	(4,600)		(5,000)	
Accruals	(400)		(350)	
Taxation	(4,200)		(3,200)	
	(9,200)		(8,550)	
Non-current Liabilities	(12,100)		(12,505)	
Total Liabilities		(21,300)		(21,055)
Net Assets		27,000		33,845
EQUITY				
Capital and Reserves		£000		£000
Share capital		18,630		22,568
Retained earnings		8,370		11,277
Total Equity		27,000		33,845

Notes (in £000s):
1. There were no sales of property, plant and equipment during the year.
2. The dividends paid during the year were £4,105. They have been deducted from retained earnings.

Required: Prepare a statement of cash flows using the indirect method for the year ended 30 September 2014; this should include the adjustment to net profit before taxation.

Appendix 7.1: Main Headings for the Cash Flow Statement (Statement of Cash Flows) for Sole Traders, Partnerships and some Non-Listed Companies under UK GAAP

A Sole Trader's, Partnership's and Non-Listed Company's	Simplified Meaning	Examples of Inflows	Examples of Outflows
Net Cash Flows from Operating Activities[1]	Cash flows from the normal trading activities of a business	i. Cash for sale of goods	i. Payments for purchases of goods ii. Expenses paid
Returns on Investments and Servicing of Finance	Cash received from investments or paid on loans	i. Interest received ii. Dividends received	i. Interest paid
Taxation	Cash paid to Government for taxation	i. Taxation refunds	i. Taxation paid
Capital Expenditure and Financial Investment	Cash flows relating to the purchase and sale of: i. property, plant and equipment ii. investments	i. Receipts for sale of property, plant and equipment e.g., motor vehicles ii. Sale of investments	i. Payments for property, plant and equipment e.g., motor vehicles ii. Purchase of investments
Acquisitions and Disposals[2]	Cash flows arising from the purchase or sale of other companies	i. Cash paid to buy another company	i. Cash received for sale of another company
Equity Dividends Paid	Dividends companies pay to shareholders	None	Dividends paid
Management of Liquid Resources[3]	Current asset investments readily turned into cash	Cash withdrawn from 7-day deposit account	Cash paid into a 7-day deposit account
Financing	Cash flows relating to the issuing or buying back of shares or loan capital	Cash received from the issue of: i. shares ii. loans	Cash paid to buy back: i. shares ii. loans

Notes:
1. Where cash flow is positive we use the term net cash inflow. Where it is negative we use net cash outflow.
2. This item mainly applies to groups of companies. They are outside the scope of this chapter.
3. For simplification, this item is not incorporated into any of the examples.

Appendix 7.2: Preparation of a Sole Trader's Cash Flow Statement Using the Direct Method Using UK Format

You have extracted the following aggregated cash figures from the accounting records of Richard Hussey, who runs a book shop. The bank has requested a cash flow statement. Prepare Hussey's cash flow statement for year ended 31 December 2013.

	£		£
Cash receipts from customers	150,000	Interest received	850
Cash payments to suppliers	60,000	Interest paid	400
Cash payments to employees	30,000	Cash from sale of motor car	3,000
Cash expenses	850	Payment for new motor car	4,350
Loan received and paid into the bank	8,150		

Richard Hussey
Cash Flow Statement Year Ended 31 December 2013

	£	£
Net Cash Inflow from Operating Activities		
Receipts from customers	150,000	
Payments to suppliers	(60,000)	
Payments to employees	(30,000)	
Expenses	(850)	59,150
Returns on Investments and Servicing of Finance		
Interest received	850	
Interest paid	(400)	450
Capital Expenditure and Financial Investment		
Sale of motor car	3,000	
Purchase of motor car	(4,350)	(1,350)
Financing		
Loan	8,150	8,150
Increase in Cash		66,400

Appendix 7.3: Preparation of the Cash Flow Statement of Any Company Ltd Using the Indirect Method Using UK GAAP

To ease understanding, we use IFRS terminology rather than that permitted under UK GAAP.

	£000
Profit before Taxation (see note below)	150
Taxation	(30)
Profit for year	120

Note:
This is after having added interest received of £15,000 to profit and having deducted interest paid of £8,000 from profit.

	Statements of Financial Position			
	31 December 2012		31 December 2013	
	£000	£000	£000	£000
ASSETS				
Non-current Assets				
Patents		30		50
Property, Plant and Equipment				
Cost	300		500	
Accumulated depreciation	(50)	250	(60)	440
Total non-current assets		280		490
Current Assets				
Inventories	50		40	
Trade receivables	20		45	
Prepayments	25		30	
Cash	45	140	40	155
Total Assets		420		645
LIABILITIES				
Current Liabilities				
Trade payables	(35)		(15)	
Accruals	(5)	(40)	(10)	(25)
Non-current Liabilities		(80)		(110)
Total Liabilities		(120)		(135)
Net assets		300		510

Appendix 7.3: Preparation of the Cash Flow Statement of Any Company Ltd Using the Indirect Method Using UK GAAP (*continued*)

EQUITY

Capital and Reserves	£000	£000
Ordinary share capital	250	360
Retained earnings	50	150
Total Equity	300	510

Notes:

1. There are no disposals of property, plant and equipment. Therefore, the increase in property, plant and equipment between 2012 and 2013 are purchases of property, plant and equipment.
2. Taxation in the income statement equals the amounts actually paid. This will not always be so.
3. Dividends paid for the year were £20,000.

Step 1: Calculation of Operating Profit

We need first to adjust net profit before taxation (£150,000) taken from profit and loss account, by adding back interest paid (£8,000) and deducting interest received (£15,000). These items are investment not operating flows. This is because we wish to determine operating or trading profit. Thus:

	£000
Net Profit before Taxation	150
Add Interest paid	8
Deduct Interest received	(15)
Operating profit	143

Step 2: Reconciliation of Operating Profit to Operating Cash Flow

This involves taking the company's operating profit and then adjusting for:

(i) Movement in working capital (e.g., increase or decrease in inventory, trade receivables, prepayments, trade payables and accruals).

(ii) Non-cash flow items such as depreciation, and profit or loss on sale of property, plant and equipment.

	£000	£000
Operating Profit		143
Add		
Decrease in inventories (1)	10	
Increase in accruals (1)	5	
Depreciation (2)	10	25
Deduct:		
Increase in trade receivables (1)	(25)	
Increase in prepayments (1)	(5)	
Decrease in trade payables (1)	(20)	(50)
Net Cash Inflow from Operating Activities		118

(1) Represents increases, or decreases, in the current assets and current liabilities sections between the two statements of financial position (i.e., movements in working capital).

(2) Difference in accumulated depreciation in the two statements of financial position represents depreciation for year (i.e., represents a non-cash flow item).

Appendix 7.3: Preparation of the Cash Flow Statement of Any Company Ltd Using the Indirect Method Using UK GAAP (*continued*)

Step 3: Cash Flow Statement year ended 31 December
This involves deducing the relevant figures in the cash flow statement by using the existing figures from the income statement and the opening and closing statements of financial position. We start from net cash inflow calculated in Step 2.

	£000	£000
Net Cash Inflow from Operating Activities		
(see above)		118
Returns on Investments and Servicing of Finance		
Interest received (1)	15	
Interest paid (1)	(8)	7
Taxation		
Taxation paid (1)	(30)	(30)
Capital Expenditure and Financial Investment		
Patents purchased (2)	(20)	
Property, plant and equipment purchased (2)	(200)	(220)
Equity Dividends Paid (1)	(20)	(20)
Financing		
Increase in non-current liabilities (2)	30	
Increase in share capital (2)	110	140
Decrease in Cash (2)		(5)

	£000
Opening Cash	45
Decrease in cash	(5)
Closing Cash	40

Notes:
1. Figure from income statement.
2. Represents increase or decrease from statement of financial position.

Some explanatory help:

1. Operating profit is adjusted for interest paid and interest received, then both are included under returns on investments and servicing of finance. In a listed company under IFRS we have included interest paid under financing flows and interest received under investing flows.
2. There are six headings recorded here rather than three using IFRS.
3. Depreciation is a non-cash flow item.
4. Taxation paid is recorded under taxation not under operating activities as under IFRS.

Appendix 7.4: Example of Statement of Cash Flows (Cash Flow Statement) Using UK GAAP (Manchester United Ltd)

Manchester United Limited
Consolidated cash flow statement

	Note	Year ended 30 June 2009		Year ended 30 June 2008	
		£000	£000	£000	£000
Net cash inflow from operating activities			112,133		94,629
Returns on investments and servicing of finance					
Interest received		1,259		1,011	
Interest paid		(1,186)		(471)	
Net cash inflow from returns on investments and servicing of finance			73		540
Taxation received/(paid)			236		(205)
Capital expenditure and financial investment					
Proceeds from sale of players' registrations		99,180		19,301	
Purchase of players' registrations		(55,220)		(45,751)	
Proceeds from sale of tangible fixed assets		28		183	
Purchase of tangible fixed assets		(3,810)		(16,754)	
Net cash inflow/(outflow) from capital expenditure and financial investment			40,178		(43,021)
Acquisitions and disposals					
Purchase of shares in subsidiary undertaking			—	(2,615)	
Net cash acquired with subsidiary undertaking			—	113	
Proceeds from sale of investment in associated company			—	1,581	
Net cash outflow from acquisitions and disposals			—		(921)

Appendix 7.4: Example of Statement of Cash Flows (Cash Flow Statement) Using UK GAAP for Manchester United (*continued*)

	£000	£000	£000	£000
Cash inflow before use of liquid resources and financing		152,620		51,022
Financing				
Increase in borrowings	25,000		8,000	
Repayment of borrowings	(25,215)		—	
Purchase of loan stock	—		(750)	
Loans to parent company	(51,620)		(70,656)	
Net cash outflow from financing		(51,835)		(63,406)
Increase/(decrease) in cash in the year 23		100,785		(12,384)

Source: Manchester United Ltd, *Annual Report and Financial Statements for the year end 30 June 2009*, p. 13.

Go online to discover the extra features for this chapter at
www.wiley.com/college/jones

Chapter 8

Interpretation of accounts

'More money has been lost reaching for yield than at the point of a gun.'

Raymond Revoe Jr, *Fortune*, 18 April 1994, *Wiley Book of Business Quotations* (1998), p. 192.

Learning Outcomes

After completing this chapter you should be able to:

- Explain the nature of accounting ratios.
- Appreciate the importance of the main accounting ratios.
- Calculate the main accounting ratios and explain their significance.
- Understand the limitations of ratio analysis.

Go online to discover the extra features for this chapter at
www.wiley.com/college/jones

Chapter Summary

- Ratio analysis is a method of evaluating the financial information presented in accounts.
- Ratio analysis is performed after the bookkeeping and preparation of the final accounts.
- There are six main types of ratio: profitability, efficiency, liquidity, gearing, cash flow and investment.
- Three important profitability ratios are return on capital employed (ROCE), gross profit ratio and net profit ratio.
- Four important efficiency ratios are trade receivables collection period, trade payables collection period, inventory turnover ratio and asset turnover ratio.
- Two important liquidity ratios are the current ratio and the quick ratio.
- Five important investment ratios are dividend yield, dividend cover, earnings per share (EPS), price earnings ratio and interest cover.
- Ratios can be viewed collectively using Z scores or pictics.
- For some predominately non-profit oriented businesses, it is appropriate to use non-standard ratios, such as performance indicators.
- Four limitations of ratios are that they must be used in context, the absolute size of the business must be considered, ratios must be calculated on a consistent and comparable basis and international comparisons must be made with care.

Introduction

The interpretation of accounts is the key to any in-depth understanding of an organisation's performance. Interpretation is basically when users evaluate the financial information, principally from the income statement and statement of financial position, so as to make judgements about issues such as profitability, efficiency, liquidity, gearing (i.e., amount of indebtedness), cash flow, and success of financial investment. The analysis is usually performed by using certain 'ratios' which take the raw accounting figures and turn them into simple indices. The aim is to try to measure and capture an organisation's performance using these ratios. This is often easier said than done!

Context

The interpretation of accounts (or ratio analysis) is carried out after the initial bookkeeping and preparation of the accounts. In other words, the transactions have been recorded in the books of account using double-entry bookkeeping and then the financial statements have been drawn up (see Figure 8.1). For this reason, the interpretation of accounts is often known as financial statement analysis. The financial statements which form the

Figure 8.1 Main Stages in Accounting Process

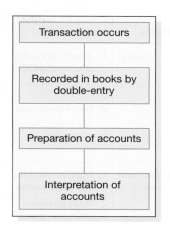

basis for ratio analysis are principally the income statement and the statement of financial position.

Overview

Two useful techniques, when interpreting a set of accounts, are (i) vertical and horizontal analysis and (ii) ratio analysis. Vertical and horizontal analysis involves comparing key figures in the financial statements. In vertical analysis, key figures (such as revenue in the income statement and total net assets in the statement of financial position) are set to 100%. Other items are then expressed as a percentage of 100. In horizontal analysis, the company's income statement and statement of financial position figures are compared across years. We return to vertical and horizontal analysis later in the chapter. For now, we focus on ratio analysis.

Broadly, ratio analysis can be divided into six major areas: profitability, efficiency, liquidity, gearing, cash flow and investment. The principal features are represented diagrammatically in Figure 8.3, but set out in more detail in Figure 8.2 on the next page. These ratios are then discussed later on in this chapter.

It is important to appreciate that there are potentially many different ratios. The actual ratios used will depend on the nature of the business and the individual preferences of users. The interpretation of accounts and the choice of ratios are thus inherently subjective. The ratios in Figure 8.2 have been chosen because generally they are appropriate for most businesses and are commonly used.

The 16 ratios, therefore, cover six main areas. Each of the above ratios can yield many more; for example, the gross profit ratio in Figure 8.2 is currently divided by revenue. However, gross profit per employee (divide by number of employees) or gross profit per share (divide by number of shares) are also possible. The fun and frustration of ratio analysis is that there are no fixed rules. In the UK, none of the ratios, except for earnings per share, is a regulatory requirement.

Figure 8.2 Principal Features of the Main Areas of the Interpretation of Accounts

Main Area	Main Source of Ratios	Main Ratios	Overview Definition
1. Profitability	Mainly derived from income statement	1. Return on capital employed (ROCE)	$\dfrac{\text{Profit before tax and loan interest}}{\text{Average capital employed}}$
		2. Gross profit ratio	$\dfrac{\text{Gross profit}}{\text{Revenue}}$
		3. Net profit ratio	$\dfrac{\text{Net profit before tax}}{\text{Revenue}}$
2. Efficiency	Mixture of income statement and statement of financial position	1. Trade receivables collection period	$\dfrac{\text{Average trade receivables}}{\text{Credit sales}}$
		2. Trade payables collection period	$\dfrac{\text{Average trade payables}}{\text{Credit purchases}}$
		3. Inventory turnover ratio	$\dfrac{\text{Cost of sales}}{\text{Average inventories}}$
		4. Asset turnover ratio	$\dfrac{\text{Revenue}}{\text{Average total assets}}$
3. Liquidity	Mainly from statement of financial position	1. Current ratio	$\dfrac{\text{Current assets}}{\text{Current liabilities}}$
		2. Quick ratio	$\dfrac{\text{Current assets–inventories}}{\text{Current liabilities}}$
4. Gearing	Mainly from statement of financial position	1. Gearing ratio	$\dfrac{\text{Long-term borrowing}}{\text{Total long-term capital}}$
5. Cash flow	Statement of cash flows	1. Cash flow ratio	$\dfrac{\text{Total cash inflows}}{\text{Total cash outflows}}$
6. Investment	Mainly share price and income statement information	1. Dividend yield	$\dfrac{\text{Dividend per ordinary share}}{\text{Share price}}$
		2. Dividend cover	$\dfrac{\text{Profit after tax and preference shares}}{\text{Ordinary dividends}}$
		3. Earnings per share	$\dfrac{\text{Profit after tax and preference dividends}}{\text{Number of ordinary shares}}$
		4. Price/earnings ratio	$\dfrac{\text{Share price}}{\text{Earnings per share}}$
		5. Interest cover	$\dfrac{\text{Profit before tax and loan interest}}{\text{Loan interest}}$

Figure 8.3 Main Ratios

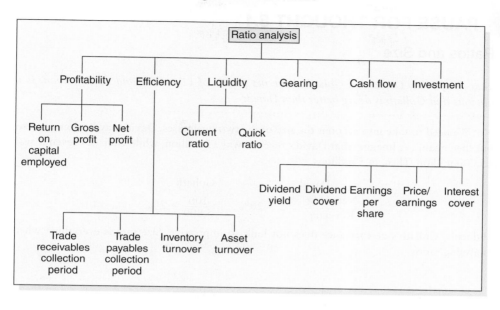

Importance of Ratios

Once the managers have prepared the accounts, then many other groups, such as investment analysts, will wish to comment on them. This is expressed in Soundbite 8.1. Different users will be interested in different ratios. For example, shareholders are primarily interested in investment ratios that measure the performance of their shares. By contrast, lenders may be interested primarily in liquidity (i.e., can the company repay its loan?). Ratios are important for three main reasons. First, they provide a quick and easily digestible snapshot of an organisation's achievements. It is much easier to glance at a set of ratios and draw conclusions from them than plough through the often quite complex financial statements. Second, ratios provide a good yardstick by which it is possible to compare one company with another (i.e., inter-firm comparisons) or to compare the same company over time (intra-firm comparisons). Third, ratio analysis takes account of size. One company may make more absolute profit than another. At first glance, it may, therefore, seem to be doing better than its competitor. However, if absolute size is taken into account, it may in fact be performing less well.

SOUNDBITE 8.1

'Captains of industry change things. We merely comment on them. Somebody has to bring the news of the relief of Mafeking.'

Angus Phaure, August, *County Natwest Business,* October 1990

Source: The Book of Business Quotations (1991), p. 13.

PAUSE FOR THOUGHT 8.1

Ratios and Size

Two companies, David and Goliath, have net profits of £1 million and £100 million. Is it obvious that Goliath is doing better than David?

No! We need to take into account the size of the two businesses. David may be doing worse, but then again . . . Imagine that David's revenue was £5 million, while Goliath's revenue was £5,000 million. Then, in £ millions,

	David	Goliath
$\dfrac{\text{Net profit}}{\text{Revenue}}$	$\dfrac{1}{5} = 20\%$	$\dfrac{100}{5,000} = 2\%$

Suddenly, Goliath's performance does not look so impressive. Size means everything when analysing ratios.

Closer Look at Main Ratios

It is now time to look in more depth at the main categories of ratio and at individual ratios. The ratios are mainly derived from the accounts of John Brown Plc. Although John Brown is a limited company, many of the ratios are also potentially usable for partnerships or sole traders. John Brown's financial statements are given at the back of this chapter as Appendix 8.1. They have been prepared for internal use and thus have more detail than in published accounts.

    Some ratios (return on capital employed, trade receivables and trade payables collection period, inventory turnover and asset turnover) use average figures from two years' accounts. In practice, two years' figures are not always available. In this case, as for John Brown, the closing figures are used on their own. When this is done, then any conclusions must be drawn cautiously. In order to place the interpretation of key ratios in context, I have, wherever the information was available, referred to figures calculated from the UK's top publicly quoted companies. As there was no one authoritative up-to-date source, I have used three main sources. First, information collected from Fame and Extel, two corporate databases, in July 2005. Second, where these sources were not available I used information from Fame and Extel November 2011. Third, I have used data from Jones and Finley (2011), which was based on a widespread sample of EU and Australian companies using IFRS. This article ('Have IFRS Made a Difference to Intra-country Financial Reporting Diversity?') was published in *The British Accounting Review*. The reader should be aware, however, that the way in which these sources calculate ratios may differ from the exact ratios in the book; they should thus be seen as guidelines rather than definitive figures.

Profitability Ratios

The profitability ratios seek to establish how profitably a business is operating. Profit is a key measure of business success and, therefore, these ratios are keenly watched by both internal users, such as management, and external users, such as shareholders. There are three main profitability ratios (return on capital employed, gross profit ratio and net profit ratio). The figures used are from John Brown Plc (see Appendix 8.1).

(i) Return on Capital Employed

This ratio considers how effectively a company uses its capital employed. It compares net profit to capital employed. A problem with this ratio is that different companies often use different versions of capital employed. At its narrowest, a company's capital employed is ordinary share capital and reserves. At its widest, it might equal ordinary share capital and reserves, preference shares, long-term loans (i.e., debentures) and current liabilities. Different definitions of capital employed necessitate different definitions of profits.

The most common definition measures *profit before interest and tax* against *long-term financing* (i.e., ordinary share capital and reserves, preference share capital and non-current liabilities). Therefore, for John Brown we have:

$$\frac{\text{Profit before tax and loan interest}}{\substack{\text{Long-term capital (ordinary share} \\ \text{capital and reserves, preference share} \\ \text{capital and non-current liabilities)}}} = \frac{50 + 10}{150 + 65 + 50 + 70} = \frac{60}{335} = 17.9\%$$

Essentially, the 17.9% indicates the return which the business earns on its capital. The key question is: could the capital be used anywhere else to gain a better return? In this example, with only one year's statement of financial position, we can only take one year's capital employed. If we have an opening and a closing statement of financial position, we can take the average capital employed over the two statements of financial position. As Real-World View 8.1 shows, this is a good return on capital, which has varied in recent years from 8.9% to 14.9%.

REAL-WORLD VIEW 8.1

Return on Capital Ratios

The return on capital varies with the economic cycle, for example, the *Investors Chronicle* in October 2011 states that:

'The latest official figures show that non-financial companies' net return on capital in the second quarter was 12.1%. Although this is below the pre-recession peak of 14.9%, it's well above the recessionary trough of 10.6%.'

In addition, it was pointed out that this is still higher than the 1990s where, for example, in 1992 it was 8.4%.

Source: The Paradox of Corporate Profits, Chris Dillow, *Investors Chronicle*, 14–20 October, 2011, p.12. Financial Times.

(ii) Gross Profit Ratio

The gross profit ratio (or gross profit divided by revenue) is a very useful ratio. It calculates the profit earned through trading. It is particularly useful in a business where inventory is purchased, marked up and then resold. For example, a retail business selling car batteries (see Figure 8.4) may well buy the batteries from the manufacturer and then add a fixed percentage as mark-up. In the case of pubs, it is traditional to mark up the purchase price of beer by 100% before reselling to customers.

In the case of John Brown, the gross profit is

$$\frac{\text{Gross profit}}{\text{Revenue}} = \frac{100}{200} = 50\%$$

This is the *direct* return that John Brown makes from buying and selling goods.

Figure 8.4 Gross Profit Illustration

Snowfield batteries buys car batteries from a wholesaler for £40 each and resells them for £60 each. What will Snowfield's gross profit be?

It will simply be revenue (£60) – purchases (£40) = gross profit (£20). Expressed as a percentage this is $\frac{20}{60} = 33.33\%$.

This is useful because Snowfield will know that its gross profit ratio should be 33.33%. If it is not, then there may be a problem, such as theft of inventory.

(iii) Net Profit Ratio

The net profit ratio (or net profit divided by revenue) is another key financial indicator. Whereas gross profit is calculated *before* taking administrative and distribution expenses into account, the net profit ratio is calculated *after* such expenses. Be careful with net profit as it is a tricky concept without a fixed meaning. Some people use it to mean profit before interest and tax, others to mean profit after interest but before tax, and still others profit after tax. For John Brown, some alternatives are:

$$\frac{\text{Net profit before taxation}}{\text{Revenue}} = \frac{50}{200} = 25\%$$

$$\frac{\text{Net profit after taxation}}{\text{Revenue}} = \frac{35}{200} = 17.5\%$$

The most popularly used alternative is net profit before taxation. This assumes that taxation is a factor that cannot be influenced by a business. This is the ratio which will be used from now on. As Real-World View 8.2 shows, most companies have traditionally, and still do today, operated on net profit margins of less than 10%. Across the top UK 250 public limited companies this ratio was 11.4% in July 2005.

REAL-WORLD VIEW 8.2

Net Profit Margins

However as we have already said profits are only likely to be a comparatively minor factor in cash flow anyway. After-tax profits in even the most spectacularly successful company will rarely run at more than about 10% of annual turnover and most companies will operate at well below this figure, say, 7% or 8% before tax.

Source: B. Warnes (1984) *The Genghis Khan Guide to Business*, Osmosis Publications London, p. 66.

Efficiency Ratios

The efficiency ratios look at how effectively a business is operating. They are primarily concerned with the efficient use of assets. Four of the main efficiency ratios are explained below (trade receivables collection period, trade payables collection period, inventory turnover and asset turnover). The first two are related in that they seek to establish how long customers take to pay and how long it takes the business to pay its suppliers. The figures used are from John Brown (see Appendix 8.1 at the end of this chapter).

(i) Trade Receivables Collection Period (Debtors Collection Period)

This ratio seeks to measure how long customers take to pay their debts. Obviously, the quicker a business collects and banks the money, the better it is for the company. This ratio can be worked out on a monthly, weekly or daily basis. This book prefers the daily basis as it is the most accurate method. The calculation for John Brown is as follows:

$$\text{Daily basis} = \frac{\text{Average trade receivables}}{\text{Credit sales per day}} = \frac{40}{200/365} = 73 \text{ days}$$

It, therefore, takes 73 days for John Brown to collect its debts. It is important to note that 'credit' sales (i.e., not cash sales) are needed for this ratio to be fully effective. This information, although available internally in most organisations, may not be readily ascertainable from the published accounts. Normally, the average of opening and closing trade receivables is used to approximate average trade receivables. When this figure is not available (as in this case), we just use closing trade receivables. Across the top 250 UK plcs it took 52 days to collect money from trade receivables in July 2005.

(ii) Trade Payables Collection Period (Creditors Collection Period)

In many ways, this is the mirror image of the trade receivables collection period. It calculates how long it takes a business to pay its trade payables. The slower a business is to pay, the longer the business has the money in the bank! As with the trade receivables collection period, we can calculate this ratio either monthly, weekly or daily. Once more, we prefer the daily basis. This is calculated below for John Brown.

$$\text{Daily basis} = \frac{\text{Average trade payables}}{\text{Credit purchases per day}} = \frac{50}{100/365} = 183 \text{ days}$$

It is usually not possible to establish accurately the figure for credit purchases from the published accounts. In John Brown, cost of sales is used as the nearest equivalent to credit purchases (remember that cost of sales is opening inventory add purchases less closing inventory). However, it should be noted that if two years' accounts are available, we can deduce purchases as the following example shows for Bamber. Bamber has opening inventory £800, closing inventory £600 and cost of sales £1,400.

	£
Opening inventory	800
Plus purchases	**1,200**
	2,000
Less Closing inventory (from year 2)	(600)
Cost of sales	**1,400**

As with the trade receivables collection ratio, strictly we should use average trade payables for the year (i.e., normally, the average of opening and closing trade payables). If this is not available, as in this case, we use closing trade payables.

It is often important to compare the trade receivables and trade payables ratios. For John Brown, this is:

$$\frac{\text{Trade receivables collection period (in days)}}{\text{Trade payables collection period (in days)}} = \frac{73 \text{ days}}{183 \text{ days}} = 0.40$$

In other words John Brown collects its cash from trade receivables in 40% of the time that it takes to pay its trade payables. The management of working capital is effective. However, this is not necessarily a good thing as supplier goodwill may be lost.

PAUSE FOR THOUGHT 8.2

Trade Receivables and Trade Payables Collection Period

Businesses whose trade receivables collection periods are much less than their trade payables collection periods are managing their working capital well. Can you think of any businesses which might be well placed to do this?

....

Businesses which sell direct to customers, generally for cash, would be prime examples. Pubs and supermarkets operate on a cash basis, or with short-term credit (cheques or credit cards). Their trade receivables collection period is very low. However, they may well take their time to pay their suppliers. If they have a high turnover of goods, they may collect the money for their goods from customers before they have even paid their suppliers.

(iii) Inventory Turnover Ratio (Stock Turnover Ratio)

This ratio effectively measures the speed with which inventory moves through the business. This varies from business to business and product to product. For example, crisps and chocolate have a high inventory turnover, while diamond rings have a low inventory turnover. Strictly this ratio compares cost of sales to average inventories. Where this figure is not available, we use the next best thing, closing inventory. Thus for John Brown, we have:

$$\frac{\text{Cost of sales}}{\text{Average inventories}} = \frac{100}{60} = 1.66 \text{ times}$$

John Brown, therefore, holds inventory for 219 days (365 ÷ 1.66) until it is sold. This is a very slow turnover.

(iv) Asset Turnover Ratio

This ratio compares revenue to total assets employed (i.e., property, plant and equipment and current assets). Businesses with a large asset infrastructure, perhaps a steel works, have lower ratios than businesses with minimal assets, such as management consultancy or dot.com businesses. Once more, where the information is available, it is best to use average total assets. For John Brown, average total assets are not available; we therefore use this year's total assets:

$$\frac{\text{Revenue}}{\text{Average total assets}} = \frac{200}{395} = 0.51 \text{ times}$$

In other words, every year John Brown generates about half of its total assets in revenue. This is very low. There are many other potential asset turnover ratios where revenue is compared to, for example, non-current assets or net assets.

If we take these three ratios together, we can gain an insight into how efficient our cash cycle is. Thus, if we hold inventory for 219 days (inventory turnover ratio) and then debtors take 73 days to pay (trade receivables collection period), all in all it takes us 292 days to receive our money, while we pay suppliers in 183 days. Some businesses can manage to receive their cash from customers before they pay them.

Liquidity Ratios

Liquidity ratios are derived from the statement of financial position and seek to test how easily a firm can pay its debts. Loan creditors, such as bankers, who have loaned money to a business, are particularly interested in these ratios. There are two main ratios (the current ratio and quick ratio). Once more we use John Brown (see Appendix 8.1).

(i) Current Ratio

This ratio tests whether the short-term assets cover the short-term liabilities. If they do not, then there will be insufficient liquid funds to pay current liabilities as they fall due. For John Brown this ratio is:

$$\frac{\text{Current assets}}{\text{Current liabilities}} = \frac{120}{60} = 2$$

In other words, the short-term assets are double the short-term liabilities. John Brown is well covered. Across the top 250 UK plcs, this ratio was 2.16 in July 2005. In other words, current assets were double current liabilities.

(ii) Quick Ratio

This is sometimes called the 'acid test' ratio. It is a measure of extreme short-term liquidity. Basically, inventories are sold, turning into trade receivables. When the debtors pay, the business gains cash. The quick ratio excludes inventory, the least liquid (i.e., the least cash-like) of the current assets, to arrive at an immediate test of a company's liquidity. If the creditors come knocking on the door for their money, can the business survive? For John Brown we have:

$$\frac{\text{Current assets} - \text{inventories}}{\text{Current liabilities}} = \frac{120 - 60}{60} = 1.0$$

For John Brown, the answer is yes. John Brown has just enough trade receivables and cash to cover its immediate liabilities. Across the top 250 UK plcs in July 2005 this ratio was 1.80.

Gearing

Like liquidity ratios, gearing ratios are derived from the statement of financial position. Gearing is also often known as leverage. Gearing effectively represents the relationship between the equity and the debt capital of a company. Essentially, equity represents the funding provided by owners (i.e., ordinary shareholders). By contrast, debt capital is that supplied by external parties (normally preference shareholders and loan holders).

So far, so good. However, the role of preference share capital and short-term liabilities is worth discussing. First, preference share capital is technically part of shareholders' funds, but preference shareholders *do not own* the company and usually receive a fixed dividend. We therefore treat them as debt. Second, current liabilities and short-term loans also finance the company. We discuss this in more detail in Chapter 19. However, generally gearing is concerned with *long-term* borrowing. Figure 8.5 now summarises shareholders' funds and long-term borrowings.

Figure 8.5 Main Elements of the Gearing Ratio

Ordinary Shareholders' Funds	Long-term Borrowings
Ordinary share capital	Preference share capital
Share premium account	Long-term loans (also known as debentures)
Revaluation reserve	
General reserve	Other non-current liabilities
Retained earnings	
Other reserves	

We can now calculate the gearing ratio for John Brown. The preferred method used in this book is to compare long-term borrowings to total long-term capital employed (i.e., equity funding plus long-term borrowings). Thus we have for John Brown:

$$\frac{\text{Long-term borrowings}}{\text{Total long-term capital}} = \frac{\text{Preference share capital and debentures}}{\substack{\text{Ordinary share capital, retained earnings and preference} \\ \text{share capital and non-current liabilities (long-term loans)}}}$$

$$= \frac{50 + 70}{150 + 65 + 50 + 70} = \frac{120}{335} = 36\%$$

In other words, 36% (or 36 pence in every £1) of John Brown is financed by long-term non-ownership capital. Essentially, the more highly geared a company, the more risky the situation for the owners when profitability is poor. This is because interest on long-term borrowings will be paid first. Thus, if profits are poor, there may be little, if anything, left to pay the dividends of ordinary shareholders. Conversely, if profits are booming, there will be relatively more profits left for the ordinary shareholders since the return to the 'lenders' is fixed. When judging the gearing ratio, it is thus important to bear in mind the overall profitability of the business. According to Jones and Finley (2011) this ratio was 72.67% in 2006 for their sample of EU and Australian companies.

Cash Flow

The cash flow ratio, unlike the other ratios we have considered so far, is prepared from the statement of cash flows, not the income statement or statement of financial position. There are many possible ratios, but the one shown here simply measures total cash inflows to total cash outflows. Figure 8.6 shows the situation using IFRS whereas Appendix 8.2 illustrates the situation using the UK GAAP cash flow statement.

Figure 8.6 The Cash Flow Ratio Using IFRS Format

Any Company Ltd has the following cash inflows and outflows in £000s.

	Inflows	Outflows
Cash Flows from Operating Activities	80	
Cash Flows from Investing Activities		205
Cash Flows from Financing Activities	120	—
Total Cash Flows	200	205
Total cash inflows	200	= 0.98
Total cash outflows	205	

Other commonly used cash flow ratios are cash flow cover (net operating cash flow divided by annual interest payments), total debt to cash flow and cash flow per share.

Investment Ratios

The investment ratios differ from the other ratios, as they focus specifically on returns to the shareholder (dividend yield, earnings per share and price/earnings ratio) or the ability of a company to sustain its dividend or interest payments (dividend cover and interest cover). The ratios once more are calculated from John Brown (see Appendix 8.1). The first four ratios covered below are mainly of concern to the shareholders. The fifth, interest cover, is of more interest to the holders of long-term loans. Many companies give details of investment ratios in their annual reports. Company Snapshot 8.1 shows the earnings per share, dividends per share and dividend cover for Manchester United from 2000 to 2004.

COMPANY SNAPSHOT 8.1

Investment Ratios

Earnings per share (pence)	7.4	11.5	9.6	5.5	4.6
Dividends per share (pence)	2.65	4.00	3.10	2.00	1.90
Dividend cover (times)	2.8	2.9	3.1	2.8	2.4

Source: Manchester United Ltd, *Annual Report 2004*, p. 81.

(i) Dividend Yield

This ratio shows how much dividend the ordinary shares earn as a proportion of their market price. The market price for the shares of leading public companies is shown daily in many newspapers, such as (in the UK) the *Financial Times*, the *Guardian*, the *Telegraph* or *The Times*. Dividend yield can be shown as net or gross of tax (dividends are paid net after deduction of tax; gross is inclusive of tax). The calculation of gross dividend varies according to the tax rate and tax rules. For simplicity, we just show the *net* dividend yield.

For John Brown, the dividend yield is:

$$\frac{\text{Dividend per ordinary share}}{\text{Share price}} = \frac{£10m \div 150m \text{ shares}}{£0.67} = \frac{0.067}{£0.67} = 10\%$$

The dividend yield is perhaps comparable to the interest at the bank or building society. However, the increase or decrease in the share price over the year should also be borne in mind. The return from the dividend combined with the movement in share price is often known as the total shareholders' return. Across the top 200 UK plcs in November 2001, the dividend yield was 4.1%.

(ii) Dividend Cover

This represents the 'safety net' for ordinary shareholders. It shows how many times profit available to pay ordinary shareholders' dividends covers the actual dividends. In other words, can the current dividend level be maintained easily? For John Brown we have:

$$\frac{\text{Profit after tax and preference dividends}}{\text{Ordinary dividends}} = \frac{30}{10} = 3.0$$

Thus, dividends are covered three times by current profits. As Company Snapshot 8.2 shows, Manchester United's dividend is well covered by profit available. Across the top 200 UK plcs in November 2001, dividend cover was 2.5.

COMPANY SNAPSHOT 8.2

Dividends

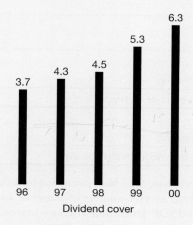

Dividend cover

Source: Manchester United Ltd, *Annual Report 2004*, p. 64.

(iii) Earnings per Share (EPS)

Earnings per share (EPS) is a key measure by which investors measure the performance of a company. Its importance is shown by the fact that it is required to be shown in the published accounts of listed companies (unlike the other ratios). It measures the earnings attributable to a particular ordinary share. For John Brown it is:

$$\frac{\text{Profit after tax and preference dividends}}{\text{Number of ordinary shares}} = \frac{30}{150} = 20\text{p}$$

Each share thus earns 20 pence. Company Snapshot 8.3 shows that GSK's EPS was 32.1p in 2010. In this case, the number of ordinary shares is adjusted for the fact that some share options may be taken up to create new shares. This is called diluted EPS. Across the top 250 UK plcs in July 2005, EPS was 32.0 pence.

(iv) Price/Earnings (P/E) Ratio

This is another key stock market measure. It uses EPS and relates it to the share price. A high ratio means a high price in relation to earnings and indicates a fast-growing, popular company in which the market has confidence. A low ratio usually indicates a slower-growing, more established company. If we look at John Brown, we have:

$$\frac{\text{Share price}}{\text{Earnings per share}} = \frac{67}{20} = 3.35$$

COMPANY SNAPSHOT 8.3

15 Earnings per Share

	2010 pence	2009 pence	2008 pence
Basic earnings per share	32.1	109.1	88.6
Adjustment for major restructuring	21.8	12.1	16.1
Basic earnings per share before major restructuring	53.9	121.2	104.7
Diluted earnings per share	31.9	108.2	88.1
Adjustment for major restructuring	21.6	12.1	16.0
Diluted earnings per share before major restructuring	53.5	120.3	104.1

Basic and adjusted earnings per share have been calculated by dividing the profit attributable to shareholders by the weighted average number of shares in issue during the period after deducting shares held by the ESOP Trusts and Treasury shares. The trustees have waived their rights to dividends on the shares held by the ESOP Trusts.

Adjusted earnings per share is calculated using results before major restructuring earnings. The calculation of results before major restructuring is described in Note 1 'Presentation of the financial statements'.

Diluted earnings per share have been calculated after adjusting the weighted average number of shares used in the basic calculation to assume the conversion of all potentially dilutive shares. A potentially dilutive share forms part of the employee share schemes where its exercise price is below the average market price of GSK shares during the period and any performance conditions attaching to the scheme have been met at the balance sheet date.

The numbers of shares used in calculating basic and diluted earnings per share are reconciled below.

Weighted average number of shares in issue	2010 millions	2009 millions	2008 millions
Basic	5,085	5,069	5,195
Dilution for share options	43	39	31
Diluted	5,128	5,108	5,226

Source: GlaxoSmithKline, *Annual Report 2010.*

This indicates that the earnings per share is covered three times by the market price. In other words, it will take more than three years for current earnings to cover the market price. Across the top 200 UK plcs in November 2000, the P/E ratio was 36.

The P/E ratio is shown in the financial pages of newspapers along with dividend yield and the share price. In Real-World View 8.3, we show details from the *Daily Telegraph* for the aerospace and defence, automobiles and parts, and banks industrial sectors. This shows that the P/E ratio for aerospace and defence ranged from 10.7 to 145.2, while for banks it was much lower, from 6.8 to 15.00. This probably reflects the more cautious attitude of the stock market to banks following the financial crisis of recent years.

REAL-WORLD VIEW 8.3

Company Share Details

AEROSPACE & DEFENCE						↓0.01%
52 week		Stock	Price	+ or −	Yld	P/E
High	Low					
pence			pence			
364	248	BAE Systems	278^1_2*	$+^3_4$	| 6.3|	10.7
736^1_2	485	Chemring ♦	518	-11^1_2	| 2.3|	11.8
245^1_2	168^1_2	Cobham Gp ♦	178	$+5^5_8$	| 3.6|	12.6
39^1_4	9	Hampson Inds	9	$-^1_4$	| 9.8|	–
136^1_4	96^3_4	Qinetiq Gp ♦	117^1_2	$+1^1_4$	| 1.4|	145.2
709^1_2	557^1_2	Rolls-Royce	709^1_2	$+9^1_2$	| 2.3|	–
1895	1305	Ultra ♦	1605	+15	| 2.2|	15.1
512^1_2	289^1_2	UMECO	289^1_2	$-^1_2$	| 6.3|	64.4
AUTOMOBILES & PARTS						↓4.92%
245	157	GKN	186	-9^1_4	| 2.8|	9.8
BANKS						↑1.34%
54^1_4	6	Bank of Ireland	8^3_4	$+^3_8$	|36.7|	–
333^1_2	138^3_4	Barclays	179^1_2	$+4^3_8$	| 3.1|	7.9
731	473^1_2	HSBC	522^1_2	$+2^1_4$	| 4.6|	15.0
71^3_4	27^1_2	Lloyds Banking Gp	33^1_4	$+1^1_8$	| –|	–
49	19^3_4	Ryl Bk Scot	24^1_2	$+^3_4$	| –|	–
859	452^3_4	Santander	535^1_2	$+11^1_2$	|10.2|	6.8
1959	1169^1_2	Standard Chart	1409	+19	| 3.1|	10.9

Source: Daily Telegraph, 20 October, 2011.

Note: The figures from left to right show the 52-week highs and lows of the share, the price on 20 October, the change since 19 July, the dividend and the P/E (price/earnings) ratio.

(v) Interest Cover

This ratio is of particular interest to those who have loaned money to the company. It shows the amount of profit available to cover the interest payable on long-term borrowings. Long-term borrowings can be defined as either preference shares and long-term loans or simply long-term loans. We will use only *long-term loans* here. This ratio is similar to dividend cover. It represents a safety net for borrowers. How much could profits fall before they failed to cover interest?

However, it is worth pointing out that interest is paid out of cash, not profit. For John Brown, we have:

$$\frac{\text{Profit before tax and loan interest}}{\text{Loan interest}} = \frac{50 + 10}{10} = 6$$

Loan interest is thus covered six times (i.e., well covered). Profits would have to fall dramatically before interest was not covered. Over the top 250 UK public limited companies in July 2005, this ratio was 23.56. Tesco's interest cover is shown in Company Snapshot 8.4. An alternative to this ratio is cash flow cover, which is net operating cash flow divided by annual interest payments.

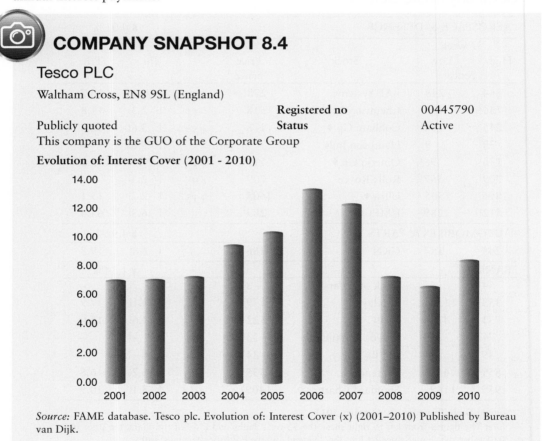

COMPANY SNAPSHOT 8.4

Tesco PLC

Waltham Cross, EN8 9SL (England)

	Registered no	00445790
Publicly quoted	**Status**	Active
This company is the GUO of the Corporate Group		

Evolution of: Interest Cover (2001 - 2010)

Source: FAME database. Tesco plc. Evolution of: Interest Cover (x) (2001–2010) Published by Bureau van Dijk.

Worked Example

Having explained 16 ratios, it is now time to work through a full example. In order to do this, we use the summarised accounts of Stevens, Turner plc in Figure 8.7 (last seen in Chapter 6). Although adapted slightly, these are essentially the accounts in Figure 6.15 for 20X1; however, we now have an extra year 20X2. The main change is that there are now two years' figures and percentages.

Figure 8.7 Illustrative Example on Interpretation of Accounts

Summarised figures for Stevens, Turner plc 20X1 and 20X2					
	20X1	20X1	20X2	20X2	(Increase/decrease)
	£000	%	£000	%	%
Income Statements					
Revenue (all credit)	350	100	450	100	+29
Cost of Sales (all credit)	(135)	(39)	(150)	(33)	+11
Gross Profit	215	61	300	67	+40
Loan interest	(8)	(2)	(10)	(2)	+25
Administrative expenses	(77)	(22)	(95)	(22)	+23
Profit before Taxation	130	37	195	43	+50
Taxation	(26)	(7)	(39)	(8)	+50
Profit for Year	104	30	156	35	+50
Statement of Financial Position					
ASSETS					
Non-current Assets					
Property, plant and equipment	600	90	611	75	+2
Intangible assets	50	7	250	31	+400
Total non-current assets	650	97	861	106	+32
Current Assets					
Inventories	25	4	42	5	+68
Trade receivables	80	12	38	5	−52
Bank	75	11	30	3	−60
	180	27	110	13	−39
Total Assets	830	124	971	119	+17
LIABILITIES					
Current Liabilities	(80)	(12)	(60)	(7)	−25
Non-current Liabilities	(80)	(12)	(100)	(12)	+25
Total Liabilities	(160)	(24)	(160)	(19)	−
Net Assets	670	100	811	100	+21
EQUITY					
Share Capital and Reserves					
Ordinary share capital (£1 each)	300	45	300	37	−
Preference share capital (£1 each)	150	22	150	18	−
	450	67	450	55	−
Reserves					
Share premium account	25	4	25	3	−
Revaluation reserve	30	4	30	4	−
General reserve	20	3	20	3	−
	75	11	75	10	
Retained earnings	154		301		
Less: Ordinary dividends	(6)		(12)		
Preference dividends	(3)		(3)		
Net retained earnings	145	22	286	35	+97
	220	33	361	45	+64
Total Equity	670	100	811	100	+21
Market Price	£1		£1.50		

Vertical and Horizontal Analysis

Before calculating the ratios it is useful to perform vertical and horizontal analysis.

Vertical Analysis

Vertical analysis is where key figures in the accounts (such as revenue, statement of financial position totals) are set to 100%. The other figures are then expressed as a percentage of 100%. For example, cost of sales for 20X1 is 135; it is thus 39% of revenue (i.e., 135 of 350). Vertical analysis is a useful way to see if any figures have changed markedly during the year. Real-World View 8.4 presents a graph using vertical analysis for Tesco's 2010 results. In this case, total assets are shown as 100%. In addition, Tesco's liquidity ratio (probably current ratio) and gearing are compared to that of other retailers.

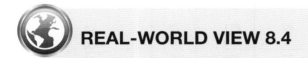

REAL-WORLD VIEW 8.4

Vertical Analysis at Tesco

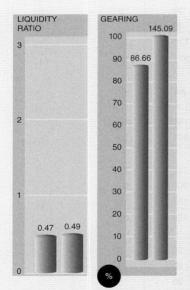

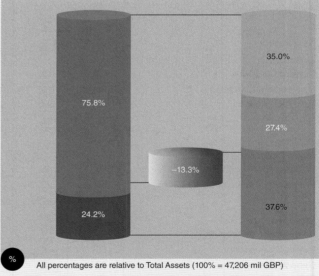

All percentages are relative to Total Assets (100% = 47,206 mil GBP)

■ Tesco PLC				
▨ PEER GROUP (502 companies)				

■ Fixed Assets	75.8%	■ Shareholders Funds	35.0%
■ Current Assets	24.2%	■ No Current Liabilities	27.4%
□ Net Current Assets	-13.3%	■ Current Liabilities	37.6%

Source: FAME Database. Tesco plc. Structure of the balance sheet 2010. Published by Bureau van Dijk.

In Stevens, Turner plc, in 20X2, we can see from the income statement that loan interest and administrative expenses represent 2% and 22% of revenue, respectively, whereas in the statement of financial position, in 20X2, property, plant and equipment represent 75% of total net assets. We need to assess whether or not these figures appear reasonable.

Horizontal Analysis

Whereas vertical analysis compares the figures within the same year, horizontal analysis compares the figures across time. Thus, for example, we see that revenue has increased from £350,000 in 20X1 to £450,000 in 20X2, a 29% increase. We need to investigate any major changes which look out of line. For example, why have there been so many changes in current assets: inventories, trade receivables, and cash have all changed markedly (i.e., inventories up 68%, trade receivables down 52% and bank down 60%)? These may represent normal trading changes, or then again...

Interpretation

We will now work through the various categories of ratio (shown in Figures 8.8 to 8.13). We present them in tables and then make some observations. When reading these it needs to be borne in mind that normally these observations would be set in the context of the industry in which the company operates and in the economic context. They should, therefore, be taken as illustrative not definitive. We will use the available data. This is most comprehensive for 20X2 (as we can use the 20X1 comparative data).

(i) Profitability Ratios

Figure 8.8 Profitability Ratios for Stevens, Turner plc 20X1 and 20X2

Ratios	20X1	20X2
1. Return on Capital Employed		
$\dfrac{\text{Profit before tax and loan interest}}{\text{Average capital employed*}}$	$\dfrac{130 + 8}{750**} = 18.4\%$	$\dfrac{195 + 10}{(911* + 750**) \div 2} = 24.7\%$
*(i.e., ordinary share capital and reserves, preference share capital and long-term capital, i.e., long-term creditors)	**(i.e., 300 + 25 + 30 + 20 + 145 + 150 + 80)	*(i.e., 300 + 25 + 30 + 20 + 286 + 150 + 100)
In 20X1, only one year-end figure is available.		**(i.e., 300 + 25 + 30 + 20 + 145 + 150 + 80)
2. Gross Profit Ratio		
$\dfrac{\text{Gross Profit}}{\text{Revenue}}$	$\dfrac{215}{350} = 61.4\%$	$\dfrac{300}{450} = 66.7\%$
3. Net Profit Ratio		
$\dfrac{\text{Net profit before tax}}{\text{Revenue}}$	$\dfrac{130}{350} = 37.1\%$	$\dfrac{195}{450} = 43.3\%$

Brief Discussion

Essentially, these profitability ratios tell us that Stevens, Turner plc's return on capital employed is running at between 18% and 25%, having increased over the year. This represents the return from the net assets of the company. Meanwhile, the business is operating on a high gross profit margin. This has also increased over the year. Finally, the net profit ratio has also increased, perhaps because the relative cost of sales has reduced.

(ii) Efficiency Ratios

Figure 8.9 Efficiency Ratios for Stevens, Turner plc 20X1 and 20X2

Ratios	20X1	20X2
1. Trade Receivables Collection Period		
$\dfrac{\text{Average trade receivables}}{\text{Credit sales per day}}$	$\dfrac{80^*}{350 \div 365} = 83$ days	$\dfrac{(80 + 38)^* \div 2}{450 \div 365} = 48$ days
	*only year-end figure available	*average of two year-end figures
2. Trade Payables Collection Period		
$\dfrac{\text{Average trade payables}}{\text{Credit purchases per day}^*}$	$\dfrac{80^*}{135 \div 365} = 216$ days	$\dfrac{(80 + 60)^* \div 2}{150 \div 365} = 170$ days
*in this case cost of sales	*only year-end figure available	*average of two year-end figures
3. Inventory Turnover Ratio		
$\dfrac{\text{Cost of sales}}{\text{Average inventories}}$	$\dfrac{135}{25^*} = 5.4$ times	$\dfrac{150}{(25 + 42)^* \div 2} = 4.48$ times
	*only year-end figure available	*average of two year-end figures
4. Asset Turnover Ratio		
$\dfrac{\text{Revenue}}{\text{Average total assets}}$	$\dfrac{350}{50 + 600 + 180^*} = 0.42$ times	$\dfrac{450}{(50 + 250) + (600 + 611)}$ $+ (180 + 110)/2^* = 0.50$ times
(i.e., intangible, property, plant and equipment and current)	*the intangible assets, property, plant and equipment and current assets figures for 20X1	*the intangible assets, property, plant and equipment and current assets figures for 20X1 and 20X2 averaged (i.e., ÷ 2)

Brief Discussion

There have been substantial reductions in the trade receivables and trade payables collection periods. Trade receivables are now paid in 48 rather than 83 days. By contrast, Stevens,

Turner pays its trade payables in 170 days not 216 days. By receiving money more quickly than paying it, Stevens, Turner is benefiting as its overall bank balance is healthier. However, it must be careful not to antagonise its suppliers as 170 days is a long time to withhold payment. Inventory is moving more slowly this year than last. However, each inventory item is still replaced 4½ times each year. Finally, the asset turnover ratio is disappointing. Revenue is considerably lower than total assets, even though there is some improvement over the year.

(iii) Liquidity Ratios

Figure 8.10 Liquidity Ratios for Stevens, Turner plc 20X1 and 20X2

Ratios	20X1	20X2
1. Current Ratio		
$\dfrac{\text{Current assets}}{\text{Current liabilities}}$	$\dfrac{180}{80} = 2.2$	$\dfrac{110}{60} = 1.8$
2. Quick Ratio		
$\dfrac{\text{Current assets} - \text{inventories}}{\text{Current liabilities}}$	$\dfrac{180 - 25}{80} = 1.9$	$\dfrac{110 - 42}{60} = 1.1$

Brief Discussion

There is a noted deterioration in both liquidity ratios. The current ratio has fallen from 2.2 to 1.8. Meanwhile, the quick ratio has declined from 1.9 to 1.1. While not immediately worrying, Stevens, Turner needs to pay attention to this.

(iv) Gearing Ratio

Figure 8.11 Gearing Ratio for Stevens, Turner plc 20X1 and 20X2

Ratio	20X1	20X2
$\dfrac{\text{Long term borrowings*}}{\text{Total long-term capital**}}$	$\dfrac{230^*}{750^{**}} = 30.7\%$	$\dfrac{250^*}{911^{**}} = 27.4\%$
*Preference shares and long-term loans (i.e., long-term creditors)	*150 + 80 = 230	*150 + 100 = 250
**Preference shares, long-term loans (i.e., long-term creditors), ordinary shares, share premium account, revaluation reserve, general reserve, retained earnings.	**150 + 80 + 300 + 25 + 30 + 20 + 145 = 750	**150 + 100 + 300 + 25 + 30 + 20 + 286 = 911

Brief Discussion
Gearing has declined over the year from 30.7% to 27.4%. In 20X2, 27.4 pence in the £ of the long-term capital employed is from borrowed money, rather than 30.7 pence last year. This change is due to the increase in retained earnings during the year.

(v) Cash Flow Ratio

Figure 8.12 Cash Flow Ratio for Stevens, Turner plc 20X1 and 20X2

From the statement of financial position and income statements in Figure 8.7, we can determine the statement of cash flows. From this statement of cash flows we can work out the cash inflows and cash outflows.

Stevens, Turner plc
Statement of Cash Flows Year Ended 31.12.20X2

	£000	£000
Cash Flows from Operating Activities		
Net Profit before Taxation and Loan Interest*		205
Add:		
Decrease in trade receivables	42	42
Deduct:		
Increase in inventories	(17)	
Decrease in trade payables	(20)	
Taxation paid	(39)	(76)
Net Cash Inflow from Operating Activities		171
Cash Flows from Investing Activities		
Purchase of intangible assets	(200)	
Purchase of property, plant and equipment	(11)	(211)
Cash Flows from Financing Activities		
Increase in loan capital	20	
Dividends paid	(15)	
Interest paid	(10)	(5)
Decrease in Cash		(45)
		£000
Opening Cash and Cash Equivalents		75
Decrease in cash		(45)
Closing Cash and Cash Equivalents		30

Therefore our cash flow ratio is:

	Cash Inflows	Cash Outflows
	£000	£000
Net Cash Inflow from Operating Activities	171	
Cash Flows from Investing Activities		211
Cash Flows from Financing Activities	5	
	176	211

$$\frac{\text{Total cash inflows}}{\text{Total cash outflows}} = \frac{171}{211} = 0.83$$

*For simplicity, we assume no depreciation.

(vi) Investment Ratios

Figure 8.13 Investment Flow Ratios for Stevens, Turner plc 20X1 and 20X2

Ratios	20X1	20X2
1. Dividend Yield		
$\dfrac{\text{Dividend per ordinary share*}}{\text{Share price}}$	$\dfrac{2^{*}}{100p} = 2\%$	$\dfrac{4^{*}}{150p} = 2.67\%$
*Net ordinary dividend divided by number shares	*6 ÷ 300 = 2p	*12 ÷ 300 = 4p
2. Dividend Cover		
$\dfrac{\text{Profit after tax and preference dividends}}{\text{Ordinary dividends}}$	$\dfrac{101}{6} = 16.8 \text{ times}$	$\dfrac{153}{12} = 12.8 \text{ times}$
3. Earnings per Share		
$\dfrac{\text{Profit after tax and preference dividends}}{\text{Number of ordinary shares}}$	$\dfrac{101}{300} = 33.7p$	$\dfrac{153}{300} = 51p$
4. Price/Earnings Ratio		
$\dfrac{\text{Share price}}{\text{Earnings per share}}$	$\dfrac{100}{33.7} = 3.0$	$\dfrac{150}{51} = 2.9$
5. Interest Cover		
$\dfrac{\text{Profit before tax and loan interest}}{\text{Loan interest}}$	$\dfrac{130 + 8}{8} = 17.2 \text{ times}$	$\dfrac{195 + 10}{10} = 20.5 \text{ times}$

Brief Discussion

More cash is flowing out than is flowing in. The main reason for this is the purchase of property, plant and equipment. The dividend yield is quite low at around 2% to 3%. However, it must be remembered that the share price has increased rapidly by 50p, and it is unusual to have strong capital growth and high dividends at the same time. Both dividend cover and interest cover are high. If necessary the company has the potential to increase dividends and interest. Earnings per share (EPS) has increased over the year and is now running at an improved 51 pence. It is this rise in EPS which may have fuelled the share price increase. The P/E ratio, however, is still very modest at 2.9.

Company Specific Ratios

The ratios provided in this chapter are widespread, but there is no standard set of ratios that are used for all companies. This makes sense as, for example, an airline will operate very differently from a mobile phone operator and ratios need to reflect this. In Company Snapshot 8.5 the key ratios and economic indicators used by Nokia, the mobile phone operator, are recorded. As can be seen, some ratios are relatively standard (e.g., return on capital employed), but some are more specialised (e.g., R&D expenditure as a % of net sales).

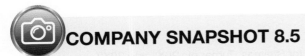

COMPANY SNAPSHOT 8.5

Key Ratios in Practice

NOKIA

Key ratios and economic indicators	2010	2009	2008	2007	2006
Net sales, EURm	42,446	40,984	50,710	51,058	41,121
Change, %	3.6	−19.2	−0.7	24.2	20.3
Exports and foreign subsidiaries, EURm	42,075	40,594	50,348	50,736	40,734
Salaries and social expenses, EURm	6,947	6,734	6,847	5,702	4,206
Operating profit, EURm	2,070	1,197	4,966	7,985	5,488
% of net sales	4.9	2.9	9.8	15.6	13.3
Financial income and expenses, EURm	−285	−265	−2	239	207
% of net Sales	0.7	0.6	—	0.5	0.5
Profit before tax EURm	1,786	962	4,970	8,268	5,723
% of net sales	4.2	2.3	9.8	16.2	13.9
Profit from continuing operations. EURm	1,850	891	3,988	7,205	4,306
% of net sales	4.4	2.2	7.9	14.1	10.5
Taxes, EURm	443	702	1,081	1,522	1,357
Dividends, EURm	1,498	1,498	1,520	2,111	1,761
Capital expenditure, EURm	679	531	889	715	650
% of net sales	1.6	1.3	1.8	1.4	1.6
Gross investments, EURm	836	683	1,166	1,017	897
% of net sales	2.0	1.7	2.3	2.0	2.2
R&D expenditure, EURm	5,863	5,909	5,968	5,647	3,897
% of net sales	13.8	14.4	11.8	11.1	9.5
Average personnel	129,355	123,171	121,723	100,534	65,324
Non-interest bearing liabilities, EURm	16,591	14,483	16,833	18,208	10,103
Interest-bearing liabilities, EURm	5,279	5,203	4,452	1,090	249
Return on capital employed, %	11.0	6.7	27.2	54.8	46.1
Return on equity, %	13.5	6.5	27.5	53.9	35.5
Equity ratio, %	42.8	41.9	42.3	46.7	54.0
Net debt to equity, %	−43	−25	−14	−62	−69

Source: Nokia, *Annual Report 2010*, p. 79.

Report Format

Students are often required to write a report on the performance of a company using ratio analysis. A report is not an essay! It has a pre-set style, usually including the following features:

- Terms of reference
- Title
- Introduction
- Major sections
- Recommendations
- Appendices

Figure 8.14 illustrates a *concise* overall report on Stevens, Turner plc for 20X1 and 20X2.

Figure 8.14 Illustrative Report on Financial Performance of Stevens, Turner plc for 20X2

Report on the Financial Performance of Stevens, Turner plc Year Ended 20X2

1.0 Terms of Reference

The Managing Director requested a report on the financial performance of Stevens, Turner plc for the year ended 20X2 using appropriate ratio analysis.

2.0 Introduction

The income statement, statement of financial position and cash flow data were used to prepare 16 ratios to assess the company's performance for 20X2. The 20X2 financial results were compared to those in 20X1. The underpinning ratios with their calculations are presented in the appendix. This report briefly covers the profitability, efficiency, liquidity, gearing, cash flow and investment ratios.

3.0 Profitability

The company has traded quite profitably over the year. This has been helped by the substantial increase in revenue (+29%), which has increased faster than cost of sales (+11%). The return on capital employed and gross profit ratios have increased over the year from 18.4% to 24.7%, and from 61.4% to 66.7%, respectively. The net profit ratio improved from 37.1% to 43.3%. This ratio is extremely good.

4.0 Efficiency

The collection of money from trade receivables is still quicker than the payment of trade payables (48 days vs 170 days), which is good for cash flow. Both collection periods have declined over the year. This means that debtors are paying quicker, but that we are also paying our trade payables quicker. The inventories are turned over 4.48 times per year, which is usual for this type of business. Finally, the asset turnover ratio appears quite low. However, once more this reflects the nature of the business.

5.0 Liquidity

Liquidity is an area to watch for the future. Both the current ratio and quick ratio have declined markedly over the year (from 2.2 to 1.8, and 1.9 to 1.1, respectively). While this is not immediately worrying, this ratio should not be allowed to slip any further. This has been caused by a fall in trade receivables and particularly by a decline in cash at the bank.

6.0 Cash flow

The cash flow ratio is 0.79. More cash is flowing out than is coming in. The main reason appears to be the purchase of property, plant and equipment. This investment has also meant that there is less cash at the bank. As a result, liquidity has fallen.

7.0 Gearing

The dependence on outside borrowing has declined during the year from 30.7% to 27.4%. This is good news. It means that if liquidity falls further, the company probably should borrow money if necessary.

8.0 Investment

Both dividends and loan interest remain well covered (respectively 12.8 times and 20.5 times). Overall, shareholders are receiving a good return for their investment. Share price has increased by 50 pence, which compensates for the low dividend yield of 2.67%. The earnings per share remains a healthy 51p (up from 33.7p). Finally, the P/E ratio has remained steady at 2.9.

9.0 Conclusions

Overall, Stevens, Turner plc has had a good year in terms of profitability, investment performance, gearing, and efficiency ratios. The one area we really need to pay attention to is cash flow and liquidity. While not immediately worrying, this area should be carefully monitored.

Appendix 1 (Extract)

1. Return on capital employed	20X1	20X2
$\dfrac{\text{Net profit before tax and loan interest}}{\text{Average capital employed}}$	$\dfrac{138}{750} = 18.4\%$	$\dfrac{205}{830} = 24.7\%$

Note: All the ratios are calculated in Figures 8.8 to 8.13.

A real report would be longer than this, but this report gives a good insight into the use of report format.

Holistic View of Ratios

So far we have looked at individual ratios. However, although useful, one ratio on its own may potentially be misleading or may even be manipulated through creative accounting. Therefore, there have been attempts to look at ratios collectively. Two main approaches are briefly discussed here.

1. The Z Score Model

The idea behind this model, which was first developed in the US, is to select ratios which when combined have a high predictive power. In the UK, an academic, Richard Taffler, developed the model using two groups of failed and non-failed companies. After a comprehensive study of accounts, he produced a model for listed industrial companies. This model proved successful in distinguishing between those companies which would go bankrupt and those companies which would not.

2. Pictics

Pictics are an ingenious way of presenting ratios. Essentially, each pictic is a face. The different elements of the face are represented by different ratios. Real-World View 8.5 demonstrates two pictics.

REAL-WORLD VIEW 8.5

Pictics

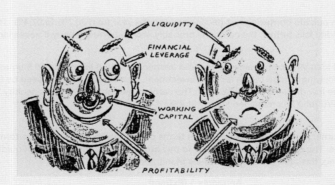

Source: Richard Taffler, Changing Face of Accountancy, *Accountancy Age,* 2 May 1996, p. 17.

The face on the left represents a successful business while that on the right is an unsuccessful business. The size of the smile represents profitability while the length of the nose represents working capital. Pictics are an easy way of presenting multi-dimensional information. Although it is easy to dismiss pictics as a joke, they have proved remarkably successful in controlled research studies.

Performance Indicators

The conventional mix of ratios may be unsuitable for some businesses, in particular those where non-financial performance is very important. Examples of such organisations include the National Health Service and the railways. Such businesses use customised performance measures, often called performance indicators. For the National Health Service, indicators such as number of operations, or bed occupancy rate, may be more important than net profit.

PAUSE FOR THOUGHT 8.3

Performance Indicators

Which performance indicators do you think would be useful when assessing the performance of individual railway operating companies?

Potentially, there are many performance indicators. For example:

- Percentage of trains late
- Miles per passenger
- Volume of freight moved
- Passengers per train
- Number of complaints
- Number of accidents

Organisations like the rail companies need to balance financial considerations (such as making profits for shareholders) with non-financial factors (such as punctuality). As Company Snapshot 8.6 shows, rail operating companies consider factors such as punctuality and UK rail customer satisfaction. They may also consider factors such as passenger and train numbers and income from fares and subsidies.

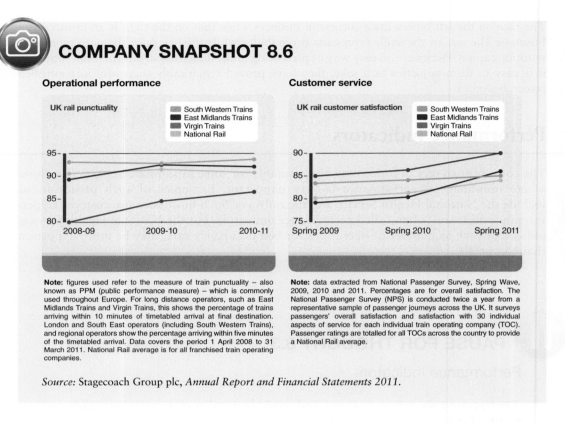

COMPANY SNAPSHOT 8.6

Operational performance

UK rail punctuality

Legend: South Western Trains, East Midlands Trains, Virgin Trains, National Rail

(y-axis: 95, 90, 85, 80; x-axis: 2008-09, 2009-10, 2010-11)

Customer service

UK rail customer satisfaction

Legend: South Western Trains, East Midlands Trains, Virgin Trains, National Rail

(y-axis: 90, 85, 80, 75; x-axis: Spring 2009, Spring 2010, Spring 2011)

Note: figures used refer to the measure of train punctuality – also known as PPM (public performance measure) – which is commonly used throughout Europe. For long distance operators, such as East Midlands Trains and Virgin Trains, this shows the percentage of trains arriving within 10 minutes of timetabled arrival at final destination. London and South East operators (including South Western Trains), and regional operators show the percentage arriving within five minutes of the timetabled arrival. Data covers the period 1 April 2008 to 31 March 2011. National Rail average is for all franchised train operating companies.

Note: data extracted from National Passenger Survey, Spring Wave, 2009, 2010 and 2011. Percentages are for overall satisfaction. The National Passenger Survey (NPS) is conducted twice a year from a representative sample of passenger journeys across the UK. It surveys passengers' overall satisfaction and satisfaction with 30 individual aspects of service for each individual train operating company (TOC). Passenger ratings are totalled for all TOCs across the country to provide a National Rail average.

Source: Stagecoach Group plc, *Annual Report and Financial Statements 2011.*

Limitations

Ratio analysis can be a useful financial tool. However, certain problems associated with ratio analysis must be appreciated.

1. Context
Ratios must be used in context. They cannot be used in isolation, but must be compared with past results or industry norms. Unless such a comparative approach is adopted, ratio analysis is fraught with danger.

2. Absolute Size
Ratios give no indication of the relative size of the result. If net profit is 10%, we do not know if this is 10% of £100 or 10% of £1 million. Both the ratio *and* the size of the organisation need to be taken into account.

3. Like with Like
We must ensure that we are comparing like with like. The accounting policies of different companies differ and this needs to be appreciated. If companies A and B, for example, use a different rate of depreciation then a net profit of 10% for company A may equal 8% for company B.

4. International Comparison

The comparison of companies in different countries is even more problematic than same-country comparisons. The economic and business infrastructure in Japan, for example, is very different from that in the US. Traditionally, this has led to the current ratio in the US being much higher than in Japan.

Despite the above limitations, ratios are widely used. As Real-World View 8.6 shows, even though these accounting ratios are based on significant assumptions and varying underlying principles, they are still commonly employed by banks, credit rating agencies and other users.

REAL-WORLD VIEW 8.6

Financial Ratios

Those of us with a grounding in accounting already know that financial information, although often (and naively) assumed to be precise, is necessarily based on significant assumptions and varying underlying principles. This means that accurate financial comparisons between companies (even those within the UK) cannot be made without a considerable amount of additional research and even restatement. In a cross-border analysis situation, the problem is further compounded by important accounting differences.

Despite this, traditional performance indicators such as profit margin, return on capital employed (ROCE), earnings per share (EPS) and the price earnings (P/E) ratio are widely published and used in decision making, often one suspects without any great attention being paid to what lies behind them. For example, banks, credit rating agencies, auditors, investment analysts, merger and acquisition teams and the financial press all use such financial ratios in their daily work.

Source: This article was published in *Management Accounting* by authors: M. Gardiner and K. Bagshaw, Financial Ratios: Can You Trust Them?, September 1997, page 30. ISSN - 0025-1682. Copyright Chartered Institute of Management Accountants (CIMA), 1997. Reproduced by Permission.

5. Validity of the Data

The reliability of the ratio analysis also depends on the reliability of the underlying data. This needs to be complete, comparable and accurate. This is particularly difficult for international comparisons.

Conclusion

Ratio analysis is a good way to gain an overview of an organisation's activities. There is a whole range of ratios on profitability, efficiency, liquidity, gearing, cash flow and investment. Taken together these ratios provide a comprehensive view of a company's financial activities.

They are used to compare a company's performance over time as well as to compare different companies' financial performance. For certain businesses, particularly those not so profit orientated, performance indicators provide a useful alternative to ratios. Performance indicators are often also used to supplement ratio analysis. When calculating ratios, care is necessary to ensure that the underlying figures have been drawn up in a consistent and comparable way. However, when used carefully, ratios are undoubtedly very useful.

 Discussion Questions

Questions with numbers in blue have answers at the back of the book.

Q1 What do you understand by ratio analysis? Distinguish between the main types of ratio analysis.

Q2 Do the advantages of ratio analysis outweigh the disadvantages? Discuss.

Q3 'Each of the main financial statements provides a distinct set of financial ratios.' Discuss this statement.

Q4 Devise a set of non-financial performance indicators which might be appropriate for monitoring:
(a) The Police
(b) The Post Office (now known as Royal Mail in the UK)

Q5 State whether the following are true or false. If false, explain why.

(a) Gross profit ratio $= \dfrac{\text{Gross profit}}{\text{Revenue}}$

(b) Net profit ratio $= \dfrac{\text{Net profit after taxation}}{\text{Average capital employed}}$

(c) Current ratio $= \dfrac{\text{Current assets} - \text{inventories}}{\text{Current liabilities}}$

(d) Debtors collection period $= \dfrac{\text{Trade receivables}}{\text{Credit sales per day}}$

(e) Asset turnover ratio $= \dfrac{\text{Revenue}}{\text{Property, plant and equipment}}$

(f) Dividend yield $= \dfrac{\text{Dividend per ordinary share}}{\text{Revenue}}$

(g) Earnings per share $= \dfrac{\text{Profit after tax and preference dividends}}{\text{Number of ordinary shares}}$

Numerical Questions

Questions with numbers in blue have answers at the back of the book.

Q1 The information below is from the accounts of John Parry, a sole trader.

Income Statement for the Year Ended 31 December 2013

	£	£
Revenue		150,000
Less *Cost of Sales*		
Opening inventory	25,000	
Add Purchases	75,000	
	100,000	
Less Closing inventory	30,000	70,000
Gross Profit		80,000
Less Expenses		30,000
Net Profit		50,000

Other information	31.12.2012	31.12.2013
	£	£
Total assets	50,000	60,000
Closing equity	300,000	500,000
Trade receivables	18,000	19,000
Trade payables	9,000	10,000

Note: All of John Parry's revenue and purchases are on credit.

Required: Calculate the following profitability and efficiency ratios:

(a) Return on capital employed
(b) Gross profit ratio
(c) Net profit ratio
(d) Trade receivables collection period
(e) Trade payables collection period
(f) Inventory turnover ratio
(g) Asset turnover ratio.

Q2 Henry Mellett has the following extracts from his statement of financial position as at 31 March 2013:

Current Assets	£
Inventory	18,213
Trade receivables	12,407
Cash	1,283
Current Liabilities	
Trade payables	14,836
Non-current liabilities	30,000
Net assets	150,000

Required: Calculate the following ratios:
(a) Current ratio   (b) Quick ratio   (c) Gearing ratio.

Q3 Jane Edwards Ltd has prepared its statement of cash flows under the direct method. It has the following main cash flows:

	£		£
Cash from customers	125,000	Dividends paid	8,000
Cash paid to employees	18,300	Taxation paid	16,000
Cash paid to suppliers	9,250	Purchase of property,	80,000
Issue of shares	29,000	plant and equipment	
Buy back loan	8,000	Sales of property, plant	35,000
		and equipment	

Required: Calculate the cash flow ratio.

Q4 From the following information for Clatworthy plc calculate the investment ratios as indicated:

	£000
Revenue	1,000
Profit before Taxation	750
(after charging loan interest of £40,000)	
Taxation	(150)
Profit for Year	600

Note: *Preference dividends for the year were £20,000 and ordinary dividends were £40,000.*

Market price ordinary shares £1.25. Number of ordinary shares in issue are 500,000.

Required:
(a) Dividend yield   (d) Price/earnings ratio
(b) Dividend cover   (e) Interest cover.
(c) Earnings per share

Q5 The abridged accounts for N.O. Hope plc are given below.

Income Statements	2012	2013
	£000	£000
Revenue	400	440
Cost of Sales	(300)	(330)
Gross Profit	100	110
Administrative expenses	(15)	(25)
Distribution expenses	(5)	(10)
Profit before Taxation	80	75
Taxation	(16)	(15)
Profit for the year	64	60

Statements of Financial Position

ASSETS

Non-current Assets	£000	£000
Property, plant and equipment	120	235
Intangible assets	20	20
Total non-current assets	140	255
Current Assets		
Inventories	80	40
Trade receivables	40	20
Bank	20	10
Total current assets	140	70
Total Assets	280	325

LIABILITIES

Current Liabilities	(70)	(75)
Non-current Liabilities	(20)	(40)
Total Liabilities	(90)	(115)
Net Assets	190	210

EQUITY

Capital and Reserves	£000	£000
Share Capital		
Ordinary share capital (£1 each)	120	125
Preference share capital (£1 each)	17	17
	137	142

Q5 N.O. Hope plc (*continued*)

	£000	£000
Reserves		
Capital reserves		
Share premium account	10	10
Revaluation reserve	10	10
Other reserves		
General reserve	8	8
Retained earnings	25	40
	53	68
Total Equity	190	210

1. Retained earnings were after taking into account dividends of £46,000 for 2012 and £45,000 for 2013.

Required: Prepare a horizontal and vertical analysis. Highlight three figures that may need further enquiry.

Q6 The following two non-listed companies, Alpha Industries and Beta Industries, operate in the same industrial sector. You have extracted the following ratios from their accounts:

	Alpha	Beta
Return on capital employed	9%	20%
Gross profit ratio	25%	25%
Net profit ratio	7%	14%
Current ratio	2.1	1.7
Quick ratio	1.7	1.3
Price/Earnings ratio	4	8
Dividend cover	2	4

Required: Compare the financial performance of the two companies. All other things being equal, which company would you expect to have the higher market price?

Q7 Anteater plc has produced the following summary accounts:

Income Statement for the Year Ended 31 December 2013

	£000
Revenue	1,000
Cost of sales	(750)
Gross Profit	250
Administrative expenses	(117)
Distribution expenses	(30)
Operating profit	103
Debenture interest	(3)
Profit before Taxation	100
Taxation	(20)
Profit for Year	80

Statement of Financial Position as at 31 December 2013

	£000	£000
ASSETS		
Non-current Assets		
Property, plant and equipment		420
Current Assets		
Inventories	40	
Trade receivables	50	
Cash	30	120
Total Assets		540
LIABILITIES		
Current Liabilities		(40)
Non-current Liabilities		(100)
Total Liabilities		(140)
Net Assets		400
EQUITY		
Capital and Reserves		
Share Capital		£000
Ordinary share capital (£1 each)		300
Preference share capital (£1 each)		20
		320

Q7 Anteater plc (*continued*)

	£000
Reserves	
Capital reserves	
Share premium account	10
Other reserves	
Retained earnings[1]	70
Total Equity	400

Share price £2.00.

[1]Note that preference dividends of £10,000 and ordinary dividends of £40,000 have been charged to retained earnings.

Required: From the above accounts prepare the following ratios:
(a) Profitability ratios
(b) Efficiency ratios
(c) Liquidity ratios
(d) Gearing ratio
(e) Investment ratios.

Q8 You are an employee of a medium-sized, light engineering company. Your managing director, Sara Potter, asks you to analyse the accounts of your company, Turn-a-Screw Ltd, with a competitor, Fix-it-Quick.

Income Statement for the Year Ended 31 December 2013

	Turn-a-Screw	Fix-it-Quick
	£000	£000
Revenue	2,500	2,800
Cost of Sales	(1,000)	(1,200)
Gross Profit	1,500	1,600
Administrative expenses (includes loan interest)	(900)	(1,170)
Distribution expenses	(250)	(200)
Profit before Taxation	350	230
Taxation	(76)	(46)
Profit for the year	274	184

Note: You have the following additional information for dividends.

	Turn-a-Screw	Fix-it-Quick
Preference dividends	(30)	(20)
Ordinary dividends	(124)	(94)

Q8 Turn-a-Screw (*continued*)

Statement of Financial Position as at 31 December 2013

	Turn-a-Screw £000	Turn-a-Screw £000	Fix-it-Quick £000	Fix-it-Quick £000
ASSETS				
Non-current assets				
Property, plant and equipment		1,820		1,765
Current Assets				
Inventories	120		115	
Trade receivables	100		115	
Cash	10	230	25	255
Total Assets		2,050		2,020
LIABILITIES				
Current Liabilities		(190)		(225)
Non-current Liabilities				
Long-term loans (10% interest)		(250)		(400)
Total Liabilities		(440)		(625)
Net Assets		1,610		1,395
EQUITY				
Capital and Reserves		£000		£000
Share Capital				
Ordinary share capital (£1 each)		850		860
Preference share capital (£0.50 each)		300		200
		1,150		1,060
Reserves				
Capital reserves				
Share premium account		125		—
Other reserves				
Retained earnings		335		335
Total equity		1,610		1,395
Share price		£1.44		£1.00

Required: Using the accounts of the two companies calculate the appropriate:

(a) Profitability ratios   (d) Gearing ratio
(b) Efficiency ratios   (e) Investment ratios.
(c) Liquidity ratios

Briefly comment on your main findings for each category.

Q9 You have been employed temporarily by a rich local businessman, Mr Long Pocket, as his assistant. He has been told at the golf club that Sunbright Enterprises plc, a locally based company, would be a good return for his money. The last five years' results are set out below.

Income Statements for the Year Ended 31 December

	2009 £000	2010 £000	2011 £000	2012 £000	2013 £000
Revenue	1,986	2,001	2,008	2,010	2,012
Cost of Sales	(1,192)	(1,221)	(1,406)	(1,306)	(1,509)
Gross Profit	794	780	602	704	503
Expenses (including loan interest)	(633)	(648)	(487)	(606)	(437)
Profit before Taxation	161	132	115	98	66
Taxation	(32)	(26)	(23)	(19)	(13)
Profit for Year	129	106	92	79	53

Statement of Financial Position as at 31 December

	2009 £000	2010 £000	2011 £000	2012 £000	2013 £000
ASSETS					
Non-current Assets					
Property, plant, and equipment	500	580	660	780	878
Current Assets					
Inventories	24	26	27	45	68
Trade receivables	112	120	121	130	134
Cash	25	24	30	21	9
Total current assets	161	170	178	196	211
Total Assets	661	750	838	976	1,089
LIABILITIES					
Current Liabilities	(83)	(90)	(111)	(126)	(210)
Non-current Liabilities (10% interest)	(100)	(110)	(120)	(130)	(150)
Total Liabilities	(183)	(200)	(231)	(256)	(360)
Net Assets	478	550	607	720	729

Q9 Sunbright Enterprises plc (*continued*)

EQUITY

Capital and Reserves	£000	£000	£000	£000	£000
Share Capital					
Ordinary share capital (£1 each)	250	250	250	300	300
Preference share capital (£1 each)	88	88	88	100	100
	338	338	338	400	400
Reserves					
Capital reserves					
Share premium account	12	12	12	25	25
Other reserves					
Retained earnings	128	200	257	295	304
Total Equity	478	550	607	720	729
Share price	£1.10	£1.08	£1.07	£1.05	£0.95

Note: You have the following details of dividends over the last five years which have been deducted from the retained earnings.

	2009	2010	2011	2012	2013
	£000	£000	£000	£000	£000
Preference dividends	(8)	(8)	(8)	(9)	(9)
Ordinary dividends	(25)	(26)	(27)	(32)	(35)

Required: Analyse the last five years' financial results for the company and calculate the appropriate ratios. Present your advice as a short report.

Note: Horizontal analysis, vertical analysis and a calculation of the cash flow ratio are not required.

Appendix 8.1: John Brown Plc

John Brown Plc has the following abridged results prepared for internal management use for the year ending 31 December 2013. The income statement and the statement of financial position are presented below.

John Brown Plc
Income Statement for the Year Ended 31 December 2013

	£m	£m
Revenue		200
Cost of sales		(100)
Gross Profit		100
Less *Expenses*		
General	40	
Loan interest	10	50
Profit before Taxation		50
Taxation		(15)
Profit for the year		35

Note: You have the following information for dividends. Preference dividends (10%) are £5m and ordinary dividends are £10m.

Appendix 8.1: John Brown Plc (*continued*)

Statement of Financial Position as at 31 December 2013

	£m	£m
ASSETS		
Non-current Assets		
Property, plant and equipment		275
Current Assets		
Inventories	60	
Trade receivables	40	
Cash	20	120
Total Assets		395
LIABILITIES		
Current Liabilities		
Trade payables		(50)
Proposed tax		(10)
		(60)
Non-current Liabilities		(70)
Total Liabilities		(130)
Net Assets		265

	£m
EQUITY	
Capital and Reserves	
Share Capital	
Ordinary share capital (1.50m £1 shares)	150
Preference share capital (50m £1 shares)	50
	200
Reserves	
Opening retained earnings	50
Retained earnings for the year	15
Closing retained earnings	65
Total Equity	265

At 31 December 2013 the market price of the ordinary shares was 67p.

Appendix 8.2: The Cash Flow Ratio Using UK GAAP

Any Company Ltd has the following cash inflows and outflows in £000s:

	Inflows	Outflows
Net Cash Inflow from Operating Activities	118	
Returns on Investments and Servicing of Finance	15	8
Taxation		30
Capital Expenditure and Financial Investment		220
Equity Dividends Paid		20
Financing	140	
Totals	273	278

Therefore, our cash flow ratio is:

$$\frac{\text{Total cash inflows}}{\text{Total cash outflows}} = \frac{273}{278} = 0.98$$

To all intents and purposes, our total cash inflows thus match our total cash outflows.

Go online to discover the extra features for this chapter at
www.wiley.com/college/jones

SECTION B

Financial Accounting:
The Context

In Section A, we looked at the accounting techniques which underpin the preparation and interpretation of the financial statements of sole traders, partnerships and limited companies. These techniques do not exist in a vacuum. In this section, we examine three crucial aspects of the context in which these accounting techniques are applied.

Chapter 9 investigates the regulatory and conceptual frameworks within which accounting operates. The regulatory framework provides a set of rules and regulations which govern accounting. The conceptual theory is broader and seeks to set out a theoretical framework to underpin accounting. Then, in Chapter 10, the main potential alternative measurement systems which can underpin the preparation of accounts are laid out. This chapter shows how using different measurement systems can yield different profits and different valuations of the statement of financial position.

The annual report, the main way in which public limited companies communicate financial information to their shareholders, is discussed in Chapter 11. This chapter outlines the nature, context and function of the annual report. Both the content and the presentation of the annual report are examined.

Chapter 9

Regulatory and conceptual frameworks

'Regulation is like salt in cooking. It's an essential ingredient – you don't want a great deal of it, but my goodness you'd better get the right amount. If you get too much or too little you'll soon know.'

Sir Kenneth Berrill, *Financial Times* (6 March 1985), *The Book of Business Quotations* (1991), p. 47.

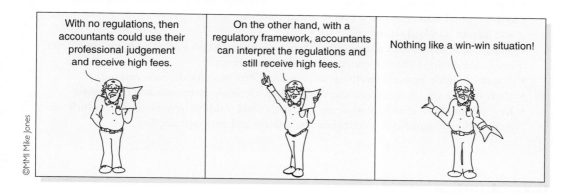

With no regulations, then accountants could use their professional judgement and receive high fees.

On the other hand, with a regulatory framework, accountants can interpret the regulations and still receive high fees.

Nothing like a win-win situation!

©MMI Mike Jones

Learning Outcomes

After completing this chapter you should be able to:

- Outline the traditional corporate model.
- Understand the regulatory framework.
- Explain corporate governance.
- Understand the conceptual framework.

Go online to discover the extra features for this chapter at
www.wiley.com/college/jones

Chapter Summary

- Directors, auditors and shareholders are the main parties in the traditional corporate model.
- The regulatory framework provides a set of rules and regulations for accounting.
- At the international level, the International Accounting Standards Board provides a broad regulatory framework for International Accounting Standards. This applies to all European listed companies, including UK companies.
- In the UK, the two main sources of regulation are the Companies Acts and accounting standards.
- Financial statements must give a true and fair view of the financial position and performance of the reporting entity.
- The UK accounting standards-setting regime operates under the Financial Reporting Council. It consists of the Codes and Standards Committee, the Accounting Council, the Audit and Assurance Council and the Financial Reporting Review Panel.
- Corporate governance is the system by which companies are directed and controlled.
- A conceptual framework is a coherent and consistent set of accounting principles which will help in standard setting.
- Some major elements in a conceptual theory are the objectives of accounting, users, user needs, information characteristics and measurement models.
- The most widely agreed objective is to provide information for decision making.
- Users include shareholders and analysts, lenders, creditors, customers and employees.
- Key information characteristics are relevance and faithful representation, which are enhanced by comparability, verifiability, timeliness and understandability.

Introduction

So far, we have looked at accounting practice – focusing on the preparation and interpretation of the financial statements of sole traders, partnerships and limited companies. In particular, we considered practical aspects of accounting such as double-entry bookkeeping, the trial balance, the income statement (profit and loss account), the statement of financial position (balance sheet), the statement of cash flows (cash flow statement) and ratio analysis. Accounting practice does not, however, take place in a vacuum. It is bounded by both a regulatory framework and a conceptual framework. These frameworks have grown up over time to bring order and fairness into accounting practice. They have been devised principally in relation to limited companies, but are also relevant to some extent to sole traders and partnerships.

The regulatory framework is essentially the set of rules and regulations which govern corporate accounting practice. At the international level, the regulatory framework is provided by the International Accounting Standards Board. This applies to all European listed companies, including UK companies. In the UK, regulations are set down mainly by government in Companies Acts and by independent private sector regulation in accounting standards. These cover small and medium-sized companies. The conceptual framework seeks to set out a theoretical and consistent set of accounting principles by which financial statements can be prepared.

Traditional Corporate Model: Directors, Auditors and Shareholders

In what I term the traditional corporate model, there are three main groups (directors, auditors and shareholders). As Figure 9.1 shows, these three groups interact. This interaction is explained in more detail below.

The directors are responsible for preparing the accounts – in practice this is usually delegated to the accounting managers. These accounts are then checked by professionally qualified accountants, the auditors. Finally, the accounts are sent to the shareholders.

1. Directors

The directors are those responsible for running the business. They are accountable to the shareholders, who in theory appoint and dismiss them. The relationship between the directors and shareholders is sometimes uneasy. The shareholders own the company, but it is the directors who run it. This relationship is often termed a 'principal–agent' relationship. The shareholders are the principals and the directors are the agents. The principals delegate the management of the company to directors. However, the directors are still responsible to the shareholders.

Figure 9.1 The Traditional Corporate Model

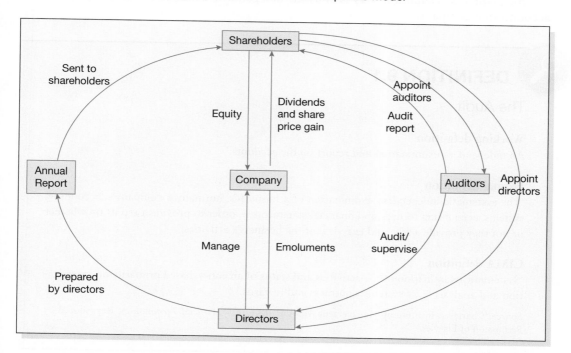

The directors are responsible for preparing the accounts which are sent to the shareholders. These accounts, prepared annually, allow the shareholders to assess the performance of the company and of the directors. They also provide information to shareholders to enable them to make share trading decisions (i.e., to hold their shares, to buy more shares or to sell their shares). As a reward for running the company, the directors receive emoluments. These may take the form of a salary, profit-related bonuses or other benefits in kind such as share options or company cars.

2. Auditors

Unfortunately, human nature being human nature, there is a problem with such arm's-length transactions. In a nutshell, how can the shareholders trust accounts prepared by the directors? For example, how can they be sure that the directors are not adopting creative accounting in order to inflate profits and thus pay themselves inflated profit-related bonuses? One way is by external auditing.

The auditors are a team of professionally qualified accountants. They are appointed by the shareholders on the recommendation of the directors. It is their job to check and report on the accounts. This checking and reporting involves extensive work verifying that the transactions have actually occurred, that they are recorded properly and that the monetary amounts in the accounts do indeed provide a true and fair view of the company's financial position and performance.

A key aspect of the external auditors is that they should be independent of management. This means, for example, that they should not be friends or relatives of management. Also, they must be careful in their provision of non-audit services and consultancy as these could potentially compromise their independence.

An audit (see Definition 9.1) is thus an independent examination and report on the accounts of a company.

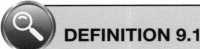

DEFINITION 9.1

The Audit

Working definition
An independent examination and report on the accounts.

Formal definition
'The systematic independent examination of a business's, normally a company's, accounting systems, accounting records and financial statements in order to provide a report on whether or not they provide a true and fair view of the business's activities.'

CIMA definition
'Systematic examination of the activities and status of an entity, based primarily on investigation and analysis of its systems, contracts and rewards.'

Source: Chartered Institute of Management Accountants (2005), *Official Terminology*. Reproduced by Permission of Elsevier.

For their time and effort the auditors are paid often quite considerable sums. The auditors prepare a formal report for shareholders. This is part of the annual report. In Company Snapshot 9.1 we attach an auditors' report prepared by PriceWaterhouseCoopers, the auditors of Rentokil, on Rentokil's 2009 accounts.

COMPANY SNAPSHOT 9.1

Report of the Auditors

Independent auditors' report to the members of Rentokil Initial plc

We have audited the financial statements of Rentokil Initial plc for the year ended 31 December 2009 set out on pages 39 to 84 and 87 to 93. The financial reporting framework that has been applied in the preparation of the group financial statements is applicable law and International Financial Reporting Standards (IFRSs) as adopted by the EU. The financial reporting framework that has been applied in the preparation of the parent company financial statements is applicable law and UK Accounting Standards (UK Generally Accepted Accounting Practice).

This report is made solely to the company's members, as a body, in accordance with sections 495, 496 and 497 of the Companies Act 2006. Our audit work has been undertaken so that we might state to the company's members those matters we are required to state to them in an auditors' report and for no other purpose. To the fullest extent permitted by law, we do not accept or assume responsibility to anyone other than the company and the company's members, as a body, for our audit work, for this report, or for the opinions we have formed.

Respective responsibilities of directors and auditors

As explained more fully in the Statement of Directors' Responsibilities set out on page 24, the directors are responsible for the preparation of the financial statements and for being satisfied that they give a true and fair view. Our responsibility is to audit the financial statements in accordance with applicable law and International Standards on Auditing (UK and Ireland). Those standards require us to comply with the Auditing Practices Board's (APB's) Ethical Standards for Auditors.

Scope of the audit of the financial statements

A description of the scope of an audit of financial statements is provided on the APB's website at http://www.frc.org.uk/apb/scope/UKP.

Opinion on financial statements

In our opinion:

- the financial statements give a true and fair view of the state of the group's and of the parent company's affairs as at 31 December 2009 and of the group's profit for the year then ended;

COMPANY SNAPSHOT 9.1 (*continued*)

- the group financial statements have been properly prepared in accordance with IFRSs as adopted by the EU;
- the parent company financial statements have been properly prepared in accordance with UK Generally Accepted Accounting Practice;
- the financial statements have been prepared in accordance with the requirements of the Companies Act 2006; and, as regards the group financial statements, Article 4 of the IAS Regulation.

Opinion on other matters prescribed by the Companies Act 2006

In our opinion:

- the part of the Directors' Remuneration Report to be audited has been properly prepared in accordance with the Companies Act 2006; and
- the information given in the Directors' Report for the financial year for which the financial statements are prepared is consistent with the financial statements.

Matters on which we are required to report by exception

We have nothing to report in respect of the following:

Under the Companies Act 2006 we are required to report to you if, in our opinion:

- adequate accounting records have not been kept by the parent company, or returns adequate for our audit have not been received from branches not visited by us; or
- the parent company financial statements and the part of the Directors' Remuneration Report to be audited are not in agreement with the accounting records and returns; or
- certain disclosures of directors' remuneration specified by law are not made; or
- we have not received all the information and explanations we require for our audit.

Under the Listing Rules we are required to review:

- the directors' statement, set out on page 30, in relation to going concern; and
- the part of the Corporate Governance Statement relating to the company's compliance with the nine provisions of the June 2008 Combined Code specified for our review.

Simon Figgis (Senior Statutory Auditor)
For and on behalf of KPMG Audit Plc, Statutory Auditor
Chartered Accountants
8 Salisbury Square
London
EC4Y 8BB
26 March 2010

Source: Rentokil Initial plc *Annual Report 2009*, p. 94.

This auditors' report thus confirms that the directors of Rentokil have prepared a set of financial statements which have given a true and fair view of the company's accounts as at 31 December 2009. This is known as a clean audit report. In this case, therefore, the auditors have not drawn the shareholders' attention to any discrepancies. A qualified auditors' report, by contrast, would be an adverse opinion on some aspect of the accounts; for example, compliance with a particular accounting standard. Shareholders of Rentokil can thus draw comfort from the fact that the auditors believe the accounts do give a true and fair view and faithfully reflect the economic performance of the company over the year.

3. Shareholders

The shareholders (in the US known as the stockholders) own the company. They have provided funding to the business in exchange for shares. Their reward is twofold. First, they may receive an annual dividend, which is simply a cash payment from the company based on profits. Second, they may benefit from any increase in the share price over the year. However, companies may make losses and share prices can go down as well as up, so this reward is not guaranteed. In the developed world, more and more companies are owned by large institutions (such as investment trusts or pension funds) rather than private shareholders.

The shareholders of the company receive an annual audited statement of the company's performance. This is called the annual report. It comprises the financial statements and also a narrative explanation of corporate performance. Included in this annual report is an auditors' report.

It is important to realise that shareholders are only liable for the equity which they contribute to a company. This equity is known as *share capital* (i.e., the capital of a company is divided into many shares). These shares limit the liability of shareholders and so we have limited liability companies. Shares, once issued, are bought or sold by shareholders on the stock market. This enables people who are not involved in the day-to-day running of the business to own shares. This division between owners and managers is often known as the divorce of ownership and control. It is a fundamental underpinning of a capitalist society.

PAUSE FOR THOUGHT 9.1

Risk and Reward

In the corporate model, each of the three groups is rewarded for its contributions. This is called the 'risk and reward model'. Can you work out each group's risk and reward?

	Contribution (risk)	Reward
Shareholders	Share capital	Dividends and increase in share price
Directors	Time and effort	Salaries, bonuses, benefits-in-kind such as cars or share options
Auditors	Time and effort	Auditors' fees

Regulatory Framework

The corporate model of directors, shareholders and auditors is one of checks and balances. The directors manage the company, receive directors' emoluments and recommend the appointment of the auditors to the shareholders. The shareholders own the company, but do not run it, and rely upon the auditors to check the accounts. Finally, the auditors are appointed by shareholders on the recommendation of the directors. They receive an auditors' fee for the work they undertake when they check the financial statements prepared by managers.

 PAUSE FOR THOUGHT 9.2

Checks and Balances

Is auditing enough to stop company directors pursuing their own interests at the expense of the shareholders?

Auditing is a powerful check on directors' self-interest. The directors prepare the accounts and the auditors check that the directors have correctly prepared them and that they give a 'true and fair' view. However, there are problems. The auditors, although technically appointed by the shareholders at the company's *annual general meeting* (i.e., a meeting called once a year to discuss a company's accounts), are recommended by directors. Auditors are also paid, often huge fees, by the company. The auditors do not wish to upset the directors and lose those fees. Given the flexibility within accounts, there is a whole range of possible accounting policies which the directors can choose. The regulatory framework helps to narrow this range of potential accounting policies and gives guidance to both directors and auditors. The auditors can, therefore, point to the rules and regulations if they feel that the directors' accounting policies are inappropriate. The regulatory framework is, therefore, a powerful ally of the auditor.

This system of checks and balances is fine, in principle. However, it is rather like having two football teams and a referee with no rules. The regulatory framework, in effect, provides a set of rules and regulations to ensure fair play. As Definition 9.2 shows, at the national level, these rules and regulations may originate from the government, the accounting standard setters or, more rarely, for listed companies, the stock exchange. The principal aim of the regulatory framework is to ensure that the financial statements present a true and fair view of the financial performance and position of the organisation.

In most countries, including the UK, the main sources of authority for the regulatory framework are either via the government through companies legislation or via accounting

DEFINITION 9.2

The National Regulatory Framework

Working definition

The set of rules and regulations which govern accounting practice, mainly prescribed by government and the accounting standard-setting bodies.

Formal definition

'The set of legal and professional requirements with which the financial statements of a company must comply. Company reporting is influenced by the requirements of law, of the accounting profession and of the Stock Exchange (for listed companies).'

Source: Chartered Institute of Management Accountants (2000), *Official Terminology.* Reproduced by Permission of Elsevier.

SOUNDBITE 9.1

Regulations

'If you destroy a free market you create a black market. If you have ten thousand regulations, you destroy all respect for the law.'

Winston S. Churchill

Source: The Book of Unusual Quotations (1959), pp. 240–41.

standard-setting bodies through accounting standards. In the UK, since 2012, this is through the Accounting Council. As Soundbite 9.1 suggests, there is a need not to overregulate. At the international level, there is a set of International Financial Reporting Standards (IFRS) issued by the International Accounting Standards Board (IASB). This is a non-governmental organisation that sets global accounting standards worldwide. The IASB is steadily growing in importance. Its standards are aimed primarily at large international companies. However, nowadays many other entities use IFRS. European listed companies must comply with IFRS.

International Accounting Standards

Over the last decade, both in the UK and in other European (and indeed non-European) countries, the role of the International Accounting Standards Board has grown in importance. The IASB has published International Accounting Standards (IAS) or International Financial Reporting Standards.

International Accounting Standards Board (IASB)

At one time, the European Union appeared to be developing its own standards. However, it has now thrown its weight behind IFRS. These are required to be used by the more than 9,000 European listed companies for their group accounts. The UK does, however, follow the European Fourth and Seventh Directive. These have been incorporated into the UK regulatory framework.

SOUNDBITE 9.2

Different Accounting Standards

'Different accounting standards are a drag on progress in much the same way as diverse languages are an inconvenience. Unlike creating a world language, creating one set of standards is achievable. Apart from the potential savings for companies with diverse international structures, complying with an internationally understood accounting paradigm opens up a wider investment audience.'

Source: Clem Chambers, Talking the Same Language, *Accountancy Age*, 3 February 2005, p. 6.

The International Accounting Standards Committee (IASC) was founded in 1973 by Sir Henry Benson to work for the improvement and harmonisation of accounting standards worldwide. Originally, there were nine members: Australia, Canada, France, Germany, Japan, Mexico, the Netherlands, the UK and Ireland, and the US. Member bodies were the national professional bodies of different countries. The IASC grew rapidly and, in 2001, 150 countries were members. The member bodies used their best endeavours to ensure that their countries followed International Accounting Standards (IAS). These were subsequently called International Financial Reporting Standards (IFRS). The IASC was reconstituted as the International Accounting Standards Board (IASB) in 2001 (to simplify matters we generally use IASB for both IASC and IASB throughout this book).

At first, the IASB merely codified the world's standards. After this initial step, the IASB began to work towards the improvement of standards. The IASB set out a restricted number of options within an accounting standard from which companies could then choose. Up until the mid-1990s, it is fair to say that the IASB made only limited progress. A threefold differentiation in the IASB's impact was possible: lesser developed countries, European countries and capital market countries. Lesser developed countries, such as Malaysia, Nigeria and Singapore, adopted IFRS because doing so was cheaper than developing their own standards. In continental Europe, the IFRS were seen both as a problem and a solution. They were a problem in that generally IFRS were seen to adopt a primarily investor-orientated approach to accounting which conflicted with the traditional continental European tax-driven, creditor-based model. They were a solution in that IFRS were preferable to US standards. Increasingly, in the early 1990s, French and German companies adopted US standards. Karel Van Hulle, Head of the EU's Accounting Unit, commented in 1995, 'It would be crazy for Europe to apply American standards, as it would be crazy for the Americans to apply European standards. We ought to develop those standards which we believe are the best for us or for our companies.' Finally, for capital market countries, such as the UK and the US, the IFRS were generally already similar to the national standards. Even so, there was a great reluctance, particularly by the US, to accept IFRS.

A breakthrough agreement came in 1995. IOSCO (The International Organisation of Securities Commissions), the body which represents the world's stock exchanges, agreed that when the IASB had developed a set of core standards, it would consider them for endorsement and would recommend them to national stock exchanges as an alternative to national standards. The advantage to IOSCO was that there would be a common currency of standards which could be used internationally. In particular, there was the hope that non-US companies could trade on the New York Stock Exchange without having to use US Generally Accepted Accounting Principles (GAAP) or provide a reconciliation to US GAAP. The IASB subsequently experienced severe problems compiling a set of core standards. However, by 2000 these were in place. The importance of the IASB is shown in Real-World View 9.1.

REAL-WORLD VIEW 9.1

Why IFRSs? Why Now?

The effective functioning of capital markets is essential to our economic well-being. In my view, a sound financial reporting infrastructure must be built on four pillars:

1. accounting standards that are consistent, comprehensive, and based on clear principles to enable financial reports to reflect underlying economic reality;
2. effective corporate governance practices, including a requirement for strong internal controls, that implement the accounting standards;
3. auditing practices that give confidence to the outside world that an entity is faithfully reflecting its economic performance and financial position; and
4. an enforcement or oversight mechanism that ensures that the principles as laid out by the accounting and auditing standards are followed.

As the world's capital markets integrate, the logic of a single set of accounting standards is evident. A single set of international standards will enhance comparability of financial information and should make the allocation of capital across borders more efficient. The development and acceptance of international standards should also reduce compliance costs for corporations and improve consistency in audit quality.

Sir David Tweedie, Chairman, International Accounting Standards Board
Testimony before the Committee of Banking, Housing and Urban Affairs of the United States Senate, Washington, 9 September 2004

Source: Deloitte, *IFRS in your pocket*, 2005, p. 2.

At the start of the new Millennium, three developments substantially enhanced the power of the IASB. First, in 2000 IOSCO allowed its members to use IFRS standards. Second, the IASC was reconstituted as the IASB in 2001 with a new chairman, Sir David Tweedie. The four main elements were: the IASC Foundation, the IASB, the Standards Advisory Council and the Standing Interpretations Committee. The IASC Foundation appoints the IASB, raises money and acts in a supervisory role. The main objectives of the IFRS foundation (IFRS, 2010) are 'to develop in the public interest, a single set of high-quality, understandable, enforceable and globally accepted financial reporting standards based upon clearly articulated principles'. To fulfil the required standards, financial statements and other reporting need to be of high quality, complete and transparent for investors and other users of financial information in the world's capital markets to make the right economic decisions. From July 2011, there was a new head of the IASB, Hans Hoogervorst, and as Real-World View 9.2 shows, the Board had a busy work programme. This workload is still continuing.

REAL-WORLD VIEW 9.2

The IASB's Workload

One of the first tasks of the new board will be to set its work programme for the next five years. By the time it does this, several very significant projects (including revenue, leases, insurance contracts and financial assets and financial liabilities) should have been completed. China, Japan, India, Canada, Brazil and several other major jurisdictions should be well on their way to International Financial Reporting Standards adoption. The Securities and Exchange Commission should have decided whether US domestic issuers should be allowed or required to use IFRS in place of US GAAP. Ideally, all the standards issued by the old board should have proved acceptable to the EU and other jurisdictions that use IFRS and to G20 ministers.

Source: D. Cairns, Where next for the IASB? *Accountancy Magazine*, February 2011, pp. 30–1. Copyright Wolters Kluwer (UK) Ltd.

The IASB sets the IFRS. At the end of 2011, there were 14 members of the IASB board with each member having one vote. As at December 2012, there were eight IFRS and 29 International Accounting Standards (IAS) (i.e., developed by the IASC) in existence. The Standards Advisory Council gives general advice and guidance to the IASB. The Standing Interpretations Committee interprets current IFRS, but also issues guidance on other accounting matters. There is also a Monitoring Board that provides a formal link between the trustees and public authorities and an advisory council which provides a forum for organisations and individuals to participate in the IASB's work. The third important development was the decision in June 2000 by the European Union that all EU listed companies would follow IFRS from 2005.

These three developments considerably enhanced the power of the IASB. By 2013, 93 countries required the use of IFRS for all listed domestic companies and many of these countries required their use by unlisted companies. The web addresses of some of these companies as well as the IASB website are given in Figure 9.2. The use of IFRS is also being encouraged by the International Federation of Accountants (IFAC). They have worked with the World Bank to ensure the global adoption of accounting and auditing standards. In many cases, the World Bank has specified the adoption of IFRS before it would grant credit. This has encouraged governments in developing countries to adopt IFRS.

Figure 9.2 Some Useful Web Addresses for Companies using International Financial Reporting Standards

Company	Nationality	Website	Sector
Gucci	Dutch	Gucci.com	Leather, Fashion
Lufthansa	German	Lufthansa.com	Airlines
Nestle	Swiss	Nestle.com	Food and Drink
Nokia	Finnish	Nokia.com	Mobile Phones
Novartis	Swiss	Novartis.com	Drug Manufacturing
Puma	German	Puma.com	Sportswear
SAS	Danish	SASgroup.net	Airlines
Swatch	Swiss	Swatch.com	Watches
UBS	Swiss	UBS.com	Banking
Volkswagen	German	Volkswagen.com	Car Manufacturing

The IFRS are continually being revised. There are, in addition, many interpretations (guidance documents) as well as the IASB's *The Conceptual Framework,* which is in the process of being updated. This framework defines the objectives of financial statements, the qualitative characteristics of financial statements and the basic elements and concepts of financial statements. IFRS, like all standards, are ultimately political in nature; as Real-World View 9.3

REAL-WORLD VIEW 9.3

A Pyrrhic Victory?

'IFRS is a good idea in principle, but the problem is the politics and whether the US gives up its sovereignty,' says Roger Barker, head of corporate governance at the Institute of Directors. 'And if too many global accounting rules are watered down in order to secure US support, IFRS will be a "pyrrhic victory",' Barker adds.

Jonathan Russell, a partner at Russell Phillips and Rees Russell and a former president of the UK 200 Group of chartered accountants and lawyers, says: 'For most small businesses, this is something that isn't even on their radar, so if and when the global accounting rules become compulsory, it will just be something else they expect their accountants to deal with.

At present at my firm I have about two clients who use international standards, which creates extra difficulties for us because we have to be familiar with UK and international GAAP.'

Big Four accounting firms appear more enthusiastic about IFRS. Pauline Wallace, UK head of public policy for PricewaterhouseCoopers, and an expert on IFRS, says that momentum towards global accounting standards appears unstoppable, and is not reliant on US support.

'The IASB has done a phenomenal job in getting its standards applied across the world,' she says. 'There is a real groundswell towards IFRS. If the US doesn't give its support for IFRS, it will be unfortunate, but it won't be a killer blow.'

Source: N. Huber, Rule the World, *Accountancy Magazine,* May 2010, p. 26. Copyright Wolters Kluwer (UK) Ltd.

shows, there has been much concern about the global rules on fair value accounting. Many critics have blamed fair value for the global financial crisis.

A consistent problem for the IASB has been the attitude of the US. Traditionally, the US has been reluctant to adopt IFRS. Although, in principle, the US favours world standards, it has several concerns about IFRS. It feels they are not as rigorous as US standards and is also worried about their enforcement. However, the shortcomings of US accounting standards revealed by US accounting scandals such as Enron and WorldCom made the IAS potentially more attractive to US regulators. In October 2003, a joint convergence project was begun by the IASB and the FASB. The aim of this project is to eliminate differences between the standards set by the IASB and FASB. Short-term convergence projects were set to be completed by 2008 with a decision by the US on convergence to follow but no decision had been made when this book went to press in 2014. Indeed, as time passes, convergence is looking less rather than more likely. The US market still does not accept IFRS at present without reconciliation to US GAAP.

PAUSE FOR THOUGHT 9.3

US Acceptance of IAS Standards

Cynics argue that it is in the US's interests deliberately to delay accepting International Accounting Standards. Why do you think this might be?

US standards are probably the most advanced of any country in the world. The US is also the richest country in the world and a source of potential capital for companies from other countries. To gain access to US finance, many overseas companies list on the US Stock Exchange. However, to do this they must adopt US standards or provide reconciliations to US standards. As time passes, more foreign companies adopt US standards. Cynics, therefore, believe that the US may be playing a waiting game. The longer the US delays approving IAS, the more foreign companies will list on the US exchange. These cynics argue, therefore, that it is in the US's interests to delay accepting IAS.

From a UK perspective, the Accounting Council, which sets standards for UK domestic non-listed companies, has accepted, in principle, the need for eventual international harmonisation. The current policy is to depart from an international consensus only when there are particular legal or tax difficulties or when the UK believes the international approach is wrong. Recently, there have been important efforts to harmonise UK and IAS standards in key areas such as goodwill, taxation and pensions. The UK is also harmonising its accounting practices with those currently used in the US. The Accounting Council has also agreed, in principle, that IFRS should be used for all publicly accountable entities.

Regulatory Framework in the UK

Most countries have a national regulatory framework that exists alongside IFRS. For example, in the UK there are two main sources of authority for regulation: the Companies Acts and accounting standards. There are some additional requirements from the Stock

Exchange for listed companies, but given their relative unimportance, they are not discussed further here.

In the UK, as in most countries, the regulatory framework has evolved over time. As accounting has grown more complex, so has the regulatory framework which governs it. At first, the only requirements that companies followed were those of the Companies Acts. However, in 1970 the first accounting standards set by the Accounting Standards Steering Committee were issued. Today, UK companies must adhere both to the requirements of Companies Acts and to accounting standards. For non-listed companies these are set by the Accounting Council (formerly the Accounting Standards Board (ASB)), for listed companies by the International Accounting Standards Board. The UK accounting standards are increasingly becoming less influential. However, from 2016 the smallest UK companies will continue to use a simplified version of UK standards, while other non-listed companies will use a standard based on IFRS for small and medium-sized enterprises (IFRS for SMEs). Alternatively, these companies can adopt IFRS. The overall aim of this regulatory framework is to protect the interests of all those involved in the corporate model. Specifically, there is a need to provide a 'true and fair view' of a company's affairs.

True and Fair View

Section 404 of the 2006 Companies Act requires that for companies following the Companies Acts Group Accounts (rather than IFRS Group Accounts): 'the accounts must give a true and fair view of the state of affairs as at the end of the financial year, and the profit or loss for the financial year, of the undertakings included in the consolidation as a whole, so far as concerns members of the company'. The 'true and fair' concept is thus of overriding importance. Unfortunately, it is a particularly nebulous concept which has no easy definition. A working definition is, however, suggested in Definition 9.3 below. In essence, there is a presumption that the accounts will reflect the underpinning economic reality. Generations of accountants have struggled unsuccessfully to pin down the exact meaning of the phrase. In general, to achieve a true and fair view, accounts should comply with the Companies Acts and accounting standards.

Occasionally, however, where compliance with the law would not give a true and fair view, a company may override the legal requirements. However, the company would have to demonstrate clearly why this was necessary.

DEFINITION 9.3

Working Definition of a 'True and Fair View'

A set of financial statements which faithfully, accurately and truly reflects the underlying economic transactions of an organisation.

Companies Acts

Companies Acts are Acts of Parliament which lay down the legal requirements for companies including regulations for accounting. There has been a succession of Companies Acts which have gradually increased the reporting requirements placed on UK companies. Initially, the Companies Acts provided only a broad legislative framework. However, later Companies Acts (CAs), especially the CA 1981, have imposed a significant regulatory burden on UK companies. The CA 1981 introduced the European Fourth Directive into UK law. Effectively, this Directive was the result of a deal between the United Kingdom and other European

Union members. The United Kingdom exported the true and fair view concept, but imported substantial detailed legislation and standardised formats for the income statement (profit and loss account) and statements of financial position (balance sheets). The CA 1981, therefore, introduced a much more prescriptive 'European' accounting regulatory framework into the UK. The latest Companies Act is the CA 2006 which has introduced IFRS into British law. Group Accounts may be prepared in accordance with Section 404 (Companies Act Group Accounts) or in accordance with international accounting standards (IFRS Group Accounts).

Accounting Standards

Whereas Companies Acts are governmental in origin, accounting standards are set by non-governmental bodies. Accounting standards were introduced, as Real-World View 9.4 indicates, to improve the quality of UK financial reporting.

REAL-WORLD VIEW 9.4

Introduction of Accounting Standards

Inflation accounting was, in fact, only one part of a bigger move towards accounting standards – a move that was itself controversial. Standards had been proposed a few years earlier to limit the scope for judgement in the preparation of accounts. They were the profession's response to a huge City row when GEC chief executive Arnold Weinstock restated the profits of AEI, a company he had just taken over, from mega millions down to zero.

The City was outraged and demanded more certainty in accounts so it could have more faith in public profit figures.

Standards were the result and, though taken for granted now, many saw them as the death knell for the profession, precisely because they limited the scope for professional judgement. Many believed the profession had been permanently diminished when its ability to make judgements was curtailed.

Source: Anthony Hilton, Demands for Change, *Accountancy Age*, 11 November 2004, p. 25.

At the international level, International Financial Reporting Standards (IFRS) are set by the International Accounting Standards Board. These are now mandatory for all European listed companies in their group accounts. However, there have been ongoing discussions between the IASB and the US Financial Accounting Standards Board (FASB) about convergence. UK non-listed companies may still follow UK accounting standards.

The UK's accounting setting regime has evolved over time. The current regulatory framework was set up in 1990, reorganised in 2004 and then again in July 2012. In 2004, the structure consisted of a Financial Reporting Council which supervised five boards regulating accounting, accountants and auditing: the Auditing Practices Board, Accounting Standards Board, Financial Reporting and Review Panel, Investigation and Discipline board and Professional Oversight

Board. The new FRC structure set up in July 2012 is shown in Figure 9.3. The main elements that concern accounting are the Codes and Standards Committee, the Accounting Council, the Financial Reporting Review Panel and the Audit and Assurance Council.

There was much concern in the accounting community about the abolition of the Accounting Standards Board. Effectively, it has been replaced by the Accounting Council.

Figure 9.3 UK's Regulatory Framework

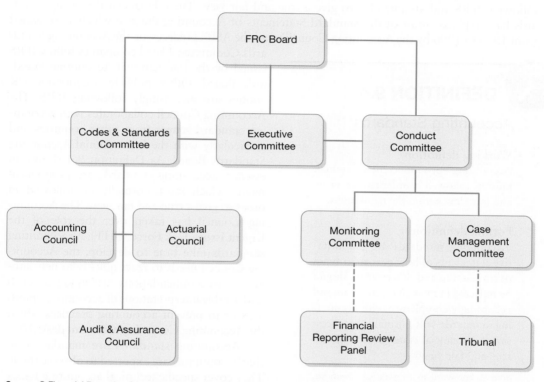

1. Financial Reporting Council (FRC)

The Financial Reporting Council is a supervisory body which ensures that the overall system is working. As can be seen in Figure 9.3, the FRC supervises a Codes and Standards Committee, an Executive Committee and a Conduct Committee. The main accounting functions come under the Codes and Standards Committee in terms of the Accounting Council and Audit and Assurance Council. In addition, the Financial Reporting Review Panel comes under the Monitoring Committee. These are discussed more fully below.

2. Codes and Standards Committee

This was established in 2012. It is responsible for advising the FRC board on monitoring an effective framework of UK codes and standards for corporate governance, stewardship, accounting, auditing and assurance and actuarial technical standards. This board is advised by the Accounting Council (including accounting and accounting narratives), the Audit and Assurance Council, and the Actuarial Council.

3. Accounting Council

The Accounting Council took over from the ASB in 2012. It is the engine of the accounting standards process. In the UK, accounting standards are called Financial Reporting Standards (FRS). The Accounting Council issues FRS which are applicable to the accounts of all UK companies not following IFRS and are intended to give a true and fair view. These Financial Reporting Standards have replaced most of the Standard Statements of Accounting Practice which were issued from 1970 to 1990 by the Accounting Council's and the ASB's predecessor, the Accounting Standards Committee. Listed companies follow IFRS issued by the International Accounting Standards Board. Other publicly accountable UK entities are increasingly following IFRS. The Accounting Council collaborates with accounting standard setters from other countries and particularly with the International Accounting Standards Board. As Definition 9.4 shows, in essence, accounting standards are pronouncements which must normally be followed in order to give a true and fair view. The Accounting Council has taken over the role of the Urgent Issues Task Force (UITF). As accounting standards take time to develop, the Accounting Council needs to react quickly to new situations. Recommendations are made to curb undesirable interpretations of accounting standards or to prevent accounting practices which the Accounting Council considers undesirable.

Accounting standards are mandatory in that accountants are expected to observe them. They cover specific technical accounting issues such as inventory, depreciation, and research and development. These standards essentially aim to improve the quality of accounting in the UK. They narrow the areas of difference and variety in accounting practice, set out minimum disclosure standards and disclose the accounting principles upon which the accounts are based. Overall, accounting standards provide a comprehensive set of guidelines which preparers and auditors can use when drawing up and verifying the financial statements.

DEFINITION 9.4

Accounting Standards

Working definition
Accounting pronouncements which must be followed in order to give a true and fair view within the regulations.

Formal definition
'Accounting standards are authoritative statements of how particular types of transaction and other events should be reflected in financial statements and accordingly compliance with accounting standards will normally be necessary for financial statements to give a true and fair view.'

Source: Foreword to *Accounting Standards*, Accounting Standards Board (1993), para. 16.

4. Audit and Assurance Council

This body, created in 2012, advises the FRC board and the Codes and Standards Committee on audit and assurance matters.

5. The Financial Reporting Review Panel (FRRP)

The FRRP investigates contentious departures from accounting standards. It reports to the Monitoring Committee. It is the 'detective' arm of the regulatory framework. The FRRP questions the directors of the companies investigated. The last resort of the FRRP is to take miscreant companies to court to force them to revise their accounts. However, so far the threat of court action has been enough. The FRRP began as a reactive body only responding to complaints. However, recently the FRRP has become more proactive as Real-World View 9.5 explains.

REAL-WORLD VIEW 9.5
FRRP

When it was set up in 1990 to deal with the scandals of the eighties, the government had decided that self-regulation was the best option. It is a strategy that Sir Bryan describes as highly successful 'because the people in the system knew they had to make it work because of the alternative'.

But since Enron, Parmalat et al, the pressure's on to up the ante. Enhancements include a new proactive approach to uncovering accounting cock-ups in the books of listed UK companies, with 300 sets of accounts slated for investigation by the Financial Reporting Review Panel (FRRP) this year.

Source: Insider, *Accountancy Age,* 1 April 2004, p. 15.

In 2005, for example, the FRRP investigated the accounts of MG Rover. This company was run by four businessmen and then subsequently collapsed. There were suspicions of accounting impropriety and, therefore, the FRRP looked into its finances. As Real-World View 9.6 shows, this triggered a government enquiry.

REAL-WORLD VIEW 9.6
FRRP and MG Rover

The Phoenix Four, the Midlands businessmen behind the collapsed MG Rover Group, are to be investigated by the Department of Trade and Industry, which has set up an independent inquiry into the affairs of the former car maker.

The inquiry was announced yesterday by Alan Johnson, the Trade and Industry Secretary. He ordered the inquiry after receiving an initial report into the company's finances by the Financial Reporting and Review Panel (FRRP), part of the accountancy watchdog, the Financial Reporting Council.

A clean bill of health for MG Rover, and its associated companies, would have left the Government little choice but to close the case. But Mr Johnson said the FRRP report 'raises a number of questions that need to be answered'. He said the public interest demanded a more detailed account of what went on at MG Rover Group, which collapsed into administration in April with the loss of more than 5000 jobs.

Source: Damian Reece, DTI Opens MG Rover Investigation, *Financial Times,* 1 June 2005, p. 57.

Corporate Governance

From the 1990s, corporate governance has grown in importance. Effectively, corporate governance is the system by which companies are directed and controlled (see Real-World View 9.7).

REAL-WORLD VIEW 9.7

Corporate Governance

Corporate governance is the way in which companies are directed and controlled. Boards of directors are responsible for corporate governance. Shareholders appoint the directors and the auditors and satisfy themselves that there is appropriate governance structure. The responsibilities of the board include the company's strategy aims, supervising the management and stewardship. They thus supervise operational aspects and are accountable to shareholders. The board's actions are subject to laws, regulations and to shareholders in the Annual General Meeting.

The financial aspects of corporate governance relate to the setting and implementation of financial policy. This will include financial controls and financial reporting.

Source: Derived from the *Report of the Committee on the Financial Assets of Corporate Governance* (1992), Gee and Co., p. 15.

The financial aspects of corporate governance relate principally to internal controls, the way in which the board of directors functions and the process by which the directors report to the shareholders on the activities and progress of the company. Corporate governance came to prominence in the UK after the failure of Polly Peck, which went insolvent after a major fraudulent misstatement of the accounts. The Cadbury Committee resulted and in 1992 made several recommendations such as the separation of the CEO and Chairman, that there should be non-executive directors and that there should be an audit committee. Several other committees followed in the UK, including the Greenbury Committee (1995) on executive compensation, the Hampel Committee (1998), which recommended a combined code, and the Turnbull Committee (1999), which suggested directors should be responsible for financial and auditing controls. In addition, since 2003 there have been several other reports. The Higgs review focused on the role of non-executive directors. Myners looked at the role of institutional investors and the Walker review focused on the banking industry. Then in 2010 a Stewardship Code was issued by the Financial Reporting Council.

SOUNDBITE 9.3

Corporate Governance

'Sarbanes-Oxley was brought in to ward off any future Enrons by, effectively, creating a vast network of internal controls and regulations that would, the legislators intended, make Enron-scale corporate deceptions impossible.'

Source: Robert Bruce, Winds of Change, *Accountancy Magazine*, February 2010, p. 27.

The continuing interest in corporate governance arises in part for two reasons. First, there have been some unexpected failures of major companies such as Polly Peck, Maxwell Communications, WorldCom, Enron and Parmalat. In the US, in particular, this has led to the Sarbanes-Oxley Act (see Soundbite 9.3). The Sarbanes-Oxley Act was the US government's response to Enron and WorldCom. Since 2004, all US companies have submitted details of their internal control systems to the US Security Exchange Council (SEC). These control systems are also audited. Second, there have been extensive criticisms in the press of 'fat-cat' directors. These directors, often of privatised companies (i.e., companies which were previously state-owned and run), are generally perceived to be paying themselves huge and unwarranted salaries.

As a result of the Cadbury Committee and other subsequent committees, there were attempts to tighten up corporate governance in the UK. In particular, there was a concern with the amount of information companies disclosed, with the role of non-executive directors (i.e., directors appointed from outside the company), with directors' remuneration, with audit committees (committees ideally controlled by non-executive directors which oversee the appointment of external auditors and deal with their reports), with relations with institutional investors and with systems of internal financial control set up by management.

Companies are very concerned to demonstrate their good corporate governance structure. In the UK, the Financial Reporting Council in 2012 revised the UK's Corporate Governance Code. This sets out principles of good corporate governance. Public companies need to disclose how they have complied with the code. Marks and Spencer plc, for example, has aligned its governance with the themes in this Code: leadership's effectiveness, accountability, communication and remuneration. Marks and Spencer has outlined its governance structure in its 2010 annual report (see Company Snapshot 9.2).

COMPANY SNAPSHOT 9.2

Governance Structures: Marks and Spencer

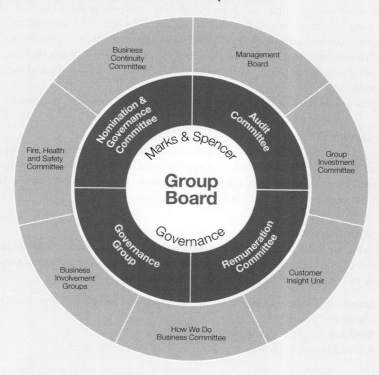

Source: Marks and Spencer plc, *Annual Report and Financial Statements 2010.*

In the annual report, companies now set out extensive details of directors' remuneration and disclose information about corporate governance. The auditors review these corporate governance elements to check that they comply with the principles of good governance and code of best practice as set out in the London Stock Exchange's rules. Company Snapshot 9.3 presents part of J.D. Wetherspoon's corporate governance statement which relates to internal control. The directors acknowledge their responsibility to establish controls such as those to protect against the unauthorised use of assets.

Internationally, there are two main approaches to corporate governance: rules-based and principles-based. The US adopts a rules-based approach as set out in the Sarbanes-Oxley Act. By contrast, the UK takes a more principles-based approach. Companies in the UK comply with the regulations or explain why they are not complying (usually termed a comply or explain approach).

COMPANY SNAPSHOT 9.3

Corporate Governance

Nomination committee

A formal nomination committee has been established, comprising John Herring (chairman), Debra van Gene, Elizabeth McMeikan and Sir Richard Beckett. The nomination committee meets as appropriate and considers all possible board appointments and also the re-election of directors, both executive and non-executive. No director is involved in any decision about his or her own re-appointment. Under the terms of the Code, one of the members of the committee was not independent.

The terms of reference of the nomination committee are available on request.

Company secretary

All directors have access to the advice of the company secretary, responsible to the board for ensuring that procedures are followed. The appointment and removal of the company secretary is reserved for consideration by the board as a whole. Procedures are in place for seeking independent professional advice, at the Company's expense.

Relations with shareholders

The board takes considerable measures to ensure that all board members are kept aware of both the views of major shareholders and changes in the major shareholdings of the Company. Efforts made to accomplish effective communication include:

- Annual general meeting, considered to be an important forum for shareholders to raise questions with the board
- Regular feedback from the Company's stockbrokers
- Interim, full and ongoing announcements circulated to shareholders

COMPANY SNAPSHOT 9.3 (*continued*)

- Any significant changes in shareholder movement being notified to the board by the company secretary, when necessary
- The company secretary maintaining procedures and agreements for all announcements to the City
- A programme of regular meetings between investors and directors of the Company, including the senior independent director, as appropriate
- The capital structure of the company is described in note 24 to the accounts.

Risk management

The board is responsible for the Company's risk-management process.

The internal audit department, in conjunction with the management of the business functions, produces a risk register annually. This register has been compiled by the business using a series of facilitated control and risk self-assessment workshops, run in conjunction with internal audit. These workshops were run with senior management from the key business functions.

The identified risks are assessed based on the likelihood of a risk occurring and the potential impact to the business, should the risk occur. The head of internal audit determines and reviews the risk assessment process and will communicate the timetable annually.

The risk register is presented to the audit committee every six months, with a schedule of audit work agreed on, on a rolling basis. The purpose of this work is to review, on behalf of the Company and board, those key risks and the systems of control necessary to manage such risks.

The results of this work are reported back to relevant senior management and the audit committee. Where recommendations are made for changes in systems or processes to reduce risk, internal audit will follow up regularly to ensure that the recommendations are implemented.

Internal control

During the year, the Company and the board continued to support and invest in resource to provide an internal audit and risk-management function. The system of internal control and risk mitigation is deeply embedded in the operations and the Company culture. The board is responsible for maintaining a sound system of internal control and reviewing its effectiveness. The function can only manage, rather than entirely eliminate, the risk of failure to achieve business objectives. It can provide only reasonable and not absolute assurance against material misstatement or loss. Ongoing reviews, assessments and management of significant risks took place throughout the year under review and up to the date of the approval of the annual report and accords with the Turnbull Guidance (Guidance on Internal Control).

The Company has an internal audit function which is discharged as follows:

- Regular audits of the Company stock
- Unannounced visits to retail units
- Monitoring systems which control the Company cash
- Health & safety visits, ensuring compliance with Company procedures

COMPANY SNAPSHOT 9.3 (*continued*)

- Reviewing and assessing the impact of legislative and regulatory change
- Annually reviewing the Company's strategy, including a review of risks facing the business
- Risk-management process, identifying key risks facing the business (Company Risk Register).

The Company has key controls, as follows:

- Clearly defined authority limits and controls over cash-handling, purchasing commitments and capital expenditure
- Comprehensive budgeting process, with a detailed 12-month operating plan and a mid-term financial plan, both approved by the board
- Business results are reported weekly (for key times), with a monthly comprehensive report in full and compared with budget
- Forecasts are prepared regularly throughout the year, for review by the board
- Complex treasury instruments are not used; decisions on treasury matters are reserved by the board
- Regular reviews of the amount of external insurance which it obtains, bearing in mind the availability of such cover, its costs and the likelihood of the risks involved
- Regular evaluation of processes and controls in relation to the Company's financial reporting requirements.

The directors confirm that they have reviewed the effectiveness of the system of internal control. Directors' insurance cover is maintained.

Keith Down
Company Secretary
10 September 2010

Source: J.D. Wetherspoon plc, *Annual Report and Accounts 2010*, p. 68.

Conceptual Framework

DEFINITION 9.5

Conceptual Framework

The development of a coherent and consistent set of accounting principles which underpin the preparation and presentation of financial statements.

Since the 1960s, standard-setting bodies (such as the Financial Accounting Standards Board (FASB), in the USA, the International Accounting Standards Board (IASB) and the Accounting Standards Board (1990–2012) in the UK) have sought to develop a conceptual framework or statement of principles which will underpin accounting practice. As Definition 9.5 shows, the basic idea of a conceptual framework is to create a set of fundamental accounting principles which will help in standard setting.

A major achievement of the search for a conceptual theory has been the emergence of the decision-making model. There is a need to provide decision-useful information to investors. In accounting, a conceptual framework has developed over time. In 1989, the IASC published a *Framework for the Preparation and Presentation of Financial Statements*. The aim of the conceptual framework is to assist the IASB in developing standards, help other standard setters and assist preparers, auditors and users in interpreting and understanding financial statements. The six essential components of a conceptual framework are broadly agreed by all three major standard-setting bodies: objectives, users, user needs, elements of financial statements, information characteristics and measurement principles with concepts of capital maintenance. These components are briefly discussed below. The various elements of the financial statements such as financial position (assets, liabilities, and equity) and performance (income and expenses), have been discussed already in Section A. The IASB updated its conceptual framework and its latest version was published in 2010. However, at the end of 2013 it produced a Discussion Paper on the Conceptual Framework. The results of this discussion were not known at the time this work went to press.

1. Objectives

The IASB broadly sees the objective of financial accounting as the provision of financial information about an organisation that is useful to a range of users, such as existing and potential investors, lenders or creditors when they are seeking to make decisions. These decisions may be, for example, buying or selling shares or giving loans. This replaces the previous objective that had been agreed by the US Financial Accounting Standards Board (FASB) and the International Accounting Standards Board (IASB) in 1999. This approach to accounting is widely known as the decision-making model (see Figure 9.4). In other words, the basic idea of accounting is to provide accounting information to users which fulfils their needs, thus enabling them to make decisions. Encompassed within this broad definition is the idea that financial statements show how the managers have accounted for the resources entrusted to them by the shareholders. This accountability is often called stewardship. To enable stewardship and decision making, the information must have certain information characteristics and use a consistent measurement model.

Figure 9.4 Decision-Making Model

In the UK, the ASB (1990–2012) had developed a Statement of Principles. The Statement takes a broader definition of the objectives of financial reporting than either the FASB or the IASB. 'The objective of financial statements is to provide information about the reporting entity's financial position, performance and changes in financial position that is useful to a wide range of users for assessing the stewardship of the entity's management and for making economic decisions' (Accounting Standards Board, *Statement of Principles*, 1999). Thus, the ASB (now the Accounting Council) sees the *objective of financial reporting* as (i) the *stewardship of management* and (ii) *making economic decisions.*

Stewardship and decision making are discussed in more depth in Chapter 11. However, at this stage it is important to introduce them. Stewardship is all about accountability. It seeks to make the directors accountable to the shareholders for their stewardship or management of the company. Corporate governance is one modern aspect of stewardship. Decision making, by contrast, focuses on the need for shareholders to make economic decisions, such as to buy or sell their shares. As performance measurement and decision making have grown in importance, so has the income statement. In a sense, decision making and stewardship are linked, as information is provided to shareholders so that they can make decisions about the directors' stewardship of the company. There has been much debate as to whether stewardship or decision making should be given primacy when drawing up financial statements.

Essentially, stewardship and decision making are user-driven and take the view that accounting should give a 'true and fair' view of a company's accounts. By contrast, the public relations view suggests that there are behavioural reasons why managers might seek to prepare accounts that favour their own self-interest. Self-interest and 'true and fair' may well conflict. In this section, we focus only on the officially recognised roles of accounting (stewardship and decision making). Discussion of the public relations role and the conflicting multiple accounting objectives is covered in Chapter 11.

PAUSE FOR THOUGHT 9.4

Stewardship and Decision Making

Why are assets and liabilities most important for stewardship, but profits most important for decision making?

Stewardship is about making individuals accountable for assets and liabilities. In particular, stewardship focuses on the physical existence of assets and seeks to prevent their loss and/or fraud. Stewardship is, therefore, about keeping track of assets rather than evaluating how efficiently they are used.

Decision making is primarily concerned with monitoring performance. Therefore, it is primarily concerned with whether or not a business has made a profit. It is less concerned with tracking assets.

2. Users

The main users are usually considered to be the present and future shareholders. Indeed, shareholders are the only group required by law to be sent an annual report. Shareholders comprise individual and institutional shareholders. Besides shareholders, there are a number of other users. In its most recent version of the Conceptual Framework (2010), the IASB focuses on existing and potential investors, lenders and other creditors. However, before this version the IASB identified a wider set of users including:

- lenders, such as banks or loan creditors
- suppliers and other trade creditors (i.e., trade payables)
- employees and employee organisations
- customers
- governments and their agencies
- general public
- analysts and advisers.

In addition to this list we can add:

- academics
- management
- pressure groups such as Friends of the Earth.

Broadly, we can see that this list is broadly the same as that discussed in Chapter 1 (see Figure 1.3). In Chapter 1, however, we distinguished between internal users (management and employees) and external users (the rest). All of these users will need the information to appraise the performance of management and also to make decisions.

Generally the accounts are pitched at the shareholders. Their primary requirement is to acquire economic information so that they can make economic decisions. Satisfying the interests of shareholders is generally thought to cover the main concerns of the other groups. The annual report adopts a general purpose reporting model. This provides a comprehensive set of information targeted at all users. It does not, therefore, specifically target the needs of one user group.

3. User Needs

User needs vary. However, commonly users will want answers to questions such as:

- How well is management running the company?
- How profitable is the organisation?
- How much cash does it have in the bank?
- Is it likely to keep trading?

The IASB looks at the needs of external users and believes that user needs will be focused on economic decisions such as to:

- Decide to buy, hold or sell shares
- Assess the stewardship or accountability of management
- Assess the ability of the entity to pay the wages

- Assess the security for monies lent
- Determine tax policy
- Determine distributable profits and dividends
- Prepare and use national income statistics
- Regulate an entity's activities.

In order to answer these questions, users will need information on the profitability, liquidity, efficiency and gearing of the company. This is normally provided in the three key financial statements: the income statement, the statement of financial position and the statement of cash flows. Users will also be interested in the softer, qualitative information provided, for example, in accounting narratives such as the chairman's statement.

4. Qualitative Information Characteristics

In order to be useful to users, the financial information needs to possess certain characteristics. The UK's Accounting Standards Board, now replaced by the Accounting Council, focuses on four principal characteristics: relevance, reliability, comparability and understandability. The ASB then classified these characteristics into those relating to content (relevance and reliability) and those relating to presentation (comparability and understandability) (see Figure 9.5).

Figure 9.5 Overview of Information Characteristics (Accounting Council)

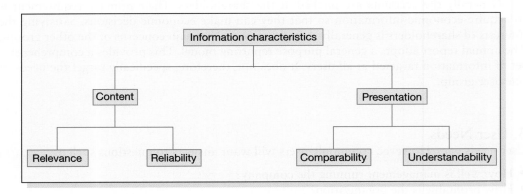

This approach was also adopted by the IASB, but it has now refined its position. The IASB now sees two fundamental qualitative characteristics: relevance and faithful representation. There are then a further four characteristics that enhance relevance and faithful representation: comparability, verifiability, timeliness and understandability (see Figure 9.6).

Figure 9.6 Overview of Information Characteristics (IASB)

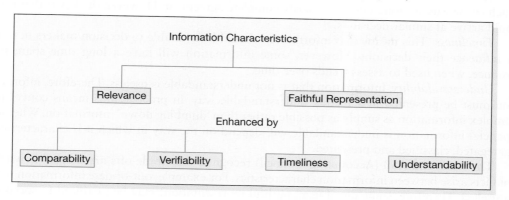

The major change in the latest conceptual framework is the replacement of reliability by representational faithfulness. The IASB abandoned 'reliability' because it believed there was a lack of common understanding of the term.

A. Fundamental Qualitative Characteristics

Relevance. Relevant information is that which affects users' economic decisions. Relevance is a prerequisite of usefulness. Examples of relevance are information that helps to predict future events or to confirm or correct past events. The relevance of financial information in the financial statements crucially depends on its materiality. If information is immaterial (i.e., will not affect users' decisions), then, in practice, it does not need to be reported. Materiality is thus best considered as a threshold or cut-off point rather than being a primary qualitative information characteristic in its own right.

Faithful Representation. Financial reports represent economic phenomena in numbers and words. Like relevance, faithful representation is a prerequisite of usefulness. Three characteristics underpin information that is representationally faithful (i.e., information that validly describes the underlying events). First, information must be complete in that all necessary information should be included. Second, reliable information must be neutral; i.e., not biased. Third, faithful representation dictates that there are no errors or omissions in the information. The IASB did not see substance over form as a separate component of faithful representation. This was because a legal form which did not represent economic substance automatically violated representational faithfulness.

B. Supplementary Enhancing Qualitative Characteristics

Comparability. Accounts should be prepared on a consistent basis and should disclose accounting policies. This will then allow users to make inter-company comparisons and intra-company comparisons over time.

Verifiability. This means that different knowledgeable and independent observers could reach consensus, although not necessarily complete agreement. However, the key is that they could arrive at similar decisions.

Timeliness. This means that information should be available to decision makers in time to influence their decisions. However, some information will have a long time span; for instance, when used to assess trends over time.

Understandability. Information that is not understandable is useless. Therefore, information must be presented in a readily understandable way. In practice, this means conveying complex information as simply as possible rather than 'dumbing down' information. Whether financial information is understandable will depend on the way in which it is characterised, aggregated, classified and presented.

The IASB and ASB (Accounting Council) recognise that trade-offs are inevitable where conflicts arise between information characteristics. For example, out-of-date information may be useless. Therefore, some detail (e.g., faithful representation) may be sacrificed to speed of reporting (e.g., timeliness). In addition, the benefits derived from information should exceed the costs of providing it. Cost is described by the IASB as a pervasive constraint.

Prudence

Another concept which was, at one time, thought to underpin reliability is prudence. Prudent information is where assets or income are not deliberately overstated or expenses and liabilities deliberately understated. There is currently much discussion about prudence. On the one hand some believe that prudence is a sensible counter-balance against the potential over-optimism of managers. Others, by contrast, argue that a prudent view mitigates against an objective view of a business. However, the IASB has omitted prudence from its latest version of the conceptual framework. It considers that prudence would be inconsistent as it would introduce bias. It has subsequently modified its position, considering prudence as the exercise of caution when making judgements under conditions of uncertainty. It should, however, not allow under- or over-estimates of liabilities or income.

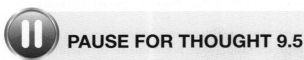

PAUSE FOR THOUGHT 9.5

The Debate about Prudence

Prudence is a much debated concept. There are two main views. Many commentators believe that prudence is very useful as it balances the managerial tendency to provide over-optimistic accounts. It is, therefore, a valuable safeguard for creditors and shareholders. This is certainly the view of the UK's House of Lords Committee which investigated banks and bank auditing in 2011. By contrast, others, including the IASB, think that accounts should be neutral and without bias. Therefore, as prudence introduces a negative bias into the accounts, it should not underpin accounts. The House of Lords Report criticised IFRS as an 'inferior system' which inhibited the auditors' ability to exercise judgement.

....

Both sides feel strongly!! Which view do you support?

5. Measurement Model

The objectives, users, user needs and information characteristics have proved relatively easy to agree upon. However, the choice of an appropriate measurement model for profit measurement and asset determination has caused much controversy. The measurement basis that underpins financial statements remains a modified form of historical cost. In other words, income, expenses, assets and liabilities are recorded at the date of their original monetary transaction. Unfortunately, although historical cost is relatively well understood and easy to understand, it understates assets and overstates profits, especially in times of inflation. Most commentators agree that historical cost, therefore, is flawed. However, there is no consensus on a suitable replacement. The alternative measurement models are more fully discussed in Chapter 10.

PAUSE FOR THOUGHT 9.6

Critics of the Conceptual Framework

The conceptual framework has been criticised for not achieving very much and being a social document rather than a theory document. What do you think these criticisms mean and are they fair?

The conceptual framework has brought into being the decision-making model. However, there is little agreement on the appropriate measurement model for accounting. In other words, should we continue to use historical cost or should we move towards some alternative measurement model that perhaps accounts for the effects of inflation? Critics have seen this failure to agree on a measurement model as a severe blow to the authority of the conceptual framework. In addition, there is concern that the conceptual framework has not really developed a theoretically coherent and consistent set of accounting principles at all. These critics argue that the conceptual framework is primarily descriptive – just describing what already exists. A descriptive framework is not a theoretical framework. Finally, some critics argue that the real reason for the search for a conceptual framework is to legitimise and support the notion of a standard-setting regime independent of government. The conceptual framework should thus be seen as a social document which supports the existence of an independent accounting profession.

Conclusion

In order to appreciate accounting practice properly, we need to understand the regulatory and conceptual frameworks within which it operates. These frameworks were primarily devised for published financial statements, such as those in the corporate annual report. The regulatory framework is the set of rules and regulations which governs corporate accounting practice. The International Accounting Standards Board sets International Financial Reporting Standards. These are followed by all European listed companies, including UK companies. The two major strands of the UK's regulatory framework are the Companies Acts and accounting standards. The UK's accounting standards regulatory framework consists of five elements: the Financial Reporting Council, the Codes and Standards Committee, the Accounting Council, the Audit and Assurance Council and the Financial Reporting Review Panel. Corporate governance is the system by which companies are governed.

A conceptual framework is an attempt to create a set of fundamental accounting principles which will help standard setting. A major achievement of the search for a conceptual framework has been the emergence of the decision-making model. The essence of this is that the objective of financial statements is to provide financial information useful to a wide range of users for making economic decisions. A second objective is to provide financial information for assessing the stewardship of managers. In order to be useful, the IASB believes this information must have relevance and faithful representation enhanced by comparability, verifiability, timeliness and understandability. Although there is general agreement on the essentials of a decision-making model, there is little consensus on which measurement model should underpin the decision-making process.

Selected Reading

The references below will give you further background. They are roughly divided into those on the regulatory framework and those on the conceptual framework.

Regulatory Framework

Bartlett, S.A. and M.J. Jones (1997) Annual Reporting Disclosures 1970–90: An Exemplification, *Accounting, Business and Financial History*, Vol. 7, No. 1, pp. 61–80.
This article looks at how the accounts of one firm, H.P. Bulmers (Holdings) plc, the cider makers, were affected by changes in the regulations from 1970 to 1990.
International GAAP 2012: Generally Accepted Accounting Practice under International Financial Reporting Standards, Ernst and Young 2012. A very thorough and complete look at IFRS.
Solomon, J.F. (2007) *Corporate Governance and Accountability*, John Wiley and Sons Ltd, Chichester.
Provides an overview of corporate governance.

The Combined Code (1998) London Stock Exchange, June.
> This provides a comprehensive set of recommendations arising from the various corporate governance reports (i.e., Cadbury, Greenbury, Hampel). UK-listed companies now follow these.

The Financial Aspects of Corporate Governance (The Cadbury Committee Report) (1992), Gee and Co.
> The first, and arguably the most influential, report into corporate governance. Authoritative.

UK and International GAAP (2004), Ernst and Young, Butterworth.
> Provides a very comprehensive guide to UK and IFRS standards as well as to the ASB's *Statement of Principles*. This guide is updated annually.

Conceptual Framework

Outlines of Potential Conceptual Frameworks by Professional Bodies

Accounting Standards Board (1999) Statement of Principles, *Accountancy*.
> This synopsis offers a good, quick insight into current thinking in the UK about a conceptual theory. The Accounting Council has taken over responsibility for this.

Accounting Standards Setting Committee (ASSC) (1975) *The Corporate Report* (London).
> A benchmark report which outlined the Committee's – at the time groundbreaking – thoughts about the theory of accounting. Easy to read.

Financial Accounting Standards Board (FASB) (1978), *Statement of Financial Accounting Concepts No. 1, Objectives of Financial Reporting by Business Enterprises* (Stanford, FASB).
> Offers an insight into the US view of a conceptual theory.

International Accounting Standards Board (IASB) (2000), *Framework for the Preparation and Presentation of Financial Statements* in International Accounting Standards, 2000.
> The IASB's early thoughts on a conceptual theory.

International Accounting Standards Board (IASB) (2010), *Conceptual Framework for Financial Reporting*.
> A very influential document outlining the IASB's views.

International Accounting Standards Board (2013), *A Review of the Conceptual Framework for Financial Reporting, IASB Discussion Paper*.
> A very useful document outlining the main points of discussion.

International GAAP (2012), *Generally Accepted Accounting Practices under International Financial Reporting Standards*, Ernst and Young, 2012.
> Provides a useful overview.

Discussion Questions

Questions with numbers in blue have answers at the back of the book.

Q1 What is the role of directors, shareholders and auditors in the corporate model?

Q2 What is the decision-making model? Assess its reasonableness.

Q3 Discuss the view that if a regulatory framework did not exist, it would have to be invented.

Q4 Companies often disclose 'voluntary' information over and above that which they are required to do. Why do you think they do this?

Q5 What is a conceptual framework and why do you think so much effort has been expended to try to find one?

Go online to discover the extra features for this chapter at
www.wiley.com/college/jones

Chapter 10

Measurement systems

'What is a Cynic? A man who knows the price of everything and the value of nothing.'

Oscar Wilde, *Lady Windermere's Fan* (1892), *Wiley Book of Business Quotations* (1998), p. 349.

Learning Outcomes

After completing this chapter you should be able to:

- Explore the importance of accounting measurement systems.
- Critically evaluate historical costing.
- Investigate the alternatives to historical costing.

Go online to discover the extra features for this chapter at
www.wiley.com/college/jones

Chapter Summary

- Measurement systems determine asset valuation and profit measurement.
- The capital maintenance concept is concerned with maintaining the capital of a company.
- Historical cost, which records items at their original cost, is the most widely used measurement system.
- Current purchasing power adjusts historical cost for changes in the purchasing power of money (i.e., inflation).
- Replacement cost is based on the cost of replacing assets.
- Realisable value is based on the orderly sale value of the assets.
- Present value is based on the present value of the discounted net cash inflows of an asset.
- Modifications to historical cost are the valuing of inventory at the lower of cost or net realisable value or, in the UK, the revaluation of property, plant and equipment.
- Fair value is based on the amount that a market participant would pay for the assets.

Introduction

SOUNDBITE 10.1

Measurement

'What you measure is what you get.'

Robert S. Kaplan and David P. Norton, *Harvard Business Review*, January–February, 1992

Source: The Wiley Book of Business Quotations (1998), p. 295.

Measurement systems underpin not only profit, but also asset valuation. Essentially, a measurement system is the way in which the elements in the accounts are valued. Traditionally, historical cost has been the accepted measurement system. Income, expenses, assets and liabilities have been recorded in the accounting system at cost at the time that they were first recognised. Unfortunately, historical cost, although easy to use, has several severe limitations; for example, it does not take inflation into account. However, although the limitations of historical cost accounting are well known, accountants have been unable to agree on any of the main alternatives such as current purchasing power, replacement cost, realisable value, present value or fair value. A variety of measurement systems are, therefore, used.

Overview

Measurement systems are the processes by which the monetary amounts of items in the financial statement are determined. These systems are fundamental to the determination of profit and to the measurement of net assets. In essence, the measurement system determines the values obtained. Potentially, there are six major measurement systems: historical cost, current purchasing power, replacement cost, realisable value, present value and fair value (see Figure 10.1).

Figure 10.1 The Alternative Measurement Systems

Measurement System	Explanation	Capital Maintenance System
Historical Cost Systems		
i. *Historical cost*	Monetary amounts recorded at the date of original transaction.	Financial capital maintenance.
ii. *Current purchasing power*	Historical cost adjusted by general changes in purchasing power of money (e.g., inflation), often measured using the retail price index (RPI).	Financial capital maintenance.
Current Value Systems		
i. *Replacement cost*	Assets valued at the amounts needed to replace them with an equivalent asset.	Physical capital maintenance.
ii. *Realisable value*	Assets valued at the amount they would fetch in an orderly sale.	Physical capital maintenance.
iii. *Present value*	Assets valued at the discounted present values of future cash inflows.	Physical capital maintenance.
iv. *Fair value*	Assets valued at the amount that a market participant would pay for them.	Physical capital maintenance.

Measurement systems are underpinned by the idea of capital maintenance (see Figure 10.2). Capital maintenance determines that a profit is made only after capital is maintained. This capital can be monetary (monetary capital maintenance) or physical (physical capital maintenance).

Figure 10.2 Capital Maintenance Concepts

What exactly is a capital maintenance concept and why is it important?

A capital maintenance concept is essentially a way of determining whether the 'capital' of a business has improved, deteriorated or stayed the same over a period of time. There are two main capital maintenance concepts (*financial capital maintenance* and *physical capital maintenance*).

Under financial capital maintenance we are primarily concerned with monetary measurement; in particular, the measurement of the net assets. This is true using both historical cost and current purchasing power. For example, under *historical cost* the capital maintenance unit is based on actual monetary units (i.e., actual pounds in the UK). Under *current purchasing power*, it is actual pounds adjusted by the rate of inflation. In both cases, if our closing net assets (as measured in £s) are higher than our opening net assets we make a profit.

Under physical capital maintenance, the physical productive capacity (i.e. operating capacity of the business) must be maintained. For example, can we still produce the same amount of goods or services at the end of a period as we could at the start? We maintain the operating capacity in terms of *replacement costs, realisable values, fair values* or *present values* (i.e., discounted future cash flows). For example, under replacement cost, we are concerned with valuing the operating capacity of the business at the replacement cost of individual assets and liabilities.

Historical cost and current purchasing power both stem from the normal bookkeeping practice of recording transactions at the date they occur in monetary amounts. For current purchasing power, these amounts are then adjusted by the general changes in the purchasing power of money. Under both measurement systems the concern is to maintain the monetary amount of the enterprise's net assets. In both cases, we are therefore concerned with financial capital maintenance. *Replacement cost, realisable value, present value and fair value are sometimes known as current value systems.* They seek to maintain the physical (or operating) capital of the enterprise. The first three systems differ in how they seek to do this. Replacement cost measures assets at the amount it would cost to *replace* them with an equivalent asset. Realisable value (also known as net realisable value or settlement value) measures assets at their sale value. Present value measures the business at the present values of the future net cash flows. These three current value systems can be combined into a 'value to the business' model.

A fourth measurement system, fair value, has recently grown in influence. This is sometimes known as a mark-to-market model as it seeks to capture an asset's market value. These market values may be based on quoted prices in active markets. Fair value is most usually associated with valuing complex financial instruments such as those used by financial institutions. It is similar to realisable value, but ignores transaction costs and takes a market-based rather than an entity perspective. It takes into account a market participant's ability to generate economic benefits by using the asset in the best way possible. It can be defined as the price that will be received when selling the asset or that is paid to transfer a liability between players in the market. See Definition 10.1 for a formal definition of fair value. Fair value has been a particularly contentious topic as many commentators have suggested that fair value accounting facilitated the asset bubble which led to the global financial crisis. This is because the asset valuation was based on rising property prices. As property prices rose, so did the value of the company's assets. Both became overinflated and when the property prices fell, so did the company's assets, which many think exacerbated the financial collapse. Given its dependence on market prices, fair value is crucially dependent on the reliability of active markets. A detailed description of fair value and the value to the business model (sometimes called current value accounting) are beyond the scope of this book.

DEFINITION 10.1

Fair Value

Fair value can be defined as the market value of an asset when it would be sold or a liability when disposed of in a normally functioning market.

It is, however, important to realise two fundamental points. First, historical cost still remains the most common measurement basis adopted by enterprises. Second, although historical cost is much criticised, there is no consensus about which measurement system, if any, should replace it. Disagreement on measurement systems is where attempts to arrive at a consensual conceptual theory have all foundered.

Measurement Systems

In this section, we discuss two of the most important measurement systems: historical cost and replacement cost. Readers interested in the other three measurement systems are referred to more advanced texts such as Geoffrey Whittington's *Inflation Accounting: An Introduction to the Debate*.

Historical Cost

Historical cost has always been the most widely used measurement system. Essentially, transactions are recorded in the books of account at the date the transaction occurred. This original cost is maintained in the books of account and not updated for any future changes in value that might occur. To illustrate, if we paid £5,000 for a building in 1980, this will be the cost that is shown in the statement of financial position when we prepare our accounts in 2014. This is even when the building has increased in value to say £500,000 through inflation. The depreciation will be based on the original value of the asset (i.e., £5,000 not £500,000).

The main strength of historical cost is that it is objective. In other words, you can objectively verify the original cost of the asset. You only need to refer to the original invoice. In addition, historical cost is very easy to use and to understand. Finally, historical cost enables businesses to keep track of their assets.

There is, however, one crucial problem with historical cost. It uses a fixed monetary capital maintenance system, which does not take inflation into account. This failure to take into account changing prices can cause severe problems. In particular, as Soundbite 10.2 shows, it may not accurately value a company's worth.

SOUNDBITE 10.2

Historical Cost Accounting's Limitations

'Historical cost-based financial reporting is not the most efficient way of reflecting a company's true value.'

Mike Starr, Chairman of American Institute of Certified Public Accountants Committee on Enhanced Business Reporting

Source: Nicholas Neveling, Consortium Urges Reporting Reforms, *Accountancy Age*, 17 February 2005, p. 11.

Replacement Cost

Replacement cost attempts to place a realistic value on the assets of a company. It is concerned with maintaining the operating capacity of a business. Essentially, replacement cost asks the question: what would it cost to replace the existing business assets with identical, equivalent assets at today's prices?

Replacement cost is an alternative method of measuring the assets and profits of a business rather than principally a method of tackling inflation. In the Netherlands, replacement costing was successfully used by many businesses, such as Heineken. As Company Snapshot 10.1 shows, Heineken in 2004 valued its property, plant and equipment at replacement cost based on expert valuation. Dutch companies are still permitted to use replacement costing under

Dutch law. However, Heineken, like all European listed companies, now uses IFRS and has, therefore, discontinued replacement costing in its more recent accounts. Indeed, the problem for the Dutch is not so much the difficulties of using replacement cost, but of convincing the rest of the world that it is a worthwhile system.

PAUSE FOR THOUGHT 10.1

Historical Cost and Asset-Rich Companies

The statements of financial position of asset-rich companies, such as banks, may not reflect their true asset values, if prepared under historical cost accounting. Why do you think this might be?

....

If we take banks and building societies as examples of asset-rich companies, these businesses have substantial amounts of prime location property. Almost in every town, banks occupy key properties in central locations. These properties were also often acquired many years ago, indeed possibly centuries ago. Using strict historical cost, these buildings would be recorded in the statement of financial position at very low amounts. This is because over time, money values have changed. If a prime site was purchased for £1,000 in 1700, that might have been worth a lot then. Today, it might be worth say £400 million. Thus, property, plant and equipment will be radically understated, unless revalued.

COMPANY SNAPSHOT 10.1

Replacement Cost and Heineken

Property, Plant and Equipment (Tangible Fixed Assets)
Except for land, which is not depreciated, tangible fixed assets are stated at replacement cost less accumulated depreciation. The following average useful lives are used for depreciation purposes:

Buildings	30–40 years
Plant and equipment	10–30 years
Other fixed assets	5–10 years

The replacement cost is based on appraisals by internal and external experts, taking into account technical and economic developments. Other factors taken into account include the experience gained in the construction of breweries throughout the world. Grants received in respect of investments in tangible fixed assets are deducted from the amount of the investment. Projects under construction are included at cost.

Source: Heineken, *Annual Report 2004*, pp. 84–5. Copyright Heineken H.V.

The main problem with replacement cost is that although the concept is very simple, in practice it is often difficult to arrive at an objective value for the replacement assets. However, in many cases specific indices are available for certain classes of assets, allowing more accurate valuations.

Deficiencies of Historical Cost Accounting

Figure 10.3 on the next page shows how historical cost accounting can give a misleading impression of the profit for the year and of the value of assets in the statement of financial position. In particular, strictly following historical cost will have the effect of:

(i)   encouraging companies to pay out more dividends to shareholders than is wise,
(ii) making companies appear more profitable than they really are, and
(iii) impairing the ability of companies to replace their assets.

In practice, many UK companies now use a modified form of historical cost accounting. This involves revaluing property, often every five years. Depreciation is then based on the revised valuation. However, in some other countries, such as the US, Germany and France, there is still a closer adherence to historical cost.

Illustrative Example of Different Measurement Systems

In Figure 10.4 on page 317, we pull together some of the threads and show how the valuation of an individual asset can vary considerably depending upon the chosen measurement system.

We can, therefore, see that different measurement systems give different asset valuations There are thus six different valuations ranging from £2,500 to £9,947. Realisable value, which is an exit value, gives the lowest valuation at £2,500 while present value, which looks to the future earnings of the company, is £9,947.

The most objective of the measurement systems are probably historical cost and current purchasing power.

	£
• Historical cost	6,000
• Current purchasing power	7,200
• Realisable value	2,500
• Replacement cost	4,000
• Present value	9,947
• Fair value	3,000

It is important to note that, in practice, each measurement system itself could potentially yield many different asset valuations, depending on the underlying assumptions and estimations. For example, present value is crucially dependent on the estimated discount rate (10%), the estimated future cash flows (£4,000), and the timing of those cash flows.

Figure 10.3 The Deficiencies of Historical Cost Accounting

A company's only asset is a building, purchased 10 years ago for £200,000. The replacement cost for an equivalent building is now £2,000,000. The company, which deals only in cash, has profits of £100,000 per annum before depreciation; it distributes 50% of its profits as dividends. The asset is depreciated over 20 years.

(i) Historical Cost Accounts in year 10

Income Statement		Statement of Financial Position	
	£		£
Profit before depreciation	100,000	Property, plant and equipment	200,000
Depreciation	(10,000)	Accumulated depreciation	(100,000)
Profit for year	90,000	Total property, plant and equipment	100,000
		Cash	550,000
		Net assets	650,000

(a) Over the first ten years, the company's net cash inflow is £1,000,000 (£100,000 × 10), minus £450,000 in dividends leaving £550,000 cash in the company. This looks healthy.

(b) The shareholders are happy receiving an annual dividend.

(c) Return on capital employed (taking closing net assets) is:

$$\frac{£90,000}{£650,000} = 13.8\%$$

Everything, therefore, seems pretty good. Unfortunately, the company has only £650,000 in net assets, which is not enough to replace the property, plant and equipment that will cost £2,000,000.

(ii) Replacement Cost Accounts in year 10

Income Statement		Statement of Financial Position	
	£		£
Profit before depreciation	100,000	Property, plant and equipment	2,000,000
Depreciation	(100,000)	Accumulated depreciation	(1,000,000)
Profit for year	–	Total property, plant and equipment	1,000,000
		Cash	1,000,000
		Net assets	2,000,000

(a) In this case, the company makes no profit because the increased depreciation has wiped out all the profits. There is no profit out of which to pay dividends. If the company had paid out dividends during the 10 years, it would have no money left to replace the property, plant and equipment.

(b) The net worth has risen considerably. This is a plus for the company. However, not paying out dividends is a considerable minus.

(c) There is no return on capital employed!

Suddenly, everything appears less rosy. However, the firm can continue in business because it can just about replace its property, plant and equipment (in actual fact, its net assets equal the amount needed to replace the property, plant and equipment). This assumes that the building could be sold for £1,000,000.

Figure 10.4 Example of Different Measurement Systems

JoJo bought a second-hand van two years ago for £10,000. She expects to keep the van for five years. The used van guide states the van is now worth £2,500. If sold, the general price in an active market for such vans is £3,000. Replacement cost for a van in a similar condition is £4,000. The future net cash flows will be £4,000 for the next three years (assume the cash flows occur at the end of the year) and she can borrow money at 10%. The retail price index was 100 when the van was bought and it is 120 now.

	Appropriate value £
Historical Cost	
We base our calculations on the original historical cost of £10,000.	
Using straight line depreciation (£10,000 ÷ 5) = £2,000 p.a.	
Thus, £10,000 − £4,000 (*two years' depreciation*)	6,000
Current Purchasing Power	
We base our calculation on the original historical cost less depreciation. In the calculation above, this was £10,000 – £4,000 = £6,000. We then adjust this for inflation. This is measured using the retail price index, which has increased from 100 to 120.	
£6,000 × $\dfrac{Closing\ RPI}{Opening\ RPI}\left(\dfrac{120}{100}\right)$	7,200
Realisable Value	
In this case, our calculations are based upon the amount of money we would receive for the van if we sold it.	
Used van guide	2,500
Replacement Cost	
In this case, we base our calculations on the amount it would cost to replace the van with a similar asset in a similar condition.	
Similar value asset	4,000
Present Value	
Here, we are interested in looking at the future cash flows generated by the asset. We then discount them back to today's value (see Chapter 17 for further information about discounting).	

£	Discount Factor*	£
4,000	0.9091	3,636
4,000	0.8264	3,306
4,000	0.7513	3,005
		9,947

	9,947
Fair Value	
Fair value: with Fair Value we are interested in the current price which this asset would reach in an active market. We ignore transaction cases. This is similar to net realisable value.	
	3,000

*10% interest discounted back, assumes cash flow is on the last day of each year.

Real Life

The merits of historical cost accounting and the advantages and disadvantages of the competing alternative measurement systems have been debated vigorously for at least 40 years. However, most companies worldwide still mainly use historical cost. Fair value is now, however, used more often, particularly by banks and financial institutions.

This is not to say that experimentation has not occurred. In the Netherlands, for example, Philips, one of the world's leading companies, used replacement cost accounting for over a generation. Finally, Philips abandoned replacement cost, not because of replacement cost's inadequacies, but because of the failure of international financial analysts to understand Philips' accounts. There are, however, still non-listed companies in the Netherlands which use replacement cost. In the UK too, there were a few companies, usually ex-privatised utilities with extensive infrastructure assets, such as British Gas, which until recently used replacement costs.

In both the UK and the US in the 1970s, there were serious attempts to replace historical cost accounting initially with current purchasing power, but later with current value accounting (a mixture of the three current value systems). These methods were thought to be superior to historical cost accounting when dealing with inflation, which was at that time quite high. They were also believed to provide a more realistic valuation of company assets. In the end these attempts failed. The reasons for their failure were quite complex. However, in general, accountants preferred the objectivity of a tried-and-tested, if somewhat flawed, historical cost system to the subjectivity of the new systems. In addition, rates of inflation fell.

The role of accounting measurement in the recent global credit crunch has aroused a lot of attention. This is particularly true of the role of fair value. When the value of financial assets declined then their fair value reduced and so did the valuation of the companies. Whereas some onlookers felt that accounting measurement was only measuring what had happened, others felt that accounting measurement had contributed to the economic problems by eroding company value.

Although the backbone of the accounts is historical cost, there is some limited use of alternative measurement systems. This is usually combined with alternative measurement systems. Inventories are typically valued at the lower of cost and net realisable value. Marketable securities and financial instruments are often valued at market value/fair value. As we pointed out earlier, many UK companies revalue their property every five years. This is particularly common in companies that have a great deal of property, such as hotel chains. However, this periodic revaluation of property means that UK accounts are prepared on a different basis to those in countries, such as France (using French domestic principles) or the US, where periodic revaluations are not permitted. Revaluations are, however, permitted under IFRS.

Conclusion

Different measurement systems will give different figures in the accounts for profit and net assets. The mostly widely used measurement system, historical cost, records and carries transactions in the accounts at their original amounts. Historical cost, however, does not deal well with changes in asset values resulting from, for example, inflation. There are four other traditional main measurement systems (current purchasing power, replacement cost, realisable value, present value). Current purchasing power adjusts historical cost for general changes in the purchasing power of money. Replacement cost records assets at the amounts needed to replace them with equivalent assets. Realisable value records assets at the amounts they would fetch in an orderly sale. Finally, present value discounts future cash inflows to today's monetary values. Although historical cost is the backbone of the accounting measurement systems, there are departures from it, such as the valuation of inventory at the lower of cost or realisable value. In particular, in the UK, many companies revalue their property. A relatively recent new measurement system is fair value, the price the asset would rate in an active market. This is similar to net realisable value. The role of fair value in the credit crunch has been hotly debated.

Selected Reading

The topic of accounting measurement systems can be extremely complex. The first two readings below have been deliberately selected because they are quite accessible to students. Students wishing for a fuller insight into the debate are referred to the book by Geoffrey Whittington below.

1. Accounting Standards Steering Committee (1975), *The Corporate Report*, Section 7, pp. 61–73.
   Although now 40 years old, this report provides a very good, easy-to-read, introduction to the topic.
2. International Accounting Standards Board (IASB) (2011), 'Conceptual Framework', in *International Financial Reporting* (2011), paras 4.54–4.65.
   It presents more modern thinking on the topics and is reasonably easy to follow.

For the Enthusiast

Whittington, G. (1983) *Inflation Accounting: An Introduction to the Debate* (Cambridge University Press).
   For students who enjoy a challenge. Gives a thorough grounding of the inflation debate, which is at the heart of choosing different measurement systems.

Discussion Questions

Questions with numbers in blue have answers at the back of the book.

Q1 'Accounting measurement systems are the skeleton of the accounting body.' Critically evaluate this statement.

Q2 Why is historical cost still so widely used, if it is so deeply flawed?

Q3 What is the difference between a financial capital maintenance concept and a physical capital maintenance concept?

Q4 Why do many UK companies revalue their property? How might this affect profit? Why is this practice unusual internationally?

Go online to discover the extra features for this chapter at
www.wiley.com/college/jones

Chapter 11

The annual report

'It is a yearly struggle: the conflict between public relations experts determined to put a sunny face on somewhat drearier figures, and those determined to tell it like it is, no matter how many "warts" there are on the year's story. The annual report is a vital instrument designed – ideally – to tell the story of a company, its objectives, where the company succeeded or failed, and what the company intends to do next year.'

Kirsty Simpson, 'Glossy, expensive and useless', *Australian Accountant*, September 1997, pp. 16–18.

Learning Outcomes

After completing this chapter you should be able to:

- Explain the nature of the annual report.
- Outline the multiple, conflicting objectives of the annual report.
- Discuss the main contents of the annual report.
- Evaluate how the annual report is used for impression management.

Go online to discover the extra features for this chapter at
www.wiley.com/college/jones

Chapter Summary

- The annual report is a key corporate financial communication document.
- It is an essential part of corporate governance.
- It serves multiple, and sometimes conflicting, roles of stewardship/accountability, decision making and public relations.
- It comprises key audited financial statements: income statement (i.e., profit and loss account), statement of financial position (i.e., balance sheet), and statement of cash flows (i.e., cash flow statement).
- It normally includes at least 22 identifiable sections.
- It includes important non-audited sections such as the chairman's statement.
- Most important companies provide group accounts.
- Goodwill is an important intangible asset in many group accounts.
- Managers use the annual report for impression management.

Introduction

The annual report is well entrenched as a core feature of corporate life. This yearly-produced document is the main channel by which directors report corporate annual performance to their shareholders. All leading companies world wide produce an annual report. In the UK, both listed and unlisted companies produce one. Many other organisations, such as the British Broadcasting Corporation, now also produce their own versions of the annual report. Indeed, in the UK the Labour Government produced the first governmental annual report in 1998. Traditionally, the annual report was a purely statutory document. The modern annual report, however, now has multiple functions, including a public relations role. Modern reports comprise a mixture of voluntary and statutory, audited and unaudited, narrative and non-narrative, financial and non-financial information. They are also governed by a regulatory framework which includes Companies Acts and accounting standards. The modern annual report has become a complex and sophisticated business document. In particular, European listed companies now follow International Financial Reporting Standards. As most publicly available annual reports are those of listed companies, the terminology laid down by the IASB will be used in this chapter.

Definition

In essence, an annual report is a document produced to fulfil the duty of the directors to report to shareholders. It is produced annually and is a mixture of financial and non-financial information. As Definition 11.1 shows, it is a report containing both audited financial information and unaudited, non-financial information.

DEFINITION 11.1

Annual Report

Working definition

A report produced annually by companies comprising both financial and non-financial information.

Formal definition

'A document produced annually by companies designed to portray a 'true and fair' view of the company's annual performance, with audited financial statements prepared in accordance with companies legislation and other regulatory requirements, and also containing other non-financial information.'

CIMA definition

'Package of information including a management report, an auditor's report and a set of financial statements with supportive notes. In the case of companies these are drawn up for a period which is called the accounting reference period, the last day of which is known as the reporting date.'

Source: Chartered Institute of Management Accountants (2005), *Official Terminology*. Reproduced by Permission of Elsevier.

Context

The annual report has evolved over time into an important communications document, especially for large publicly listed companies. Surveys have consistently shown that it is one of the most important sources of financial information. It plays a critical confirmatory role. The earliest annual reports arose out of the need to make directors accountable to their shareholders. The main financial statement was the statement of financial position. In order to ensure that the financial statements fairly represented corporate performance, the annual report was audited. The annual report, therefore, has always played a key role in the control of the directors by the shareholders. The central role of the annual report in external reporting can be seen in Figure 11.1.

In essence, the directors are responsible for the preparation of the financial statements from the accounting records. The actual preparation is normally carried out by accounting staff. An annual report is then compiled, often with the help of a company's public relations department and graphic designers. These graphic designers are responsible for the layout and design of the annual report (providing, for example, colourful graphs and photographs). The annual report's financial content is then audited and disseminated

Figure 11.1 The Annual Report

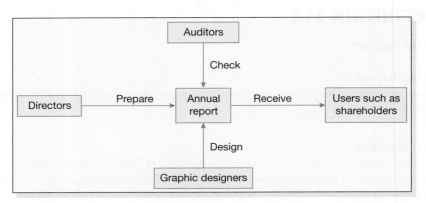

to the main users, principally the shareholders. As discussed in Chapter 9, much of the annual report is mandated by a regulatory framework consisting principally of the requirements of the Companies Acts and accounting standards.

Multiple Roles

The annual report is a social as well as a financial document. Therefore, as society evolves, so does the annual report. The earliest annual reports were stewardship documents. Today's annual report is much more complex, being an amalgam of stewardship and accountability, decision making and public relations. These concepts are discussed below. The first two roles are those traditionally recognised by standard setters. Although it is important to realise that nowadays the IASB prefers decision making rather than stewardship. However, the public relations role is more driven by preparer self-interest.

(i) Stewardship and Accountability

Effectively, stewardship involves the directors reporting their actions to the shareholders. This reflects the origins of financial reporting. In the middle ages, the stewards who managed the estates used to render an annual account of the master's assets (for example, livestock and cereals) to the lord of the manor. The main aim of the accounts, or annual statement, was thus for the lord of the manor to keep a check on the steward's activities. In particular, there was a concern that the steward should not defraud the lord of the manor. An important aspect of stewardship is this accountability. Accountability is traditionally seen as referring to the control and safeguarding of the assets of a company.

Gradually, as the economy became more sophisticated so did the accountability mechanisms. At first, there was a rudimentary statement of assets and liabilities, showing how much the organisation owned and owed. This gradually evolved into the modern statement of financial position. However, the fundamental aim was still to account for the assets and liabilities of the organisation. Accountability tended to diminish in importance with the rise of decision making.

An important modern aspect of stewardship is corporate governance. Essentially, in both Europe and the US, several well-publicised corporate financial scandals (e.g., Polly Peck, Maxwell) led to a growing concern with monitoring the activities of directors. In addition, the privatisation of the utilities created considerable concern over the salaries of so-called 'fat-cat directors'. Real-World Views 11.1 and 11.2 discuss this issue. As can be seen, this issue is apparently perennial and refuses to go away. The committees which looked at corporate governance in the 1990s all stressed the role that corporate financial communication could play in increasing directors' accountability to shareholders. The accounting scandals such as Enron and WorldCom in the US and Parmalat in Italy have reawakened interest in corporate governance. There has been increasing concern with auditor independence and the need for effective audit committees.

REAL-WORLD VIEW 11.1

Directors' Pay: The Continuing Debate

Directors' pay has long been a problem for politicians in the UK. For example, Alex Brummer stated that Stephen Byers, a UK politician, had called for world-class salaries for world-class performance. However, as Brummer pointed out at the time:

'The trouble is that it fits only a handful of the executives and companies in the Guardian's pay survey. Of the 35 or so directors in the million-pounds-plus pay club only a handful – such as those at the drugs companies SmithKline Beecham and Glaxo Wellcome – deliver a world class product.'

Brummer further pointed out that others, for example, Bob Mendelsohn of Royal and Sun Alliance took home £2.4 million without being world class.

Since then directors' pay fuelled by generous remuneration schemes sanctioned by generous remuneration committees have continued to soar. A particular bone of contention has been bank bonuses where bankers, widely seen as failing society and causing the global financial crisis, are still walking away with huge salaries. This caused a rare shareholders revolt at Barclays in 2012.

Source: Alex Brummer, Time is Up for World Class Waffle, *The Guardian*, 20 July 1999.

REAL-WORLD VIEW 11.2

Director's Pay:

Bob Diamond, the new boss of Barclays, has refused to bow to MPs' demands that he waives his 2010 bonus, which could be as much as £8m.

Speaking yesterday, Mr Diamond said he had forgone his bonus in 2008 and 2009 and would decide 'with my family' whether to do so again. He added: 'There was a period of remorse and apology for banks and I think that period needs to be over.'

In a lengthy and sometimes irascible session before the Treasury Select Committee, Mr Diamond attacked the MPs for being 'wrong and unfair' about British banks.

'I really resent the fact that you refer to this as blackjack or casino banking or rogue trading,' he said. 'It's wrong, it's unfair, it's a poor choice of words. We have some fantastically strong financial institutions in this country and frankly they deserve better.'

The banker had been called to appear before the committee to discuss bank competition, but was mostly grilled on pay, leading him to make an impassioned defence of the industry.

He warned that the government could not expect bonuses to be 'isolated' and targeted for regulation and 'assume it won't have consequences'.

He told the MPs that shareholders had not asked for information about this year's bonus pool but were 'very involved' in the process.

Source: Louise Armistead and Harry Wilson, MPs try to shame Barclays boss on pay, *Daily Telegraph*, 12 January 2011, p. 23.

PAUSE FOR THOUGHT 11.1

'Fat Cat' Directors

There has been a great furore about the salaries of 'fat-cat' directors. What justification do you think they tend to give for their salaries? What do their critics argue?

The directors' view

Conventionally, directors argue that they are doing a complex and difficult job. They are running world-class businesses and they, therefore, need to be paid world-class salaries. They also create and add shareholder value because of increased share prices and, therefore, they deserve to be well paid.

The critics' view

Yes, but if the directors are paid on the basis of performance, then we would expect them not to get big bonuses when their organisations are doing less well. However, generally this does not happen. Also, much of the increase in share prices that directors ascribe to themselves is often caused by a general rise in the stock market. This debate has intensified because of the financial crisis and credit crunch. Many believe it is unfair, for example, for bankers to pay themselves big salaries when they are widely perceived to be responsible for the current economic downturn.

(ii) Decision Making

In the twentieth century, decision making has increasingly replaced stewardship as the main role of accounting. This reflects wider developments in society, business and accounting. In particular, decision making is associated with the rise of the modern industrial company.

Industrialisation led to increasingly sophisticated businesses and to the creation of the limited liability company with its divorce of ownership and control. Shareholders were no longer involved in the day-to-day running of the business. They were primarily interested in increases in the value of their share price and in any dividends they received. These dividends were based on profits. Consequently, the income statement became more important relative to the statement of financial position. The primary interest of shareholders shifted from cash and assets to profit. Thus, performance measurement and decision making replaced asset management and stewardship as the prime objective of financial information.

PAUSE FOR THOUGHT 11.2

Engines of Capitalism

Limited liability companies have been called the engines of capitalism. Why do you think this is so?

....

Effectively, limited liability companies are very good at allowing capital to be allocated throughout an economy. There are several advantages to investors. First, they can invest in many companies, not just one. Second, they can sell their shares very easily, assuming a buyer can be found. Third, they stand to lose only the amount of capital they have originally invested. Their personal assets are thus safe.

These new shareholder concerns were officially recognised by two reports in the 1960s and 1970s in the US and the UK. Both reports, *A Statement of Basic Accounting Theory* (American Accounting Association, 1966) in the US and *The Corporate Report* (Accounting Standards Steering Committee, 1975) in the UK, proved turning points in the development of accounting. Before then stewardship had been the generally acknowledged role of accounting. After them, decision-usefulness was generally recognised as the prime criterion. In a sense, decision making and stewardship are linked, for shareholders need to make decisions about how well the directors have managed the company.

In a nutshell, the purpose of the annual report was recognised to be:

> 'to communicate economic measurements of and information about the resources and performance of the reporting entity useful to those having reasonable rights to such information.' (*The Corporate Report*, 1975, para. 3.2)

The decision-making model had been born!

As Definition 11.2 shows, the modern objective of accounting is still recognised as providing users with information so that they can make decisions.

For the shareholder, these economic decisions might involve the purchase or sale of shares. Other users will have different concerns. For example, banks might be principally interested in whether or not to lend a company more money.

DEFINITION 11.2

Decision-Making Objective of Annual Report

Working definition
Providing users, especially shareholders, with financial information so that they can make decisions such as buying or selling their shares.

Formal definition
The IASB broadly sees the objective of financial accounting as the provision of financial information about an organisation that is useful to a range of users, such as existing and potential investors, lenders or creditors, when they are seeking to make decisions. The decisions may be, for example, buying or selling shares or giving loans.

(iii) Public Relations Role

The public relations role reflects the annual report's development over the last 20 years as a major marketing tool. Company management has come to realise that the annual report represents an unrivalled opportunity to 'sell' the corporate image. In part, this only reflects human nature. We all wish to look good. It is a rare person who never attempts to massage the truth; for example, at a job interview. The public relations role of annual reports does, however, provoke strong reactions by some commentators (see Real-World View 11.3).

REAL-WORLD VIEW 11.3

Public Relations and the Annual Report

Queen Isabella was said to have washed only three times in her life, and only once voluntarily. That was when she was married. The other two times were at her birth and death. No wonder Columbus left to discover a new world. Why this olfactory analysis of history? Because this is the time of year when we are inundated with corporate annual reports, and in most of them the letter to the shareholders smells as wretched as Queen Isabella must have.

One of the sad truths about malodorous things is that people tend to get used to them in time. But I'll never become accustomed to the public-relations pap I read in most annual reports. Every year tens of thousands of stale, vapid, and uninspired letters to shareholders appear in elaborate annual reports. They are printed on expensive paper whose gloss and sheen are exceeded only by the glitzy words of the professional PR writer who ghosted the message. They will be read by shareholders who don't understand them – or believe them. Quite often they are hype. Sometimes they are dull. Some are boastful, others apologetic. And they are generally ambiguous.

Source: Sal Marino, *Industry Week,* 5 May 1997, p. 12.

Conflicting Objectives

The standard-setting organisations generally only recognise the first two objectives of financial statements (also by implication of annual reports): stewardship and decision making. Indeed, there is currently heated debate within the accounting community about the relative importance of stewardship vis-à-vis decision making. In effect, these two objectives clash with the public relations role. This is because the stewardship and decision-making roles rely upon the notion of providing a neutral and objective view of the company. However, the public relations view is where managers seek to present a favourable, not a neutral, view of a company's activities. This causes stress, particularly if a company did not perform as well as market analysts had predicted. In these cases, as we see in Chapter 12, there is great pressure for the company management to indulge in impression management.

 PAUSE FOR THOUGHT 11.3

Stewardship or Decision Making

There are broadly two schools of thought about the basic objectives of accounting. First, there are those who think that accounting is all about decision making. This is generally the line followed by the IASB. Others, however, are less convinced. For example, Professor David Myddelton ('Yesterday', *Accountancy Magazine*, March 2010, p. 22) disagrees with the modern-day assumption that the primary purpose of company accounts is decision-usefulness for investors, and presents three main reasons for doing so:

'First, companies publish their accounts much later than nearly all of the many other sources of information for investors. Second, Modern Portfolio Theory of investment implies that a fully-diversified investor need not care much about the results of any specific company. Asset allocation and portfolio re-balancing are far more important.'

And his third reason concludes:

'. . . the vast majority of entities producing accounts do not have investors who are even remotely considering buying or selling shares in them.'

Some commentators often think that more credence should be given to accountability. In particular, that directors should be accountable to their shareholders. The Accounting Community is thus divided.

So what do you think? Should accounting be primarily about decision making?

Main Contents of the Annual Report

Every annual report is unique. The average annual report ranges from about 40–80 pages with many having substantially more pages. Indeed, some annual reports, such as HSBC, run into hundreds of pages. Perhaps unsurprisingly, therefore, the modern annual report is often criticised for being too complex. A company's report presents a wide variety of corporate financial and non-financial information. The traditional financial statements (e.g., statement of financial position, statement of comprehensive income (or income statement and statement of comprehensive income), statement of cash flows) and accompanying financial information (such as notes to accounts) are normally audited. Other parts, such as the chairman's statement, are not. Nowadays, they are also normally positioned at the back of the annual report with the more contextual qualitative information such as the chairman's statement appearing at the front. However, auditors generally review this qualitative information to ensure it is consistent with the audited accounts. In addition, the report is a mixture of voluntary and mandatory (i.e., prescribed by regulation) information, and narrative and non-narrative information. In Figure 11.2, the main sections of a typical annual report are outlined. Although based on UK financial reporting practice, in the main these sections are also found in most European listed companies.

Figure 11.2 Main Sections of a Typical Annual Report

Section	Audited	Narrative (N)	Mandatory (M)
	Formally	Non-Narrative (NN)	Voluntary (V)
1. Statement of comprehensive income (or income statement and statement of comprehensive income)	Yes	NN	M
2. Statement of financial position	Yes	NN	M
3. Statement of cash flows	Yes	NN	M
4. Statement of changes in equity	Yes	NN	M
5. Note on reconciliation of net cash flow to movement in net debt	Yes	NN	M
6. Note on historical cost profits and losses	Yes	NN	M
7. Accounting policies	Yes	N	M
8. Notes to the accounts	Yes	N	M
9. Principal subsidiaries	No	N	M
10. Business Review	No	N	M
11. Chairman's statement	No	N	V
12. Directors' report	No	N	M
13. Review of operations	No	N	V
14. Social and environmental accounting statement	No	N	V
15. Statement of corporate governance	No	N	M
16. Directors' Remuneration Report	No	N	M
17. Auditors' report	Not applicable	N	M

Figure 11.2 Main Sections of a Typical Annual Report (*continued*)

	Formally	*Non-Narrative (NN)*	*Voluntary (V)*
18. Statement of directors' responsibilities for the financial statements	No	N	M
19. Shareholder information	No	N	V
20. Highlights	No	NN	V
21. Historical summary	No	NN	V
22. Shareholder analysis	No	NN	V

A growing trend is for companies to produce multiple reports. Some companies produce an annual report, which contains only financial statements aimed at sophisticated investors, and another report entitled 'Annual Review', which contains simplified financial information and discussion. Companies also may produce separate environmental, corporate responsibility or sustainability reports. These deal with non-financial matters. For example, the environmental report might deal with issues such as pollution, recycling and biodiversity. This is particularly true of large listed companies both in the UK, Europe and the US. Indeed a recent development is the International Integrated Reporting Committee (IIRC), an influential group of business leaders, academics, accountants and regulators who aim to develop a global reporting framework that embraces environmental and financial issues. Integrated reporting is particularly advanced in South Africa where companies produce a separate integrated report that has financial information side by side with environmental data. In addition, many companies produce web-based financial information. For simplicity, however, we assume for the rest of this chapter that a company produces only the traditional annual report.

The main sections of the annual report can be divided into audited and non-audited statements. These are shown in Figure 11.3 and discussed below. In the text, various illustrative figures are included from the annual report of Tesco, a UK listed company, and from the annual report of the Finnish listed company, Nokia.

The Audited Statements

Nine audited financial sections are normally included by most UK companies in their annual reports. The first three (the statement of comprehensive income (see Chapter 3), the statement of financial position (see Chapter 4) and the statement of cash flows (see Chapter 7)) have already been covered in depth earlier. As Soundbite 11.1 shows, they are still very important despite the growth in non-audited material. They are, therefore, only lightly touched on here. The remaining audited statements are all comparatively recent. They can be divided into subsidiary statements and explanatory material. All the sections are presented in a relatively standard way, following guidance laid down in the Companies Acts and accounting standards.

Figure 11.3 Overview of the Annual Report

Contents				
Audited			**Non-audited**	
Main statements	Subsidiary Statements	Explanatory material	Narrative	Non-narrative
1. Statement of comprehensive income (SOCI) (or income statement and statement of comprehensive income) 2. Statement of financial position 3. Statement of cash flows	4. Statement of changes in equity 5. Note on reconciliation of net cash flow to movement in net debt 6. Note on historical cost profits and losses	7. Accounting policies 8. Notes to the accounts 9. Principal subsidiaries	10. Business Review 11. Chairman's statement 12. Directors' report 13. Review of operations 14. Social and environmental accounting statement 15. Statement of corporate governance 16. Directors' remuneration report 17. Auditors' report 18. Statement of directors' responsibilities for the financial statements 19. Shareholder information	20. Highlights 21. Historical summary 22. Shareholder analysis

Main Statements
1. Statement of Comprehensive Income (SOCI) or Income Statement and Statement of Comprehensive Income (also known as Profit and Loss Account). The statement of comprehensive income is widely recognised as one of the two primary financial statements. It focuses on the revenue earned and expenses incurred by the business during the accounting period as well as non-trading items. Importantly, this is not the same as cash received and cash paid. European listed companies follow guidelines for the SOCI as laid down by IAS 1 *Presentation of Financial Statements.* UK non-listed companies usually follow UK Financial Reporting Standard FRS 142, Chapter 5: SOCI and the Income Statement, although they may choose to follow IFRS. An illustration of the income statement for AstraZeneca is given in Company Snapshot 6.3 in Chapter 6.

SOUNDBITE 11.1

The Accounting Numbers

'For all their flaws – and I accept that some can be rather colourful – the numbers in reports and accounts do give you a good solid picture of how the company has actually performed – the cashflow, the strength of the balance sheet, the level of debt.'

Source: Ian Fraser, More than Words, *Accountancy Magazine*, November 2009, p. 39.

The SOCI may be presented as one statement; alternatively it can be presented as two statements: first, the income statement dealing with trading items and arriving at profit for the year and second, the statement of comprehensive income dealing with other items. Practice varies between companies with some companies producing just one statement of comprehensive income whereas others present an income statement and then a statement of comprehensive income. *In this book, we generally present the income statement as one statement*. Other non-trading items are typically outside the scope of this book. As one statement, the statement of comprehensive income deals with profit from trading as well as dealing with *non-trading gains and losses* in a unified statement. The SOCI attempts to highlight all shareholder gains and losses (i.e., not just those from trading). These gains and losses might, for example, be surpluses on property revaluation. Alternatively, as in the case of Tesco in 2010 (see Company Snapshot 11.1), there may be a gain on foreign currency translations, losses on pensions or losses on hedging (insuring against) cash flows. Tesco's statement of

COMPANY SNAPSHOT 11.1

Statement of Comprehensive Income

Group statement of comprehensive income

Year ended 27 February 2010	notes	52 weeks 2010 £m	53 weeks 2009 Restated* £m
Change in fair value of available-for-sale financial assets and investments		1	3
Currency translation differences		343	(275)
Total loss on defined benefit pension schemes	28	(322)	(629)
(Losses)/gains on cash flow hedges:			
Net fair value (losses)/gains		(168)	505
Reclassified and reported in the Group Income Statement		5	(334)
Tax relating to components of other comprehensive income	6	54	375
Total other comprehensive income		(87)	(355)
Profit for the year		2,336	2,138
Total comprehensive income for the year		2,249	1,783
Attributable to:			
Owners of the parent		2,222	1,784
Minority interests		27	(1)
		2,249	1,783

*See note 1 Accounting policies.

Source: Tesco PLC, *Annual Report and Financial Statements 2010*, p. 71.

comprehensive income just shows the non-trading gains and losses. Tesco also produced a separate income statement.

2. *The Statement of Financial Position*. It is much debated whether the statement of financial position or the income statement are the most important for decision making. The statement of financial position focuses on assets, liabilities and shareholders' funds (i.e., equity or capital employed) at a particular point in time (the reporting date). The statement of financial position, along with the income statement, is prepared from the trial balance. The statement of financial position is commonly used to assess the liquidity of a company, whereas the income statement focuses on profit. An illustration of the statement of financial position for AstraZeneca is given in Company Snapshot 6.4 in Chapter 6.

3. *Statement of Cash Flows*. Unlike the previous two statements, which use the matching basis and are prepared from the trial balance, the statement of cash flows is usually prepared by deduction from the income statement and statements of financial position. It is a relatively new statement; for example, introduced in the UK in 1991. The objective of the statement of cash flows is to report and categorise cash inflows and outflows during a particular period. In Company Snapshot 11.2, Tesco PLC's Statement of Cash Flows for 2010 is given (note that Tesco still prefer to use the old UK GAAP terminology, cash flow statement).

COMPANY SNAPSHOT 11.2

Tesco PLC's Cash Flow Statement (Statement of Cash Flows)

Year ended 27 February 2010	notes	52 weeks 2010 £m	53 weeks 2009 £m
Cash flows from operating activities			
Cash generated from operations	31	5,947	4,978
Interest paid		(690)	(562)
Corporation tax paid		(512)	(456)
Net cash from operating activities		4,745	3,960
Cash flows from investing activities			
Acquisition of subsidiaries, net of cash acquired		(65)	(1,275)
Proceeds from sale of property, plant and equipment		1,820	994
Purchase of property, plant and equipment and investment property		(2,855)	(4,487)
Proceeds from sale of intangible assets		4	–
Purchase of intangible assets		(163)	(220)
Increase in loans to joint ventures		(45)	(242)
Investments in joint ventures and associates		(4)	(30)

COMPANY SNAPSHOT 11.2 (*Continued*)

Year ended 27 February 2010	notes	52 weeks 2010 £m	53 weeks 2009 £m
Investments in short-term and other investments		(1,918)	(1,233)
Proceeds from sale of short-term investments		1,233	360
Dividends received		35	69
Interest received		81	90
Net cash used in investing activities		(1,877)	(5,974)
Cash flows from financing activities			
Proceeds from issue of ordinary share capital		167	130
Increase in borrowings		862	7,387
Repayment of borrowings		(3,601)	(2,733)
Repayment of obligations under finance leases		(41)	(18)
Dividends paid		(968)	(883)
Dividends paid to minority interests		(2)	(3)
Own shares purchased		(24)	(265)
Net cash from financing activities		(3,607)	(3,615)
Net (decrease) increase in cash and cash equivalents		(739)	1,601
Cash and cash equivalents at beginning of year		3,509	1,788
Effect of foreign exchange rate changes		49	120
Cash and cash equivalents at end of year	19	2,819	3,509

Source: Tesco PLC, *Annual Report and Financial Statements 2010*, p. 74.

Subsidiary Statements

4. Statement of Changes in Equity. This statement highlights major changes to the ownership claims of shareholders. These include profit (or loss) for the year, annual dividends and new share capital. In Tesco's statement of changes in equity (Company Snapshot 11.3), Tesco has chosen to show all the changes in other comprehensive income (thus replicating the information shown in the statement of comprehensive income in Company Snapshot 11.1) and then show the share and dividend movements. It could have just begun with the total comprehensive income of £2,249 m.

5. Note on Reconciliation of Net Cash Flow to Movement in Net Debt. This statement seeks to reconcile the increase in cash flow calculated from the statement of cash flows to the net debt. As Tesco's 2010 statement (Company Snapshot 11.4) shows, it specifies increases and decreases in debt and cash flow.

COMPANY SNAPSHOT 11.3

Tesco PLC's Statement of Changes in Equity

	Issued share capital £m	Share premium £m	Other reserves £m	Capital redemption reserve £m	Hedging reserve £m	Translation reserve £m	Treasury shares £m	Retained earnings £m	Total £m	Minority interest £m	Total equity £m
	ATTRIBUTABLE TO OWNERS OF THE PARENT										
At 28 February 2009 (restated*)	395	4,638	40	13	175	173	(229)	7,644	12,849	57	12,906
Profit for the year	–	–	–	–	–	–	–	2,327	2,327	9	2,336
Other comprehensive income											
Change in fair value of available-for-sale financial assets	–	–	–	–	–	–	–	1	1	–	1
Currency translation differences	–	–	–	–	–	325	–	–	325	18	343
Loss on defined benefit schemes	–	–	–	–	–	(2)	–	(320)	(322)	–	(322)
Loss on cash flow hedges	–	–	–	–	(163)	–	–	–	(163)	–	(163)
Tax on components of other comprehensive income	–	–	–	–	–	(33)	–	87	54	–	54
Total other comprehensive income	–	–	–	–	(163)	290	–	(232)	(105)	18	(87)
Total comprehensive income	–	–	–	–	(163)	290	–	2,095	2,222	27	2,249
Transactions with owners											
Purchase of treasury shares	–	–	–	–	–	–	(24)	–	(24)	–	(24)
Share-based paymens	–	–	–	–	–	–	73	168	241	–	241
Issue of shares	4	163	–	–	–	–	–	–	167	–	167
Purchase of minority interest	–	–	–	–	–	–	–	91	91	3	94
Dividends paid to minority interests	–	–	–	–	–	–	–	–	–	(2)	(2)
Dividends authorised in the year	–	–	–	–	–	–	–	(968)	(968)	–	(968)
Tax on items charged to equity	–	–	–	–	–	–	–	18	18	–	18
Transactions with owners	4	163	–	–	–	–	49	(691)	(475)	1	(474)
At 27 February 2010	399	4,801	40	13	12	463	(180)	9,048	14,596	85	14,681
At 23 February 2008	393	4,511	40	12	4	245	(204)	6,814	11,815	87	11,902
IFRIC 13 restatement	–	–	–	–	–	–	–	(29)	(29)	–	(29)
At 23 February 2008 (restated*)	393	4,511	40	12	4	245	(204)	6,785	11,786	87	11,873
Profit for the year	–	–	–	–	–	–	–	2,133	2,133	5	2,138

COMPANY SNAPSHOT 11.3 (Continued)

	Issued share capital £m	Share premium £m	Other reserves £m	Capital redemption reserve £m	Hedging reserve £m	Translation reserve £m	Treasury shares £m	Retained earnings £m	Total £m	Minority interest £m	Total equity £m
			ATTRIBUTABLE TO OWNERS OF THE PARENT								
Other comprehensive income											
Change in fair value of available-for-sale investments	–	–	–	–	–	–	–	3	3	–	3
Currency translation differences	–	–	–	–	–	(269)	–	–	(269)	(6)	(275)
Loss on defined benefit schemes	–	–	–	–	–	(2)	–	(627)	(629)	–	(629)
Gains on cash flow hedges	–	–	–	–	171	–	–	–	171		171
Tax on components of other comprehensive income	–	–	–	–	–	199	–	176	375	–	375
Total other comprehensive income	–	–	–	–	171	(72)	–	(448)	(349)	(6)	(355)
Total comprehensive income	–	–	–	–	171	(72)	–	1,685	1,784	(1)	1,783
Transaction with owners											
Purchase of treasury shares	–	–	–	–	–	–	(165)	–	(165)	–	(165)
Share-based payments	–	–	–	–	–	–	140	68	208	–	208
Issue of shares	3	127	–	–	–	–	–	–	130	–	130
Share buy-backs	(1)	–	–	1	–	–	–	–	–	–	–
Purchase of minority interest	–	–	–	–	–	–	–	–	–	(26)	(26)
Dividends paid to minority interests	–	–	–	–	–	–	–	–	–	(3)	(3)
Fair value reserve arising on acquisition of Tesco Bank	–	–	–	–	–	–	–	(71)	(71)	–	(71)
Dividends authorised in the year	–	–	–	–	–	–	–	(883)	(883)	–	(883)
Tax on items charged to equity	–	–	–	–	–	–	–	60	60	–	60
Transaction with owners	2	127	–	1	–	–	(25)	(826)	(721)	(29)	(750)
At 28 February 2009 (restated*)	395	4,638	40	13	175	173	(229)	7,644	12,849	57	12,906

* See note 1 Accounting policies.

Source: Tesco PLC, *Annual Report and Financial Statements 2010*, p. 73.

COMPANY SNAPSHOT 11.4

Tesco PLC's Reconciliation of Net Cash Flow to Movement in Net Debt Note

Year ended 27 February 2010	note	52 weeks 2010 £M	53 weeks 2009 £M
Net (decrease)/increase in cash and cash equivalents		(739)	1,601
Investment in Tesco Bank		(230)	–
Elimination of net increase in Tesco bank cash and cash equivalents		(167)	(37)
Debt acquired on acquistion of Homever		–	(611)
Transfer of joint venture loan receivable on acquisition of Tesco Bank		–	(91)
Net cash inflow (outflow) from debt and lease financing		2,780	(4,636)
Dividend received from Tesco Bank		150	–
Increase in short-term investments		81	873
Increase in joint venture loan receivables		45	242
Other non-cash movements		(249)	(759)
Decrease/(increase) in net debt in the year		1,671	(3,418)
Opening net debt	32	(9,600)	(6,182)
Closing net debt	32	(7,929)	(9,600)

NB. The reconciliation of net cash flow to movement in net debt note is not a primary statement and does not form part of the cash flow statement and forms part of the notes to the financial statements.

Source: Tesco PLC, *Annual Report and Financial Statements 2010*, p. 74.

6. *Note on Historical Cost Profits and Losses.* If the accounts are prepared under the historical cost convention then the original cost of assets is recorded in the accounts. However, sometimes assets, particularly property, will be revalued. These assets are not then included in the accounts at their original purchase price. Depreciation on the revalued property will then be more than on the original cost. This note records any such differences caused by departures from the historical cost convention. Tesco records its property, plant and equipment at cost so there is no note on historical cost profits and losses.

Explanatory Material
7. *Accounting Policies.* Companies must describe the accounting policies they use to prepare the financial statements. The flexibility inherent within accounting means that

companies have a choice of accounting policies in areas such as foreign currencies, goodwill, pensions, sales and inventories. Different accounting policies will result in different accounting figures. Nokia's policy on inventories is given as an illustration (see Company Snapshot 11.5).

COMPANY SNAPSHOT 11.5

Policy on Inventories

Inventories are stated at the lower of cost or net realisable value. Cost is determined using standard cost, which approximates actual cost, on a FIFO (first in first out) basis. Net realisable value is the amount that can be realised from the sale of the inventory in the normal course of business after allowing for the costs of realisation.

In addition to the cost of materials and direct labour, an appropriate proportion of production overhead is included in the inventory values.

An allowance is recorded for excess inventory and obsolescence based on the lower of cost or net realisable value.

Source: Nokia, *Annual Report 2010*, p. 24. Reproduced by permission.

8. *Notes to the Accounts*. These notes provide additional information about items in the accounts. They are often quite extensive. For example, in Tesco's 2014 annual report the main financial statements take up five pages, but the 35 notes take up a further 47 pages. These notes flesh out the detail of the three main financial statements. They cover a variety of topics. For example, the first six Tesco notes cover prior year adjustment, segmental analysis, operating profit, employee profit-sharing, profit on ordinary activities before taxation, and employment costs. The notes to accounts can be crucial. 'The numbers are just part of the story. The balance sheet is just a snapshot. It captures some of the picture but not all of it so that's why the notes to the accounts are important' (Jill Treanor, *The Guardian*, 6 March 2000, p. 28).

9. *Principal Subsidiaries*. Most large companies consist of many individual companies arranged as the parent (or holding company) and its subsidiaries. Collectively, they are known as groups (see later in this chapter for a fuller explanation of groups). In the case of a group, there will be a listing of the parent (i.e., main) company's subsidiary companies (i.e., normally those companies where over 50% of the shares are owned by the parent company) and associate companies (normally where between 20% and 50% of shares are owned by the parent company).

The Non-Audited Sections

The amount of non-audited information in annual reports has mushroomed over the last 30 years. It has caught even experienced observers by surprise. Narrative information has grown in importance over the last generation until as Deloitte (2010) point out, almost half of the annual report is narrative (see Real-World View 11.4).

REAL-WORLD VIEW 11.4

Accounting Narratives

The balance of narrative versus financial statements as a proportion of the total annual report has shifted slightly from the prior year. As shown in figure 2, below, financial statements now represent on average 2% more of the total report than last year at 48% (2008: 46%). The overall shift is to an increase in length of the financial statements. The larger companies continue to devote more of the report to narrative information than the middle and smaller companies, with total narrative of 56%, 50% and 45% respectively (2008: 59%, 51% and 47% respectively). The relative decline between 2008 and 2009 may be due to the factors referred to above regarding information being moved to company websites or separate reports.

Figure 2 What is the balance of narrative and financial reporting in the annual report?

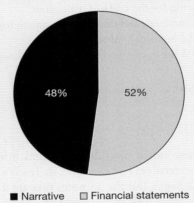

■ Narrative   ☐ Financial statements

Source: Deloitte (2010) *A Telling Performance, Surveying Narrative Reporting in Annual Reports.*

SOUNDBITE 11.2

Narrative Reporting

'Indeed, the financial statements are becoming a technical appendix, play a supporting role to a evolving narrative.'

Source: Michael Power, *Accountancy Magazine*, February 2011, Pantomime Accounting, p. 22.

The non-audited information is extremely varied, but can be broadly divided into narrative and non-narrative information. The *narrative* information consists mainly of the chairman's statement, the directors' report, the business review and the auditors' report. As Soundbite 11.2 shows, some argue that narrative reporting is now the key driver in an annual report. By contrast, the *non-narrative* information mainly comprises the highlights and the historical summary. Although these sections are not audited, the auditor is required to review the non-narrative information to see if there are material misstatements or material inconsistencies with the financial statements. If there are, the auditors consider whether any information needs to be amended. Unfortunately, all this is very subjective and, in reality, little guidance is given to auditors.

Narrative Sections

10. Business Review. The operating and financial review (OFR) represented a major innovation in UK financial reporting. For the first time, regulators formally recognised the importance of qualitative, non-financial information. It enabled companies to provide a formalised, structured and narrative explanation of financial performance. The ASB introduced the OFR as a voluntary statement in 1993. It had two parts: first, the operating review which discusses items such as a company's operating results, profit and dividends; second, the financial review which covers items such as capital structure and treasury policy. The OFR aimed to provide investors with more relevant information. In an interesting example of government interference in UK accounting, the Government in November 2005 decided to abolish the proposed mandatory status of the OFR. This is discussed in Pause for Thought 11.4. It has been replaced with a European piece of legislation, the Business Review. This is a narrative report and covers items such as the company's strategy, its business model, its investment policies and its future plans.

PAUSE FOR THOUGHT 11.4

The Operating and Financial Review (OFR)

The Operating and Financial Review is a document that was originally suggested by the UK's Accounting Standards Board. It was a document whereby companies could present an extended narrative on areas such as risks or social and environmental information. It was going to be made mandatory but then the Labour Government scrapped it. The Coalition Government in 2010, however, planned to reinstate it.

So what would you do? Scrap it or reinstate it?

11. Chairman's Statement. This is the longest-established accounting narrative. It is provided voluntarily by nearly all companies. The chairman's statement provides a personalised overview of the company's performance over the past year. Most chairman's statements cover strategy, the financial performance and future prospects. It is also traditional for the chairman to thank the employees and retiring directors.

12. Directors' Report. The directors' report is prescribed by law. Its principal objective is to supplement the financial information with information that is considered vital for a full appre-

PAUSE FOR THOUGHT 11.5

Auditing the Accounting Narratives

Auditors check that the accounts give a true and fair view of the company's performance.

What difficulties do you think an auditor might have if called upon to audit the narrative sections of the annual report, such as the chairman's statement?

The main difficulty is deciding how to audit the written word. Usually, auditors audit figures. They can thus objectively trace these back to originating documentation. The problem with accounting narratives is that they are very subjective. How do you audit phrases such as 'We have had a good year' or 'Profit has increased substantially'?

ciation of the company's activities. Items presented here (or elsewhere in the accounts – an increasingly common practice) might include any changes in the company's activities, proposed dividends, and charitable and political gifts.

13. *Review of Operations.* This section forms a natural complement to the chairman's statement. Whereas the chairman provides the overview, the chief executive reviews the individual business operations, often quite extensively. Normally, the chief executive discusses, in turn, each individual business or geographical segment.

SOUNDBITE 11.3

Sustainability Information

'Accounting mechanisms have not, for the moment at least, kept pace with our requirements for sustainability information.'

Prince Charles

Source: Accountancy Age, 2 June 2005, p. 12.

14. *Social and Environmental Accounting Statement.* A growing number of companies are reporting social and environmental, social responsibility or sustainability information. For example, over 70% of the UK's top 350 listed companies report such information. This information is largely voluntary. Increasingly, companies are producing separate stand-alone environmental reports or sustainability reports. There is also a trend towards integrated reporting (i.e., combining financial and non-financial environmental information in one single report). However, they may also include sections in their annual report. For example, J.D. Wetherspoon's in 2010 included a corporate social responsibility section in its 2010 annual report. This covered, inter alia, responsible drink retailing, the environment, and community and charitable activities.

15. Statement of Corporate Governance. This statement arises out of the drive to make directors more accountable to their shareholders. The corporate governance statement is governed by stock market requirements. The issues usually covered are risk management, treasury management, internal controls, going concern and auditors. A major objective is to present a full and frank discussion of the directors' remuneration. Contained within this section is often a Directors' Remuneration Report. However, growing numbers of companies record this separately.

16. Directors' Remuneration Report. This includes details of directors' pay. It may include details of the remuneration committee, the remuneration policy and the main components of the directors' pay (for example: basic salary, incentives, bonuses, share options and performance-related pay). There is also a graph showing the company's total shareholder return with an appropriate stock market index (see Company Snapshot 11.6 for Tesco PLC's 2010 performance graph). This is headed total shareholder return. It compares Tesco's share price against the FTSE 100 and Eurofirst Food and Drug Index over a ten-year period. Tesco is shown to out perform these other indices. This graph helps shareholders to compare directors' remuneration to company performance.

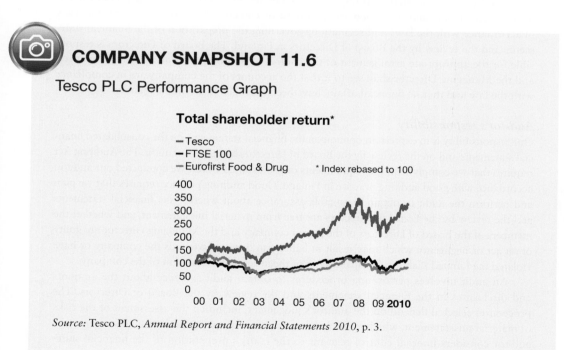

COMPANY SNAPSHOT 11.6

Tesco PLC Performance Graph

Total shareholder return*

- Tesco
- FTSE 100
- Eurofirst Food & Drug   * Index rebased to 100

Source: Tesco PLC, *Annual Report and Financial Statements 2010*, p. 3.

17. Auditors' Report. The audit is an independent examination of the financial statements. An example of an auditors' report for Nokia, a Finnish company, is given in Company Snapshot 11.7. An example of a UK company's audit report is given for Rentokil in Company Snapshot 9.1.

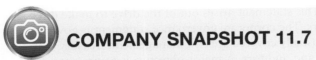

COMPANY SNAPSHOT 11.7

Independent Auditors' Report

To the Annual General Meeting of Nokia Corporation

We have audited the accounting records, the financial statements, the review by the Board of Directors and the administration of Nokia Corporation for the year ended 31 December 2010. The financial statements comprise the consolidated statement of financial position, income statement, statement of comprehensive income, cash flow statement, statement of changes in shareholder's equity and notes to the consolidated financial statements, as well as the parent company's balance sheet, income statement, cash flow statement and notes to the financial statements.

Responsibility of the Board of Directors and the Managing Director

The Board of Directors and the Managing Director are responsible for the preparation of consolidated financial statements that give a true and fair view in accordance with International Financial Reporting Standards (IFRS) as adopted by the EU, as well as for the preparation of financial statements and the review by the Board of Directors that give a true and fair view in accordance with the laws and regulations governing the preparation of the financial statements and the review by the Board of Directors in Finland. The Board of Directors is responsible for the appropriate arrangement of the control of the company's accounts and finances, and the Managing Director shall see to it that the accounts of the company are in compliance with the law and that its financial affairs have been arranged in a reliable manner.

Auditor's responsibility

Our responsibility is to express an opinion on the financial statements, on the consolidated financial statements and on the review by the Board of Directors based on our audit. The Auditing Act requires that we comply with the requirements of professional ethics. We conducted our audit in accordance with good auditing practice in Finland. Good auditing practice requires that we plan and perform the audit to obtain reasonable assurance about whether the financial statements and the review by the Board of Directors are free from material misstatement, and whether the members of the Board of Directors of the parent company and the Managing Director are guilty of an act or negligence which may result in liability in damages towards the company or have violated the Limited Liability Companies Act or the articles of association of the company.

An audit involves performing procedures to obtain audit evidence about the amounts and disclosures in the financial statements and the review by the Board of Directors. The procedures selected depend on the auditor's judgement, including the assessment of the risks of material misstatement, whether due to fraud or error. In making those risk assessments, the auditor considers internal control relevant to the entity's preparation of the financial statements and the review by the Board of Directors that give a true and fair view in order to design audit procedures that are appropriate in the circumstances, but not for the purpose of expressing an opinion on the effectiveness of the company's internal control. An audit also includes evaluating the appropriateness of accounting policies used and the reasonableness of

COMPANY SNAPSHOT 11.7 (*continued*)

accounting estimates made by management, as well as evaluating the overall presentation of the financial statements and the review by the Board of Directors.

We believe that the audit evidence we have obtained is sufficient and appropriate to provide a basis for our audit opinion.

Opinion on the consolidated financial statements

In our opinion, the consolidated financial statements give a true and fair view of the financial position, financial performance, and cash flows of the group in accordance with International Financial Reporting Standards (IFRS) as adopted by the EU.

Opinion on the company's financial statements and the review by the Board of Directors

In our opinion, the financial statements and the review by the Board of Directors give a true and fair view of both the consolidated and the parent company's financial performance and financial position in accordance with the laws and regulations governing the preparation of the financial statements and the review by the Board of Directors in Finland. The information in the review by the Board of Directors is consistent with the information in the financial statements.

Other opinions

We support that the financial statements should be adopted. The proposal by the Board of Directors regarding the distribution of the profit shown in the balance sheet is in compliance with the Limited Liability Companies Act. We support that the Members of the Board of Directors and the Managing Director should be discharged from liability for the financial period audited by us.

Helsinki, March 11, 2011

PricewaterhouseCoopers Oy
Authorised Public Accountants

Merja Lindh
Authorised Public Account

Source: Nokia, *Annual Report 2010*, p. 82. Reproduced by permission.

Companies are legally required to publish the auditors' report. In essence, the report states whether the financial statements present a 'true and fair view' of the company's activities over the previous financial year. It sets out the respective responsibilities of directors and auditors as well as spelling out the work carried out to arrive at the auditors' opinion.

The auditors' report thus outlines the respective responsibilities of directors and auditors, the basis of the audit opinion and how the auditors arrived at their opinion. PricewaterhouseCoopers, the auditors of Nokia, are one of the world's leading auditing partnerships.

18. *Statement of Directors' Responsibilities for the Financial Statements.* This statement (see Company Snapshot 11.8) was introduced because of a general misconception by the general public of the purpose of an audit compared with the actual nature of an audit as

COMPANY SNAPSHOT 11.8

Statement of Directors' Responsibilities

The Directors are required by the Companies Act 2006 to prepare financial statements for each financial year which give a true and fair view of the state of affairs of the company and the Group as at the end of the financial year and of the profit or loss for the financial year. Under that law the Directors are required to prepare the Group financial statements in accordance with International Financial Reporting Standards (IFRSs) as endorsed by the European Union (EU) and have elected to prepare the Company financial statements in accordance with UK Accounting Standards.

In preparing the Group and Company financial statements, the Directors are required to:

- select suitable accounting policies and then apply them consistently;
- make reasonable and prudent judgements and estimates;
- for the Group financial statements, state whether they have been prepared in accordance with IFRS, as endorsed by the EU;
- for the Company financial statements state whether applicable UK Accounting Standards have been followed; and
- prepare the financial statements on the going concern basis, unless it is inappropriate to presume that the Group and the Company will continue in business.

The Directors confirm that they have complied with the above requirements in preparing the financial statements.

The Directors are responsible for keeping proper accounting records which disclose with reasonable accuracy at any time, the financial position of the Company and the Group, and which enable them to ensure that the financial statements and the Directors' Remuneration Report comply with the Companies Act 2006, and as regards the Group financial statements, Article 4 of the IAS Regulation.

The Business Review includes a fair review of the business and important events impacting it, as well as a description of the principal risks and uncertainties of the business.

The Directors are responsible for the maintenance and integrity of the Annual Review and Summary Financial Statement and Annual Report and Financial Statements published on the Group's corporate website. Legislation in the UK concerning the preparation and dissemination of financial statements may differ from legislation in other jurisdictions.

The Directors have general responsibility for taking such steps as are reasonably open to them to safeguard the assets of the Group and of the Company and to prevent and detect fraud and other irregularities.

Source: Tesco PLC, *Annual Report and Financial Statement 2010*, p. 68.

understood by auditors. The directors must spell out their responsibilities which include (i) keeping proper accounting records; (ii) preparing financial statements in accordance with the Companies Act 2006; (iii) selecting suitable accounting policies consistently; (iv) stating whether Group and Company financial statements are following appropriate standards; (v) preparing the financial statements under the going concern basis and (vi) making reasonable and prudent judgements and estimates.

In the case of Tesco, in 2010, it is noteworthy that the Group financial statements are prepared following IFRS, as endorsed by the EU, while the parent company accounts are still prepared following UK GAAP.

19. Shareholder Information. Companies increasingly include a variety of shareholder information. This might, for example, include a financial calendar, share price details, shareholder analysis (see item 22) or notice of the AGM. The information may be narrative or non-narrative in nature.

Non-Narrative Sections

20. Highlights. This very popular feature normally occurs at the start of the annual report, often accompanied by graphs of selected figures. This section provides an at-a-glance summary of selected figures and ratios.

In Tesco's report (Company Snapshot 11.9), for example, group sales, group profit, profit before tax, earnings per share, dividend per share, group enterprise value (market capitalisation plus net debt) and return on capital employed are the financial ratios highlighted. The financial highlights may be seen as an abridged version of the historical summary.

21. Historical Summary. The historical summary is a voluntary recommendation of the stock exchange. Indeed, in the UK, it is one of the very few regulations set out by the stock

COMPANY SNAPSHOT 11.9

Financial Highlights

Group sales (including VAT)*	+6.8%
Underlying profit before tax	+10.1%
Group profit before tax	+10.4%
Underlying diluted earnings per share**	+9.1%
Diluted earnings per share	+9.8%
Dividend per share	+9.1%

All growth figures reported on a 52-week basis.

COMPANY SNAPSHOT 11.9 (*continued*)

52 weeks ended 27 February 2010	2009/10	2008/9‡	
		52 weeks	53 weeks
Group sales (£m) (including VAT)*	62,537	58,570	59,426
Group revenue (£m) (excluding VAT)	56,910	53,115	53,898
Group trading profit (£m)	3,412	3,039	3,086
Underlying profit before tax (£m)	3,395	3,083	3,124
Group profit before tax (£m)	3,176	2,876	2,917
Underlying diluted earnings per share (p)	31.66	28.50	28.87
Dividend per share (p)	13.05	—	11.96
Group enterprise value (£bn) (market capitalisation plus net debt)	41.4	—	35.9
Return on capital employed	12.1%	—	12.8%

* Group sales (inc. VAT) excludes the accounting impact of IFRIC 13 (Customer Loyalty Programmes).
** Growth in underlying diluted EPS calculated on a constant tax rate basis.
‡ Restated for the impact of IFRIC 13 and IFRS 2.

Source: Tesco PLC, *Annual Report and Financial Statements 2010*, Inside Cover.

exchange. Usually, companies choose to present five years of selected data from both the statement of financial position and the income statement.

22. *Shareholder Analysis*. In many ways this item supplements item 19, shareholder information. It provides detailed analysis of the shareholders, for example, by size of shareholding.

These 22 items are by no means exhaustive; for example, J.D. Wetherspoon's plc, the pub chain, provides a list of its Directors, officers and advisers.

Presentation

The style of the annual report is becoming much more important. Companies are increasingly presenting key financial information as graphs rather than as tables. This information is voluntary and generally often supplements the mandatory information. Many companies use graphs to provide oases of colour and interest in otherwise dry statutory documents. In many cases, the graphs are presented at the front along with the highlights.

Tesco, for example, in 1999 provided five-year graphs of group sales, group operating profit, earnings per share, and operating cash flow and capital expenditure (see Company Snapshot 11.10).

Photographs are also common in annual reports. These may be of employees or products. However, often they act as 'mood music' with no obvious relationship to the actual content of the report.

The increased use of the Internet provides many opportunities for companies to present their annual reports on their websites. Many companies are now experimenting with this new presentational format, often using varied presentational methods. Figure 11.4 on page 350 gives some well-known company websites and students are encouraged to visit them.

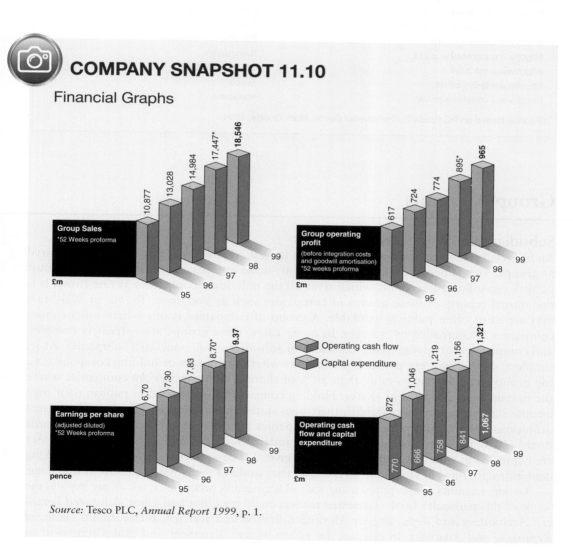

COMPANY SNAPSHOT 11.10

Financial Graphs

Source: Tesco PLC, *Annual Report 1999*, p. 1.

Figure 11.4 Well-Known Company Websites

Internet Address	Description
(a) Information on Companies	
http://www.annualreports.com	Annual reports of US firms
http://www.companiesonline.com	Identifies US companies
http://www.ukdirectory.com	UK websites by sector
(b) 10 Company Web Sites	
http://www.bp.com	British Petroleum
http://www.bt.com	British Telecom
http://www.british-airways.com	British Airways
http://www.marks-and-spencer.co.uk	Marks & Spencer
http://www.manutd.com	Manchester United
http://www.sainsburys.co.uk	Sainsbury's
http://www.gsk.com	GlaxoSmithKline
http://www.tesco.co.uk	Tesco
http://www.vodafone.co.uk	Vodafone

Source: Based on PC Guide 2: *The Internet Guide*, Mark Goode, 2004.

Group Accounts

Subsidiary and Associated Companies

An interesting feature of most of the world's largest companies is that they are structured as groups. This is because companies often buy other companies. All the companies must publish consolidated accounts which treat all the individual companies as one entity. It is the annual reports of these groups of companies such as Vodafone, Toyota or Wal-Mart that are most often publicly available. A group of companies is one where one or more companies is controlled by another. In many cases, these groups are extremely complex and complicated involving many hundreds of subsidiary and associated companies. At its simplest, *subsidiaries* are normally companies where the parent or holding company (i.e., top group company) owns more than 50% of shares and *associates* are companies where the parent owns 20–50% of shares. Holding companies do not need to publish their own income statement, but must publish their own statement of financial position. The formal definitions of subsidiary and associated companies provided by the Accounting Standards Board (ASB), the International Accounting Standards Board (IASB) and the Companies Act are expressed in complex language. They are given for completeness. However, the working definitions provided in Definition 11.3 are all that students really need to know at this stage.

Group accounts are prepared using special accounting procedures, which are beyond the scope of this particular book (interested readers could try Elliot and Elliot, *Advanced Financial Accounting and Reporting*, or Alexander, Britton and Jorrisen, *International Financial Reporting and Analysis*). In essence, the group income statement and group statement of

DEFINITION 11.3

1. Subsidiary Company

Working definition

A company where more than half the shares are owned by another company or which is effectively controlled by another company, or is a subsidiary of a subsidiary.

2. Associated Company

Working definition

A company in which 20–50% of the shares are owned by another company or one in which another company has a significant influence.

financial position attempt to portray the whole group's performance and financial position rather than that of individual companies.

Thus, in Figure 11.5, the group comprises seven companies. Company A is the parent company and owns over 50% of companies B and C, making them subsidiaries. Company B also owns more than 50% of the shares of companies B1 and B2. Companies B1 and B2 thus become sub-subsidiaries of Company A. These four companies (B, C, B1 and B2) are therefore consolidated as subsidiaries using normal accounting procedures. In addition, appropriate proportions of companies D and E are taken into the group accounts since these two companies are associates as between 20% and 50% of the shares are held. Overall, therefore, we have the aggregate financial performance of the whole group. One group set of financial statements is prepared. It is these group accounts that are normally published in the annual report.

Figure 11.5 Example of Group Structure

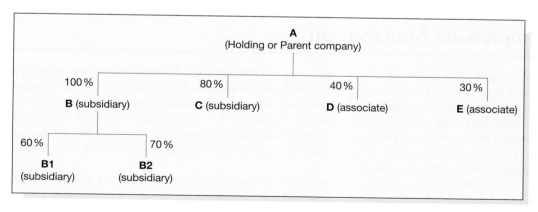

Goodwill

Goodwill is a particular feature of group companies. Goodwill is known as an intangible asset (i.e., one that you cannot touch). Goodwill, in accounting terms, is only recognised when one company takes over another. It represents the value of the whole business over and above the value of its individual assets and liabilities. This can often be quite considerable. European listed companies follow International Financial Reporting Standard 3 which states that goodwill is shown as an asset on the statement of financial position. It is then reviewed every year to see if the goodwill has lost value. If it has lost value, this value will be written off to the income statement. That annual review is called an impairment test. For UK non-listed companies, the UK standard requires a different treatment. The preferred treatment is that companies should write off goodwill to the income statement annually over a period of up to 20 years. This process of writing off goodwill is called amortisation. It is similar to depreciation. Non-listed companies are also permitted, if they can make a case, to write off goodwill over a period of greater than 20 years or even not at all.

PAUSE FOR THOUGHT 11.6

Group Accounts

Nowadays, most leading companies must prepare group accounts. Can you think of any problems they might encounter?

There are many! Many companies will have hundreds of subsidiaries. All the information must be supplied to head office. At head office, it must all be collected and collated. Different subsidiaries may have different year-end accounting dates, or operate in different countries using different accounting policies and different currencies. Some of the subsidiaries will have been acquired or sold, or the shareholdings of the parent company will have changed, during the year. All these are potential problems.

Impression Management

Managers have significant incentives to try to influence the financial reporting process in their own favour. These incentives may be financial and non-financial. Financially, managers may be keen, for example, to maximise their own remuneration. If remuneration is based on profits, they may seek to adopt accounting policies that will increase rather than decrease profits. In non-financial terms, managers, like all human beings, will try to portray themselves in a good light. This may result, for example, in managers selectively disclosing only positive features of the annual performance.

In this section, three illustrative examples of impression management are discussed: creative accounting, narrative enhancement and use of graphs.

PAUSE FOR THOUGHT 11.7

Impression Management

Can you think of any non-accounting situations where human beings indulge in impression management?

There are many, just to take two: interviews and dating. At an interview, normal, sane candidates try to give a good impression of themselves in order to get the job. This may involve trying to stress their good points and downplay their bad points. When dating, you try to look good to impress your partner. Once more, most normal people will try to present themselves in a favourable light. You want to impress your dates not repel them.

Creative Accounting

Creative accounting will be dealt with more fully in Chapter 12. Put simply, creative accounting is the name given to the process whereby managers use the flexibility inherent within the accounting process to manipulate the accounting numbers. Flexibility within the accounting system is abundant. By itself, flexibility allows managers to choose those accounting policies that will give a true and fair view of the company's activities. However, there are also oppor-

PAUSE FOR THOUGHT 11.8

Inventory and Creative Accounting

A company has one asset, inventory. Its abridged statement of financial position is set out below.

	£		£
Inventory	50,000	Equity	30,000
		Retained earnings	20,000
	50,000		50,000

If the company revalues its inventory to £60,000, what will happen to profit?
The answer is that profit increases by £10,000, as the new statement of financial position shows.

	£		£
Inventory	60,000	Equity	30,000
		Profit	30,000
	60,000		60,000

tunities for managers to choose policies which portray themselves in a good light. The worst excesses are covered by the regulatory framework. To see how the flexibility within accounting can alter profit, we take inventory and depreciation as examples.

Inventory
In accounting terms:

$$\text{Assets} - \text{Liabilities} = \text{Equity}$$

In other words, if assets increase so will equity. As equity includes retained earnings, if we increase inventory we will increase retained earnings. Inventory is an easy asset to manipulate, if we wish to increase our profits. We could, for example, do an extremely thorough stocktake at the end of one year, recording and valuing items which normally would have been overlooked.

Depreciation
Depreciation is the expense incurred when property, plant and equipment is written down in value over its useful life. Unfortunately, estimates of useful lives vary. For example, if an asset has an estimated useful life of five years then depreciation, using a straight line basis, would be 20% per year. If the asset's estimated useful life was ten years, depreciation would be 10% per year. In other words, by extending the useful life, we halve the depreciation rate and halve the amount that is treated as an expense in the income statement. Managers can thus alter profit by choosing a particular rate of depreciation. They would argue that they are more fairly reflecting the useful life of the asset.

Narrative Enhancement
Narrative enhancement occurs when managements use the narrative parts of the annual report to convey a more favourable impression of performance than is actually warranted. They may do this by omitting key data or stressing certain elements. Many companies stress, for example, their 'good' environmental performance. Indeed, social and environmental disclosures are nowadays exceedingly common. Since such disclosures are voluntary and reviewed rather than audited, there is great potential for companies to indulge in narrative enhancement. This can be seen from Real-World View 11.5. In this, the news reported by Australian corporations is overwhelmingly positive, which is unlikely to be true in reality.

Graphs
Graphs are a voluntary presentational medium. Used well they are exceedingly effective. However, they also present managers with significant opportunities to manage the presentation of the annual report. For example, a variety of research studies show that managers are exceedingly selective in their use of graphs. They tend to display time-series trend graphs when performance is good, with these graphs presenting a rising trend of corporate performance. By contrast, when the results are poor, graphs are omitted.

Even when included, there is a potential for graphical misuse. The increase in the height of the graph should be proportionate to the increase in the data. However, graphs are often drawn more favourably than is warranted. For example, graphs may be (and often are) drawn with non-zero axes that enhance the perception of growth. Or graphs may simply be drawn inaccurately.

REAL-WORLD VIEW 11.5

Environmental Accounting

An interesting example of narrative measurement is given by Craig Deegan and Ben Gordon. They studied the environmental disclosure practices of Australian corporations.

The number of positive and negative words of environmental disclosure in annual reports from 1980 to 1991 are recorded for 25 companies. They find:

	1980	1985	1988	1991
Mean positive disclosure	12	14	20	105
Mean negative disclosure	0	0	0	7

They conclude:

'The environmental disclosures are typically self-laudatory, with little or no negative disclosures being made by all firms in the study.'

Source: Craig Deegan and Ben Gordon (1996), A Study of the Environmental Disclosure Practices of Australian Corporations, *Accounting and Business Research*, Vol 26, Issue 3, p. 198. Taylor & Francis.

Currently, graphs are not regulated; therefore companies are free to use them creatively. An interesting example is shown in Company Snapshot 11.11. These five graphs represent the financial performance of Polly Peck. This company had spectacular results just before the company collapsed into a totally unexpected bankruptcy. Although not inaccurately drawn, they do present a very effective, and misleading, display. Who could guess that this company was about to fail? Certainly not the investors or even the auditors. Polly Peck is one of Britain's most important business scandals.

Conclusion

The annual report is a key part of the process by which managers report to their shareholders. It is central to the corporate governance process. There are three overlapping objectives: stewardship and accountability, decision making and public relations. The annual report is built around three core audited financial statements: the income statement, the statement of financial position and the statement of cash flows. However, in the UK another six important audited financial statements are normally present: statement of changes in equity; note on reconciliation of net cash flow to movement on net debt; note on historical cost profits and losses; accounting policies; notes to the accounts; and the principal subsidiaries. Most large enterprises are groups consisting of subsidiary and associated companies. The main accounts are therefore group accounts.

The modern annual report also consists of non-audited sections. These can be divided into narratives and non-narratives. In the UK, the ten narratives comprise the chairman's statement, the business review, the directors' report, the review of operations, the social and environmen-

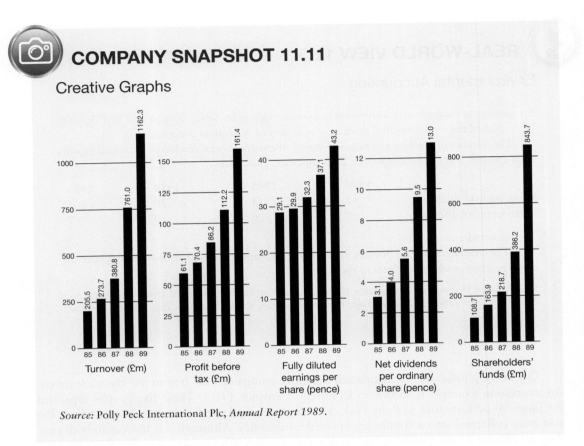

COMPANY SNAPSHOT 11.11

Creative Graphs

Source: Polly Peck International Plc, *Annual Report 1989*.

tal accounting statement, the statement of corporate governance, the directors' remuneration report, the auditors' report, the statement of directors' responsibilities for the financial statements and shareholder information. The three non-narratives are the highlights, the historical summary and the shareholder analysis. As well as these sections, the modern annual report commonly uses graphs and photographs to enhance its presentation. Managements face many incentives to influence the financial reporting process in their favour. This can be done, for example, through creative accounting, narrative enhancement or the use of graphs.

Selected Reading

Unfortunately, there is no one book or article which really covers the modern annual report. Readers are referred to the following four sources which cover some valuable material.

1. Deloitte Touche Tohmatsu (2009) *A Telling Performance: Surveying Narrative Reporting in Annual Reports.*
   This publication takes a good look at the rapid growth of the narrative parts of the annual report.

2. Deegan, C. and Gordon, B. (1996) 'A Study of Environmental Disclosure Practices of Australian Companies', *Accounting and Business Research*, Vol. 26, No. 5, pp. 187–99. This article provides an interesting insight into how individual companies accentuate the good news and downplay bad news of their environmental activities.

3. The full Companies Act 2006 can be seen at http://www.legislation.gov.uk/ukpga/ 2006/46/contents. At this site there are also all the previous Companies Acts. Deloitte have produced a guide which specifically covers the Companies Acts. It is available at http://www.pwc.co.uk/eng/publications/practical_guide_to_companies_act_2006.html.

4. McKinstry, S. (1996) 'Designing the Annual Reports of Burton plc from 1930 to 1994', *Accounting, Organizations and Society*, Vol. 21, No. 1, pp. 89–111. This rather heavyweight article looks at how one company's annual reports have changed over time, concentrating particularly on the public relations aspects.

Discussion Questions

Questions with numbers in blue have answers at the back of the book.

Q1 Explain the role that the annual report plays in the corporate governance process.

Q2 Evaluate the stewardship/accountability, decision making and public relations roles of the annual report and identify any possible conflicts.

Q3 In your opinion, what are the six most important sections of the annual report. Why have you chosen these sections?

Q4 Why do companies prepare group accounts?

Q5 What do you understand by the term 'impression management'? Why do you think that managers might use the annual report for impression management?

Go online to discover the extra features for this chapter at
www.wiley.com/college/jones

SECTION C

Management
Accounting

So far, we have looked at financial accounting. Financial accounting is much more publicly visible than management accounting. Management accounting takes place within businesses and is essential to the running of a business. It can be usefully divided into (1) cost accounting, which includes costing (Chapter 13), and planning, control and performance (Chapters 14 and 15), and (2) short-term decision making (Chapter 16). In Section D on Business Finance we cover long-term decision making (Chapter 17).

This section investigates some major issues involved in management accounting. In Chapter 12, there is a brief introduction into the nature of management accounting and also of finance. Much of the terminology is introduced and an overview of the rest of the book is provided. Chapters 13, 14 and 15 look at cost accounting, one of the two main streams of management accounting. In Chapter 13, the role of costing in inventory valuation and pricing is investigated. The cost allocation process is then outlined together with the use of different costing methods in different industries. Both traditional absorption costing and the more modern activity-based costing are discussed. Chapters 14 and 15 look at planning, control and performance. Chapter 14 sets out the cost control technique of budgeting. The different types of budget are briefly discussed. Responsibility accounting is also discussed. Then in Chapter 15 standard costing is explored. The individual variances are explained and a worked example is shown. Chapter 16 investigates the managerial techniques (such as break-even analysis and contribution analysis) used for short-term operational decision making.

Note on Terminology

With the growth in the use and importance of the International Accounting Standards Board, we now use the terminology of the International Financial Reporting Standards for ease of understanding and consistency.

Chapter 12

Introduction to management accounting and finance

'Jones was loyal to his staff, and diplomatic, but clearly had been bewildered by what he found when he arrived. "Well, we've only just got an audited balance sheet [statement of financial position] for 1998," he said, "We just don't have any contemporary operating or financial data on which to make management decisions in this airline at the moment. It's the old garbage-in, garbage-out syndrome." '

Graham Jones commenting on the Greek airline company, *Olympic Airlines*
Source: Matthew Gwyther, Icarus Descending, *Management Today*, January 2000, pp. 52–3.

Learning Outcomes

After completing this chapter you should be able to:

- Explain the nature and importance of management accounting.
- Outline the relationship between financial accounting and management accounting.
- Explain the relationship between management accounting and finance.
- Explain the main branches of cost accounting and decision making.
- Explain the main branches of finance.
- Discuss cost minimisation and revenue maximisation.
- Understand some of the major terms used in management accounting.

 Go online to discover the extra features for this chapter at
www.wiley.com/college/jones

Chapter Summary

- Management accounting is the provision of accounting information to management to help with costing, with planning, control and performance and with decision making.
- Whereas the main focus of financial accounting is external, management accounting is internally focused.
- Management accounting has its origins in costing; however, nowadays costing is less important as new areas such as strategic management accounting develop.
- Management accounting can be broadly divided into cost accounting (costing; planning, control and performance) and decision making.
- Costing consists of recovering costs for pricing and for the valuation of inventory.
- Planning, control and performance are concerned with planning and controlling future costs using budgeting and standard costing as well as evaluating performance.
- Decision making involves short-term decision making and strategic management accounting.
- Finance consists of capital budgeting, sources of finance and management of working capital.
- Traditionally, management accounting has been criticised for focusing on minimising costs rather than maximising revenue.
- Increasingly, management accounting is making use of digital technology and sophisticated software applications.

 PAUSE FOR THOUGHT 12.1

Management Accounting

Why do you think management accounting is so called?

Management accounting is a relatively new term and has been in widespread use only since the 1950s. The term combines management and accounting. It suggests that accountants have a managerial role within the company. They are, in effect, more than just a functional specialist group. The term management accounting has come, therefore, to represent all the management and accounting activities carried out by accountants within a business. This involves not only costing, and planning, control and performance, but also managerial decision making.

Introduction

Management accounting is concerned with the internal accounting within a business. Essentially, it is the provision of both financial and non-financial information to managers so that they can manage costs and make decisions. The decision-making aspect overlaps with finance in terms of long-term decision making. Capital investment appraisal can be treated as part of either management accounting or finance. In this book, we will treat it as part of finance as it is financed by external sources. In many ways, therefore, management accounting is less straightforward than financial accounting. Management accounting varies markedly from business to business and management accountants, in effect, carry around a toolkit of techniques, their 'tools of the trade'. The purpose of this section is to try to explain these techniques and to fit them into an overall picture of management accounting. By contrast, finance, as well as including investment appraisal, will include the raising of external finance and management of working capital.

Context

The management accountant works within a business. The focus of management accounting is thus internal rather than external. In this book, we simplify the formal definition (see Definition 12.1) and take the purpose of management accounting as being to provide managers with accounting information in order to help with costing, with planning, control and performance and with decision making. As the formal, official definition shows, management accounting concerns business strategy, planning and control, decision making, efficient resource usage, performance improvement, safeguarding assets, corporate governance and internal control.

DEFINITION 12.1

Management Accounting

Working definition
The provision of financial and non-financial information to management for costing, for planning, control and performance, and for decision making.

Formal definition
'Management accounting is the application of the principles of accounting and financial management to create, protect, preserve and increase value so as to deliver that value to the stakeholders of for-profit and not-for-profit enterprises, in the public and private sectors. Management accounting is an integral part of management. It requires the identification, generation, presentation, interpretation and use of information relevant to:

- Inform strategic decisions and formulate business strategy;
- Plan long, medium and short-run operations;
- Determine capital structure and fund that structure;
- Design reward strategies for executives and shareholders;

- Inform operational decisions;
- Control operations and ensure the efficient use of resources;
- Measure and report financial and non-financial performance to management and other stakeholders;
- Implement corporate governance procedures, risk management and internal controls.'

Source: Chartered Institute of Management Accountants (2005), *Official Terminology*. Reproduced by Permission of Elsevier.

In essence, costing concerns (1) setting a price for a product or service so that a profit is made and (2) arriving at a correct valuation for inventory. Planning, control and performance involve planning and controlling future costs using budgeting and standard costing as well as performance evaluation. Decision making involves managers solving problems using various problem-solving techniques.

PAUSE FOR THOUGHT 12.2

Problem Solving

Can you think of five problems the management accountant may need to solve?

The list is potentially endless. However, here are ten.

1. What products or services should be sold?
2. How much should be sold?
3. Should a product be made in-house or bought in?
4. Should the firm continue manufacturing the product?
5. At what level of production will a profit be made?
6. Which products or services are most profitable?
7. How can a firm minimise its costs?
8. How can the firm maximise revenue?
9. Which areas should the firm diversify into?
10. When will a new product break even?

Relationship with Financial Accounting

The orientation of management accounting is completely different to that of financial accounting. As Figure 12.1 shows, financial accounting is concerned with providing information (such

Figure 12.1 Relationship between Financial and Management Accounting

Financial Accounting	*Management Accounting*
1. Aims to provide information principally for external users, such as shareholders.	1. Aims to provide information for internal users such as management.
2. Concerned with recording information using double-entry bookkeeping.	2. Not so concerned with recording. Information is needed for costing, for planning, control and performance, for decision making etc.
3. Works within a statutory context.	
4. Main statements are the statement of financial position and income statement.	3. There is no statutory context.
	4. Not so concerned with preparing financial statements.
5. Basically looks back to the past.	
6. The end product is the annual reporting package in a standardised format.	5. Looks to the future.
	6. Different businesses produce very different management information.

as the statement of financial position and income statement) to shareholders about past events. Management accountants will also be interested in such information, often on a monthly basis.

However, management accountants will also require a broader range of internal management information for costing, for planning, control and performance, and for decision making. Importantly, whereas financial accounting works within a statutory context, management accounting does not. Management accounting is thus much more varied and customised than financial accounting.

Financial accounting, in fact, has influenced the development of management accounting. Management accounting emerged much later than financial accounting. Indeed, early management accountants were primarily cost accountants.

Armstrong and Jones (1992) argue that management accountants have been involved in a 'collective mobility' project where cost accountants have redefined themselves as management accountants dealing with wider management accounting and strategic management issues. In part, this has been an attempt to move away from costing, which was perceived as low status, and to emulate the Institute of Chartered Accountants in England and Wales, which was considered as high status.

Perhaps because of its comparatively humble origins, management accounting has often been seen as subservient to financial accounting. Johnson and Kaplan (1987) argued in *Relevance Lost* that most management accounting practices had been developed by 1925 and that since then there has been comparatively little innovation. Under this view, management accounting has major problems. In particular, product costing is distorted, decision-making information becomes unreliable and management accounting reflects external reporting requirements rather than modern management needs.

Opinions differ on the current relevance of management accounting. However, it is true that management accounting has struggled to adapt to changes in the business environment. In particular, it has been relatively slow to adapt to the decline of manufacturing industry and the rise of the service economy in the UK and US (see Figure 12.2). These difficulties are likely to be exacerbated by the rise of knowledge-based companies. Management accounting is also struggling to adapt to globalisation and technological change. As we will see, however, new management techniques have arisen (such as activity-based costing, strategic management accounting and just-in-time stock valuation) which seek to address the criticisms of management accounting.

Figure 12.2 The Information Age

Two main types of employment structures seem to be present in the information, knowledge-based economy. One is the "service economy model", epitomised by the United Kingdom, US and Canada. This is characterised by a rapid phasing out of manufacturing employment after 1970, as the pace of informatisation has accelerated. Having witnessed the elimination of almost all agricultural employment, this model emphasises a new employment structure where differentiation among service activities becomes the key element for analysing and structuring working arrangements. This model emphasises capital management services over producer services and keeps expanding the social service sector largely because of dramatic rises in healthcare jobs. There is to a lesser extent an increase in education employment. This model of the economy is also characterised by expansion of managerial work, including a considerable number of middle managers. This model arose following the neo-liberal, non-interventionist economic policies of the Thatcher and Reagan administrations in the 1980s, when in the midst of world turmoil the manufacturing and trade bases of the UK and US economies were radically changed.

Source: C. Farnham (2005), *Managing in a Strategic Business Context,* p. 63. Chartered Institute of Personnel and Development.

Relationship between Management Accounting and Finance

The management accountant will also often be involved in infrastructural projects. These are long-term projects such as building a factory. There are two aspects to this. First, a project needs to be evaluated. This may be seen as capital investment appraisal. The management accountant will also need to manage the finances of the business. This can be divided into the raising of external finance through loans or shares. Alternatively, it will involve the management of working capital. This is an efficient use of the current assets (inventories, trade receivables and cash) and the current liabilities (trade payables) of a business.

Overview

The diversity of management accounting makes it difficult to separate out individual strands. However, this book broadly splits management accounting and finance into two: cost accounting and decision making

1. **Cost Accounting.** This involves:
   (i) *Costing* (Chapter 13) (recovering costs as a basis for pricing and for inventory valuation), and
   (ii) *Planning, control and performance* (Chapters 14 and 15) (i.e., planning and controlling future costs using budgeting and standard costing).
   Cost accounting is a common term used to embrace both costing, and planning, control and performance. Definition 12.2 shows two formal definitions of cost accounting.

DEFINITION 12.2

Cost Accounting

Working definition
The determination of actual and standard costs, budgeting and standard costing.

Formal definition
1. 'The classification, recording and appropriate allocation of expenditure in order to determine the total cost of products or services.'
      This earlier definition by ICMA is a good description of cost recovery.
2. 'Gathering of cost information and its attachment to cost objects, the establishment of budgets, standard costs and actual costs of operations, processes, activities or products; and the analysis of variances, profitability or the social use of funds. The use of the term "*costing*" is not recommended except with a qualifying adjective, e.g. standard costing.'
      This CIMA (2005) definition embraces both cost accounting, and planning, control and performance.

Source: Chartered Institute of Management Accountants (2005), *Official Terminology*. Reproduced by Permission of Elsevier.

The first is by the Institute of Cost and Management Accountants (ICMA), the predecessor body of the author of the second definition, the Chartered Institute of Management Accountants (CIMA) in 2005. It is interesting to see that the definition has widened considerably over time. In particular, the more recent CIMA definition now explicitly mentions budgeting and standard costing.

2. **Decision Making.**
   (i) *Short-term decision making* (Chapter 16) management accounting involves operational or day-to-day decision making (such as break-even analysis).
   (ii) *Long-term decision making* i.e., strategic management accounting (for coverage of this see the companion book *Accounting* by Michael Jones).

Finance

The financial aspects of a business can be divided into three major parts:

1. **Long-term Decisions**
   (i) *Capital budgeting* (Chapter 17) i.e., investment appraisal, which can also be seen as part of long-term decision making.
   (ii) *Raising of external funds* (Chapter 18) i.e., the raising of share capital or loan capital which can be used to finance the long-term infrastructural decisions of the business.
2. **Short-term Decisions**
   (iii) *Efficient management of working capital* (Chapter 19) i.e., the effective and efficient use of the inventory, trade receivables, cash and trade payables of the business.

It is important, however, to appreciate that, in practice, this split although useful is somewhat arbitrary. For example, short-term decision making could be seen as a part of cost accounting as it is based on marginal costing (i.e., it excludes fixed costs).

These two major areas are shown in Figure 12.3. The major areas shown in Figure 12.3 are discussed briefly below and then more fully discussed in the chapters that follow. Key terms that underpin management accounting are introduced. These new terms are highlighted in **bold** in the text and a full definition is then provided in Definitions 12.3 and 12.4 which follow the same order as in the text. These terms are more fully discussed later in the book.

Cost Accounting

Costing (Chapter 13)

Costing has its origins in manufacturing industry. The basic idea underpinning costing is cost recovery (i.e., the need to recover all the **costs** of making a product into the price of the final product). Broadly, cost recovery is achieved using a technique called **total absorption costing**. Total absorption costing seeks to recover both **direct costs** and **indirect costs** into a product or service. This form of costing thus seeks to establish the total costs of a product so that they can be recovered in the final selling price. As well as costing for pricing, costing is used for inventory valuation. In this case, either **absorption costing** or **marginal costing** is used. However, it should be remembered that for inventory valuation for financial reporting purposes, inventories are usually valued using absorption costing.

Different industries will have different costing systems. For example, medicinal tablets will necessitate batch costing, while shipbuilding uses contract costing. A more modern technique called activity-based costing is sometimes used.

Figure 12.3 Overview of Management Accounting and Finance

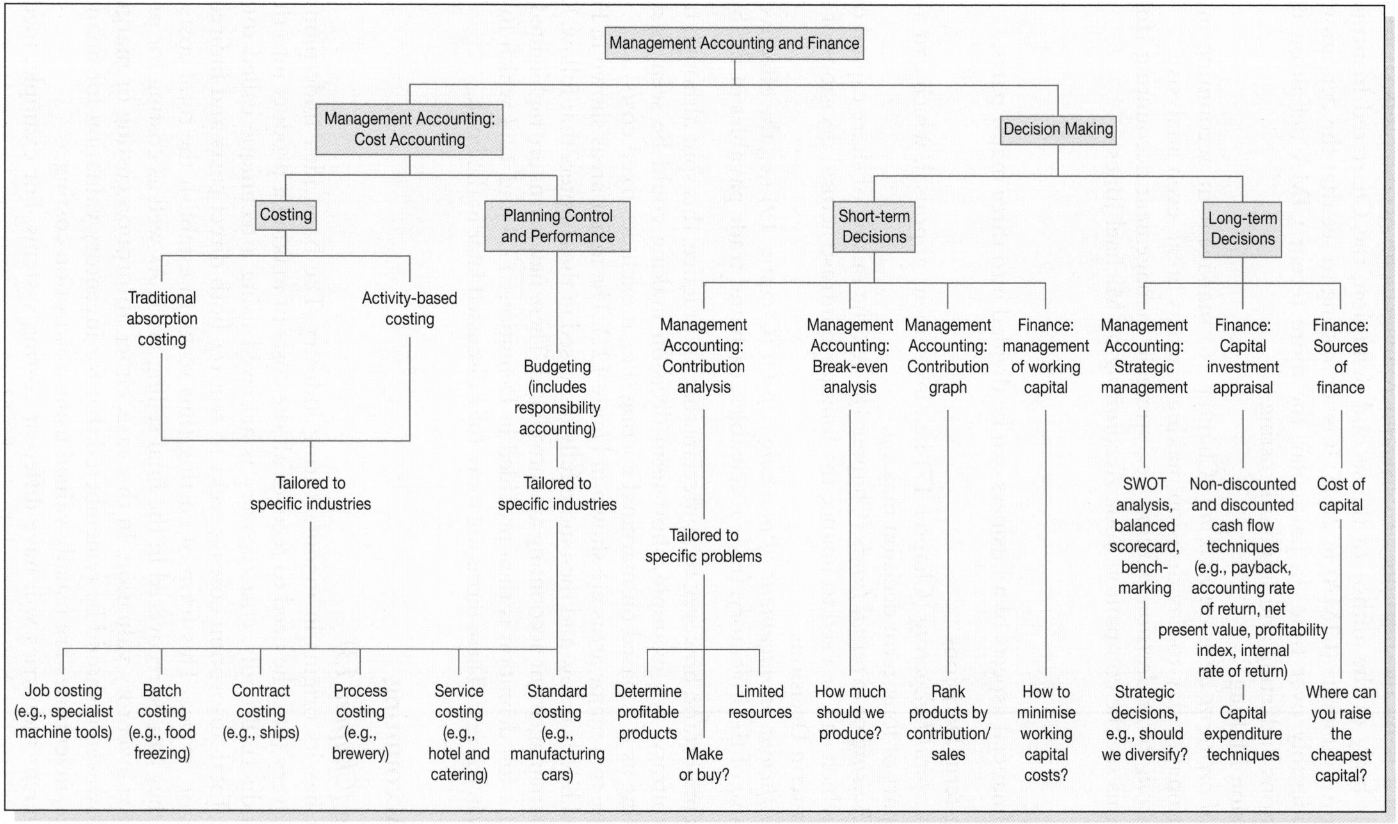

DEFINITION 12.3

The Basic Building Blocks of Management Accounting and Finance: Some Key Cost Accounting Terms

i. Costing

Cost. A cost is simply an item of expenditure (planned or actually incurred).

Total absorption costing. This form of costing is used to recover all the costs (both direct and indirect) incurred by a company into the price of the final product or service.

Direct costs. Direct costs are those costs that can be directly identified and attributed to a product or service; for example, the amount of direct labour that is incurred making a product. Sometimes these costs are called *product costs*.

Indirect costs. Indirect costs are those costs that cannot be directly identified and attributed to a product or service; examples are administrative, selling and distribution costs. These costs are totalled and then recovered into the product or service in an indirect way. For example, if there were £10,000 administrative costs and 10,000 products, each product might be allocated £1 of administrative costs. Indirect costs are often called *overheads* or *period costs*.

Absorption costing. Absorption costing is the form of costing used for valuing inventory for external financial reporting. It recovers the costs of all the overheads that can be directly attributed to a product or service. However, unlike marginal costing, which can sometimes be used for inventory valuation, it includes both fixed and variable production overheads.

Marginal costing. Marginal costing excludes fixed costs from the costing process. It focuses on revenue, variable costs and contribution. Fixed costs are written off against contribution. It can be used for decision making or for valuing inventory. When valuing inventory only variable production overheads are included in the inventory valuation. (See Definition 12.4 for explanations of *fixed costs, variable costs* and *contribution*.) Marginal costing is called contribution analysis when used for decision making.

ii. Planning, Control and Performance Evaluation

Controllable costs. Costs that a manager can influence and that the manager can be held responsible for.

Uncontrollable costs. Costs that a manager cannot influence and that the manager cannot be held responsible for.

Standard costs. Standard costs are individual cost elements (such as direct materials, direct labour and variable overheads) which are estimated in advance. Normally, the quantity and the price of each cost element are estimated separately. Actual costs are then compared with standard costs to determine variances.

Variances. Variances are the differences between the budgeted costs and the actual costs in both budgeting and standard costing. These variances are then investigated by management.

Planning, Control and Performance (Chapters 14 and 15)

Planning, control and performance aim to control current costs and plan for the control of future costs as well as evaluate performance. Two essential management control systems (i.e., systems that provide information for managerial planning, control and performance evaluation) are budgeting and standard costing.

- *Budgeting* (Chapter 14). Budgeting involves setting future targets. Actual results are then compared with these budgeted results. Any differences will be investigated. Budgets may be used as part of responsibility accounting. In such systems, a distinction is often made between **controllable costs** and **uncontrollable costs**.
- *Standard costing* (Chapter 15) is a standardised version of budgeting. Standard costing involves using preset costs for direct labour, direct materials and overheads. Actual costs are then compared with the **standard costs**. Any **variances** are then investigated.

Decision Making

Decision making involves choosing between alternatives. When making a choice it is essential to consider only those costs that are relevant to the actual decision, i.e., *relevant costs*. To match the structure of the book, we divide decision making into management accounting and finance. In simple terms, management accounting deals primarily with short-term decision making, while sources of finance deals mainly with long-term decision making.

(i) Management Accounting

Short-Term Decisions (Chapter 16)

In many ways, distinguishing between short-term operational decisions and long-term strategic decisions is somewhat arbitrary. It is, however, an essential managerial task as Soundbite 12.1 shows. It provides a useful basic distinction. Short-term decisions are dealt with in Chapter 16. Chapter 19 on managing working capital also covers some short-term financing. Long-term decisions are covered in Section D on finance, in Chapter 17 on capital investment appraisal and Chapter 18 on sources of finance, respectively.

SOUNDBITE 12.1

Short and Long-term Planning

'The real issue for most businesses is being able to juggle the link between the short and long-term effectively.'

Source: Gillian Lees, Building World-class Businesses for the Long Term, *Global Accountant*, September/October 2011, p. 26.

Businesses face many short-term decisions. Essentially, decision making is about choice. Businesses need to make numerous decisions. For example, should a business make a product itself or buy in the product? Should a business continue making or providing a product or service? At what price will a product break even (i.e., make neither a profit nor a loss)? These decisions are solved using various problem-solving techniques such as break-even analysis and contribution analysis. In such short-term decisions, it is essential to distinguish between **fixed costs** and **variable costs**.

A key aspect of short-term decision making is contribution. Contribution is sales less variable costs. In other words, fixed costs are excluded. Contribution is at the heart of two common management accounting techniques: **break-even analysis** and **contribution analysis**. This area of management accounting is sometimes called cost-volume-profit analysis.

Cost Behaviour

A key aspect of costing and a prerequisite of effective decision making is the determination of how costs vary with activity. In essence, as Definition 12.4 shows, at its simplest there are fixed costs and variable costs. Where costs do not increase with increasing activity, for example depreciation or insurance, they are fixed costs. Where they do change with increased activity they are variable costs. In some cases, however, the costs for a certain activity may be partly fixed and partly variable. For example, where there is a fixed charge for electricity and then payment is per unit. In this case, we have semi-variable costs. These costs are shown diagrammatically in Figure 12.4. Fixed costs may also be stepped; in other words, at a certain activity level, they may increase.

DEFINITION 12.4

The Basic Building Blocks of Management Accounting and Finance: Some Key Decision-Making Terms

Short-Term Decisions

Fixed costs. Fixed costs are those costs that *will not vary* with production or revenue (for example, insurance) in an accounting period. They will not, therefore, be affected by short-term decisions such as whether or not production is increased.

Variable costs. Variable costs, however, *will vary* with production and revenue (for example, the metered cost of electricity). Short-term decision making is primarily concerned with variable costs. Revenue less variable costs gives *contribution*, a useful concept in short-term decision making.

Break-even analysis. Break-even analysis involves calculating the point at which a product makes neither a profit nor a loss. Fixed costs are divided by the contribution per unit (i.e., revenue less variable costs divided by number of products). This gives the break-even point.

Contribution analysis. When there is more than one product, this technique is useful in determining which product is the most profitable. It compares the relative contribution of each product. This can also be called cost-volume-profit analysis.

Long-Term Decisions

Discounted cash flow. Discounted cash flow discounts the future expected cash inflows and outflows of a potential project back to their present value today. Decisions can then be made on whether or not to go ahead with the project.

Figure 12.4 Fixed, Variable and Semi-variable Costs

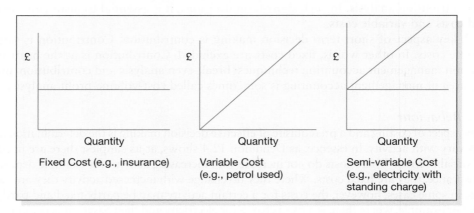

The behaviour of costs is important because it feeds through into cost per unit. Essentially, the more units you produce, the less fixed cost per unit. The more units you produce, however, does not affect your variable cost per unit which remains the same. Finally, total cost (i.e., fixed and variable costs together) will decline over the quantity produced. This cost behaviour is shown in Figure 12.5.

Figure 12.5 Fixed, Variable and Total Cost per Unit

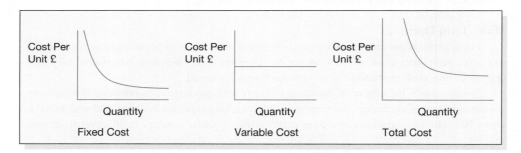

Long-term Decisions

Strategic Management Accounting

Whereas costing represents the oldest branch of management accounting, strategic management accounting represents the newest. Strategic management accounting represents a response to criticisms that management accounting is outdated and lacking in innovation. Using strategic management accounting, the management accountant relates the activities of the firm to the wider external environment. Strategic management is thus concerned with the long-term strategic direction of the firm. Strategic management accounting is considered quite sophisticated and is **outside the scope of this introductory book**. Students interested in this topic could look at the companion book by Michael Jones on *Accounting*.

PAUSE FOR THOUGHT 12.3

Cost Accounting and Management Accounting

A distinction is sometimes made between cost accounting and management accounting. What do you see as the essential difference?

Management accounting has its origins in cost accounting. However, gradually cost accounting and management accounting have been seen as distinct. Cost accounting is seen, at its narrowest, as focusing on cost collection and cost recovery and more widely as cost recovery and control. However, management accounting is viewed as a much broader term which not only encompasses cost accounting, but also involves decision making and, more recently, strategic management accounting. Cost accounting is thus typically portrayed as routine and low level, whereas management accounting is seen as a higher-level activity.

(ii) Finance

The financial aspects of this book are dealt with in Chapters 17, 18 and 19. Capital investment appraisal (Chapter 17) and sources of finance (Chapter 18) can broadly be classified under long-term decision making while the management of working capital (Chapter 19) can be seen as potentially concerned with short-term decisions.

Long-term Decisions

Capital Investment Appraisal (Chapter 17)
Capital budgeting involves the financial evaluation of future projects. This evaluation is carried out by using various techniques such as payback, the accounting rate of return, net present value, the profitability index and the internal rate of return. Under net present value, the profitability index and the internal rate of return, the technique of **discounted cash flow** analysis is used.

Sources of Finance (Chapter 18)
The topic of business finance is immense. In this chapter, we look at the sources and methods of raising long-term finance. Long-term financing of the business involves the choice between internal financing through retained profits and external financing through either leasing, loans or share capital. Share capital is normally raised via a rights issue, a public issue or a placing. The workings of the stock market are explored with an examination of the primary and secondary markets, the main market and the AIM market. The concept of the efficient market is also explained (Chapter 18). Finally, in Chapter 18, the rate and calculation of cost of capital is explained.

Short-term Decisions

Management of Working Capital (Chapter 19)
This covers the internal generation of funds. In the short term, the management of working capital involves the management accountants in a series of short-term decisions about the

optimal level of inventory and trade receivables. This may use a series of techniques such as Materials Requirement Planning (MRP), Economic Order Quantity (EOQ) and Just-in-Time for optimising inventory. Meanwhile, debt factoring and invoice discounting can be used to reduce the cost of trade receivables.

PAUSE FOR THOUGHT 12.4

Short-Term vs Long-Term Decisions

What do you think are the essential differences between short-term and long-term decisions?

Short-term decisions are operational, day-to-day decisions which typically involve the firm's internal environment. For example, what quantity of a particular product should we make or what should be the price of a particular product.

By contrast, long-term decisions are strategic, non-operational decisions. These typically involve a firm's external environment. So, for example, they may involve the need to diversify or the need to make acquisitions and disposals. Alternatively, they might evaluate whether a long-term capital investment is worthwhile.

Cost Minimisation and Revenue Maximisation

The management accountant can make a business more efficient through cost minimisation or revenue maximisation. Cost minimisation attempts to reduce costs. However, as stated in Real-World View 12.1, this needs to be done in a controlled way. This may be achieved by tight budgetary control or cutting back on expenditure.

REAL-WORLD VIEW 12.1

Cost Savings

'In order to have any chance of containing costs in a sustainable way you have to know what you're doing. . . . If you don't know your starting point, how will you know where you can make savings.'

Source: Andrew Stone, Keep your eye on the big picture for savings, *Daily Telegraph,* Wednesday, August 2010, p. B12.

SOUNDBITE 12.2

Sales Maximisation

'Legend tells of the traveller who went into a county store and found the shelves lined with bags of salt. "You must sell a lot of salt," said the traveller, "Nah," said the storekeeper. "I can't sell no salt at all. But the feller who sells me salt – boy, can *he* sell salt".'

Martin Mayer (1974), *The Bankers*

Source: The Executive's Book of Quotations (1994), p. 255. Oxford University Press.

Some authors argue strongly that management accounting needs to refocus on revenue maximisation. In part, revenue maximisation is achieved through the new focus on strategic management accounting which looks outwards to the external environment rather than inwards. Substantial opportunities arise to adopt new techniques such as customer database mining. This latter technique looks at customer databases and seeks to extract from them customer data which will expand the business's revenue.

Management accountants have often been criticised for being overly concerned with cost cutting (see, for example, Lesley Jackson, H.P. Bulmer Holding plc's UK Finance Director, in Real-World View 12.2).

REAL-WORLD VIEW 12.2

Cost Minimisation

Jackson's time as general commercial manager gave her the opportunity to look at a business from a different angle. She says it made her a better accountant.

'A lot of accountants tend to look at cost minimalisation and low risk. They tend to have a more conservative mindset. I became slightly more maverick in this sense,' she says.

It was this broader outlook on business and varied skills-sets that gave Jackson the edge over other candidates for the role at Bulmers.

Source: Michelle Perry, Brewing up a Profit, *Accountancy Age*, 3 May 2001, p. 20.

Use of Computers and Impact of Digital Technology

The theory and practice of management accounting and finance is shown in the next seven chapters. In practice, for most of the techniques shown, a dedicated computer program would be used. Alternatively, a spreadsheet could be set up so as to handle the calculations. These programs enable complicated and often complex real-life situations to be modelled. However, it is essential to be able to appreciate which figures should be input into the computer. As Peter Williams states:

'While it may be possible for any company with a PC to produce a set of management information using relatively low-cost accounting software, there is no guarantee that the output will be true and fair.' (*Accountancy Age*, 2 March 2000, p. 23)

Digital technology affects all businesses. Management accounting changes and adapts to this as Alnoor Bhimani shows in Real-World View 12.3.

REAL-WORLD VIEW 12.3

Levels of Digital Impact on Economic Activities

'Novel products and new services emerge at a pace that closely matches the rate of technological advances. The use of digital technologies hastens the rate of innovation and the speed at which new product offerings evolve. The advent of digitization has given rise to information goods such as e-books, digital music recordings, and mobile messaging platforms among others. Information-intensive services such as web-based airline bookings and car rental reservation systems and Internet-based courier-tracking facilities are now common-place. They provide benefits to consumers (value-makers) who guide the activities of firms (value-makers), which, in turn, seek to benefit commercially from these innovations. For many industries, digitization as part of technological offerings and processes underpin the extent of value creation and the basis of exchange. Management accounting information can be useful in value creation monitoring and reporting and to align changes in the types of costs incurred with revenues generated within increasingly digitized contexts.'

Source: A. Bhimani, (2006), 'Management Accounting and Digitization,' *Contemporary Issues in Management Accounting,* Oxford University Press.

There are many sophisticated IT systems that have grown up over recent years which help management run their businesses. Enterprise Resource Planning Systems (ERPS) are one of the most well known. These cover a whole range of integrated program covering both financial accounting and management accounting functions. The basic transactional data is entered once and then is available for use by employees, including management accountants, across the company.

Art not a Science

It must be remembered that management accounting is an art not a science. Much of management accounting is involved in looking to the future. As such, it deals with the inherent uncertainty that the future inevitably brings. Key activities, such as costing, budgeting and capital investment appraisal, involve forecasts and estimates. In many cases, managers will run multiple versions of their estimates to see how sensitive their estimates are to changes to basic parameters such as volume or price. This is often known as sensitivity analysis.

Changing Nature of Management Accounting

Management accounting techniques are changing over time. Some of these changes are dictated by changes in the business environment such as the long-term decline in manufacturing industry and the rise of the service sector. Other factors involve the increasing use of information technology and the rise of e-commerce. Up-to-date information is often difficult to get. However, specific techniques such as activty-based costing are increasing rapidly.

There are also many other varied techniques such as decision trees where you map all the options. You can then assign probabilities and amounts to these and calculate what you think is the optimal result.

Conclusion

Management accounting is the internal accounting function of a firm. Finance is concerned with the raising of money for businesses and with the way those funds are used. Management accounting can be divided into cost accounting (costing; planning, control and performance) and decision making (short-term and long-term). In costing, the two main aspects are pricing and inventory valuation. In planning, control and performance, budgeting and standard costing are used. Short-term decision making is used to determine the most profitable course of action for operational decisions. Finance is mainly concerned with decision making. Unlike management accounting, which is mainly concerned with short-term decisions, finance is mainly concerned with long-term decisions. It involves capital appraisal, the sources of external funds and the management of working capital.

Selected Reading

Armstrong, P. and Jones, C. (1992) The Decline of Operational Expertise in the Knowledge-base of Management Accounting: An examination of some post-war trends in the qualifying requirements of the Chartered Institute of Management Accountants, *Management Accounting Research*, Vol. 3, pp. 53–75.

An interesting look at how the management accounting profession has gradually changed over time. Originally concerned with costing, it now has a much wider focus.

Bhimani, A. (2005) *Contemporary Issues in Management Accounting* (Oxford University Press).

This book contains 19 chapters that give useful insights into many aspects of management accounting.

Drury, C. (2005) *Management and Cost Accounting* (Thomson Learning: London).
    This is a comprehensive text on management and cost accounting. Once students have mastered the basics, this represents a good book for future reading.
Johnson, T. and Kaplan, R.S. (1987) *Relevance Lost: The Rise and Fall of Management Accounting* (Harvard University Press).
    A benchmarking book which triggered a relook at management accounting. After this book a new management accounting emerged consisting of topics such as activity-based costing and strategic management accounting.
Kaplan, R.S. (1984), Yesterday's Accounting Undermines Production, *Harvard Business Review*, July/August, pp. 95–101.
    This provides a good overview of the problems with traditional management accounting.

Discussion Questions

Questions with numbers in blue have answers at the back of the book.

Q1 What are the main branches of management accounting and what are their main functions?

Q2 Why do you think that management accounting has been so keen to lose its costing image?

Q3 What are the following types of cost and why are they important?
(a) Direct cost
(b) Indirect cost
(c) Fixed cost
(d) Variable cost
(e) Standard cost

Q4 The management accountant has been described as a professional with a toolkit of techniques. How fair a description do you think this is?

Q5 Why have management accountants been criticised for being cost minimisers and how might they be revenue maximisers?

Q6 Is finance all about decision-making?

Q7 State whether the following statements are true or false. If false explain why.
(a) The two main branches of management accounting are cost accounting and decision making.
(b) Total absorption costing is where all the overheads incurred by a company are recovered in the valuation of inventory.
(c) The difference between absorption costing and marginal costing as a form of costing for inventory valuation is that absorption costing includes direct materials, direct labour and all production overheads. By contrast, marginal costing only includes direct materials, direct labour and all *variable* production overheads. Marginal costing, therefore, excludes fixed production overheads.
(d) Finance is only concerned with long-term infrastructural decisions.
(e) Discounted cash flow discounts the future expected cash flows of a project back to their present-day monetary values.

 Go online to discover the extra features for this chapter at
www.wiley.com/college/jones

Chapter 13

Costing

'Watch the costs and the profits will take care of themselves.'

Andrew Carnegie, quoted in R. Sobel and D.B. Silicia (1986), *The Entrepreneurs – An American Adventure* (Houghton Mifflin)
Source: Wiley Book of Business Quotations (1998), p. 89.

Learning Outcomes

After completing this chapter you should be able to:

- Explain the nature and importance of costing.
- Discuss the process of traditional costing.
- Understand the nature of activity-based costing.
- Distinguish between different costing systems.
- Discuss target costing.

Go online to discover the extra features for this chapter at
www.wiley.com/college/jones

Chapter Summary

- Costing is a subset of cost accounting and is used as a basis for inventory valuation and for cost-plus pricing.
- There are direct costs and indirect costs or overheads.
- The six stages in traditional cost recovery are:
  (1) recording costs
  (2) classifying costs
  (3) allocating indirect costs to departments
  (4) reapportioning costs from service to productive departments
  (5) calculating an overhead recovery rate, and
  (6) absorbing costs into products and services.
- Activity-based costing is a sophisticated version of cost recovery which uses cost allocation drivers based on activities to allocate costs.
- Different industries have different costing methods such as job costing, batch costing, standard costing, contract costing, process costing and service costing.
- Non-production overheads are included in cost-plus pricing, but not in inventory valuation.
- In inventory valuation, either all production costs (absorption costing) or only variable production costs (marginal costing) can be allocated.
- Target costing, developed by the Japanese, is based on market prices and set at the pre-production stage.
- Companies in trouble often cut costs, such as labour costs, in order to improve their profitability.

Introduction

Management accounting can be broadly divided into cost accounting and decision making. In turn, cost accounting has two major strands: (1) costing, and (2) planning, control and performance. Costing involves ascertaining all the costs of a product or service so as to form the basis for pricing and for inventory valuation. The first management accountants were essentially cost accountants. Their job was to make sure that manufactured products were priced so as fully to recover all the costs incurred in making them. This process of recording, classifying, allocating the costs and then absorbing those costs into individual products and services still remains the basis of cost recovery. However, the traditional methods of cost recovery were geared up for manufacturing industries and assumed that overhead costs were relatively small. The decline of manufacturing industry, the increasing importance of overhead costs and the rise of service industries has caused a need to rethink some of the basics of cost recovery. In particular, the technique of activity-based costing has gained in popularity.

Importance of Cost Accounting

In this book, we take cost accounting to involve two main parts. The first is costing, which is the process of determining the actual costs of products and services. This usually looks to the past. And the second is costing for planning, control and performance where expected costs are determined for future periods either through budgeting or standard costing.

Costs are the essential building blocks for both financial and management accounting. In costing, costs represent *actual* items of expenditure. In budgeting and standard costing, costs represent *future* (expected) items of expenditure. Costs represent a major building block of management accounting. In financial accounting, it is important to match costs against revenue to determine profit.

An important part of this matching process in manufacturing industry is the allocation of production costs to inventory. Either all production costs (absorption costing) or variable production costs (marginal costing) can be allocated. Sometimes marginal costing is termed variable costing. In Figure 13.1, we use absorption costing, in which all the production costs are allocated to inventory. These costs will be included in the cost of opening inventory in the next accounting period and then matched against revenue to determine profit. Later on, in Figure 13.14, both absorption and marginal costing are shown for comparative purposes.

Figure 13.1 Allocation of Costs to Inventory Using Absorption Costing

Stockco manufactures only toys. The direct costs of manufacturing 1,000 toys is £1,000. Total production overheads for the toys (for example, factory light and heat) are £500. At the end of the year 200 toys are in inventory. What is the cost of the closing inventory?

	1,000 units £	Per unit £
Direct costs	1,000	1.00
Production overheads	500	0.50
	1,500	1.50

The closing inventory is thus 200 @ £1.50 = £300

Another extremely important function of costing is as a basis for pricing. The selling price of a product is key to making a profit. In many businesses, the fundamental economic law is that the cheaper the price of the goods, the more goods will be sold.

In practice, there are two methods of pricing: market pricing and cost-plus pricing. In market pricing, the focus is external. The prices charged by competitors are examined together with the amount that customers are willing to pay. In cost-plus pricing, by contrast, the focus is internal. The total costs of making the product are established (i.e., all the direct costs and all the indirect costs or overheads) and then a profit percentage or profit mark-up is added. When setting prices, companies will bear in mind both the costs of making the product and also the amount for which competitor products are selling. At certain times firms will adopt different pricing strategies. For example, a company may discount its prices to boost revenue.

PAUSE FOR THOUGHT 13.1

Cost-Plus Pricing

What is the purpose of cost-plus pricing and how can it prove dangerous in a competitive market?

....

Cost-plus pricing seeks to recover all the overheads into a product or service. However, it is only as good as the method chosen to recover the overheads and the estimates made. The problem is that prices are often set by the market rather than by the company. A company may determine the cost of a product and then its selling price. However, in a competitive market, this price may be higher than competitors' prices or be more than customers wish to pay. When adopting cost-plus pricing it is always important to perform a reality check and ask: can we really sell the product or service at this price? In practice, therefore, it is advisable to use both cost-plus pricing and market pricing together.

In general, companies strive to keep their costs as low as possible. Those companies that can do this, such as Wal-Mart, the American retailer that purchased Asda, have a key competitive advantage (see Real-World View 13.1).

REAL-WORLD VIEW 13.1

Costing as Competitive Advantage

Richard Tomkins (Marketing Value for Money) presents an insightful look at the cost bases of supermarkets. He points out that a typical Tesco superstore sells about 36,000 lines, while a Wal-Mart store sells about 100,000 lines. He quotes Mr Ettenberg, chairman of Customer Strategies World-wide, a US retail consultancy, as saying:

'The fact that they're in groceries, that they're in pharmaceuticals, that they're in general merchandise – all of that is a by-product of their ability to construct a process that has all the costs taken out from it right from the very beginning.'

This enables them to build a low-cost distribution system.

Source: Richard Tomkins, Marketing Value for Money, *Financial Times*, 14 May 1999.

Types of Cost

A cost is simply an amount of expenditure which can be attributed to a product or service. It is possible to distinguish between two main types of cost: **direct costs** and **indirect costs**. Definition 12.3 in the last chapter provides definitions of these. Direct costs are simply those that **can** be directly attributed to a product or service. Indirect costs are those that **cannot** be directly attributed. Indirect costs are also known as overheads. In manufacturing industry, direct costs have declined over time while indirect costs have risen. This makes costing more difficult. Figures 13.2 (below) and 13.3 on the next page demonstrate two cost structures for a manufactured product and for a service product, respectively. In both cases, we are totalling all our costs so that we can recover them into the final selling price. This is known as **total absorption costing**. This should be distinguished from absorption costing and marginal costing which, as we have just discussed, are used for inventory valuation, not for pricing.

Figure 13.2 Cost Structure for a Manufactured Product (for Example, a Computer)

	£	Examples
Direct materials	50*	Plastics, steel
Direct labour	120*	Manufacturing labour
Direct expenses	10*	Royalties
Prime Cost	180	
Production overheads	60†	Supervisors' wages
Production Cost	240	
Administrative overheads	50†	Staff costs, office expenses
Selling and distribution overheads	60†	Advertising
Total Cost	350	
Profit	50	
Selling Price	400	

*Direct costs, i.e., those that can be directly attributed to the product

†Indirect costs, i.e., those that cannot be directly attributed to the product

Essentially, a proportion of the cost of the manufactured product can be directly attributed. The direct materials are those such as the plastic, steel and glass that are actually used to make the product. The direct labour is the labour cost actually incurred in making the product. The direct expenses are royalties paid per product manufactured. These three costs (direct materials, direct labour and direct expenses) are known as the **prime cost. The remaining costs are all overheads.**

The production overheads are those associated with the production process. Examples are supervisors' wages or the electricity used in the factory area. By contrast, administrative overheads (for example, staff costs, office expenses, accountants' fees) and selling and distribution overheads (for example, transport and advertising) are incurred outside the production area. An essential element

SOUNDBITE 13.1

Cost Control

'"Control" is the muscle behind every expenses policy. Implementing a strategy for streamlining costs is only as effective as your ability to execute, monitor and evaluate it.'

Source: B. Walsh, Developing a Robust Expenses Policy Can Pay Rich Dividends for Companies, *Accountancy*, March 2011, p. 48.

of costing is that as we move further away from the direct provision of a product or service, it becomes more difficult to allocate the costs fairly. Thus, it is easiest to allocate the direct costs, but most difficult to allocate the administrative costs. Company Snapshot 13.1 shows that administrative expenses can be substantial. For Google Ireland Ltd, for example, administrative expenses represented 78% of sales.

COMPANY SNAPSHOT 13.1

Administrative Expenses

The 2009 Google Ireland Ltd accounts show the company turned over €7.9bn in Europe for the year ending 2009 and a profit of just €45m after 'administrative expenses' of €5.46bn were stripped out.

Administrative expenses largely refer to royalties (or a licence fee) Google pays its Bermuda HQ for the right to operate.

Notes to the accounts show 'administrative expenses' rose significantly between 2008 and 2009 – by €794m – because of increases in headcount, sales and marketing and the 'royalties paid as a result of increases in recorded turnover'.

Source: L. O'Carroll, US investigates Google Tax Strategies, *The Guardian*, 14 October 2011. Copyright Guardian News & Media Ltd 2011.

A key aspect of cost control is the need to reduce costs, particularly in times of economic downturn.

In Figure 13.3, we use the example of a computer helpline, which callers phone to receive advice. In this case, the only direct costs will probably be direct labour. The administrative, selling and distribution costs will be proportionately higher. The key problem in cost

Figure 13.3 Cost Structure for a Service Product (for Example, the Cost per Customer Call for a Computer Helpline)

	£	Examples
Direct labour	4*	Telephone operator
Prime Cost	4	
Administrative expenses	5†	Management, office expenses
Selling and distribution costs	4†	Advertising, marketing
Total Cost	13	
Profit	2	
Selling Price	15	

*Direct costs, i.e., those that can be directly attributed to the service

†Indirect costs, i.e., those that cannot be directly attributed to the service

recovery is thus how to recover the overheads. Direct costs can be directly allocated to a cost unit (i.e., an individual product or service unit, such as a customer's phone call). However, indirect costs have to be totalled and then divided up amongst all the cost units. This is much more problematic.

PAUSE FOR THOUGHT 13.2

Manufacturing a Television

From the following information can you work out the cost and selling price of each television using total absorption costing?

(i)   Direct materials £25; direct labour £50; direct expenses £3 per television.
(ii) £18,000 production overheads; £14,000 administrative expenses; and £15,000 selling and distribution costs.
(iii) 1,000 televisions produced. Profit mark-up of 20% on total cost.

	£
We would thus have:	
Direct materials	25
Direct labour	50
Direct expenses	3
Prime Cost	78
Production overheads (N1)	18
Production Cost	96
Administrative expenses (N1)	14
Selling and distribution costs (N1)	15
Total Cost	125
Profit (20% × £125, i.e., 20% mark-up on cost)	25
Selling Price	150

N1: To work out overheads per television, divide the total overheads by number of televisions produced.

$$\text{Production overheads} \quad = \frac{£18,000}{1,000} = \quad £18 \text{ per television}$$

$$\text{Administrative expenses} \quad = \frac{£14,000}{1,000} = \quad £14 \text{ per television}$$

$$\text{Selling and distribution costs} \quad = \frac{£15,000}{1,000} = \quad £15 \text{ per television}$$

In this case, we are thus absorbing all the overheads into the product whether they represent direct overheads or indirect overheads (such as production, administrative or selling and distribution expenses).

Traditional Costing

The aim of costing is simply to recover (also known as 'to absorb') the costs into an identifiable product or service so as to form the basis for pricing and inventory valuation. In pricing, all the overheads are recovered. For inventory valuation, only those overheads directly related to the production of inventory can be recovered (i.e., direct costs and attributable production overheads). In the next two sections, we look at total absorption costing for pricing, using traditional costing and activity-based costing. In traditional cost recovery or cost absorption, there are six major steps. We will then look at activity-based costing, which is a more modern way of tackling cost recovery. Both traditional total absorption costing and activity-based costing can be used in manufacturing or non-manufacturing industries.

In manufacturing industry, total absorption costing means recovering all the costs from those departments in which products are manufactured (**production departments**) and from those that supply support activities such as catering, administration, or selling and distribution (**service support departments**) into the cost of the end product. In service industries, we recover all the costs from those departments that deliver the final service to customers (**service delivery departments**) and from the service support departments. We set out below the six steps for recovering costs into products (see Figure 13.4). Diagrammatically, this process is illustrated in Figure 13.5 on the next page. **However, exactly the same process would be used for recovering costs into services.**

Figure 13.4 Six Steps in Traditional Total Absorption Costing

1. Record all the costs.
2. Classify all the costs.
3. Allocate all the indirect costs to the departments of a business.
4. Reallocate costs from service support departments to production departments.
5. Calculate an overhead recovery rate.
6. Absorb both the direct costs and the indirect costs (or overheads) into individual products.

REAL-WORLD VIEW 13.2

Pricing Long-Term Contracts

'Cardiff is the cause,' said Weir. 'The race to finish for the October kick-off has caused further unexpected costs.'

Weir blamed the tender process: 'It was a guaranteed maximum price job and we got the bidding wrong. We have delivered a super project, but a financial disaster.'

Last year John Laing had exceptional losses of £26m on the stadium. There may be more to come, 'but not on the same scale,' said Weir.

'We have a four-cylinder business firing on three. We are taking action to get construction right.'

Source: Cardiff Stadium a Penalty for Laing, Roger Nuttall, *The Express*, 10 September 1999.

In essence, businesses need to make a profit. Revenue, therefore, needs to exceed the total costs incurred in making a product. Businesses are thus very keen to ascertain their costs so that they can set a reasonable price for their products. Sometimes, especially for long-term contracts or one-off jobs, this can prove very difficult. For example, Cardiff's Millennium stadium used for international rugby matches, although a triumph of construction and well known internationally, was a financial disaster for John Laing (see Real-World View 13.2).

Figure 13.5 Diagrammatic Representation of Traditional Total Absorption Costing

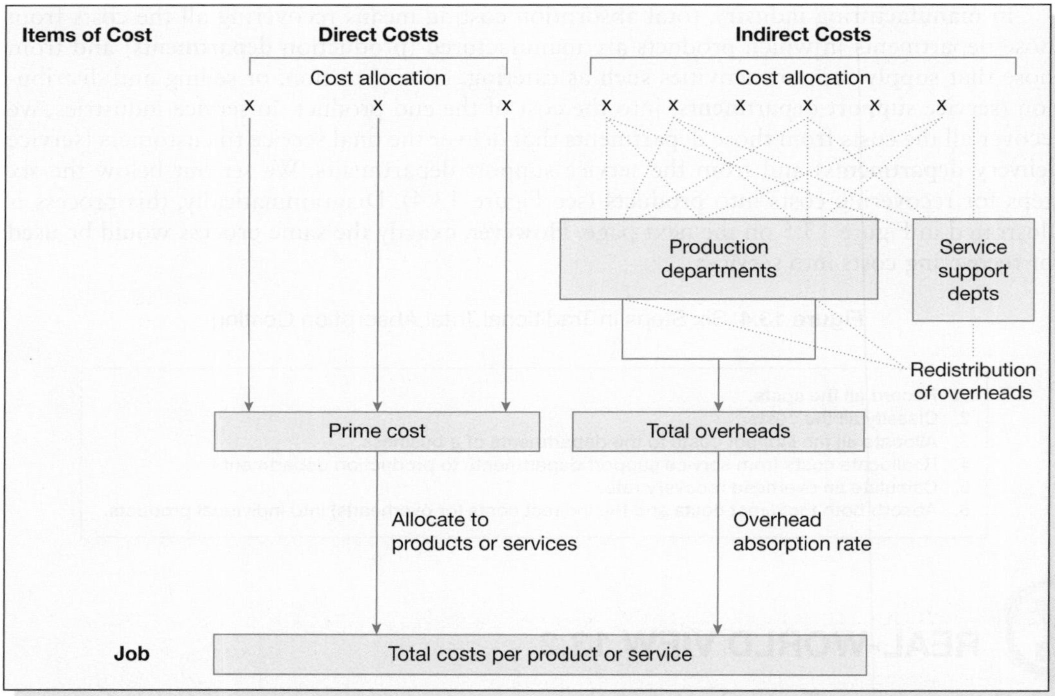

Step 1: Recording

The first step in cost recovery is to record all the costs. It is important to appreciate that many businesses have integrated financial accounting and management accounting systems. There is thus no need to keep separate records for both financial accounting and management accounting. Direct costs, such as direct materials and direct labour, can be directly traced to individual products or services. For example, in manufacturing industries, a job may have a job card on which the direct material and direct labour incurred is recorded.

Indirect costs, such as rent or administrative costs, are much more difficult to record. There are two main problems: estimation and total amount. The first problem is that it is unlikely that the actual costs will be known until the end of a period. Transport costs, for example, may be known only after the journeys have been made. They will, therefore, have to be estimated.

The second problem is that the total costs are recorded centrally. They must then be allocated to products.

Step 2: Classification

This involves categorising and grouping the costs before allocating them to departments. We may, for example, need to calculate the total rent or total costs for light and heat.

Step 3: Allocate indirect costs to departments

Direct costs can be directly traced to goods or services. For overheads, the process is indirect. The key to overhead allocation is to find an appropriate basis for allocation. These are called allocation bases or cost drivers. Figure 13.6 shows some possible allocation bases for various types of cost.

Figure 13.6 Departmental Allocation Bases

Types of Cost	*Possible Allocation Bases*
Power	Number of machine hours
Depreciation, insurance	Value of property, plant and equipment
Canteen, office expenses	Relative area of floor space
Rent, business rates, light and heat	Number of employees

Step 4: Reallocate service support department costs to production departments

Once all the costs are allocated, we must reallocate them to the production departments. This is because we need to recover these costs into *specific products* which are *made* only in the *production departments*.

Step 5: Overhead recovery rate

Once we have allocated our costs to production departments, we need to absorb these costs into the final product. We must choose a suitable recovery rate. The choice of rate reflects the nature of the activity and could be any of the following (or even others):

- Rate per unit
- Rate per direct labour hour
- Rate per machine hour
- Rate per £ materials
- Rate per £ direct labour
- Rate per £ prime cost.

Figure 13.7 illustrates this process.

Figure 13.7 Overhead Recovery Rate

A firm has £12,000 indirect costs in department F. It also has the following data available:

	£	
Direct materials	30,000	240,000 units produced
Direct labour	70,000	6,000 direct labour hours are used
Prime Cost	100,000	50,000 machine hours are used

Calculate the various overhead recovery rates discussed previously in step 5.

The various overhead recovery rates are:

1. Per unit $= \dfrac{£12,000}{240,000} =$ £0.05 per unit

2. Per direct labour hour $= \dfrac{£12,000}{6,000} =$ £2.00 per labour hour

3. Per machine hour $= \dfrac{£12,000}{50,000} =$ £0.24 per machine hour

4. Per £ material $= \dfrac{£12,000}{30,000} =$ £0.40 per £ material

5. Per £ labour $= \dfrac{£12,000}{70,000} =$ £0.17 per £ labour

6. Per £ prime cost $= \dfrac{£12,000}{100,000} =$ £0.12 per £ prime cost

In practice, only one of these six overhead recovery rates would be used, most likely direct labour hours.

Step 6: Absorption of costs into products

Once we have calculated an absorption rate we can absorb our costs. In practice, there will be many products of varying size and complexity. Figure 13.8 illustrates how we would now recover our costs into products.

Figure 13.8 Recovery into Specific Jobs

If, for example, the following Job X007 was one of the 200,000 units produced and we recover our overheads *per direct labour hour* then we might have the following situation.

Job X007		£
Direct materials	(10 kilos at £2)	20
Direct labour	(12 hours at £12)	144
Prime Cost		164

The direct materials are directly recovered into the job; we must now recover the indirect costs. We recover into our product 12 hours at £2.00 per hour (as calculated in Figure 13.7) = £24.00.

	£
Our total cost is therefore	
Prime Cost	164
Overheads	24
Total Cost	188
Profit: 25% mark-up on cost	47
Selling Price	235

Comprehensive Example

In Figure 13.9, a comprehensive example of cost recovery looks at all six steps in the cost recovery process.

Figure 13.9 Comprehensive Cost Recovery Example

Millennium plc has the following three departments:

- A. Production
- B. Production
- C. Service support

Type of Cost	Proposed Basis of Apportionment	£
Rent and business rates	Floor area	4,000
Repairs and maintenance	Amount actually spent	1,000
Canteen	Number of employees	500
Depreciation	Cost of fixed assets	2,100
		7,600

It is estimated that:

(i) Department A has a floor area of 4,000 sq.ft., Department B has a floor area of 3,000 sq.ft., and Department C has a floor area of 1,000 sq.ft.

(ii) The following direct labour hours will be used: A (2,000 hours), B (3,000 hours), and C (300 hours)

(iii) Department A has 50 employees, Department B 30 employees and Department C 20 employees

(iv) Department A has machinery costing £15,000, Department B has £25,000 machinery and Department C has £30,000 machinery

(v) The wage rates are £11 per hour for A, £12 per hour for B, and £10 per hour for C

(vi) Repairs are to be A £200; B £300; C £500.

It is estimated that 70% of Department C's facilities are used by Department A, and 30% by Department B, and that C's direct material and direct labour for the year will be £3,000 and £1,500. The overheads will be recovered by reference to the amount of direct labour hours used.

Millennium plc wishes to prepare a quotation for the following job C206. Profit is to be at 25% on cost.

Direct material	£400
Direct labour	Department A 20 hours
	Department B 10 hours

We have already recorded (step 1), and classified (step 2) our information so the next stage (step 3) is to allocate our indirect costs (i.e., overheads) to departments.

Step 3: Overhead Allocation to Departments

Type of Cost	Allocation	Total £	A £	B £	C £
C's direct labour	Traced directly (Helpnote 1)	3,000			3,000
C's direct material	Traced directly (Helpnote 1)	1,500			1,500
Rent and business rates (calculation shown below in Helpnote point 2)	Area (4,000: 3,000: 1,000)	4,000	2,000	1,500	500
Repairs and maintenance	Actual	1,000	200	300	500
Canteen	No. of employees (50: 30: 20)	500	250	150	100
Depreciation	Cost of fixed assets (15,000: 25,000: 30,000)	2,100	450	750	900
Total		12,100	2,900	2,700	6,500

Figure 13.9 Comprehensive Cost Recovery Example (*continued*)

Helpnotes:

1. We must include our direct labour and direct materials for Department C in our calculations of the overhead allocation rate because although direct for Department C, they are indirect for Departments A and B, which are the production departments.

2. The allocations for each type of cost are made by allocating each cost across the departments in proportion to the total cost. For example, the rent and business rates total area is 8,000 sq.ft. Thus:
   A (4,000/8,000) × £4,000 = £2,000.
   B (3,000/8,000) × £4,000 = £1,500, and
   C (1,000/8,000) × £4,000 = £500

Step 4: Reallocate Service Support Department Costs to Production Departments

The next stage is to reallocate the service support department costs to the production departments. Since 70% of C is used by A, and 30% by B, it is only fair to reallocate them in this proportion.

	Total	A	B	C
	£	£	£	£
Total overheads	12,100	2,900	2,700	6,500
Reallocation %		70%	30%	(100%)
		4,550	1,950	(6,500)
New total	12,100	7,450	4,650	

If there were more service support departments, we would have to continue to reallocate the costs until they were all absorbed into production departments. In this case the allocation is finished.

Step 5: Calculate an Overhead Recovery Rate

It is now time to work out an overhead recovery rate.

	Total	A	B
	£	£	£
Total overheads	12,100	7,450	4,650
Direct labour hours		2,000	3,000
Recovery rate		3.73	1.55

Step 6: Absorption of Costs into Products

Finally, we must absorb both our direct and indirect costs into our products as a basis for pricing.

Job C206

		£
Direct labour	A. 20 hours at £11	220.00
	B. 10 hours at £12	120.00
Direct material		400.00
Prime Cost		740.00
Overheads	A. 20 hours at £3.73	74.60
	B. 10 hours at £1.55	15.50
Total Cost		830.10
25% mark-up on cost		207.52
Selling Price		1,037.62

Total absorption costing (as we have just demonstrated in Figure 13.9) is where we try to recover all our overheads (direct and indirect) into a product or service. It forms the basis of job, contract, batch, process and service costing.

PAUSE FOR THOUGHT 13.3

Traditional Product Costing

Traditional product costing usually uses either direct machine hours or direct labour hours to determine its overhead recovery rate. Can you see any problems with this in a service and knowledge-based economy?

In manufacturing industry, products are made intensively using machines and direct labour. It makes sense, therefore, to recover overheads using those measures. However, in service industries or knowledge-based industries, products or services may have very little direct labour input and do not use machines. The financial services industry or Internet companies, for example, have very few industrial machines or direct labour. In this case, machine hours and labour hours become, at best, irrelevant and, at worst, very dangerous when pricing goods or services. In these and other industries new methods of allocating cost are necessary. The stimulus to find these new methods has led to the development of activity-based costing. This seeks to establish activities as a basis for allocating overheads.

Activity-Based Costing

Traditional total absorption costing was developed in manufacturing industries. In these industries, there are usually substantial quantities of machine hours or direct labour hours. These volume-related allocation bases are used to allocate overheads. However, recently, traditional absorption costing has been criticised for failing to respond to the new post-manufacturing industrial environment and for lacking sophistication. Allocation using direct cost bases often, therefore, fails to reflect the true distribution of the costs. It is argued that this leads to inaccurate pricing.

Activity-based costing aims to remedy these defects. It is based on the premise that activities that occur within a firm cause overhead costs. By identifying these activities, a firm can achieve a range of benefits, including the ability to cost products more accurately. Essentially, activity-based costing is a more sophisticated version of the traditional product costing system. There is a six-stage process (see Figure 13.10).

Figure 13.10 Six Steps in Activity-Based Costing

1. Record all the costs.
2. Classify all the costs.
3. Identify activities.
4. Identify cost drivers and allocate overheads to them.
5. Calculate activity-cost driver rates.
6. Absorb both the direct costs and indirect costs into a product or service.

We will now work through these six steps. The process is portrayed graphically in Figure 13.11.

Figure 13.11 Diagrammatic Representation of Activity-Based Costing

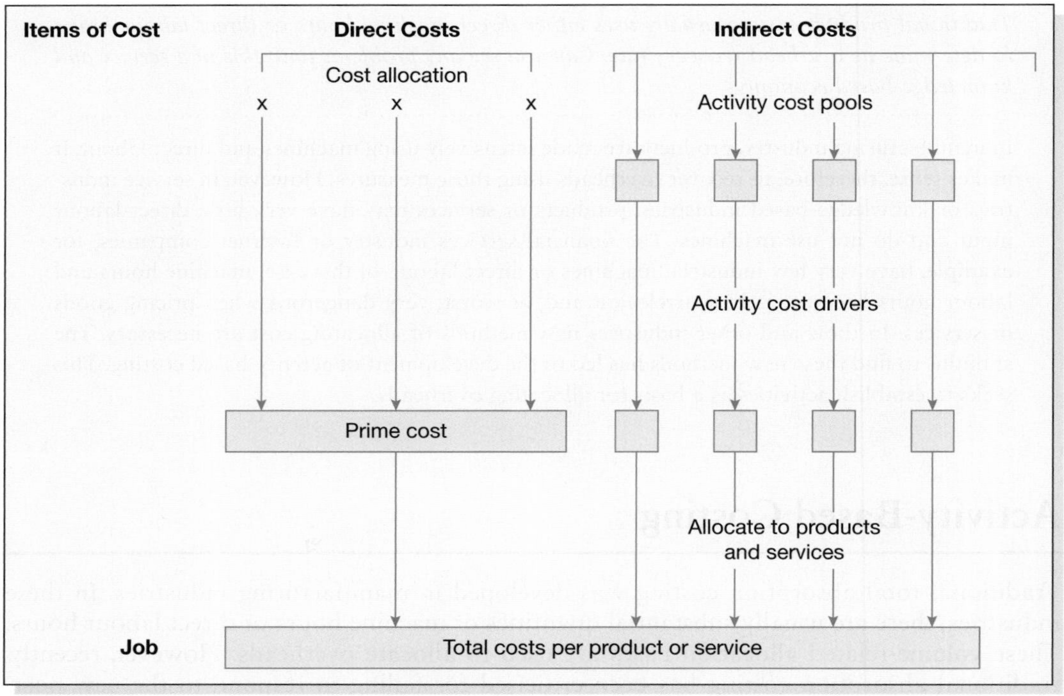

Steps 1 and 2
The first two steps are the same as for traditional costing.

Step 3: Identify activities
The firm identifies those activities that determine overhead costs. Production is one such activity.

Step 4: Identify cost drivers and allocate appropriate overheads to them
Activity-based accounting seeks to link cost recovery to cost behaviour. Activity-cost drivers determine cost behaviour. Activity-cost drivers for a production department, for example, might be the number of purchase orders, the number of set-ups, maintenance hours, the number of inspections, the number of despatches, machine hours or direct labour hours.

Step 5: Calculate activity-cost driver rates
Here, for each activity driver we calculate an appropriate cost driver rate. This is the total costs for a cost driver divided by the number of activities. An example might be £2,000 total costs for material inspections divided by 250 material inspections.

Step 6: Absorb both direct and indirect costs into a product or service

This process is similar to traditional product costing. The total costs are allocated to products using activity cost drivers; they are then divided by the number of products.

In Figure 13.12 an activity-based costing example is given for Fireco. This has two products (A and B) and four activity-cost drivers have been identified (set-ups, purchase orders, inspections and sales invoices.

Figure 13.12 Activity-Based Costing Example

Fireco has the following costs: for setting up machinery £8,000, for ordering material £3,000, for inspecting the material £2,000 and sales ledger expenses £8,000. Selling price is cost plus 25%. There is also the following information:

	A £	B £
Direct materials	8,000	7,000
Direct labour	10,000	15,000
Number of set-ups	20	30
Number of purchase orders	4,000	1,000
Number of inspections	100	150
Number of sales invoices processed	7,000	3,000
Number of products	16,000	10,000

What would be the activity-cost driver rates, total cost and selling price?

As we have already completed steps 1–4 (recording, classifying, and identifying cost drivers with associated overheads), we can proceed to step 5, calculating the activity cost-driver rates.

Step 5: Calculation of Activity-Cost Driver Rates

Activity	Set-ups	Purchase orders	Inspections	Sales ledger
Cost	£8,000	£3,000	£2,000	£8,000
Cost driver	50 set-ups	5,000 purchase orders	250 inspections	10,000 sales ledger
Cost per unit of cost driver	£160	£0.60	£8.00	£0.80

Here we simply divided the total costs of each activity by the total number of the activities. There are, for example, 20 set-ups for A and 30 set-ups for B making 50 set-ups in total. We divide this into the total cost of £8,000 to arrive at £160 per set-up.

Step 6: Absorb both the Direct and Indirect Costs into the Products

Activity	Set-ups	Purchase orders	Inspections	Sales	Total costs
A	20 × £160 = £3,200	4,000 × £0.60 = £2,400	100 × £8.00 = £800	7,000 × £0.80 = £5,600	£12,000
B	30 × £160 = £4,800	1,000 × £0.60 = £600	150 × £8.00 = £1,200	3,000 × £0.80 = £2,400	£9,000
Total	£8,000	£3,000	£2,000	£8,000	£21,000

Here, we multiplied the cost per unit of cost driver by the number of cost drivers. For example, we have 20 set-ups (i.e., number of cost drivers) for A and 30 set-ups (i.e., number of cost drivers) for B. Each set-up costs £160 (i.e., cost per unit of cost driver).

Figure 13.12 Activity-Based Costing Example (*continued*)

	A £	B £
Total overhead costs	12,000	9,000
Number of products	16,000	10,000
Overhead per product	£0.75	£0.90

Here, we took the total overhead costs for A (£12,000) and for B (£9,000) and divided by the number of products to arrive at the overhead per product. We can now prepare the product cost statements for products A and B. Direct materials and direct labour are calculated by dividing the total costs for each product by the total number of products (i.e., for A's direct materials, we divide £8,000 by 16,000 products).

	A Product cost £	B Product cost £
Direct materials	0.50	0.70
Direct labour	0.62	1.50
Prime Cost	1.12	2.20
Overheads	0.75	0.90
Total Cost	1.87	3.10
Profit (25% mark-up on cost)	0.47	0.78
Sales Price	2.34	3.88

Activity-based costing is thus a more sophisticated version of traditional product costing. It can give more accurate and reliable information. It also significantly increases the company's ability to manage costs and is suitable for both manufacturing and service companies. However, importantly, it involves much more time and effort to set up than traditional product costing and may not be suitable for all companies. In Figure 13.13, we show the difference between the two systems diagrammatically.

Figure 13.13 Traditional Costing Versus ABC

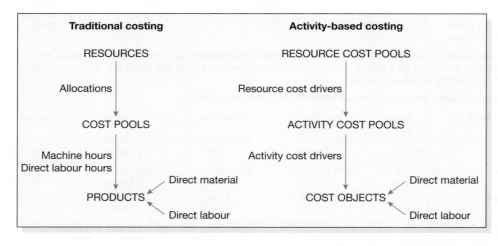

Source: E. Labro (2005), Analytics of Costing System Design in A. Bhimani, *Contemporary Issues in Management Accounting* (2005), Oxford University Press, p. 219.

Costing for Inventory Valuation

Non-Production Overheads

It is important to distinguish between costing as a basis of pricing, which we have just looked at, and costing as the basis for inventory valuation. The key difference is in the treatment of non-production overheads.

PAUSE FOR THOUGHT 13.4

Non-Production Overheads

Why are administrative, sales and marketing costs not included as overheads in inventory valuation?

The problem of non-production overheads is a tricky one. The administrative, sales and marketing costs, for example, are required when calculating the total cost of a product as a basis for pricing. However, they should not be included when calculating an inventory valuation. The reason is that these costs are not incurred in actually making the product. It would, therefore, be incorrect to include them in the cost of the product. These non-production costs are often called period costs. This is because they are allocated to the *period* not the *product*.

When valuing inventory it is permissible to include production overheads, but not non-production overheads. This is shown in John Laing's annual report in Company Snapshot 13.2. However, for cost-plus pricing we need to take into account all overheads. These include non-production overheads such as sales, administrative and marketing expenses. As Figure 13.14 on the next page shows, there can be quite a difference.

COMPANY SNAPSHOT 13.2

Production Overheads

Inventories

Inventories are stated at the lower of cost, including production overheads, and net realisable value.

Source: John Laing plc, *Annual Report and Accounts 2005*, p. 83.

Figure 13.14 Costing for Inventory Valuation and for Cost-Plus Pricing

A product has the following cost structure. 100,000 products are manufactured.

	Inventory valuation (Marginal costing)	Inventory valuation (Absorption costing)	Cost-plus pricing (Total absorption costing)
	£000	£000	£000
Direct materials	10	10	10
Direct labour	25	25	25
Prime Cost	35	35	35
Variable production overheads	10	10	10
Fixed production overheads	–	5	5
Total Production Costs	45	50	50
Administrative costs			10
Marketing costs			8
Sales costs			7
Total Cost			75
Profit: 33.3% mark-up on cost			25
Selling Price			100

At what value should each item be recorded in inventory and what is the selling price per item?

i. *Inventory* using marginal costing $\dfrac{£45,000}{100,000} = 0.45\text{p}$

ii. *Inventory* using absorption costing $\dfrac{£50,000}{100,000} = 0.50\text{p}$

iii. *Selling price* using total absorption costing $\dfrac{£100,000}{100,000} = £1.00$

Helpnote: Using **marginal costing,** only the **variable production overheads** that can be attributed are included in the inventory valuation. In **absorption costing,** we include **all the production overheads.** It is absorption costing that is used for inventory valuation in **financial reporting.** In **total absorption costing,** we recover **all the costs** into the product's final selling price.

Different inventory valuation measures: FIFO, LIFO, AVCO

The inclusion of production overheads in finished goods inventory is one key problem in inventory valuation. Another difficulty, which primarily concerns raw material inventory, is the choice of inventory valuation methods. There are three main methods: FIFO (first-in-first-out), LIFO (last-in-first-out) and AVCO (average cost). All three are permitted in management accounting and for inventory valuation in the financial accounts in the US. However, in the UK, and under IFRS, only FIFO and AVCO are permitted for inventory valuation in financial accounting.

Inventory valuation is not quite as easy as it may at first seem. It depends on which assumptions you make about the inventory sold. Is the inventory you buy in first, the first to be sold (first-in-first-out (FIFO))? Or is the inventory you buy in last, sold first (last-in-first-out (LIFO))? If the purchase price of inventory changes then this assumption matters.

In Figure 13.15, we investigate an example of the impact that using FIFO or LIFO has upon the valuation of raw materials inventory. We also include a third method, AVCO (average cost), which takes the average purchase price of the goods as their cost of sale.

Figure 13.15 FIFO, LIFO and AVCO Inventory Valuation Methods

Inventory co purchases its inventory on the first day of the month. It starts with no inventory. Its purchases and revenue over the first three months are as follows:

		Kilos	Cost per kilo	Total cost
January 1	Purchases	10,000	£1.00	£10,000
February 1	Purchases	15,000	£1.50	£22,500
March 1	Purchases	20,000	£2.00	£40,000
		45,000		£72,500
March 31	Revenue	(35,000)		
March 31	Closing inventory	10,000		

What is the closing inventory valuation using FIFO, LIFO and AVCO?

(i) FIFO: Here, the first inventory purchased is the first sold. The 35,000 kilos sold, therefore, used up all the January inventory (10,000 kilos), and the February inventory (15,000 kilos), and (10,000 kilos) of the March inventory. We, therefore, have left in inventory 10,000 kilos of material valued at the March purchase price of £2.00 per kilo. Closing inventory is, therefore, 10,000 × £2 = £20,000.

(ii) LIFO: Here the last inventory purchased is assumed to be the first to be sold. The 35,000 kilos sold, therefore, used up:

20,000	kilos from March
15,000	kilos from February
35,000	

We, therefore, have remaining 10,000 kilos from January at £1 per kilo = £10,000.

(iii) AVCO: Here the inventory value is pooled and the average cost of purchase is taken as the cost of the goods sold. We purchased 45,000 kilos for £72,500 (i.e., £1.611 per kilo). The cost of our inventory is, therefore, 10,000 kilos × average cost £1.611 = £16,110.

We can, therefore, see that our inventory *valuations* vary considerably.

	£
FIFO	20,000
LIFO	10,000
AVCO	16,110

It should be appreciated that inventory valuation is distinct from physical inventory management. In most businesses, good business practice dictates that you usually physically issue the oldest inventory first (i.e., adopt FIFO). However, in inventory valuation you are allowed to choose what is acceptable under the regulations.

PAUSE FOR THOUGHT 13.5

FIFO, LIFO and AVCO and Cost of Sales

Do you think that using a different inventory valuation method in Figure 13.14 would affect cost of sales or profit?

Yes!! Whichever valuation method is used, both cost of sales and profit are affected. Essentially, the cost of purchases will be split between inventory and cost of sales.

	Total cost	Cost of sales	Inventory
	£	£	£
FIFO	72,500	52,500 (N1)	20,000
LIFO	72,500	62,500 (N2)	10,000
AVCO	72,500	56,390 (N3)	16,110

(N1) FIFO represents:			£
	January	10,000 kilos at £1.00	10,000
	February	15,000 kilos at £1.50	22,500
	March	10,000 kilos at £2.00	20,000
			52,500

(N2) LIFO represents:			£
	February	15,000 kilos at £1.50	22,500
	March	20,000 kilos at £2.00	40,000
			62,500

(N3) AVCO represents:		£
	35,000 kilos at £1.611	56,390

Profit is affected because if cost of sales is less, inventory, and thus profit, is higher and vice versa. In this case, using FIFO will show the greatest profit as its cost of sales is lowest. LIFO will show the lowest profit. AVCO is in the middle!

Different Costing Methods for Different Industries

So far we have focused mainly on allocating costs to individual jobs in manufacturing. However, job costing is not appropriate in many situations. Different industries have different costing problems. To solve these problems different types of costing have evolved. In order to give a flavour of this, we look below at four industries (see Figure 13.16).

Figure 13.16 Overview of Different Industries' Costing Methods

Industry	Costing Method
1. Manufacturing in batches	Batch costing
2. Shipbuilding	Contract costing
3. Brewery	Process costing
4. Hotel and catering	Service costing

1. Batch Costing

Batch costing is where a number of items of a similar nature are processed together. There is thus not one discrete job. Batch costing can be used in a variety of situations, such as manufacture of medicinal tablets (as shown in Figure 13.17).

Figure 13.17 Batch Costing

A run of 50,000 tablets are made for batch number x1.11. There are 2,000 defective tablets and 50 tablets per box. Overheads are recovered on the basis of £6 per labour hour. The material was 3 kg at £5.00 per kg, and labour rate A 6 hours at £9.00, and rate B 7 hours at £10.00.

	£
The costing statement might look as follows:	
Direct materials (3 kg at £5.00)	15.00
Direct labour (13 hours: A 6 at £9	54.00
B 7 at £10)	70.00
Prime Cost	139.00
Overheads (13 hours at £6)	78.00
Total Cost	217.00
Boxes (48,000 ÷ 50)	960
Cost per box	22.6p

2. Contract Costing

A contract can be looked at as a very long job or a job lasting more than one year. It occurs in big construction industries such as shipbuilding and aircraft building. A long-term contract extends over more than one year and creates the problem of when to take profit. If we have a three-year contract, do we take all our profit at the start of our contract, at the end, or equally throughout the three years?

The answer has gradually evolved over the years, and there are now certain recognised guidelines for taking a profit or loss. Generally, losses should be taken as soon as it is realised they will occur. By contrast, profits should be taken so as to reflect the proportion of the work carried out. This is shown in Company Snapshot 13.3, which shows John Laing's accounting policy for long-term contracts.

COMPANY SNAPSHOT 13.3

Long-Term Contracts

Revenue recognition in the Group's management companies is determined by reference to the following policies:

- long-term facilities management contracts are accounted for in accordance with IAS11 'Construction Contracts'. Revenues and profits recognised are determined by reference to services provided in the period, adjusted to reflect the forecast level of profitability at the end of the contract period.
- fees receivable in respect of management services agreements with PFI/PPP Project Companies are recognised evenly over the period of the agreement; and
- income arising in respect of recoveries of bid costs on financial close of PFI/PPP Project Companies is recognised as invoiced. Revenue excludes the value of intra-group transactions and VAT and includes the Group's revenue derived from the provision of services to joint ventures by Group subsidiaries.

When it is probable that the expected outcome over the life of a facilities management or management services contract will result in a net outflow of economic benefits or overall loss, a provision is recognised immediately. The provision is determined based on the net present value of the expected future cash inflows and outflows.

Source: John Laing plc, *Annual Report and Accounts 2010,* Accounting Policies, p. 94.

In practice, allocating profits can be very complex. There are no set rules. We will use a simplified formula: *Profit to be taken = % contract complete × total estimated contract profit × 2/3.* Usually, the customer and the supplier will negotiate and set a price for a contract in advance. Figure 13.18 provides an illustrative example.

Figure 13.18 Contract Costing

O&P Ferries requires a new ferry to be built. It asks Londonside Shipbuilders for a quotation. Londonside looks at its costs and decides that the ship will cost £4 million direct materials, £4 million direct labour and £5 million indirect overheads. They then quote O&P Ferries £19 million for the job. They aim to complete the job in 3 years. Londonside therefore estimate a £6 million profit (£19 million less £13 million). When should they take the profit?

The answer is that the situation is reviewed as the contract progresses, and profit taken according to the formula given earlier. For example, if we have the following costs:

In £ millions	Year 1		Year 2		Year 3	
	£	£	£	£	£	£
Contract Price (Remains fixed)		19		19		19
Costs Incurred to Date						
Direct materials	2		3		5	
Direct labour	2		2		5	
Indirect overheads	2		3		6	
Total costs incurred to date	6		8		16	
Estimated future costs	8		5		–	
Total Costs (estimated and incurred)		14		13		16
Estimated Profit		5		6		3
% Contract complete		6/14ths		8/13ths		Complete

At the end of year 3 the contract is finished therefore the estimated profit will be the actual profit.

So if we apply our formula we can see how it works:

	% contract complete	×	Total estimated contract profit	×	$\frac{2}{3}$		This year's profit £	Total estimated profit to date £
Year 1	$\frac{6}{14}$	×	£5m	×	$\frac{2}{3}$	= £1.43m	£1.43m	£1.43m
Year 2	$\frac{8}{13}$	×	£6m	×	$\frac{2}{3}$	= £2.46m	£1.03m	£2.46m

We take an additional £1.03 million in year 2 (i.e., the profit to date, £2.46m, less year 1's profit, £1.43m).

							This year's profit	Total estimated profit to date
Year 3							£0.54m	£3.0m

In year 3, we know the actual profit is £3 million. We can therefore take all the profit not taken so far. This is £3 million – £2.46 (already taken) = £0.54 million.

3. Process Costing

Process costing is used in industries with a continuous production process; e.g., beer brewing. Products are passed from one department to another, and then processed further. At any one point in time, therefore, many of the products will only be partially complete. To deal with this problem of partially completed products, the concept of equivalent units has developed. At the end of a process, if we partially finish units then we take the percentage of completion and convert to fully completed equivalent units. If, for example, (see Figure 13.19) we have 1,000 litres of beer that are half way through the beer-making process, this would equal 500 litres fully complete (i.e., there would be the equivalent of 500 litres).

Figure 13.19 Process Costing

A firm manufactures beer. There are two processes A and B. There are 1,000 litres of opening inventory of beer for process B, the fermentation stage (the product has already been through process A). They are 50% complete. During the year 650 litres are finished and transferred (i.e., completed). The closing work in progress consists of 800 litres, 75% completed. The costs incurred in that process during that year are £15,000.

To find out the cost per litre, we must first find out how many litres are effectively produced during the period. We can do this by deduction. First of all we can establish the total inventory that was completed by the end of the year. This will equal the inventory we have finished and transferred (650 litres) plus the closing inventory (800 litres, 75% complete, equals 600 litres). From this 1,250 litres we need to take the opening inventory (1,000 litres, 50% complete, equals 500 litres). We have, therefore, our effective production of 750 litres.* The cost is then £15,000 divided by the 750 equivalent litres, equals £20 per litre.

	Equivalent litres
Finished and transferred	650
Closing inventory (800 × 75%)	600
Total completed	1,250
Opening inventory (1,000 × 50%)	(500)
Effective production	750

Therefore, using 'equivalent' litres our cost per litre for process B is:

$$\frac{£15,000}{750} = £20$$

4. Service Costing

Service costing concerns services such as canteens. In large businesses, for example, canteens might be run as independent operating units that have to make a profit. The cost of a particular service is simply the total costs for the service divided by the number of services provided. Service costing uses the same principles as job costing. In Figure 13.20 an example of service costing for canteens is shown. It can be seen that roast dinners cost £2.60 and salads £1.35.

Figure 13.20 Service Costing for Canteens

A canteen serves 10,000 meals: 6,000 are roast dinners and 4,000 salads. The roast dinners are bought in for £2.50 each and the salads for £1.25. The canteen costs are £1,000. They are apportioned across the number of meals served. What is the cost of each meal?

	Roast Dinners £	Salads £
Bought-in price	2.50	1.25
Overheads per meal $\left(\dfrac{£1,000}{10,000} = 0.10p\right)$	0.10	0.10
	2.60	1.35

Target Costing

So far we have focused principally on cost-plus pricing. However, the Japanese have introduced a concept called target costing, which focuses on market prices. Essentially, a price is set with reference to market conditions and customer purchasing patterns. A target profit is then deducted to arrive at a target cost. This target cost is set in order to allow a company to achieve a certain market share and a certain profit. The target profit is set before the product is manufactured.

The costs are then examined and re-examined in order to make the target cost. Often this is done by breaking down the product into many individual components and costing them separately. The product may be divided into many functions using 'functional analysis'. Functions may include attractiveness, durability, reliability and style among other things. Each function is priced. Target costing may also be used in conjunction with life cycle costing. Life cycle costing involves tracing all the costs of a product over their entire life cycle. Target costing will be the first stage in this process.

Cost-Cutting

A final key reason why it is essential for a business to have a good knowledge of its costs is for cost-cutting. As we mentioned in Chapter 12, the two major ways to improve profitability are by improving revenue or by cutting costs. Whereas improving revenue is a long-term solution, cost-cutting is a short-term solution. It is particularly useful when a business is in trouble. It is perhaps the most common business response as Real-World View 13.3 shows. By announcing cost-cutting measures, the business signals to the City and to its investors that it is serious about improving its profitability. Unfortunately, one of the most important elements of most companies' costs is labour. Therefore, companies often shed labour. When doing this, companies may run into trouble with trade unions or with politicians. As Real-World View 13.3 shows, US companies were responding to the financial downturn in 2011 by cutting costs.

REAL-WORLD VIEW 13.3

Cutting Costs

When company profits decline then a company strategy commonly adopted by CEOs is to cut costs rather than to expand sales. This was certainly the case in the US after the financial crisis according to Reuters.

'Those who went so far as to say demand was slowing down generally said they were reacting in the way corporate America always does in times of crisis – cutting costs.'

Source: Reuters (Scott Malone, Martinne Geller, Liana Baker), 26 October 2011, *Insight:* In tough times, Wall Street watches CEO word games.

As an alternative to cutting labour costs, companies sometimes attempt to cut other costs such as training or research and development. By doing this, companies may sacrifice long-term profitability for short-term profitability.

Conclusion

Costing is an important part of management accounting. It involves recording, classifying, allocating and absorbing costs into individual products and services. Cost recovery is used to value inventory by including production overheads and for cost-plus pricing by determining the total costs of a product or service. Traditionally, overheads have been allocated to products or services primarily using volume-based measures such as direct labour hours or machine hours. However, more recently, activity-based measures such as number of purchase orders processed have been used. Different industries use different costing systems such as batch costing, contract costing, process costing and service costing. Target costing, based on a product's market price, has been developed in Japan. Businesses in trouble often cut costs, such as labour, in order to try to improve their profitability.

Discussion Questions

Questions with numbers in blue have answers at the back of the book.

Q1 What is costing and why is it important?

Q2 Compare and contrast the traditional and the more modern activity-based approaches to costing.

Q3 Overhead recovery is the most difficult part of cost recovery. Discuss.

Q4 Target costing combines the advantages of both market pricing and cost-plus pricing. Discuss.

Q5 State whether the following statements are true or false. If false, explain why.
(a) A cost is an actual past expenditure.
(b) When recovering costs for pricing we use total absorption costing. However, for inventory valuation we use absorption costing or marginal costing.
(c) When using traditional total absorption costing it is important to identify activity cost drivers.
(d) In process costing, if we had 100 units that were 50% complete, this would equal 50 equivalent units.
(e) In inventory valuation, marginal costing is normally used in valuing inventory in financial reporting.

Numerical Questions

Questions with numbers in blue have answers at the back of the book.

Q1 Sorter has the following costs:
(a) Machine workers' wages
(b) Cost clerks' wages
(c) Purchase of raw materials
(d) Machine repairs
(e) Finance director's salary
(f) Office cleaners
(g) Delivery van staff's wages
(h) Managing director's car expenses
(i) Depreciation on office furniture
(j) Computer running expenses for office
(k) Loan interest
(l) Auditors' fees
(m) Depreciation on machinery
(n) Advertising costs
(o) Electricity for machines
(p) Bank charges

Q1 Sorter has the following costs (*continued*)
Required: An analysis of Sorter's costs between:

(i)   Direct materials
(ii) Direct labour
(iii) Production overheads

(iv) Administrative expenses
(v) Selling and distribution costs

Q2 Costa has the following costs:

	£
Salaries of administrative employees	90,800
Wages of factory supervisors	120,000
Computer overhead expenses	9,000
($^2/_3$ in factory, $^1/_3$ in administration)	
Interest on loans	3,000
Wages: selling and distribution	18,300
Salaries: marketing	25,000
Royalties	3,600
Raw materials used in production	320,000
Depreciation: Machinery used for production	8,000
Office fixtures and fittings	4,200
Delivery vans	3,500
Buildings ($^1/_2$ factory; $^1/_4$ office; $^1/_4$ sales)	10,000
Labour costs directly connected with production	200,000
Other production overheads	70,000
Commission paid to sales force	1,200

Required: A determination of Costa's:

(i)   prime cost
(ii) production cost
(iii) total cost

Q3 Makemore has three departments: Departments A and B are production and Department C is a service support department. It apportions its overheads as follows (see brackets):

		£
Supervisors' salaries	(number of employees)	25,000
Computer advisory	(number of employees)	18,000
Rent and business rates	(floor area)	20,000
Depreciation on machinery	(cost)	21,000
Repairs	(actual spend)	4,000
		88,000

You have the following information:
(a) Department A 1,000 employees, B 2,000 employees, C 500 employees.
(b) Department A 10,000 sq.feet, B 6,000 sq.feet, and C 4,000 sq.feet.
(c) Department A machinery costs £30,000, B machinery costs £15,000.
(d) Repairs are £2,800, £1,100 and £100, respectively, for departments A, B and C.
(e) Department C's facilities will be reallocated 60% for A and 40% for B.

(f)	Department A	Department B
Direct labour hours	80,000	40,000
Machine hours	100,000	200,000

Required: An apportionment of the overheads to products A and B
(i) using direct labour hours, and
(ii) using machine hours.

Q4 Flight has two products, the 'Takeoff' and the 'Landing'. They go through two departments and incur the following costs:

		Takeoff		Landing	
Dept. A –	Direct labour	10 hours	£10 per hour	9 hours	£7 per hour
	Direct materials	10 kilos	£5 per kilo	7 kilos	£12 per kilo
Dept. B –	Direct labour	8 hours	£12 per hour	5 hours	£8 per hour
	Direct materials	5 kilos	£15 per kilo	6 kilos	£10 per kilo

Takeoff's indirect overheads are absorbed at £7 per labour hour for Dept. A and £5 per hour Dept. B.
Landing's indirect overheads are absorbed at £6 per labour hour for Dept. A and £4 per hour for Dept. B.
Selling price is to be 20% on cost.

Required: The prices for which Flight should sell 'Takeoff' and 'Landing'.

Q5 An up-market catering company, Spicemeals, organises banquets and high-class catering functions. A particular function for the Blue Devils university dining club has the following costs for 100 guests.

100 starters	at	£1.00 each
50 main meals	at	£3.00 each
50 main meals	at	£2.50 each
200 desserts	at	£1.50 each
200 bottles of wine	at	£5.00 each
100 coffees	at	£0.20 each

Direct labour:				
	Supervisory	8 hours	at	£15.00
	Food preparation	30 hours	at	£8.00
	Waitressing	200 hours	at	£9.00

Overheads relating to this job based on total hours are recovered at £1.10 per hour. There are £180,000 general overheads within the business and about 300 functions. Profit is to be 15% on cost.

Required: The price Spicemeals should charge for this function and the amount for each guest.

Q6 A medicinal product 'Supertab' is produced in batches. Batch number X308 has the following costs:

Direct labour: Grade				
	1	200 hours	at	£8.00
	2	50 hours	at	£9.00
	3	25 hours	at	£15.00
Direct materials: Type	A	10 kilos	at	£8.00
	B	5 kilos	at	£10.00
	C	3 kilos	at	£15.00

Production overheads are based on labour hours at £3 per hour. 20,000 tablets are produced, but there is a wastage of 10%. Non-production overheads are £15,000 for the month. There are usually 250 batches produced per month. There are 50 tablets in a container. The selling price will be 25% on cost.

Required: What is the selling price of each container?

Q7 Dodo Airways has agreed a tender for a new aircraft at £20m. The company making the product has the following cost structure for this long-term contract.

	Tender		Year 1		Year 2		Year 3	
	£m	£m	£m	£m	£m	£m	£m	£m
Sales price		20		20		20		20
Direct materials	3		1		2		4.5	
Direct labour	8		2		5		8.0	
Overheads	4	15	1	4	2	9	4.5	17
Profit		5		16		11		3
Estimated costs to complete				12		7		–

Required: What is the profit Dodo should take every year? Use the formula given in this chapter (see page 402).

Q8 Serveco is a home-service computer company. There are two levels of computer service offered: basic and enhanced service. You have the following details on each.

	Basic	Enhanced
Total basic call out time	25,000 hours	37,500 hours
Total travelling time	25,000 hours	5,000 hours
Parts serviced/replaced	50,000	100,000
Technical support (mins)	75,000	100,000
Service documentation (units)	100,000	25,000
Number of call-outs	50,000	10,000

You have the following costs:

	Basic	Enhanced	Total
Basic computer operatives' labour	£20 per hour	£25 per hour	
Spare parts installed			£100,000
Technical support cost			£125,000
Service documentation cost			£300,000

Serveco requires a profit mark-up of cost plus 25%.

Required: Calculate an appropriate standard call-out charge for the basic and enhanced services using activity-based costing.

Q9 A company, Rugger, manufactures two products: the Try and the Conversion. The company has traditionally allocated its production overhead costs on the basis of the 100,000 direct hours used in the manufacturing department. Direct labour costs £10 per hour. The company is now considering using activity-based costing. Details of the overheads and cost drivers are as follows:

Production Overheads	Total Cost (£)	Cost Driver	Total
(a) Manufacturing	10,000	Assembly-line hours	100,000 hours
(b) Materials handling	60,000	Number of stores notes	1,500 notes
(c) Inspection	40,000	Number of inspections	600 inspections
(d) Set-ups	5,000	Number of set-ups	500 set-ups

You have the following information about the products.

	Try	Conversion
Number of units	15,000	2,500
Assembly-line hours (direct labour) per unit	6 hours	4 hours
Direct materials per unit	£8	£100
Number of stores notes	600	900
Number of inspections	257	343
Number of set-ups	200	300

Required: Calculate a product cost using:
(i) traditional total absorption costing, recovering overheads using direct labour hours;
(ii) activity-based costing, and then
(iii) comment on any differences.

Chapter 14

Planning, control and performance: Budgeting

'The budget is God.'

Slogan at Japanese Company, Topcom (*Economist*, 13 January 1996)
Source: *The Wiley Book of Business Quotations* (1998), p. 90.

Learning Outcomes

After completing this chapter you should be able to:

- Explain the nature and importance of budgeting.
- Outline the most important budgets.
- Prepare the major budgets and a master budget.
- Discuss the behavioural implications of budgets.

Go online to discover the extra features for this chapter at
www.wiley.com/college/jones

Chapter Summary

- The two major branches of cost accounting are costing, and planning, control and performance.
- Budgeting is a key element of planning, control and performance.
- Budgets are ways of turning a firm's strategic objectives into practical reality.
- Most businesses prepare, at the minimum, a cash budget.
- Large businesses may also prepare a revenue, a trade receivables and a trade payables budget.
- Manufacturing businesses may prepare a raw materials, a production cost and a finished goods budget.
- Individual budgets fit into a budgeted income statement and a budgeted statement of financial position.
- Budgeting has behavioural implications for the motivation of employees.
- Some behavioural aspects of budgets are spending to budget, padding the budget and creative budgeting.
- Responsibility accounting may involve budget centres and performance measurement.

Introduction

Cost accounting can be divided into costing, and planning, control and performance. Budgeting and standard costing are the major parts of planning, control and performance. Budgeting, or budgetary control, is a key part of businesses' planning for the future. A budget is essentially a plan for the future. Budgets are thus set in advance as a way to quantify a firm's objectives. Actual performance is then monitored against budgeted performance. For small businesses, the cash budget is often the only budget. Larger businesses, by contrast, are likely to have a complex set of interrelating budgets. These build up into a budgeted income statement and a budgeted statement of financial position. Although usually set for a year, budgets are also linked to the longer-term strategic objectives of an organisation.

Management Accounting Control Systems

A business needs systems to control its activities. Budgeting and standard costing are two essential management control systems that enable a business to run effectively. They represent an assemblage of management accounting techniques which enable a business to plan, monitor and control ongoing financial activities. A particular aspect of a management accounting control system is that it is often set up to facilitate performance evaluation. Performance evaluation involves evaluating the performance of either individuals or departments. A key facet of performance evaluation is whether it is possible to allocate responsibility and whether the costs are controllable or uncontrollable.

Nature of Budgeting

In many ways, it would be surprising if businesses did not budget. For budgeting is part of our normal everyday lives. Whether it is a shopping trip, a university term or a night out on the town, we all generally have an informal budget of the amount we wish to spend. Businesses merely have a more formal version of this 'informal' personal budget.

PAUSE FOR THOUGHT 14.1

Personal Budgets

You are planning to jet off for an Easter break in the Mediterranean sun. What sort of items would you include in your holiday budget?

There would be a range of items, for example:

- transport costs to and from the airport
- cost of flight to Mediterranean
- cost of hotel
- cost of meals

- spending money
- entertainment money
- money for gifts

All these together would contribute to your holiday budget.

SOUNDBITE 14.1

Budgeting

'While most managers dislike having to deal with them, budgets are nevertheless essential to the management and control of an organization. Indeed, budgets are one of the most important tools management has for leading an organization toward its goals.'

Source: Christopher Bart (1988), Budgeting Gamesmanship, *Accounting of Management Executive*, p. 285. Reprinted in S.M. Young, *Readings in Management Accounting*, Third Edition, 2001.

Planning, control and performance is one of the two major branches of cost accounting. This is shown in Figure 14.1.

Standard costing is, in reality, a more tightly controlled and specialised type of budget. Although often associated with manufacturing industry, standard costs can, in fact, be used in a wide range of businesses.

Budgeting can be viewed as a way of turning a firm's long-term strategic objectives into reality. As Figure 14.2 shows, a business's objectives are turned into forecasts and plans. These plans are then compared with the actual results and performance is evaluated.

In small businesses, this process may be relatively informal. However, for large

Figure 14.1 Main Branches of Cost Accounting

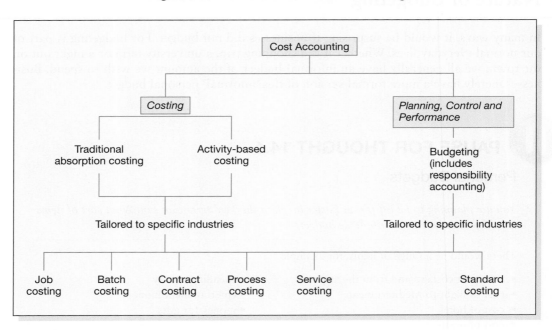

businesses there will be a complex budgeting process. The period of a budget varies. Often there is an annual budget broken down into smaller periods such as months or even weeks.

Figure 14.2 The Budgeting Process

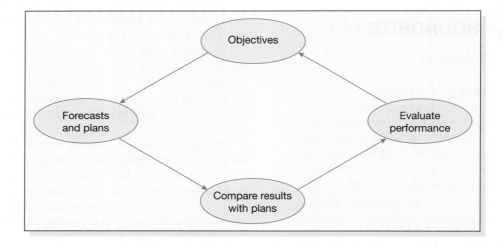

As Definition 14.1 shows, a budget is a quantitative financial plan: which sets out a business's targets.

DEFINITION 14.1

Budget

Working definition
A future plan which sets out a business's financial targets.
Formal definition
'Quantitative expression of a plan for a defined period of time. It may include planned sales volumes and revenues, resource quantities, costs and expenses, assets, liabilities and cash flows.'

Source: Chartered Institute of Management Accountants (2005), *Official Terminology*. Reproduced by Permission of Elsevier.

Four major aspects of budgets are planning, coordinating, motivation and control. Budgets, therefore, combine both technical and behavioural features. Budgets can be used for performance evaluation. These behavioural aspects and performance evaluation are discussed more fully later in the chapter.

(i) Planning

This involves setting out a comprehensive plan appropriate to the business. For small businesses, this may mean a cash budget. For larger businesses, there will probably be a formalised and sophisticated budgeting system. Planning enables businesses to balance their short-term operations with their future intended activities.

(ii) Coordinating

A key aspect of the budgetary process is that it relates the various activities of a company to each other. Therefore, revenue is related to purchases, and purchases to production. This needs to be done so that, for example, the correct amount of inventory is held. The business can be viewed as an interlocking whole.

(iii) Motivation

By setting targets, the budget has important motivational aspects. If the targets are too hard, they can be demotivating. If too easy, they will not provide any motivation at all. The motivational aspects of budget setting can be very helpful to businesses, but, as we will see later, they can also lead to behavioural responses from employers such as padding the budget.

(iv) Control

This is achieved through a system of making individual managers responsible for individual budgets. When actual results are compared against target results, individual managers will be asked to explain any differences (or variances). The manager's performance is then evaluated. Budgets, as Real-World View 14.1 shows, are an indispensable form of administrative control and accountability. Formal performance evaluation mechanisms such as responsibility accounting are often introduced.

REAL-WORLD VIEW 14.1

Budgetary Control and Responsibility

Budgetary control and responsibility accounting have been the foundation of management control systems design and use in most business (and other) organizations for many years. But whereas in the 1960s and 1970s such systems were almost exclusively based on management accounting information, more recently we have seen a recognition that a wider set of tools are required involving both the use of a range of non-financial performance measures and alternative concepts of accountability such as value chain management. Nevertheless, the focus remains on accountability arrangements within and outside organizations, and on taking a broad, holistic approach to the management of organizational performance.

Source: D. Otley (2006), Trends in budgeting control and responsibility accounting, in A. Bhimani, *Contemporary Issues in Management Accounting*, Oxford University Press, p. 291.

In large businesses, budgets are generally set by a budgetary committee. This will normally involve managers from many different departments. The sales manager, for example, may provide information on likely future revenue, which will form the basis of the revenue budget. However, it is important that individual budgets are meshed together to provide a coordinated and coherent plan. As Soundbite 14.2 shows, the starting point for this year's budget is usually last year's budget. A form of budgeting called **zero based budgeting** assumes the activities are being incurred for the first time. This approach forces businesses to look at all activities from scratch and see if they are necessary. It is very time-consuming, but can be particularly useful as a one-off exercise which necessitates managers reviewing all activities of the business as if for the first time. The budgetary process is normally ongoing, however, with meetings during the year to review progress against the current budget and to set future budgets.

SOUNDBITE 14.2

Last Year's Budget

'The largest determining factor of the size and content of this year's budget is last year's budget.'

Aaron Wildavsky, *The Politics of the Budgetary Process*, 1964

Source: The Executive's Book of Quotations (1994), p. 39. Oxford University Press.

Although budgets are set within the business, external factors will often constrain them. A key external constraint is demand. It is futile for a company to plan to make ten million motorised skateboards if there is demand for only five million. Indeed, potential revenue is the principal factor that limits the expansion of many businesses. Usually, the revenue budget is determined first. Some businesses employ a **materials requirement planning** (MRP) system. Based on revenue demand, MRP coordinates production and purchasing to ensure the optimal flow of raw materials and optimal level of raw material inventory. Another important budgetary constraint in manufacturing industry is production capacity. It is useless planning to sell ten million motorised skateboards if the production capacity is only five million. A key element of the budgetary process is thus harmonising demand and supply.

Nowadays, it is rare for businesses not to have budgets. As Figure 14.3 shows, budgets have many advantages. The chief disadvantages are that budgets can be inflexible and create behavioural problems. Budgets can be inflexible if set for a year. It is common to revise budgets regularly to take account of new circumstances. This is easier when they are prepared using spreadsheets. The behavioural problems may be created, for example, when individuals attempt to manipulate the budgeting process in their own interest. This is discussed later.

Figure 14.3 The Benefits of Budgeting

- Strategic planning can be more easily linked to management decisions
- Standards can be set to aid performance evaluation
- Plans can be set in financial terms
- Managers can be made responsible for budgets
- Budgets encourage cooperation and coordination

PAUSE FOR THOUGHT 14.2

Budgets

Budgets are often said to create inflexibility as they are typically set for a year in advance. Can you think of any ways to overcome this inflexibility?

This inflexibility can be dealt with in two ways: rolling budgets and flexible budgets. With rolling budgets, the budget is updated every month. There is then a new twelve-month budget. The problem with rolling budgets is that it takes a lot of time and effort to update budgets regularly. Flexible budgets attempt to deal with inflexibility by setting a range of budgets with different activity levels. So a company might budget for servicing 100,000, 150,000 or 200,000 customers. In this case, there would, in effect, be three budgets for three different levels of business activity.

Cash Budget

The cash budget is probably the most important of all budgets. Almost all companies prepare one. Indeed, banks will often insist on a cash budget before they lend money to small businesses. For a sole trader, the cash budget is often as important as the income statement and statement of financial position. It reflects the need to balance profitability and liquidity. There are similarities, but also differences, between the cash budget and the statement of cash flows that we saw in Chapter 7. They are similar in that both the cash budget and statement of cash flows chart the flows of cash within a business. The differences arise in that the statement of cash flows is normally prepared in a standardised format in accordance with accounting regulations and looks backwards in time. By contrast, the cash budget is not in a standardised format and unlike the statement of cash flows looks forward in time.

Essentially, the cash budget looks into the future. Figure 14.4 gives the format of the cash budget. We start with the opening cash balance. Receipts are then recorded; for example, cash received from cash sales, from trade receivables or from the sale of property, plant and equipment. Cash payments are then listed; for example, cash purchases of goods, payments for trade payables or expenses paid. Receipts less payments provide the monthly cash flow. Opening cash and cash flow determine the closing cash balance. It is important to realise that depreciation is not a cash flow and does not, therefore, appear in a cash budget.

Figure 14.4 The Format of a Cash Budget

	Jan. £	Feb. £	March £	April £	May £	June £	Total £
Opening cash	X	X	X	X	X	X	X
Add *Receipts*							
Trade receivables	X	X	X	X	X	X	X
	X	X	X	X	X	X	X
Less *Payments*							
Payments for goods	X	X	X	X	X	X	X
Expenses	X	X	X	X	X	X	X
Other payments	X	X	X	X	X	X	X
	X	X	X	X	X	X	X
Cash flow	Y	Y	Y	Y	Y	Y	Y
Closing cash	X	X	X	X	X	X	X

In Figure 14.5 on the next page, we show an actual example of how in practice a cash budget is constructed.

Other Budgets

A business may have numerous other budgets. Indeed, each department of a large business is likely to have a budget. In this section, we will look at three key budgets common to many businesses: revenue budget, trade receivables budget and trade payables budget. In the next section, we will look at three additional budgets that are commonly found in manufacturing businesses: raw materials budget, finished goods budget and production cost budget. Finally, we will bring the budgets together in a comprehensive example.

Figure 14.5 Illustrative Example of a Cash Budget

Jason Chan has £12,000 in a business bank account. His projections for the first six months trading are as follows.

(i) Credit sales will be: January £8,800, February £8,800, March £9,000, April £12,500, May £20,200, June £30,000. The revenue is received in the month following sale.

(ii) Goods supplied on credit will be: January £7,000, February £10,000, March £9,800, April £10,400, May £7,000, June £8,000. Trade payables are paid one month in arrears.

(iii) Loan receivable 1 March £4,000 to be repaid in full plus £400 interest on 1 June.

(iv) Drawing £500 per month.

Prepare the cash budget.

	Jan. £	Feb. £	March £	April £	May £	June £	Total £
Opening cash	12,000	11,500	12,800	15,100	13,800	15,400	12,000
Add *Receipts*							
Trade receivables		8,800	8,800	9,000	12,500	20,200	59,300
Loan received			4,000				4,000
	–	8,800	12,800	9,000	12,500	20,200	63,300
Less *Payments*							
Payments for goods		7,000	10,000	9,800	10,400	7,000	44,200
Loan repayment						4,400	4,400
Drawings	500	500	500	500	500	500	3,000
	500	7,500	10,500	10,300	10,900	11,900	51,600
Cash flow	(500)	1,300	2,300	(1,300)	1,600	8,300	11,700
Closing cash	11,500	12,800	15,100	13,800	15,400	23,700	23,700

Helpnotes:

(i) The receipts of trade receivables and payments of trade payables are thus running one month behind actual revenue and actual purchases, respectively. Thus, for example, the debtors will pay the £30,000 of revenue made in June in July and they are, therefore, not recorded in this budget.

(ii) The cash flow column is simply total receipts less total payments. Cash outflows (where receipts are less than payments) are recorded in brackets.

(i) Revenue Budget

The revenue budget is determined by examining how much the business is likely to sell during the forthcoming period. Figure 14.6 provides an example. Revenue budgets, like many other budgets, can be initially expressed in units before being converted to £s. In many businesses, the revenue budget is the key budget as it determines the other budgets. The revenue budget is, therefore, often set first.

(ii) Trade Receivables Budget

The trade receivables budget begins with opening trade receivables (often taken from the opening statement of financial position) to which are added credit sales (often taken from the revenue budget). Cash receipts are then deducted, leaving closing trade receivables. An example of the format for a trade receivables budget is provided in Figures 14.7 and 14.8.

Figure 14.6 Example of a Revenue Budget

A business has two products, Alpha and Omega. It is anticipated that revenue of the Alpha will run at 500 units throughout January to June. However, the Omega will start at 1,000 units and rise by 100 units per month. Each Alpha sells at £35, each Omega sells at £50. Prepare the revenue budget.

	Jan. £	Feb. £	March £	April £	May £	June £	Total £
Alpha	17,500	17,500	17,500	17,500	17,500	17,500	105,000
Omega	50,000	55,000	60,000	65,000	70,000	75,000	375,000
Total revenue	67,500	72,500	77,500	82,500	87,500	92,500	480,000

Figure 14.7 Format of a Trade Receivables Budget

	Jan. £	Feb. £	March £	April £	May £	June £	Total £
Opening trade receivables	X	X	X	X	X	X	X
Credit sales	X	X	X	X	X	X	X
	X	X	X	X	X	X	X
Cash received for trade receivables	(X)	(X)	(X)	(X)	(X)	(X)	(X)
Closing trade receivables	X	X	X	X	X	X	X

Figure 14.8 Example of a Trade Receivables Budget

Sara Peters has opening trade receivables of £800. These are received one month in arrears. Revenue is forecast to be £900 in January, rising by £200 per month. Prepare the trade receivables budget.

	Jan. £	Feb. £	March £	April £	May £	June £	Total £
Opening trade receivables	800	900	1,100	1,300	1,500	1,700	800
Credit sales	900	1,100	1,300	1,500	1,700	1,900	8,400
	1,700	2,000	2,400	2,800	3,200	3,600	9,200
Cash received	(800)	(900)	(1,100)	(1,300)	(1,500)	(1,700)	(7,300)
Closing trade receivables	900	1,100	1,300	1,500	1,700	1,900	1,900

(iii) Trade Payables Budget

In many ways, the trade payables budget is the mirror image of the trade receivables budget. It starts with opening trade payables (often taken from the opening statement of financial position), adds credit purchases and then deducts cash paid. The result is closing trade payables. The format for the trade payables budget is given in Figure 14.9, while Figure 14.10 provides an illustrative example.

Figure 14.9 Format of a Trade Payables Budget

	Jan. £	Feb. £	March £	April £	May £	June £	Total £
Opening trade payables	X	X	X	X	X	X	X
Credit purchases	X	X	X	X	X	X	X
	X	X	X	X	X	X	X
Cash paid to trade payables	(X)	(X)	(X)	(X)	(X)	(X)	(X)
Closing trade payables	X	X	X	X	X	X	X

Figure 14.10 Example of a Trade Payables Budget

Jon Matthews has opening trade payables of £1,200. Trade payables are expected to be paid one month in arrears. In January, purchases are forecast to be £9,000, rising by £100 per month. Prepare the trade payables budget.

	Jan. £	Feb. £	March £	April £	May £	June £	Total £
Opening trade payables	1,200	9,000	9,100	9,200	9,300	9,400	1,200
Credit purchases	9,000	9,100	9,200	9,300	9,400	9,500	55,500
	10,200	18,100	18,300	18,500	18,700	18,900	56,700
Cash paid	(1,200)	(9,000)	(9,100)	(9,200)	(9,300)	(9,400)	(47,200)
Closing trade payables	9,000	9,100	9,200	9,300	9,400	9,500	9,500

Manufacturing Budgets

Manufacturing companies normally hold more inventory than other businesses. It is, therefore, common to find three additional budgets: a production cost budget, a raw materials budget and a finished goods budget. Often these budgets are expressed in units, which are then converted into £s. For ease of understanding, we express them here only in financial terms.

(i) Production Cost Budget

The production cost budget, as its name suggests, estimates the cost of production. This involves direct labour, direct materials and production overheads. There may often be sub-budgets for each of these items. The production cost format is shown in Figure 14.11, while Figure 14.12 shows an example. Once the production cost is determined, the finished goods budget can be prepared. It is important to realise that the budgeted production levels are generally determined by the amount the business can sell.

Figure 14.11 Format of a Production Cost Budget

	Jan.	Feb.	March	April	May	June	Total
	£	£	£	£	£	£	£
Direct materials	X	X	X	X	X	X	X
Direct labour	X	X	X	X	X	X	X
Production overheads	X	X	X	X	X	X	X
	X	X	X	X	X	X	X

Figure 14.12 Example of a Production Cost Budget

Ray Anderson has the following forecast details from his production department. Direct materials are £6 per unit, direct labour is £8 per unit and production overheads are £4 per unit. 1,000 units will be made in January, rising by 100 units per month. Prepare the production cost budget.

	Jan.	Feb.	March	April	May	June	Total
	£	£	£	£	£	£	£
Direct materials	6,000	6,600	7,200	7,800	8,400	9,000	45,000
Direct labour	8,000	8,800	9,600	10,400	11,200	12,000	60,000
Production overheads	4,000	4,400	4,800	5,200	5,600	6,000	30,000
	18,000	19,800	21,600	23,400	25,200	27,000	135,000
Units	1,000	1,100	1,200	1,300	1,400	1,500	7,500

(ii) Raw Materials Budget

The raw materials budget is particularly useful as it provides a forecast of how much raw material the company needs to buy. This can supply the purchases figure for the trade payables budget. The raw materials budget format is shown in Figure 14.13. It starts with opening inventory of raw materials (often taken from the opening statement of financial position); purchases are then added. The amount used in production is then subtracted, arriving at closing inventory. An example is shown in Figure 14.14.

(iii) Finished Goods Budget

The finished goods budget is similar to the raw materials budget except it deals with finished goods. As Figure 14.15 shows, it starts with the opening inventory of finished goods (often

Figure 14.13 Format of a Raw Materials Budget

	Jan. £	Feb. £	March £	April £	May £	June £	Total £
Opening inventory of raw materials	X	X	X	X	X	X	X
Purchases	X	X	X	X	X	X	X
	X	X	X	X	X	X	X
Used in production	(X)	(X)	(X)	(X)	(X)	(X)	(X)
Closing inventory of raw materials	X	X	X	X	X	X	X

Figure 14.14 Example of a Raw Materials Budget

Dai Jones has opening raw materials inventory of £1,200. Purchases of raw materials will be £600 in January, increasing by £75 per month. Production will be 400 units per month using £2 raw material per unit. Prepare the raw materials budget.

	Jan. £	Feb. £	March £	April £	May £	June £	Total £
Opening inventory of raw materials	1,200	1,000	875	825	850	950	1,200
Purchases	600	675	750	825	900	975	4,725
	1,800	1,675	1,625	1,650	1,750	1,925	5,925
Used in production	(800)	(800)	(800)	(800)	(800)	(800)	(4,800)
Closing inventory of raw materials	1,000	875	825	850	950	1,125	1,125

Figure 14.15 Format of a Finished Goods Budget

	Jan. £	Feb. £	March £	April £	May £	June £	Total £
Opening inventory of finished goods	X	X	X	X	X	X	X
Produced	X	X	X	X	X	X	X
	X	X	X	X	X	X	X
Cost of sales	(X)	(X)	(X)	(X)	(X)	(X)	(X)
Closing inventory of finished goods	X	X	X	X	X	X	X

taken from the statement of financial position); the amount produced is then added (from the production cost budget). The cost of sales (i.e., cost of the goods sold) is then deducted. Finally, it finishes with the closing inventory of finished goods. The finished goods budget is useful for keeping a check on whether the business is producing sufficient goods to meet demand. Figure 14.16 gives an example of a finished goods budget.

Figure 14.16 Example of a Finished Goods Budget

Ranjit Patel has £8,000 of finished good inventory in January. 1,000 units per month will be produced at a product cost of £10 each. Revenue will be £10,000 in January, rising by £1,000 per month. Gross profit is 25% of revenue. Prepare the finished goods budget.

	Jan. £	Feb. £	March £	April £	May £	June £	Total £
Opening inventory of finished goods	8,000	10,500	12,250	13,250	13,500	13,000	8,000
Produced	10,000	10,000	10,000	10,000	10,000	10,000	60,000
	18,000	20,500	22,250	23,250	23,500	23,000	68,000
Cost of sales*	(7,500)	(8,250)	(9,000)	(9,750)	(10,500)	(11,250)	(56,250)
Closing inventory of finished goods	10,500	12,250	13,250	13,500	13,000	11,750	11,750
*Cost of sales is 75% of sales	10,000	11,000	12,000	13,000	14,000	15,000	75,000

Comprehensive Budgeting Example

Once all the budgets have been prepared, it is important to gain an overview of how the business is expected to perform. Normally, a budgeted income statement and budgeted statement of financial position are drawn up. This is often called a master budget. The full process is now illustrated using the example of Jacobs Engineering (see Figure 14.17), a manufacturing company. A manufacturing company is used so as to illustrate the full range of budgets discussed in this chapter. From Figure 14.17, the interlocking nature of the budgetary process can be seen. To take one example, for the trade receivables budget: the totals from the revenue budget are fed into the trade receivables budget as credit sales, while the cash received from trade receivables in the cash budget also appears in the trade receivables budget.

An overview of the whole process is presented in Figure 14.18. This shows how the various budgets interlock. It must be appreciated that Figure 14.18 does not include all possible budgets (for example, many businesses have labour, selling and administration budgets). However, Figure 14.18 does give a good appreciation of the basic budgetary flows.

After the budgetary period, the actual results are compared against the budgeted results. Any differences between the two sets of results will be investigated and action taken, if appropriate. This basic principle of investigating why any variances have occurred is common in both budgeting and standard costing.

Figure 14.17 Comprehensive Budgeting Example

Jacobs Engineering is a small manufacturing company. There are the following forecast summarised details.

Jacobs Engineering Ltd

Statement of Financial Position (Abridged) as at 31 December 20X1

	£	£
ASSETS		
Non-current Assets		
Property, plant and equipment		100,000
Current Assets		
Trade receivables (Nov. £13,000, Dec £14,000)		27,000
Inventory of raw materials		10,000
Inventory of finished goods		15,000
Total Assets		152,000
Current Liabilities		
Trade payables (Nov. £12,000, Dec. £13,000)		(25,000)
Bank overdraft		(7,000)
Total Liabilities		(32,000)
Net Assets		120,000

	£
EQUITY	
Capital and Reserves	
Share Capital	
Ordinary share capital	90,000
Reserves	
Retained earnings	30,000
Total Equity	120,000

Notes:
1. Depreciation is 10% straight line basis per year.
2. Purchases will be £10,000 in January, increasing by £300 per month. They are payable two months after purchase.
3. Revenue will be 450 units of product A at average production cost plus 25% and 500 units of product B at average production cost plus 20%. Trade receivables will be received two months in arrears.
4. Average production cost *per unit* remains the same as last year and is the same for product A and product B. It consists of direct materials £10, direct labour £7, production overheads £3. Both direct labour and production overheads will be paid in the month used. Production 1,000 units per month.
5. Non-production expenses are £4,000 per month, and will be paid in the month incurred.

Required: Prepare the revenue budget, cash budget, trade receivables budget, trade payables budget, production cost budget, finished goods budget, raw materials budget, budgeted income statement and budgeted statement of financial position for six months ending 30 June 20X2.

Revenue Budget

	Jan. £	Feb. £	March £	April £	May £	June £	Total £
Product A*	11,250	11,250	11,250	11,250	11,250	11,250	67,500
Product B**	12,000	12,000	12,000	12,000	12,000	12,000	72,000
	23,250	23,250	23,250	23,250	23,250	23,250	139,500

* 450 units × £20 average production cost (i.e., direct materials £10, direct labour £7 and production overhead £3) plus 25%

** 500 units × £20 average production cost (i.e., direct materials £10, direct labour £7 and production overhead £3) plus 20%

Figure 14.17 Comprehensive Budgeting Example (*continued*)

Cash Budget

	Jan. £	Feb. £	March £	April £	May £	June £	Total £
Opening cash	(7,000)	(20,000)	(33,000)	(33,750)	(34,800)	(36,150)	(7,000)
Add Receipts							
Trade receivables	13,000	14,000	23,250	23,250	23,250	23,250	120,000
	13,000	14,000	23,250	23,250	23,250	23,250	120,000
Less Payments							
Payment for goods	12,000	13,000	10,000	10,300	10,600	10,900	66,800
Non-production expenses	4,000	4,000	4,000	4,000	4,000	4,000	24,000
Direct labour	7,000	7,000	7,000	7,000	7,000	7,000	42,000
Production overheads	3,000	3,000	3,000	3,000	3,000	3,000	18,000
	26,000	27,000	24,000	24,300	24,600	24,900	150,800
Cash flow	(13,000)	(13,000)	(750)	(1,050)	(1,350)	(1,650)	(30,800)
Closing cash	(20,000)	(33,000)	(33,750)	(34,800)	(36,150)	(37,800)	(37,800)

Trade Receivables Budget

	Jan. £	Feb. £	March £	April £	May £	June £	Total £
Opening trade receivables	27,000	37,250	46,500	46,500	46,500	46,500	27,000
Credit sales	23,250	23,250	23,250	23,250	23,250	23,250	139,500
	50,250	60,500	69,750	69,750	69,750	69,750	166,500
Cash received	(13,000)	(14,000)	(23,250)	(23,250)	23,250)	(23,250)	(120,000)
Closing trade receivables	37,250	46,500	46,500	46,500	46,500	46,500	46,500

Trade Payables Budget

	Jan. £	Feb. £	March £	April £	May £	June £	Total £
Opening trade payables	25,000	23,000	20,300	20,900	21,500	22,100	25,000
Credit purchases	10,000	10,300	10,600	10,900	11,200	11,500	64,500
	35,000	33,300	30,900	31,800	32,700	33,600	89,500
Cash paid	(12,000)	(13,000)	(10,000)	(10,300)	(10,600)	(10,900)	(66,800)
Closing trade payables	23,000	20,300	20,900	21,500	22,100	22,700	22,700

Production Cost Budget

	Jan. £	Feb. £	March £	April £	May £	June £	Total £
Diect materials	10,000	10,000	10,000	10,000	10,000	10,000	60,000
Direct labour	7,000	7,000	7,000	7,000	7,000	7,000	42,000
Production overheads	3,000	3,000	3,000	3,000	3,000	3,000	18,000
	20,000	20,000	20,000	20,000	20,000	20,000	120,000

Figure 14.17 Comprehensive Budgeting Example (*continued*)

Finished Goods Budget

	Jan. £	Feb. £	March £	April £	May £	June £	Total £
Opening inventory of finished goods	15,000	16,000	17,000	18,000	19,000	20,000	15,000
Produced	20,000	20,000	20,000	20,000	20,000	20,000	120,000
	35,000	36,000	37,000	38,000	39,000	40,000	135,000
Cost of sales*	(19,000)	(19,000)	(19,000)	(19,000)	(19,000)	(19,000)	(114,000)
Closing inventory of finished goods	16,000	17,000	18,000	19,000	20,000	21,000	21,000

*(950 units × £20)

Raw Materials Budget

	Jan. £	Feb. £	March £	April £	May £	June £	Total £
Opening inventory of raw materials	10,000	10,000	10,300	10,900	11,800	13,000	10,000
Purchases	10,000	10,300	10,600	10,900	11,200	11,500	64,500
	20,000	20,300	20,900	21,800	23,000	24,500	74,500
Used in production*	(10,000)	(10,000)	(10,000)	(10,000)	(10,000)	(10,000)	(60,000)
Closing inventory of raw materials	10,000	10,300	10,900	11,800	13,000	14,500	14,500

*1,000 units per month × £10 direct materials.

Jacobs Ltd Engineering
Budgeted Income Statement
for six months ending 30 June 20X2

	£	£	Source budget
Revenue		139,500	Revenue
Less *Cost of Sales*		114,000	Finished goods
Gross Profit		25,500	
Less *Expenses*			
Depreciation	10,000		
Expenses	24,000	34,000	
Net Loss		(8,500)	

Jacobs Ltd Engineering
Budgeted Statement of Financial Position as at 30 June 20X2

	Cost £	Accumulated depreciation £	Net book value £	Source Budget
ASSETS				
Non-current Assets				
Property, plant and equipment	100,000	(10,000)	90,000	

Figure 14.17 Comprehensive Budgeting Example (*continued*)

	£	£	
Current Assets			
Trade receivables	46,500		Trade receivables
Inventory of raw materials	14,500		Raw materials
Inventory of finished goods	21,000	82,000	Finished goods
Total Assets		172,000	
LIABILITIES			
Current Liabilities			
Trade payables	(22,700)		Trade payables
Bank overdraft	(37,800)		Cash
Total Liabilities		(60,500)	
Net Assets		111,500	
EQUITY			
Share Capital and Reserves		£	Opening statement
Share Capital		90,000	of financial position
Ordinary share capital			
Reserves			Opening statement
Retained earnings	30,000		of financial position
			Income statement
Less: Retained loss for year	(8,500)	21,500	
Total Equity		111,500	

Figure 14.18 Budgeting Overview

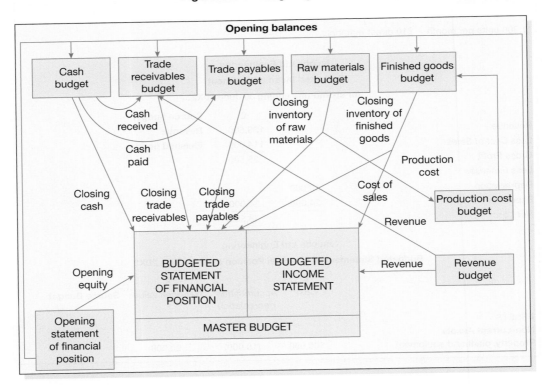

Behavioural Aspects of Budgeting

It is important to realise that there are several, sometimes competing, functions of budgets; for example, planning, coordinating, motivation and control. Budgeting is thus a mixture of technical (planning and coordinating) and behavioural (motivation and control) aspects. In short, budgets affect the behaviour of individuals within firms.

SOUNDBITE 14.3

Importance of budgets

'While most managers dislike having to deal with them, budgets are nevertheless essential to the management and control of an organisation. Indeed, budgets are one of the most important tools management has for leading an organisation toward its goals.'

Source: C.K. Bart (1988), Budgeting Gamesmanship in S.M. Young (2001), *Readings in Management Accounting*, p. 217.

The budgetary process is all about setting targets and individuals meeting those targets. As Real-World View 14.2 shows, a senior supply chain manager demonstrates that managers strive, using all possible means, to meet their targets.

REAL-WORLD VIEW 14.2

Meeting Targets

I try to make sure I hit the target so if we had to spend more on air freight we find it somewhere else . . . if there is a variance you are expected to offset it with something else. For instance, next year I fully expect currency to go adverse. Does that mean to say that we will get lower targets? No . . . if I was to sit back here and say: 'Well, currency has hit me, I can't do anything', I wouldn't be in the job for very long. The thing is not to sit there and say: 'All the world is against me' . . . Find another way.

Source: Reprinted from *Accounting, Organizations and Society*, Vol. 35, by authors: N. Frow, D. Marginson and S. Ogden, 'Continuous' Budgeting: Reconciling Budget Flexibility With Budgeting Control. page 454, Copyright 2010, with permission from Elsevier.

The problem is that an optimal target for the business is not necessarily optimal for the individual employee. Conflicts of interest, therefore, arise between the individual and the company. It may, for example, be in a company's interests to set a very demanding budget. However, it is not necessarily in the employee's interests. Budgets can, therefore, have powerful motivational or demotivational effects. For employees, in particular, budgets are often treated with great suspicion. Top managers often use budgets deliberately as a motivational tool. Managers lower down in the organisation often develop strategies to cope with imposed budgets (see Real-World View 14.3).

REAL-WORLD VIEW 14.3

The Games that Product Managers Play

Although they never referred to them as 'games' per se, the product managers interviewed were not wanting for a rather extensive lexicon to describe their budgeting manipulations. 'Cushion,' 'slush fund,' 'hedge,' 'flexibility,' 'cookie jar,' 'hip/back pocket,' 'pad,' 'kitty,' 'secret reserve,' 'war chest,' and 'contingency' were just some of the colourful terms used to label the games that managers played with their financial forecasts and budgets. For the most part, however, all of these terms could be used interchangeably.

Source: C.K. Bart (1988), Budgeting Gamesmanship, in S.M. Young (2001), *Readings in Management Accounting*, p. 218.

SOUNDBITE 14.4

Balancing Budgetary Needs

'Attempting to use a budget system to give effective short-term control whilst encouraging managers to make accurate estimates of future outcomes has long been recognised as a knife-edge that managers need to walk.'

Source: D. Otley (2006) Trends in Budgetary control and responsibility accounting, in A. Bhimani, *Contemporary Issues in Management Accounting*, Oxford University Press, p. 292.

To demonstrate the behavioural impact of budgeting, we look below at three behavioural practices associated with budgeting: spending to budget, padding the budget and creative budgeting.

(i) Spending to Budget

Many companies allocate their expense budget for the year. If the budget is not spent, then the department loses the money. This is a double whammy as often next year's budget is based on this year's. So an underspend this year will also result in less to spend next year. It is in managers' individual interests (but not necessarily in the firm's interests) to avoid this. Managers, therefore, will spend money at the last minute on items such as recarpeting of offices. This is the idea behind the cartoon at the start of this chapter!

PAUSE FOR THOUGHT 14.3

Spending to Budget

Jane Morris has a department and was allocated £120,000 to spend for year ended 31 December 2013. In 2014, the budget is based on the 2013 budget plus 10% inflation. She spends prudently so that by 1 December 2013 she has spent £90,000. Normal expenditure would be a further £10,000. Thus, she would have spent £100,000 in total. What might she do?

Well, it is possible she might give the £20,000 (£120,000–£100,000) unspent back to head office. However, this will result in only £110,000 (£100,000 + 10%) next year. More likely she will try to spend the surplus. For example, buy:

- a new computer
- new office furniture
- new carpets.

(ii) Padding the Budget

Budgets are set by people. Therefore, there is a great temptation for individuals to try to create slack in the system to give themselves some leeway. For example, *you might think* that your department's revenue next year will be £120,000 and the expenses will be £90,000. Therefore, you think you will make £30,000 profit. However, at the budgetary committee *you might argue* that your revenue will be only £110,000 and your expenses will be £100,000. You are, therefore, attempting to set the budget so that your profit is £10,000 (i.e., £110,000 – £100,000). You have, therefore, built in £20,000 budgetary slack (£30,000 profit [true estimated position] less £10,000 profit [argued position]). Real-World View 14.4 demonstrates the behavioural aspects involved in padding the budget.

REAL-WORLD VIEW 14.4

Padding the Budget

Another condition identified as facilitating budgeting games was the time constraints imposed on senior management during the product plan review period. As one manager put it:

> 'Senior management just doesn't have the time
> for checking every number you put into your
> plans . . . . So one strategy is to "pad" everything.
> if you're lucky, you'll still have 50% of your
> cushions after the plan reviews.'

Source: C.K. Bart (1988), Budgetary Gamesmanship, in S.M. Young (2001), *Readings in Management Accounting*, p. 219.

Figure 14.19 Creative Budgeting

Jasper Grant gets a bonus of £1,000 if he meets his budgeted profit of £100,000 for the year ending in December. At the end of November, he has the following information.

	£
Sales commission to date	200,000
Extra sales commission estimated for December	25,000
Expenses to date	97,000
Expenses to be incurred	
: Weekly press advertising	3,000
: Repairs	8,000
: Necessary expenses	25,000

How can Jasper meet budget?

At the moment, Jasper's situation is as follows:

	£
Sales commission (£200,000 + £25,000)	225,000
Less: *Expenses* (£97,000 incurred + £36,000 anticipated)	133,000
Actual Profit	92,000
Budgeted Profit	100,000
Budgetary Shortfall	(8,000)

Jasper would, therefore, fail to meet his budgeted profit.

However, if the advertising and repairs were deferred until the next period, Jasper would make the budget. So he might be tempted to defer them.

	£
Sales commission	225,000
Less: Expenses to date	97,000
Necessary expenses	25,000
Actual Profit	103,000
Budgeted Profit	100,000
Surplus over Budget	3,000

Jasper would, therefore, gain his bonus as he would meet his target. However, what is good for Jasper is not necessarily good for his firm. By not advertising or having repairs done quickly, it is likely that the long-term productivity of the firm will suffer.

(iii) Creative Budgeting

If departmental managers are rewarded on the basis of the profit their department makes, then they may indulge in creative budgeting. Creative budgeting may, for example, involve deferring expenditure planned for this year until next year (see, for example, Figure 14.19).

Responsibility Accounting

The behavioural aspects of budgeting can be utilised when designing responsibility accounting systems. In such systems, organisations are divided into budgetary areas, known as responsibility centres. Managers are held accountable for the activities within these centres. As Figure 14.20 shows, there are different sorts of responsibility centre.

Figure 14.20 Responsibility Centres and Managerial Accountability

Responsibility Centre	Managerial Accountability
Revenue Centre	Revenues
Cost Centre	Costs
Profit Centre	Revenues, costs and thus profits
Investment Centre	Revenues and costs (i.e., profits) and investment (i.e., non-current assets and net current assets)

A revenue centre is totally focused on revenue and exists, for example, in situations where sales managers may be responsible for revenue in their own regions. Cost centres, by contrast, are where the manager just deals with costs; for example, a purchases manager. In profit centres and investment centres, the managers have more responsibility. In investment centres, in particular, managers will have particular autonomy and these centres are usually at subsidiary or group rather than departmental level.

Managers of investment centres thus have more responsibility than those of profit centres, who in turn have more responsibility than managers of cost or revenue centres. A key aspect of responsibility accounting is that the manager is responsible for controllable costs, but not uncontrollable costs. Controllable costs are simply those costs that a manager can be expected to influence. An uncontrollable cost is one over which the manager has no control; for example, price rises of purchases caused by suppliers increasing their product prices or adverse movements in exchange rates making the costs of importing goods more expensive.

Responsibility accounting is a way of monitoring the activities of managers and judging their performance. The budgeted costs, revenues and profits are compared with the actual results. Managers can be rewarded or penalised accordingly, often by the payment or non-payment of bonuses.

Investment centres are often evaluated using specific performance measures. Three of the most common are Return on Investment (ROI), Residual Income (RI) and Return on Sales (ROS). These three ratios are outlined in Figure 14.21.

These three ratios all have strengths and weaknesses. Return on Sales is quite simple. However, it does not take into account the investment a company has made in its operations and, therefore, is quite limited in practice. An alternative term for Return on Sales is Return on Revenue. However, Return on Sales (ROS) is used in this book as this is still the most widely used term. Return on Investment is more sophisticated and provides a useful indicator of the firm's profitability. However, it does not take into account a company's desired return on capital. Residual Income, by contrast, does and indicates the profits a company makes over its minimum return.

Figure 14.21 Three Performance Measures

Ratio	Definition	Comments
(i) Return on Investment (ROI)	$\dfrac{\text{Profit before interest and tax}}{\text{Average capital employed}}$	Simple, but often investment difficult to determine (usually defined as non-current assets plus net current assets). Does not take size into account. Similar to return on capital employed.
(ii) Residual Income (RI)	Income − (required rate of return × investment, i.e., capital employed)	Quite simple: can use quite an arbitrary rate of return.
(iii) Return on Sales (ROS)	$\dfrac{\textit{Operating profit}}{\text{Revenue}}$	Quite simple. Definition of profit may be difficult. Similar to net profit ratio.

Below, in Figure 14.22, is an example of how these particular measures may be used in practice. The example of three divisions of an international car hire firm is used, HireCarCo. These are based in London, Paris and Berlin.

Figure 14.22 Performance Measures for Three Divisions

HireCarCo has three operating divisions in London, Paris and Berlin. Each acts as a broadly independent investment centre. The key figures are set out below

	London	Paris	Berlin
	£m	£m	£m
Investment	1,000,000	800,000	600,000
	£m	£m	£m
Revenue	500,000	350,000	200,000
Costs	(300,000)	(180,000)	(120,000)
Operating profit	200,000	170,000	80,000

Required: **Calculate**
a) Return on Investment (ROI)
b) Residual Income (RI) − assuming the required rate of return is 10%
c) Return on Sales (ROS)

	London	Paris	Berlin
i) Return on Investment			
$\dfrac{\text{Operating Profit}}{\text{Investment}}$	$\dfrac{£200,000}{£1,000,000} = 20\%$	$\dfrac{£170,000}{£800,000} = 21.2\%$	$\dfrac{£80,000}{£600,000} = 13.3\%$
ii) Residual Income			
Income − (Required Rate of Return × Investment)	£200,000 − (£1,000,000 × 10%) = £100,000	£170,000 − (£800,000 × 10%) = £90,000	£80,000 − (£600,000 × 10%) = £20,000
iii) Return on Sales			
$\dfrac{\text{Operating Profit}}{\text{Revenue}}$	$\dfrac{£200,000}{£500,000} = 40\%$	$\dfrac{£170,000}{£350,000} = 48.6\%$	$\dfrac{£80,000}{£200,000} = 40\%$

From the results, it can be seen that measured by return on investment and return on sales, the manager of the Paris branch would be judged to be performing the best. However, in absolute terms, the London manager has done best, having the highest residual income.

Conclusion

Budgeting is planning for the future. This is important as a business needs to compare its actual performance against its targets. Most businesses prepare a cash budget and large businesses often prepare a complex set of interlocking budgets which culminate in a budgeted income statement and a budgeted statement of financial position. Budgets have a human as well as a technical side. As well as being useful for planning and coordination, budgets are used to motivate and monitor individuals. Budgets are often used as the basis for performance evaluation. Sometimes, therefore, the interests of individuals and businesses may conflict.

 Discussion Questions

Questions with numbers in blue have answers at the back of the book.

Q1 What are the advantages and disadvantages of budgeting?

Q2 Why do some people think that the cash budget is the most important budget? Do you agree?

Q3 The behavioural aspects of budgeting are often overlooked, but are extremely important. Do you agree?

Q4 State whether the following statements are true or false. If false, explain why.
  (a) The four main aspects of budgets are planning, coordinating, control and motivation.
  (b) The commonest limiting factor in the budgeting process is production.
  (c) A master budget is formed by feeding in the results from all the other budgets.
  (d) Depreciation is commonly found in a cash budget.
  (e) Spending to budget, padding the budget and creative budgeting are all common behavioural responses to budgeting.

Numerical Questions

Questions with numbers in blue have answers at the back of the book.

Q1 Jill Lee starts her business on 1 January with £15,000 in the bank. Her plans for the first six months are as follows.

(a) Payments for goods will be made one month after purchase:

January	February	March	April	May	June
£21,000	£19,500	£18,500	£23,400	£25,900	£31,100

(b) All revenue consists of cash sales:

January	February	March	April	May	June
£25,200	£27,100	£21,200	£20,250	£48,300	£37,500

(c) Expenses will be £12,000 in January and will rise by 10% per month. They will be paid in the month incurred.

Required: Prepare Jill Lee's cash budget from 1 January to 30 June.

Q2 John Rees has the following information for the six months 1 July to 31 December.
(a) Opening cash balance 1 July £8,600
(b) Sales at £25 per unit:

	April	May	June	July	Aug.	Sept.	Oct.	Nov.	Dec.
Units	100	130	150	180	200	210	220	240	280

Trade receivables will be paid two months after the customers have bought the goods.
(c) Production in units:

	April	May	June	July	Aug.	Sept.	Oct.	Nov.	Dec.	Jan.
Units	140	140	140	180	200	190	200	210	260	200

(d) Raw materials costing £10 per unit are delivered in the month of production and will be paid for three months after the goods are used in production.
(e) Direct labour of £6 per unit will be payable in the same month as production.
(f) Other variable production expenses will be £6 per unit. Two-thirds of this cost will be paid for in the same month as production and one-third in the month following production.
(g) Other expenses of £200 per month will be paid one month in arrears. These expenses have been at this rate for the past two years.
(h) A machine will be bought and paid for in September for £8,000.
(i) John Rees plans to borrow £4,500 from a relative in December. This will be banked immediately.

Required: Prepare John Rees's cash budget from 1 July to 31 December.

Q3 Fly-by-Night plc has the following revenue forecasts for the revenue for two products: the Moon and the Star.
  (a) The Moon will sell 1,000 units in January, rising by 50 units per month. From January to March each Moon will sell at £20, with the price rising to £25 from April to June.
  (b) The Star will sell 2,000 units in January, rising by 100 units per month. Each Star will sell at £10.

Required: Prepare the revenue budget for Fly-by-Night from January to June.

Q4 David Ingo has opening trade receivables of £2,400 (November £1,400, December £1,000). The trade receivables will be received two months in arrears. Credit sales in January will be £1,000, rising by 10% per month.

Required: Prepare D. Ingo's trade receivables budget for January to June.

Q5 Thomas Iger has opening trade payables of £2,900 (£400 October, £1,200 November, £1,300 December). Trade payables will be paid three months in arrears. Credit purchases in January will be £2,000, rising by £200 per month until March and then suffering a 10% decline in April and remaining constant.

Required: Prepare T. Iger's trade payables budget for January to June.

Q6 Brenda Ear will have production costs per unit of £5 raw materials, £5.50 direct labour and £2 variable overheads. Production will be 700 units in January, rising by 50 units per month.

Required: Prepare B. Ear's production cost budget for January to June.

Q7 Roger Abbit has £1,000 opening inventory of raw materials. Purchases will be £900 in January, rising by £200 per month. Production will be 240 units from January to March at £4 raw materials per unit, rising to 250 units per month at £5 raw materials per unit from April to June.

Required: Prepare R. Abbit's raw materials budget for January to June.

Q8 Freddie Ox has £9,000 of opening finished goods inventory. In July, 1,500 units will be produced at a production cost of £10 each. Production will increase at 100 units per month; production cost remains steady. Revenue will be £15,000 in July, rising by £1,500 per month. Gross profit is 20% of revenue.

Required: Prepare F. Ox's finished goods budget for July–December.

Q9 Asia is a small non-listed manufacturing company. There are the following details:

Asia Ltd
Abridged Statement of Financial Position as at 31 December 20X1

	£	£
ASSETS		
Non-current assets		
Property, plant and equipment		99,500
Current Assets		
Trade receivables (Nov. £10,000, Dec. £11,000)	21,000	
Inventory (raw materials)	10,000	
Inventory (finished goods)	9,500	40,500
Total Assets		140,000
LIABILITIES		
Current Liabilities		
Trade payables (Nov. £3,500, Dec. £3,500)	(7,000)	
Bank	(8,000)	
Total Liabilities		(15,000)
Net Assets		125,000
		£
EQUITY		
Share Capital and Reserves		
Share Capital		
Ordinary share capital		103,000
Reserves		
Retained earnings		22,000
Total Equity		125,000

Notes:

1. Property, plant and equipment are at cost. Depreciation is at 10% straight line basis per year.
2. Purchases will be £4,800 in January, increasing by £200 per month. They will be paid two months after purchase.
3. Revenue will be £15,000 in January, increasing by £400 per month. Trade receivables are received two months in arrears. They will be based on market price with no formal mark-up from gross profit.
4. Production cost per unit will be: direct materials £12; direct labour £10; production overheads £2 (direct labour and production overheads will be paid in the month incurred). Production 400 units per month. Revenue is 380 units per month.
5. Expenses will run at £6,000 per month. They will be paid in the month incurred.

Q9 Asia Ltd (*continued*)

Required: Prepare the revenue budget, cash budget, trade receivables budget, trade payables budget, production cost budget, raw materials budget, finished goods budget, the income statement and statement of financial position for six months ending 30 June 20X2.

Q10 Peter Jenkins manages a department and has the following budget for the year.

	£	£
Revenue		100,000
Discretionary costs:		
Purchases	(20,000)	
Advertising	(10,000)	
Training	(8,000)	
Repairs	(19,000)	(57,000)
		43,000
Non-discretionary costs:		
Labour (split equally throughout the year)		(18,000)
Profit		25,000

Peter receives a budget of 10% of profit for any quarter in which he makes a minimum profit of £8,000. If he makes less than £8,000 profit, he receives no bonus. In any quarter in which he makes a loss he will earn no profit, but will not incur a penalty.

Required: Calculate the maximum and minimum bonuses Peter could expect. Assume Peter has *complete discretion* about when the revenue will be earned and when the discretionary costs will be incurred.

Q11 All Sunshine Enterprises runs a hire car service in three locations: London, Oslo and Stockholm. The three operating divisions have the following results for the year.

	London £m	Oslo £m	Stockholm £m
Investment	2,000,000	1,000,000	500,000
	£m	£m	£m
Revenue	1,500,000	800,000	300,000
Costs	(800,000)	(400,000)	(135,000)
Operating profit	700,000	400,000	165,000

Required:
Calculate:
i)   Return on Investment (ROI)
ii) Residual Income (RI) – assuming the required rate of return is 12%
iii) Return on Sales (ROS)*

*Can be called Return on Revenue

Which is the best relative measure for each division?

Go online to discover the extra features for this chapter at
www.wiley.com/college/jones

Chapter 15
Planning, control and performance: Standard costing

'No amount of planning will ever replace dumb luck.'

Anonymous
Source: The Executive's Book of Quotations (1994), p. 217.

Learning Outcomes

After completing this chapter you should be able to:

- Explain the nature and importance of standard costing.
- Outline the most important variances.
- Calculate variances and prepare a standard costing operating statement.
- Interpret the variances.

Go online to discover the extra features for this chapter at
www.wiley.com/college/jones

Chapter Summary

- Costing, and planning, control and performance are the two main branches of cost accounting.
- Standard costing, along with budgeting, is one of the key aspects of planning, control and performance.
- Standard costing is a sophisticated form of budgeting based on predetermined costs for cost elements such as direct labour or direct materials.
- There are sales and cost variances.
- Variances are deviations of the actual results from the standard results.
- Standard cost variances can be divided into quantity variances and price variances.
- There are direct materials, direct labour, variable overheads and fixed overheads cost variances.
- Standard cost variances are investigated to see why they have occurred.

Introduction

Cost accounting has two main branches: costing, and planning, control and performance. Standard costing, along with budgeting, is one of the two parts of planning, control and performance. Standard costing can be seen as a more specialised and formal type of budgeting. A particular feature of standard costing is the breakdown of costs into various cost components such as direct labour, direct materials, variable overheads and fixed overheads. In standard costing, **expected (or standard) sales or costs are compared against actual sales or costs.** Any differences between them (called **variances**) are then investigated. In management accounting, the normal terminology is 'sales' rather than 'revenue' variances and this is the convention we use in this book. Variances are divided into those based on quantity and those based on prices. Standard costing, therefore, links the future (i.e., expected costs) to the past (i.e., costs that were actually incurred). Standard costing has proved a useful planning and control tool in many industries. However, standard costing, as Soundbite 15.1 shows, has limitations in times of change.

SOUNDBITE 15.1

Limitations of Standard Costing

'One shortcoming of standard costs for companies seeking continuous improvement, for example, is that they presuppose the goal is to optimize efficiency within a given state of operating conditions rather than to strive for ongoing improvement.'

Source: R. Drtina, S. Hoeger and J. Schaub, Continuous Budgeting at The HON Company, *Management Accounting*, January 1996, in S. Mark Young, *Readings in Management Accounting* (2001), Prentice Hall, p. 214.

Nature of Standard Costing

Standard costing is a sophisticated form of budgeting. Standard costing was originally developed in manufacturing industries in order to control costs. Essentially, standard costing involves investigating, often in some detail, the distinct costing elements which make up a product such as direct materials, direct labour, variable overheads and fixed overheads. After this investigation the costs which should be incurred in making a product or service are determined (see Definition 15.1). For example, a table might be expected to be made using eight hours of direct labour and three metres of wood. These become the standard quantities for making a table.

DEFINITION 15.1

Standard Cost

Working definition

A predetermined calculation of the costs that *should* be incurred in making a product.

Formal definition

'The planned unit cost of the products, components or services produced in a period. The standard cost may be determined on a number of bases. The main uses of standard costs are in performance measurement, control, stock [inventory] valuation and in the establishment of selling prices.'

Source: Chartered Institute of Management Accountants (2000), *Official Terminology*. Reproduced by Permission of Elsevier.

After a table is made, the direct labour and direct materials actually used are compared with the standard. For example, if nine hours are taken rather than eight, this is one hour worse than standard. However, if two metres of wood rather than three metres are used, this is one metre better than standard.

These differences from standard are called variances, which may be favourable (i.e., we have performed better than expected) or unfavourable (i.e., we have performed worse than expected). Unfavourable variances are sometimes called adverse variances. The essence of a good standard costing system is to establish the reason for any variances. Although standard costing is associated with manufacturing industry, it can be adopted in other industries, such as hotel and catering. Just as in normal budgeting, managers are often rewarded on the basis of whether they have met their targets or standards. Real-World View 15.1 gives an example of this in a budgetary context.

Setting standards involves making a decision about whether you are aiming for ideal, attainable or normal standards. They are all different. There is no such thing as a perfect standard. Ideal standards are those which would be attained in an ideal world. Unfortunately, the real world differs from the ideal world. Attainable standards are more realistic and can be reached with effort. Normal standards are those which a business usually attains. Attainable standards are the standards most often used by organisations.

REAL-WORLD VIEW 15.1

A Manager under Pressure

Some of the more successful managers here last year are the ones that really got their profit targets as low as possible and then 'exceeded plans' in terms of results. Unfortunately, last year I called my numbers realistically and am now being penalised in terms of my bonus. You might say, though, that last year I was young and innocent. This year I'm older and wiser!

Source: C.K. Bart (1988), Budgeting Gamesmanship, Academy of Management Executive, pp. 285–94, reprinted in S.M. Young (2001), *Readings in Management Accounting,* Prentice Hall, p. 220.

Standards are usually set by industrial engineers in conjunction with accountants. This often causes friction with the workers who are actually monitored by the standards. Real-World View 15.2 gives a flavour of these tensions. Although dating from the last century, this has a contemporary feel about it.

REAL-WORLD VIEW 15.2

Setting the Standards

Remember those bastards are out to screw you, and that's all they got to think about. They'll stay up half the night figuring out how to beat you out of a dime. They figure you're going to try to fool them, so they make allowances for that. They set [rates] low enough to allow for what you do. It's up to you to figure out how to fool them more than they allow for . . .

Source: W.P. Whyte (1955), *Money and Motivation,* pp. 15–16, as quoted in A. Hopwood (1974), *Accounting and Human Behaviour,* p. 6.

Standard Cost Variances

In order to explain how standard costing works, the illustration of manufacturing a table is continued. In a succession of examples, more detail is gradually introduced. Figure 15.1 introduces the basic overview information for Alan Carpenter who is setting up a furniture business. In May, he makes a prototype table. To simplify the presentation in the figures, *favourable* variances are shorted to 'Fav'. and *unfavourable* variances to 'Unfav'.

Before the prototype table was actually made, Alan Carpenter thought it would cost £20 and that he could sell it for £30. He, therefore, anticipated a profit of £10. In actual fact, the table was sold for £33. Carpenter thus made £3 more sales than anticipated. However, the table cost £22 (£2 more than anticipated). Overall, therefore, actual profit is £11 rather than the predicted standard profit of £10. Carpenter benefits £3 from selling well, but loses £2

Figure 15.1 Overview of Standard Costs for Alan Carpenter for May

	Standard	Actual	Variance	
	£	£	£	
Revenue	30	33	3	Fav.
Costs	20	22	(2)	Unfav.
Profit	10	11	1	Fav.

through excessive costs. There is an overall favourable sales variance of £3, and an overall unfavourable cost variance of £2 which gives a £1 favourable profit variance.

We now expand the example and look at Alan Carpenter's operations for June. In June he anticipates making and selling 10 tables. In actual fact, he makes and sells only nine tables (see Figure 15.2).

Figure 15.2 Standard Costs for Alan Carpenter for June

	Budget 10 Tables	Actual 9 Tables
	£	£
Revenue	300	290
Costs	200	170
Profit	100	120

Calculation of variances

i. Flex the Budget

	Budget 10 Tables	Flexed Budget 9 Tables	Actual 9 Tables	Variance	
	£	£	£	£	
Revenue	300	270	290	20	Fav.
Costs	200	180	170	10	Fav.
Profit	100	90	120	30	Fav.

ii. Calculate Variances

		£	
Budgeted Profit		100	
Sales quantity variance (1 table at £10 profit)		(10)	Unfav.
Budgeted profit for actual production		90	
Sales price variance		20	Fav.
Cost variance		10	Fav.
Actual Profit		120	

Before calculating the variances, we must flex the budget. Flexing the budget simply means adjusting the budget to take into account the *actual quantity produced*. We need to do this because we need to calculate the costs *which would have been incurred if we actually made* nine tables. If we made only nine tables, we would logically expect to incur costs for nine rather than ten tables. In addition, we would expect to sell nine not ten tables. The budget must, therefore, be calculated on the basis of the nine actual tables made rather than the ten predicted.

PAUSE FOR THOUGHT 15.1

Flexing the Budget

Why would it be so misleading if we failed to flex our budget?

If we failed to flex our budget then we would not compare like with like. For example, we would be trying to compare costs based on an output of ten tables with costs incurred actually making nine tables. We need to adjust for this, otherwise the budget will be distorted.

By making nine rather than ten tables, the profit for one table is lost. This was £10 (as there was £100 profit for ten tables). There is thus a £10 drop in profits. This is called a **sales quantity variance**. (Note that we are *assuming*, at this stage, that all the *costs will vary in direct relation to the number of tables*.) We can now compare the sales and costs actually earned and incurred for nine tables with those that were expected to be earned and incurred. As Figure 15.2 shows, the nine tables were expected to sell for £270, but were actually sold for £290. In other words, we received £20 more than we had anticipated for our tables. This was the **sales price variance**. Note that the sales quantity variance is caused by lost profit. By contrast, the sales price variance is caused by the fact we are selling the tables for more than we anticipated. There is thus a **favourable sales price variance** of £20. The budgeted cost for nine tables was £180. However, the actual cost incurred is only £170. There is thus a favourable cost variance of £10. The difference between the budgeted profit of £100 and the actual profit of £120 can be explained by these three variances (unfavourable sales quantity variance (£10), favourable sales price variance (£20) and favourable cost variance (£10)).

So far, we have seen that it is important to flex the budget, and looked at the sales volume variance and the sales price variance. It is now time to look in more detail at the cost variances. When looking at cost variances, it is important to distinguish between variable and fixed costs. As we saw in Chapter 12, variable costs are those costs that directly vary with a product or service (for example, direct materials, direct labour or production overheads). The more products made, the more the variable costs. Thus, if it costs £20 to make one table, it will cost £200 to make ten tables. Fixed costs, however, do not vary. You will pay the buildings insurance of £10 per month whether you make one table or 100 tables. In continuing the Alan Carpenter example, the costs are now divided into fixed and variable. In effect, therefore, we are using a variable costing system where a firm's costs are not allocated to inventory. In an absorption costing system where inventory would be valued, there would need to be an additional variance, a volume variance. However, as these variables are not very useful for controlling or analysing a company's activities, they are not considered further here.

Essentially, *all the variable costs* (direct materials, direct labour, and variable overheads) *have two elements – price and quantity*. For example, when making a table we might predict using the following standard prices and standard quantities:

	Price		*Quantity*
Direct labour	£5 per hour	for	2 hours
Direct materials	£1 per metre	for	5 metres of wood
Variable overheads (incurred on basis of direct labour hours)	£2 per hour	for	2 hours

When our actual price and actual quantity vary from standard, we will have price and quantity variances. In other words, the overall cost variances for direct labour, direct materials and variable overheads can be divided into a quantity and a price variance. **Price variances** are caused when the **standard price** of a product *differs* from the **actual price. Quantity variances** are caused when the **standard quantity** *differs* from the **actual quantity.** These differences between the standard and the actual quantity when multiplied by standard price will give us the overall quantity variance. Favourable variances are where we have done better than expected; unfavourable variances are where we have done worse than expected. For fixed overheads, which do not vary with production, we compare the actual fixed overheads incurred with the standard. We call this difference the fixed overheads quantity variance.

An overview of all these variances is given in Figure 15.3, and in Figure 15.4 the main elements of all the variances are summarised. For simplification, this book uses the terms price and quantity variances throughout. Often, however, more technical terminology is used (these alternative technical terms are shown in the second column of Figure 15.4).

Figure 15.3 Diagram of Main Variances

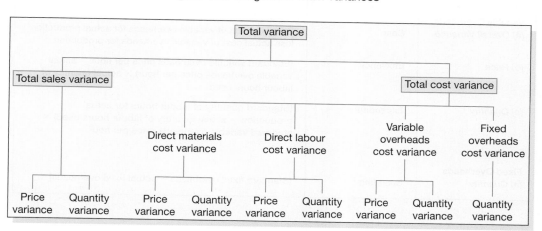

Figure 15.4 Calculation of the Main Variances

Variances	Technical Name	Calculation
i. SALES		
(a) Overall Variance	Sales	Not usual to calculate an overall sales variance as it is more meaningful to calculate the results in terms of contribution
(b) Price	Price	(Standard price per unit − actual price per unit) × actual quantity of units sold
(c) Quantity	Volume	(Standard quantity of units sold − actual quantity of units sold) × standard contribution unit
ii. COSTS		
Direct Materials		
(a) Overall Variance	Cost	Standard cost of materials for actual production less actual cost of materials used in production
(b) Price	Price	(Standard price per unit of material − actual price per unit of material) × actual quantity of materials used.
(c) Quantity	Usage	(Standard quantity of materials for actual production − actual quantity of materials used) × standard material price per unit of materials
Direct Labour		
(a) Overall Variance	Cost	Standard cost of labour for actual production less actual cost of labour used in production
(b) Price	Rate	(Standard price per hour − actual price per hour) × actual quantity of labour hours used
(c) Quantity	Efficiency	(Standard quantity of labour hours for actual production − actual quantity of labour hours used) × standard labour price per hour
Variable Overheads		
(a) Overall Variance	Cost	Standard cost of variable overheads for actual production less actual cost of variable overheads for production
(b) Price	Efficiency	(Standard variable overheads price per hour − actual variable overheads price per hour) × actual quantity of labour hours used
(c) Quantity	Expenditure	(Standard quantity of labour hours for actual production − actual quantity of labour hours used) × standard variable overheads price per hour
Fixed Overheads		
(a) Quantity	Spending	(Standard fixed overheads − actual fixed overheads)

Figure 15.4 Calculation of the Main Variances (*continued*)

Helpnote

At first sight this table looks daunting. However, in essence the way we calculate all the overall variances, price variances and quantity variances is remarkably similar. The key essentials are explained below. *Note that in standard costing, standard refers to the budget.*

i. Overall Variances

Here we are interested in comparing the budgeted cost of the actual items we produce (**standard cost of actual production**) with the actual cost of items we produce (**actual cost of production**). The only variation is whether we are talking about direct materials, direct labour or variable overheads. The overall variance can be split into **price and quantity variances**. There is no overall variance for sales or fixed overheads. It is important to realise that, in practice, the **overall variance is normally calculated just by flexing the budget.** The difference between the flexed budget and the actual results gives the overall variance.

ii. Price Variances

Here we are interested in comparing the **standard price for the actual quantity used or sold** with the **actual price for the actual quantity used or sold**. The only variation is whether we are relating this to sales, direct materials, direct labour or variable overheads. For variable overheads we use the actual quantity of labour hours used, as we are recovering variable overheads using labour hours. There is no price variance for fixed overheads. The standard formula is:

(Standard price − actual price) × actual quantity used or sold

iii. Quantity Variances

In this case, we are interested in comparing the budgeted cost of the actual items produced or sold (**standard cost of actual production or standard quantity for sales**) with the actual quantity produced or sold (**actual quantity used or sold**). This gives us the quantity difference. This is then multiplied by the standard contribution per item for the sales variance and by the standard price per unit (**normally, metres or hours**) for the other variances. The only variation is whether we are considering the standard price of direct materials, direct labour or variable overheads or the standard selling price. For variable overheads, we use the standard quantity of labour hours and the actual quantity of labour hours used as we are recovering variable overheads using labour hours. The standard formula is:

Standard quantity of actual production (or, for sales, standard quantity for sales) less actual quantity used (or, for sales, actual quantity sold) × standard price (or, for sales, standard contribution per item)

For fixed overheads, the quantity variance is simply standard fixed overheads less actual fixed overheads.

In order to see how these variances all interlock, we now expand the Alan Carpenter example (see Figure 15.5).

Using Figure 15.5, we now calculate the variances in two steps: flexing the budget and calculating the individual variances.

Flexing the Budget

Note that fixed overheads are not flexed! This is because by their very nature they do not vary with production. The flexed budget is used in the calculation of variances so that the levels of activity are the same and can be used as a basis for meaningful comparisons.

Figure 15.5 Worked Example: Alan Carpenter's Standard Costs for June

i. Standard Cost per Table	£	£
Selling Price		30
Direct materials: 5 metres of wood at £1 per metre	(5)	
Direct labour: 2 hours at £5 per hour	(10)	
Variable overheads (recovered on labour hours):		
2 hours at £2 per hour	(4)	
Fixed overheads: £10 in total divided by 10 tables	(1)	(20)
Budgeted Profit		10

ii. Budgeted (i.e., standard) Results for June: 10 Tables	£	£
Selling Price		300
Direct materials: 50 metres of wood at £1 per metre	(50)	
Direct labour: 20 hours at £5 per hour	(100)	
Variable overheads: 20 hours at £2 per hour	(40)	
Fixed overheads	(10)	(200)
Budgeted Profit		100

iii. Actual Results for June: 9 Tables	£	£
Selling Price		290
Direct materials: 44 metres of wood at £1.20 per metre	(52.80)	
Direct labour: 16 hours at £4.50	(72.00)	
Variable overheads	(33.00)	
Fixed overheads	(12.20)	(170)
Actual Profit		120

	Budget (i.e., standard)		Flexed Budget (i.e., standard quantity of actual production)		Actual Results		Overall Variances	
	10 Tables		9 Tables		9 Tables			
	£	£	£	£	£	£	£	
Revenue		300		270		290.00	20.00	Fav.
Direct materials	(50)		(45)		(52.80)		(7.80)	Unfav.
Direct labour	(100)		(90)		(72.00)		18.00	Fav.
Variable overheads	(40)	(190)	(36)	(171)	(33.00)	(157.80)	3.00	Fav.
Contribution*		110		99		132.20		
Fixed overheads		(10)		(10)		(12.20)	(2.20)	Unfav.
Profit		100		89		120.00		

*This is sometimes known as profit before fixed overheads.

By flexing the budget, *we have automatically calculated (1) the sales price variance, and (2) the overall cost variances* for direct materials, direct labour and variable overheads. It is important to note that the *flexed budget gives us the standard quantity of the actual production*. The cost variances will then be broken down into the individual price and quantity variances (see Figure 15.6). However, *first* we need to calculate the sales quantity variance.

Calculating Individual Variances

(a) Sales Quantity Variance

Standard quantity

of units sold	—	actual quantity of units sold	×	contribution*	
10	—	9	×	£11	= £ 11 Unfav.**

Notes:

*This is budgeted profit before fixed overheads (£110) divided by the budgeted number of tables (10). Therefore, we have, £110 ÷ 10 = £11. Note that this is calculated *before* fixed overheads. This is because fixed overheads will remain the same whatever the value of sales. They must be excluded from the calculation and their variance calculated separately.

**This represents the difference between the budgeted profit (£100) less the flexed budget (£89). *In practice, this is the easiest way to calculate this variance.*

(b) Individual Price and Quantity Variances

When we calculate the price and quantity variances based on our flexed budget, we can use the standard price and quantity formulas given below (see Figure 15.6). We then need to remember that the standard price for sales is the standard selling price per unit, for direct materials it is the price per unit of direct materials used and so on. For quantity we need to remember that we are concerned with the standard quantity of materials, labour, etc. Figure 15.6 is based on Figure 15.5 and our flexed budget.

Figure 15.6 Calculation of Individual Price and Quantity Variances for Alan Carpenter

Overall Variance =	Price Variance +		Quantity Variance	
	(standard price – actual price sold or used) × actual quantity sold or used		*(standard quantity of actual production – actual quantity used) × standard price*	
	Price calculations	**Notes**	**Quantity calculations**	**Notes**
(a) Sales i. Sales price Note the sales quantity variance is automatically given by flexing the budget	(£30 – £32.22*) × 9 tables = **£20 Fav.** *£290 sold ÷ 9 tables sold = (£32.22)	**(1)**	ii. Sales quantity See calculation above (a) for sales quantity variance	**(2)**
(b) Direct Materials Overall (£7.80) Unfav.	(£1– £1.20 × 44 metres = (£8.80) Unfav. = **(£8.80) Unfav.**	**(3)** +	(45 metres – 44 metres) × £1 = £1 Fav. £1 Fav.	**(4)**
(c) Direct Labour Overall £18 Fav.	(£5 – £4.50) × 16 hours = £8 Fav. = **£8 Fav.**	**(5)** +	(18 hours – 16 hours) × £5 = £10 Fav. £10 Fav.	**(6)**
(d) Variable Overheads Overall £3 Fav.	(£2.00 – £2.06*) × 16 hours = (£1) Unfav. *£33 actual at 16 hours = £2.06 per hour = **(£1) Unfav.**	**(7)** +	(18 hours – 16 hours) × £2 = £4 Fav. £4 Fav.	**(8)**
(e) Fixed Overheads Overall (£2.20) Unfav.	**=**		Standard less actual £10 – £12.20 = (£2.20) Unfav. (£2.20) Unfav.	**(9)**

Figure 15.6 Calculation of Individual Price and Quantity Variances for Alan Carpenter (*continued*)

Notes:
1. **Sales Price Variance:** The standard selling price is £30 per unit. However, we sell at £32.22 per table (£290 ÷ 9). Therefore, overall, across the nine tables, we make £20 (9 × £2.22) more than we expected.
2. **Sales Quantity Variance:** The standard quantity expected to be sold was ten tables. We actually sold nine tables. Therefore, we lose the contribution on one table of £11. This was the overall contribution expected of £110 divided by the standard quantity of ten tables.
3. **Direct Materials Price Variance:** The standard price (£1.00) per metre is less than the actual price (£1.20) paid per metre by £0.20 pence per metre. As 44 metres were used this results in an unfavourable variance of £8.80.
4. **Direct Materials Quantity Variance:** The standard quantity to make nine tables is 45 metres. However, only 44 were actually used. As the standard price was £1 per metre, Alan Carpenter gains £1, which is a favourable variance.
5. **Direct Labour Price Variance:** The standard price (£5.00) per labour hour is greater than the actual price paid (£4.50). As 16 labour hours were used, the result is an £8 favourable variance.
6. **Direct Labour Quantity Variance:** The standard quantity to make nine tables is 18 hours. Alan Carpenter has taken 16 hours. As the standard price per labour hour is £5, there is a £10 favourable variance.
7. **Variable Overhead Price Variance:** The standard recovery rate is £2.00 per hour. However, Alan Carpenter has recovered £33 in the 16 hours actually worked (i.e., £2.0625 per hour). Given the 16 hours worked, this results in an overall over-recovery of £1 (i.e., 16 × £0.0625). In other words, we expected to recover £32, but we actually recovered £33 (16 hours × £2.06). We thus recovered £1 more than expected, which is unfavourable.
8. **Variable Overheads Quantity Variance:** It was anticipated that 18 hours would be used to recover variable overheads for 9 tables. In actual fact, 16 hours were used. Since £2 per hour is recovered, there is an under-recovery of £4. This is favourable.
9. **Fixed Overhead Volume Variance:** The fixed overhead was expected to be £10. In fact, it was £12.20. This is £2.20 more than expected. Therefore, we have a £2.20 unfavourable variance.

We can now draw up a standard cost reconciliation statement. This statement reconciles the budgeted profit of £100 to the actual profit of £120.

Alan Carpenter: Standard Cost Reconciliation Statement for June				
	£	£	£	
Budgeted Profit			100	
Sales quantity variance			(11)	Unfav.
Budgeted Profit at Actual Sales			89	
	Fav.	Unfav.		
Variances	£	£		
Sales price	20			
Direct materials price		8.80		
Direct materials quantity	1			
Direct labour price	8			
Direct labour quantity	10			
Variable overhead price		1.00		
Variable overhead quantity	4			
Fixed overhead variance		2.20		
	43	12.00	31	Fav.
Actual Profit			120	

Interpretation of Variances

A key aspect of both budgeting and standard costing is the investigation of variances. In Figure 15.7 we look at some possible reasons for variances.

Figure 15.7 Possible Causes of Variances

Variance	Favourable	Unfavourable
1. Sales Quantity	We sell more than we expect because of • good market conditions • good marketing.	We sell less than we expect because of • poor market conditions • bad marketing.
2. Sales Price	We sell at a higher price than expected because of • unexpected market demand • good economy.	We sell at a lower price than expected because of • tough competition • poor economy.
3. Direct Materials Quantity	We use more material than expected because of • poor-quality material • sloppy production.	We use less material than expected because of • high-quality material • efficient production.
4. Direct Materials Price	Our material costs are more than expected because of • a price rise.	Our material costs are less than we expect because • we find an alternative cheaper supplier.
5. Direct Labour Quantity	We use more labour than we expected because of • inefficient cheaper workers who take longer • labour problems.	We use less labour than expected because of • efficient workers who are quicker.
6. Fixed Overheads	The overall costs are more than expected because of • inflation.	The overhead costs are less than expected because • we change to a cheaper source.

SOUNDBITE 15.2

Behavioural Aspects of Standards

'All persons concerned with setting standards are striving to gain some measure of personal control over factors which are important in their organisational lives.'

Source: A. Hopwood (1974), *Accounting and Human Behaviour*, pp. 6–7.

These variances represent differences in what actually happened to what we expected to happen. It must be remembered that variances are only as good as the original budgets or standards that are set. Therefore, if unrealistic, incorrect or unattainable standards are set, this will create misleading variances. As we saw earlier, setting the original standards can often cause severe tensions between the standard setters and the employees. In standard costing a more sophisticated, systematic approach is taken to the investigation of variances than in budgeting.

The nature of variable overheads means that these variances are tied into the basis of absorption (for example, direct labour hours). The causes for the variable overhead variances will, therefore, tend to reflect those for the direct labour hours. It is not, therefore, particularly meaningful to investigate the reasons for these variances separately. Variable overheads have, therefore, been excluded from Figure 15.7. When interpreting variances it is important to distinguish between those factors that are controllable (such as the amount of labour used) and those that are not controllable (such as supplier price rises or price rises caused by changes in foreign currency). Non-financial considerations such as risk and customer satisfaction are also important.

PAUSE FOR THOUGHT 15.2

Compensating Variances

Why might there be compensating variances? For example, an unfavourable material quantity variance, but a favourable material price variance.

Sometimes the quantity and price variances are interconnected. For example, we plan to make a product and we budget for a high-quality material. If we then substitute a low-quality material, it will be likely to cost less. However, we will need to use more. Therefore, we would have an unfavourable material quantity variance, but a favourable price variance.

Conclusion

Standard costing is a sophisticated form of budgeting. It was originally used in manufacturing industries, but is now much more widespread. Standard costing involves predetermining the cost of the various elements of a product or service (such as selling price, direct materials, direct labour and variable overheads). These standard costs are then compared with the actual costs and any differences, called variances, investigated. These variances are split into price and quantity variances. Standard costing allows costs to be monitored very closely. In many businesses, it is thus a very useful form of planning, control and performance. However, it is important to appreciate the fact that budgeting and standard costing, although key elements of planning, control and performance, have their limitations and can actually change, and indeed influence, performance. This is neatly demonstrated in Real-World View 15.3 with which we conclude this section.

REAL-WORLD VIEW 15.3

What You Measure is What You Get

Despite such long-standing and clear delineations of the limits of performance measurement, contemporary discussions of the results of performance measurement initiatives frequently conclude with a wry smile and the acknowledgement that once again this is a case where 'you get what you measure'. As with the term 'creative accounting', however, this expression reflects an ironic acknowledgement of the limits of our abilities to control behaviour through performance measurement, not of our success.

Source: T. Ahrens and S. Chapman (2006), New measures in performance management, in A. Bhimani, *Contemporary Issues in Management Accounting*, p. 1.

Discussion Questions

Questions with numbers in blue have answers at the back of the book.

Q1 'Setting the standards is the most difficult part of standard costing.' What considerations should be taken into account when setting standards?

Q2 'Standard costing is good for planning and control, but unless great care is taken can often be very demotivational.' Discuss.

Q3 Standard costing is more about control than motivation. Do you agree with this statement?

Q4 'The key to standard setting is providing a good, fair initial set of standards.' Discuss.

Q5 State whether the following statements are true or false. If false, explain why.
  (a) Favourable cost variances are where actual costs are less than standard costs.
  (b) Flexing the budget means adjusting the budget to take into account the actual prices incurred.
  (c) Price and quantity variances are the main constituents of the overall cost variances.
  (d) The direct materials price variance is: (standard price per unit of material − actual price per unit of material) × actual quantity of materials used.
  (e) The direct labour quantity variance is: (standard price of labour hours for actual production − actual price of labour hours used) × standard labour price per hour.

Numerical Questions

Questions with numbers in blue have answers at the back of the book.

Q1 Stuffed restaurant has the following results for December.

	Budget	Actual
Number of meals	10,000	12,000
	£	£
Price per meal	10.00	10.60
Food cost	30,000	37,200
Labour cost	35,000	36,000
Variable overheads	5,000	6,000
Fixed overheads	3,000	3,100

Required:
(i) Calculate the flexed budget.
(ii) Calculate the sales price variance.
(iii) Calculate the overall cost variances for materials, labour, variable overheads and fixed overheads (note: you do not have enough information to calculate the more detailed price and quantity variances).
(iv) Calculate the sales quantity variance.
(v) Discuss the variances. In particular, highlight what extra information might be needed.

Q2 Engines Incorporated, a small engineering company, has the following results for April for its product, the Widget. It budgeted to sell 12,500 widgets at £9.00 each. However, 16,000 widgets were actually sold at £8.80 each. The budgeted and actual costs are given below.

	Budget	Actual
Number of widgets	12,500	16,000
	£	£
Price per widget	9.00	8.80
Direct materials	40,000	42,000
Labour cost	32,000	29,000
Variable overheads	6,000	8,000
Fixed overheads	8,000	10,000

Required:
(i) Calculate the flexed budget.
(ii) Calculate the sales price and sales quantity variances.

Q2 Engines Incorporated (*continued*)

(iii) Calculate the overall cost variances for materials, labour, variable over-heads and fixed overheads (note: you do not have enough information to calculate the more detailed price and quantity variances).

(iv) Discuss the variances. In particular, highlight what extra information might be needed for a more detailed investigation.

Q3 Birch Manufacturing makes bookcases. The company has the following details of its June production.

	Estimated	Actual
Number of bookcases	10,000	11,000
Metres of wood	100,000	120,000
Price per metre	0.50p	0.49p

Required: Calculate the:
(i) overall direct materials cost variance
(ii) direct materials price variance
(iii) direct materials quantity variance.

Q4 Sweatshop has the following details of direct labour used to make tracksuits for July.
(a) Standard: 550 sweatshirts at 2 hours at £5.50 per hour.
(b) Actual production: 500 sweatshirts at 1,050 hours for £5,880.

Required: Calculate the:
(i) overall direct labour cost variance
(ii) direct labour price variance
(iii) direct labour quantity variance.

Q5 Toycare manufactures puzzle games. It has the following details of its March production.

	Estimated	Actual
Number of puzzle games	11,000	12,000
Kilos of raw materials	5,500	4,800
Price per kilo	0.45p	0.46p
Direct labour (hours)	6,600	4,800
Direct labour price per hour	£5.50	£5.30

Required: Calculate the:
(i) overall direct materials cost variance
(ii) direct materials price variance
(iii) direct materials quantity variance
(iv) overall direct labour cost variance
(v) direct labour price variance
(vi) direct labour quantity variance.

Q6 Wonderworld has the following details for its variable overheads for August for its Teleporter. Each Teleporter is expected to take two labour hours and variable overheads are expected to be £2.50 per labour hour. Wonderworld expects to make 100,000 teleporters. In actual fact, it makes 110,000 teleporters using 230,000 labour hours. Its budgeted fixed overheads were £10,000. However, it actually spends £9,800 on fixed overheads. Actual variable overheads are £517,500.

Required: Calculate the:
(i) overall variable overheads cost variance
(ii) variable overheads price variance
(iii) variable overheads quantity variance
(iv) fixed overheads variance.

Q7 Special Manufacturers has the following details for its variable overheads for July on its Startrek product. Each Startrek is expected to take three labour hours and variable overheads are expected to be £4.25 per labour hour. The firm expects to make 200,000 Startreks. In actual fact, it makes 180,000 Startreks using 630,000 labour hours. Its budgeted fixed overheads were £25,000. However, it actually spends £23,000 on fixed overheads. Actual variable overheads are £2,800,000.

Required: Calculate the:
(i) overall variable overheads cost variance
(ii) variable overheads price variance
(iii) variable overheads quantity variance
(iv) fixed overheads variance.

Q8 Peter Peacock plc manufactures a subcomponent for the car industry. There are the following details for August:
(a) *Budgeted data*
Revenue: 200,000 subcomponents at £2.80 each
Direct labour: 40,000 hours at £7.25 per hour
Direct materials: 100,000 sheets of metal at £1.25 each
Variable overheads: £40,000 recovered at £1.00 per direct labour hour
Fixed overheads: £68,000
(b) *Actual data*
220,000 subcomponents were actually sold and produced
Revenue: 220,000 subcomponents at £2.78 each
Direct labour: 43,500 hours at £7.30 per hour
Direct material: 125,000 sheets of metal at £1.20
Variable overheads: £42,500
Fixed overheads: £67,000

Required:
(i) Calculate the flexed budget and overall variances.
(ii) Calculate the individual price and quantity variances.
(iii) Calculate a standard cost reconciliation statement for August.
(iv) Comment on the results.

Q9 Supersonic plc manufactures an assembly mounting for the aircraft industry. In July, it was expected that 80,000 assembly mountings would be sold at £18.80 each. In actual fact, 76,000 assembly mountings were sold for £20.00 each. The cost data are provided below.

	Budgeted data	Actual data
Direct materials	200,000 sheets of metal at £2.10 each	150,000 sheets of metal at £2.20 each
Direct labour	50,000 hours at £8.00 per hour	51,000 hours at £7.50 per hour
Variable overheads	£45,000 recovered at £0.90 per direct labour hour	£41,000
Fixed overheads	£78,000	£80,000

Required:
(i) Calculate the flexed budget and overall variances.
(ii) Calculate the individual price and quantity variances.
(iii) Calculate a standard cost reconciliation statement for July.
(iv) Comment on the results.

Go online to discover the extra features for this chapter at
www.wiley.com/college/jones

Chapter 16

Short-term decision making

'So there I was, fresh from the annual meeting of the Society for Judgement and Decision Making, and behaving like Buridan's Ass – the imaginary creature which starved midway between two troughs of hay because it couldn't decide which to go for.'

Source: Peter Aytan, Ditherer's Dilemma, *New Scientist*, 12 February 2000, p. 47.

Learning Outcomes

After completing this chapter you should be able to:

- Explain the nature of short-term business decisions.
- Understand the concept of contribution analysis.
- Investigate some of the decisions for which contribution analysis is useful.
- Draw up break-even charts and contribution graphs.

Go online to discover the extra features for this chapter at
www.wiley.com/college/jones

Chapter Summary

- In business, decision making involves choosing between alternatives and involves looking forward, using relevant information and financial evaluation.
- Businesses face a range of short-term decisions such as how to maximise limited resources.
- It is useful to distinguish between costs that vary with production or sales (variable costs) and costs that do not (fixed costs).
- Revenue less variable costs equals contribution.
- Contribution less fixed costs equals net profit.
- Contribution and contribution per unit are useful when making short-term business decisions.
- Contribution analysis can help determine which products or services are most profitable, which are making losses, whether to buy externally rather than make internally and how to maximise the use of a limited resource.
- Throughput accounting attempts to remove bottlenecks from a production system; it treats direct labour and variable overheads as fixed.
- Break-even analysis shows the point at which a product makes neither a profit nor a loss.
- Both break-even charts and contribution graphs are useful ways of portraying business information.

Introduction

Businesses, like individuals, are continually involved in decision making. A decision is simply a choice between alternatives. It is forward looking. Business decisions may be long-term strategic ones about raising long-term finance or capital expenditure. Alternatively, the decisions may be short-term, day-to-day, operational ones, such as whether to continue making a particular product. This particular chapter looks at short-term decisions. When making short-term decisions, it is important to consider only factors relevant to the decision. Depreciation, for example, will not generally change whatever the short-term decision. It is not, therefore, included in the short-term decision-making calculations.

Decision Making

Individuals make decisions all the time. These may be short-term decisions: Shall we go out or stay in? If we go out, do we go for a meal, to the cinema or to a pub? Or long-term decisions: Shall we get married? Shall we buy a house? These decisions involve choosing between various competing alternatives.

Managers also make continual decisions about the short-term and long-term future. Shall we make a new product or not? Which product shall we make: A or B? Figure 16.1 gives

Figure 16.1 Some Short-Term Managerial Decisions

> • Which products should the business continue to make this year?
> • Which departments should the business close down this year?
> • How should the business maximise limited resources this year?
> • At what level of production does the business currently break even?
> • How can the business maximise current profits?

some examples of short-term business decisions. However, it is important to note the context. For example, discontinuing a product or department can have long-term consequences.

Whatever the nature of the decision, informed business decision making will share certain characteristics, such as being forward-looking, using relevant information and involving financial evaluation.

(a) Forward-looking

Decisions look to the future and, therefore, require forward-looking information. Past costs that have no ongoing implications for the future are irrelevant. These costs are sometimes known as **sunk costs** and should be *excluded from decision making*.

(b) Relevant Information

When choosing between alternatives, we are concerned only with information which is relevant to the particular decision. For example, after arriving in the centre of town by taxi, you are trying to choose between going to the cinema or pub. The taxi fare is a sunk cost which is not relevant to your decision. You cannot alter the past. *Relevant costs and revenues are, therefore, those costs and revenues that will affect a decision. Sunk costs are non-relevant costs.*

To make an informed decision, only relevant information is needed. This information may be financial or non-financial. The non-financial information will normally, however, have indirect financial consequences. For example, a drop in the birth rate may have financial consequences for suppliers of baby products.

(c) Financial Evaluation

In business, effective decision making will involve financial evaluation. This means gathering the relevant facts and then working out the financial benefits and costs of the various alternatives. There are a variety of techniques available to do this, which we will be discussing in subsequent chapters.

Decisions may have **opportunity costs**. *Opportunity costs are the potential benefit lost by rejecting the best alternative course of action.* If you work in the union bar at £9 per hour and the next best alternative is the university bookshop at £7 per hour, then the opportunity cost is £7 per hour. This is because you forgo the chance of working in the bookshop at £7 per hour. However, from the above, it should not be assumed that business decision making is always wholly rational. As we all know, many factors, not all of them rational, enter into real-life decision making (see Real-World View 16.1).

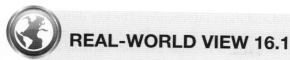

REAL-WORLD VIEW 16.1

Decision Making

The upshot? Although you might think that asking what you want should be the flip side of asking what you don't want, it isn't. When you reject something you focus more on the negative features; when you select something you're focusing on the positive. So whether it's an ice cream or a prospective employee, deciding what (or who) you want by a process of rational elimination may not actually give you what you want. There is no simple panacea to ease the pain of choice other than passing the buck, of course (hence the irksome cliché: 'No, you decide').

As for you sadistic purveyors of all this choice, don't get too smug. When Sheena Sethi-Iyengar, from the Massachusetts Institute of Technology, set up a tasting counter for exotic jams in a grocery, she found that too much choice can be bad for business. More customers stopped to sample from a 24-jam counter than from a 6-jam counter. But only 3 per cent bought any jam when 24 were on offer, compared with 30 per cent when there were 6 to choose from.

Source: Peter Aytan, Ditherer's Dilemma, *New Scientist*, 12 February 2000, vol. 165, no 2225, p. 471. © 2000 Reed Business Information Ltd, England Reproduced by Permission. http://www.newscientist .com/article/mg16522254.700-ditherers-dilemma.html.

Contribution Analysis

When making short-term decisions, a technique called contribution analysis has evolved. This technique has several distinctive features (see Figure 16.2).

Figure 16.2 Key Features of Contribution Analysis

- Distinction between those costs that are the same whatever the level of production or service (**fixed costs**) and those that vary with the level of production or service (**variable costs**).
- Profit is no longer the main criterion by which decisions are judged. The key criterion becomes *contribution to fixed costs.*
- Calculations are often performed on the basis of **unit costs** rather than in total.
- Contribution analysis focuses on the *extra cost of making an extra product* or providing an extra unit of service.

It is now important to look more closely at the key elements of contribution analysis: fixed costs, variable costs and contribution. The analysis and interaction of these elements is sometimes called cost-profit-volume analysis. In this book, the term contribution analysis is used because it is considered easier to understand and more informative. The key difference between profit and contribution is that when determining profit you do not split the costs between fixed and variable costs. Contribution, however, is revenue less only variable costs. It is, therefore, necessary to analyse costs into those that are fixed and those that are variable. In practice, this may prove very difficult and is obviously subjective.

(i) Fixed Costs

Fixed costs *do not change* if we sell more or fewer products or services. *They are thus irrelevant for short-term decisions*. For a business, fixed costs might be business rates, depreciation, insurance or rent. On a normal household telephone bill, for example, the fixed cost is the amount of the rental. It should be stressed that fixed costs will not change over the short term, but over the long term all costs will change (see Pause for Thought 16.1).

 PAUSE FOR THOUGHT 16.1

Fixed Costs

In the long run all fixed costs are variable. Why do you think this is so?

This is because at some stage the underlying conditions will change. For example, at a certain production level it will be necessary to buy extra machines; this will necessitate extra depreciation and insurance, both normally fixed costs. Alternatively, if a factory closes then even the fixed costs will no longer be incurred.

(ii) Variable Costs

These costs *do vary* with the level of production or service provided. *They are thus relevant for short-term decisions*. If we take a business, variable costs might be direct labour, direct materials, or overheads directly linked to service or production. In practice, it may be difficult to ascertain which costs are fixed and which are variable. In addition, some costs will have elements of both a fixed and variable nature. For example, an electricity bill has a fixed standing charge and then an amount per unit of electricity used. However, to simplify matters, we shall treat costs as either fixed or variable.

(iii) Contribution

Contribution to fixed overheads, or contribution in short, is simply revenue less variable costs. If revenue is greater than variable costs, it means that for each product made or service provided, the business contributes to its fixed overheads. Once a business's fixed overheads are covered, a profit will be made.

Contribution, as we shall see, is a very useful technique which enables businesses to choose the most profitable goods and services. Contribution analysis is sometimes called **marginal costing**. This comes from economics where a marginal cost is the *extra cost or 'incremental' cost needed to produce one more good or service*. Figure 16.3 demonstrates how contribution analysis works.

Figure 16.3 Demonstration of Contribution Analysis

Clueless has two products (X and Y) and the following abridged income statement.

	£	£
Revenue		100,000
Less: *Costs*		
Direct materials	25,000	
Direct labour	35,000	
Overheads	20,000	80,000
Net Profit		20,000

Which of the two products is the most profitable?

To answer this question, we need additional information about X and Y and about which costs are fixed and which are variable. We can then use contribution analysis.

Additional information	**X**	**Y**
Sales units	1,000	2,000
	£	£
Revenue	50,000	50,000
Direct materials	15,000	10,000
Direct labour	20,000	15,000
Variable overheads	7,000	3,000
Fixed overheads	10,000	

Contribution Analysis

	X (1,000 units)				Y (2,000 units)			
	Per unit		Total		Per unit		Total	
	£	£	£	£	£	£	£	£
Revenue		50		50,000		25		50,000
Less: *Costs*								
Direct materials	15		15,000		5.0		10,000	
Direct labour	20		20,000		7.5		15,000	
Variable overheads	7	42	7,000	42,000	1.5	14	3,000	28,000
Contribution		8		8,000		11		22,000
X's contribution								8,000
Total Contribution								30,000
Fixed overheads								(10,000)
Net Profit								20,000

We can thus see that:
1. X makes a contribution of £8 per unit, while Y makes a contribution of £11 per unit.
2. X contributes £8,000 to fixed overheads, while Y contributes £22,000 to fixed overheads.

The contribution data in Figure 16.3 can be used to answer a series of 'what if' questions, varying the levels of sales for X and Y. Contribution analysis is thus very versatile (as Figure 16.4 shows).

Figure 16.4 'What if' Questions for Products X and Y

(i) What if the revenue of X and Y doubles?
(ii) What if the revenue of X and Y halves?

(i) If the revenue of X and Y doubles, the contribution would double. Thus:

	£
X (Existing contribution £8,000)	16,000
Y (Existing contribution £22,000)	44,000
	60,000
Fixed overheads	(10,000)
Net Profit	50,000

(ii) If the revenue of X and Y halves the contribution will halve. Thus:

	£
X (Existing contribution £8,000)	4,000
Y (Existing contribution £22,000)	11,000
	15,000
Fixed overheads	(10,000)
Net Profit	5,000

Helpnote:
The net profit (originally £20,000) increases and decreases by more than the direct increase or decrease in revenue units. The contribution varies in line with revenue, but fixed overheads do not vary. The overall net profit, in turn, therefore does not alter in direct proportion to the change in revenue or contribution.

Cost Behaviour
Understanding cost behaviour is extremely important as it affects not only contribution, but profit. Let us take the example of Costbehav Ltd which manufactures widgets. It is planning production for the next year. It is considering five levels of production: 10,000, 20,000, 30,000, 40,000 or 50,000 units per year. Sales will be £2 per unit. Fixed costs are £200,000 whereas variable costs are £10 per unit. How would contribution and profit vary with production?

It can be seen by looking at Figure 16.5 that contribution per unit and variable costs per unit remain constant. However, fixed costs per unit decline from £20 to £4 while total costs fall from £30 per unit to £14 per unit. As a result profit per unit increases from a loss of £10 at 10,000 units to a profit of £6 per unit at 50,000 units.

Figure 16.5 Cost Behaviour

Units	10,000	20,000	30,000	40,000	50,000
	£	£	£	£	£
Revenue	200,000	400,000	600,000	800,000	1,000,000
Variable costs	(100,000)	(200,000)	(300,000)	(400,000)	(500,000)
Contribution	100,000	200,000	300,000	400,000	500,000
Fixed costs	(200,000)	(200,000)	(200,000)	(200,000)	(200,000)
Profit/(loss)	(100,000)	–	100,000	200,000	300,000
Contribution per unit	£10	£10	£10	£10	£10
Profit (loss) per unit	(£10)	(–)	£3.33	£5	£6
Variable costs per unit	£10	£10	£10	£10	£10
Fixed costs per unit	£20	£10	£6.67	£5	£4
Total costs per unit	£30	£20	£16.67	£15	£14

Decisions, Decisions

Contribution analysis can be used in a range of possible situations. All these involve the basic business questions:

- Are we maximising the firm's contribution by producing the most profitable products?
- Is the product making a positive contribution to the firm? If not, cease production.
- Should we make the products in-house?
- Are we making the most of limited resources?

Although the decisions are different, the basic approach is the same (see Helpnote 16.1). In all cases, we are seeking to maximise a company's contribution.

HELPNOTE 16.1

Basic Contribution Approach to Decision Making

1. Separate the costs into fixed and variable.
2. Allocate revenue and costs to different products.
3. Calculate contribution (revenue less variable cost) for each product:
   (a) in total; (b) where appropriate, per unit or per unit of limiting factor.

It is important to realise that contribution analysis provides a rational approach to decision making. However, it should not be seen as providing a definitive answer. In the end, making the right decision will also involve an element of judgement. This is the sentiment expressed in Soundbite 16.1.

SOUNDBITE 16.1

Decision Making is Crucial

'Making the right decision is crucial in the world of business. It comes as no surprise that companies spend a lot of their training budgets on developing their staff's decision making techniques. If you make a well considered decision you will lead your team to success. On the other hand, a poor decision can end in failure.'

British Council: www.british-council.org/learnenglish

Source: As reprinted in *Global Accountant Magazine*, July/August 2011, p. 32. British Council.

An interesting example relates to Lego, the children's retail company. In 2005, Lego cut the number of colours by half and reduced the number of stock-keeping units to £6,500. As Real-World View 16.2 shows, this produced tremendous results for Lego.

REAL-WORLD VIEW 16.2

Reducing Product Ranges

Results for customer: While customers saw the number of product options reduced and were asked to change their ordering habits, they obtained a substantial improvement in customer service. On-time delivery rose from 62 per cent in 2005 to 92 per cent in 2008.

Customers rated Lego as a 'best in class' supplier and Lego won a European supply chain excellence award. Those customers were now asking their other suppliers to use Lego as the benchmark for excellence.

The result for Lego: Sales increased from 2005 to 2008 by 35 per cent and profitability in 2008 was an all-time record. The fixed cost base had been reduced from 75 per cent to 33 per cent.

Source: The case study: Lego, *Financial Times*, 25 November 2010, p. 16. Copyright IMD. (Carlos Cordon, Ralf Seifert and Edwin Wellian).

(i) Determining the Most Profitable Products

If a company makes a range of products or services, we can use contribution analysis to see which are the most profitable (see Figure 16.6).

(ii) Should We Cease Production of Any Products?

The key here is to see whether or not any products or services are making a negative contribution. If they are, this will decrease our overall contribution.

Figure 16.6 Determining the Most Profitable Products or Services

A garage provides its customers with three services: the basic service, the deluxe service and the superdeluxe service. It has the following details.

	Selling price £	Direct labour £	Direct materials £
Basic	75	35	10
Deluxe	95	45	12
Superdeluxe	120	65	14

Variable overheads are 50% direct labour. Fixed overheads are £1,000 per month. Which services are the most profitable?

We need to calculate *per unit*

	Basic £	Basic £	Deluxe £	Deluxe £	Superdeluxe £	Superdeluxe £
Sales Price		75.00		95.00		120.00
Less: *Variable costs*						
Direct materials	10.00		12.00		14.00	
Direct labour	35.00		45.00		65.00	
Variable overheads	17.50		22.50		32.50	
Total variable costs		62.50		79.50		111.50
Contribution		12.50		15.50		8.50
Ranked by profitability		2		1		3

The deluxe service is the most profitable (£15.50 contribution per unit), followed by the basic service (£12.50 contribution per unit) and the superdeluxe (£8.50 contribution per unit). Note that we do not take fixed costs into account. This is because they are irrelevant to the decision.

PAUSE FOR THOUGHT 16.2

Negative Contribution

Why should we discontinue any product or service with a negative contribution?

Products and services with negative contribution are bad news. This means that every extra product or service makes no contribution to our fixed costs. In actual fact, the more products or services we provide, the greater our loss. This is because our variable costs per unit are greater than the selling price per unit.

Let us take the example in Figure 16.7.

A key aspect of discontinuing a product is the identification of complementary goods (e.g., eggs and bacon, fish and chips) where if you discontinue one product then you will lose sales of the other.

Figure 16.7 Dropping Loss-Making Products

We have the following information for Dolly, which makes three sweets: the mixtures, the sweeteners and the gobsuckers.

	£	£
Current Revenue		
Mixtures (100,000 at 50p)		50,000
Sweeteners (200,000 at 20p)		40,000
Gobsuckers (400,000 at 10p)		40,000
		130,000
Less: *Costs*		
Direct materials	50,000	
Direct labour	40,000	
Variable overheads	20,000	
Fixed overheads	10,000	
Total costs		120,000
Net Profit		10,000

The variable costs are split between the products: 50% to mixtures, 25% to sweeteners and 25% to gobsuckers.
Are all these products profitable? If not, what is the effect on profit of dropping the unprofitable one?

We need to rearrange our information to identify contribution per sweet.

	Mixtures		Sweeteners		Gobsuckers	
	£	£	£	£	£	£
Revenue		50,000		40,000		40,000
Less: *Variable costs:*						
Direct materials	25,000		12,500		12,500	
Direct labour	20,000		10,000		10,000	
Variable overheads	10,000	55,000	5,000	27,500	5,000	27,500
Contribution		(5,000)		12,500		12,500
Total Contribution ((£5,000) + £12,500 + £12,500)						20,000
Fixed overheads						(10,000)
Net Profit						10,000

Sweeteners and gobsuckers thus make positive contributions of £12,500 each and are therefore profitable. By contrast, mixtures makes a negative contribution of £5,000. If we drop mixtures, profit increases by £5,000. We can see this below.

	£
Sweeteners	12,500
Gobsuckers	12,500
Total Contribution	25,000
Less: Fixed overheads	(10,000)
Net Profit	15,000

(iii) The Make or Buy Decision

Here we need to compare the cost of providing goods or services internally with the cost of buying in the goods or services. We compare the variable costs of making them internally with the external costs. Businesses often outsource (i.e., buy in) their non-essential activities. In Real-World View 16.3, the role of outsourcing is discussed after the British General Election of May 2010.

REAL-WORLD VIEW 16.3

British Airways and Outsourcing

Outsourcing is a popular way in which companies can attempt to cut their costs. Although the sector in the UK suffered following the May 2010 election, J. Ficenec (2011) shows outsourcing has subsequently increased in the UK with, for example, back-office outsourcing expert Capita announcing a £1.1bn of major contracts in the first six months of 2011.

'These new opportunities and the increase in business activity come as the government desperately tries to get its finances under control.'

Source: J. Ficenec (2011) Outsourcing Austerity, *Investors Chronicle* (14–20 October, p. 54). Financial Times.

This sort of decision is also often faced by local governments in tendering or contracting out services such as cleaning (see Figure 16.8).

Figure 16.8 The Make or Buy Decision

A local government is looking at a particular cleaning contract. One of the existing local government departments has bid for a particular contract, with the following costs.

	£
Direct materials	28
Direct labour, 25 hours at £8.50	
Variable overheads	12

Speedyclean, a private company, has offered to do the contract for £250. Should we accept?

Internally	£
Direct materials	28.00
Direct labour (25 hours at £8.50)	212.50
Variable overheads	12.00
	252.50
Externally	250.00

Yes, on pure cost grounds it should be awarded externally to Speedyclean.

However, as Pause for Thought 16.3 shows, other factors should be considered.

PAUSE FOR THOUGHT 16.3

Other Factors in Make or Buy Decisions

What other factors, apart from the costs, should you take into account in make and buy decisions?

In practice, make or buy decisions can involve many other factors. For example:

- Have the internal employees other work?
- Is the external price sustainable over time?
- Do we want to be dependent on an external provider?
- Will we be able to take action against the external provider if there is a deficient service?
- What consequences will awarding the contract externally have for morale, staff turnover?

(iv) Maximising a Limiting Factor

Businesses often face a situation where one of the key resource inputs is a limiting factor on production. For example, the quantity of direct materials may be limited or labour hours may be restricted. The basic idea, in this case, is to *maximise the contribution of the limiting factor*. Figure 16.9 demonstrates this concept for a hotel which has three restaurants, but a limited amount of direct labour hours.

Figure 16.9 Maximising Contribution per Limiting Factor

A hotel has three restaurants (Snack, Bistro and Formal). There are only 1,150 labour hours available at £10 per hour. If the restaurants opened normally for the coming week then 1,300 hours would be used: 400 hours for Snack, 500 hours for Bistro and 400 hours for Formal. Under normal opening you expect the following:

	Snack 2,000		Bistro 3,000		Formal 2,000	
Customers	£	£	£	£	£	£
Revenue		10,000		12,000		16,000
Less: Costs						
Direct materials	2,000		2,500		7,500	
Direct labour	4,000		5,000		4,000	
Variable overheads	1,000		1,250		2,000	
Fixed overheads*	2,000	9,000	3,000	11,750	2,000	15,500
Net Profit		1,000		250		500

*Allocated by number of customers

You are required to maximise profit.

Figure 16.9 Maximising Contribution per Limiting Factor (*continued*)

To maximise profit, we need to **maximise our contribution per unit of limiting resource**, i.e., labour hours. We need to maximise this as *labour is limited to 1,150 hours*. We must, therefore, first determine our overall contribution and the contribution per labour hour.

Labour hours	Snack 400		Bistro 500		Formal 400	
	£	£	£	£	£	£
Revenue		10,000		12,000		16,000
Less: *Variable costs*						
Direct materials	2,000		2,500		7,500	
Direct labour	4,000		5,000		4,000	
Variable overheads	1,000	7,000	1,250	8,750	2,000	13,500
Contribution		3,000		3,250		2,500

Contribution per labour hour:

$$\text{Contribution} \quad \frac{£3,000}{400 \text{ hours}} = £7.50 \qquad \frac{£3,250}{500 \text{ hours}} = £6.50 \qquad \frac{£2,500}{400 \text{ hours}} = £6.25$$

Above, we have divided the coming week's contribution by the number of labour hours available. We ought, therefore, to use our labour first in the Snack, then in the Bistro, and only lastly on the Formal restaurant. This is because our contribution is greatest for the Snack at £7.50 per hour, next for the Bistro at £6.50 per hour and least for the Formal at £6.25 per hour. Our maximum profit (to the nearest £) is therefore:

			£
Snack	400 hours (i.e. the Snack's capacity)	× £7.50	3,000
Bistro	500 hours (i.e. the Bistro's capacity)	× £6.50	3,250
Formal	250 hours (i.e. the balance)	× £6.25	1,563
1,150 hours			7,813
Less: Fixed costs			(7,000)
Net Profit			813

Any other allocation would result in less profit. For example, if we allocated the hours according to *maximum contribution per customer* (i.e., in the order Snack (£1.50), Formal (£1.25), Bistro (£1.08)).

			£
Snack	400 hours (i.e. Snack's capacity)	× £7.50	3,000
Formal	400 hours (i.e. Formal's capacity)	× £6.25	2,500
Bistro	350 hours (i.e. Balance)	× £6.50	2,275
1,150 hours			7,775
Less: Fixed costs			(7,000)
Net Profit			775

Throughput Accounting

Throughput accounting is a relatively new approach to production management and uses a variant of contribution per limiting factor. This approach looks at a production system from the perspective of capacity constraint or bottlenecks. It essentially asks: what are a system's main bottlenecks? For instance, is it shortage of machine hours in a certain department? Every effort is then made to eliminate the bottlenecks. Goldratt and Cox in *The Goal* (1992) look at throughput contribution (defined as revenue less direct materials) as a key measure. Interestingly, therefore, all other costs are treated as fixed. Thus, direct labour and variable overheads are seen as fixed overheads in this system. Figure 16.10 provides an example of a throughput operating statement. The throughput contribution is £40,000 (i.e., revenue of £105,000 less direct materials at £65,000).

Figure 16.10 Throughput Accounting

Sanderson Engineering has the following details from its accounting records for January.

	£000		£000
Revenue	105,000	Production overheads	10,000
Direct materials	65,000	Administrative expenses	6,000
Direct labour	18,000	Selling and distribution expenses	5,000

Prepare a throughput accounting statement.

Sanderson Engineering Throughput Accounting Statement for January.

	£000	£000
Revenue		105,000
Direct materials		(65,000)
Throughput Contribution		40,000
Direct labour	(18,000)	
Production overheads	(10,000)	
Administrative expenses	(6,000)	
Selling and distribution expenses	(5,000)	(39,000)
Net Profit		1,000

Throughput analysis, just like contribution per limiting factor, could be used to allocate production if there was a production bottleneck. Let's just assume that three products (A, B and C) go through many processes, but process B's hours are limited. In this case, one would calculate out the contribution per process B hour, using the additional data in Figure 16.11.

Figure 16.11 shows that A has the greatest contribution, but more important the greatest contribution per process hour. It pays, therefore, to focus on product As then product B and finally product C.

Figure 16.11 Example of Throughput Accounting

Products	£ Contribution	Number	Throughput Contribution per unit	Process B hours	Contribution per process hour
A	15,000	1,000	£15.00	3	£5.00
B	13,000	2,000	£6.50	2	£3.25
C	12,000	3,000	£4.00	4	£1.00
	40,000				

Break-Even Analysis

The contribution concept is particularly useful when determining the break-even point of a firm. The break-even point is simply that point at which a firm makes neither a profit nor a loss. A firm's break-even point can be expressed as follows:

$$\text{Revenue} - \text{Variable costs} - \text{Fixed costs} = 0$$

In other words, the break-even point is the point where contribution equals fixed costs. We can find the break-even point in units by dividing fixed costs by contribution per unit. Figures 16.12 and 16.13 show how the break-even point works.

Figure 16.12 The Essentials of Break-Even Analysis

Break-Even Point	Contribution	Break-Even Point in Units
The point at which a business makes neither a profit nor a loss	Revenue – Variable costs	$\dfrac{\text{Fixed costs}}{\text{Contribution per unit}}$

Figure 16.13 An Example of Break-Even Analysis

A restaurateur, William Bunter, has expected revenue of 15,000 meals at £20 each. His variable costs are £8 per meal. If the fixed costs are £120,000, what is the break-even point? What is sales revenue at break-even profit?

We, therefore, have

$$\frac{\text{Fixed costs}}{\substack{\text{Contribution per unit (i.e., meal)}\\ \text{(Revenue – variable cost per unit (i.e., meal))}}} = \frac{£120,000}{£20 - £8} = \frac{£120,000}{£12} = 10,000 \text{ meals}$$

Sales revenue at break-even is thus 10,000 × £20 = £200,000.

Assumptions of Break-Even Analysis

The beauty of break-even analysis is that it is comparatively straightforward. However, break-even analysis is underpinned by several key assumptions. Perhaps the main one is **linearity**. Linearity assumes that the behaviour of the revenue and costs will remain constant despite increases in the level of revenue. Revenue and variable costs are assumed always to be strictly variable and fixed costs are assumed to be strictly fixed. For instance, in Figure 16.11 it is assumed that revenue will remain at £20 per meal, variable costs will remain at £8 per meal and fixed costs will remain at £120,000, whether we sell 1,000 meals, 10,000 meals or 100,000 meals. In practice, it is more likely that these costs will be fixed or variable within a particular range of activity (often called the **relevant range**). The break-even point also implies a precision which is perhaps unwarranted. A better description might be the break-even area. In practice, break-even analysis suffers from the same problems as contribution analysis more generally. In particular, it is difficult for accounting to estimate variable or fixed costs.

Other Uses of Break-Even Analysis

Break-even analysis can also form the basis of more sophisticated analyses such as (i) calculating the margin of safety, (ii) 'what-if' analysis or (iii) graphical analysis.

(i) Margin of Safety – Purposes and Limitations

Bunter may wish to calculate how much he has sold over and above the break-even point. It can be seen as a company's comfort zone, the amount of revenue which the company could lose before it starts making a loss. This is called the margin of safety. Bunter's margin of safety is calculated using a general formula:

$$\frac{\text{Actual units sold } - \text{ units at break-even point}}{\text{Actual units}}$$

The break-even point can be calculated in either (a) units (i.e., in this case, meals) or (b) money. Therefore:

(a) Bunter's margin of safety (units) $= \dfrac{15,000 - 10,000}{10,000} = 50\%$

(b) Bunter's margin of safety (£s) $= \dfrac{£300,000 - £200,000}{£200,000} = 50\%$

(ii) What-if Analysis

The break-even point can also be used as a basis for 'what-if' analysis. For instance, we know that each unit sold in excess of the break-even point adds one unit's contribution to profit. Similarly, each unit less than the break-even point creates a loss of one unit's contribution. So, we can easily answer questions such as 'what is the profit or loss if Bunter sells (a) 8,000 meals or (b) 13,000 meals?'

(a) **8,000 meals.** This is 2,000 meals fewer than the break-even point of 10,000 meals. The loss is, therefore, 2,000 meals × contribution per meal. Thus, 2,000 meals × £12 contribution per meal (revenue £20 − £8 variable cost) = £24,000 loss.

(b) **13,000 meals.** This is 3,000 meals more than the break-even point of 10,000 meals. The profit is thus 3,000 meals × £12 contribution per meal (revenue £20 − £8 variable cost) = £36,000 profit.

The break-even point is a very flexible concept and provides potentially rewarding insights into business.

(iii) Graphical Break-Even Point
Another benefit of break-even analysis is that it can be shown on a graph (see Figure 16.14).

Figure 16.14 Graphical Break-Even Point

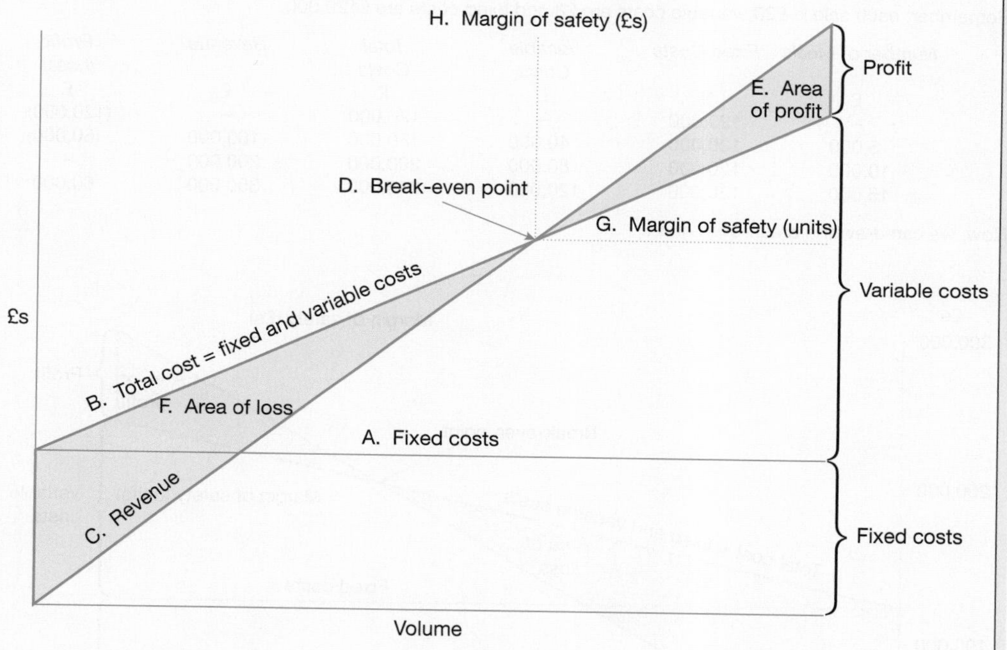

On the graph, it is important to note the following points:

A. **Fixed costs.** This is a straight horizontal line.
B. **Variable costs (total cost).** This is a straight line which starts on the vertical Y axis and 'piggybacks' the fixed cost line.
   Effectively, the variable cost line also represents the **total cost (fixed cost plus variable costs).**
C. **Revenue.** The revenue line starts at the origin and then climbs steadily.
D. **Break-even point.** This is the point where the revenue line (C) and the total cost line (B) (i.e., variable costs or total cost line) cross.
E. **Area of profit.** This is where the revenue line (C) is higher than the total cost line (B). A profit is thus being made.
F. **Area of loss.** This is where the revenue line (C) is lower than the total cost line (B). There is thus a loss.
G. **Margin of safety (units).** This is the difference between current revenue and the revenue needed to break even in units.
H. **Margin of safety (£s).** This is the difference between current revenue and the revenue needed to break even in £s.

Figure 16.15 is the graph for William Bunter. Sales are set at four levels: 0 meals; 5,000 meals; 10,000 meals; and 15,000 meals. Break-even point is 10,000 meals.

Figure 16.15 Bunter's Break-Even Chart

First, we need to work out the figures to graph.
Remember: each sale is £20, variable costs are £8 and fixed costs are £120,000.

Number of Meals	Fixed Costs	Variable Costs	Total Costs	Revenue	Profit (Loss)
£	£	£	£	£	£
–	120,000	–	120,000	–	(120,000)
5,000	120,000	40,000	160,000	100,000	(60,000)
10,000	120,000	80,000	200,000	200,000	–
15,000	120,000	120,000	240,000	300,000	60,000

Now, we can draw the break-even chart.

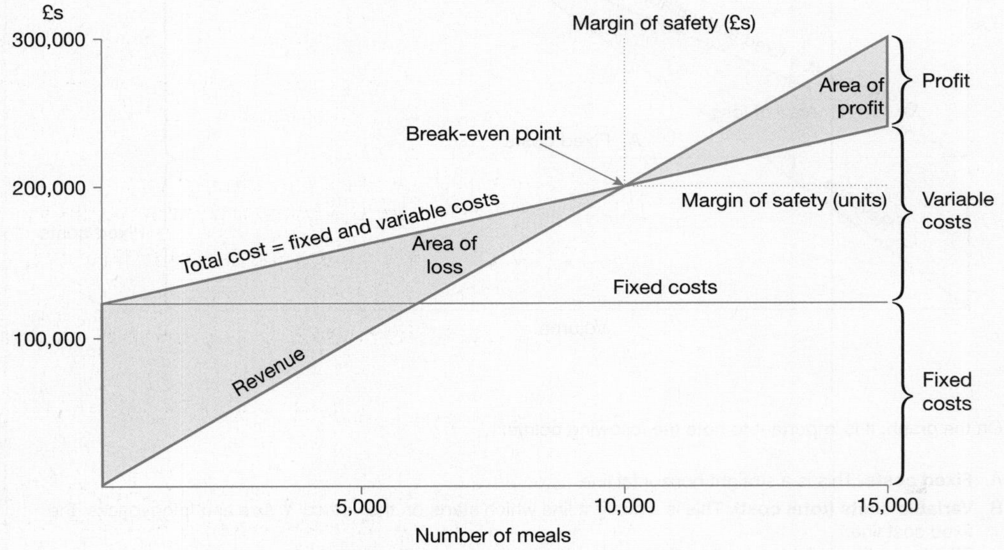

(iv) Contribution to Revenue

Another useful technique is to evaluate different products using their contribution to revenue. Thus, if we had three different products, we could rank them by their contribution to revenue as in Figure 16.16. This is often called contribution to sales, but for consistency and ease of understanding, contribution to revenue is used.

In this case our most profitable product is thus C with a contribution to revenue of 66.67%.

Figure 16.16 Ranking Products Using Contribution to Revenue (Sales)

	Revenue	Variable Costs	Contribution	Contribution to Revenue (Sales)		Ranking
	£	£	£	%		
A	10,000	5,000	5,000	50	(£5,000/£10,000)	2
B	20,000	15,000	5,000	25	(£5,000/£20,000)	3
C	30,000	10,000	20,000	66.67	(£20,000/£30,000)	1
	60,000	30,000	30,000			

Contribution Graph

Contribution to revenue can also be graphed. This overcomes a limitation of the break-even chart in that it can be used for only one product. A contribution graph (see Figure 16.17) is sometimes called a *profit/volume chart*. However, in this book we use the term contribution graph as it is easier to understand. A contribution graph looks a bit like a set of rugby posts! It is based on the idea that each unit sold generates one unit's contribution. Initially, this contribution covers fixed costs and then generates a profit. The horizontal line represents level of revenue (either in units or £s). Above the horizontal line is profit, while below the line is loss. The diagonal line represents contribution. In effect, it is the cumulative profit or

Figure 16.17 Contribution Graph

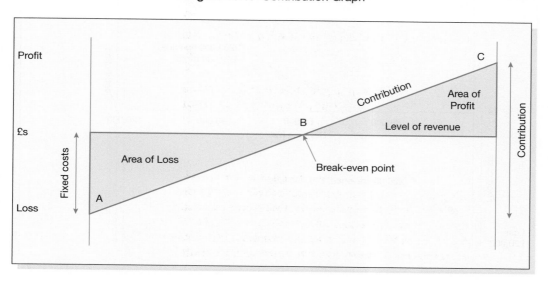

Figure 16.18 Contribution Graph for a Department Store

Department	Revenue	Variable Costs	Contribution	Contribution/Revenue (Sales) Ratio		Ranking
	£	£	£	%		
Toys	20,000	10,000	10,000	50	(£10,000/£20,000)	1
Clothes	40,000	30,000	10,000	25	(£10,000/£40,000)	3
CDs	60,000	40,000	20,000	33⅓	(£20,000/£60,000)	2
Total	120,000	80,000	40,000	33⅓	(£40,000/£120,000)	
Fixed costs			(20,000)			
Net Profit			20,000			

Using this information draw a contribution graph.

First we draw up a cumulative profit/loss table ranked by the highest contribution/revenue ratio. The cumulative profit/loss is simply cumulative contribution less fixed costs.

	Cumulative Revenue	Cumulative Contribution	Cumulative Profit/(Loss)
	£	£	£
Fixed costs			(20,000)
Toys	20,000	10,000	(10,000)
CDs	80,000	30,000	10,000
Clothes	120,000	40,000	20,000

We are now in a position to draw up a graph.

loss plotted against cumulative revenue. So when there is no revenue there is a loss (point A). This loss is, in effect, the total fixed costs. The company then breaks even at point B. At this point contribution equals fixed costs. Above point B each unit sold adds one unit of contribution to the company's profit. Finally, point C represents maximum cumulative revenue and maximum contribution.

The relationship between contribution and revenue is defined as $\frac{\text{Contribution}}{\text{Revenue (Sales)}}$.

Sometimes this is known as the profit/volume ratio. This ratio provides an easy way of comparing the contributions of different products. We take, as an example, a department store which has three departments: toys, clothes and CDs (see Figure 16.18).

In many industries, there are substantial fixed costs. In the retail industry, for example, as Real-World View 16.4 shows, the concept of break-even becomes very important.

REAL-WORLD VIEW 16.4

Fixed Costs and Supermarkets

Richard Tomkins (Marketing Value for Money) commented on the UK supermarket chains of Asda, Safeway, Sainsbury and Tesco. 'All of these supermarkets have substantial fixed costs. They depend on volume of sales. So that if one supermarket cuts their costs, the others are forced to follow. If they don't they are worried that their volumes will fall to below break-even point.'

Source: Richard Tomkins, Marketing Value for Money, *Financial Times*, 14 May 1999.

Conclusion

Businesses constantly face short-term decisions such as how to maximise a limited resource. When making these decisions it is useful to distinguish between fixed and variable costs. Fixed costs do not, in the short run, change with either production or revenue (for example, insurance or depreciation). Variable costs, by contrast, do change when the production volume or revenue volume changes (examples are direct materials and direct labour). Revenue (sales) less variable costs gives contribution. Contribution is a useful accounting concept. By calculating contribution we can, for example, determine which products are the most profitable. Break-even analysis is another useful concept that builds on contribution analysis. The break-even point is the point at which a business makes neither a profit nor a loss. It is determined by dividing fixed costs by the contribution per unit. The break-even chart shows the break-even point graphically. The contribution graph is a useful way of graphing the profit or loss of one or more products.

Discussion Questions

Questions with numbers in blue have answers at the back of the book.

Q1 Distinguish between fixed and variable costs. Why are fixed costs irrelevant when making a choice between certain alternatives such as whether to produce more of product A or of product B?

Q2 What is contribution per unit and why is it so useful in short-term decision making?

Q3 What are the strengths and weaknesses of break-even analysis?

Q4 State whether the following statements are true or false. If false, explain why.
   (a) Fixed costs are those that do not vary with long-term changes in the level of revenue or production.
   (b) Contribution is revenue less variable costs.
   (c) Break-even point is $\dfrac{\text{Variable costs}}{\text{Contribution per unit}}$
   (d) Contribution/revenue (sales) ratio is $\dfrac{\text{Profit}}{\text{Revenue (Sales)}}$
   (e) Non-financial items are not important in decision making.

 Numerical Questions

Questions with numbers in blue have answers at the back of the book.

Q1 Jungle Animals makes 10 model animals with the following cost structure.

	Selling Price £	Direct Labour £	Direct Materials £	Variable Overheads £
Alligators	1.00	0.50	0.20	0.35
Bears	1.20	0.60	0.10	0.30
Cougars	1.10	0.66	0.15	0.33
Donkeys	1.15	0.60	0.18	0.30
Eagles	1.20	0.56	0.12	0.28
Foxes	0.90	0.50	0.10	0.25
Giraffes	1.05	0.40	0.25	0.20
Hyenas	1.25	0.56	0.10	0.28
Iguanas	0.95	0.40	0.12	0.20
Jackals	0.80	0.40	0.13	0.20

Q1 Jungle Animals (*continued*)

Required:

(i)   Calculate the contribution per toy.
(ii) Calculate the contribution/revenue (sales) ratio per toy.
(iii) Which two toys bring in the greatest contribution?
(iv) Which three toys have the highest contribution/revenue (sales) ratio?
(v)   Which two toys would you not manufacture at all?

Q2 An insurance company, Riskmore, has four divisions: car, home, personal and miscellaneous. These four divisions account, respectively, for 40%, 30%, 20% and 10% of revenue and 25% each of the variable costs. Riskmore has the following summary income statement.

	£
Revenue	200,000
Less: *Costs*	
Variable costs	100,000
Fixed costs	50,000
Net Profit	50,000

Required: Calculate the profitability of the divisions.

Q3 Scrooge Ltd is looking to outsource its accounts department. Ghost Ltd has approached Scrooge and offered to provide the service for £190,000. Scrooge Ltd ascertains the following costs are involved internally:

Clerical labour	10,000 hours at £8
Supervisory labour	6,000 hours at £10
Direct materials	£25,000
Variable overheads	£3 per clerical labour hour
Fixed overheads	£8,000

Required: Calculate whether or not Scrooge Ltd should accept Ghost's bid. State any assumptions you have made and other factors you might take into account.

Q4 A large hotel, The Open Umbrella, has two kiosks. One sells sweets and is open 35 hours per week. The second sells newspapers and magazines and is open 55 hours per week. Unfortunately, next week labour is restricted to 70 hours. Labour is £10 per hour. Last week's results when both were fully open and 90 labour hours were available are set out below.

	Kiosk 1 (Sweets)		Kiosk 2 (Newspapers)	
	£	£	£	£
Revenue		1,075		1,475
Less: *Costs*				
Direct labour	350		550	
Direct materials	600		700	
Variable overheads	70	1,020	110	1,360
Contribution		55		115

Required: How would you maximise the profits using the 70 labour hours available?

Q5 Globeco makes four geographical board quiz games: France, Germany, UK and US. Globeco has the following recent results.

	France		Germany		UK		US	
Units sold	1,000		1,500		4,000		6,000	
	£	£	£	£	£	£	£	£
Revenue		2,000		3,000		12,000		24,000
Less: *Variable Costs*								
Direct labour	800		1,350		6,000		15,600	
Direct materials	200		300		1,300		1,400	
Variable overheads	80		135		600		1,560	
Fixed overheads (equal allocation)	1,000		1,000		1,000		1,000	
		2,080		2,785		8,900		19,560
Net Profit (loss)		(80)		215		3,100		4,440

Q5 Globeco (*continued*)

For next year, there are only 1,500 direct labour hours available. Last year there were 2,375 direct labour hours. Direct labour is paid at £10 per hour. The maximum revenue (in units) is predicted to be 2,000 France, 3,500 Germany, 6,000 UK and 8,000 US.

Required: Calculate the most profitable production schedule, given that direct labour hours, the limiting factor, are restricted to 3,000 hours.

Q6 Freya manufactures heavy-duty hammers. They each cost £4 in direct materials and £3 in variable expenses. They sell for £10 each. Fixed costs are £30,000. Currently 20,000 hammers are sold.

Required:
(i)   What is the break-even point?
(ii) What is the profit if the number of hammers sold is:
      (a) 4,000   (b) 14,000?
(iii) What is the current margin of safety in (a) units and (b) £s?
(iv) Draw a break-even chart.

Q7 Colin Xiao runs a restaurant which serves 10,000 customers a month. Each customer spends £20, variable costs per customer are £15. Fixed costs are £10,000.

Required:
(i)   What are the current break-even point and margin of safety in £s?
(ii) Calculate the new break-even point and margin of safety in £s if the average spend per customer is:
      (a) £17   (b) £19   (c) £25

Assume all other factors remain the same.

Q8 A computer hardware distributor, Modem, has three branches in Cardiff, Edinburgh and London. It has the following financial details.

	Revenue £	Direct Labour £	Other Variable Overheads £
Cardiff	200,000	60,000	105,000
Edinburgh	300,000	80,000	150,000
London	1,000,000	350,000	520,000

Head office fixed overheads are £150,000.

Required:
(i)   Calculate the contribution/revenue ratios.
(ii) Draw the contribution graph.

Go online to discover the extra features for this chapter at
www.wiley.com/college/jones

SECTION D

Business Finance

We have now looked at both the techniques and context of financial accounting and management accounting. In this section, we now look at company finance. Company finance is essential to the successful running of a business. We divide it into three chapters. Chapter 17 will look at long-term decision making. Then Chapter 18 looks at the sources of capital with Chapter 19, the final chapter in the book, investigating the management of working capital.

The three chapters in this section thus look at different aspects of the financial management of a company. In Chapter 17 we look at capital investment. The main capital investment appraisal techniques such as payback period, accounting rate of return, net present value, profitability index and internal rate of return (IRR) are evaluated. This is followed by two chapters which look at the sources of capital a business may use to finance its activities. In the first chapter, Chapter 18, the main external sources of finance are investigated covering particularly the stock exchange, share capital and loan capital. The cost of capital is also discussed. Then, in Chapter 19, the focus shifts to the way in which a business finances itself internally through the efficient use of working capital. The various ways in which a business can maximise the efficient use of inventory, trade receivables, cash and trade payables are discussed.

SECTION D

Business
Finance

Chapter 17
Long-term decision making: Capital investment appraisal

'There are no maps to the future.'

A.J.P. Taylor

Over the years, many sophisticated capital investment techniques have been perfected.

We can for example use the easy-to-calculate payback method or the highly-regarded discounted cashflow method.

Nonetheless, in our business, we prefer a less scientific technique.

OK, so heads, we invest; tails, we don't

©MMI Mike Jones

Learning Outcomes

After completing this chapter you should be able to:

- Introduce and explain the nature of capital investment.
- Outline the main capital investment appraisal techniques.
- Appreciate the time value of money.
- Explain the use of discounting.

Go online to discover the extra features for this chapter at
www.wiley.com/college/jones

Chapter Summary

- Capital investment decisions are long-term, strategic decisions, such as building a new factory.
- Capital investment decisions involve initial cash outflows and then subsequent cash inflows.
- Many assumptions underpin these cash inflows and outflows.
- There are five main capital investment techniques. Two (payback and accounting rate of return) do not take into account the time value of money. Three do (net present value, profitability index and internal rate of return).
- Payback is the simplest method. It measures how long it takes for a company to recover its initial investment.
- The accounting rate of return uses profit not cash flow and measures the annual profit over the initial capital investment.
- The profitability index is similar to Net Present Value (NPV). It compares the total NPV cash flows with the initial investment.
- Net present value discounts estimated future cash flows back to today's values.
- Internal rate of return establishes the discount rate at which the project breaks even.
- Sensitivity analysis is often used to model future possible alternative situations.

Introduction

Management accounting can be divided into cost recovery and control, and decision making. In turn, decision making consists of short-term and long-term decisions. Whereas strategic management sets the overall framework within which the long-term decisions are made, capital investment appraisal involves long-term choices about specific investments in future projects. These projects may include, for example, investment in new products or new infrastructure assets. Without this investment in the future, firms would not survive in the long term. However, capital investment decisions are extremely difficult as they include a considerable amount of crystal ball gazing. This chapter looks at five techniques (the payback period, the accounting rate of return, net present value, the profitability index and the internal rate of return) which management accountants use to help them peer into the future.

Nature of Capital Investment

Capital investment is essential for the long-term survival of a business. Existing property, plant and equipment, for example, wears out and needs replacing. The capital investment decision operationalises the strategic, long-term plans of a business. As Figure 17.1 shows, long-term capital expenditure decisions can be distinguished from short-term decisions by their time span, topic, nature and level of expenditure, by the external factors taken into account and by the techniques used.

Figure 17.1 Comparison of Short-Term Decisions and Long-Term Capital Investment Decisions

Characteristic	Short-Term	Long-Term
1. Time Span	Maximum 1 to 2 years, mostly present situation	Upwards from 2 years
2. Topic	Usually concerned with current operating decision, e.g., discontinue present product	Concerned with future expenditure decisions, e.g., build new factory
3. Nature	Operational	Strategic
4. Level of Expenditure	Small to medium	Medium to great
5. External Factors	Generally not so important	Very important, especially interest rate, inflation rate
6. Sample Techniques	Contribution analysis, break-even analysis	Payback, accounting rate of return, net present value, and internal rate of return

Capital budgeting is a term which is often used for capital investment decisions. As Real-World View 17.1 shows, there is a distinct difference between capital and operating expenditures.

REAL-WORLD VIEW 17.1

Capital and Operating Expenditures

Capital budgeting refers to the planning and control process associated with capital expenditures. Capital expenditures, often referred to as capital investments, are expenditures for projects not intended for immediate consumption. Accordingly, capital expenditures increase, or at least maintain, the capital assets of an organization. The term capital assets as used above, refers to what economists usually call capital goods ... Accountants usually refer to capital assets as fixed assets [property, plant and equipment].

In contrast to capital expenditures, operating expenditures relate to items that will only benefit the current operating period. Technically speaking, capital and operating expenditures are costs in that they both require the use of resources. Operating expenditures are usually thought of as an expense because the resources are consumed during the current period and the associated benefits are also assumed to be derived during the current period. Capital expenditures are treated as investments because the resources, or at least part of them, are not consumed during the current period and the benefits derived from such resources are received over more than the current period. However, the proportion of capital investments consumed (i.e., the proportion of capital consumption) during the acquisition period becomes an operating expenditure.

Source: Abridged from L.A. Gordon, M.P. Loeb and C.Y. Tseng (2005), Capital budgeting and informational impediments: a management accounting perspective in A. Bhimani *Contemporary Issues in Management Accounting.*

Capital investment decisions are thus usually long-term decisions, which may sometimes look 10 or 20 years into the future. They are often the biggest expenditure decisions that a business faces. Some examples of capital investment decisions might be deciding whether or not to build a new factory or whether to expand into a new product range. A football club, such as Manchester United, for example, might have to decide whether or not to build a new stadium. A common capital expenditure decision will involve choosing between alternatives. For example, which of three particular stadiums should we build? Or which products should we currently develop for the future? These decisions are particularly important given the fast-changing world.

A key problem with any capital investment decision is taking into account all the external factors and correctly forecasting future conditions. As the quotation by A.J.P. Taylor at the start of the chapter stated: 'There are no maps to the future.' In Real-World View 17.2 Peter Aytan wonders why everything takes longer to finish and costs more than originally budgeted.

REAL-WORLD VIEW 17.2

Forecasting the Future

Trouble ahead

Why does everything take longer to finish and cost more than we think it will? The Channel Tunnel was supposed to cost £2.6 billion. In fact, the final bill came to £15 billion. The Jubilee Line extension to the London Underground cost £3.5 billion, about four times the original estimate. There are many other examples: the London Eye, the Channel Tunnel rail link.

This is not an exclusively British disease. In 1957, engineers forecast that the Sydney Opera House would be finished in 1963 at a cost of A$7 million. A scaled-down version costing A$102 million finally opened in 1973. In 1969, the mayor of Montreal announced that the 1976 Olympics would cost C$120 million and 'can no more have a deficit than a man can have a baby'. Yet the stadium roof alone – which was not finished until 13 years after the games – cost C$120 million.

Source: Trouble Ahead, Peter Aytan, *New Scientist*, 29 April 2000, vol. 166, no. 2236, p. 43. © 2000 Reed Business Information Ltd, England. Reproduced by permission. http://www.newscientist.com/article/mg16622364.600-trouble-ahead.html

The basic decision is simply whether or not a particular capital investment decision is worthwhile. In business, this decision is usually made by comparing the initial cash outflows associated with the capital investment with the later cash inflows. We can distinguish between the initial investment, net cash operating flows for succeeding years and other cash flows.

(i) Initial Investment

This is our initial capital expenditure. It will usually involve capital outflows on infrastructure assets (for example, buildings or new plant and machinery) or on working capital. This initial expenditure is needed so that the business can expand.

PAUSE FOR THOUGHT 17.1

A Football Club's New Stadium

A football club is contemplating building a new stadium. What external factors should it take into account?

....

There are countless factors. Below are some that might be considered.

- How much will the stadium cost?
- How many extra spectators can the new stadium hold?
- How much can be charged per spectator?
- How many years will the stadium last?
- What is the net financial effect when compared with the present stadium?
- How confident is the club about future attendance at matches?

(ii) Net Cash Flows

These represent the operating cash flows expected from the project once the infrastructure assets are in place. Normally, we talk about annual net cash flow. This is simply the cash inflows less the cash outflows calculated over a year. For convenience, *cash flows are usually assumed to occur at the end of the year.*

(iii) Other Flows

These involve other non-operating cash flows. For example, the taxation benefits from the initial capital expenditure or the cash inflow from scrap.

PAUSE FOR THOUGHT 17.2

Assumptions in Capital Investment Decisions

A big problem in any capital investment decision is the assumptions that underpin it. Can you think of any of these?

....

- Costs of initial outlay
- Tax effects
- Cost of capital
- Inflation
- Cash inflows and outflows over period of project.

These, in turn, may depend on pricing policy, external demand, value of production etc.

Capital Investment Appraisal Techniques

Capital investment decisions (i.e., the capital budgeting process) need to be planned and coordinated (see Soundbite 17.1). Probably the key way by which this can be done is using capital investment appraisal techniques.

SOUNDBITE 17.1

Capital Budgeting

'Capital budgeting serves to plan, coordinate, and motivate activities throughout an organisation. The budgeting process defines a set of rules to govern the way in which managers at different levels of the hierarchy produce and share information about investment projects.'

Source: T. Pfeiffer and G. Schneider (2010) Capital Budgeting, Information Timing, and the Value of Abandonment Options, *Management Accounting Research*, 21, p. 238.

The five main techniques used in capital investment decisions are payback period, accounting rate of return, net present value, profitability index and internal rate of return. An overview of these five techniques is presented in Figure 17.2. These techniques are then discussed further. However, it is important to appreciate that, in practice, multiple approaches are used and that different companies will use the techniques in different ways.

Figure 17.2 Five Main Types of Investment Appraisal Techniques

Feature	Payback Period	Accounting Rate of Return	Net Present Value	Profitability Index	Internal Rate of Return
Nature	Measures time period in which cumulative cash inflows overtake cumulative cash outflows	Assesses profitability of initial investment	Discounts future cash flows to present	Measures the cash flows against the initial investment (i.e., variation of net present value)	Determines the rate of return at which a project breaks even
Ease of use	Very easy	Easy	May be difficult	Concept easy, calculations may be difficult	Quite difficult
Takes time value of money into account	No	No	Yes	Yes	Yes
Main assumptions	Value and volume of cash flows	Reliability of annual profits	Value and volume of cash flows, cost of capital	Value and volume of cash flows, cost of capital	Value and volume of cash flows, cost of capital
Focus	Cash flows	Profits	Cash flows	Cash flows	Cash flows

It is important to realise that the payback period and the accounting rate of return take into account only the *actual* cash inflows and outflows. However, net present value, the profitability index and the accounting rate of return take into account the *time value of money*.

PAUSE FOR THOUGHT 17.3

Time Value of Money

Why do you think it is important to take into account the time value of money?

There is an old saying that time is money! In the case of long-term capital investment decisions, it certainly is. Would you prefer £100 now or £100 in 10 years' time? That one is easy! But what about £100 now or £150 in five years' time? There is a need to standardise money in today's terms. To do this, we need to attribute a time value to money. In practice, we take this time value to be the rate at which a company could borrow money. This is called the cost of capital. If our cost of capital is 10%, we say that £100 today equals £110 in one year's time, £121 in two years' time and so on. If we know the cost of capital of future cash flows we can, therefore, discount them back to today's cash flows.

As Real-World View 17.3 shows, amounts spent yesterday can mean huge sums today. Compounding is the opposite of discounting! If we discounted the $136,000,000,000 dollars back from 1876 to 1607 using a 10% discount rate, we should arrive at nearly one dollar (nearly because compounding and discounting are not quite symmetrical).

REAL-WORLD VIEW 17.3

Compound Growth

Compound Interest

From a speech in Congress more than 100 years ago:

It has been supposed here that had America been purchased in 1607 for $1, and payment secured by bond, payable, with interest annually compounded, in 1876 at ten percent, the amount would be – I have not verified the calculation – the very snug little sum of $136,000,000,000; five times as much as the country will sell for today. It is very much like supposing that if Adam and Eve have continued to multiply and replenish once in two years until the present time, and all their descendants had lived and had been equally prolific, then, saying nothing about twins and triplets, there would now be actually alive upon the earth, a quantity of human beings in solid measure more than thirteen and one-fourth times the bulk of the entire planet.

Source: Peter Hay (1988), *The Book of Business Anecdotes*, Harrap Ltd, London, p. 10.

Each of the five capital investment appraisal techniques is examined using the information in Figure 17.3.

Figure 17.3 Illustrative Example of a Financial Service Company Wishing to Invest in a New Online Banking Service

The Everfriendly Bank is contemplating launching a new online banking service, called the Falcon. There are three alternative approaches, each involving £20 million initial outlay. In this case, cash inflows can be taken to be the same as profit. Cost of capital is 10%.

Year	A	B	C
Cash flows	£000	£000	£000
0 (i.e., now)	(20,000)	(20,000)	(20,000)
1	4,000	8,000	8,000
2	4,000	6,000	8,000
3	8,000	6,000	6,000
4	6,000	3,000	6,000
5	6,000	2,000	3,000

Helpnote: The cash outflow is traditionally recorded as being in year 0 (i.e., today) in brackets. The cash inflows occur from year 1 onwards and are conventionally taken at the end of the year. To simplify matters, in this example, cash inflows have been taken to be the same as net profit. Finally, cost of capital can be taken as the amount that it cost the Everfriendly Bank to borrow money.

Payback Period

The payback period (see Definition 17.1) is a relatively straightforward method of investment appraisal. It simply measures the cumulative cash inflows against the cumulative cash outflows until the project recovers its initial investment. The payback method is useful for

DEFINITION 17.1

Payback Period

The payback period simply measures the cumulative cash inflows against the cumulative cash outflows. The point at which they coincide is the payback point.

Specific advantages

1. Easy to use and understand.
2. Conservative.

Specific disadvantages

1. Fails to take into account cash flows after payback.
2. Does not take into account the time value of money.

Figure 17.4 Payback Using Everfriendly Bank

Year	Projects		
	A	B	C
	£000	£000	£000
0 (i.e., now) Cash outflows	(20,000)	(20,000)	(20,000)
Cumulative cash inflows			
1	4,000	8,000	8,000
2	8,000	14,000	16,000
3	16,000	**20,000**	**22,000**
4	**22,000**	23,000	28,000
5	28,000	25,000	31,000
Payback year	3.67 years*	3 years	2.67 years*

* For these two projects, payback will be two-thirds of the way through a year. This is because (taking project A to illustrate) after three years our cumulative inflows are £16 million and after four years they are £22 million. Assuming, and it is a big assumption, a steady cash flow, we reach payback point after two-thirds of a year (i.e., £4 million needed for payback, divided by £6 million cash inflows).

screening projects for an early return on the investment. Ideally, it should be complemented by another method such as net present value. In a study of 14 UK, US and Japanese companies, Carr, Kolehmainen and Mitchell (*Management Accounting*, 2010, pp. 167–84) found that payback was frequently used with the payback target being between 2.5 to 5 years.

Taking Everfriendly Bank's Falcon project, when do we recover the £20 million? Figure 17.4 shows this is after 3.67 years for project A, 3 years for project B and 2.67 years for project C.

Payback is a relatively straightforward investment technique. It is simple to understand and apply, and promotes a policy of caution in the investment decision. The business always chooses the investment which pays off the initial investment the most quickly. However, although useful, payback has certain crucial limitations.

PAUSE FOR THOUGHT 17.4

Limitations of Payback

Can you think of any limitations of payback?

Two of the most important limitations of payback are that it ignores both cash flows after the payback and the time value of money. Thus, a project may have a slow payback period, but have substantial cash flows once it is established. These will not be taken into account. In addition, cash flows in later years are treated as being the same value as cash flows in early years. This ignores the time value of money and may distort the capital investment decision.

Accounting Rate of Return

This method, unlike the other three methods, focuses on the profitability of the project, rather than its cash flow. At its simplest, cash flows less depreciation will equal profit. Thus it is distinctly different in orientation from the other methods. The basic definition of the accounting rate of return is:

$$\text{Accounting rate of return} = \frac{\text{Average annual profit}}{\text{Capital investment}}$$

However, once we look more closely we run into potential problems. What exactly do we mean by 'profit' and 'capital investment'? For profit, do we take into account interest, taxation and depreciation? For capital investment, do we take the initial capital investment or the average capital employed over its life? Different firms will use different versions of this ratio. In this book, profit before interest and taxation, and initial capital investment are preferred (see Definition 17.2). This is because it is similar to conventional accounting ratios and seems logical! However, a common alternative is average capital investment. The accounting rate of return is easy to understand and use. Its main disadvantages are that profit and capital investment have many possible definitions and, like payback, the accounting rate of return does not take into account the time value of money.

DEFINITION 17.2

Accounting Rate of Return

Accounting rate of return is a capital investment appraisal method which assesses the viability of a project using annual profit and initial capital invested. There are several ways of defining it. For example, the average annual profit divided by the average capital investment. Our preferred definition is:

$$\frac{\text{Average annual profit before interest and taxation}}{\text{Initial capital investment}}$$

Specific advantages

1. Takes the whole life of a project.
2. Similar to normal accounting ratios.

Specific disadvantages

1. Many definitions of profit and capital investment possible.
2. Does not consider the time value of money.
3. Measures an initial cash flow using a profit measure.

In Figure 17.5, we provide an example of the calculation of the Accounting Rate of Return and show how revenue and expenses differ from cash received and cash paid.

Figure 17.5 Accounting Rate of Return

Cagliari plc is thinking of investing £1 million each in the Melis and the Gaia. The company's cost of capital is 8%. The management accountant estimates the following future financial figures for the Melis.

Years	Revenue (cash and credit)	Cash Received	Expenses (cash and credit)	Expenses (paid)	Depreciation
	£	£	£	£	£
1	500,000	450,000	320,000	290,000	80,000
2	550,000	500,000	350,000	340,000	80,000
3	600,000	550,000	410,000	400,000	80,000
4	650,000	600,000	460,000	440,000	80,000
5	700,000	650,000	490,000	480,000	80,000

Determine for the Melis and the Gaia:

(i)   The cash flows

(ii)   The profit

(iii)   The accounting rate of return

(i)   The cash flows for the Melis is:

Year	Cash Received	Cash Paid	Net
	£	£	£
1	450,000	290,000	160,000
2	500,000	340,000	160,000
3	550,000	400,000	150,000
4	600,000	440,000	160,000
5	650,000	480,000	170,000
Total	2,750,000	1,950,000	800,000

(ii)   The profit for the Melis is:

Year	Revenue	Expenses	Depreciation	Profit
	£	£	£	£
1	500,000	320,000	80,000	100,000
2	550,000	350,000	80,000	120,000
3	600,000	410,000	80,000	110,000
4	650,000	460,000	80,000	110,000
5	700,000	490,000	80,000	130,000
Total	3,000,000	2,030,000	400,000	570,000

The management accountant estimates the following future financial figures for the Gaia.

Years	Revenue (cash and credit) £	Cash Received £	Expenses (cash and credit) £	Expenses (paid) £	Depreciation £
1	400,000	380,000	380,000	350,000	80,000
2	550,000	530,000	400,000	380,000	80,000
3	660,000	650,000	420,000	410,000	80,000
4	680,000	630,000	470,000	450,000	80,000
5	750,000	730,000	500,000	480,000	80,000

Determine:

(i)   The cash flows for the Gaia are:

Year	Cash Received £	Cash Paid £	Net £
1	380,000	350,000	30,000
2	530,000	380,000	150,000
3	650,000	410,000	240,000
4	630,000	450,000	180,000
5	730,000	480,000	250,000
Total	2,920,000	2,070,000	850,000

(ii)   The profit for the Gaia is:

Year	Revenue £	Expenses £	Depreciation £	Profit £
1	400,000	380,000	80,000	(60,000)
2	550,000	400,000	80,000	70,000
3	660,000	420,000	80,000	160,000
4	680,000	470,000	80,000	130,000
5	750,000	500,000	80,000	170,000
Total	3,040,000	2,170,000	400,000	470,000

(iii)   The Accounting Rate of Return is:

	Melis	Gaia
$\dfrac{\text{Average amount paid before interest and taxation}}{\text{Initial Capital Investment}}$ =	£114,000*	£94,000**
	£1,000,000	£1,000,000
	= 11.4%	= 9.4%

* = £570,000/5

** = £47,000/5

As the company's cost of capital is 8%, the company can invest in both as its accounting rate of return is greater than 8%. Note the difference between cash flow and income/expenses. Thus for Gaia there are the following differences: cash received (£2,920,000) and revenue (£3,040,000) and cash paid (£2,070,000) and expenses (£2,170,000). In practice, the company is likely to also perform discounted cash flow.

The accounting rate of return is applied to the Everfriendly Bank in Figure 17.6.

Figure 17.6 Accounting Rate of Return Using Everfriendly Bank

	Project Cash Flows		
	A	**B**	**C**
Year	£000	£000	£000
0 (i.e., now) Cash outflows	(20,000)	(20,000)	(20,000)
Net cash inflows (note)			
1	4,000	8,000	8,000
2	4,000	6,000	8,000
3	8,000	6,000	6,000
4	6,000	3,000	6,000
5	6,000	2,000	3,000
Total	28,000	25,000	31,000

	A	B	C
Average profit	£28,000,000	£25,000,000	£31,000,000
	5 years	5 years	5 years
	= 5,600,000	= 5,000,000	= 6,200,000
Our accounting rate of return is therefore:	£5,600,000	£5,000,000	£6,200,000
	£20,000,000	£20,000,000	£20,000,000
	= 28%	= 25%	= 31%

We would, therefore, choose project C because its accounting rate of return is the highest.

Note: In this case, cash inflow equals net profit. This will not always be the case. They must, for example, be adjusted for depreciation.

Returns on investment are treated very seriously by businesses. In Real-World View 17.4, Vodafone has a projected rate of return of at least 15% on its capital investment. However, it is not absolutely clear from the press extract whether it has used the accounting rate of return.

REAL-WORLD VIEW 17.4

Rates of Return

Rates of Return are of key interest to businesses. Dan Roberts looked at Vodafone AirTouch. Its finance director Ken Hydon indicated that its estimated future rate of return was at least 15% and added that:

'Although the £6 bn cost of Vodafone's new UK licence will be spread over its 20-year lifespan, most of the estimated £4 bn network spending and handset subsidy will be required in the first four or five years.'

Source: Dan Roberts, Telecommunications group releases internal targets to counter criticism it overpaid for licence, *Financial Times*, 31 May 2000.

Net Present Value

The net present value, profitability index and internal rate of return can be distinguished from the payback period and accounting rate of return because they take into account the time value of money. Essentially, time is money. If you invest £100 in a bank or building society and the interest rate is 10%, the £100 is worth £110 in one year's time (100 × 1.10), and £121 in two years' time (100 × 1.10², or 110 × 1.10).

We can use the same principle to work backwards. If we have £110 in the bank in a year's time with a 10% interest rate, it will be worth £100 today (£110 × 0.9091, i.e., 100 ÷ 110). Similarly, £121 in two years' time would be worth £100 today (£121 × 0.8264, i.e., 100 ÷ 121).

PAUSE FOR THOUGHT 17.5

Discounting

You are approached by your best friend, who asks you to lend her £1,000. She promises to give you back £1,200 in two years' time. Your money is in a two-year fixed ecological bond and earns 6%. Putting friendship aside, do you lend her the money?

To work this out, we need to compare like with like. We could work forwards (i.e., multiplying £1,000 by the 6% earned over two years (1.06²) = £1,123.60). £1,000 today is worth £1,123.60 in two years' time. Or more conventionally, we work back from the future using the time value of money, in this case 6%.

$$\text{Thus, £1,200 in one year's time} = £1,200 \times (100/106, \text{ i.e., } 0.9434)$$
$$= £1,132.08 \text{ today}$$

$$\text{While £1,200 in two years' time} = £1,200 \times (100/112.36, \text{ i.e., } 106 \times 1.06)$$
$$= £1,200 \times 0.8900$$
$$= £1,068 \text{ today}$$

Therefore, as £1,200 in two years' time is the equivalent of £1,068 today you should accept your friend's offer as this is £68 more than you currently have.

Fortunately, we do not have to calculate discount rates all the time! We use discount tables (see Appendix 17.1 at the end of this chapter). So to obtain a 10% interest rate in two years' time, we look up the number of years (two) and the discount rate (10%). We then find a discount factor of 0.8264!

As Definition 17.3 shows, net present value uses the discounting principle to work out the value in today's money of future expected cash flows. Cash flows are normally determined by the rate at the end of the year. The cost of capital is used as the discount rate. Conventionally, the cost of capital is taken as the rate at which the business can borrow money. However, the estimation of the cost of capital can be quite difficult. In Chapter 18 we look in more detail at how companies can derive their cost of capital. Cost of capital is a key element of capital investment appraisal. Essentially, a business is seeking to earn a higher return from new projects than its cost of capital. If this is achieved, the projects will be viable. If not, they are unviable.

DEFINITION 17.3

Net Present Value

Net present value is a capital investment appraisal technique which discounts future expected cash flows to today's monetary values using an appropriate cost of capital.

Specific advantages

1. Looks at all the cash flows.
2. Takes into account the value of money.

Specific disadvantages

1. Estimation of the cost of capital may be difficult.
2. Assumes all cash flows occur at the end of a period (normally a year).
3. Can be complex.

Behavioural factors can also play their part in making a decision. For instance, Graham Cleverly (*Managers and Magic*, 1971, p. 86) commented:

> If a company decides it will only go ahead with projects that show a discounted return on investment of better than 15 per cent, anyone putting forward a project will ensure that the accompanying figures indicate a better than 15 per cent return.

Additionally, he went on to state:

> If the criterion is raised to 20 per cent, the figures will be improved accordingly. And there is no way in which the person analysing the project can contest those figures – unless he can find a flaw in the performance of the projection rituals.

Figure 17.7 applies net present value to the Everfriendly Bank using the cost of capital of 10% as the discount rate.

Figure 17.7 Net Present Value as Applied to the Everfriendly Bank

| | Project Cash Flows | | | Discount Rate | Discounted Cash Flows | | |
	A	B	C	10%	A	B	C
	£000	£000	£000		£000	£000	£000
Year							
0 (i.e., now)	(20,000)	(20,000)	(20,000)	1	(20,000)	(20,000)	(20,000)
1	4,000	8,000	8,000	0.9091	3,636	7,273	7,273
2	4,000	6,000	8,000	0.8264	3,306	4,958	6,611
3	8,000	6,000	6,000	0.7513	6,010	4,508	4,508
4	6,000	3,000	6,000	0.6830	4,098	2,049	4,098
5	6,000	2,000	3,000	0.6209	3,725	1,242	1,863
Total discounted cash flows					20,775	20,030	24,353
Net Present Value (NPV)					775	30	4,353

All three projects have a positive net present value and, therefore, are worth carrying out. However, project C has the highest NPV and thus should be chosen if funds are limited.

When using net present value, it is useful to follow the steps in Helpnote 17.1.

HELPNOTE 17.1

Calculating Net Present Value

1. Calculate initial cash flows.
2. Choose a discount rate (usually given), normally based on the company's cost of capital.
3. Discount original cash flows using discount rate.
4. Match discounted cash flows against initial investment to arrive at net present value.
5. Positive net present values are good investments. Negative ones are poor investments.
6. Choose the highest net present value. This is the project that will most increase the shareholders' wealth.

PAUSE FOR THOUGHT 17.6

Discount Tables

Using the discount tables given in Appendix 17.1, what are the following discount factors:
(i) 8% at 5 years, (ii) 12% at 8 years, (iii) 15% at 10 years, (iv) 20% at 6 years, and
(v) 9% at 9 years.

From Appendix 17.1, we have
(i) 0.6806; (ii) 0.4039; (iii) 0.2472; (iv) 0.3349; (v) 0.4604

In practice, calculating net present values becomes very complicated. For example, you have to take into account taxation, inflation etc. However, net present value is a very versatile technique, allowing you to determine which projects are worth investing in and to choose between competing projects.

Profitability Index

In a sense, the profitability index can be seen as an extension of NPV. It uses the figures derived from NPV calculations to produce a simple index that can be used to evaluate profits. It can thus be seen as a method of interpreting NPV. The Profitability Index is normally defined as:

$$\frac{\text{Present value of cash inflows}}{\text{Initial investment}}$$

If the cash flows are more than the initial investment, the index is, therefore, above 1. The project should thus be accepted. By contrast, if the cash flows are less than the initial investment, the index is less than 1. The project should thus be rejected. If we look at the Everfriendly Bank then we have the following situation (see Figure 17.8).

Figure 17.8 Profitability Index for Everfriendly Bank

	A	B	C
Discounted cash flows	£20,775	£20,030	£24,353
Initial investment	£20,000	£20,000	£20,000
Profitability index	1.04	1.002	1.22

In this case, using the company's cost of capital as the discount rate, we would choose project C as the profitability index is the highest. However, in cases where the NPV of the cash flows gave a different result from the profitability index, we would go with the investment which generated the greatest NPV in terms of cash flow. The profitability index can be useful in circumstances where it is necessary to choose between many different projects with positive NPVs; for example, when funds are short. Usually, we use the company's cost of capital as the discount rate.

Internal Rate of Return (IRR)

The internal rate of return is a more sophisticated discounting technique than net present value. As Definition 17.4 shows, it can be defined as the rate of discount required to give a net present value of zero. Another way of looking at this is the maximum rate of interest that a company can afford to pay without suffering a loss on the project. Projects are accepted if the company's cost of capital is less than the IRR. Similarly, projects are rejected if the company's cost of capital is higher than the IRR. The advantages of the internal rate of return are that it takes into account the time value of money and calculates a break-even rate of return. However, it is complex and difficult to understand. In a study of 14 UK, US and Japanese companies, Carr, Kolehmainen and Mitchell (*Management Accounting*, 2010, pp. 167–84) found that across 14 UK, US and Japanese companies the average IRR target ranged from 16–22% with a premium over cost of capital of between 6.3% and 9.5%.

DEFINITION 17.4

The Internal Rate of Return (IRR)

'Annual percentage return achieved by a project at which the sum of the discounted cash inflows over the life of the project is equal to the sum of the discounted cash outflows. It pays a company to invest in a project if it can borrow money for less than the IRR (CIMA (2005) *Official Terminology*).

Specific advantages	Specific disadvantages
1. Uses time value of money.	1. Difficult to understand.
2. Determines the break-even rate of return.	2. No need to select a specific discount rate.
3. Looks at all the cash flows.	3. Complex, often needing a computer.
	4. In certain situations, gives misleading results (for example, where there are unconventional cash flows).'

Source: Chartered Institute of Management Accountants (2005), *Official Terminology*. Reproduced by Permission of Elsevier.

When calculating the IRR, there are four main steps. These are shown in Helpnote 17.2.

HELPNOTE 17.2

Calculating the Internal Rate of Return (IRR)

1. Calculate a positive NPV for all projects.
2. Calculate a negative NPV for all projects. Use trial and error. The higher the discount rate, the lower the NPV.
3. Calculate out the IRR using the formula:

$$\text{IRR} = \text{Lowest discount rate} + \text{difference in discount rates} \times \frac{\text{lowest discount rate NPV}}{\text{difference in NPVs}}$$

4. Choose the project with the highest IRR. When evaluating a single project, the project will be chosen when its IRR is higher than the company's cost of capital.

The relationship of the internal rate of return to net present value is shown in Figure 17.9 and the internal rate of return is then applied to the Everfriendly Bank in Figure 17.10.

Figure 17.9 Relationship Between the Net Present Value and Internal Rate of Return

A project has the following net present values (NPVs).

£2,000,000 NPV at 10% discount rate.
(£1,000,000) NPV at 15% discount rate.
What is the internal rate of return?

We can find the internal rate of return either (i) *diagrammatically* or (ii) *mathematically* by a process called interpolation.

(i) Diagrammatically

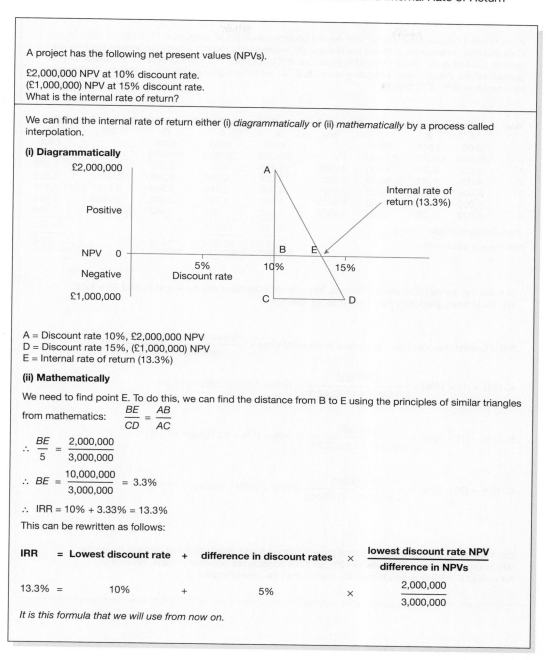

A = Discount rate 10%, £2,000,000 NPV
D = Discount rate 15%, (£1,000,000) NPV
E = Internal rate of return (13.3%)

(ii) Mathematically

We need to find point E. To do this, we can find the distance from B to E using the principles of similar triangles from mathematics: $\dfrac{BE}{CD} = \dfrac{AB}{AC}$

$\therefore \dfrac{BE}{5} = \dfrac{2,000,000}{3,000,000}$

$\therefore BE = \dfrac{10,000,000}{3,000,000} = 3.3\%$

$\therefore$ IRR = 10% + 3.33% = 13.3%

This can be rewritten as follows:

IRR	= Lowest discount rate	+	difference in discount rates	×	lowest discount rate NPV
					difference in NPVs
13.3% =	10%	+	5%	×	2,000,000
					3,000,000

It is this formula that we will use from now on.

Figure 17.10 Internal Rate of Return as Applied to the Everfriendly Bank

From Figure 17.7, we know that at 10% our net present values are all positive, A £775,000, B £30,000 and C £4,353,000. To solve the problem mathematically, we need to ascertain a negative present value for each project. So, first of all, we try 15%. 15% produced A (£1,824,000), B (£1,852,000) and C £1,874,000 in net present values. We still need a negative value for C. So we run a higher discount rate 20% for C. This gives us a negative NPV of (£207,000).

Year	Project Cash Flows			Discount Rate 15%	Discounted Cash Flows (DCF)			Discount Rate 20%	DCF C
	A	B	C		A	B	C		C
	£000	£000	£000		£000	£000	£000		£000
0	(20,000)	(20,000)	(20,000)	1	(20,000)	(20,000)	(20,000)	1	(20,000)
1	4,000	8,000	8,000	0.8696	3,478	6,957	6,957	0.8333	6,666
2	4,000	6,000	8,000	0.7561	3,024	4,537	6,049	0.6944	5,555
3	8,000	6,000	6,000	0.6575	5,260	3,945	3,945	0.5787	3,472
4	6,000	3,000	6,000	0.5718	3,431	1,715	3,431	0.4823	2,894
5	6,000	2,000	3,000	0.4972	2,983	994	1,492	0.4019	1,206
Total discounted cash inflows					18,176	18,148	21,874		19,793
Net Present Value (NPV)					(1,824)	(1,852)	1,874		(207)

To solve this we can now use our formula. We use 15% discount rate for A and B, and 20% for C. We could have used 20% for all three as an alternative.

$$IRR = \text{Lowest discount rate} + \text{difference in discount rates} \times \frac{\text{lowest discount rate NPV}}{\text{difference in NPVs}}$$

$$A. \ 10\% + (15 - 10\%) \times \frac{£775,000}{£775,000 + £1,824,000} = 10\% + (5\% \times 0.2982) = 11.5\%$$

$$B. \ 10\% + (15 - 10\%) \times \frac{£30,000}{£30,000 + £1,852,000} = 10\% + (5\% \times 0.01594) = 10.1\%$$

$$C. \ 10\% + (20 - 10\%) \times \frac{£4,353,000}{£4,353,000 + £207,000} = 10\% + (10\% \times 0.9546) = 19.6\%$$

Our ranking for the IRR method is thus project C, then A and, finally, B. As all projects have IRRs which exceed our cost of capital of 10%, all three projects are potentially viable. However, for project B the IRR is only marginally greater than the cost of capital of 10%.

The IRR can be a very useful technique. However, the complexity is often off-putting. In practice, students will be pleased to learn that the calculations to arrive at the IRR are generally done using a computer program. Normally, the results from NPV and IRR will be consistent. However, in some cases, such as projects with unconventional cash flows (e.g., alternating cash inflows and outflows), the NPV and IRR may give different results. In these cases, NPV is probably the most reliable. This is particularly true when there are mutually exclusive projects with a different IRR.

If there were a clash between the results from the different methods then it would be difficult to choose. Different businesses will prefer different methods depending on their priorities. I would probably choose net present value as the superior method. This is because it takes into account the time value of money, is more reliable, and is easier to understand and use than the internal rate of return.

Now that we have calculated the results for the Everfriendly Bank using all four methods, we can compare them (see Figure 17.11). Project C is clearly the superior method.

Before we leave the capital investment appraisal techniques, it is important to reiterate that the results achieved will only be as good as the assumptions that underpin them. This is powerfully expressed by Graham Cleverly (1971) on p. 86 of *Managers and Magic*:

> Where the validity of one's original information is suspect, performing ever more sophisticated calculations seems pointless. Nonetheless, there can hardly be a company in which new projects are not required to be subjected to a ritual calculation of the 'internal rate of return', 'net present value', 'payback period' or some other criterion of profitability.

However, in the majority of cases those involved are themselves not convinced of the validity of the data.

Figure 17.11 Comparison of the Projects for Everfriendly Bank Using the Four Capital Methods

	Projects		
	A	B	C
Payback Period	3.67 years	3 years	2.67 years
Ranking	3	2	1
Accounting Rate of Return	28%	25%	31%
Ranking	2	3	1
Net present Value	£775,000	£30,000	£4,353,000
Ranking	2	3	1
Profitability Index	1.04	1.002	1.22
Ranking	2	3	1
Internal Rate of Return	11.5%	10.1%	19.6%
Ranking	2	3	1

Project C is the superior project using all methods, so we could choose project C.

Other Factors

There are many other factors that affect capital investment appraisal. Below we discuss three of the most important: sensitivity analysis, inflation and non-cash flow items.

1. Sensitivity analysis

The assumptions underpinning the capital investment decision mean that it is often sensible to undertake some form of **sensitivity analysis**. Sensitivity analysis involves modelling the future to see if alternative scenarios will change the investment decision. For example, a project's estimated cash outflow might be £10 million, its estimated inflows might be £6 million and its cost of capital might be 10%. All three of these parameters would be altered to assess any impact upon the overall results.

2. Inflation

The effects of inflation should also be included in any future capital investment model. Inflation means that a pound in a year's time will not buy as much as a pound today, as the price of goods will have risen. Therefore, we need to adjust for inflation. This can be done in two ways.

(i) *By adjusting future cash flow.* Under this method, we increase the future cash flows by the expected rate of inflation. If inflation was 3% over a year we would, therefore, increase an expected cash flow of £100 million by 3% to £103 million. We would then discount these adjusted flows as normal.

(ii) *By adjusting the discount rate.* If we were using a discount rate of 10%, we would deduct the inflation rate. If inflation was 3%, we would then discount the future cash flows at 7%.

3. Non-cash flow items

As we saw in Chapter 7, cash flow and profit are distinctly different. Discounted cash flows are based on cash flows not on accounting profit. In order to arrive at forecast cash flows from forecast profit we must, therefore, adjust the profit for non-cash flow items. In particular, we need to add back depreciation. Depreciation is not a cash flow item. We should also adjust for any other non-cash flow items such as profit or losses on the sale of assets. Finally, we might adjust for capital allowances, which are allowed by the taxation authorities as a replacement for depreciation.

Conclusion

Capital investment appraisal methods are used to assess the viability of long-term investment decisions. Capital investment projects might be a football club building a new stadium or a company building a new factory. Capital investment decisions are long-term and often very expensive. It is, therefore, very important to test their viability. Five capital investment appraisal methods are commonly used: payback period; accounting rate of return; net present value; profitability index and internal rate of return. Unlike the last three, the first two do not take into account the time value of money. The payback period simply assesses how long it takes a company's cumulative cash inflows to outstrip its initial investment. The accounting rate of return assesses the profitability of a project using average annual profit over initial capital investment. Net present value discounts back estimated future cash flows to today's values using cost of capital as a discount rate. The profitability index compares the NPVs of the cash flows with the initial investment. Finally, internal rate of return establishes the discount rate at which a project breaks even. All five appraisal methods are based on many assumptions about future cash flows. These assumptions are often tested using sensitivity analysis.

Discussion Questions

Questions with numbers in blue have answers at the back of the book.

Q1 (a) Why do you think capital investment is necessary for companies?
(b) What sort of possible capital investment might there be in:
  (i)   the shipping industry?
  (ii) the hotel and catering industry?
  (iii) manufacturing industry?

Q2 Discuss the general problems that underpin capital investment appraisal.

Q3 Briefly outline the five main capital investment appraisal techniques and then discuss the specific advantages and disadvantages of each technique.

Q4 Why is time money?

Q5 State whether the following statements are true or false. If false, explain why.
(a) The five main capital investment appraisal techniques are payback period, accounting rate of return, net present value, profitability index and internal rate of return.
(b) The payback period and net present value techniques generally use discounted cash flows.
(c) The accounting rate of return is the only investment appraisal technique that focuses on profits not cash flows.
(d) The discount rate normally used to discount cash flows is the interest rate charged by the Bank of England.
(e) Sensitivity analysis involves modelling future alternative scenarios and assessing their impact upon the results of capital investment appraisal techniques.

Numerical Questions

Questions with numbers in blue have answers at the back of the book.
These questions gradually increase in difficulty. Students may find question 6, in particular, testing.

Q1 What are the appropriate discount factors for the following?
  (i)   5 years at 10% cost of capital   (iv) 4 years at 12% cost of capital
  (ii)   6 years at 9% cost of capital   (v)   3 years at 14% cost of capital
  (iii) 8 years at 13% cost of capital   (vi) 10 years at 20% cost of capital

Q2 A company, Fairground, has a choice between investing in one of three projects: the Rocket, the Carousel or the Dipper. The cost of capital is 8%. There are the following cash flows.

	Rocket £	Carousel £	Dipper £
Initial outlay	(18,000)	(18,000)	(18,000)
Cash inflow			
Year 1	8,000	6,000	10,000
Year 2	8,000	4,000	6,000
Year 3	8,000	14,000	5,000

Required: An evaluation of Fairground's projects using:
(i)   the payback period
(ii) the accounting rate of return (assume cash flows are equivalent to profits)
(iii) net present value
(iv) profitability index
(v)   the internal rate of return.

Q3 Wetday is evaluating three projects: the Storm, the Cloud and the Downpour. The company's cost of capital is 12%. These projects have the following cash flows.

Year	Storm £	Cloud £	Downpour £
0 (Initial outlay)	(18,000)	(12,000)	(13,000)
Cash inflow			
1	4,000	5,000	4,000
2	5,000	2,000	4,000
3	6,000	3,000	4,000
4	7,000	2,500	4,000
5	8,000	3,000	4,000

Required: Calculate:
(i)   the payback period
(ii) the accounting rate of return (assume cash flows equal profits)
(iii) the net present value
(iv) the internal rate of return.

Q4 A company, Choosewell, has £30,000 to spend on capital investment projects. It is currently evaluating three projects. The initial capital outlay is on a piece of machinery that has a four-year life. Its cost of capital is 9%.

	Ready		Steady		Go	
	£		£		£	
Initial capital outlay	(30,000)		(15,000)		(15,000)	
	Inflows	Outflows	Inflows	Outflows	Inflows	Outflows
Year	£	£	£	£	£	£
1	36,000	24,000	25,000	16,000	16,000	8,000
2	36,000	14,000	18,000	11,000	13,000	6,500
3	32,000	26,000	17,000	12,000	12,000	6,000
4	4,000	5,000	3,000	4,000	6,000	6,000

Required: Calculate:
(i)   the payback period
(ii) the accounting rate of return
(iii) the net present value
(iv) profitability index
(v)   the internal rate of return.

Q5 A football club, Manpool, is considering investing in a new stadium. There are the following expected capital outlays and cash inflows for two prospective stadiums.

Year	Bowl £000	Superbowl £000
Outlays		
0	(1,000)	(1,000)
1	(1,000)	(1,000)
Net inflows		
1	50	300
2	100	300
3	150	300
4	200	300
5	250	300
6	300	300
7	350	300
8	400	300
9	450	300
10	500	300

Assume the football club can borrow money at respectively:

(a) 5%   (b) 8%   (c) 10%

Required:
(i)   Which stadium should be built and at which rate using net present value?
(ii) What is the internal rate of return for the two stadiums?

Q6 A company, Myopia, has the following details for its new potential product, the Telescope.

Year	Capital Outlay	Capital Inflow	Revenue	Interest	Expenses (Excludes Depreciation)	Taxation
	£	£	£	£	£	£
0	(700,000)	–	–	–	–	–
1			340,000	20,000	(40,000)	–
2			270,000	20,000	(130,000)	(4,500)
3			320,000	20,000	(160,000)	(18,375)
4			345,000	20,000	(185,000)	(24,281)
5			430,500	20,000	(205,000)	(48,361)
6			330,300	20,000	(160,300)	(35,033)
7			200,600	20,000	(100,100)	(16,825)
8			145,300	20,000	(46,500)	(18,034)
9			85,200	20,000	(28,100)	(6,925)
10		5,000	38,600	20,000	(8,300)	–

Myopia's cost of capital is 10%. The capital outlay is for the Jodrell machine which will last 10 years. The capital inflow of £5,000 is the scrap value after 10 years.

Required: Calculate:
(i)   the payback period
(ii) the accounting rate of return
(iii) the net present value
(iv) profitability index
(v)   the internal rate of return.

Helpnote. In this question, which has a different format from those encountered so far, it is first necessary to calculate *profit before interest and tax* (i.e., revenue less expenses and depreciation). After this we need to adjust for interest, taxation, depreciation (based on the initial capital outlay) and other cash flows to arrive at a final cash flow figure.

Go online to discover the extra features for this chapter at
www.wiley.com/college/jones

Appendix 17.1: Present Value of £1 at Compound Interest Rate $(1 + r)$

Years (n)					Interest rates (r)					
	1%	2%	3%	4%	5%	6%	7%	8%	9%	10%
1	0.9901	0.9804	0.9709	0.9615	0.9524	0.9434	0.9346	0.9259	0.9174	0.9091
2	0.9803	0.9612	0.9426	0.9246	0.9070	0.8900	0.8734	0.8573	0.8417	0.8264
3	0.9706	0.9423	0.9151	0.8890	0.8638	0.8396	0.8163	0.7938	0.7722	0.7513
4	0.9610	0.9238	0.8885	0.8548	0.8227	0.7921	0.7629	0.7350	0.7084	0.6830
5	0.9515	0.9057	0.8626	0.8219	0.7835	0.7473	0.7130	0.6806	0.6499	0.6209
6	0.9420	0.8880	0.8375	0.7903	0.7462	0.7050	0.6663	0.6302	0.5963	0.5645
7	0.9327	0.8706	0.8131	0.7599	0.7107	0.6651	0.6227	0.5835	0.5470	0.5132
8	0.9235	0.8535	0.7894	0.7307	0.6768	0.6274	0.5820	0.5403	0.5019	0.4665
9	0.9143	0.8368	0.7664	0.7026	0.6446	0.5919	0.5439	0.5002	0.4604	0.4241
10	0.9053	0.8203	0.7441	0.6756	0.6139	0.5584	0.5083	0.4632	0.4224	0.3855

Years (n)					Interest rates (r)					
	11%	12%	13%	14%	15%	16%	17%	18%	19%	20%
1	0.9009	0.8929	0.8850	0.8772	0.8696	0.8621	0.8547	0.8475	0.8403	0.8333
2	0.8116	0.7972	0.7831	0.7695	0.7561	0.7432	0.7305	0.7182	0.7062	0.6944
3	0.7312	0.7118	0.6931	0.6750	0.6575	0.6407	0.6244	0.6086	0.5934	0.5787
4	0.6587	0.6355	0.6133	0.5921	0.5718	0.5523	0.5337	0.5158	0.4987	0.4823
5	0.5935	0.5674	0.5428	0.5194	0.4972	0.4761	0.4561	0.4371	0.4190	0.4019
6	0.5346	0.5066	0.4803	0.4556	0.4323	0.4104	0.3898	0.3704	0.3521	0.3349
7	0.4817	0.4523	0.4251	0.3996	0.3759	0.3538	0.3332	0.3139	0.2959	0.2791
8	0.4339	0.4039	0.3762	0.3506	0.3269	0.3050	0.2848	0.2660	0.2487	0.2326
9	0.3909	0.3606	0.3329	0.3075	0.2843	0.2630	0.2434	0.2255	0.2090	0.1938
10	0.3522	0.3220	0.2946	0.2697	0.2472	0.2267	0.2080	0.1911	0.1756	0.1615

Helpnote: This table shows what the value of £1 today will be in the future, assuming different interest rates. Therefore, £1 today will be worth 90.91 pence in one year's time if the interest rate is 10%. If you are given cash flows at a future time, you need to use the interest rates in the table to adjust them to today's monetary value. Thus, if we have £5,000 in five years' time and our interest rate is 10%, then, using the table, this will be worth £5,000 × 0.6209 or £3,104 in today's money.

Chapter 18

The sources of finance

Learning Outcomes

After completing this chapter you should be able to:

- Explain the nature and importance of sources of finance.
- Explain the workings of the Stock Exchange.
- Analyse the ways in which the long-term finance of a company may be provided.
- Understand the concept of the cost of capital.

Go online to discover the extra features for this chapter at
www.wiley.com/college/jones

Chapter Summary

- Sources of finance are vital to the survival and growth of a business.
- There are internally and externally generated sources of finance.
- Sources of finance can be short-term or long-term.
- Short-term and long-term sources of finance are normally matched with current assets and long-term, infrastructure assets, respectively.
- Retained profits are where a company finances itself from internal funds.
- Stock exchanges, including the London Stock Exchange, are vital sources of finance.
- There are primary and secondary markets for shares and on the London Stock Exchange a main market and an Alternative Investment Market.
- Stock markets are generally held to be efficient.
- Three major sources of external long-term financing are leasing, share capital and long-term loans.
- Leasing involves a company using, but not owning, an asset.
- Share capital is provided by shareholders who own the company and receive dividends.
- Share capital can be divided into outsiders (professional investors and retail investors) and inside equity investors.
- Loan capital providers do not own the company and receive interest.
- Loan capital can be divided into private and public debt.
- Small and medium-sized businesses have different financing needs, often supplied by venture capitalists and business angels.
- Cost of capital is the effective rate at which a company can raise finance.

Introduction

Sources of finance are vital to a business. They allow it to survive and grow. Sources of finance may be raised internally and externally. The efficient use of working capital is an important internal, short-term source of funds, while retained profits can be an important internal, long-term source. External funds may also be short-term or long-term. Bank loans, trade payables and debt factoring are examples of external short-term finance. External long-term sources allow businesses to carry out their long-term strategic aims. The stock market provides an active source of capital for companies. Share capital and loan capital are examples of long-term finance. Every business aims to optimise its use of funds. This involves minimising short-term borrowings and financing long-term infrastructure investments as cheaply as possible. Small and medium-sized businesses have different financing needs to large businesses, often supplied by venture capitalists and business angels.

Nature of Sources of Finance

Sources of finance may be generated internally or raised externally. These sources of finance may be short-term or long-term. If short-term, they will typically be associated with operational activities involving the financing of working capital (such as inventory, trade receivables or cash). If long-term, they will typically be associated with funding longer-term infrastructure assets, such as the purchase of land and buildings.

Normally, it is considered a mistake to borrow short and use long (e.g., use bank overdrafts for long-term purposes). For instance, if a bank overdraft was used to finance a new building, then the company would be in trouble if the bank suddenly withdrew the overdraft facility. Firms thus strive to fund their current assets through current liabilities. As Figure 18.1 shows, *internal* sources of finance may be generated over the *short term* through the efficient management of working capital, or over the *long term* by reinvesting retained profits.

Figure 18.1 Overview of Sources of Finance

	Short term (less than 2 years)	**Long term (over 2 years)**
Internal (within firm)	(a) Efficient cash management	(a) Retained profits
	(b) Efficient trade receivables management	
	(c) Efficient inventory management	
External (outside firm)	(a) Bank overdraft	(a) Leasing
	(b) Bank loans	(b) Share capital (equity)
	(c) Trade payables (creditors)	(c) Long-term borrowing (debt)
	(d) Invoice discounting	
	(e) Debt factoring	
	(f) Sale and leaseback	

External sources of capital may be raised in the *short term* by cash overdrafts, bank loans, the use of trade payables, invoice discounting, debt factoring or sale and leaseback. Over the *longer term* the three most important external sources of finance are leasing, share capital and long-term borrowing. Although 'short term' is defined as less than two years, this is, in fact, very arbitrary. For example, some leases may be for less than two years while bank overdrafts and bank loans will sometimes be for more than two years. However, this division provides a useful and convenient simplification. It is also, however, important to appreciate that most short-term funding will continue over a much longer period as, for example, one trade payable, bank overdraft or bank loan replaces another.

As can be seen in Figure 18.1, broadly the funding of a firm can be categorised as constituting the efficient management of assets and the sources of funding. The efficient management of assets comprises efficient cash management, efficient trade receivables management and efficient inventory management as well as retained profits. The sources of finance comprise bank funding, current liabilities trade payables, invoice discounting, debt factoring, sale and leaseback, leasing, share capital and long-term borrowing. An analysis of the key external providers of finance (the use of information by capital providers) suggests that the three main capital providers in the US and EU are equity, debt and current liabilities. Shareholders' equity can broadly be seen as share capital (outside professional investors, outside retail investors and inside users, e.g., family), non-current liabilities as long-term borrowing or debt (banks or bonds) and current liabilities (broadly trade payables or creditors). This is set out in Figure 18.2. The figures for the US, the EU and then separately for the UK are given.

Figure 18.2 Overview of Key Capital Providers in the US and EU

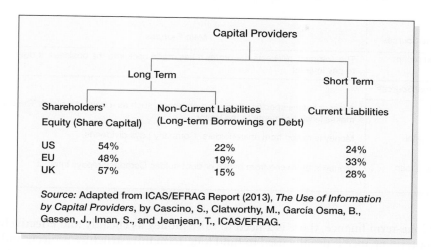

Source: Adapted from ICAS/EFRAG Report (2013), *The Use of Information by Capital Providers*, by Cascino, S., Clatworthy, M., García Osma, B., Gassen, J., Iman, S., and Jeanjean, T., ICAS/EFRAG.

As can be seen, shareholders' equity is the main source of funds. It comprises about 50% of funding. Non-current liabilities (debt) is about 20% and current liabilities (trade payables) ranges from 24% in the US to 33% in Europe. Cascino et al. (2013) point out that this pattern of funding varies from country to country. They, for example, compare the UK and Portugal. Thus, Portugal relies much more on current liabilities (40%) and non-current liabilities (debt) (33%) than on shareholders' equity (27%). These different patterns lead to different priorities. Thus, in the UK the priority will be on paying dividends while in Portugal it will be on repaying suppliers and funding debt.

These three capital providers will be dealt with in more detail later in the book. Share capital and long-term borrowings will be dealt with later on in this chapter, given their long-term nature. Meanwhile, trade payables, given their short-term nature, will be dealt with in Chapter 19 on the management of working capital.

Long-Term Financing

There are potentially four main sources of long-term finance: retained profits; leasing; share capital and loan capital (see Figures 18.3 and 18.4).

Figure 18.3 Overview of Sources of Long-Term Finance

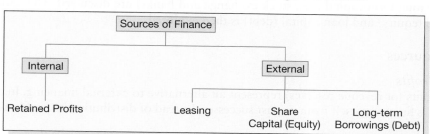

Figure 18.4 Sources of Long-Term Finance

(i) Internal Sources	Main Features
Retained profits	The company reinvests the profits it has made back into the business. It does not have to pay interest.
(ii) External Sources	
Leasing	A lessor leases specific assets to a company, such as a train or a plane. The company makes lease payments to the lessor.
Share capital	Money is raised from shareholders. Company pays dividends.
Long-term loan	Money is borrowed from banks or debt holder. Company repays interest.

For long-term finance, there is a need to raise money as cheaply and effectively as possible. Long-term finance is usually used to fund long-term infrastructure projects and can often be daunting, given the huge sums involved. The most important two sources of long-term funds are share capital, also known as equity, and long-term loans, also known as debt.

Size of Business

External sources of finance can roughly be divided into two: the acquisition of assets and the acquisition of capital. The acquisition of assets is, in effect, the direct leasing of assets by a company, such as cars or property. This is done through leasing companies or property management companies. This can be seen as a normal business transaction. The acquisition of capital is more direct – the cash provided can be used for any purpose, including the purchase of assets. The acquisition of cash is usually through institutions such as the stock market (shares and corporate bonds) or through banks.

As a business grows, its source of funding will also generally change. The nature of the funding to a large extent is, therefore, determined by the structure of a business: sole trader, partnership, unlisted company or listed company. Small businesses will often rely at first on family or friends. As they grow, they will seek alternative sources of finance so that when they are large listed companies, they will generally rely primarily on share capital and loan capital. Firm size also affects the bargaining power of companies. Larger firms often have both the resources and the bargaining power to drive better financing deals than smaller firms. Thus, they usually will be able to obtain a lower cost of capital.

We will review the four main sources of funding below; we then look at the needs of small and medium-sized businesses. Leasing is outlined first and then the main institutions that provide long-term capital (i.e., stock exchange and banks) are discussed. The nature of share capital (equity) and loan capital (debt) is then explored.

Internal Sources

Retained Profits

Retained profits (or revenue reserves) represent an alternative to external financing. In effect, the business is financing itself from its past successes. Instead of distributing its profits as dividends, the company invests them for the future. Shareholders thus lose out today, but hope to gain tomorrow. As the company grows using its retained profits, it will in the future make more profits, distribute more dividends and then have a higher share price. In theory, that is!

In many businesses, retained profits represent the main source of long-term finance. It is important to realise that retained profits, themselves, are not directly equivalent to cash. They represent, in effect, retained assets which may, but importantly may not, be cash. However, indirectly they represent the cash dividends that the company could have paid out to shareholders. Retained profits are particularly useful in times when interest rates are high.

 PAUSE FOR THOUGHT 18.1

Retained Profits

What might be a limitation of using only retained funds as a source of long-term finance?

Retained profits are an easy resource for a company to draw upon. There is, however, one major limitation: a company can only grow by its own efforts and when funds are available. Therefore, growth may be very slow. The situation is similar to buying a house: you could save up for 25 years and then buy a house. Or you could buy one immediately by taking out a mortgage. Most people, understandably, prefer not to wait.

External Sources

(a) Leasing

In principle, the leasing of a company's assets is no different to an individual hiring a car or a television for personal usage. The property, initially at least, remains the property of the lessor. The lessee pays for the lease over a period of time. Depending on the nature of the property, the asset may eventually become the property of the lessee or remain, forever, the property of the lessor.

The main advantage of leasing is that the company leasing the asset does not immediately need to find the capital investment. The company can use the asset without buying it. This is particularly useful where the leased asset will directly generate revenue which is then used to pay the leasing company. Many of the tax benefits of leasing assets have now been curtailed. However, leasing remains an attractive way of financing assets such as cars, buses, trains or planes. Normally, leasing is tied to specific assets.

In the end, the company leasing the assets will pay more for them than buying them outright. The additional payments are how the leasing companies make their money. Leases are usually used for medium or long-term asset financing. Hire purchase or credit sales, which share many of the general principles of leases, are sometimes used for medium to short-term financing.

Strictly, leasing is a source of assets rather than a source of finance. It does not result in an inflow of money. However, it is treated as a source of finance because if the asset had been bought outright, not leased, the business would have needed to fund the original purchase. Long-term leasing can be considered equivalent to debt. The asset is purchased by the lessor, but used and paid for by the lessee, including an interest payment. Long-term leases must be disclosed on the statement of financial position. There is a recent trend where businesses that own property portfolios sell them for cash. They then lease back the original properties. For example, in 1999 Marks and Spencer was in talks to sell and lease back its prime sites such as at Oxford Circus (Morrison, *Sunday Telegraph*, 21 March 1999).

Institutional Sources of Funds

Stock Exchanges

(i) The Institutional Setting

Stock exchanges are a major method by which companies can raise funds via share capital or loans. Most developed countries and many developing countries have stock exchanges which aim to provide finance for their domestic economies. Large stock exchanges such as the London Stock Exchange or the New York Stock Exchange also service a global market. The importance of a country's stock exchange depends upon the structure of a country's economy. In any country, a key question for any company is how to finance its operations. In countries such as France and Germany, there is a much greater dependence on debt finance than in, for example, the UK and the US. The relative worldwide importance of the stock exchange (where equity is traded and raised) can be seen in Figure 18.5.

The presence of a strong equity stock market, such as in the US or the UK, leads countries to have an investor and an economic reality-orientated accounting system. There is a focus on profitability, and the importance of auditing increases. By contrast, a strong debt market is historically associated with the increased importance of banks. Thus, Germany, whose

Figure 18.5 Relative Strength of Selected Major Stock Exchanges as at January 2009

Country (Region)	Exchange	Domestic Companies	Market Capitalisation of Domestic Companies ($bn)
		No.	£bn
Europe	Euronext	1,013	1,863
Germany	Deutsche Börse	742	937
Spain	BME	3,517	871
United Kingdom	London	2,399	1,758
Canada	Toronto	3,747	998
United States:	NASDAQ	2,602	2,204
	New York	2,910	9,363
China:	Hong Kong	1,252	1,238
	Shanghai	864	1,557
India	Bombay	4,925	613
Japan	Tokyo	2,373	2,923
Australia	Australian	1,918	587

Source: Data from The World Federation of Exchanges. Pearson Education.

economy is larger than that of the UK, has a much smaller stock market. As a consequence, much more of the funding for industry comes inevitably from loan finance.

It can be seen that the US stock exchange is by far the most important in terms of market capitalisation followed by Japan, Europe and the UK. The Chinese stock market is increasing very quickly. The London Stock Exchange is also very important, particularly as an international stock exchange with companies from over 60 countries listed.

The origins of the London Stock Exchange can be traced back to the coffee houses of the seventeenth century where traders first met. Stock exchanges have developed as they provide useful mechanisms by which companies and governments can raise money. Stock exchanges, for example, help governments raise money for large infrastructure projects or in the past for wars. They also provide a channel for individuals in an economy to save money either as personal investments or in investment trusts or pension funds. And, finally, they have many advantages for companies. They allow them to grow, to avoid an over-dependency on bank finance and to engage in acquisition and merger activities.

As well as serving the national economy, stock exchanges in countries like the UK and the US are important homes for overseas capital. Companies overseas may come to London or New York simply because the markets in their own country may not serve their needs or because they wish to diversify. With the growth of international trade, most large companies both produce and sell in many countries. If this is the case, then when a company's subsidiaries need to borrow money, perhaps to build a new factory, then they may borrow in the currency of the country in which the factory is located. This will avoid the need to convert the borrowed funds into the local currency. Raising money in the local market can also signal the company's commitment to that market.

(ii) Primary and Secondary Markets

There is a basic distinction between primary and secondary markets. Indeed, they follow on from each other. A primary market is when a company, government or international organisation needs to raise finance. It will come to the market with a share issue or bond issue. Investors will buy these shares or bonds. The issuer will receive their money. However, the beauty of the stock exchange is that these shares or bonds are then traded. This encourages investors to buy them in the first place, thus benefiting the original issuer. The new purchaser of these shares or bonds is hoping to sell them for more than they were purchased. In this case, the investor makes a profit. The buying and selling is recorded and a price is set – generally when demand and supply meet. On the world's stock exchanges prices are, therefore, set for major shares and bonds. In the UK, the 100 top companies by market capitalisation (i.e., the market value of all of a company's issued share capital) is known as the FTSE 100 index (the footsie). There are also other indices such as the FTSE 250 or the FTSE small cap index. The FTSE 100 index is announced on a daily basis and is a key measure of the health of the British economy.

(iii) London Stock Exchange: Main Market and AIM

On the London Stock Exchange there are two main markets for shares: the Main Market and the Alternative Investment Market (AIM). The Main Market has many well-established, international companies. The London market is one of the most international in the world.

The AIM is a market especially designed for smaller growing companies. Many of these companies are new to the market and may be supported by venture capital. Some of the companies on the AIM will progress to the main market.

Shares on both markets are bought and sold with investors seeking to make a profit. However, investing in the stock market is not risk free. Shares may go down as well as up. Shares in the AIM market are generally more risky than those in the main market as they are often less liquid and the volume of trading may be lower.

As well as shares, a variety of other products are traded on the London Stock Exchange. These include bonds issued by companies or governments. Whereas shares pay dividends, bonds pay a usually fixed rate of interest. In addition, other products such as derivatives are traded.

(iv) Listing

It is not always the correct decision for a company to get listed on a stock market. It is a case of balancing the advantages with the disadvantages. The main advantages are threefold. First, there is easier access to finance for new products. Second, the company's profile will be enhanced and it may gain a national/international reputation. Third, the company's value will more than likely increase and as a result so will the owner's wealth. Indeed, some shares can be sold and the owner can benefit personally.

However, there are some disadvantages. First, it will become easier for the original owners to lose control; for example, by a takeover. The more shares that are issued, the more likely that they will be bought by outsiders. If they are bought by institutional investors, for example, these investors may wish to intervene in the company if they feel it is not being run correctly. For example, the institutional investors may feel the company's strategy is wrong. Second, the firm becomes more high profile and this may result in enhanced media attention. Finally, the costs of obtaining a listing are expensive and the regulatory burden also increases.

(v) International Market

The main stock exchanges provide not only a domestic market but also an international market for raising money. This is particularly true of the London Stock Exchange.

PAUSE FOR THOUGHT 18.2

Overseas Listing

You are a small Internet company in a small developing company with a great new technology. Your main markets are in Europe and you need a substantial investment. Discuss the pros and cons of a Listing on the London Stock Exchange.

Pros
- Access to a ready source of funds.
- Close to final market of the company so no cash currency conversion costs.
- Funds in home market may be limited.

Cons
- May be expensive.
- Not home environment.

(vi) Stock Market Efficiency

The essence of a stock market is the buying and selling of shares at a fair price. A fair price is difficult to determine but, in effect, seeks to reflect the worth of the company. In an efficient capital market, the prices of the traded shares will reflect all publicly available information. Shares will automatically adjust to these prices as new information is made available. This is commonly known as the efficient market hypothesis (EMH). There has been considerable debate about whether stock markets are efficient and at what level. For example, the weak form of the EMH states that current share prices reflect historical information. There has been considerable testing of the EMH. Although generally there is support for the EMH, there is also evidence that it does not work in all situations. These situations are particularly interesting to investors since they provide opportunities for them to make money.

(vii) The Bond Market

As well as an active market in company shares, there is an active market in corporate bonds. There are different forms of loans. Corporate bonds are often traded on the Stock Exchange. They are rather like shares as they are divided into individual tradable units. To make bonds more attractive they are often convertible into ordinary shares. This gives the holder of the bonds potentially a future equity stake in the company.

(b) Share Capital

Apart from reserves, there are two main types of corporate long-term capital: share capital and loan capital. These can be termed capital providers. Cascino et al. (2013) identify five types of capital providers as shown in Figure 18.6.

As can be seen, there are three different types of share capital providers (outside professionals, outside retail investors, inside equity investors) and two different types of long-term capital providers (private debt and public debt). The three types of share capital providers are

Figure 18.6 Capital Providers

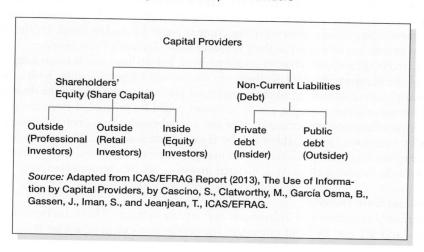

Source: Adapted from ICAS/EFRAG Report (2013), The Use of Information by Capital Providers, by Cascino, S., Clatworthy, M., García Osma, B., Gassen, J., Iman, S., and Jeanjean, T., ICAS/EFRAG.

discussed below and the two types of long-term capital providers are discussed in Section C on Loan Capital.

(i) Outside Professional Investors

Professional investors are often called institutional investors. They are, in effect, usually indirect investors in the sense that they manage funds on behalf of third parties. They collect large sums of money and then invest them in, for example, shares, bonds or property. The most important professional investors are pension funds and insurance companies. Typically, they manage portfolios. For example, a pension fund manages the accumulated funds provided by private individuals who have paid money into a pension fund over a long period of time so as to save up for a pension in retirement. Insurance companies collect money that individuals pay to protect themselves against accident, theft or natural disaster. Institutional investors are typically the largest investors in the stock market. They are seeking to invest in the most profitable products. They are thus interested in key financial indicators such as profit or cash flow. Professional investors are interested in the financial statements as well as meetings with management. They use the information that they collect to make financial decisions, such as whether to buy, hold or sell shares. Professional investors are particularly important in the United Kingdom, but are growing in importance in all countries with active stock markets. Their buying and selling of shares is a major determinant of the fixing of the market price.

(ii) Outside Retail Investors

These investors are often private individuals. They own and manage their own portfolios. They are significant owners of shares. However, their needs and influence differ considerably from those of the professional investors. Retail investors typically are price takers rather than price setters – their intervention in the market does not affect the trading price of the shares. They typically do not rely on the published financial statements. They rely more on newspapers, brokers or personal contacts. In addition, they place more weight on the Chairman's statements. Retail investors are particularly common in the US.

(iii) Inside Equity Investors

These investors, unlike the outside investors, have a direct and vested interest in the company. The investors are typically in management positions or employees. Often these investors are the original owners who gained shares when the company was formed or listed. Or they have been given shares as bonuses or as part of their remuneration. Typically these investors are relatively unsophisticated in their approach to financial matters, but do have inside knowledge of the performance of the company. In the UK, there are special insider trading rules which aim to stop inside investors taking advantage of their privileged position in the firm to the disadvantage of the outside investors. For example, inside investors might be prevented from buying and selling shares around the announcement date of the annual results. It is probably true to say that as the size of a company grows, there will be fewer inside investors. Whereas in Anglo-Saxon countries external investors predominate, in many European countries, such as France, and in other areas of the world, such as Asia, internal investors are much more common.

Investment and Unit Trusts

Both institutional investors and individuals may invest in trusts. These are institutions which pool money and are run by fund managers for profit. For example, a unit trust is an open-ended investment whose value is represented by the underlying assets (i.e., the number of units multiplied by their price). There is an annual management charge. There are usually restrictions on the amount of share capital that can be held in individual companies. Both investment and unit trusts are popular as they are less risky than investing into individual stocks and shares. The trusts will hold a portfolio of shares. The main disadvantage is the management fees.

Share capital is divided into ordinary shares and preference shares. Both sets of shareholders are paid dividends. However, while ordinary shareholders are owners, preference shareholders are not (Chapter 8 provides a fuller discussion of these issues).

When a company wishes to raise substantial sums of new money, the normal choice is either raising share capital or loan capital. Freeserve, the Internet service provider, for example, chose a stock market flotation raising an anticipated £1.9 billion from shares.

There are three main methods by which a company may raise share capital: rights issue, public issue and placing. The main features of these alternatives are listed in Figure 18.7.

Figure 18.7 Types of Share Issue

Type	Main Feature
Rights Issue	Existing shareholders can buy more shares in proportion to their existing holdings.
Public Issue	Company itself directly offers shares to the public. A prospectus containing the company's details is issued. The shares may be issued at a fixed price or open to tender (i.e., bidding). A variation on the public issue is the offer for sale. The company sells the new issue of shares to a financial institution which then issues them on the company's behalf.
Placing	A company coming to the market for the first time may allow underwriters to 'place' shares with certain financial institutions. These institutions will then hold them or sell them.

A **rights issue** is therefore an issue to existing shareholders. In June 2001, for example, British Telecom asked its *existing* shareholders for £5.9 billion extra cash. Rights issues are a continual fact of corporate life. They are regularly reported in the financial press. For example in 2011, Lamprell, a UK company, sought to acquire Maritime Industrial Services for £208 million, £139 million being from a rights issue. *The Investors Chronicle* recommended that investors should take up this rights issue.

By contrast, **public issues** and **placings** involve new shareholders. The public issue is distinguished from the placing chiefly by the fact that the shares are 'open' to public purchase rather than being privately allocated. In all three types of share issue, the company receives the amount that the shareholders pay for the shares. This money can then be used to finance expansion or on any other corporate activity. Stock market issues can make entrepreneurs potentially very rich. Real-World View 18.1 looks at the placing by Arbuthnot Banking Group of a quarter of its shares in the Alternative Investment Market of the UK Stock Exchange. This flotation is aimed at raising money to strengthen its retail subsidiary, the Secure Trust's loan book and also for possible future acquisitions.

REAL-WORLD VIEW 18.1

Placing

ARBUTHNOT Banking Group is to float its retail subsidiary, Secure Trust Bank, at 720p per share, valuing it at £102m, via a placing of almost a quarter of its equity next week on AIM. The remaining 75.5pc stake will be retained by Arbuthnot, which is controlled by Henry Angest, the multi-millionaire and Conservative Party donor. The flotation should raise £25m, with the £9.8m proceeds from the sale of new shares to be used for 'significant expansion' of Secure Trust's loan book and possible acquisitions. Paul Lynam, Secure Trust's chief executive, said: 'We have grown the loan book in the last 12 months to the end of June by almost 100pc on the back of a 47pc increase in our customers. We have more people looking to borrow from us than we have had the capital available to support. The retail bank lends in motor finance, retail point of sale and personal unsecured lending. Its half-year pre-tax profits this year were £5m. Arbuthnot will use the £12.4m proceeds from selling existing shares, and a £3.4m dividend from Secure Trust, to increase Arbuthnot's capital and develop strategic plans.

Source: E. Gosden (2011), Secure Trust Bank valued at £102m. *Daily Telegraph*, 29 October 2011, p. 35.

(c) Loan Capital

Loan capital is long-term borrowing. The holders of the loans are paid loan interest. Long-term loans are often known as **debentures**. Loan capital can chiefly be distinguished from ordinary share capital by five features. First, loan interest is a *deduction* from profits *not*, like dividends, a *distribution* of profits. Second, loan capital, unlike ordinary share capital, is commonly repaid. Third, unlike ordinary shareholders, the holders of loan capital do not own the company. Fourth, interest on loans may be allowable for tax purposes. And, finally, most loans will be secured either on the general assets of the company or on specific assets, such as land and buildings. In other words, if the company fails, the loan holders have first call on the company's assets. For example, in Real-World View 18.2, the debenture holders of Enterprise Inns are in the position whereby they are holding over 500 pubs as security. They will be able to sell the assets of the company to recover their loans.

REAL-WORLD VIEW 18.2

Security over Assets

I would advise continuing to hold a position in the Enterprise Inns 6.5 per cent 2018 bond. Operating profit continues to cover interest payments, albeit by a low multiple of 1.7 times and, importantly, bondholders have the security of a claim on over 500 pubs. While this is no great help in terms of servicing the debt, this debenture-like feature will help the recovery of the asset in the event of the company folding. On balance, I am happy to hold the security, but I am aware that over the medium-term the risk to the bond price is on the downside.

Source: Mark Glowrey, 'Enterprise Inns' last orders', 9–14 September 2011.

Sometimes convertible loans are issued which may be converted into ordinary shares at a specified future date.

Loans and debt have always attracted humorists, as Real-World Views 18.3 and 18.4 show.

REAL-WORLD VIEW 18.3

Loans

The Importance of Being Seen

Around the turn of the century a speculator by the name of Charles Flint got into financial difficulties. He had a slight acquaintance with J.P. Morgan, Sr., and decided to touch him for a loan. Morgan asked him to come for a stroll around the Battery in lower Manhattan. The two men discussed the weather in some detail, and other pressing matters, when finally, after about an hour or so, the exasperated Flint burst out: 'But Mr. Morgan, how about the million dollars I need to borrow?'

Morgan held out his hand to say goodbye: 'Oh, I don't think you'll have any trouble getting it now that we have been seen together.'

Source: Peter Hay (1988), *The Book of Business Anecdotes*, Harrap Ltd, London, p. 5.

REAL-WORLD VIEW 18.4

Debt

Stratagem

A moneylender complained to Baron Rothschild that he had lent 10,000 francs to a man who had gone off to Constantinople without a written acknowledgement of his debt.

'Write to him and demand back 50,000 francs,' advised the baron.

'But he only owes me 10,000,' said the moneylender.

'Exactly, and he will write and tell you so in a hurry. And that's how you will have acknowledgement of his debt.'

Source: Peter Hay (1988), *The Book of Business Anecdotes*, Harrap Ltd, London, p. 5.

As we saw in Figure 18.6, long-term capital or debt can be divided into private and public debt.

(i) Private Debt

Private debt can be seen as broadly bank debt. The company makes a one-to-one contract with a bank for a loan. This contract will usually include lots of detailed covenants between the company and the bank. These covenants will be based on financial information; for instance, there may be restrictions placed on the company's gearing ratio. The number of years of the loan and other details will be negotiated between the company and the bank. There may be limitations provided on additional borrowing by other third-party lenders.

Banks provide loans to companies. This debt capital is utilised both by small and large companies. Like corporate bonds, bank loans will carry rates of interest. The interest is paid by the bank. Bank loans are often called term loans as they are usually repayable after a fixed period of time. The terms of the loan are determined after discussion between the bank and the company. They may be secured on specific assets in which case they are often, in effect, mortgages. Or they could be unsecured. This is where they are secured on the general assets of the company rather than on any one particular asset.

(ii) Public Debt

Public debt differs in character from private debt as it is typically funding through the issuance of corporate bonds. The bond holders will receive remuneration by way of interest rather than dividends. These bonds will normally be for a set period of time. They can usually be bought and sold on the open market.

Another different form of international finance is the Eurobond. A Eurobond is a bond issued in the international capital market. These bonds are not specifically part of European Union financing. The bonds are often denominated in dollars. A consortium of originating banks will organise the issue, placing the bonds into the public domain. Other banks and institutions will decide whether or not to participate in the issue. They will then take up the bonds and keep them themselves or sell them on to clients. Interest is paid at an agreed rate. Again the Eurobond provides a source of capital for the original issuer and a source of income for the subsequent purchasers.

As we saw in Chapter 8, the relationship between ordinary share capital and a company's fixed interest funds (long-term loans and preference shares) is known as gearing. Gearing is particularly important when assessing the viability of a company's capital structure. Banks are particularly concerned with gearing when they lend money to companies.

Small and Medium-Sized Businesses

Small and medium-sized businesses face different problems in raising capital to listed companies. Listed companies are generally much bigger in terms of capital, revenue and number of employees. They will have established a reputation. For small businesses, however, which are often under-capitalised and very small in operational terms, there may be problems attracting capital. Indeed, many small businesses often struggle to obtain finance with many being forced into liquidation. Starting your own business is often a dream for many people, but it is also very risky.

Small businesses, such as sole traders or partnerships, will generally start with funding from one of three main sources: family, friends or the bank. Family money may, for example, be from savings or from other sources such as a redundancy or very commonly provided by taking out a second mortgage. Friends will supply money usually guaranteed on the company's assets or for a share in the profits. Finally, a bank overdraft or loan is frequently used, secured on the company's assets.

This money is often used to supply the infrastructural assets of the business, such as the property, or working capital, such as inventory. However, as the business grows, it may find itself struggling to expand – for example, to buy new premises or to employ more workers. The business then has a problem. Often this can be solved by increased bank loans. However, in some cases this is not enough. This is when sole traders or partnerships may convert into unlisted, private companies. The company may then resort to venture capital or to business angels.

(a) Venture Capital

Venture capital is a high-risk investment. It is capital that is targeted at small and medium-sized businesses that have run out of bank funding, but are not yet ready to consider a listing. There are advantages, but there also disadvantages to venture capital.

PAUSE FOR THOUGHT 18.3

You are a small company that has been trading for 6 years. You have been offered an investment of £100,000 by Ventcap.

What do you think the advantages and disadvantages of accepting Ventcap's offer are?

Although each venture capital offer will vary, it is likely that some of the following will apply.

Advantages
- Secure investment.
- Instant £100,000.

Disadvantages
- Ventcap is likely to take an equity stake in the company, which will dilute your ownership.
- Ventcap may well demand a seat on the board, which will affect your control of the company.

In essence, therefore, in venture capital the necessary funding will be provided, but the company will no longer be as free and independent as it was before. At the end of an agreed period (usually between 5 and 10 years), the venture capitalist is likely to sell its stake. By its very nature, venture capital is riskier than normal investment. However, there are potentially high rewards to the venture capitalist if the investment is successful. The venture capitalists are, therefore, in a sense, speculating that they can use their experience to pick winners!

(b) Business Angels

This is similar to venture capital. However, in this case the potential investors are individuals. Often they are themselves successful investors. Business angels have been popularised by the *Dragons' Den* TV programme where investors may lend money to individuals who convince them they have sound business plans. As with venture capitalists, business angels usually take a minority equity stake in the business. They also generally take an active part in the running of the company. So once again the small company gets an influx of capital – but at a price.

(c) Government Help

The final source of help for small businesses is from the government. In the UK, the government assists companies through the Enterprise Finance Guarantee Scheme, which helps businesses by providing a loan for a maximum of 10 years. The scheme was launched in 2008. It is designed to help small businesses and provide bank loans of up to £1 million. Its main aim is to provide businesses with working capital. The borrower pays interest.

Structure of the Business

As businesses grow, their structure will change as will the underlying source of finance. The nature of the capital providers will depend on the structure of the business. Thus, sole traders and partnerships will rely upon money from the owners of the businesses, supplemented by loans from friends or family or from the bank. This money will be sufficient when the business is small or even medium-sized. However, as the business grows, there will be a need to attract more outside investors as private debt and inside users will not be enough. Private limited companies will raise money by issuing shares. These will usually be held mainly by inside equity investors such as the directors and trading will be restricted. Private limited companies will also rely on private debt supplied by banks. The major changes come when a private limited company wishes to be listed on the stock market. This will require a share issue such as a public issue or placing. As a result, there will be a growth in outside investors. As the business grows, the shares will be publicly traded and the inside investors generally become less influential shareholders. There may also be public debt.

Cost of Capital

From the details of a company's different sources of finance, it is possible to determine its cost of capital (see Definition 18.1). In essence, the cost of capital is simply the cost at which a business raises funds. Companies aim to arrive at an optimal cost of capital. Cost of capital is often used as a discount rate in investment appraisal decisions. The two main sources of funds are debt (from long-term loans) and equity (from share capital). Normally, debt finance will be cheaper than equity. Each source of finance will have an associated cost of capital. However, it is important to calculate the business's overall cost of capital (known as the weighted average cost of capital or WACC).

WACC is the cost of capital normally used as the discount rate in capital investment appraisal (see Chapter 17). However, it should be borne in mind that individual projects will often be financed using different sources of finance which will not necessarily be the company's WACC. WACC is perhaps best seen as the company's targeted sustainable cost of capital. The same principles can be adopted for personal finance and for business. The proportion of the debt is multiplied by the effective cost of capital for each source. The cost of capital for debt finance is normally taken after taking into account the effect of interest. We take the examples of Deborah Ebt, a student, in Figure 18.8 and Costco plc in Figure 18.9.

DEFINITION 18.1

Weighted Average Cost of Capital (WACC)

'The average cost of the company's finance (including equity, debentures and bank loans) weighted according to the proportion each element bears to the total pool of capital.
Weighting is usually based on market valuations, current yields and costs after tax.

Example

Capital	Market Value	= Rate
Equity	$8M × 10%	= $0.8M
Debt	$4M × 8.45%	= $0.338M
Total	$12M	$1.138M

Weighted average cost 9.483% ($1.138 million/$12 million).

The weighted average cost of capital is often used as the measure to be used as the hurdle rate for investment decisions or as the measure to be minimised in order to find the capital structure for the company.'

Source: Chartered Institute of Management Accountants (2005), *Official Terminology.* Reproduced by Permission of Elsevier.

Figure 18.8 Calculation of Cost of Capital for a Student, D. Ebt

D. Ebt finances her college course as follows:

General expenses, by credit card	£3,000 at 25% interest per annum	
Accommodation, by bank loan	£4,000 at 10% interest per annum	
Car, by loan from uncle	£3,000 at 5% interest per annum	

What is D. Ebt's overall weighted average cost of capital?

Source of Finance	Proportion	Cost of Capital	Weighted Average Cost of Capital (WACC)
	£	%	%	%
Credit card	3,000	30	25	7.5
Bank loan	4,000	40	10	4.0
Personal loan	3,000	30	5	1.5
	10,000	100		13.0

Helpnote

The weighted average cost of capital is the proportion of total debt financed by loan source multiplied by interest rate. Therefore, for credit cards (£3,000/£10,000) × 25% = 7.5%. The cost of capital for each source of finance is simply the interest rate.

Figure 18.9 Example of a Company's Cost of Capital

Costco plc has 800,000 £1 ordinary shares currently quoted on the stock market at £2.50 each. It pays a dividend of 20p per share. Costco also has £200,000 worth of debt capital currently worth £1,000,000 on the stock market. The loan interest payable is 60,000.

Calculate Costco plc's weighted average cost of capital.

Source of Finance	Market Value	Proportion %	Cost of capital	Weighted Average Cost of Capital (WACC)
Equity	£2,000,000	66.67	8% (£0.20 ÷ £2.50)	5.3%
Debt	£1,000,000	33.33	6% (£60,000 ÷ £1,000,000)	2.0%
	£3,000,000	100.00		7.3%

The cost of capital is thus 7.3%.

Helpnote
We need to take the *market value* of the capital, not the original nominal value of the capital, as this is the value that the capital is *currently worth*. The cost of equity capital is simply the dividend divided by the share price and the cost of debt capital is the interest payable divided by the market price of the debt.

As Soundbite 18.1 below shows, cost of capital is an important business concept.

SOUNDBITE 18.1

Cost of Capital

'Business is the most important engine for social change in our society . . . And you're not going to transform society until you transform business. But you're not going to transform business by pretending it's not a business. Business means profit. You've got to earn your cost of capital. They didn't do it in the former Soviet Union, that's why it's former.'

Lawrence Perlman, *Twin Cities Business Monthly* (November 1994)

Source: The Wiley Book of Business Quotations (1998), p. 69. Reproduced by permission of John Wiley & Sons Ltd.

Figure 18.8 thus shows that overall the weighted average cost of capital is 13% for D. Ebt. The most expensive source of finance was the credit card and the cheapest was the personal loan.

Figure 18.9 thus indicates that overall the weighted average cost of capital is 7.3%. The equity capital constitutes most of this (i.e. 5.3%).

The cost of capital is a potentially complex and difficult subject. However, the basic idea is simple: the company is trying to find the optimal mix of debt and equity which will enable it to fund its business at the lowest possible cost. Investors show great interest in a company's cost of capital (see Real-World View 18.5).

REAL-WORLD VIEW 18.5

Railtrack's Cost of Capital

Cost of capital is a troublesome concept whose calculations vary from company to company. Bearbull, for example, looks at Railtrack's cost of capital and concludes that:

'As for cost of capital, it's a matter of guesswork – or the capital-asset pricing model – to calculate the figure in the first place. However, the rail regulator reckons that Railtrack's cost of capital is close to 7.5 per cent before both tax and inflation . . .'

According to Bearbull that means that Railtrack's total shareholder return would be 10% in addition to a dividend yield of 2.8%.

Source: Playing Monopoly, Bearbull, *The Investors Chronicle*, 4 August 2000, p. 18. Financial Times.

Conclusion

Sources of finance are essential to a business if it is going to grow and survive. We can distinguish between short-term and long-term sources of finance. Long-term sources of capital are used to fund the long-term activities of a business. The four main sources are an internal source (retained profits) and three external sources (leasing, share capital and loan capital). Share capital can be divided into outside professional investors, outside retail investors and inside equity investors. Loan capital can be seen as private debt (i.e., insider finance from banks and public debt (i.e., outsider finance from bond holders). Retained profits are not borrowings but, in effect, represent undistributed profits ploughed back into the business. Leasing involves a company using an asset, but not owning it. Shareholders own the company and are paid dividends. Loan capital providers do not own the company and are paid loan interest. A key function of managing long-term finance is to minimise a company's cost of capital, which is the effective rate at which a company can raise funds. Shares and bonds are often traded on international stock exchanges such as the London Stock Exchange. There are primary markets where the initial capital is raised and secondary markets where subsequent trading is conducted. On the London Stock Exchange there is the main market for large well-established companies and the Alternative Investment Market (AIM) for smaller companies. Stock markets are generally held to be efficient in that prices reflect historically available information. There is also an active Corporate Bond Market and a Eurobond Market. Smaller businesses have different financing needs and sometimes rely on business angels and venture capitalists.

Discussion Questions

Questions with numbers in blue have answers at the back of the book.

Q1 Why are the sources of finance available to a firm so important? What are the main sources of finance and which activities of a business might they finance?

Q2 What is the efficient market hypothesis?

Q3 What are the advantages and disadvantages of retained funds, debt and equity as methods of funding a business?

Q4 What is the weighted average cost of capital and why is it an important concept in business finance?

Q5 State whether the following statements are true or false. If false, explain why.
  (a) Long-term sources of finance are usually used to finance working capital.
  (b) There are four external long-term sources of finance: retained profits, leasing, share capital and loan capital.
  (c) A rights issue, a public issue and a placing are three major ways in which a company can raise share capital.
  (d) There are two main markets on the London Stock Exchange: the Main Exchange and Secondary Exchange.
  (e) EMH stands for effective market hypothesis.

Numerical Questions

Questions with numbers in blue have answers at the back of the book.

Q1 Albatross plc has the following information about its capital:

Source of Finance	Current Market Value	Present Cost of Capital
£million %		
Ordinary shares	4	12
Preference shares	1	10
Long-term loan	3	8

Required: What is Albatross's weighted average cost of capital?

Q2 Nebula plc is looking at its sources of finance. It collects the following details. Currently, there are 500,000 ordinary shares in issue, with a market price of £1.50 and a current dividend of £0.30. The number of preference shares in issue is 300,000, with a market price of £1.00 and a dividend of 15p. There are £200,000 of long-term debentures carrying 12% interest. These are currently trading at £220,000.

Required: Calculate Nebula's weighted average cost of capital.

Go online to discover the extra features for this chapter at
www.wiley.com/college/jones

Chapter 19

The management of working capital

'It doesn't take very long to screw up a company. Two, three months should do it. All it takes is some excess inventory, some negligence in collecting, and some ignorance about where you are.'

Source: Mary Baechler in *Inc.*, October (1994) quoted in *The Wiley Book of Business Quotations* (1998), p. 86.

Learning Outcomes

After completing this chapter you should be able to:

- Explain the nature and importance of working capital.
- Discuss the nature of short-term financing.
- Understand how to manage inventories, trade receivables, cash and trade payables.

Go online to discover the extra features for this chapter at
www.wiley.com/college/jones

Chapter Summary

- Working capital is how a company funds its short-term operations.
- Working capital can be defined as current assets less current liabilities.
- Companies will usually match short-term borrowings with short-term uses of capital.
- Short-term internal sources of finance concern the more efficient use of cash, trade receivables and inventory.
- Techniques for the internal management of working capital involve the trade receivables collection model, the economic order quantity and just-in-time inventory management.
- Short-term external sources of finance include a bank overdraft, a bank loan, trade payables, debt factoring, invoice discounting, and the sale and buy back of inventory.

Introduction

A business needs to fund its activities. These funds can be raised internally or externally. As we saw in Chapter 18, common forms of external financing are leasing, share capital, bonds and long-term loans. External financing is often long term in nature. By contrast, internal financing is normally much more short term. Internal financing is also different in nature. In essence it can be seen as using the working capital (current assets and liabilities) as efficiently as possible. Second, as well as efficient usage there is some dependence on external bodies such as banks or debt factoring companies. Trade payables are also an important source of short-term funding. They, along with equity and debt capital, are the three most important external capital providers.

Working Capital

Working capital can be seen as the engine of a business. It enables the business to survive from day to day. Working capital can be defined as current assets less current liabilities. These are, therefore, inventories, trade receivables and cash less trade payables and any short-term loans (often defined as less than two years).

The individual elements of working capital are interrelated. At their simplest, for example, inventories and cash are directly linked. So if we buy raw materials on credit then we will temporarily save cash, while if we sell inventories on credit then our cash will not immediately increase. This is because the money is tied up in, respectively, trade payables and trade receivables.

The amount and type of working capital vary from business to business. Thus, a knowledge-based industry may have a low level of inventory, while a traditional manufacturing business may have high levels of inventory. Retail stores, for example, typically carry high levels of inventory.

As we saw in Chapter 4, there is a working capital cycle (see Figure 4.7). Traditionally, this starts with cash that is paid to trade payables so that they will provide goods (inventory).

This inventory is then turned from raw material inventory into finished good inventory. These finished goods are then sold to customers, creating trade receivables. These trade receivables are then turned back into cash when the debtors pay the trade receivables. There is also cash paid out for wages and expenses. A healthy business will end up with more cash at the end of the working capital cycle than it had at the start.

Working capital is usually distinguished from non-current assets and non-current liabilities as being short-term. However, it is important to appreciate that while individual debtors and creditors are indeed short-term, the company will continually be selling goods, receiving money, buying goods and paying money. Therefore, in this sense, working capital itself is very long-term although its individual elements may be short-term.

Managing Working Capital

The essential idea of managing working capital is to use it as efficiently as possible. In essence, this will involve trying to minimise the amount of money tied up in working capital. As Figure 19.1 shows, the different elements of working capital need to be managed differently.

Figure 19.1 Managing Working Capital

Elements	Main Problems
1. Cash	Maintaining sufficient cash to pay trade payables, employees etc.
	Minimising the use of overdrafts.
2. Trade Receivables	Determining appropriate credit levels.
	Collecting debts as quickly as possible.
	Establishing a discount policy if necessary.
	Credit control.
3. Inventories	What is the appropriate level for raw materials and finished goods that balances holding sufficient inventory against the problems of stock outs?
4. Trade Payables	Making sure there is enough money available to pay the trade payables.

Planning and Evaluating Working Capital

There are various tools that can be used when planning working capital and then evaluating its efficiency. We look here at the two main ones: budgeting and ratio analysis.

(a) Budgeting

A company will usually include a set of budgets for the main aspects of working capital. These are outlined in more detail in Chapter 14, on budgeting. The five budgets that are most important directly to planning the individual elements of working capital are the cash budget, the trade receivables budget, the raw materials budget, the finished goods budget and the trade payables budget. The cash budget is reasonably complicated as it will include all the anticipated cash receipts and payments. However, the other four budgets are quite simple. The trade receivables and trade payables budgets are, in effect, mirror images. They start with the opening balances, add new credit sales/credit purchases and then deduct cash received and cash paid to arrive at the opening balance. The raw materials and finished goods budgets are also similar. They start with the opening inventories, add respectively purchases/production and then deduct raw materials and finished goods used in production/ cost of sales to arrive at the closing inventories. The only other common budget is the production cost budget, which determines the direct materials, direct labour and production overheads. This is then fed into the finished goods budget. Budgets are produced typically on a six months' basis.

(b) Ratio Analysis

A common way of assessing how efficiently the individual elements of working capital are performing is shown using ratios. These are discussed in more detail in Chapter 8. The main ratios for working capital are summarised in Figure 19.2. Detailed calculations are shown in Chapter 8.

Figure 19.2 Main Working Capital Ratios

Working Capital Element	Ratio	Ratio as at July 2005[1]
Current Ratio	Current assets / Current liabilities	2.16
Quick Ratio	Current assets – inventories / Current liabilities	1.80
Trade Receivables Collection Period	Average trade receivables / Credit sales per day	52 days
Trade Payables Collection Period	Average trade payables / Credit purchases per day	–
Inventory	Cost of sales / Average inventories	–

[1]Taken from Fame and Excel databases.

These ratios can be used to collectively assess the status of the company's working capital. The current ratio is most usually thought to be safest over 1.0 so that current assets exceed current liabilities. The quick ratio is often seen as desirable at above 0.7. If a company thinks its current ratio or quick ratio is too low, it could inject money into the business through a long-term loan. However, usually this is not desirable as normally it is not considered sensible to finance operating activities, such as production, through long-term borrowing. Long-term borrowing is generally reserved for capital expenditure such as the purchase of a new factory.

There are no general overall guidelines for the other ratios as they vary from business to business. However, the trade receivables and trade payables ratios are often matched. In theory, it should take as long to pay your creditors as your debtors take to pay you. However, in practice this is not always the case. In particular, many smaller suppliers, such as individual

PAUSE FOR THOUGHT 19.1

Matching Short- and Long-Term Financing

It is often considered a mistake to 'borrow short and use long' or 'to borrow long and use short'. What do you think this might mean? And why could it be a mistake?

Borrowing short and using long might be, for example, using a bank overdraft to finance a major infrastructural project. By contrast, borrowing long and using short would be, for example, to raise a long-term loan or share capital to finance the purchase of inventory. In both cases, there is a mismatch between the external source of funds and its internal use. For example, in the first instance, if the bank withdrew its overdraft facility, the company would be in real trouble with its infrastructural project. In the second instance, there is a long-term liability generated for a short-term financing need (i.e., the purchase of inventory). In the longer term, this is unsustainable.

farmers, feel that their large customers, such as big supermarkets, set very long credit periods which small suppliers such as farmers are forced to pay if they want to remain suppliers.

Short-Term Financing

Short-term financing is often called the management of working capital (current assets less current liabilities). One of the main aims is to reduce the amount of short-term finance that companies need to borrow for their day-to-day operations. The more money that is tied up in current assets, the more capital is needed to finance those current assets. Essentially, as well as using its working capital as efficiently as possible, a company may use short-term borrowings to finance its inventory, trade receivables or cash needs.

Figure 19.3 provides an overview of a company's short-term internal and external sources of finance. This includes *internal* management techniques for the efficient management of working capital (for example, trade receivables collection model, the economic order quantity and the just-in-time inventory model). The external sources of funds can be divided into those that are direct sources of funds, such as bank overdrafts or bank loans and trade payables (these are capital providers), and indirect sources of funds, such as invoice discounting, invoice factoring and sale and leaseback that are generated from the use of assets such as trade receivables or inventory to raise external funds.

Internal Financing
Companies will try to minimise their levels of working capital so as to avoid short-term borrowings. In this section, we look at the main elements of efficient working capital management and three important techniques used to control working capital levels. In Chapter 4, we looked at the working capital cycle.

Figure 19.3 Overview of Short-Term Sources of Finance

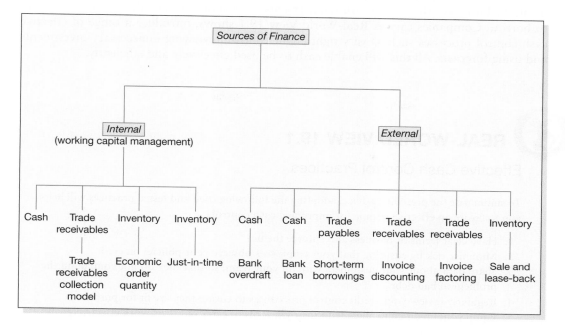

SOUNDBITE 19.1

Good Cash Control

'Wise FDs are taking some very valuable lessons forward into the recovery and showing a renewed respect for the importance of good cash control. They are committed to streamlining and automating their finance processes, improving the quality of management information, and gaining a clearer understanding of customers and suppliers.'

Source: Showing Cash Who's Boss, www.iris.co.uk/exchequer (Iris Accounting and Business Solutions), 2011.

(a) Cash

As we saw in Chapter 7, cash is the lifeblood of a business. Companies need cash to survive. As Soundbite 19.1 shows, good cash control is crucial especially in hard economic times.

Businesses will try to keep enough cash to manage their day-to-day business operations (e.g., purchase inventory and pay trade payables), but not to maintain excessive amounts of cash. Businesses prepare cash budgets (see Chapter 14), which enable them to forecast the levels of cash that they will need to finance their operations. They may also use the liquidity and quick ratios to assess their level of cash (see Chapter 8). If, despite careful cash management, the business's short-term cash requirements are insufficient then the business will have to borrow. Companies can, as Real-World View 19.1 shows, introduce a range of effective cash control processes such as very tight credit control, reviewing unnecessary investments and using forecasts. All this will enable cash to be used effectively and efficiently.

REAL-WORLD VIEW 19.1

Effective Cash Control Practices

To summarise the preceding advice, adopting the following tried and tested practices will help you to create an effective regime for improving cash control.

1. Have clear terms of business and enforce them.
2. Minimise risk by ensuring that your employees observe your policies on credit.
3. Share data about your customers with all your team, so that they do not compound the problem of bad debt.
4. Regularly review your credit control procedures to ensure they are fit for purpose.
5. Equip your credit controllers with the right tools to carry out their work effectively with minimum effort.
6. Free time for higher value work by using automation to help you manage by exception.
7. Use "paperless" technology to reduce costs while sharpening your credit processes.
8. Use eBanking to streamline and accelerate payments into your account.
9. Free up cash by reviewing and eliminating unnecessary investment across your business.
10. Constantly monitor your cash position, using technology to quickly generate meaningful reports.
11. Use cash flow as a business intelligence tool and stay alert to events that threaten your profitability.
12. Accurately forecast and manage your cash flow, so you know the position today and in six months' time.
13. Build your cash flow targets into your HR performance management processes.

Source: Showing Cash Who's Boss, www.iris.co.uk/exchequer (Iris Accounting and Business Solutions). 2011.

(b) Trade Receivables

Trade receivables management is a key activity within a firm. It is often called credit control. Trade receivables result from the sale of goods on credit. There is, therefore, the need to monitor carefully the receipts from trade receivables to see that they are in full and on time.

There will often be a separate department of a business concerned with credit control. The credit control department will, for example, establish credit limits for new customers, monitor the age of debts and chase up bad debts. In particular, they may draw up a trade receivables age schedule. This will profile the age of the debts and allow old debts to be quickly identified.

The credit control department will look at each customer and ideally should use discretion in determining the length of the credit period. The length of credit can vary depending on the product, the seller's liquidity position, the buyer's financial position and cash discounts. For example, an expensive product like a car might be sold over several years, whereas office stationery might be paid for in cash. If the seller is short of cash, the seller may be more reluctant to sell on credit. Whereas, if the buyer is short of cash then the buyer may not be able to buy the product at all without an extended credit period. Finally, if a discount is given then it will usually be for a cash payment. Obviously, cash is preferred to credit as it is immediate and there is no doubt about whether the debtor will pay.

PAUSE FOR THOUGHT 19.2

Advantages and Disadvantage of Credit

What do you think the advantages and disadvantages of offering credit are?

The simplest advantage is that you will increase revenue. More customers will buy your products. The disadvantages are, however, often quite substantial. The first is that the longer the credit period, the higher the risk of non-payment. The second is that the credit control department can often be quite expensive to run. The final disadvantage is that the company is without cash for longer. This will, for example, mean that it will lose out on interest receivable or even have to pay for interest on an overdraft.

When setting credit limits, the credit control department may follow certain procedures. It may, for example:

1. Run a credit check on a potential customer to establish its creditworthiness. This could involve a number of steps that are set out below.
2. Evaluate the past record of the customer in terms of prompt payment. This can be assessed for existing customers through past records.
3. Review the customer's past accounts (available, for example, from Company's House). This can be used for new customers. Company's House keeps records of past accounts.
4. Obtain a reference. This may be from a bank or from other past suppliers who have dealt with the customer.
5. Assess the honesty of the customer. This can be done via personal acquaintance, but also by asking business contacts.
6. Obtain the opinion of a specialist credit rating agency (often known as a credit bureau). This will provide a credit check and information on past creditworthiness. The credit rating agency will, however, normally charge for this.

7. Look at the Register of County Court Judgments. This will show whether any judgments against the customer for non-payment have been made.

Based on these credit checks, the company can decide whether or not to trade with the customer and what terms it might wish to offer. There are thus a lot of administrative costs involved in giving credit. Indeed, the credit collection process is continually trying to balance the costs of collection with the benefits of giving extended credit periods. This may involve using a trade receivables collection model.

Trade Receivables Collection Model

This is a useful technique designed to maintain the most efficient level of trade receivables for a company. A trade receivables collection model balances the extra revenue generated by increased revenue with the increased costs associated with extra revenue (i.e., credit control costs, bad debts and the delay in receiving money). The model assumes that the more credit granted, the greater the revenue. However, this extra revenue is offset by increased bad debts as the business sells to less trustworthy customers. Whether the delay in receipts means that the business receives less interest or pays out more interest depends on whether or not the bank account is overdrawn. Usually, the cost of capital (i.e., effectively, the company's borrowing rate: see Chapter 18) is used to calculate the financial costs of the delayed receipts. Figure 19.4 illustrates the trade receivables collection model.

(c) Inventory

For many businesses, especially for manufacturing businesses, inventory is often an extremely important asset. Inventory is needed to create a buffer against excess demand, to protect against rising prices or against a potential shortage of raw materials and to balance revenue and production.

Inventory control is concerned not primarily with valuing inventory (see Chapter 13), but with protecting the inventory physically and ensuring that the optimal level is held. Inventory may be stolen or may deteriorate. For many businesses, such as supermarkets, the battle against theft and deterioration is never-ending. A week-old lettuce in a supermarket is not a pleasant asset!! For supermarkets, inventory can also be a competitive advantage (see Real-World View 19.2). Woolworth, a UK company, went on to build a nationwide chain of shops and proved very successful for over a century until its demise in the credit crunch in 2010.

REAL-WORLD VIEW 19.2

Inventory

A Way to Look at It
'When F.W. Woolworth opened his first store, a merchant on the same street tried to fight the new competition. He hung out a big sign: "Doing business in this same spot for over fifty years". The next day Woolworth also put out a sign. It read: "Established a week ago; no old stock [inventory]".'

Source: Peter Hay (1988), *The Book of Business Anecdotes*, Harrap Ltd, London, p. 275.

Figure 19.4 Trade Receivables Collection Model

Bruce Bowhill is the finance director of a business with current revenue of £240,000. If credit rises, so do bad debts. The contribution is 20%, the cost of capital is 15%, the credit control costs are £10,000 per annum at all levels of revenue.

Credit	Annual revenue	Bad Debts
Nil	£240,000	–
1 month	£320,000	1%
2 months	£500,000	5%
3 months	£650,000	10%

What is the most favourable level of revenue?

We need to balance the increased contribution earned by increased revenue with the increased costs of easier credit (i.e., credit control, bad debts and cost of capital).

	Nil credit £	1 month £	2 months £	3 months £
Revenue	240,000	320,000	500,000	650,000
Contribution 20%	48,000	64,000	100,000	130,000
Cost of credit control		(10,000)	(10,000)	(10,000)
Bad debts 1% revenue		(3,200)		
5% revenue			(25,000)	
10% revenue				(65,000)
Cost of capital relating to delay in payment: 15% of average trade receivables*		(4,000)	(12,500)	(24,375)
Revised Contribution	48,000	46,800	52,500**	30,625

*Average trade receivables per month
= £26,667   (£320,000 ÷ 12) (1 month)
= £83,333   (£500,000 ÷ 6)   (2 months)
= £162,500   (£650,000 ÷ 4)   (3 months)

**The optimal level is thus two months as it has the highest revised contribution.

Three common techniques associated with efficient inventory control are materials requirement planning and/or the economic order quantity model and just-in-time inventory management.

(i) Materials Requirement Planning (MRP) and Economic Order Quantity (EOQ). Material requirements planning (see Definition 19.1) is a sophisticated approach designed to coordinate the production process, particularly the purchase of raw materials. It was devised in the 1960s as a computerised program designed to coordinate the acquisition of materials.

This program has subsequently been updated to include other areas of corporate activity such as finance, logistics, engineering and marketing (MRPII) (see Definition 19.1). MRP can be used in conjunction with EOQ, which is a way of determining the optimal size of inventory that is required by a company.

DEFINITION 19.1

Material Requirements Planning (MRP) and Manufacturing Resource Planning (MRPII)

Material requirements planning (MRP)
'System that converts a product schedule into a listing of materials and components required to meet that schedule, so that adequate stock [inventory] levels are maintained and items are available when needed.'

Manufacturing resource planning (MRPII)
'Expansion of material requirements planning (MRP) to give a broader approach than MRP to the planning and scheduling of resources, embracing areas such as finance, logistics, engineering and marketing.'

Source: Chartered Institute of Management Accountants (2005), *Official Terminology*. Reproduced by Permission of Elsevier.

The EOQ model seeks to determine the optimal order quantity needed to minimise the costs of ordering and holding inventory. These costs are the costs of placing the order and the carrying costs. Carrying costs are those costs incurred in keeping an item in inventory, such as insurance, obsolescence, interest on borrowed money or clerical/security costs. The costs of ordering inventory are mainly the clerical costs. The EOQ can be determined either graphically or algebraically. Figure 19.5 on the next page demonstrates both methods. A key assumption underpinning the EOQ model is that the inventory is used in production at a steady rate. A much simpler but effective method of stock control is called the 'two bins system'. In essence, once one bin is used up then an order is placed to replenish this bin, while the other bin is used up.

(ii) Just-in-Time. Just-in-time was developed in Japan, where it has proved an effective method of inventory control. As Definition 19.2 shows, there are various types of just-in-time (i.e., production and purchasing).

Just-in-time seeks to minimise inventory holding costs by the careful timing of deliveries and efficient organisation of production schedules. At its best, just-in-time works by delivering inventory just before it is used. The amount of inventory is thus kept to a minimum and inventory holding costs are also minimised. In order to do this, there is a need for a very streamlined and efficient production and delivery service. The concept behind just-in-time has been borrowed

Figure 19.5 Economic Order Quantity

Tree plc has the following information about the Twig, one of its inventory items. The Twig has an average yearly use in production of 5,000 items. Each Twig costs £1 and the company's cost of capital is 10% per annum. For each Twig, insurance costs are 2p per annum, storage costs are 2p per annum and the cost of obsolescence is 1p. The ordering costs are £60 per order.

i. Graphical Solution

We must first compile a table of costs at various order levels. For example, at an order quantity of 500, Tree needs 10 orders per annum (i.e., to buy 5,000 Twigs) which would give a total order cost of £600. The average quantity in inventory (250) will be half the order quantity (500). As it costs 15 pence to carry an item, the total carrying cost will be £37.50 (i.e., 250 × 15p). Finally, the total cost will be £637.50 (total order cost £600 plus total carrying cost £37.50).

Order quantity (Q)	Average number of orders per annum	Order cost	Total order cost	Average quantity in inventory	Carrying cost per item of inventory	Total carrying cost	Total cost
			(1)	(2)	(3)	(4)	(5)
		£	£		£	£	£
500	10	60	600	250	0.15	37.50	637.50
1,000	5	60	300	500	0.15	75.00	375.00
2,000	2.5	60	150	1,000	0.15	150.00	300.00
2,500	2	60	120	1,250	0.15	187.50	307.50
5,000	1	60	60	2,500	0.15	375.00	435.00

Notes from table:
(1) Number of orders per annum multiplied by order cost.
(2) This represents half the order quantity. It assumes steady usage and instant delivery of inventory.
(3) Cost of capital 10p (10% × £1), insurance 2p, storage 2p, obsolescence 1p. All per item.
(4) Average quantity in inventory (2) multiplied by the carrying cost of £0.15 (3).
(5) Total order cost (1) and total carrying cost (4).

The graph can now be drawn with order quantity on the horizontal axis and annual costs along the vertical axis. The intersection of carrying cost and ordering cost represents the optimal re-order level. The optimal order quantity is thus close to 2,000.

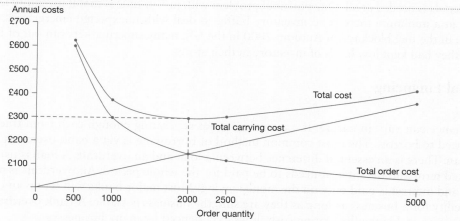

ii. Algebraic Solution

Fortunately, there is no need to know how to derive this formula, just apply it.

$$Q = \sqrt{\frac{2AC}{i}}$$ where Q = economic order quantity
A = average annual usage
C = cost of each order being placed
i = carrying cost per unit per annum

$$\therefore Q = \sqrt{\frac{2 \times 5,000 \times 60}{0.15}} = 2,000 \text{ Twigs}$$

DEFINITION 19.2

Just-in-time (JIT)

'System whose objective is to produce or to procure products or components as they are required by a customer or for use, rather than for stock.

Just-in-time system. Pull system, which responds to demand in contrast to a *push* system, in which stocks act as buffers between the different elements of the system such as purchasing, production and sales.

Just-in-time production. Production system which is driven by demand for finished products, whereby each component on a production line is produced only when needed for the next stage.

Just-in-time purchasing. Purchasing system in which material purchases are contracted so that the receipt and usage of material, to the maximum extent possible, coincide.'

Source: Chartered Institute of Management Accountants (2005), *Official Terminology.* Reproduced by permission of Elsevier.

NB: This definition still uses stock rather than inventory. Either is permissible.

by many UK and US firms. Taken to its logical extreme, just-in-time means that no inventory of raw materials is needed at all. One potential problem with just-in-time is that if inventory levels are kept at a minimum there is no inventory buffer to deal with unexpected emergencies. For example, in the fuel blockade of Autumn 2000 in the UK, many supermarkets ran out of food because they had kept low levels of inventory in their stores.

External Financing

(a) Cash

Bank finance can vary in nature. If a company is not generating enough cash from trading, it may need to borrow. The most common method of borrowing is via a bank overdraft or a bank loan. There is an essential difference between a loan and an overdraft. A loan is usually for a fixed term and the interest needs to be paid for the whole period. An overdraft is more flexible and interest is paid only on the money owing. Most major banks will set up an overdraft facility for a business as long as they are sure the business is viable. A bank overdraft is a good way to tackle the fluctuating cash flows experienced by many businesses.

The exact terms of individual bank loans will vary. However, essentially a loan is for a set period of years and this may well be more than two years. The rate of interest on a loan will normally be lower than on a bank overdraft. Loans may be secured on business assets, for example specific assets, such as inventory or motor vehicles. This resembles an individual borrowing money from a building society or bank to purchase a house and securing the mortgage on the house. A loan may also have covenants attached to it, such as specifying a

PAUSE FOR THOUGHT 19.3

Bank Overdrafts

A bank overdraft represents a flexible way for a business to raise money. Can you think of drawbacks?

....

Overdrafts usually carry relatively high rates of interest. Overdrafts often carry variable rates of interest and are subject to a limit, which should not be exceeded without authorisation from the bank. They can be withdrawn at very short notice and are normally repayable on demand. Generally, interest is determined by time period and security. The shorter the time period, the higher the interest rate typically paid. In addition, if the loan is not secured on an asset (i.e., is unsecured) the rate of interest charged will once again be higher. Small businesses without a track record may often find it difficult to get a bank overdraft. Even when an overdraft is granted, the bank may insist that it is secured against the company's assets.

ratio of debt to equity that the firm is expected to adhere to, restricting payment of dividends to shareholders or restricting the issuance of future debt to third parties.

In the UK, companies are more dependent on short-term financing than in some other European countries, such as Germany. Indeed, it is often said that German banks are long-term investors, whereas UK banks are short-term. UK companies can borrow from a variety of UK banks. The most well known are the high street banks such as Barclays, HSBC, Lloyds and the National Westminster. However, there are also other banks, such as accepting houses. Accepting houses guarantee bills of exchange which are offered for sale by the UK Treasury every week. UK companies can also borrow from international banks. Bank finance is nowadays global. Each country will have its own banks. However, there are also many global banks which will conduct operations internationally. As we saw in Chapter 18, this form of financing is sometimes termed private debt.

The cost of borrowing varies depending upon the length of the loan, the purpose and the individual circumstances. Banks generally lend on the basis of some security. This might, for example, be property, plant and equipment or general net assets. However, there is always the residual problem of bad debts. Indeed, the global financial crisis revealed that many leading banks had loaned money on the basis of inadequate security. To avoid bad debts, banks have over the years developed various credit scoring systems. These seek to assess the creditworthiness of individual companies.

(b) Trade Payables

Trade payables are a source of finance as until they are paid, the creditors are effectively loaning money to the business. In some businesses, creditors will be paid after 120 days which represents, in effect, a loan to the company for 4 months. Most companies buy and sell on credit; therefore, trade payables become a very important source of finance. As we saw in Chapter 18, Cascino et al. (2013) in the use of information by capital providers, estimated that across Europe and the US about 33% and 24% of capital provided was from current liabilities (trade payables), thus making it the second biggest source after share capital (equity). Despite this, the role that trade payables play in financing firms is often overlooked. It is a truism to relate that one company's debtor is another company's creditor. There is thus a complicated network of accounts receivable and accounts payable. Large buyers often exploit their purchasing power over smaller suppliers and gain extended credit. In the UK, for example, there has been concern in 2014 that some government departments in the UK are not paying small suppliers promptly. As a result, this is hindering the growth and development of those small companies. The whole determination of a company's credit policy can be quite complex. It has been discussed earlier in this chapter under our discussion on trade receivables and internal financing. The policy can be dependent on a variety of financial and non-financial factors such as industry standards.

(c) Trade Receivables

Since trade receivables are an asset, it is possible to raise money against them. This is done by debt factoring or invoice discounting.

(i) *Debt factoring.* Debt factoring is, in effect, the subcontracting of trade receivables. Many department stores, for example, find it convenient to subcontract their credit sales to debt factoring companies. The advantage to the business is twofold. First, it does not have to employ staff to chase up the trade receivables. Second, it receives an advance of money from the factoring organisation. There are, however, potential problems with factoring. The debt factoring company is not a charity and will charge a fee, for example 4% of revenue, for its services. In addition, the debt factoring company will charge interest on any cash advances to the company. Finally, the company will lose the management of its customer database to an external party. As Soundbite 19.2 shows, debt factoring has traditionally been viewed with some suspicion.

(ii) *Invoice discounting.* Invoice discounting, in effect, is a loan secured on trade receivables. The financial institution will grant an advance (for example, 75%) on outstanding sales invoices (i.e., trade receivables). Invoice discounting can be a one-off, or a continuing, arrangement. An important advantage of invoice discounting over debt factoring is that the credit control function is not contracted out. The company, therefore, keeps control over its records of trade receivables. Figure 19.6 compares debt factoring with invoice discounting.

The aim of trade receivables management is simply to collect money from trade receivables as soon as possible.

For an optimal cash balance, with no considerations of fairness, a business will benefit if it can accelerate its receipts and delay its payments. Receipts from customers and payments to suppliers are measured using the trade receivables/trade payables collection period ratio (see Chapter 8).

SOUNDBITE 19.2

Debt Factoring

'Handing over your sales ledger to a factor was once viewed in the same league as Dr Faustus flogging his soul off to the devil – a path of illusory rides that would lead only to inevitable business ruin and damnation.'

Jerry Frank, *No Longer a Deal with the Devil*

Source: *Accountancy Age*, 18 May 2000, p. 27.

Figure 19.6 Comparison of Debt Factoring and Invoice Discounting

Element	Debt Factoring	Invoice Discounting
Loan from financial institution	Yes	Yes
Sales ledger (i.e., keeping records of debtors)	Management by financial institution	Managed by company
Time period	Continuing	Usually one-off, but can be continuing

(d) Inventory

As with trade receivables, it is sometimes possible to borrow against inventory. However, the time period is longer. Inventory needs to be sold, then the trade receivables need to pay. Inventory is not, therefore, such an attractive basis for lending for the financial institutions. However, in certain circumstances, financial institutions may be prepared to buy the inventory now and then sell it back to the company at a later date.

PAUSE FOR THOUGHT 19.4

Sale and Buy Back of Inventory

Can you think of any businesses where it may take such a long time for inventory to convert to cash that businesses may sell their inventory to third parties?

The classic example of sale and buy back occurs in the wine and spirit business. It takes a long time for a good whisky to mature. A finance company may, therefore, be prepared to buy the inventory from the whisky distillery and then sell it back at a higher price at a future time. In effect, there is a loan secured against the whisky and the retailer will be paying an interest/service charge to the finance company.

Another example might be in the construction industry. Here the financial institution may be prepared to loan the construction company money in advance. The money is secured on the work-in-progress which the construction company has already completed. The construction company repays the loan when it receives money from the customers. It will repay the original amount plus what is, in effect, an interest or service charge.

Conclusion

Working capital can be defined as current assets less current liabilities. Short-term financing concerns the management of working capital: cash, trade receivables and inventory. This may involve the more efficient use of working capital using various techniques such as the trade receivables collection model and the economic order quantity model. Alternatively, it may involve raising loans from the bank by an overdraft, or loans secured on trade receivables by debt factoring, or by the sale and leaseback of inventory. It can also involve using trade payables as a supplier of capital. Companies will often use budgeting and ratio analysis to evaluate how efficiently they are using their working capital. Normally a company will finance its short capital needs by short-term capital rather than long-term borrowing. There are a variety of different bank loans possible. Companies will often set up a credit control department to assess potential customers' credit risks and to set credit limits for its customers.

 Discussion Questions

Questions with numbers in blue have answers at the back of the book.

Q1 What is working capital and how might a company try to manage it?

Q2 How might a company try to plan and evaluate its working capital?

Q3 Why would a company funding an infrastructure project of ten years in length be unlikely to use a short-term loan or overdraft to finance it?

Q4 State whether the following statements are true or false. If false, explain why.
   (a) A trade receivables collection model seeks the efficient management of trade receivables by balancing the benefits of extra credit sales against the extra costs of those sales.
   (b) Two common techniques of inventory control are the economic order quantity model and the just-in-time approach.
   (c) Working capital is current assets less current liabilities.
   (d) The current ratio should normally be under 1.
   (e) Bank overdrafts are more flexible than loans and are available on fixed term.

Numerical Questions

Questions with numbers in blue have answers at the back of the book.

Q1 Lathe plc is a small manufacturing firm. It buys in a subcomponent, the Tweak, for £1.50. The cost of insurance and storage per Tweak are £0.40 and £0.50 per item per year, respectively. It costs £25 for each order. The annual quantity purchased is 20,000.

Required:
(i) What is the economic order quantity? Solve this (a) graphically and (b) algebraically.
(ii) What are the total costs per annum at this level?

Q2 A bookshop, Bookworm, buys 2,500 copies of the book *Deep Heat* per year. It costs the bookshop £0.80 per annum to carry the book as inventory and £20 to prepare a new order.

Required:
(i) The total costs if orders are 1, 2, 5, 10 and 20 times per year.
(ii) The economic order quantity. An algebraic solution only is required.

Q3 Winter Brollies wishes to revise its credit collection policy. Currently it has £500,000 revenue, a credit policy of 25 days and an average collection period of 20 days. 1% of debtors default. Credit control costs are £5,000 for 25 days and 30 days; £6,000 for 60 days and 90 days. There is the following potential forecast for revenues:

Credit Period (Days)	Average Collection Period (Days)	New Annual Revenue (£)	Bad Debts (%)
30	25	600,000	2
60	55	700,000	4
90	85	800,000	8

The cost of capital is 10% and the average contribution is 20% on selling price. Assume 360 days in year.

Required: Advise Winter Brollies whether or not it should revise its credit policy.

Go online to discover the extra features for this chapter at
www.wiley.com/college/jones

Glossary of Key Accounting and Finance Terms

This glossary contains most of the key accounting terms that students are likely to encounter. Words highlighted in bold are explained elsewhere in the glossary.

Absorption costing
The form of costing used for valuing inventory for external financial reporting. All the overheads which can be attributed to a product are recovered. Unlike **marginal costing**, which can sometimes be used for inventory valuation, absorption costing includes both fixed and variable production overheads.

Acid test ratio
See **quick ratio**.

Accounting
The provision of information to managers and owners so they can make business decisions.

Accounting concept
A principle underpinning the preparation of accounting information.

Accounting Council
The Accounting Council took over from the **ASB** in 2012. It is the body which now sets UK accounting standards under the **Accounting Council**. The Accounting Council has taken over the role of the Urgent Issues Task Force (UITF).

Accounting equation
The basic premise that **assets** equal **liabilities**.

Accounting period
The time period for which the accounts are prepared. Audited financial statements are usually prepared for a year.

Accounting policies
The specific accounting methods selected and followed by a company in areas such as **revenue**, foreign currencies, inventories, goodwill and pensions.

Accounting rate of return
A method of **capital investment appraisal** which assesses the viability of a project using annual profit and initial capital invested.

Accounting standards
Accounting pronouncements which set out the disclosure and measurement rules businesses must follow to give a **true and fair view** when drawing up accounts.

Accounting Standards Board (ASB)
Until 2012, when it was replaced by the **Accounting Council**, this body set the UK's accounting standards.

Accruals
The amounts owed to the suppliers of services at the statement of financial position date, for expenses such as telephone or light and heat.

Accruals concept
See **matching concept**.

Accumulated depreciation
The total depreciation on **property, plant and equipment** including this year's and prior years' depreciation.

Activity-based costing
A cost recovery technique which identifies key activities and key activity **cost drivers**.

Alternative Investment Market (AIM)
On the London Stock Exchange where the newer, smaller companies are traded.

Annual report
A report produced annually by a **company** comprising both financial and non-financial information.

Appropriation account
The sharing out of partners' profit after net profit has been calculated in the **income statement**.

Asset turnover ratio
A ratio which compares **revenue** to total assets employed.

Assets
Essentially, items owned or leased by a business. Assets may be tangible or intangible, current or non-current. Assets bring economic benefits through either sale (for example, inventory) or use (for example, a car).

Associated company
A company in which 20–50% of the shares are owned by another company or in which another company has a significant influence.

Attainable standard cost
A **standard cost** which can be reached with effort.

Audit and Assurance Council
This body, created in 2012, advises the FRC board and the **Codes and Standards Committee** on audit and assurance matters.

Auditors
A team of professionally qualified accountants *independent* of a company. Appointed by the **shareholders** on the recommendation of the **directors**, the auditors check and report on the accounts prepared by the directors.

Auditors' report
A statement in a company's **annual report** which states whether the financial statements present a '**true and fair view**' of the company's activities over the previous financial year.

Authorised share capital
The amount of **share capital** that a company is *allowed* to issue to its shareholders.

Average cost (AVCO)
A method of inventory valuation where inventory is valued at the average purchase price (see also **first-in-first-out** and **last-in-first-out**).

Bad debts
Those debts that will definitely not be paid. They are an **expense** in the **income statement** and are written off **trade receivables** in the **statement of financial position**.

Balance off
In **double-entry bookkeeping**, the accounts are balanced off and the figures for **assets** and **liabilities** are carried forward to the next period. In effect, this signals the end of an **accounting period**.

Balance sheet – Alternative name for Statement of financial position
A financial statement which is a snapshot of a business at a particular point in time. It records the **assets, liabilities** and **equity** of a business. Assets less liabilities equal equity. Equity is the owners' interest in the business.

Bank overdraft
A business or individual owes the bank money.

Batch costing
A number of items of a similar nature are processed and costed together (e.g., baking bread).

Bookkeeping

The preparation of the basic accounts. Monetary transactions are entered into the books of account. A **trial balance** is then extracted, and an **income statement** and a **statement of financial position** are prepared.

Break-even analysis

Break-even analysis involves calculating the point at which a product or service makes neither a profit nor a loss. **Fixed costs** are divided by the contribution per unit giving the **break-even point**.

Break-even point

The point at which a firm makes neither a profit nor a loss. A firm's break-even point can be expressed as: **Revenue** – variable costs – fixed costs = 0.

Budget

A future plan which sets out a business's financial targets.

Budgeting

Budgeting involves setting future targets. Actual results are then compared with budgeted results. Any **variances** are then investigated.

Business review

Required by European legislation and incorporated into the 2006 Companies Act. Businesses give a narrative view of, for example, their strategies and business models.

Business angel

Someone who provides capital for a small company in return for an equity stake and often a seat on the board.

Called-up share capital

The amount of **issued share capital** that is fully paid up by **shareholders**. For example, a share may be issued for £1.50 and paid in three equal instalments. After two instalments the called-up share capital is £1.

Capital

An alternative to **equity** often used for sole traders, partnerships or private limited companies.

Capital expenditure

A payment to purchase an **asset** with a long life such as **property, plant and equipment**.

Capital expenditure and financial investment

In a **statement of cash flows** prepared under UK accounting standards, cash flows relating to the purchase and sale of **property, plant and equipment** and **investments**.

Capital investment appraisal

A method of evaluating long-term **capital expenditure decisions**.

Capital investment decisions
Usually long-term decisions (such as building a new factory).

Capital maintenance concept
A way of determining whether the 'equity' of a business has improved, deteriorated or stayed the same over a period of time. There is both financial and physical capital maintenance.

Capital reserves
Reserves not distributable to shareholders as dividends (e.g., the share premium account or revaluation reserve).

Carriage inwards
The cost of delivering raw materials. Refers to the days when goods were delivered by horse and carriage.

Carriage outwards
The cost of delivering the finished goods. Refers to the days when goods were delivered by horse and carriage.

Carrying costs
Costs such as insurance, obsolescence, interest on borrowed money or clerical/security costs incurred in holding inventory.

Cash and bank
The actual money held by the business either at the business as cash or at the bank.

Cash and cash equivalent
This is cash at bank and cash held in short-term (say up to 30 days) deposit accounts.

Cash at bank
Money deposited with a bank.

Cash book
In large businesses, a separate book which records cash and cheque transactions.

Cash budget
This budget records the projected inflows and outflows of cash.

Cash flow statement
Alternative name for the statement of cash flows used under UK GAAP. A financial statement which shows the cash inflows and outflows of a business.

Chairman's statement
A statement in a company's annual report which provides a personalised overview of the company's performance over the past year. It generally covers strategy, financial performance and future prospects.

Codes and Standards Committee

Established in 2012. It is responsible for advising the FRC board on monitoring an effective framework of UK codes and standards for corporate governance, stewardship, accounting, auditing and assurance and actuarial technical standards. This board is advised by the **Accounting Council**.

Companies Acts

Acts of Parliament which lay down the legal requirements for companies including accounting regulations.

Company

A business enterprise where the **shareholders** have **limited liability**.

Conceptual framework

A coherent and consistent set of accounting principles which underpin the preparation and presentation of financial statements.

Consistency concept

An accounting principle which states similar items should be treated similarly from year to year.

Contract costing

A form of **costing** in which costs are allocated to contracts (i.e., usually big jobs which occur in construction industries such as shipbuilding). A long-term contract extends over more than one year and creates the problem of when to take profit.

Contribution

Contribution to fixed overheads, or contribution in short, is **revenue** less **variable costs**.

Contribution analysis

A technique for short-term decision making where **fixed costs, variable costs** and **contribution** are analysed. The objective is to maximise a company's contribution (and thus profit) when choosing between different operating decisions.

Contribution graph

A graph which plots cumulative contribution against cumulative **revenue**. Also called a profit/volume graph.

Controllable cost

A cost that a manager can influence and that a manager can be held responsible for.

Corporate bond

A bond issued to investors by a company that pays a rate of interest.

Corporate governance
The system by which companies are directed and controlled. The financial aspects of corporate governance relate principally to internal control and the way in which the board of directors functions and reports to the shareholders on the activities and progress of the company.

Cost
An item of expenditure (planned or actually incurred).

Cost accounting
Essentially, **costing** and **planning and control**.

Cost allocation
The process by which **indirect costs** are recovered into total cost or into inventory.

Cost centre
In **responsibility accounting**, where a manager is held responsible for costs.

Cost driver
In **activity-based costing**, a factor causing a change in an activity's costs.

Cost minimisation
Minimising cost either by tight budgetary control or cutting back on expenditure.

Cost of capital
The interest rate at which a business raises funds.

Cost of sales
Essentially the cost of directly providing the **revenue**.

Cost recovery
The process by which costs are recovered into a product or service to form the basis of pricing or inventory valuation.

Cost-volume-profit analysis
A **management accounting** technique which looks at the effect of changes in fixed costs, variable costs and **revenue** on profit. Also called **contribution analysis**.

Costing
Recovering **costs** as a basis for pricing and inventory valuation.

Creative accounting
Using the flexibility within accounting to manage the measurement and presentation of the accounts so that they serve the interests of the preparers.

Credit
An entry on the right-hand side of a 'T' account. Records principally increases in **liabilities, equity** or **income**. May also record decreases in **assets** or **expenses**.

Credit control
Controlling **trade receivables** by establishing credit limits for new customers, monitoring the age of debts and chasing up **bad debts**.

Creditors
Alternative name for trade payables. Amounts owed to trade suppliers for goods supplied on credit, but not yet paid.

Creditors budget
An alternative name for the **trade payables budget**. This **budget** forecasts the level of future trade payables. It keeps a running balance of the **trade payables** by adding purchases and deducting cash payments.

Creditors collection period
An alternative term for the **trade payables** collection period (sometimes used for sole traders, partnerships and non-listed companies). Measures how long a business takes to pay its **trade payables** by relating the **trade payables** to cost of sales.

Current assets
Those **assets** (e.g., **inventories, trade receivables** and **cash**) that a company uses in its day-to-day operations.

Current liabilities
The liabilities that a business uses in its day-to-day operations (e.g., **trade payables**).

Current purchasing power
A **measurement system** where historical cost is adjusted by general changes in the purchasing power of money (e.g., inflation), often measured using the retail price index (RPI).

Current ratio
A short-term test of liquidity which determines whether short-term **assets** cover short-term **liabilities**.

Debenture
Another name for a **long-term loan**. Debentures may be **secured** or **unsecured loans**.

Debit
An entry on the left-hand side of a 'T' account. Records principally increases in either **assets** or **expenses**. May also record decreases in **liabilities, equity** or **income**.

Debt factoring

Where the **trade receivables** are subcontracted to a third party who is paid to manage them.

Debtors

An alternative term for **trade receivables** sometimes used for sole traders, partnerships or non-listed companies. When there are credit sales, but the customers have not yet paid.

Debtors age schedule

An alternative name for **trade receivables age schedule** for sole traders, partnerships or non-listed companies. A credit control technique which profiles the age of the debts and allows old debts to be quickly identified.

Debtors budget

An alternative name for the **trade receivables** budget for sole traders, partnerships or non-listed companies. This **budget** forecasts the level of future **trade receivables**. It keeps a running balance of trade receivables by adding **revenue** and deducting cash received.

Debtors collection model

An alternative name for the **trade receivables collection model** (for sole traders, partnerships or non-listed companies). A technique for managing **working capital** which seeks to maintain the most efficient level of **trade receivables** for a company. It balances the extra revenue generated by increased **revenue** with the increased costs associated with extra **revenue** (e.g., credit control costs, bad debts and the delay in receiving money).

Debtors collection period

An alternative name for the **trade receivables collection period**. A ratio which measures how long customers take to pay their debts by relating **trade receivables** to **revenue**.

Decision-making in management accounting

The choice between alternatives. Only **relevant costs and revenues** should be considered.

Decision-making objective of financial reporting

Providing users, especially shareholders, with financial information so that they can make decisions such as whether to buy or sell shares.

Depreciation

Depreciation attempts to match a proportion of the original cost of the **property, plant and equipment** to the **accounting period** in which the property, plant and equipment were used up as an annual expense.

Direct costs

Costs directly identifiable and attributable to a product or service (e.g., the amount of direct labour or direct materials incurred). Sometimes called **product costs**.

Direct labour overall variance
Standard cost of labour for actual production less actual cost of labour used in production.

Direct labour price variance
(Standard price per hour – actual price per hour) × actual quantity of labour used.

Direct labour quantity variance
(Standard quantity of labour hours for actual production – actual quantity of labour hours used) × standard labour price per hour.

Direct materials overall variance
Standard cost of materials for actual production less actual cost of materials used in production.

Direct materials price variance
(Standard price per unit of material – actual price per unit of material) × actual quantity of materials used.

Direct materials quantity variance
(Standard price per unit of material – actual price per unit of material) × actual quantity of materials used.

Direct method of preparing the statement of cash flows
Classifies *operating* cash flows by function or type of activity (e.g., receipts from customers).

Directors
Those responsible for running the business. Accountable to the **shareholders** who, in theory, appoint and dismiss them.

Directors' remuneration report
A statement in an **annual report** in which companies include details of their directors' pay.

Directors' report
A narrative statement in an **annual report**. It supplements the financial information with information considered important for a full appreciation of a company's activities.

Discount allowed
A reduction in the selling price of a good or service allowed by the business to customers for prompt payment. Treated as an **expense**.

Discount factor
A factor by which future cash flows are discounted to arrive at today's monetary value.

Discount received

A reduction in the purchase price of a good or service granted to a business from the supplier for paying promptly. Treated as an **income**.

Discounted cash flow

The future expected cash inflows and outflows of a potential project discounted back to their present value today to see whether or not proposed projects are viable.

Dividend

A cash payment to shareholders rewarding them for investing money in a company.

Dividend cover

A ratio showing how many times profit available to pay ordinary dividends covers actual dividends.

Dividend yield

A ratio showing how much dividend ordinary shares earn as a proportion of market price.

Double-entry bookkeeping

A way of systematically recording the financial transactions of a company so that each transaction is recorded twice.

Doubtful debts

Debts which may or may not be paid. Usually, businesses estimate a certain proportion of their debts as doubtful.

Drawings

Money which a **sole trader** or partner takes out of a business as living expenses. It is, in effect, the owner's salary and is really a withdrawal of capital.

Earnings per share (EPS)

A key ratio by which investors measure the performance of a company.

Economic order quantity (EOQ)

A technique for managing **working capital**. The optimal EOQ is calculated so as to minimise the costs of ordering and holding inventory.

Efficiency ratios

Ratios which show how efficiently a business uses its assets.

Efficient market hypothesis

The idea of an efficient market hypothesis is that the price of traded shares will reflect available information and this provides a fair reflection of a company's underlying value.

Enterprise Finance Guarantee Scheme
A government scheme which helps businesses by providing a loan in return for interest.

Enterprise Resource Planning Systems (ERPS)
Enterprise Resource Planning Systems (ERPS) cover a whole range of integrated program that embrace both financial accounting and management accounting functions.

Entity concept
A business has a distinct and separate identity from its owner. This is obvious in the case of a large limited company where **shareholders** own the company and managers manage the company. However, there is also a distinction between a **sole trader's** or **partnership's** personal and business assets.

Equity
Equity represents the owner's interest in the business. In effect, equity is a liability as it is owed by the business to the owner (e.g., **sole trader**, partner or **shareholder**). Equity is the assets of a business less its liabilities to third parties. Equity is accumulated wealth and is increased by profit, but reduced by losses.

Equivalent units
In **process costing**, partially finished units are converted to fully completed equivalent units by estimating the percentage of completion.

Eurobond
A bond issued on the international capital market.

Expenses
The day-to-day **costs** incurred in running a business; e.g., telephone, business rates and wages. Expenses are expenses even if goods and services are consumed, but not yet paid. Expenses are, therefore, different from cash paid.

Fair value
The price that will be received when selling an asset or that is paid to transfer a liability in a market.

Financial accounting
The provision of financial information on a business's financial performance targeted at external users, such as shareholders. It includes not only **double-entry bookkeeping**, but also the preparation and interpretation of the financial accounts.

Financial capital maintenance concept
This concept is primarily concerned with **monetary measurement**; in particular, the measurement of the net assets.

Financial Reporting Council (FRC)
The Financial Reporting Council is a supervisory body which ensures that the overall system is working. The FRC supervises a **Codes and Standards Committee**, an Executive Committee and

a Conduct Committee. The main accounting functions come under the codes and standards committee in terms of the **Accounting Council** and **Audit and Assurance Council**. In addition, the **Financial Reporting Review Panel** comes under the monitoring committee. These are discussed more fully under the relevant entries.

Financial Reporting Review Panel (FRRP)
The FRRP investigates contentious departures from accounting standards and is part of the UK's standard-setting regime.

Financing cash flows
In a **statement of cash flows**, they relate to the issuing or buying back of shares or loan capital.

Finished goods inventory
The final inventory after the manufacturing process is completed; for example, finished tables. The cost includes materials and other manufacturing costs (e.g., labour and manufacturing overheads).

First-in-first-out (FIFO)
A method of inventory valuation where the inventory bought first is the first to be sold. See also **average cost** and **last-in-first-out**.

Fixed assets
The term for property, plant and equipment sometimes used in sole traders, partnerships and non-listed companies. Infrastructure assets used to run the business long-term and *not* used in day-to-day production. Include **non-current assets** (e.g., motor vehicles, land and buildings, fixtures and fittings, plant and machinery) and **intangible fixed assets** (e.g., goodwill).

Fixed costs
Costs that *do not vary* with production or sales (for example, insurance) in an **accounting period** and are not affected by short-term decisions. Often called fixed overheads.

Fixed overheads
See **fixed costs**.

Fixed overheads quantity variance
Standard fixed overheads – actual fixed overheads.

Flexing the budget
Adjusting the **budget** to account for the *actual quantity produced*.

Free cash flow
Cash flow from operations after deducting interest, tax preference dividends and ongoing capital expenditure. This, however, excludes strategic capital expenditure and ordinary share dividends.

FTSE (Financial Times Stock Exchange)
Lists the prices of shares on the London Stock Market.

GAAP (Generally Accepted Accounting Practices)
The body of standards and accounting regulations that make up a complete set of accounting rules and regulations, usually for a country. Often referred to as UK GAAP and US GAAP.

Gearing
The relationship between a company's ordinary shareholders' funds and the debt capital.

General reserve
A **revenue reserve** created to deal with general, unspecified contingencies such as inflation.

Going concern concept
The business will continue into the foreseeable future. **Assets, liabilities, incomes** and **expenses** are measured on this basis.

Goodwill
In takeovers, the purchase price less the amount paid for the net assets. It represents the value placed on the earning power of a business over and above its **net asset** value.

Gross profit
Revenue less **cost of sales**.

Gross profit ratio
This ratio relates the profit earned through trading to **revenue**.

Historical cost
A **measurement system** where monetary amounts are recorded at the date of original transaction.

Historical cost convention
The amount recorded in the accounts will be the *original* amount paid for a good or service.

Horizontal analysis
A form of ratio analysis which compares the figures in the accounts across time. It is used to investigate trends in the data.

Ideal standards
In **standard costing**, standards attained in an ideal world.

Impression management
Managers try to influence the financial reporting process in their own favour. Includes both **creative accounting** and **narrative enhancement**.

Income

The revenue earned by a business; e.g., **revenue**. Income is income, even if goods and services have been delivered but customers have yet to pay. Income thus differs from cash received.

Income receivable

Receivable by the business from a third party; e.g., **dividends** receivable (from companies) or interest receivable (from the bank).

Income statement

A financial statement which records the **income** and **expenses** of a business over the **accounting period**, normally a year. **Income** less **expenses** equals **profit**. By contrast, where expenses are greater than income, losses will occur. The balance from the income statement is transferred annually to the **statement of financial position** where it becomes part of **revenue reserves**. The term **income statement** is used for a listed company.

Indirect costs

Those costs *not* directly identifiable *nor* attributable to a product or service; e.g., administrative, and selling and distribution costs. These costs are totalled and then recovered indirectly into the product or service. Also called **indirect overheads** or **period costs**.

Indirect method of preparing a statement of cash flows

Operating cash flow is derived from the **income statement** and **statement of financial position** and not classified directly by function (such as receipts from **revenue**).

Indirect overheads

See **indirect costs**.

Intangible assets

Non-current assets one cannot touch, unlike **tangible non-current assets** (such as land and buildings). Most common in **companies**.

Interest cover

A ratio showing the amount of profit available to cover the **interest payable** on long-term borrowings.

Interest payable

An expense related especially to bank loans. When paid becomes interest paid.

Internal rate of return (IRR)

A **capital investment appraisal** technique. The internal rate of return represents the discount rate required to give a **net present value** of zero. It pays a company to invest in a project if it can borrow money for less than the IRR.

International Accounting Standards Board (IASB)
An international body founded in 1973 to work for the improvement and harmonisation of accounting standards worldwide. Originally called the International Accounting Standards Committee.

International Financial Reporting Standards (IFRS)
The accounting standards produced by the **International Accounting Standards Board**. The standards are now widely used for listed companies in, for example, Europe and Australia.

Interpretation of accounts
The evaluation of financial information, principally from the **income statement** and **statement of financial position**, so as to make judgements about profitability, efficiency, liquidity, gearing, cash flow, and the success of a financial investment. Sometimes called **ratio analysis**.

Inventory
Goods purchased and awaiting use (**raw materials**) or produced and awaiting sale (**finished goods**). Measures the time it takes for inventory to move through the business.

Inventory turnover ratio
An alternative to **stock turnover ratio** sometimes used for sole traders, partnerships and non-listed companies.

Investment centre
In **responsibility accounting**, where a manager is held responsible for the revenues, costs (i.e., profits) and investment.

Investment ratios
Measures the returns to the shareholder (**dividend yield, earnings per share** and **price/earnings ratio**) or the ability of a company to sustain its dividend or interest payments (**dividend cover** and **interest cover**).

Investments
Assets such as stocks and **shares**.

Invoice discounting
The sale of **trade receivables** to a third party for immediate cash.

Issued share capital
The share capital *actually* issued by a **company**.

Job costing
The recovery of costs into a specific product or service.

Just-in-time

A method of inventory control developed in Japan. It seeks to minimise inventory holding costs by the careful timing of deliveries and efficient organisation of production schedules. At its best, just-in-time delivers inventory just before it is used.

Last-in-first-out (LIFO)

A method of inventory valuation where the last inventory purchased is the first sold. See also **average cost** and **first-in-first-out**.

Leasing

Where the **assets** are owned by a third party which the business pays to use them.

Liabilities

Amounts the business owes (e.g., trade payables, bank loan). They can be short-term or long-term, third-party liabilities or equity (i.e., liability owed by the business to the owner).

Limited liability

Shareholders are only liable to lose the amount of money they initially invested.

Limiting factor

Where production is constrained by a particular shortage of a key element; e.g., a restricted number of labour hours.

Liquidity ratios

Ratios derived from the **statement of financial position** that measure how easily a firm can pay its debts.

Listed company

A **company** quoted on a stock exchange.

Loan capital

Money loaned to a company by third parties who do not own the company and are entitled to interest *not* dividends.

Loans

Amounts borrowed from third parties, such as a bank.

Long-term creditors

An alternative term for non-current liabilities sometimes used in sole traders', partnerships' or non-listed companies' accounts.

Long-term loan

A loan, such as a bank loan, not repayable within a year. Sometimes called a **debenture**.

Main market
On the London Stock Exchange where the well-established companies are traded.

Management accounting
The provision of both financial and non-financial information to managers for **cost accounting, planning, control and performance, and decision making.** It is thus concerned with the internal accounting of a business.

Management accounting control system
An assemblage of management control techniques which enable a business to plan, monitor and control ongoing financial activities. In addition, management control systems facilitate performance evaluation. **Budgeting** and **standard costing** are examples of management accounting control systems.

Margin of safety
In **break-even analysis,** the difference between current **revenue** and break-even **revenue.**

Marginal costing
Marginal costing excludes fixed overheads from the costing process. It focuses on **revenue, variable costs** and **contribution. Fixed costs** are written off against contribution. It can be used for decision making or for valuing inventory. When valuing inventory only variable production overheads are included in the inventory valuation.

Market value
The value shares fetch on the open market; i.e., their trading value. This may differ significantly from their **nominal value.**

Master budget
The overall budgeted **statement of financial position** and **income statement** prepared from the individual **budgets.**

Matching concept
Recognises **income** and **expenses** when accrued (i.e., earned or incurred) rather than when money is received or paid. Income is matched with any associated expenses to determine the appropriate profit or loss. Also known as the accruals concept.

Materials requirement planning (MRP) system
An MRP system is based on sales demand and coordinates production and purchasing to ensure the optimal flow of raw materials and optimal level of **raw material inventories.**

Measurement systems
The processes by which the monetary amounts of items in the financial statements are determined. Such systems are fundamental to the determination of **profit** and to the measurement of **net assets.** There are six major measurement systems: fair value, **historical cost, current purchasing power, replacement cost, realisable value** and **present value.**

Monetary measurement convention

Only items measurable in financial terms (for example, pounds or dollars) are included in the accounts. Atmospheric pollution is thus excluded, as it has no measurable financial value.

Narrative enhancement

Managers use the narrative parts of the **annual report** to convey a more favourable impression of performance than is actually warranted; e.g., by omitting key data or stressing certain elements.

Net assets

Total assets less **non-current liabilities** and **current liabilities**.

Net book value

The cost of **tangible property, plant and equipment** less accumulated depreciation.

Net cash flow from operating activities

In a **statement of cash flows**, cash flows from the normal trading activities of a business when prepared using UK GAAP.

Net present value

A **capital investment appraisal** technique which discounts future expected cash flows to today's monetary values using an appropriate cost of capital.

Net profit

Revenue less **cost of sales** less **expenses**.

Net profit ratio

A ratio which relates **profit** after **expenses** (i.e., **net profit**) to **revenue**.

Net realisable value

See **realisable value**.

Nominal value

The face value of the shares when originally issued.

Non-current assets

The term which covers both tangible and intangible long-term assets such as **property, plant and equipment** and **goodwill**.

Non-current liabilities

Amounts borrowed from third parties and repayable after a year. The most common are **long-term loans**.

Normal standards

In **standard costing**, standards which a business usually attains.

Note on historical cost profits and losses
A statement in the **annual report** which records any differences caused by departures from the **historical cost convention** (e.g., revaluation and subsequent depreciation of **property, plant** and **equipment**).

Notes to the accounts
In a company's **annual report,** they provide additional information about items in the accounts.

Objective of financial statements
To provide information about the financial position, performance and changes in financial position of an enterprise useful to a wide range of **users** in making decisions.

Operating and financial review
A statement in a company's **annual report,** originally developed by the United Kingdom's Accounting Standards Board, which enables companies to provide a formalised, structured and narrative explanation of financial performance. It was abolished as a piece of mandatory legislation in 2006 and replaced with the Business review.

Operating cash flow
In a **statement of cash flows,** operating profit adjusted for movements in **working capital** and non-cash flow items such as **depreciation.**

Operating profit
Net profit before taxation adjusted for interest paid and interest received.

Opportunity cost
The potential benefit lost by rejecting the best alternative course of action.

Ordinary (equity) share capital
Share capital issued to the **shareholders,** who own the company and are entitled to ordinary **dividends.**

Overall variances
In **standard costing,** the budgeted cost of the actual items produced (*standard cost of actual production*) is compared with the actual cost of items produced (*actual cost of production*).

Overheads
See **indirect costs.**

Padding the budget
In **budget** setting, where individuals try to create slack to give themselves some room for manoeuvre.

Partnership
Business enterprises run by more than one person, whose liability is normally unlimited.

Partnership capital accounts
The long-term equity invested into a partnership by the individual partners.

Partnership current accounts
The partners' share of the profits of the business. The main elements are the opening balances, salaries, profit for year, drawings and closing balances.

Patents
An **intangible asset** resulting from expenditure to protect rights to an invention.

Payback method
A method of **capital investment appraisal** which measures the cumulative cash inflows against the cumulative cash outflows to determine when a project will pay for itself.

Performance evaluation
The monitoring and motivation of individuals often in **responsibility accounting** systems.

Period costs
See **indirect costs**.

Periodicity convention
Accounts are prepared for a set period of time; i.e., an accounting period.

Physical capital maintenance concept
This concept is concerned with maintaining the physical productive capacity (i.e., operating capacity) of the business.

Planning, control and performance
The planning and control of future costs as well as the evaluation of performance using **budgeting** and **standard costing**. An abbreviated form of planning, control and performance evaluation.

Preference share capital
Share capital issued to **shareholders** who are *not* owners of the company and who are entitled to fixed dividends.

Prepayment
The amount paid in advance to the suppliers of services; e.g., prepaid insurance.

Present value
A **measurement system** where future cash inflows are discounted back to present-day values.

Price/earnings ratio
A ratio which measures **earnings per share** against share price.

Price variances
In **standard costing,** the *standard* price for the *actual* quantity used or sold is compared with the *actual* price for the *actual* quantity used or sold.

Primary market
A market where shares and bonds are initially issued.

Prime cost
Direct materials, direct labour and direct expenses totalled.

Private debt
Debt which involves a company and a bank.

Private limited company
A company where trading in shares is restricted.

Process costing
Used in industries with a continuous production process (e.g., beer brewing) where products progress from one department to another.

Product costs
See **direct costs.**

Production cost budget
This **budget** estimates the future cost of production, incorporating direct labour, direct materials and production overheads.

Production departments
Where products are manufactured.

Profit
Revenue less purchases and **expenses.**

Profit and loss account
A financial statement which records the **income** and **expenses** of a business over the **accounting period,** normally a year. **Income** less **expenses** equals **profit.** By contrast, where expenses are greater than income, losses will occur. The balance from the profit and loss account (income statement) is transferred annually to the **statement of financial position** where it becomes part of **revenue reserves.** The term **income statement** is used for a listed company and also is an alternative term for sole traders, partnerships and non-listed companies.

Profit centre

In **responsibility accounting**, where a manager is held responsible for the revenues and costs and thus profits.

Profitability ratios

They establish how profitably a business is performing.

Profit/volume chart

See **contribution graph**.

Property, plant and equipment

Infrastructure assets used to run the business long-term and *not* used in day-to-day production. Includes **tangible non-current assets** (e.g., motor vehicles, land and buildings, fixtures and fittings, plant and machinery) and **intangible assets** (e.g., **goodwill**).

Provision for doubtful debts

Those debts a business is dubious of collecting. Deducted from **trade receivables** in the **statement of financial position**. Only *increases* or *decreases* in the provision are entered in the **income statement**.

Prudence concept

Income and **profit** should only be recorded in the books when an inflow of cash is certain. By contrast, any **liabilities** should be provided as soon as they are recognised, even though the amount may be uncertain. Introduces an element of caution into accounting. The IASB is ambivalent about prudence as it is concerned that prudence conflicts with the idea of neutral and unbiased accounting.

Public debt

Where a company issues bonds which are then traded on the open market.

Public limited company

A **company** where shares are bought and sold by the general public.

Quantity variances

The budgeted cost of the actual items produced or sold (*standard cost of actual production* or *standard quantity sold*) is compared with the actual quantity produced or sold (*actual quantity used or sold*).

Quick ratio

Measures extreme short-term liquidity; i.e., **current assets** (excluding **inventory**) against **current liabilities**. Sometimes called the 'acid test ratio'.

Ratio analysis

See **interpretation of accounts**.

Raw material inventory

Inventory purchased and ready for use; e.g., a carpenter with wood awaiting manufacture into tables.

Raw materials budget

This **budget** forecasts the future quantities of raw materials required. May supply the purchases figure for the **trade payables budget**.

Realisable value

A **measurement system** where assets are valued at what they would fetch in an orderly sale. Also known as net realisable value.

Reconciliation of movements in shareholders' funds

A financial statement in the **annual report** which highlights major changes to the wealth of shareholders such as profit (or loss) for the year, annual dividends and new share capital.

Reducing balance method of depreciation

A set percentage of **depreciation** is written off the **net book value** of **property, plant and equipment** every year.

Regulatory framework

The set of rules and regulations which govern accounting practice, mainly prescribed by government and the accounting standard-setting bodies.

Relevance

Relevant information affects **users'** economic decisions. Relevance is a prerequisite of usefulness and, for example, helps to predict future events or to confirm or correct past events.

Relevant costs and revenues

Costs that will affect a decision (as opposed to non-relevant costs, which will not).

Reliability

Reliable information is free from material error and is unbiased.

Replacement cost

A **measurement system** where assets are valued at the amounts needed to replace them with an equivalent asset.

Reserves

The accumulated profits (**revenue reserves**) or capital gains (**capital reserves**) to shareholders.

Residual income

A ratio often used in **performance evaluation** in which a required rate of return on investment is deducted from income.

Responsibility accounting systems

Where an organisation is divided into budgetary areas for which individuals are held responsible. The budgetary areas may be known as **revenue centres, cost centres, profit centres,** or **investment centres.**

Retained profits

The **profit** a company has not distributed via **dividends.** An alternative to external financing. In effect, the business finances itself from its past successes.

Return on capital employed

A ratio looking at how effectively a company uses its capital (**equity**). It compares **net profit** to capital employed. The most common definition measures **profit** before tax and **debenture** interest against long-term capital (i.e., **ordinary share capital** and **reserves, preference share capital** and **long-term loans**).

Return on investment

A ratio often used in **performance evaluation** which relates income to investment.

Return on sales

A ratio often used in **performance evaluation** which relates operating profit to **revenue.** Can be called 'Return on revenue'.

Returns on investments and servicing of finance

In a **cash flow statement** prepared under UK GAAP, cash received from investments or paid on loans.

Revaluation reserve

A **capital reserve** created when **property, plant and equipment** are revalued to more than the original amount for which they were purchased. The revaluation is a gain to the shareholders.

Revenue

Income earned from selling goods and other activities.

Revenue budget

This **budget** estimates the future quantity of **revenue.**

Revenue centre

In **responsibility accounting,** where a manager is held responsible for the revenues.

Revenue expenditure

Payments for a current year's good or service such as purchases for resale or telephone expenses.

Revenue reserves
Reserves potentially distributable to shareholders as **dividends**; e.g., the **retained earnings, general reserve.**

Reverse engineering
A detailed analysis of competitors' products to see how they are made.

Review of operations
In a company's **annual report,** a narrative where the chief executive reviews the individual business operations.

Rights issue
Current **shareholders** are given the right to subscribe to new shares in proportion to their current holdings.

Sale and leaseback
Companies sell their **tangible non-current assets** to a third party and then lease them back.

Sales
Income earned from selling goods. Also known as **revenue.**

Sales budget
Alternative name for revenue budget which estimates the future quantity of revenue.

Sales price variance
(Standard price per unit – actual price per unit) × actual quantity of units sold.

Sales quantity variance
(Standard quantity of units sold – actual quantity of units sold) × standard contribution per unit.

Secondary market
A market where shares and bonds are subsequently traded.

Secured loans
Loans guaranteed (i.e., secured) by the **assets** of the company.

Securities Exchange Commission (SEC)
An independent regulatory institution in the US with quasi-judicial powers. US **listed companies** must file a detailed annual form, called the 10–K, with the SEC.

Sensitivity analysis
Involves modelling the future to see if alternative scenarios will change an investment decision.

Service costing

Service costing concerns specific services such as canteens run as independent operations. The cost of a particular service is the total costs for the service divided by the number of service units.

Service delivery departments

Departments in service industries that deliver the final service to customers.

Service support departments

Departments that supply support activities such as catering, administration, or selling and distribution.

Share capital

The total capital of the business is divided into shares. Literally a 'share' in the capital of the business.

Share options

Directors or employees are allowed to buy shares at a set price. They can then sell them for a higher price at a future date if the share price rises.

Share premium account

A **capital reserve** created when new shares are issued for more than their **nominal value**. For example, for shares issued for £150,000 with a nominal value of £100,000, the share premium account is £50,000.

Shareholders

The owners of the company who provide share capital by way of shares.

Social and environmental accounting statement

A voluntary statement produced by companies in their **annual report** dealing with social and environmental issues such as sustainable development.

Sole trader

A business enterprise run by a sole owner whose liability is unlimited.

Spending to budget

Departments ensure they spend their allocated **budgets**. If they do not, the department may lose the money.

Standard cost

A standard cost is the individual cost elements of a product or service (such as direct materials, direct labour and variable overheads) that are estimated in advance. Normally, the quantity and the price of each cost element are estimated separately. Actual costs are then compared with standard costs to determine **variances**.

Standard costing

A standardised version of **budgeting**. Standard costing uses preset costs for direct labour, direct materials and overheads. Actual costs are then compared with the standard costs. Any **variances** are then investigated.

Statement of cash flows

A financial statement which shows the cash inflows and outflows of a business.

Statement of changes in equity

An alternative term to the **statement of total recognised gains and losses** and **reconciliation of movements in shareholders' funds** as produced by a listed company.

Statement of comprehensive income (SOCI)

Followed by UK listed companies, it presents the income as a combined statement dealing with trading income and then income from other sources. Companies can also produce two statements (an income statement for trading items and the SOCI for other income).

Statement of directors' responsibilities for the financial statements

A statement in a company's **annual report** where directors spell out their responsibilities including (i) keeping proper accounting records; (ii) preparing financial statements in accordance with the Companies Act 2006; (iii) applying appropriate accounting policies; and (iv) following all applicable accounting standards.

Statement of financial position

A financial statement which is a snapshot of a business at a particular point in time. It records the **assets, liabilities** and **equity** of a business. Assets less liabilities equal equity. **Equity** is the owners' interest in the business.

Statement of total recognised gains and losses (STRGL)

A financial statement in the **annual report** which attempts to highlight all shareholder gains and losses and not just those from trading. The STRGL begins with the **profit** from the **income statement** and then adjusts for *non-trading gains and losses*.

Stewardship

Making individuals accountable for **assets** and **liabilities**. Stewardship focuses on the physical monitoring of assets and the prevention of loss and fraud rather than evaluating how efficiently the assets are used.

Stock

An alternative to inventory often used for sole traders, partnerships or private limited companies. Goods purchased and awaiting use (**raw materials**) or produced and awaiting sale (**finished goods**).

Stock turnover ratio

An alternative to **inventory turnover ratio** sometimes used for sole traders, partnerships and non-listed companies. Measures the time taken for inventory to move through a business.

Straight-line method of depreciation

The same amount of **depreciation** is written off the **tangible non-current assets** every year.

Strategic management accounting

A form of **management accounting** which considers an organisation's internal and external environments.

Subsidiary company

A **company** where more than half of the shares are owned by another company or which is effectively controlled by another company, or is a subsidiary of a subsidiary.

Sunk cost

A past cost with no ongoing implications for the future. It should thus be *excluded from decision making* as it is a non-relevant cost.

'T' account (ledger account)

Each page of each book of account has a **debit** side (left-hand side) and a **credit** side (right-hand side). This division of the page is called a 'T' account.

'T' Account (ledger account)	
Assets and expenses on the left-hand side DEBIT	Incomes, liabilities and equity on the right-hand side CREDIT

Tangible non-current assets

Non-current assets one can touch (e.g., land and buildings, plant and machinery, motor vehicles, fixtures and fittings). Tangible non-current assets are known as **property, plant and equipment** in **listed companies**.

Target costing

A price is set with reference to market conditions and customer purchasing patterns. A target profit is then deducted to arrive at a target cost.

Third-party liabilities

Amounts owing to third parties. They can be short-term (e.g., **trade payables**, bank overdraft) or long-term (e.g., a bank loan).

Throughput accounting

This uses a variant of contribution per limiting factor to determine a production system's main bottlenecks (e.g., shortage of machine hours in a certain department).

Total absorption costing

Both **direct costs** and **indirect costs** are absorbed into a product or service so as to recover the total costs in the final selling price.

Total shareholders' funds
The **share capital** and **reserves** owned by both the ordinary and preference shareholders.

Trade payables
Amounts owed to trade suppliers for goods supplied on credit, but not yet paid.

Trade payables budget
An alternative term for creditors budget. This **budget** forecasts the level of future trade payables. It keeps a running balance of trade payables by adding purchases and deducting cash payments.

Trade payables collection period
An alternative term for creditors collection period. This budget forecasts the level of future trade payables

Trade receivables
An alternative term for debtors. When sales are made on credit, but the customers have not yet paid.

Trade receivables age schedule
An alternative name for debtors age schedule. A credit control technique which profiles the age of the debts and allow old debts to be quickly identified.

Trade receivables budget
An alternative name for debtors budget. This **budget** forecasts the level of future trade receivables. It keeps a running balance of trade receivables by adding **revenue** and deducting cash received.

Trade receivables collection model
A technique for managing **working capital** which seeks to maintain the most efficient level of **trade receivables** for a company. It balances the extra revenue generated by increased **revenue** with the increased costs associated with extra **revenue** (e.g., credit control costs, bad debts and the delay in receiving money).

Trade receivables collection period
A ratio which measures how long customers take to pay their debts by relating trade receivables to **revenue**.

Trading and profit and loss account
The formal name for the full income statement prepared by a **sole trader**.

Trading and profit and loss and appropriation account
The formal name for the income statement prepared by a **company** or a **partnership**.

Trial balance
A listing of debit and credit balances to check the correctness of the **double-entry book-keeping** system.

True and fair view
Difficult to define but, essentially, a set of financial statements which faithfully, accurately and truly reflect the underlying economic transactions of the organisation.

Uncontrollable cost
A cost that a manager cannot influence and that the manager cannot be held responsible for.

Unsecured loans
Loans which are not guaranteed (i.e., secured) by a company's **assets**.

Urgent Issues Task Force (UITF)
The UITF is part of the UK's standard-setting process. It makes recommendations to curb undesirable interpretations of existing accounting standards or prevent accounting practices which the **Accounting Standards Council** considers undesirable.

Users
Those with an interest in using accounting information, such as shareholders, lenders, suppliers and other trade payables, customers, government, the public, management and employees.

Variable costs
These costs vary with production and **revenue** (for example, the metered cost of electricity). Short-term decision making is primarily concerned with variable costs.

Variable overheads overall variance
Standard cost of variable overheads for actual production less actual cost of variable overheads for production.

Variable overheads price variance
(Standard variable overheads price per hour – actual variable overheads price per hour) $\times$ actual quantity of labour hours used.

Variable overheads quantity variance
(Standard quantity of labour hours for actual production – actual quantity of labour hours used) $\times$ standard variable overheads price per hour.

Variance
The difference between the budgeted costs and the actual costs in both **budgeting** and **standard costing**.

Venture capital

Capital provided by a venture capitalist who invests in a small company in return for an equity stake and often a seat on the board.

Vertical analysis

In **ratio analysis,** vertical analysis is where key figures in the accounts (such as **revenue, statement of financial position** totals) are set to 100%.

Work-in-progress inventory

Partially completed inventory (sometimes called stock-in-process) which is neither **raw materials** nor **finished goods.**

Working capital

Current assets less **current liabilities** (in effect, the operating capital of a business).

Zero-based budgeting

A **budget** based on the premise that the activities are being incurred for the first time.

Appendix: Answers

Chapter 1: Discussion *Answers*

The answers provide some outline points for discussion.

A1 Accounting is important because it is the language of business and provides a means of effective and understandable business communication. The general terminology of business is thus accounting-driven. Concepts such as profit and cash flow are accounting terms. In addition, accounting provides the backbone of a business's information system. It provides figures for performance measurement, for monitoring, planning and control and gives an infrastructure for decision making. It enables businesses to answer key questions about past business performance and future business policy.

A3 There are many differences. The six listed below will do for starters!

    (a) Financial accounting is designed to provide information on a business's recent financial performance and is targeted at external users such as shareholders. However, the information is also often used by managers. By contrast, management accounting is much more internally focused and is used solely by managers.

    (b) Financial accounting operates within a regulatory framework set out by accounting standards and the Companies Acts. There is no such framework for management accounting.

    (c) The main work of financial accounting is preparing financial statements such as the statement of financial position and income statement. By contrast, management accounting uses a wider range of techniques for planning, control and performance, and for decision making.

    (d) Financial accounting is based upon double-entry bookkeeping, while management accounting is not.

    (e) Financial accounting looks backwards, while management accounting is forward looking.

    (f) The end product of financial accounting is a standardised set of financial statements. By contrast, management accounting is very varied. Its output depends on the needs of its users.

A6 A company needs to raise finance in the most optimal way it can. Finance is needed for both the short-term and the long-term needs of a company. Short-term needs involve the management of working capital. In effect, this is the inventory, cash, trade receivables and trade payables of a business. They need to be used in the most efficient way possible. The external sources of funds are most often share capital provided by shareholders or loans given by banks. These capital funds are often invested in infrastructural projects such as building a new factory. This is often called investment appraisal.

Chapter 2: Discussion *Answers*

The answers provide some outline points for discussion.

A1 Financial accounting is essentially the provision of financial information to users for decision making. More formally, the IASB broadly sees the objective of financial accounting as the provision of financial information about an organisation that is useful to a range of users, such as existing and potential investors, lenders or creditors when they are seeking to make decisions. These decisions may, for example, be buying or selling shares or giving loans.

In other words, financial accounting provides financial information (such as assets, liabilities, equity, expenses and income) to users (such as shareholders). This is useful because they can assess how well the managers run the company. On the basis of their assessment of the stewardship of management, they can make business decisions; for example, shareholders can decide whether or not to keep or sell their shares. Financial accounting is central to any understanding of business. It provides the basic language for assessing a business's performance. Unless we understand financial accounting, it is difficult to see how we can truly understand business. It would be like trying to drive a car without taking driving lessons. For non-specialists, a knowledge of financial accounting will help them to operate effectively in a business world.

A5 Double-entry bookkeeping is the essential underpinning of accounting. It provides an efficient mechanism by which organisations can record their financial transactions. For instance, large companies, such as Tesco or British Petroleum, may have millions of transactions per year. Double-entry bookkeeping provides a useful way of consolidating these. In a sense, therefore, the double-entry process permits organisations to make order from chaos. Double-entry bookkeeping enables the preparation of a trial balance. This, in turn, permits the construction of the income statement account and the statement of financial position.

A6 True or false?
   (a) *True.* Assets show what a business owns, while liabilities show what a business owes.
   (b) *False.* The profit and loss account does show income earned and expenses incurred. However, net assets are the assets less liabilities which are shown in the statement of financial position. Income less expenses equals profit.
   (c) *False.* Stewardship used to be the main objective up until about the 1960s. However, now decision making is generally recognised as the main objective.
   (d) *True.* This is because of the entity concept where the business is separate from the owner. Therefore, business assets, liabilities, income and expenses must be separated from private ones.
   (e) *True.* This is because the matching concept seeks to match income and expenses to the accounting period in which they arise. There is thus accounting symmetry. By contrast, prudence dictates that although income should be matched to the year in which it is earned, any liabilities should be taken as soon as they are recognised.

This means that if it is known that a liability would be incurred, say, in three years' time, it would be included in the current accounting period. There is thus accounting asymmetry. The two principles thus clash.

(f) *True*. All transactions can be classified as either debits (assets and expenses) or credits (incomes and liabilities).

Chapter 2: Numerical *Answers*

A1 Sharon Taylor

Income Statement (Profit and Loss Account)

	£	£
Revenue		8,000
Less *Expenses*		
General expenses	4,000	
Trading expenses	3,000	7,000
Net Profit		1,000

Statement of Financial Position (Balance Sheet)

	£
Assets	15,000
Liabilities	(3,000)
Net Assets	12,000

EQUITY

	£
Opening equity	11,000
Add Profit	1,000
Closing equity	12,000

Statement of Cash Flows

	£
Cash inflows	10,000
Cash outflows	(12,000)
Net cash outflow	(2,000)

A3 (i) Assets = Liabilities   £25,000 = £25,000

(ii) Assets = Liabilities + Equity   £25,000 = £15,000 + £10,000

(iii) Assets = Liabilities + Equity + Profit   £40,000 = £15,000 + £10,000 + £15,000

(iv) Assets = Liabilities + Equity + (Income − Expenses)   £40,000 = £15,000 + £10,000 + (£60,000 − £45,000)

(v) Assets + Expenses = Liabilities + Equity + Income   £40,000 + £45,000 = £15,000 + £10,000 + £60,000

(vi)

'T' Account		'T' Account	
Assets + Expenses	Liabilities + Equity + Income	£40,000 + £45,000 = £85,000	£15,000 + £10,000 + £60,000 = £85,000

A4

	Account	Debit	Account	Credit
(a)	Wages	Increases an expense	Bank	Decreases an asset
(b)	Bank	Increases an asset	Equity	Increases equity
(c)	Hotel	Increases an asset	Bank	Decreases an asset
(d)	Electricity	Increases an expense	Bank	Decreases an asset
(e)	Bank	Increases an asset	Revenue	Increases income
(f)	Purchases	Increases an expense	A. Taylor (trade payable)	Increases a liability

Chapter 3: Discussion *Answers*

The answers provide some outline points for discussion.

A1 The income statement is used by a variety of users for a variety of purposes. Sole traders and partnerships use it to determine how well they are doing. They will want to know if the business is making a profit. This will enable them to make decisions such as how much they should take by way of salary (commonly called drawings). Similarly, the tax authorities will use the income statement as a starting point to calculate the tax that these businesses owe the government.

For the shareholders of a limited company, profit enables them to assess the performance of the company's management. Shareholders can then make decisions about their investments. Company directors, on the other hand, may use profits to work out the dividends payable to shareholders, or to calculate their own profit-related bonuses. In short, profit has multiple uses.

A5 **True or false?**
(a) *False.* Profit is income earned less expenses incurred.
(b) *True.*
(c) *False.* Revenue returns are returns by customers.
(d) *True.*
(e) *True.*

Chapter 3: Numerical *Answers*

A1 Joan Smith

Joan Smith
Income Statement for the Year Ended 31 December 2013

	£	£
Revenue		100,000
Less *Cost of Sales*		
Opening inventory	10,000	
Add Purchases	60,000	
	70,000	
Less Closing inventory	5,000	65,000
Gross Profit		35,000
Less *Expenses*		
General expenses	10,000	
Other expenses	8,000	18,000
Net Profit		17,000

A2 Dale Reynolds

Dale Reynolds
Trading Account Section of Income Statement for the Year Ended 31 December 2013

	£	£	£
Revenue			50,000
Less Revenue returns			1,000
			49,000
Less *Cost of Sales*			
Opening inventory		5,000	
Add Purchases	25,000		
Less Purchases returns	2,000		
	23,000		
Add Carriage inwards	1,000	24,000	
		29,000	
Less Closing inventory		8,000	21,000
Gross Profit			28,000

Chapter 4: Discussion *Answers*

The answers provide some outline points for discussion.

A1 The statement of financial position and income statement are indeed complementary. Both are prepared from a trial balance. The statement of financial position takes the assets, liabilities and equity, and arranges them into a position statement. By contrast, the income statement takes the income and expenses and arranges them into a performance statement. The statement of financial position represents a snapshot of the business at a certain point in time. The income statement represents a period, usually a month or a year. The statement of financial position deals with liquidity, while the income statement deals with performance. Both together, therefore, provide a complementary picture of an organisation both at a particular point in time and over a period.

A5   True or false?
   (a)   *True.*
   (b)   *False.* Inventory and bank are indeed current assets, but trade payables are current liabilities.
   (c)   *False.* Total net assets are non-current assets (i.e. intangible assets and property, plant and equipment) and current assets less current liabilities, and non-current liabilities.
   (d)   *True.*
   (e)   *False.* An accrual is an expense owing; for example, an unpaid telephone bill. An amount prepaid (for example, rent paid in advance) is a prepayment.

Chapter 4: Numerical *Answers*

A1   **Jane Bricker**

Jane Bricker
Capital Employed as at 31 December 2013

Equity	£
Opening equity	5,000
Add Profit	12,000
	17,000
Less Drawings	7,000
Closing equity	10,000

A2   **Alpa Shah**

Alpa Shah
Net Assets as at 30 June 2014

ASSETS	£
Non-current Liabilities	100,000
Current Assets	50,000
Total Assets	150,000
Total Liabilities	
Current Liabilities	(30,000)
Non-current Liabilities	(20,000)
Total Liabilities	(50,000)
Net Assets	100,000

Chapter 5: Discussion *Answer*

The answer provides some outline points for discussion.

A1 A sole trader is where only one person owns the business. For example, a retailer, such as a baker, might be a sole trader. It is important for sole traders to prepare accounts for several reasons. First, as a basis for assessing their own financial performance. This indicates whether they can take out more wages (known as drawings), whether they can expand or pay their workers more. Second, the tax authorities need to be assured that the profit figure, which is the basis for assessing tax, has been properly prepared. And third, if any money has been borrowed, for example, from the bank, then the bankers will be interested in assessing performance.

Chapter 5: Numerical *Answers*

A1 **M. Anet**

M. Anet
Income Statement for the Year Ended 31 December 2013

	£	£
Revenue		25,000
Less Cost of Sales		
Purchases		15,000
Gross Profit		10,000
Less Expenses		
Electricity	1,500	
Wages	2,500	4,000
Net Profit		6,000

M. Anet
Statement of Financial Position as at 31 December 2013

	£
ASSETS	
Non-current Assets	
Property, Plant and Equipment	
Hotel	40,000
Van	10,000
Total non-current assets	50,000
Current Assets	
Bank	8,000
A. Brush (trade receivable)	400
Total current assets	8,400
Total Assets	58,400

A1 **M. Anet** (*continued*)

	£
LIABILITIES	
Current Liabilities	
A. Painter (trade payable)	(500)
Non-current Liabilities	–
Total Liabilities	(500)
Net Assets	57,900

	£
EQUITY	
Opening equity	51,900
Add Net profit	6,000
Closing equity	57,900

A2 **P. Icasso**

P. Icasso
Income Statement for the Year Ended 31 March 2014

	£	£
Revenue		35,000
Less Revenue returns		3,000
		32,000
Less Cost of Sales		
Purchases	25,000	
Less purchase returns	4,000	21,000
Gross Profit		11,000
Less Expenses		
Electricity	1,000	
Advertising	800	1,800
Net Profit		9,200

P. Icasso
Statement of Financial Position as at 31 March 2014

	£
ASSETS	
Non-current Assets	
Property, Plant and Equipment	
Hotel	50,000
Van	8,000
Total non-current assets	58,000
Current Assets	
Bank	9,000
Shah (trade receivable)	1,250
Chan (trade receivable)	2,250
Total current assets	12,500
Total Assets	70,500

A2 P. Icasso (*continued*)

LIABILITIES £

Current Liabilities

Jones (trade payable) (1,250)

Non-current Liabilities –

Total Liabilities (1,250)

Net Assets 69,250

£

EQUITY

Opening equity 60,050

Add Net profit 9,200

Closing equity 69,250

A3 R. Ubens

R. Ubens
Income Statement for the Year Ended 31 December 2013

	£	£	£
Revenue			88,000
Less Revenue returns			800
			87,200
Less Cost of Sales			
Opening inventory		3,600	
Add Purchases	66,000		
Less Purchase returns	1,200	64,800	
		68,400	
Less Closing inventory		4,000	64,400
Gross Profit			22,800
Less Expenses			
Electricity		1,500	
Advertising		300	
Printing and stationery		50	
Telephone		650	
Rent and rates		1,200	
Postage		150	3,850
Net Profit			18,950

R. Ubens
Statement of Financial Position as at 31 December 2013

	£
ASSETS	
Non-current Assets	
Property, Plant and Equipment	
Building	20,400
Motor van	3,500
Total non-current assets	23,900

A3 R. Ubens (*continued*)

	£
Current Assets	
Inventory	4,000
Bank	4,400
Trade receivables	2,600
Total current assets	11,000
	34,900
LIABILITIES	
Current Liabilities	
Trade Payables	(3,800)
Non-current Liabilities	–
Total Liabilities	(3,800)
Net Assets	31,100
	£
EQUITY	
Opening equity	19,950
Add Net profit	18,950
	38,900
Less Drawings	7,800
Closing equity	31,100

A4 C. Onstable

Income Statement (extracts)		Statement of Financial Position (extracts)	
Expenses		**Current assets**	
Rent	£2,880 (i.e., 12 × £240)	Prepayments	£840*
Insurance	£360 (£480 − £120)	*(Rent 3 × £240 = £720; Insurance £120)	

A5 V. Gogh

V. Gogh
Income Statement for the Year Ended 31 December 2013

	£	£	£
Revenue			40,000
Less Revenue returns			500
			39,500
Less *Cost of Sales*			
Opening inventory		5,500	
Purchases	25,000		
Less Purchases returns	450	24,550	
		30,050	
Less Closing inventory		9,000	21,050
Gross Profit			18,450

A5 V. Gogh (*continued*)

	£	£
Less *Expenses*		
Business rates	1,000	
Rent	400	
Telephone	450	
Insurance	750	
General expenses	150	
Electricity	700	
Wages	10,500	13,950
Net Profit		4,500

	£
ASSETS	
Non-Current assets	
Property, Plant and Equipment	
Shop	9,000
Motor car	8,500
Total non-current assets	17,500
Current Assets	
Inventory	9,000
Bank	1,300
Trade receivables	3,500
Prepayments	200
Total current assets	14,000
Total Assets	31,500
LIABILITIES	
Current Liabilities	
Trade payables	(1,500)
Accruals	(350)
Total current liabilities	(1,850)
Non-current Liabilities	(3,700)
Total Liabilities	(5,550)
Net Assets	25,950

	£
EQUITY	
Opening equity	34,350
Add Net profit	4,500
	38,850
Less Drawings	12,900
Closing equity	25,950

A6 L. Da Vinci

L. Da Vinci
Income Statement for the Year Ended 30 September 2014

	£	£	£
Revenue			105,000
Less Revenue returns			8,000
			97,000
Less Cost of Sales			
Opening inventory		6,500	
Add Purchases	70,000		
Less Purchase returns	1,800		
	68,200		
Add Carriage inwards	250	68,450	
		74,950	
Less Closing inventory		7,000	67,950
Gross Profit			29,050
Less Expenses			
Discounts allowed		300	
Electricity		2,025	
Telephone		500	
Wages		32,500	
Insurance		200	
Rent		1,000	
Business rates		1,000	37,525
Net loss			(8,475)

L. Da Vinci
Statement of Financial Position as at 30 September 2014

	£
ASSETS	
Non-current Assets	
Property, Plant and Equipment	
Business premises	18,000
Motor van	7,500
Computer	1,500
Total non-current assets	27,000
Current Assets	
Inventory	7,000
Trade receivables	12,000
Bank	1,800
Prepayments	275
Total current assets	21,075
Total Assets	48,075

A6 L. Da Vinci (*continued*)

	£
LIABILITIES	
Current Liabilities	
Trade payables	(13,000)
Accruals	(1,375)
Total current liabilities	(14,375)
Non-current Liabilities	(6,600)
Total Liabilities	(20,975)
Net assets	27,100

	£
EQUITY	
Opening equity	44,075
Less Net loss	8,475
	35,600
Less Drawings	8,500
Closing equity	27,100

A7 H. Ogarth

Income Statement for the year ended 31 December 2013 (extracts)

Expenses	£
Depreciation on buildings	10,000
Depreciation on machinery	3,000
Depreciation on motor van	2000
	15,000

Statement of Financial Position (extracts)	£ Cost	£ Accumulated depreciation	£ Net book value
Property, Plant and Equipment			
Buildings	100,000	(10,000)	90,000
Machinery	50,000	(3,000)	47,000
Motor van	20,000	(2,000)	18,000
	170,000	(15,000)	155,000

Chapter 6: Discussion *Answers*

The answers provide some outline points for discussion.

A1 These three forms of business enterprise fit various niches. The sole trader form is good for very small businesses, such as a window cleaner, carpenter or small shopkeeper. There is a limited amount of equity needed and the individual can do most of the work. The accounting records needed for this type of business are not extensive. Partnerships are useful where the business is a little more complicated. They are suitable for situations where more than one person works together. There is then a need to sort out each partner's share of equity and profits. Companies are useful where a lot of equity is needed. Thus, they are particularly suitable for medium-sized and large businesses. They are particularly appropriate when raising money externally because of the concept of limited liability. As shareholders are only liable for the amount of their initial investments, they will be keener to invest as their potential losses will be limited.

A5 True or false?
(a) *False*. Drawings are withdrawal of equity by the partners; they are found in the partners' current accounts.
(b) *True*.
(c) *False*. Nominal value is the face value of the shares, normally the amount the shares were originally issued at. Market value is their stock-market value.
(d) *False*. Unsecured loans are secured on the general assets of the business. It is secured loans which are attached to specific assets.
(e) *False*. Reserves are accumulated profits and cannot directly be spent. Only cash can be spent.

Chapter 6: Numerical *Answers*

A1 Tom and Thumb

Tom and Thumb
Income Statement for Year Ended 31 December 2013

		£	£
Net Profit before Appropriation			100,000
Less Salaries:			
Tom		10,000	
Thumb		30,000	40,000
			60,000
Profits:			
Tom	3	45,000	
Thumb	1	15,000	60,000

Tom and Thumb
Statement of Financial Position as at 31 December 2013

Equity	£	£	£
	Tom	Thumb	
Capital Accounts	8,000	6,000	14,000
Current Accounts			

A1 Tom and Thumb (*continued*)

	£	£	
Opening balances	3,000	(1,000)	
Add:			
Salaries	10,000	30,000	
Profit share	45,000	15,000	
	58,000	44,000	
Less Drawings	25,000	30,000	
Closing balances	33,000	14,000	47,000
Total Partners' Funds			61,000

A2 J.Waite and P. Watcher

J. Waite and P. Watcher
Income Statement for the Year Ended 30 November 2014

		£	£
Revenue			350,000
Less Cost of Sales			
Opening inventory		9,000	
Add Purchases		245,000	
		254,000	
Less Closing inventory		15,000	239,000
Gross Profit			111,000
Less Expenses			
Depreciation:			
Land and buildings		2,000	
Motor vehicles		3,000	
Electricity		3,406	
Wages		14,870	
Rent and business rates		6,960	
Telephone		1,350	
Interest on loan		2,800	
Other expenses		5,500	39,886
Net Profit before Appropriation			71,114
Less Salaries:			
Waite		18,000	
Watcher		16,000	34,000
			37,114
Profits:			
Waite	3	22,268	
Watcher	2	14,846	37,114

A2 J. Waite and P. Watcher (*continued*)

J. Waite and P. Watcher
Statement of Financial Position as at 30 November 2014

ASSETS	£	£	£
Non-Current Assets	Cost	*Accumulated depreciation*	*Net book value*
Property, Plant and Equipment			
Land and Buildings	166,313	(2,000)	164,313
Motor vehicles	65,000	(3,000)	62,000
	231,313	(5,000)	226,313
Current Assets			
Inventory			15,000
Trade receivables			12,000
Bank			6,501
Total current assets			33,501
Total Assets			259,814
LIABILITIES			
Current Liabilities			
Trade payables			(18,500)
Accruals			(300)
Total current liabilities			(18,800)
Non-current Liabilities			(28,000)
Total Liabilities			(46,800)
Net Assets			213,014

	Waite	Watcher	
EQUITY	£	£	£
Capital Accounts	88,000	64,000	152,000
Current Accounts			
Opening Balances	(2,500)	12,000	
Add:			
Salaries	18,000	16,000	
Profit share	22,268	14,846	
	37,768	42,846	
Less Drawings	13,300	6,300	
Closing balances	24,468	36,546	61,014
Total Partners' Funds			213,014

A5   Red Devils Ltd

Red Devils Ltd
Statement of Comprehensive Income and Retained Earnings for the Year Ended 30 November 2014 (unpublished)

	£	£
Revenue		[As per Accounts of Sole
Less Cost of Sales		Trader or Partnership]
Gross Profit		150,000
Less Expenses		
Debenture interest	14,000	
General expenses	22,100	
Directors' fees	19,200	
Auditors' fees	7,500	62,800
Profit before Taxation		87,200
Taxation		(17,440)
Profit after Taxation		69,760
Dividends on ordinary shares	(25,000)	
Dividends on preference shares	(9,000)	
Transfer to general reserve[1]	(3,500)	(37,500)
Retained Profit		32,260

1. The transfer to general reserve could also be done in the statement of financial position.

Red Devils Ltd
Statement of Financial Position as at 30 November 2013

	£
ASSETS	
Non-current Assets	
Property, Plant and Equipment	680,900
Current Assets	
Inventories	105,000
Trade receivables	4,700
Bank	5,300
Total current assets	115,000
Total Assets	795,900
LIABILITIES	
Current Liabilities	
Trade payables	(46,200)
Taxation	(17,440)
Auditors' fees	(7,500)
Debenture interest	(14,000)

A5   Red Devils Ltd (*continued*)

		£
Total current liabilities		(85,140)
Non-current Liabilities		(200,000)
Total Liabilities		(285,140)
Net Assets		510,760

Share Capital and Reserves	Authorised	Issued
Share Capital	£	£
Ordinary share capital (£1 each)	400,000	250,000
6% preference shares	150,000	150,000
	550,000	400,000

Reserves		
Capital reserves		
Share premium account		55,000
Other reserves		
Opening general reserve	11,000	
Transfer for year	3,500	
Closing general reserve		14,500
Opening retained earnings	9,000	
Retained earnings for year	32,260	
Closing retained earnings		41,260	55,760
Total equity			510,760

A6   Superprofit Ltd

Superprofit Ltd
Statement of Comprehensive Income and Retained Profits (Income Statement)
for the Year Ended 31 December 2013

	£000	£000	£000
Revenue			351
Less *Cost of Sales*			
Opening inventories		23	
Add Purchases		182	
		205	
Less Closing inventories		26	179
Gross Profit			172
Less *Expenses*			
Depreciation:			
Land and buildings		18	
Motor vehicles		7	
Auditors' fees		2	

A6 Superprofit Ltd (*continued*)

	£000	£000
Loan interest	4	
Electricity	12	
Insurance	3	
Wages	24	
Light and heat	8	
Telephone	5	
Other expenses	26	109
Profit before Taxation		63
Taxation		(13)
Net Profit after Taxation		50
Ordinary dividends	(9)	
Preference dividends	(3)	(12)
Retained Profit		38

Superprofit Ltd
Statement of Financial Position as at 31 December 2013

	£000 Cost	£000 *Accumulated depreciation*	£000 *Net book value*
ASSETS			
Non-current Assets			
Intangible Assets			
Patents			12
Property, Plant and Equipment			
Land and buildings	378	(18)	360
Motor vehicles	47	(7)	40
	425	(25)	400
Total non-current assets			412
Current Assets			
Inventories			26
Trade receivables			18
Bank			31
Total current assets			75
Total Assets			487
LIABILITIES			
Current Liabilities			
Trade payables			(45)
Taxation payable			(13)
Other accruals (see note below)			(6)
			(64)

A6 Superprofit Ltd (continued)

	£000	£000	£000
Non-current Liabilities			(32)
Total Liabilities			(96)
Net Assets			391

Share Capital and Reserves		
Share Capital	Authorised	Issued
Ordinary share capital	250	210
Preference share capital	50	25
	300	235

Reserves

	£000	£000	£000
Capital reserves			
Share premium account		40	
Other reserves			
Revaluation reserve		35	
General reserve		15	
Opening retained earnings	28		
Retained earnings for year	38		
Closing retained earnings		66	156
Total Equity			391

Note: Loan interest (£4) and auditors' fees (£2)

A9 Stock High plc

Stock High plc

Statement of Comprehensive Income for the Year Ended 31 March 2014

	Notes	£000
Revenue		1,250
Cost of Sales		(400)
Gross Profit		850
Administrative expenses		(216)
Distribution expenses		(230)
Profit before Taxation		404
Taxation		(94)
Profit for year		310

Stock High plc

Statement of Financial Position as at 31 March 2014

	Notes	£000
ASSETS		
Non-current Assets		
Property, Plant and Equipment	1	814
Intangible Assets	2	50
Total non-current assets		864

A9 Stock High plc (*continued*)

		£000
Current Assets		
Inventories		20
Trade receivables		100
Bank		22
Total current assets		142
Total Assets		1,006
LIABILITIES		
Current Liabilities	3	(20)
Non-current Liabilities		(60)
Total Liabilities		(80)
Net Assets		926
EQUITY		
Capital and Reserves	4	750
Called-up share capital	5	550
Share premium account		25
Other reserves	6	55
Retained earnings		296
Total Equity		926

Stock High plc
Statement of Changes in Equity as at 31 March 2014

	£000
Balance as at 1 April 2013	36
Retained earnings for year	310
Less: Dividends	(50)
Balance as at 31 March 2014	296

Notes:

1. Property, Plant and Equipment

	£000 Cost	£000 Accumulated depreciation	£000 Net book value
Land and buildings	800	(156)	644
Motor vehicles	400	(230)	170
	1,200	(386)	814

2. Intangible Assets

Patents	50
	50

3. Current Liabilities

Trade payables	12
Taxation	8
	20

A9 Stock High plc (*continued*)

	£000
4. Authorised Share Capital	
Ordinary share capital (£1)	600
Preference share capital (£1)	150
	750
5. Called-up Share Capital	
Ordinary share capital	450
Preference share capital	100
	550
6. Other Reserves	
Revaluation reserve	30
General reserve	25
	55

Chapter 7: Discussion *Answers*

The answers provide some outline points for discussion.

A1 Cash is king because it is central to the operations of a business. Unless you generate cash, you cannot pay employees, suppliers or expenses, or buy new property, plant and equipment. The end result of a lack of cash is the closure of a business. Cash is also objective. There is very little subjectivity involved in estimating cash. Either you have cash or you don't! With profits, however, there is much more subjectivity. Often one can alter the accounting policies of a business; for example, use a different rate of depreciation and thus alter the amount of profit. It is not as easy to manipulate cash.

A5 **True or false?**
   (a) *False.* It is true that both items are non-cash flow items and that depreciation is added back to operating profit. However, profit from the sale of property, plant and equipment is deducted from operating profit.
   (b) *False.* Inventory and trade receivables are items of working capital. However, property, plant and equipment are not.
   (c) *True.*
   (d) *True.*
   (e) *False.* It is much more commonly used than the direct method.

Chapter 7: Numerical *Answers*

A1 Bingo

Included in income statement	Included in statement of cash flows
(a) Not in full IFRS, but in IFRS for SMEs	Yes
(b) No	Yes, financing
(c) Yes	No

(d) Yes   Yes, Cash flows from operating activities
(e) No   Yes, Cash flows from investing activities
(f) No   Yes, Cash flows from investing activities
(g) No   Yes, Cash flows from investing activities
(h) Yes, part of charge for year   No
(i) No   Yes, Cash flows from financing activities
(j) Yes   Yes, Cash flows from investing activities

A2   Peter Piper

Peter Piper
Statement of Cash Flows for the Year Ended 31 December 2013

	£	£
Cash Flows From Operating Activities		
Receipts from customers	250,000	
Payments to suppliers	(175,000)	
Payments to employees	(55,000)	
Expenses	(10,000)	10,000
Cash Flows from Investing Activities		
Interest received	1,150	
Sale of property	25,000	
Purchase of office equipment	(15,000)	11,150
Cash Flows from Financing Activities		
Loan repaid	(25,000)	
Interest paid	(350)	(25,350)
Decrease in Cash		(4,200)

A4   D. Rink

D. Rink
Reconciliation of Operating Profit to Operating Cash Flow
Year Ended 31 December 2013

	£	£
Operating Profit		95,000
Add:		
Decrease in inventories	3,000	
Decrease in prepayments	1,500	
Increase in trade payables	300	
Increase in accruals	250	
Depreciation	8,000	13,050
Deduct:		
Increase in trade receivables	(1,150)	
Profit on sale of property, plant and equipment	(3,500)	(4,650)
Net Cash Inflow from Operating Activities		103,400

A6   Grow Hire Ltd

Grow Hire Ltd
Statement of Cash Flows for the Year Ended 31 December 2013

	£000	£000
Net Profit before Taxation		112,000
Add:		
Interest paid	6,500	
Decrease in inventories	2,000	
Decrease in trade receivables	7,000	
Increase in accruals	1,000	
Depreciation (£44,000 – £28,000)	16,000	32,500
Deduct:		
Taxation paid	(33,600)	
Decrease in trade payables	(25,000)	
Interest received	(13,000)	(71,600)
Cash Flows from Operating Activities		72,900
Cash Flows from Investing Activities		
Patents purchased	(34,200)	
Property, plant and equipment purchased	(20,000)	
Interest received	13,000	(41,200)
Cash Flows from Financing Activities		
Equity dividends paid	(35,800)	
Increase in non-current liabilities	12,000	
Increase in share capital	1,600	
Interest paid	(6,500)	(28,700)
Increase in Cash		3,000

	£000
Opening Cash	7,000
Increase in cash	3,000
Closing Cash	10,000

A8   Expenso plc

Expenso plc
Statement of Cash Flows for the Year Ended 30 September 2014

	£000	£000
Cash Flows from Operating Activities		
Net profit before Taxation		10,017
Add:		
Interest paid	85	
Increase in trade payables	400	
Depreciation	2,500	2,985
Deduct:		
Taxation paid	(4,005)	
Interest received	(868)	

A8   **Expenso plc** (*continued*)

	£000	£000
Decrease in accruals	(50)	
Increase in inventories	(3,600)	
Increase in trade receivables	(1,300)	(9,823)
Cash Flows from Operating Activities		3,179
Cash Flows from Investing Activities		
Interest received	868	
Land and buildings purchased	(6,000)	
Plant and machinery purchased	(5,000)	
Patents purchased	(500)	(10,632)
Cash Flows from Financing Activities		
Equity dividends paid	(4,105)	
Increase in non-current liabilities	405	
Increase in share capital	3,938	
Interest paid	(85)	153
Decrease in Cash		(7,300)
		£000
Opening Cash		8,800
Decrease in cash		(7,300)
Closing Cash		1,500

Note: We needed to calculate taxation paid (in £000s).

Opening accrual + Income statement − Amount paid = Closing accrual

Taxation   £4,200   +   £3,005   −   £4,005   =   £3,200

Or alternatively,

		Taxation paid		
	£			£
Paid	4,005		Bal. b/f	4,200
Bal. c/f	3,200		Income statement	3,005
	7,205			7,205

Chapter 8: Discussion *Answers*

The answers provide some outline points for discussion.

A1   Ratio analysis is simply the distillation of the figures in the accounts into certain key ratios so that a user can more easily interpret a company's performance. Ratio analysis is also known as financial statement analysis or the interpretation of accounts. There are traditionally thought to be six main types of ratios:

   (a)   *Profitability ratios*: Generally derived from the income statement, they seek to determine how profitable the business has been. Main ratios: return on capital employed, gross profit, net profit.

(b) *Efficiency ratios*: Compare the income statement to the statement of financial position figures. Try to work out how efficiently the company is utilising its assets and liabilities. Main ratios: trade receivables collection period, trade payables collection period, inventory turnover and asset turnover ratio.

(c) *Liquidity*: Assess the short-term cash position of the company. They are derived from the statement of financial position. Main ratios: current ratio and quick ratio.

(d) *Gearing*: Looks at the relationship between the owners' capital and the borrowed capital. This ratio is derived from the statement of financial position.

(e) *Cash flow*: This ratio seeks to measure how the company's cash inflows and cash outflows compare. The cash flow ratio, unlike the other ratios, is derived from the statement of cash flows.

(f) *Investment ratios*: These ratios are used by investors to determine how well their shares are performing. They generally compare share price with dividend or earnings information. The five main ratios are: dividend yield, dividend cover, earnings per share, price/earnings ratio and interest cover.

A5 True or false?

(a) *True.*

(b) *False.* More usually: $\text{Net profit} = \dfrac{\text{Net profit before taxation}}{\text{Revenue}}$

(c) *False.* $\text{Current ratio} = \dfrac{\text{Current assets}}{\text{Current liabilities}}$. The ratio given was the quick ratio.

(d) *True.*

(e) *False.* This is actually the property, plant and equipment turnover ratio.

$\text{Asset turnover ratio} = \dfrac{\text{Revenue}}{\text{Total assets}}$

(f) *False.* $\text{Dividend yield} = \dfrac{\text{Dividend per ordinary share}}{\text{Share price}}$

(g) *True.*

Chapter 8: Numerical *Answers*

A1 John Parry

The ratios below are calculated in £s.

(a) Return on capital employed
$$= \frac{\text{Net profit}^*}{\text{Capital employed}^{**}}$$
$$= \frac{50,000}{(300,000 + 500,000) \div 2} = 12.5\%$$

*For sole traders, tax is not an issue.
**We take average for year.

(b) Gross profit ratio
$$= \frac{\text{Gross profit}}{\text{Revenue}} = \frac{80,000}{150,000} = 53.3\%$$

(c) Net profit ratio
$$= \frac{\text{Net profit}^*}{\text{Revenue}} = \frac{50,000}{150,000} = 33.3\%$$

*For sole traders, tax is not an issue

A1 John Parry (*continued*)

(d) Trade receivables collection period $= \dfrac{\text{Average trade receivables}}{\text{Credit sales per day}}$

$= \dfrac{(18,000 + 19,000) \div 2}{150,000 \div 365} = 45 \text{ days}$

(e) Trade payables collection period $= \dfrac{\text{Average trade payables}}{\text{Credit purchases per day}}$

$= \dfrac{(9,000 + 10,000) \div 2}{75,000 \div 365} = 46 \text{ days}$

(f) Inventory turnover ratio $= \dfrac{\text{Cost of sales}}{\text{Average inventories}}$

$= \dfrac{70,000}{(25,000 + 30,000) \div 2} = 2.5 \text{ times}$

(g) Asset turnover ratio $= \dfrac{\text{Revenue}}{\text{Average total assets}}$

$= \dfrac{150,000}{(50,000 + 60,000) \div 2} = 2.7 \text{ times}$

A2 Henry Mellett

£

(a) Current ratio $= \dfrac{\text{Current assets}}{\text{Current liabilities}} = \dfrac{31,903}{14,836} = 2.2 \text{ times}$

(b) Quick ratio $= \dfrac{\text{Current assets} - \text{inventories}}{\text{Current liabilities}} = \dfrac{31,903 - 18,213}{14,836} = 0.9 \text{ times}$

(c) Gearing ratio $= \dfrac{\text{Long-term borrowings}}{\text{Total long-term capital*}} = \dfrac{30,000}{150,000 + 30,000} = 16.7\%$

*Remember, total net assets are equivalent to shareholders' funds.

A3 Jane Edwards

	Cash inflows	Cash outflows
	£	£
Customers	125,000	
Issue of shares	29,000	
Sale of property, plant and equipment	35,000	
Employees		18,300
Suppliers		9,250
Buy back loan		8,000
Dividends		8,000
Taxation		16,000
Purchase of property, plant and equipment		80,000
	189,000	139,550

Cash flow ratio $= \dfrac{\text{Total cash inflows}}{\text{Total cash outflows}} = \dfrac{£189,000}{£139,550} = 1.35$

A4 Clatworthy plc

£000*

(a) Dividend yield $= \dfrac{\text{Dividend per ordinary share}}{\text{Share price (in £s)}} = \dfrac{40 \div 500}{1.25} = 6.4\%$

(b) Dividend cover $= \dfrac{\text{Profit after tax and preference dividends}}{\text{Ordinary dividends}} = \dfrac{580}{40} = 14.5 \text{ times}$

(c) Earnings per share $= \dfrac{\text{Profit after tax and preference dividends}}{\text{Number of ordinary shares}} = \dfrac{580}{500} = £1.16$

(d) Price/earnings ratio $= \dfrac{\text{Share price}}{\text{Earnings per share}} = \dfrac{1.25}{1.16} = 1.08$

(e) Interest cover $= \dfrac{\text{Profit before tax and loan interest}}{\text{Loan interest}} = \dfrac{790}{40} = 19.8 \text{ times}$

*Except for price/earnings ratio.

A7 Anteater plc

The ratios below are calculated from the accounts. There is insufficient information for the average return on capital employed and the efficiency ratios. The closing year figure is, therefore, taken from the balance sheet. This is indicated by a single asterisk. Except where indicated, calculations are in £000s.

(a) Profitability ratios	Ratio	Calculations (£000s)	
Return on capital employed	Net profit before tax and loan interest/ Average capital employed*	(100 + 3)/500*	= 20.6%
		* = 300 + 20 + 10 + 70 + 100	
Gross profit ratio	Gross profit/Revenue	250/1,000	= 25%
Net profit ratio	Net profit before tax/Revenue	100/1,000	= 10%
(b) Efficiency ratios			
Trade receivables collection period	Average trade receivables*/ Credit sales per day	50/(1,000 ÷ 365)	= 18.3 days
Trade payables collection period	Average trade payables*/ Credit purchases per day (cost of sales taken)	40/(750 ÷ 365)	= 19.5 days
Inventory turnover ratio	Cost of sales/Average inventories*	750/40 = 18.8 times	
Asset turnover ratio	Revenue/Average total assets*	1,000/(420 + 120)	= 1.8 times
(c) Liquidity ratios			
Current ratio	Current assets/Current liabilities	120/40 = 3.0	
Quick ratio	Current assets − inventories/ Current liabilities	(120 − 40)/40	= 2.0
(d) Gearing ratio			
Gearing	Long-term borrowings/Total long-term capital	(100 + 20)/ (400 + 100)	= 24%

A7 **Anteater plc** (*continued*)

(e) **Investment ratios**

Dividend yield	Dividend per ordinary share/ Share price (in £s)	(40 ÷ 300)|2.00	= 6.7%
Dividend cover	Profit after tax and preference dividends/Ordinary dividends	70|40	= 1.75
Earnings per share	Profit after tax and preference dividends/Number of ordinary shares	70|300	= 23.3p
Price/earnings ratio **Calculation in pence.	Share price/Earnings per share**	200|23.3	= 8.6
Interest cover	Profit before tax and loan interest/ Loan interest	103|3	= 34.3

Chapter 9: Discussion *Answers*

The answers provide some outline points for discussion.

A1 The role of the three is complementary.
   (a) The directors run the business and prepare the accounts. They invest their labour and are rewarded, for example, by salaries and bonuses.
   (b) The shareholders own the business and make decisions partly on the basis of the accounts they receive. They invest their equity and are rewarded, hopefully, by dividends and an increase in share price.
   (c) The auditors check that the directors have prepared accounts that provide a 'true and fair' view of the company's performance over the year. They invest their labour and are rewarded by the auditors' fees. They are independent of the directors and, in theory, are responsible to the shareholders.

A2 The IASB broadly sees the objective of financial accounting as the provision of financial information about an organisation that is useful to a range of users, such as existing and potential investors, lenders or creditors when they are seeking to make decisions. These decisions may, for example, be buying or selling shares or giving loans.

   In other words, financial accounting provides financial information (such as assets, liabilities, equity, expenses and income) to users (such as shareholders). This is useful because they can assess how well the managers run the company. On the basis of their assessment of the stewardship of management, they can make business decisions; for example, shareholders can decide whether or not to keep or sell their shares. Financial accounting is central to any understanding of business. It provides the basic language for assessing a business's performance. Unless we understand financial accounting, it is difficult to see how we can truly understand business. It would be like trying to drive a car without taking driving lessons. For non-specialists, a knowledge of financial accounting will help them to operate effectively in a business world.

This appears reasonable as far as it goes. However, critics argue that the decision-making model has several flaws. First, it assumes that one set of financial statements is appropriate for all users. Second, what is appropriate for shareholders is assumed to be appropriate for all users. Third, the focus on decision making neglects other important aspects such as stewardship. And finally, and most radically, the decision-making model focuses on financial information, thus ignoring non-financial aspects such as the environment.

Chapter 10: Discussion *Answers*

The answers provide some outline points for discussion.

A1 An accounting measurement system is a method of determining the monetary amounts in the accounts. Different measurement systems will result in different valuations for net assets. This in turn will cause profit to be different. The measurement of assets and the determination of profit is key to the preparation of accounts. However, different accounting measurement systems can cause wide variation in both net assets and net profit. Thus, it is probably not unreasonable to call accounting measurement systems the skeleton that underpins the accounting body. The accounting measurement systems will determine the basic parameters of the accounting results.

A2 Historical cost is still widely used internationally. Indeed, it is certainly much more popular than the alternative measurement bases. However, historical cost has been widely criticised. In particular, there is concern that it fails to reflect changing asset values resulting from inflation or technological change. There has, therefore, been extensive debate over alternative measurement systems, most obviously by the Financial Accounting Standards Board in the US, the Accounting Standards Board in the UK and the International Accounting Standards Board. All these bodies have wrestled with alternative measurement systems, seeing them as essential to framing a successful conceptual theory for accounting.

So far, there has been little agreement on an alternative system. The first reason is that historical cost is widely used, easy to understand and objective. Users are, therefore, reluctant to abandon it. This is particularly true when the alternatives are often not easy to understand or use and are often subjective. In addition, the main incentive to change was the high level of inflation in the Western world, particularly in the UK and the US in the 1970s. However, more recently inflation rates have fallen and with them interest in alternatives to historical cost.

Chapter 11: Discussion *Answers*

The answers provide some outline points for discussion.

A1 The annual report plays a central role in corporate governance. Essentially, it is a key mechanism by which the directors report to the shareholders and other users on their stewardship of the company. The directors prepare the financial statements, which provide information on income and expenses, assets, liabilities and equity, so that shareholders can monitor the activities of the directors. This monitoring allows the shareholders to see that the managers are not abusing their position; for example, by paying themselves great salaries at the expense of the shareholders. In order to ensure that the accounts are true and fair, the auditors audit the financial statements. These financial statements will be included in an annual report along with other financial and non-financial information. The annual report itself is often prepared by design consultants.

A2 These three roles have the following functions:

(i) *Stewardship and accountability*

The directors provide information to the shareholders so that they can monitor the directors' activities. This has grown out of ideas of accountability (i.e., the control and safeguarding of corporate assets). The idea has been extended to corporate governance; in particular, the monitoring of directors' remuneration. The IASB takes the view that stewardship is a subset of decision making. However, other interested parties see it as an objective in its own right.

(ii) *Decision making*

The decision-making aim is 'to communicate economic measures of, and information about, the resources and performance of the reporting entity useful to those having reasonable rights to such information' (*The Corporate Report*, 1975). The aim, therefore, in essence, is to provide users, such as shareholders, with information so that they can make decisions, such as buying or selling shares.

(iii) *Public relations*

The public relations objective of the annual report is simply recognising the incentives that management has to use the annual report to show the results in a good light. It is often associated with the idea of the annual report as a marketing tool. The clash between these three objectives is that while the first two (accountability and decision making) are based on the idea of a true and fair view, public relations is not about truth and fairness. Public relations attempts to depart from truth and fairness to show the company in the best possible light.

Chapter 12: Discussion *Answers*

The answers provide some outline points for discussion.

A1	*Branches*	*Functions*
	(1) Cost Accounting	
	(i) *Costing*	To recover costs as a basis for pricing and for inventory valuation.
	(ii) *Planning, Control and Performance*	

A1 (*continued*)

(a) Budgeting	To plan and control future costs and engage in performance evaluation through budgeting.
(b) Standard costing	To plan and control future costs and engage in performance evaluation through standard costing.

(2) Decision Making

(i) *Short-term Decisions*	To make short-term decisions (such as whether to make a product) using techniques such as contribution analysis and break-even analysis.
(ii) *Long-term Decisions*	
Strategic management	To make decisions of a strategic nature such as whether or not to diversify the business.

A6 Finance certainly has decision making as a central aspect of its activities. There are several major aspects. First, finance concerns the appraisal of long-term infrastructural decisions. These may be, for example, the building of a factory or a major project. These can be appraised using techniques such as discounted cash flow, internal rate of return, payback or the profitability index. The decision here is whether to undertake the investment decision. Second, finance is about the provision of these long-term funds. This will involve the raising of funds, perhaps on the stock market. This might be share capital or via the issuance of long-term bonds. The decision here is where to raise the money and how much is needed. Third, finance consists of short-term financing. This is normally to manage working capital. Money can, for example, be raised from banks or from debt factors. Short-term finance also involves looking at the most efficient ways of using current assets (e.g., inventory, trade receivables and cash) and current liabilities (e.g., trade payables). Short-term financing, therefore, also involves making lots of decisions.

A7 **True or false?**
(a) *True.*
(b) *False.* Total absorption costing is where all the costs incurred by a company are totalled so that they can be recovered into the product or service's final selling price.
(c) *True.*
(d) *False.* Whereas finance does concern long-term infrastructural decisions, it also includes short-term decisions such as those to do with the raising of working capital.
(e) *True.*

Chapter 13: Discussion *Answers*

The answers provide some outline points for discussion.

A1 Costing is the process of recording, classifying, allocating and then absorbing costs into individual products and services. Costing is particularly important for two main reasons: inventory valuation and pricing. In inventory valuation, the aim is to recover the costs incurred in producing a good. The costs of inventory valuation thus include direct materials, direct labour, direct expenses and appropriate production overheads. In absorption costing, we include all production overheads, both fixed and variable. In marginal costing, we include only variable production overheads. In effect, financial accounting drives the inventory valuation process. This is because external reporting regulations allow attributable production overheads (i.e., allow absorption costing) to be included in inventory. For pricing, all the overheads (both production and non-production, i.e., total absorption costing) are included in the cost before a percentage is added for profit. Thus the total cost may include direct materials, direct labour, direct expenses, production and non-production overheads. Nowadays, with the decline of manufacturing industry, there has been a decline in the importance of direct costs and an increase in the importance of indirect costs or overheads.

A5 True or false?
  (a) *False*. It is true that a cost can be an actual past expenditure. However, it is important to appreciate that a cost can also be an estimated, future expenditure.
  (b) *True*.
  (c) *False*. We identify activity cost drivers in activity-based costing.
  (d) *True*.
  (e) *False*. No, in financial reporting we use absorption costing.

Chapter 13: Numerical *Answers*

A1 Sorter

(i) Direct materials	*c* (purchase of raw materials)
(ii) Direct labour	*a* (machine workers' wages)
(iii) Production overheads	*b* (cost clerks' wages)∗ Assumes cost clerks are based in factory, *d* (machine repairs), *m* (depreciation on machinery), *o* (electricity for machines)
(iv) Administrative expenses	*e* (finance director's salary), *f* (office cleaners), *h* (managing director's car expenses), *i* (depreciation on office furniture), *j* (computer running expenses for office), *k* (loan interest), *l* (auditors' fees), *p* (bank charges)
(v) Selling and distribution costs	*g* (delivery van staff's wages), *n* (advertising costs)

A2 Costa

Costa
Costing Statement for Costa

	£	£	£
Direct materials			320,000
Direct labour			200,000
Royalties			3,600
(i) Prime Cost			523,600
Production Overheads			
Factory supervisors' wages		120,000	
Depreciation (£8,000 + £5,000)		13,000	
Computer overheads		6,000	
Other overheads		70,000	209,000
(ii) Production Cost			732,600
Other Costs			
Administrative Expenses			
Administrative salaries	90,800		
Depreciation (£4,200 + £2,500)	6,700		
Computer overheads	3,000		
Interest on loans	3,000	103,500	
Selling and Distribution Costs			
Wages	18,300		
Marketing salaries	25,000		
Commission	1,200		
Depreciation (£3,500 + £2,500)	6,000	50,500	154,000
(iii) Total Cost			886,600

A3 Makemore

Makemore
Overhead Allocation Statement

	Total £	Ratio Split	A £	B £	C £
Supervisors' salaries	25,000	1,000:2,000:500	7,143	14,286	3,571
Computer advisory	18,000	1,000:2,000:500	5,143	10,286	2,571
Rent and business rates	20,000	10,000:6,000:4,000	10,000	6,000	4,000
Depreciation	21,000	30,000:15,000	14,000	7,000	–
Repairs	4,000		2,800	1,100	100
Allocated	88,000		39,086	38,672	10,242
Reallocation of service support department C's costs			60%	40%	(100%)
			6,145	4,097	(10,242)
Total Allocation	88,000		45,231	42,769	–

A3 Makemore (*continued*)

	A £	B £	C £
(i) Labour hours	$\frac{£45,231}{80,000}$	$\frac{£42,769}{40,000}$	
Rate per hour	= £0.57	£1.07	
(ii) Machine hours	$\frac{£45,231}{100,000}$	$\frac{£42,769}{200,000}$	
Rate per hour	=£0.45	£0.21	

A8 Serveco

Calculate activity-cost driver rates

Activity	Spare Parts Installed	Technical Support	Service Documentation	
Cost	£100,000	£125,000	£300,000	
Cost driver	150,000 parts	175,000 minutes	125,000 units	
Cost per unit of Cost driver	£0.667	£0.7143	£2.4	
Costs absorbed to services				*Total cost*
Basic	50,000 × £0.667	75,000 × £0.7143	100,000 × £2.4	
	= £33,333	= £53,572	= £240,000	£326,905
Enhanced	100,000 × £0.667	100,000 × £0.7143	25,000 × £2.4	
	= £66,667	= £71,428	= £60,000	£198,095
Total costs	£100,000	£125,000	£300,000	£525,000
Total overhead costs	*Total overheads*	*Call-outs*	*Overheads per call-out*	
Basic	£326,905	50,000	£6.54	
Enhanced	£198,095	10,000	£19.81	

Call-Out Cost/Charge

	Basic £		Enhanced £	
Labour hours (including travelling time)	20.00	$\frac{(25,000 + 25,000) \times £20}{50,000 \text{ call-outs}}$	106.25	$\frac{(37,500 + 5,000) \times £25}{10,000 \text{ call-outs}}$
Overheads	6.54		19.81	
Total Cost	26.54		126.06	
Profit: 25% mark-up on cost	6.63		31.51	
Call-out Charge	33.17		157.57	

Note: Some of the calculations have been rounded in this answer.

Chapter 14: Discussion *Answers*

The answers provide some outline points for discussion.

A1   A major advantage of budgeting is that it requires you to predict the future in economic terms. You can plan ahead and buy in extra resources and schedule workloads. In addition, budgeting enables you to predict your future performance. You can then tell how well or how badly you are actually doing against your predicted budget. Finally, budgeting has an important responsibility and control function. You can put somebody in charge of the budget, make them responsible and so control future activities. Variances from budget can thus be investigated.

    The major disadvantages of budgets are that they may be constraining and dysfunctional to the organisation. The constraint is caused by the budget perhaps setting a straitjacket which inhibits innovation and the adoption of inflexible business policies. The dysfunctional nature of budgeting is that the objectives of the individual may not necessarily be the same as that of the organisation. Individuals may, therefore, seek to 'pad' their budgets or manage them to their own personal advantage.

A4   **True or false?**
   (a)   *True.*
   (b)   *False.* Although sometimes production is a limiting factor, the commonest limiting factor is demand.
   (c)   *True.*
   (d)   *False.* Depreciation is never found in a cash budget as it does not represent a cash flow.
   (e)   *True.*

Chapter 14: Numerical *Answers*

A1   **Jill Lee**

Jill Lee
Cash Budget for Six Months Ending June

	Jan. £	Feb. £	March £	April £	May £	June £	Total £
Opening cash	15,000	28,200	21,100	8,280	(5,942)	1,389	15,000
Add *Receipts*							
Revenue	25,200	27,100	21,200	20,250	48,300	37,500	179,550
	25,200	27,100	21,200	20,250	48,300	37,500	179,550
Less Payments							
Goods	–	21,000	19,500	18,500	23,400	25,900	108,300
Expenses	12,000	13,200	14,520	15,972	17,569	19,326	92,587
	12,000	34,200	34,020	34,472	40,969	45,226	200,887
Cash flow	13,200	(7,100)	(12,820)	(14,222)	7,331	(7,726)	(21,337)
Closing cash	28,200	21,100	8,280	(5,942)	1,389	(6,337)	(6,337)

A3 Fly-by-Night

Fly-by-Night
Revenue Budget for Six Months Ending June

	Jan. £	Feb. £	March £	April £	May £	June £	Total £
Moon (1)	20,000	21,000	22,000	28,750	30,000	31,250	153,000
Star (2)	20,000	21,000	22,000	23,000	24,000	25,000	135,000
	40,000	42,000	44,000	51,750	54,000	56,250	288,000
(1) Moon (units)	1,000	1,050	1,100	1,150	1,200	1,250	6,750
(2) Star (units)	2,000	2,100	2,200	2,300	2,400	2,500	13,500

Helpnote: Multiply the units by the price per unit.

A4 D. Ingo

D. Ingo
Trade Receivables Budget for Six Months Ending June

	Jan. £	Feb. £	March £	April £	May £	June £	Total £
Opening trade receivables	2,400	2,000	2,100	2,310	2,541	2,795	2,400
Credit sales	1,000	1,100	1,210	1,331	1,464	1,610	7,715
	3,400	3,100	3,310	3,641	4,005	4,405	10,115
Cash received	(1,400)	(1,000)	(1,000)	(1,100)	(1,210)	(1,331)	(7,041)
Closing trade receivables	2,000	2,100	2,310	2,541	2,795	3,074	3,074

A6 B. Ear

B. Ear
Production Cost Budget Six Months Ending June

	Jan. £	Feb. £	March £	April £	May £	June £	Total £
Raw materials	3,500	3,750	4,000	4,250	4,500	4,750	24,750
Direct labour	3,850	4,125	4,400	4,675	4,950	5,225	27,225
Variable overheads	1,400	1,500	1,600	1,700	1,800	1,900	9,900
	8,750	9,375	10,000	10,625	11,250	11,875	61,875
Units	700	750	800	850	900	950	4,950

A7 R. Abbit

R. Abbit
Raw Materials Budget Six Months Ending June

	Jan. £	Feb. £	March £	April £	May £	June £	Total £
Opening inventory	1,000	940	1,080	1,420	1,670	2,120	1,000
Purchases	900	1,100	1,300	1,500	1,700	1,900	8,400
	1,900	2,040	2,380	2,920	3,370	4,020	9,400
Used in production	(960)	(960)	(960)	(1,250)	(1,250)	(1,250)	(6,630)
Closing inventory	940	1,080	1,420	1,670	2,120	2,770	2,770

A11 All Sunshine Enterprises

	London	Oslo	Stockholm
(i) Return on Investment			
$\dfrac{\text{Income}}{\text{Investment}}$	$\dfrac{£700,000}{£2,000,000} = 35\%$	$\dfrac{£400,000}{£1,000,000} = 40\%$	$\dfrac{£165,000}{£500,000} = 33\%$
(ii) Residual Income			
Income − (Required rates of return × investment)	£700,000 − (12% × £2,000,000)	£400,000 − (12% × £1,000,000)	£165,000 − (12% × £500,000)
	= £460,000	= £280,000	= £105,000
(iii) Return on Sales*			
$\dfrac{\text{Operating profit}}{\text{Revenue}}$	$\dfrac{£700,000}{£1,500,000}$	$\dfrac{£400,000}{£800,000}$	$\dfrac{£165,000}{£300,000}$
	= 46.7%	= 50%	= 55%

Therefore, Return on Investment gives Oslo 40% and is its best relative measure. Residual Income gives London £460,000 and is its best relative measure. Return on Sales gives Stockholm 55% and is its best relative measure.

*Can be called Return on Revenue.

Chapter 15: Discussion *Answers*

The answers provide some outline points for discussion.

A1 Setting the standards involves first of all making a decision about whether one is aiming for ideal, attainable or normal standards. Ideal standards are those that can be reached if everything goes perfectly. Attainable standards are those that can be reached with a little effort. Normal standards are those that are based on past experience and that the business normally meets. Attainable standards are probably the best because they include a motivational element.

The two main elements of a standard are quantity (i.e., hours, materials) and price (i.e., hourly rate, price per kilo). It follows, therefore, that we need to consider the factors that influence quantity and price. These might be based on past experience, prevailing market conditions and future expectations. For instance, if a firm were setting labour standards it might base its labour quantity standard on the hours taken in the past less an improvement element. The labour price standard might be based on the prevailing wage rate with an amount built in for any wage increases.

A5 True or false?
(a) *True.*
(b) *False.* Flexing the budget means adjusting the budget to take into account the actual quantity produced.
(c) *True.*
(d) *True.*
(e) *False.* The direct labour quantity variance is: (standard *quantity* of labour hours for actual production − actual *quantity* of labour hours used) × standard labour price per hour.

Chapter 15: Numerical *Answers*

A1 Stuffed

(i–iii)

	Budget	Flexed Budget	Actual	Sales Price and Overall Cost Variances*	
Number of customers	10,000	12,000	12,000		
	£	£	£	£	
Revenue	100,000	120,000	127,200	7,200	Fav.
Food cost					
(i.e., materials cost)	(30,000)	(36,000)	(37,200)	(1,200)	Unfav.
Labour cost	(35,000)	(42,000)	(36,000)	6,000	Fav.
Variable overheads	(5,000)	(6,000)	(6,000)	–	
Contribution	30,000	36,000	48,000	12,000	Fav.
Fixed overheads	(3,000)	(3,000)**	(3,100)	(100)	Unfav.
Profit	27,000	33,000	44,900	11,900	Fav.

Helpnotes

*The sales price variance is £7,200 Fav. The overall cost variances are food cost (i.e., direct materials) variance £1,200 Unfav., labour cost variance £6,000 Fav., zero overall variable overheads cost variance, and £100 Unfav. fixed overhead variance.

**Remember, fixed costs remain unchanged whatever the level of activity. We do not, therefore, flex these.

(iv) *Sales Quantity Variance* = (standard quantity of meals sold − actual quantity of meals sold) × standard contribution per unit = 10,000 − 12,000 × (£30,000 ÷ 10,000) = £6,000 Fav.

Note this is simply the flexed profit (£33,000) less the original budget (£27,000) = £6,000 Fav.

A1 Stuffed (*continued*)

(v) (a) *Sales Variances*. Both are favourable. 2,000 more customers visited the restaurant than anticipated. They paid £0.60 more per meal than expected.
  (b) *Material Cost*. We paid £1,200 more than expected. This may be due to increased prices or increased quantity used. We need more information on this.
  (c) *Labour Cost*. We paid £6,000 less than expected. Either we paid less per hour or we used fewer hours than expected. We need more information.
  (d) *Variable Overheads*. These were as budgeted.
  (e) *Fixed Overheads*. These were slightly more (£100 more) than expected.

A3 Birch Manufacturing

	£	
(i) Overall Direct Materials Variance		
Standard cost of materials for actual production (10 metres of wood* at 50p × 11,000)	55,000	
Actual cost of materials used in production (120,000 metres × 0.49 pence)	58,800	
	(3,800)	Unfav.

*Each bookcase is estimated to take 10 metres of wood (100,000 metres ÷ 10,000 bookcases)

	£	
(ii) Direct Materials Price Variance		
(standard price per unit of material − actual price per unit of material) × actual quantity of materials used = (50p − 49p) × 120,000 metres	1,200	Fav.
(iii) Direct Materials Quantity Variance		
(standard quantity of materials for actual production − actual quantity of materials used) × standard material price per unit = (11,000 × 10 metres − 120,000 metres) × 0.50p	(5,000)	Unfav.
	(3,800)	Unfav.

A4 Sweatshop

	£	
(i) Overall Direct Labour Variance		
Standard cost of labour for actual production (500 sweatshirts at 2 hours) × £5.50	5,500	
Actual cost of labour used in production	5,880	
	(380)	Unfav.

	£	
(ii) Direct Labour Price Variance		
(standard labour price per hour − actual price per hour) × actual quantity of labour used = (£5.50 − £5.60*) × 1,050 hours	(105)	Unfav.

*£5,880 labour cost divided by 1,050 hours

A8 Sweatshop (*continued*)

(iii) Direct Labour Quantity Variance

(Standard quantity of labour hours for actual production − actual
  quantity of labour hours used)
  × standard labour price per hour
  = (2 hours × 500 sweatshirts − 1,050 hours) × £5.50 per hour   (275)   Unfav.

                                                                    (380)   Unfav.

A6 Wonderworld

(i) Overall Variable Overheads Cost Variance

	£
Standard cost of variable overheads for actual production (110,000 teleporters at 2 labour hours at £2.50)	550,000
Actual cost of variable overheads for production	517,500
	32,500 Fav.

(ii) Variable Overheads Price Variance

(standard variable overheads price per hour − actual variable   £
  overheads price per hour) × actual quantity of labour hours used
  = (£2.50 − £2.25)* × 230,000   57,500   Fav.

*variable overheads £517,500 ÷ 230,000 actual labour hours

(iii) Variable Overheads Quantity Variance

(standard quantity of labour hours for actual production −
  actual quantity of labour hours used) × standard variable
  overheads price per hour
  = (110,000 × 2 hours − 230,000 hours) × £2.50   (25,000)   Unfav.

                                                                    32,500   Fav.

(iv) Fixed Overheads Variance

Standard fixed overheads less actual fixed overheads   £
  = £10,000 − £9,800   200   Fav.

A8 Peter Peacock plc
August's results

(i) Flexed budget

	Budget *(i.e., standard)*	*Flexed* *Budget* *(i.e., standard* *quantity of* *actual* *production)*	*Actual*	*Sales Price* *and Overall* *Cost* *Variances*	
Volume	200,000	220,000	220,000		
	£	£	£	£	
Revenue	560,000	616,000	611,600	(4,400)	Unfav.
Direct materials	(125,000)	(137,500)	(150,000)	(12,500)	Unfav.

A8 Peter Peacock plc (*continued*)

	Budget £	Flexed £	Actual £	Variances £	
Direct labour	(290,000)	(319,000)	(317,550)	1,450	Fav.
Variable overheads	(40,000)	(44,000)	(42,500)	1,500	Fav.
Contribution	105,000	115,500	101,550	(13,950)	Unfav.
Fixed overheads	(68,000)	(68,000)	(67,000)	1,000	Fav.
Profit	37,000	47,500	34,550	(12,950)	Unfav.

(ii) Individual Variances: Sales

Sales Quantity Variance
(Standard quantity of units sold − actual quantity of units sold) × standard contribution

£

(200,000 − 220,000) × 0.525* = 10,500 Fav.**

$$*\frac{\text{Contribution}}{\text{Budgeted sales volume}} = \frac{105,000}{200,000}$$

**Represents budgeted profit £37,000 − flexed budget profit £47,500

Sales Price Variance
This can be taken direct from the flexed budget, or it can be calculated as follows:
(standard selling price − actual selling price per unit) × actual quantity of units sold
(£2.80 − £2.78) × 220,000 = (£4,400) Unfav.

Costs

Price	**Quantity**
(standard price − actual price per unit) × actual quantity	*(standard quantity of actual production − actual quantity) × standard price*
Direct Material Variances	
(£1.25 per sheet − £1.20 per sheet) × 125,000 sheets = £6,250 Fav.	(220,000 subcomponents × 0.50 sheets per subcomponent* gives 110,000 sheets − 125,000 sheets) × £1.25 = (£18,750) Unfav.
	*100,000 sheets ÷ 200,000 subcomponents. This gives the amount of material per subcomponent.
Direct Labour Variances	
(£7.25 per hour − £7.30 per hour) × 43,500 hours = (£2,175) Unfav.	(220,000 subcomponents × 0.20 hours* gives 44,000 hours − 43,500 hours) × £7.25 = £3,625 Fav.
	*40,000 hours ÷ 200,000 subcomponents. This gives the amount of the labour per subcomponent

A8 Peter Peacock plc *(continued)*

Variable Overhead Variances

(£1.00 per hour − £0.977 per hour)*   (220,000 subcomponents × 0.20 hours* gives
× 43,500 hours = £1,000 Fav.   44,000 hours − 43,500 hours) × £1.00
*£42,500 variable overheads ÷   = £500 Fav.
43,500 hours   *40,000 hours ÷ 200,000 subcomponents.
                                                      This gives the amount of labour per subcomponent
                                                      and we are recovering our variable overheads on
                                                      the labour hours.

Fixed Overheads   £68,000 standard fixed overheads − £67,000
                                          actual fixed overheads = £1,000 Fav.

(iii)

Peter Peacock plc
Standard Cost Reconciliation Statement for August

	£	£	£	
Budgeted Profit			37,000	
Sales quantity variance			10,500	Fav.
Budgeted profit at actual sales			47,500	
Variances	*Fav.*	*Unfav.*		
Sales price		4,400		
Direct materials price	6,250			
Direct materials quantity		18,750		
Direct labour price		2,175		
Direct labour quantity	3,625			
Variable overheads price	1,000			
Variable overheads quantity	500			
Fixed overheads variance	1,000			
	12,375	25,325	(12,950)	
Actual Profit			34,550	

(iv) The actual profit for Peacock is £2,450 less than budgeted (£37,000 − £34,550). Peacock has actually sold 20,000 more units than anticipated, creating a favourable sales quantity variance of £10,500. However, it has done this by reducing the price slightly so there is an unfavourable sales price variance.

On the cost variances, there is a favourable direct materials price variance (£6,250) as the sheets are cheaper than anticipated. However, more sheets were used than anticipated, possibly because they were poorer quality. There is thus an unfavourable quantity variance of £18,750. The labour price variance of £2,175 is unfavourable since Peacock paid £7.30 per hour rather than the budgeted £7.25. However, perhaps because a better quality of labour was used, and fewer hours were used creating a favourable quantity variance of £3,625. For variable overheads, less overheads than anticipated were incurred creating a favourable price variance of £1,000. Also because of the fewer hours used, less overheads were recovered into the product causing a favourable quantity variance. Finally, fixed overheads were less than anticipated.

Chapter 16: Discussion *Answers*

The answers provide some outline points for discussion.

A1 Fixed costs are those costs, like depreciation or insurance, which do not vary with production or revenue. They remain fixed whatever the level of production or revenue. This is not universally true as at a certain point, such as acquiring a new machine, fixed costs will vary. However, it is a reasonable working assumption.

Variable costs, by contrast, are those costs that do vary with production or revenue. If we make more products or provide more services, then our variable costs will increase. Conversely, if we make fewer products or provide fewer services, then our variable costs will decrease.

Fixed costs are irrelevant for decision making because they will be incurred whatever the decision. They are fixed within the relevant range of activity. For example, insurance and depreciation will not vary whether we choose to produce more of product A or more of product B. We should, therefore, ignore these costs when making decisions.

A4 **True or false?**

(a) *False.* Wrong time horizon. Fixed costs do *not* vary with short-term changes in the level of revenue or production.

(b) *True.*

(c) *False.* Wrong numerator. Break-even point is $\dfrac{\text{Fixed costs}}{\text{Contribution per unit}}$

(d) *False.* Contribution/revenue (sales) ratio is $\dfrac{\text{Contribution}}{\text{Revenue (sales)}}$

(e) *False.* Non-financial items do not feature directly in the calculations, but they are extremely important.

Chapter 16: Numerical *Answers*

A1 Jungle Animals

(i), (ii)	Selling Price	Variable Costs	Contribution	Contribution/ Revenue (Sales) Ratio
	£	£	£	%
Alligators	1.00	1.05	(0.05)	(5.0)
Bears	1.20	1.00	0.20	16.7
Cougars	1.10	1.14	(0.04)	(3.6)
Donkeys	1.15	1.08	0.07	6.1
Eagles	1.20	0.96	0.24	20.0
Foxes	0.90	0.85	0.05	5.6
Giraffes	1.05	0.85	0.20	19.0
Hyenas	1.25	0.94	0.31	24.8
Iguanas	0.95	0.72	0.23	24.2
Jackals	0.80	0.73	0.07	8.8

A1 **Jungle Animals** (*continued*)

(iii) The two toys with the highest contribution are Hyenas (£0.31 contribution) and Eagles (£0.24 contribution).

(iv) The three toys with the highest contribution/revenue (sales) ratio are Hyenas (24.8%), Iguanas (24.2%) and Eagles (20%).

(v) Alligators and Cougars have a negative contribution so we would not make them.

A3 **Scrooge**

Internal bid:	£
Clerical labour	80,000
Supervisory labour	60,000
Direct materials	25,000
Variable overheads	30,000
	195,000
External bid	(190,000)
Thus saving by buying in	5,000

So on the straight accounting calculation Scrooge would outsource. The chief assumption is that all the labour is indeed variable and can be laid off or redeployed easily. Other factors are the impact upon industrial relations, long-term implications and confidentiality. The outside bid is marginally superior. However, when these other factors are taken into account it may be better to go with the status quo.

A6 **Freya**

(i)

Contribution per hammer	£	£
Revenue		10
Less: *Variable Costs*		
Direct materials	4	
Variable expenses	3	7
Contribution		3

Break-even point: $\dfrac{\text{Fixed costs}}{\text{Contribution per unit}} = \dfrac{£30,000}{£3} = 10,000 \text{ hammers}$

(ii) (a) If 4,000 sold

Contribution (4,000 × £3) =	£12,000
Fixed costs	(£30,000)
Loss	(£18,000)

(b) If 14,000 sold

Contribution (14,000 × £3) =	£42,000
Fixed costs	(£30,000)
Profit	£12,000

(iii) Current margin of safety

(a) Units (i.e., Hammers): $\dfrac{\text{Actual hammers sold} - \text{hammers at break-even}}{\text{Hammers at break-even}}$

$= \dfrac{20,000 - 10,000}{10,000} = 100\%$

(b) £s: $\dfrac{\text{Actual revenue} - \text{revenue at break-even}}{\text{Revenue at break-even}}$

$= \dfrac{200,000 - 100,000}{100,000} = 100\%$

A8 Freya (continued)

(iv) Break-even chart

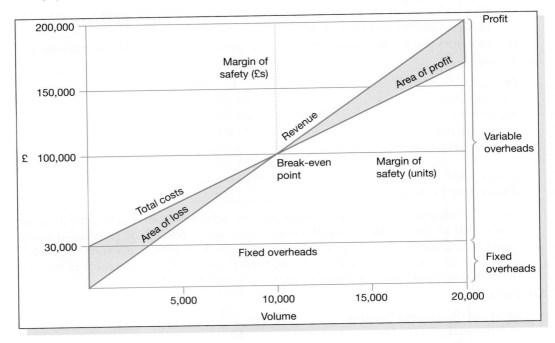

A8 Modem

(i)

Branch	Revenue £	Variable Costs £	Contribution £	Contribution/ Revenue Ratio %	Ranking
Cardiff	200,000	165,000	35,000	17.5 (£35, 000/£200,000)	2
Edinburgh	300,000	230,000	70,000	23.3 (£70, 000/£300,000)	1
London	1,000,000	870,000	130,000	13.0 (£130,000/£1,000,000)	3
	1,500,000	1,265,000	235,000		
Fixed costs			(150,000)		
Net Profit			85,000		

(ii) Cumulative profit table in contribution/revenue ratio ranking:

	Cumulative Revenue £	Cumulative Contribution £	Cumulative Profit/Loss £
Fixed costs			(150,000)
Edinburgh	300,000	70,000	(80,000)
Cardiff	500,000	105,000	(45,000)
London	1,500,000	235,000	85,000

A8 Modem (*continued*)

Modem's Contribution/Revenue Graph

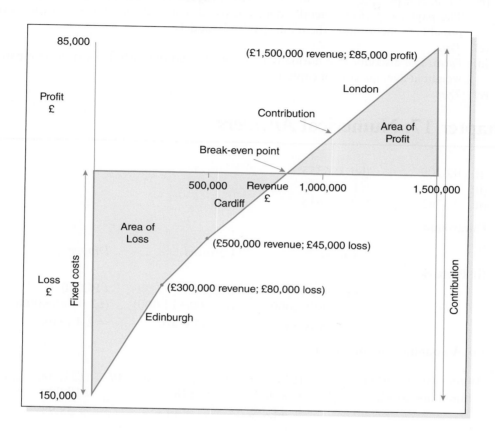

Chapter 17: Discussion *Answers*

The answers provide some outline points for discussion.

A1 **(a)** Capital investment is necessary for the development of a company's infrastructure. Companies also expand or reorientate their strategic direction. Therefore, they need to invest in infrastructure assets, such as factories or plant and machinery. Essentially, in a competitive business world, companies will either grow or stagnate. If they stagnate, they will be likely to be taken over.

    (b) **(i)** Ships or equipment for making ships such as dry docks, cranes, heavy equipment etc.

        (ii) New hotels or refurbishment of old ones.

        (iii) New factories, plant and machinery, computer technology.

A5 True or false?

(a) *True.*

(b) *False.* Net present value and the internal rate of return use discounted cash flows. The payback period generally does not use discounted cash flows. It is, however, possible to incorporate them into payback models.

(c) *True.*

(d) *False.* The discount rate normally used for discounting cash flows is the company's weighted average cost of capital.

(e) *True.*

Chapter 17: Numerical *Answers*

A1 (i) 0.6209   (iv) 0.6355
(ii) 0.5983   (v) 0.6750
(iii) 0.3762   (vi) 0.1615

A2 Fairground

	Rocket	Carousel	Dipper
(i) Payback	£16,000 +	£10,000 +	£16,000 +
	(£2,000/£8,000)	(£8,000/£14,000)	(£2,000/£5,000)
	= 2.25 years	= 2.57 years	= 2.4 years

(ii) Accounting rate of return

Annual average profit/	(£24,000 ÷ 3)/	(£24,000 ÷ 3)/	(£21,000 ÷ 3)/
Initial investment	£18,000	£18,000	£18,000
	= 44.4%	= 44.4%	= 38.9%

(iii) Net present value

Year	Rocket £	Carousel £	Dipper £	Discount Rate 8%	Rocket £	Carousel £	Dipper £
0	(18,000)	(18,000)	(18,000)	1	(18,000)	(18,000)	(18,000)
1	8,000	6,000	10,000	0.9259	7,407	5,555	9,259
2	8,000	4,000	6,000	0.8573	6,858	3,429	5,144
3	8,000	14,000	5,000	0.7938	6,350	11,113	3,969
Net Present Value (NPV)					2,615	2,097	372

(iv) Profitability Index

	Rocket £	Carousel £	Dipper £
NPV	(20,615)	(20,097)	(18,372)
Initial Investment	18,000	18,000	18,000
Profitability index	1.15	1.12	1.02

So on (i)–(iii) we would choose the Rocket on all criteria as our project.

A2 **Fairground** (*continued*)

(v) **Internal rate of return (IRR):** choose 18% to achieve a negative NPV.

Net present value Year	Rocket £	Carousel £	Dipper £	Discount Rate 18%	Rocket £	Carousel £	Dipper £
0	(18,000)	(18,000)	(18,000)	1	(18,000)	(18,000)	(18,000)
1	8,000	6,000	10,000	0.8475	6,780	5,085	8,475
2	8,000	4,000	6,000	0.7182	5,746	2,873	4,309
3	8,000	14,000	5,000	0.6086	4,869	8,520	3,043
Net Present Value (NPV)					(605)	(1,522)	(2,173)

Therefore, calculate IRR using formula:

IRR = Lowest discount rate + difference in discount rates $\times \dfrac{\text{lowest discount rate NPV}}{\text{difference in NPVs}}$

$$\text{Rocket} \quad = \quad 8\% + \left(10\% \times \frac{£2,615}{£2,615 + £605}\right) \quad = 16.1\%$$

$$\text{Carousel} \quad = \quad 8\% + \left(10\% \times \frac{£2,097}{£2,097 + £1,522}\right) = 13.8\%$$

$$\text{Dipper} \quad = \quad 8\% + \left(10\% \times \frac{£372}{£372 + £2,173}\right) \quad = 9.5\%$$

Therefore, as our cost of capital (8%) is less than the IRR, we could potentially undertake all the projects. We would choose to invest in Rocket because it has the highest IRR. Rocket is the preferred project under all five methods.

A3 **Wetday**

	Storm	Cloud	Downpour
(i) **Payback**	£15,000 + (£3,000/£7,000) = 3.43 years	£10,000 + (£2,000/£2,500) = 3.8 years	£12,000 + (£1,000/£4,000) = 3.25 years

(ii) **Accounting rate of return**

Average annual profit/ Initial investment	£6,000/£18,000 = 33.3%	£3,100/£12,000 = 25.8%	£4,000/£13,000 = 30.8%

(iii) **Net present value**

Year	Storm £	Cloud £	Downpour £	Discount Rate 12%	Storm £	Cloud £	Downpour £
0	(18,000)	(12,000)	(13,000)	1	(18,000)	(12,000)	(13,000)
1	4,000	5,000	4,000	0.8929	3,572	4,464	3,572
2	5,000	2,000	4,000	0.7972	3,986	1,594	3,189
3	6,000	3,000	4,000	0.7118	4,271	2,135	2,847

A3 Wetday (*continued*)

Year	Storm £	Cloud £	Downpour £	Discount Rate 12%	Storm £	Cloud £	Downpour £
4	7,000	2,500	4,000	0.6355	4,449	1,589	2,542
5	8,000	3,000	4,000	0.5674	4,539	1,702	2,270
Net Present Value (NPV)					2,817	(516)	1,420

Therefore, depending upon the criteria, we will choose a different project. Downpour has the quickest payback; Storm the highest accounting rate of return and NPV. Probably, therefore, we will choose Storm. We will definitely not choose Cloud, because of its negative NPV.

(iv) **Internal rate of return (IRR).** Choose 20% for Storm and Downpour to get a negative NPV. However, choose 8% for Cloud to get a positive NPV.

Year	Storm £	Cloud £	Downpour £	Discount Rate 20%	Discount Rate 8%	Storm (20%) £	Cloud (8%) £	Downpour (20%) £
0	(18,000)	(12,000)	(13,000)	1	1	(18,000)	(12,000)	(13,000)
1	4,000	5,000	4,000	0.8333	0.9259	3,333	4,629	3,333
2	5,000	2,000	4,000	0.6944	0.8573	3,472	1,715	2,778
3	6,000	3,000	4,000	0.5787	0.7938	3,472	2,381	2,315
4	7,000	2,500	4,000	0.4823	0.7350	3,376	1,837	1,929
5	8,000	3,000	4,000	0.4019	0.6806	3,215	2,042	1,608
Net Present Value (NPV)						(1,132)	604	(1,037)

Calculate IRR, using formula

$$\text{IRR} = \text{Lowest discount rate} + \text{difference in discount rates} \times \frac{\text{lowest discount rate NPV}}{\text{difference in NPVs}}$$

$$\text{Storm} \quad = \quad 12\% + \left(8\% \times \frac{£2,817}{£2,817 + £1,132}\right) = 17.7\%$$

$$\text{Cloud} \quad = \quad 8\% + \left(4\% \times \frac{£604}{£604 + £516}\right) = 10.2\%$$

$$\text{Downpour} \quad = \quad 12\% + \left(8\% \times \frac{£1,420}{£1,420 + £1,037}\right) = 16.6\%$$

As our cost of capital is 12%, we could potentially undertake Storm or Downpour. Storm has the highest IRR and we would choose this project if funds were limited. As Storm has the highest accounting rate of return, NPV and IRR, this is our preferred project.

Chapter 18: Discussion *Answers*

The answers provide some outline points for discussion.

A1 Firms are in some ways like living things. They need energy to survive and grow. In the case of living things, the energy is provided by sunlight. For firms, the energy is supplied by sources of finance. These may be short-term, like a bank overdraft, or long-term, like a long-term loan. These sources of finance enable a firm to buy inventory, carry out day-to-day operations and expand by the purchase of new property, plant and equipment. In essence, short-term finance should be used to sustain the firm's working capital, while long-term finance should fund the company's infrastructure. Some of the major sources of finance and the activities financed are outlined below:

Source of finance	Activities financed
Bank overdraft	Working capital, day-to-day operations
Debt factoring	Trade receivables
Invoice discounting	Trade receivables
Trade payables	Working capital, day-to-day operations
Sale and buy back of inventory	Inventory
Leasing	Leased assets
Retained profits	Infrastructure assets, e.g., property, plant and equipment
Share capital	Infrastructure assets, e.g., property, plant and equipment
Long-term loan	Infrastructure assets, e.g., property, plant and equipment

A2 EMH stands for efficient market hypothesis. There are various forms of this hypothesis. However, they all seek to test in one shape or form whether the price of a company's shares reflects its true value. Its true value is usually established through the analysis of information about the firm. This analysis is generally conducted by financial analysts. It is generally thought that with some anomalies the EMH holds, certainly in its weak form. In other words, the price of a share reflects all published information.

A5 **True or false?**
(a) *False.* They are normally used to finance long-term infrastructure assets.
(b) *False.* Retained profits is an internal, not an external, source of long-term finance.
(c) *True.*
(d) *False.* The two main markets are the main market and the AIM Market.
(e) *False.* EMH stands for efficient market hypothesis, which maintains that share prices will always reflect underlying information. There are various versions of this such as strong, semi-strong and weak.

Chapter 18: Numerical *Answers*

A1 Albatross

Source of Finance	Current Market Value		Present Cost of Capital	Weighted Average Cost of Capital
	£ million	%	%	%
Ordinary shares	4	50.0	12	6.00
Preference shares	1	12.5	10	1.25
Long-term loan	3	37.5	8	3.00
	8	100.0		10.25

Chapter 19: Discussion *Answers*

A2 A company might use ratio analysis and budgeting. With ratio analysis a company might use, for example, the current ratio, quick ratio, trade receivables collection period, the trade payables period or the inventory ratio. This would build up a picture of the company's performance. This would be particularly useful over time and as a basis of comparing the company's performance with its competitors. A company might use budgeting in an attempt to forecast future activities. The main budgets that might be used are the cash budget, the trade receivables and trade payables budgets, and the raw materials and finished goods budgets.

A3 This is because there is a mismatch of funding. Generally, it is considered healthy to match current funding with operational activities. Long-term funding will be reserved for infra-structural activities. In this particular case, the problem would be that the company might be in trouble at the end of the loan period if it had to repay the loan. Also, it would be in trouble if the bank recalled the overdrafts. From the bank's point of view, it would also not usually make short-term loans or overdrafts to fund long-term infrastructural projects.

A4 True or false?

(a) *True.*

(b) *True.*

(c) *True.*

(d) *False.* It is the reverse. If the current ratio was under 1 then there would be less current assets than current liabilities. This is not a good idea. The current ratio should be above 1 so that there are more current assets than liabilities.

(e) *False.* Bank overdrafts are more flexible as you have more ability to use them as you wish, but they are not usually for a fixed period of time.

Chapter 19: Numerical *Answers*

A1 Lathe

(i) (a) **Graphical Solution**

Order Quantity Q	Number of Orders per annum	Order Cost	Total Order Cost	Average Quantity in Stock	Carrying Cost	Total Carrying Cost	Total Cost
		£	£	£	£	£	£
250	80	25	2,000	125	0.90	112.50	2,112.50
500	40	25	1,000	250	0.90	225.00	1,225.00
1,000	20	25	500	500	0.90	450.00	950.00
1,500	13.33	25	333	750	0.90	675.00	1,008.00
2,000	10	25	250	1,000	0.90	900.00	1,150.00

Graphical solution: Optimal order quantity about 1,000

(i) (b) Algebraic solution:

Economic order quantity formula

$$Q = \sqrt{\frac{2AC}{i}}$$

where:

Q = Economic order quantity
A = Average annual usage
C = Cost of each order being placed
i = Carrying cost per unit per annum

$$Q = \sqrt{\frac{2 \times 20,000 \times 25}{0.9}} = 1,054 \text{ Tweaks}$$

(ii) Total costs per annum

		£
Costs of purchase	£1.50 × 1,054	1,581
Order costs	$\dfrac{20,000}{1,054} \times £25$	474
Carrying costs	$\dfrac{1,054}{2} \times 0.90$	474
Total costs		2,529

Index

abridged company accounts, 70, 153, 165
absolute size, 258
absorption costing, 369, 382, 384, 393, 449
   total, 369, 384, 387, 388, 392, 393
ACCA *see* Association of Chartered
   Certified Accountants
acceptance of IAS standards, 288
accountability, 300, 301, 324–5
accountancy, types of, 13–18
   auditing, 13–15
   bookkeeping, 15
   finance, 16
   financial accounting, 15–16
   insolvency, 16
   management accounting, 16
   fraud detection, 16
   management consultancy, 18
   taxation, 17
accountant, types of, 18–20
   professionally qualified accountants,
     18–20
   second-tier bodies, 20
accounting
   background to, 27–65
   introduction to, 1–23
accounting, language of, 30–7
   assets, 32
   statement of financial position
     (balance sheet), 34–6
   state of cash flows, 36–7
   equity (capital), 33
   expenses, 31–2
   income, 30
   income statement, 33–4
   liabilities, 32
accounting, limitations of, 21
accounting, nature of, 2–4
accounting and finance
   financial accounting and financial
     management, 5–6

importance of, 4–5
limitations of accounting, 21
nature of, 2–4
types of accountancy, 13–18
types of accountant, 18–20
users of accounts, 7–8
accounting concepts, 50–1
   accruals (matching concept), 51
   consistency, 51
   going concern, 50
   prudence, 51
accounting context, 9–12
   history, 9–10
   international accounting, 10
   organisations, 11–12
   technology, 11
accounting conventions, 49–5
Accounting Council, 292
accounting equation, 38–44, 111, 116
   and financial statements, 111
   trial balance, 42–4
accounting policies, 338–9
accounting principles, 49
   language of accounting, 30–7
   importance of financial accounting, 48
   student example, 44–8
   financial accounting, 28–30
accounting questions, 3
accounting rate of return, 492, 496–7, 500–3
accounting scandals, 82
   see also creative accounting; Enron;
     WorldCom
accounting standards, 290–1
   Accounting Council, 292
   Accounting Standards Board, 292, 298,
     300, 304
   Financial Reporting Council, 291
   Financial Reporting Review Panel, 292–3
   introduction of, 290
   Urgent Issues Task Force, 292

Accounting Standards Board, 289, 298, 304
  Statement of Principles, 300
Accounting Standards Steering Committee,
  289
accounting terms, 34
accounting treatment for limited companies,
  163–4
accruals (matching concept), 51, 80, 99,
  113, 117
  and prepayments, 117, 118
accumulated depreciation, 95
acid test ratio, 240
activities, identification of, 393, 394
activity-based costing, 367, 387, 393–6
activity-cost driver rates, calculation of,
  394
adjustments to trial balance, 116–24
  accruals, 117
  bad and doubtful debts, 119–24
  depreciation,118–19
  inventories (stock), 116–17
  prepayments, 117–18
administrative expenses, 385
after-tax profits, 237
AGM (annual general meeting), 282
AICPA *see* American Institute of Certified
  Public Accountants
allocation of indirect costs, 389
American Accounting Association, 3
American Institute of Certified Public
  Accountants, 313
annual financial accounts, 30
annual general meeting, 282
annual report, 165, 321–57
  audited statements, 331–9
  conflicting objectives of, 329
  context, 323–4
  definition, 323
  group accounts, 350–2
  impression management, 352–5
  main contents, 329–48
  multiple roles, 324–9
  narrative sections, 341–7
  non-audited sections, 339–47
  non-narrative sections, 347–8
  presentation, 348–9

annual report, roles, 324–9
  conflicting objectives, 329
  decision making, 327–8
  public relations, 328
  stewardship and accountability, 324–5
appropriate overhead allocation, 394
appropriation account, 144–6
Arbuthnot Banking Group, 529
ASB *see* Accounting Standards Board
Asda, 383, 483
asset turnover ratio, 239
asset-rich companies, 314
assets, 32
  wearing out, 80–2
associated companies, 350–1
Association of Accounting Technicians, 18
Association of Chartered Certified
  Accountants, 18, 20
assumptions *see* accounting concepts
AstraZeneca, 170–3, 209–10
Audit and Assurance Council, 292
audited statements of annual report, 331–9
  explanatory material, 338–9
  main statements, 331–5
  subsidiary statements, 335–8
auditing, 13–15
Auditing Practices Board, 279, 290
auditors, 278–81
auditors' report, 279–80, 343–4, 344–5
AVCO, 399–400
average cost (AVCO), 399–400

BA (British Airways), 473
bad debts, 98,119–23
balance sheet *see* statement of financial
  position
bank loans, 532, 533
bank overdraft, 520, 532, 544, 552, 553
bankruptcy, 144, 151, 355
banks, 553
Barclays Bank, 4
batch costing, 401
BBC (British Broadcasting Corporation),
  322
Bearbull 537
beer brewing, 404

before-tax profits, 237
being seen, 531
benefits in kind, 278
bond market 527
bonuses, 278, 343
Boo.com, 191
bookkeeping, 10, 11, 13, 15
bottlenecks, 475
break-even analysis, 367, 371, 477–81
    assumptions, 477–8
    graphical break-even point, 479–80
    margin of safety, 478
    other uses of, 478–81
    what-if analysis, 478
British Airways 473
British Broadcasting Corporation, 322
British Gas, 318
British Petroleum, 152
British Telecom, 529
Brook Brothers, 73
BT (British Telecom), 529
budget is God, 413
budget targets, meeting, 431
budgeting, 367, 413–42
    behavioural aspects, 431–4
    creative budgeting, 434
    example, 426–30
    padding the budget, 433
    spending to budget, 432–3
    working capital, 542–3
budgeting, nature of, 415–19
    control, 417
    coordinating, 417
    motivation, 417
    planning, 417
Bulmer Holdings, H.P., 375
business angels 533–4
business, language of, 2
Byers, Stephen, 325

Cadbury Committee, 294
called-up capital, 175
capital accounts, 146
capital allowances 512
capital and revenue expenditure, 82
capital budgeting 493, 496

capital employed, 101–2
    see also equity
capital expenditure, 493
capital goods 493
capital investment appraisal, 373,
        491–517
    accounting rate of return, 500–3
    assumptions, 495
    inflation, 512
    internal rate of return, 507–11
    nature of, 492–5
    net present value, 504–7
    other factors, 512
    payback period, 498–9
    profitability index, 507
    sensitivity analysis, 512
    taxation, 512
    techniques, 496–8
capital investment, nature of, 493–500
    initial investment 496
    net cash flows 497
    non-operating cash flows 497
    techniques 498–500
capital maintenance, 311–12
capital reserves, 161
capitalism, 327
Cardiff Millennium Stadium, 387
Carnegie, Andrew, 380
cash, 541, 545–6, 552–3
    bank account and, 194–8
    bank and, 99
    definition, 194
    importance of, 192–3
cash book, 194
cash budget, 419–20
cash flow, 191, 192
    vs. profit, 200
cash inflow and outflow of cash, 195
cash flow ratios, 241, 252
cash flow statement see statement of cash
        flows
cash loss vs. stated loss, 199
chairman's statement, 341
Channel Tunnel, 494
charitable gifts, 342
chartered accountants, 18–19

Chartered Institute of Management
    Accountants, 20, 29
Chartered Institute of Public Finance and
    Accountancy, 20
checks and balances, 282
choice, 370, 373
Churchill, Winston S., 283
CIMA (Chartered Institute of Management
    Accountants), 20, 29
CIPFA (Chartered Institute of Public
    Finance and Accountancy), 20
City, the, 290, 405
classification of costs, 389, 406
clerical costs, 550
Coca-Cola, 152
Codes and Standards Committee, 291–2
collective mobility, 365
Companies Acts, 10, 276, 283, 289–90, 306
    1981 289–90 1985, 87 2006 67, 71,
    152, 279, 290
company, 151
comparability, 303
compensating variances, 456
competitive advantage, costing as, 383
compound growth, 497
compound interest 497
computers, 11, 15, 375–6, 511
    helpline, 385
conceptual framework, 298–305
    content of, 302
    criticisms of, 305
    measurement model, 305
    objectives, 299–300
    qualitative information characteristics,
      302–4
    user needs, 301–2
    users, 301
conflict of interest, 432
consistency, 51
contract costing, 401–3
contracting out, 473, 554
contribution analysis, 369, 371,
    465–9
    contribution, 466–7
    fixed costs, 466
    variable costs, 466

contribution, 371, 466–7
    to revenue, 480–1
control, 417
controllable costs, 369, 435
conventions, 49–51
    entity, 49
    historical cost, 49, 50
    monetary measurement, 49
    periodicity, 50
coordination, 417
corporate bonds 522, 527, 532
corporate governance, 293–8
corporation tax, 153, 176
cost, types of, 383–6
cost accounting 366, 367–70
    costing, 367
    importance of, 382–3
    and management accounting, 373
    planning, control and performance, 370
cost behaviour, 371–2, 468, 469
cost control, 384
cost-cutting, 405–6
cost drivers, identification of, 394
cost minimisation and revenue
    maximisation, 374–5
cost of capital 505, 534–7
    behavioural implications of, 505
cost of sales, 75–6, 400
cost-plus pricing, 383
cost-profit-volume analysis, 465
cost recording, 388–9, 406
costing, 367, 366, 380–412
    activity-based costing, 393–6
    as competitive advantage, 383
    cost-cutting, 405–6
    definition, 369
    different methods for different industries,
      401–5
    importance of, 382–3
    for inventory valuation, 397–400
    target costing, 405
    traditional costing, 387–93
    types of cost, 383–6
costing methods, 401–5
    batch costing, 401
    contract costing, 401–3

process costing, 404
service costing, 404–5
costs, classification of, 389, 406
creative accounting, 353–4
depreciation, 354
inventory, 354
creative budgeting, 434
credit, advantages and disadvantages of 547
credit sales, 523
creditors *see* trade payables
creditors' collection period, 237–8
credits, 42
current accounts, 147
debit balances on, 147
current assets, 96–9
cash and bank, 99
inventories (stocks), 96–8
prepayments, 98
trade receivables (debtors), 98
current liabilities, 99–101
accruals, 99
loans, 99–101
trade payables (creditors), 99
current ratio, 239, 543
current value systems, 312
customer database mining, 375
cynicism, 309, 288

debentures, 159–60
see also loan capital
debit balances on current accounts, 147
debits, 42
debt 521, 522, 523, 531
debt factoring, 554
debtors collection period, 237
debtors *see* trade receivables
decision making, 327–8, 366, 370–4,
463–5
financial evaluation, 464
forward-looking, 464
key terms, 371
relevant information, 464
short-term decisions, 371, 462–88
and stewardship, 300
see also short-term decision making
decisions, range of, 469–75

determining most profitable products,
471
make or buy decision, 474
maximising a limited factor, 474–5
cessation of production, 470–2
definitions
accounting, 3
accounting rate of return, 500
accounting standards, 292
annual report, 322–3
assets, 90
audit, 278
balance sheet (statement of financial
position), 89–90
budget, 417
capital and revenue expenditure, 82
conceptual framework, 298
costing, 369
decision-making objective of annual
report, 328
equity, 90
expenses, 70
financial accounting, 29
income, 70
income statement (profit and loss
account), 69
internal rate of return, 508
liabilities, 90
management accounting, 363
national regulatory framework, 283
net present value, 505
ownership interest, 90
payback period, 498
standard cost, 446
subsidiaries and associated companies,
351
true and fair view, 289
Deloitte and Touche, 31
Department of Trade and Industry, 293
depreciation, 118–19, 354
measurement of, 94–5
determining most profitable product,
470
direct costs, 369, 383–6, 387, 388, 395–6
direct method of cash flow statement
preparation, 200–2

directors, 277–8
  'fat-cat', 325, 326
  pay, 325–6
  remuneration report, 343
  report, 341–2
  self-interest, 48
  view of fat-cat directors, 326
disclosure, 354
discount rate 504–5, 507
discount tables 506
discounted cash flow, 371, 373
discounting, 497, 504–5
dividend cover, 242
dividend yield, 242
dividends, 155–7
divorce of ownership and control, 152
dot.com businesses, 239
doubtful debts, 98, 119–23

earnings per share, 243
economic order quantity (EOQ), 374,
    549–50
economic reality, 289
efficiency ratios, 234–6, 250
  asset turnover ratio, 239
  creditors' collection period, 237–8
  debtors' collection period, 237
  inventory (stock) turnover ratio, 239
efficient market hypothesis (EMH) 527
Enron, 192, 293, 325
Enterprise Finance Guarantee Scheme, 534
Enterprise Inns 530
entity (capital), 33
environmental accounting, 355
EOQ (economic order quantity), 374,
    549–50
EPS (earnings per share), 243
equity, 33
  see also capital
equity employed, 101–2
estimating, 80
Eurobond 532
Everfriendly Bank's Falcon project 501
expenditure deferral, 434
expenses, 31–2, 77–9
explanatory material, 338–9

accounting policies, 338–9
  notes to the accounts, 339
  principal subsidiaries, 339
Extel, 234
external financing, 523–4, 552–5
  cash 552–3
  inventory, 555
  leasing, 523–4
  trade payables, 553–4
  trade receivables, 554

fair value, 312
faithful representation, 303
Fame, 234, 246, 248
fat-cat directors, 294–5, 326
  critics' view, 326
  directors' view, 326
FIFO, 339, 399–400
financial accounting, 6, 15–16, 28–30
  importance of, 48
  vs management accounting, 364–6
financial accounting, context of
  annual report, 321–57
  measurement systems, 309–20
  regulatory and conceptual frameworks,
    275–308
  annual report, 323–4
  management accounting, 363–4
financial accounting, techniques
  accounting background, 27–65
  balance sheet, 86–108
  cash flow statement, 190–228
  interpretation of accounts, 229–72
  partnerships and limited companies,
    141–89
  preparing financial statements,
    109–40
  profit and loss account, 66–85
financial analysts, 7
financial evaluation, 464
financial position, 103
financial ratios, 259
Financial Reporting Council, 291
Financial Reporting Review Panel, 291,
    292–3
financial statements, main, 110–11

see also balance sheet; cash flow
statement; profit and loss account
financial statements, preparation,
109–40
adjustments to trial balance, 116–24
main financial statements, 110–11
trial balance to profit and loss account
and balance sheet, 112–16
finished goods budget, 424–6
finished goods, 97
first-in-first-out *see* FIFO
fixed costs, 371, 466, 481–3
flexing the budget, 448, 451–2
football clubs
greatest assets, 104
new stadium, 495
profits, 81
see also Manchester United
forecasting the future, 494
forward-looking decision making, 464
fraud detection, 16
see also creative accounting
FRC (Financial Reporting Council), 291
Freeserve, 529
friction, 446
FRRP *see* Financial Reporting Review Panel
FTSE 100 index (the footsie), 525
fuel blockade, 552
functional analysis, 405

GAAP *see* Generally Accepted Accounting
Principles
garbage in, garbage out, 11, 361
gearing 532
gearing ratios, 240–1, 251–2
General Electric Company, 4
Generally Accepted Accounting Principles,
285
Germany, 553
GIGO, 11, 361
Glaxo-Wellcome, 325
globalisation, 365
going concern, 50
goodwill, 41, 123, 164, 352
see also bonuses; intangible assets
graphic designers, 323

graphical break-even point,
479–80
graphs, 354–5
Greenbury Committee, 294
gross profit ratio, 236
gross profit, 77
group accounts, 350–2
goodwill, 352
subsidiary and associated companies,
350–1

Hampel Committee, 294
Heineken, 313–14
Higgs Report, 294
highlights, 347–8
hire purchase, 523
historical cost, 49, 50, 311, 312
deficiencies of, 315, 316–17
historical cost convention, 49, 50
historical summary, 347–8
history of accounting, 9–10
holistic view of ratios, 256–7
pictics, 256–7
Z score model, 256
horizontal analysis, 249
horizontal format of balance sheet, 108
HSBC, 13, 33, 68, 329

IASB *see* International Accounting
Standards Board
ICAEW *see* Institute of Chartered
Accountants in England and Wales
ICAI *see* Institute of Chartered Accountants
in Ireland
ICAS *see* Institute of Chartered Accountants
of Scotland
IFRS *see* International Financial Reporting
Standards
ignorance, 540
importance
of accounting, 4
of stock valuation, 96
impression management, 354–6
creative accounting, 354–5
narrative enhancement, 355–6
income, 30

income statement and statement of
  comprehensive income *see* statement
  of comprehensive income (SOCI)
income statement *see* profit and loss account
incremental cost, 467
indirect cost allocation, 389
indirect costs, 369, 381, 383–6, 389, 395–6
indirect method of cash flow statement
  preparation, 203–14
  adjusting profit before taxation, 205
  reconciliation of operating profit, 204–14
individual price and quantity variance,
  453–4
individual variances, calculation of, 453–4
  individual price and quantity variances,
  453–4
  sales quantity variance, 453
inflation, 512
informal personal budget, 415
information characteristics of conceptual
  framework,300, 302–4
innovative accounting *see* creative accounting
inside investors 528
insolvency, 16
Institute of Chartered Accountants in
  England and Wales, 19, 22, 365
Institute of Chartered Accountants in
  Ireland, 19, 22
Institute of Chartered Accountants of
  Scotland, 19, 22
institutional investors 528
institutional sources of funds 524–30
intangible assets, 41, 123, 162–3, 352
  see also goodwill
interest cover, 245–6
internal financing, 522–3, 542–52
  cash, 545–6
  inventory, 548–52
  retained profits, 522–3
  trade receivables, 546–8
internal rate of return 498, 504, 507–11
international accounting, 10, 259
International Accounting Standards Board,
  10, 50, 51, 142, 283–8
  IAS 1, 332
  IAS 7, 195, 197–8

International Accounting Standards
  Committee (IASC), 284
International Financial Reporting
  Standards, 10, 82, 142, 283, 284–8
International Organisation of Securities
  Commissions (IOSCO), 285
interpretation of accounts *see* ratio analysis
inventory (stock), 96–8, 116–17, 354, 543,
  548–50, 555
  and creative accounting, 355
  economic order quantity 549–50
  just-in-time, 550–2
  sale and buy-back, 555
  valuation, 97, 364
inventory turnover ratio, 239
inventory valuation measures, 399–400
investment analysts, 6
investment ratios, 241–6, 253
  dividend cover, 242
  dividend yield, 242
  earnings per share, 243
  interest cover, 245–6
  price/earnings ratio, 243–5
invoice discounting, 554–5
IOSC (International Organisation
  of Securities Commissions), 285
IRR *see* internal rate of return

Japan, 259, 405, 550
  just-in-time, 550–2
  see also target costing
Johnson, H.T., 365
Jubilee Line extension, 494
just-in-time, 365, 374, 550–2

Kaplan, Robert S., 310, 365

labour costs, cutting, 405–6
Laing, John, 387, 397, 402
Lamprell, 529
last-in-first-out *see* LIFO
leaseback, 520, 544
leasing; 522, 523–4
Lego, 470
liabilities, 32
LIFO, 399–400

like with like comparison, 258

limited companies, distinctive accounting features of, 154–64
  balance sheet, 154
  dividends, 155–7
  formats and terminology, 157–9
  intangible assets, 162–3
  long-term capital, 159–62
  taxation, 155

limited companies and partnerships, 141–89
  context, 143–4
  example, 165–70
  limited companies, 150–64
  partnerships, 144–50
  profit and loss account, 70
  published accounts, 170–5

limited liability, 151

limited liability partnership (LLP), 144

linearity, 477

liquidation *see* bankruptcy

liquidity ratios, 239–40, 251
  current ratio, 239
  quick ratio, 240

listed companies, 82, 105

LLP (limited liability partnership), 144

loan capital 522, 530–2

loans, 99–101, 552, 553

London Eye, 496

London Stock Exchange, 524, 525
  Alternative Investment Market (AIM) 526–7, 529
  Main Markets 526

London Underground 496

long-term capital, 159–62, 527–8

long-term contracts
  policy, 402
  pricing, 387

long-term decision making *see* capital investment appraisal

long-term financing 521–34,, 541, 542, 544
  external 522, 523–4
  institutional sources of funds 524–30
  internal sources 522–3
  size of business 522

lord of the manor, 324

loss-making products, 472

make or buy decision, 473–4

management accounting, 6, 16, 361–79
  budgeting, 413–42
  capital investment appraisal, 491–517
  changing nature of, 377
  context, 363–4
  control systems, 414
  and cost accounting, 373
  cost minimisation and revenue maximisation, 374–5
  costing, 380–412
  definitions, 363
  key decision-making terms, 371
  overview, 366–74
  relationship with financial accounting, 364–5
  short-term decision making, 462–88
  standard costing, 443–61
  use of computers, 375–6
  sources of finance, 518–34

management accounting, overview, 366–74
  cost accounting, 366, 367–70
  cost behaviour, 371–2
  decision making, 370–4
  non-production, 397–8
  production, 397

management consultancy, 17

management of working capital, 540–57
  long-term financing, 552–5
  short-term financing, 544–52

management vs financial accounting, 364–5

manager under pressure, 446

Manchester United, 5, 95, 494
  depreciation, 95
  investment ratios, 241, 242
  merger with Manchester City, 18
  turnover, 12

manufacturing budgets, 423–6
  finished goods budget, 424–6
  production cost budget, 424
  raw materials budget, 424, 425

manufacturing industry, decline of, 381, 384

manufacturing resource planning, (MRPII), 550

margin of safety, 478

marginal costing, 367, 369, 382, 384, 467
    see also contribution analysis
Maritime Industrial Services (MIS), 527
market price, 152, 383
Marks & Spencer, 34–7, 524
    governance, 295
mark-up, 77
Massachusetts Institute of Technology, 465
matching *see* accruals
materials requirement planning (MRP), 374,
    418, 549–50
maximisation of limited factors, 474–5
Maxwell Communications, 294, 325
measurement model of conceptual
    framework, 305
measurement systems, 309–20
    alternative, 311, 318
    example, 315–17
    historical cost, 313
    overview, 310–12
    real life, 318
    replacement cost, 313–15
    types, 313–15
Memorandum of Association, 161
MG Rover, 293
Microsoft, 4
Middle Ages, 324
Milken, Michael, 102
missing assets, 104
mistrust, 7
monetary capital maintenance, 311
monetary measurement, 49
money, 29, 99
mortgages 532
motivation, 417
MRP *see* materials requirement planning

narrative enhancement, 354
narrative sections of annual report, 341–7
    auditors' report, 343–5
    business reviews, 341
    chairman's statement, 341
    directors' remuneration report, 343
    directors' report, 341–2
    operating and financial review, 341
    review of operations, 342

shareholder analysis, 347
social and environmental accounting
    statement, 342
statement of corporate governance,
    343
statement of directors' responsibilities for
    financial statements, 346–7
National Health Service, 257
national regulatory framework, 282, 283
negative contribution, 471
negative disclosure, 355
net assets, 89
net present value 498, 499, 504–7, 509,
    511
    calculation of, 506
net profit margins, 245
net profit ratio, 236–7
net profit, 79
Netherlands, 313, 318
New York Stock Exchange 524
NHS (National Health Service), 257
Nokia, 339, 343
    auditors' report, 344–5
    ratios, 253, 254
    stocks (inventories), 96, 97
nominal value, 152
non-audited sections of annual report,
    339–47
    narrative sections, 339–47
    non-narrative sections, 347–8
non-cash flow items, 204–14
non-current assets,94–6
non-narrative sections of annual report,
    347–8
    highlights, 347
    historical summary, 347–8
    shareholder analysis, 348
non-production overheads, 397–8
non-relevant costs 464
non-trading gains and losses, 332
Norton, David P., 310
Note on Historical Cost Profits and Losses,
    338
Note on Reconciliation of Net Cash Flow to
    Movement in Net Debt, 335
notes to the accounts, 339, 355

objective value, 315
Office for National Statistics, 75, 142
OFR (operating and financial review), 341
Olympic Airlines, 361
Olympic Games, Montreal, 494
ONS *see* Office for National Statistics
operating and financial review, 341
operating expenditure, 493
operating profit by adjusting profit before
    taxation, calculation of, 204
opportunity costs, 464
ordinary shares 527, 529
organisations, 11–12
outside retail investors 528
outsourcing, 473
overdrafts, 544, 552, 553
overhead recovery rate, 389–90
overheads, 369, 381, 382, 383, 384
    fixed, 444, 445, 449, 450, 466
    variable, 444, 445, 449, 451, 456, 475
overtrading, 200

P/E ratio *see* price/earnings ratio
padding the budget, 433
Parmalat, 293, 294, 325
partners, 144
    profit sharing, 146
partnerships and limited companies
        see limited companies and partnerships
passing the buck, 465
patents, 163
payback period, 496, 497, 498–9
payback, limitations of, 499
Pennon, 32
Penny Black, 161
performance evaluation, 364, 435
performance graph, 343
performance indicators, 257–8
period costs, 369
periodicity, 50
personal budgets, 415
personal finances, 51
Philips, 318
Phoenix Four, 293
physical capital maintenance, 311
pictics, 256–7

placing 529, 530
planning, 417
planning, control and performance, 366
    see also budgeting; standard costing
planning for the future *see* budgeting
political gifts, 342
Polly Peck, 294, 325
    creative accounting, 355, 356
positive cash flow, 202
positive disclosure, 355
preference shares 529
prepayments, 98, 117–18
    and accruals, 118
present value, 312
price changes, 80
price/earnings ratio, 243–5
PriceWaterhouseCoopers, 15, 279, 345
prime cost, 384
principal–agent relationship, 277
principal subsidiaries, 339
private debt 532
probability ratios, 235–7, 249–50
    gross profit ratio, 236
    net profit ratio, 236–7
    return on capital employed, 235
problem solving, 364
process costing, 404
production cost budget, 426
products making negative contribution, 471
professional accountancy bodies, 19
professional investors 528
profit, 79–82
    accruals or matching concept, 80
    changing prices, 80
    estimating, 80
    wearing out of assets, 80–2
Profit and Loss Account *see* statement of
    comprehensive income (SOCI)
profit performance, 68
profit sharing, 146
profit sharing ratio, 146
profit/volume chart, 481
profit/volume ratio, 483
profitability index 498, 499, 504, 507
property, plant and equipment, 94,
    120–1, 314

prudence, 51, 304
PSR (profit sharing ratio), 144
public debt 532
public issue 529
public relations, 328
published accounts of limited companies, 170–5
punctuality, 257

quick ratio, 240, 543
quipus, 9

rail companies, performance indicators, 257, 258
Railtrack 537
rates of return, 503
ratio analysis, 229–72, 543–4
    context, 230–1
    holistic view of ratios, 256–7
    limitations, 258–9
    main ratios 234–9
    overview, 231–3
    performance indicators, 257–8
    ratios and size, 234
    report format, 254–6
ratio analysis, limitations of, 258–9
    absolute size, 258
    context, 258
    data validity, 259
    international comparison, 259
    like with like, 258
ratios, 234–46
    cash flow ratios, 241
    company specific, 253–4
    efficiency ratios, 237–9
    gearing ratios, 240–1
    holistic view of, 256–7
    importance of, 233–4
    investment ratios, 241–6
    liquidity ratios, 239–40
    main, 234–46
    probability ratios, 235–7
    size and, 234
raw materials
    budget, 424, 425
    stock, 97

real life, 318
realisable value, 312
reallocation of service support costs, 389
receivables, provision for impairment of, 122–3
reconciliation of operating profit to operating cash flow, 204–14
    non-cash flow items, 204–14
    working capital adjustments, 204
recording *see* double-entry bookkeeping
reducing balance method of measuring depreciation, 94, 95
Registrar of Companies, 153
regulation, 283
regulatory framework, 275–308
    conceptual framework, 298–305
    corporate governance 293–8
    regulatory framework, 282–8
    traditional corporate model, 277–81
    UK, 288–93
relationship between cash and profit, 198–200
relevance, 303
relevant costs, 464
relevant information, 303, 464
relevant range, 478
reliability, 302, 303
Rentokil Initial plc, 118, 121, 279–81
replacement cost, 312, 313–15
report format, 254–6
reserves, 162, 163
residual income, 435
responsibility budgeting, 435–6
retained profits, 522–3
return on capital employed, 235
return on investment, 435
return on sales, 435
revaluation reserve, 162
revaluation, 96
revenue budget, 420, 421, 422
revenues and expenses, 33
review of operations, 342, 355
RI (residual income), 435
rights issue, 529
ringfencing, 144
risk and reward, 281

ROI (return on investment), 435
Rolls-Royce, 97
ROS (return on sales), 435
Royal Society for the Protection of Birds
    (RSPB), 4
royalties, 41

Safeway, 483
Sainsbury, J., plc, 14–15, 483
    cash flow activities, 213–14
    cost of sales, 75, 76
    dividends, 156, 157
    and fixed costs, 483
sale and buy back of inventory, 555
sales, 72–6
sales generation, 72
sales price variance, 448
sales quantity variance, 448, 453
scrap, 495
SEC see Securities Exchange Commission
Secure Trust 530
self-interest, 48, 324
sensitivity 512
sensitivity analysis, 512
service costing, 404–5
service economy model, 365
service industries, 365, 387
setting standards, 446
share capital, 38, 281, 522, 527–30
share price, 243
shareholder analysis, 348
shareholders, 281
shares and share options, 152
Shell, 68
shopping, 415
short-term decision making, 370–2, 462–88
    break-even analysis, 477–81
    contribution analysis, 466–8
    contribution graph, 481–3
    decision making, 463–5
    range of decisions, 469–75
    throughput accounting, 475–6
    vs long-term decisions, 374
short-term financing 519–21, 544–55
    external financing, 552–5
    internal financing, 544–52

small and medium-sized businesses 532–4
    venture capital 533
    business angels 534
    government help 534
SmithKline Beecham, 325
social and environmental accounting
    statement, 342
sole trades, 144
sources of finance, 373, 518–38
    cost of capital 534–7
    long-term 521–34
    nature of 519–21
    short-term 519–21
    see also management of working capital
spending to budget, 432–3
Stagecoach Group, plc, 74, 111
standard cost variances 446–54
    calculating individual variances, 453–4
    flexing the budget, 451–2
standard costing, 369, 443–61
    interpretation of variances, 455–6
    limitations, 444
    nature of, 445–6
    standard cost variances, 446–54
standardised format, 165
Standards Advisory Council, 285
standards, behavioural aspects, 455
statement of cash flows, 36–7, 190–228,
    330, 331, 334–5
    cash and the bank account, 194–8
    context, 194
    importance of cash, 192–3
    preparation of cash flow statement,
    200–14
    relationship between cash and profit,
    198–200
statement of cash flows, preparation,
    200–14
    direct method, 200–2
    indirect method, 203–14
statement of changes in equity, 335
statement of comprehensive income (SOCI),
    33, 66–85, 163, 330, 331–4
    capital and revenue expenditure, 82
    context, 67–8
    cost of sales, 75–6

statement of comprehensive income (SOCI),
      (*continued*)
   definitions, 69–70
   expenses, 77–9
   gross profit, 77
   interpretation of, 83
   layout, 71–2
   limitations of, 83
   listed companies, 82
   main components, 72–9
   net profit, 79
   other income, 77
   profit, 79–82
   revenue or sales, 72–5
statement of corporate governance, 343
statement of directors' responsibilities for
      financial statements, 346–7
statement of financial position (balance
      sheet), 34–6, 86–108, 145, 154, 164,
      330, 331, 334
   balancing, reason for, 94
   context, 88
   definitions, 89–90
   in annual report, 334
   interpretation, 104–5
   layout, 90–1
   limitations, 103–4
   listed companies, 105
   main components, 91–103
statement of financial position, components,
      91–103
   contingent liabilities, 101
   current assets, 96–9
   current liabilities, 99–101
   equity (capital employed), 101–2
   non-current assets, 94–6
   non-current liabilities, 101
Statement of Principles (ASB), 300
stewardship, 294, 300, 324–5
   and decision making, 329
stock exchanges 524–7
   institutional setting 524–5
   international market 526
   listing 526
   primary and secondary markets 525
   stock market efficiency 527

stock market flotation 529
stock turnover ratio, 239
stockholders *see* shareholders
stocks *see* inventories
straight-line method of measuring
      depreciation, 94, 95
strategic management accounting, 365, 372
stress, 329
structure
   of accounting organisations, 11
   of business 534
student loans, 47–8
subsidiaries, 350–1
subsidiary statements, 335–8
   note on reconciliation of net cash flow to
      movement in net debt, 335
   note on historical cost profits and losses,
      338
sunk costs, 464
supermarkets, 238, 483, 544
supplementary notes, 165
suspicion, 432
sustainability information, 342
Sydney Opera House, 494

T account, 39–40, 42–4
Taffler, Richard, 256
tally sticks, 9
tangible fixed assets, 314
target costing, 405
tax avoidance, 17
tax evasion, 17
taxation, 17, 155, 157, 507, 512
Taylor, A.J.P., 491, 494
technology, 11, 365
television manufacture, 386
tendering, 473
Tesco, 49, 100, 162, 483
   annual report, 331–8, 343, 349
   costing, 383
   financial graphs, 349
   financial highlights, 347–8
   fixed costs, 483
   interest cover, 246
   Note on Historical Cost Profits and
      Losses, 338

Notes to the Accounts, 339
Performance Graph, 343
Reconciliation of Net Cash Flow to
    Movement in Net Debt Note, 338
share capital, 38
Statement of Cash Flows, 334–5
Statement of Changes in Equity, 336–7
Statement of Comprehensive Income
    (SOCI),333–4
Statement of Directors' responsibilities,
    346
vertical analysis, 248
throughput accounting, 475–6
time value of money, 499
timeliness, 304
tools of the trade, 363
Topcom, 413
total absorption costing, 369, 384, 387,
    388, 392, 393
total depreciation, 95
Toyota, 152, 350
trade payables (creditors), 32, 99, 553–4
    budget, 420, 423
trade payables collection period, 237–8, 543
trade receivables, 546–8, 554
    budget, 420, 421–3
    debt factoring, 554
    invoice discounting, 554
trade receivables collection model,
    548, 549
trade receivables collection period, 237,
    238, 543
trade unions, 405
trading account, 77, 78
traditional corporate model, 277–81
    auditors, 278–81
    directors, 277–8
    shareholders, 281
traditional costing, 387–93
    absorption of costs into products, 390
    allocate indirect costs to departments, 389
    classification, 389
    overhead recovery rate, 389–90
    reallocate service support department
        costs to production departments, 389
    recording, 388–9

traditional product costing, 393
trial balance, 42–4, 112–16
    adjustments to, 116–24
    to profit and loss account, 112–16
    to statement of financial position,
        112–16
true and fair view, 292
trusts 528–9
Turnbull Committee, 294
turnover, 72, 175
Tweedie, David, 285

UBS Global Management, 192
UBS Phillips and Drew, 190, 193
UITK see Urgent Issues Task Force
uncontrollable costs, 369, 435
understandability, 304
unit trusts 528–9
United Kingdom
    accounting standards, 290–3
    Companies Acts, 288, 289–90
    regulatory framework, 288–93
    true and fair view, 289
United States
    Financial Accounting Standards Board,
        298
unprofitable products, 470–1
Urgent Issues Task Force, 292
users, accounts, 7–9

valuation of inventory, 399–400
    measures, 399–400
    non-production overheads, 397–8
value to the business model, 312
variable costs, 371, 372, 448–9, 466
variable overheads, 444, 445, 449, 451,
    456, 475
variances, 369, 446–54
    calculating individual, 450–1
    interpretation of, 455–6
venture capital 533
verifiability, 304
vertical analysis, 248–9
Vodafone, 97, 121, 350, 503
    rates of return, 503
Volkswagen, 4

WACC (weighted average cost of capital), 534, 535, 536
Wal-Mart, 350, 383
wearing out of assets, 80–2
weighted average cost of capital (WACC) 534, 535, 536
Weinstock, Arnold, 290
Welch, Jack, 192
Wetherspoon, J.D., 50, 348
    cash flow statement, 211, 212
    corporate governance, 296–8
    corporate social responsibility, 342
    dividends, 242
    internal control, 296
what-if analysis, 468, 478
whisky, 555

Wildavsky, Aaron, 418
wine and spirit business, 555
Woolworth, F.W., 548
working capital, 541–4
    planning and evaluating, 542–4
working capital adjustments, 204
working capital cycle, 541–2
working capital management, 540–57
working capital ratios, 543–4
work-in-progress, 97
WorldCom, 82, 325

Z score model, 256
zero based budgeting, 418